I0754777

The Story of God Bible Commentary Series Endorsements

"Getting a story is about more than merely enjoying it. It means hearing it, understanding it, and above all, being impacted by it. This commentary series hopes that its readers not only hear and understand the story but are impacted by it to live in as Christian a way as possible. The editors and contributors set that table very well and open up the biblical story in ways that move us to act with sensitivity and understanding. That makes hearing the story as these authors tell it well worth the time. Well done."

Darrell L. Bock
Dallas Theological Seminary

"The Story of God Bible Commentary series invites readers to probe how the message of the text relates to our situations today. Engagingly readable, it not only explores the biblical text but offers a range of applications and interesting illustrations."

Craig S. Keener
Asbury Theological Seminary

"I love The Story of God Bible Commentary series. It makes the text sing and helps us hear the story afresh."

John Ortberg
Former Pastor of Menlo Park Presbyterian Church

"In this promising new series of commentaries, believing biblical scholars bring not only their expertise but their own commitment to Jesus and insights into today's culture to the Scriptures. The result is a commentary series that is anchored in the text but lives and breathes in the world of today's church with its variegated pattern of socioeconomic, ethnic, and national diversity. Pastors, Bible study leaders, and Christians of all types who are looking for a substantive and practical guide through the Scriptures will find these volumes helpful."

Frank Thielman
Beeson Divinity School

"I'm a storyteller. Through writing and speaking I talk and teach about understanding the story of God throughout Scripture and about letting God reveal more of his story as I live it out. Thus I am thrilled to have a commentary series based on the story of God—a commentary that helps me to Listen to the Story, that Explains the Story, and then encourages me to probe how to Live the Story. A perfect tool for helping every follower of Jesus to walk in the story that God is writing for them."

Judy Douglass
Director of Women's Resources, Cru

"The Bible is the story of God and his dealings with humanity from creation to new creation. The Bible is made up more of stories than of any other literary genre. Even the psalms, proverbs, prophecies, letters, and the Apocalypse make complete sense only when set in the context of the grand narrative of the entire Bible. This commentary series breaks new ground by taking all these observations seriously. It asks commentators to listen to the text, to explain the text, and to live the text. Some of the material in these sections overlaps with introduction, detailed textual analysis and application, respectively, but only some. The most riveting and valuable parts of the commentaries are the stories that can appear in any of these sections, from any part of the globe and any part of church history, illustrating the text in any of these areas. Ideal for preaching and teaching."

Craig L. Blomberg
Denver Seminary

"Pastors and lay people will welcome this new series, which seeks to make the message of the Scriptures clear and to guide readers in appropriating biblical texts for life today."

Daniel I. Block
Wheaton College and Graduate School

"An extremely valuable and long overdue series that includes comment on the cultural context of the text, careful exegesis, and guidance on reading the whole Bible as a unity that testifies to Christ as our Savior and Lord."

Graeme Goldsworthy
author of *According to Plan*

1–2 KINGS

The Story of God Bible Commentary

1–2 KINGS

David T. Lamb

Tremper Longman III & Scot McKnight
General Editors

ZONDERVAN ACADEMIC

1–2 Kings

Requests for information should be addressed to:
Zondervan, *3900 Sparks Dr. SE, Grand Rapids, Michigan 49546*

Zondervan titles may be purchased in bulk for educational, business, fundraising, or sales promotional use. For information, please email SpecialMarkets@Zondervan.com.

ISBN 978-0-310-49096-8 (hardcover)

ISBN 978-0-310-12535-8 (ebook)

Cover design: Ron Huizinga
Cover image: iStockphoto.com
Interior typesetting: Kait Lamphere

Printed in the United States of America

21 22 23 24 25 26 27 28 29 30 31 /TRM/ 15 14 13 12 11 10 9 8 7 6 5 4 3 2 1

To all the students and friends from InterVarsity, Missio Seminary, and dozens of churches from all over the world where I've had the privilege to teach the Word of God. Your wisdom appears on every page of this book.

Old Testament series

1 ▪ Genesis—*Tremper Longman III*
2 ▪ Exodus—*Christopher J. H. Wright*
3 ▪ Leviticus—*Jerry E. Shepherd*
4 ▪ Numbers—*Jay A. Sklar*
5 ▪ Deuteronomy—*Myrto Theocharous*
6 ▪ Joshua—*Lissa M. Wray Beal*
7 ▪ Judges—*Athena E. Gorospe*
8 ▪ Ruth/Esther—*Marion Ann Taylor*
9 ▪ 1–2 Samuel—*Paul S. Evans*
10 ▪ 1–2 Kings—*David T. Lamb*
11 ▪ 1–2 Chronicles—*Carol M. Kaminski*
12 ▪ Ezra/Nehemiah—*Douglas J. Green*
13 ▪ Job—*Martin A. Shields*
14 ▪ Psalms—*Elizabeth R. Hayes*
15 ▪ Proverbs—*Ryan P. O'Dowd*
16 ▪ Ecclesiastes/Song of Songs—*George Athas*
17 ▪ Isaiah—*Mark J. Boda*
18 ▪ Jeremiah/Lamentations—*Andrew G. Shead*
19 ▪ Ezekiel—*Havilah Dharamraj*
20 ▪ Daniel—*Wendy L. Widder*
21 ▪ Minor Prophets I—*Beth M. Stovell*
22 ▪ Minor Prophets II—*Beth M. Stovell*

New Testament series

1 ▪ Matthew—*Rodney Reeves*
2 ▪ Mark—*Timothy G. Gombis*
3 ▪ Luke—*Kindalee Pfremmer DeLong*
4 ▪ John—*Nicholas Perrin*
5 ▪ Acts—*Dean Pinter*
6 ▪ Romans—*Michael F. Bird*
7 ▪ 1 Corinthians—*Justin K. Hardin*
8 ▪ 2 Corinthians—*Judith A. Diehl*
9 ▪ Galatians—*Nijay K. Gupta*
10 ▪ Ephesians—*Mark D. Roberts*
11 ▪ Philippians—*Lynn H. Cohick*
12 ▪ Colossians/Philemon—*Todd Wilson*
13 ▪ 1, 2 Thessalonians—*John Byron*
14 ▪ 1, 2 Timothy, Titus—*Marius Nel*
15 ▪ Hebrews—*Radu Gheorghita*
16 ▪ James—*Mariam J. Kamell*
17 ▪ 1 Peter—*Dennis R. Edwards*
18 ▪ 2 Peter, Jude—*C. Rosalee Velloso Ewell*
19 ▪ 1, 2, & 3 John—*Constantine R. Campbell*
20 ▪ Revelation—*Jonathan A. Moo*
21 ▪ Sermon on the Mount—*Scot McKnight*

Contents

Acknowledgments

Any project of this magnitude involves many people. I am grateful to God for all of them, for all the ways they have shaped and improved this commentary. Tremper Longman III invited me to contribute to this series, and I have deeply appreciated the various roles he has played in my life: a mentor, a sponsor, and a friend. Tremper and Myrto Theocharous provided me with substantial and perceptive feedback, which not only improved the overall quality of the writing but made me a better scholar.

The folks at Zondervan have been a great support throughout this project, overseeing the whole process (Katya Covrett), hosting me and dozens of other authors for lunches annually at biblical studies conferences, reading over my first chapter (Verlyn Verbrugge), providing me with free commentaries in this series from scholars who met deadlines better than I did, and finally working through the entire manuscript in depth and graciously offering suggestions (Nancy Erickson).

I have been given the opportunity to teach on two of my favorite prophets, Elijah and Elisha, in my Sunday school class, The Gathering, at Calvary Church of Souderton, and at several other churches, perhaps most notably, Calvary Vision Church of Blue Bell and Immanuel Church of the Nazarene in Lansdale. The Mid-Atlantic Region of Intervarsity has invited me to teach and preach in various contexts, and I have always felt welcomed, not just as a staff spouse but as a colleague and a friend. For the past fifteen years Missio Seminary has given me opportunities to teach repeatedly on the book of Kings, and more significantly, they have paid me to do what I love: to study, to teach, and to write about God's Word.

From both their positive and negative examples, the characters in the book of Kings have taught me many lessons along the way about obedience, leadership, and trusting God: David and Solomon, Ahab and Jezebel, Elijah and Elisha, Naboth and Micaiah, Jehoshaphat and Jehu, Naaman and his wife's servant girl, Jehosheba and Jehoiada, Jehoahaz and Jehoash (both sets), Pekahiah and Pekah, Tiglath-Pileser III and Sennacherib, Hezekiah and Josiah, Shaphan and Huldah, Jehoiakim and Jehoiachin.

A group of friends and family read over early drafts of chapters: Jason Armold, J. D. Atkins, Dan Brockway, Jeremy Chen, Tim Diehl, Lisa Lamb,

Nathan Lamb, Noah Lamb, Rich Lamb, Shannon Lamb, Alison Siewert, and Dan Siewert. My wife, Shannon, and two sons, Nathan and Noah, not only read over chapters, they also provided me with stories, brainstormed relevant cultural examples, listened to my struggles, and encouraged me throughout the whole process.

To my friends at Zondervan, InterVarsity, many churches, and Missio Seminary and to my family, thank you. I couldn't have completed this commentary without your support.

The Story of God Bible Commentary Series

Why another commentary series?

In the first place, no single commentary can exhaust the meaning of a biblical book. The Bible is unfathomably rich and no single commentator can explore every aspect of its message.

In addition, good commentary not only explores what the text meant in the past but also its continuing significance. In other words, the Word of God may not change, but culture does. Think of what we have seen in the last twenty years: we now communicate predominantly through the internet and email; we read our news on iPads and computers. We carry smartphones in our pockets through which we can call our friends, check the weather forecast, make dinner reservations, and get an answer to virtually any question we might have.

Today we have more readable and accurate Bible versions in English than any generation in the past. Bible distribution in the present generation has been very successful; more people own more Bibles than previous generations. However, studies have shown that while people have better access to the Bible than ever before, people aren't reading the Bibles they own, and they struggle to understand what they do read.

The Story of God Bible Commentary hopes to help people, particularly clergy but also laypeople, read the Bible with understanding not only of its ancient meaning but also of its continuing significance for us today in the twenty-first century. After all, readers of the Bible change too. These cultural shifts, our own personal developments, and the progress in intellectual questions, as well as growth in biblical studies and theology and discoveries of new texts and new paradigms for understanding the contexts of the Bible—each of these elements work on an interpreter so that the person who reads the Bible today asks different questions from different angles.

Culture shifts, but the Word of God remains. That is why we as editors of The Story of God Bible Commentary, a commentary based on the New International Version 2011 (NIV 2011), are excited to participate in this new series of commentaries on the Bible. This series is designed to speak to this generation with the same Word of God. We are asking the authors to explain what the Bible says to the sorts of readers who pick up commentaries so they can understand not only what Scripture says but what it means for today. The Bible does not change, but relating it to our culture changes constantly and in differing ways in different contexts.

As editors of the Old Testament series, we recognize that Christians have a hard time knowing exactly how to relate to the Scriptures that were written before the coming of Christ. The world of the Old Testament is a strange one to those of us who live in the West in the twenty-first century. We read about strange customs, warfare in the name of God, sacrifices, laws of ritual purity, and more and wonder whether it is worth our while or even spiritually healthy to spend time reading this portion of Scripture that is chronologically, culturally, and—seemingly—theologically distant from us.

But it is precisely here that The Story of God Commentary series Old Testament makes its most important contribution. The New Testament does not replace the Old Testament; the New Testament fulfills the Old Testament. We hear God's voice today in the Old Testament. In its pages he reveals himself to us and also his will for how we should live in a way that is pleasing to him.

Jesus himself often reminds us that the Old Testament maintains its importance to the lives of his disciples. Luke 24 describes Jesus's actions and teaching in the period between his resurrection and ascension. Strikingly, the focus of his teaching is on how his followers should read the Old Testament (here called "Moses and all the Prophets," "Scriptures," and "the law of Moses, the Prophets and Psalms"). To the two disciples on the road to Emmaus, he says:

> "How foolish you are, and how slow to believe all that the prophets have spoken! Did not the Messiah have to suffer these things and then enter his glory?" And beginning with Moses and all the Prophets, he explained to them what was said in all the Scriptures concerning himself. (Luke 24:25–27)

Then to a larger group of disciples he announces:

> "This is what I told you while I was still with you: Everything must be fulfilled that is written about me in the law of Moses, the Prophets and the Psalms." Then he opened their minds so they could understand the Scriptures. (Luke 24:44–45)

The Story of God Commentary series takes Jesus's words on this matter seriously. Indeed, it is the first series that has as one of its deliberate goals the identification of the trajectories (historical, typological, and theological) that land in Christ in the New Testament. Every commentary in the series will, in the first place, exposit the text in the context of its original reception. We will interpret it as we believe the original author intended his contemporary audience to read it. But then we will also read the text in the light of the death and resurrection of Jesus. No other commentary series does this important work consistently in every volume.

To achieve our purpose of expositing the Old Testament in its original setting and also from a New Testament perspective, each passage is examined from three angles.

Listen to the Story. We begin by listening to the text in order to hear the voice of God. We first read the passage under study. We then go on to consider the background to the passage by looking at any earlier Scripture passage that informs our understanding of the text. At this point too we will cite and discuss possible ancient Near Eastern literary connections. After all, the Bible was not written in a cultural vacuum, and an understanding of its broader ancient Near Eastern context will often enrich our reading.

Explain the Story. The authors are asked to explain each passage in light of the Bible's grand story. It is here that we will exposit the text in its original Old Testament context. This is not an academic series, so the footnotes will be limited to the kinds of books and articles to which typical Bible readers and preachers will have access. Authors are given the freedom to explain the text as they read it, though you will not be surprised to find occasional listings of other options for reading the text. The emphasis will be on providing an accessible explanation of the passage, particularly on those aspects of the text that are difficult for a modern reader to understand, with an emphasis on theological interpretation.

Live the Story. Reading the Bible is not just about discovering what it meant back then; the intent of The Story of God Bible Commentary is to probe how this text might be lived out today as that story continues to march on in the life of the church.

Here, in the spirit of Christ's words in Luke 24, we will suggest ways in which the Old Testament text anticipates the gospel. After all, as Augustine famously put it, "the New Testament is in the Old Testament concealed, the Old Testament is in the New Testament revealed." We believe that this section will be particularly important for our readers who are clergy who want to present Christ even when they are preaching from the Old Testament.

The Old Testament also provides teaching concerning how we should live today. However, the authors of this series are sensitive to the tremendous impact that Christ's coming has on how Christians appropriate the Old Testament into their lives today.

It is the hope and prayer of the editors and all the contributors that our work will encourage clergy to preach from the Old Testament and laypeople to study this wonderful, yet often strange, portion of God's Word to us today.

Tremper Longman III, general editor Old Testament
George Athas, Mark Boda, and Myrto Theocharous, editors

Abbreviations

AB	Anchor Bible
AIL	Ancient Israel and Its Literature
ANEP	*The Ancient Near East in Pictures Relating to the Old Testament.* Edited by James B. Pritchard. 2nd ed. Princeton: Princeton University Press, 1969
ANET	*Ancient Near Eastern Texts Relating to the Old Testament.* Edited by James B. Pritchard. 3rd ed. Princeton: Princeton University Press, 1969
Ant.	Josephus, *Jewish Antiquities*
AOTC	Abingdon Old Testament Commentaries
ApOTC	Apollos Old Testament Commentary
B. Bat.	Bava Batra in the Jerusalem Talmud
BAR	*Biblical Archaeology Review*
BASOR	*Bulletin of the American Schools of Oriental Research*
BBCOT	*Bible Background Commentary: Old Testament.* Edited by John H. Walton, Victor H. Matthews, and Mark W. Chavalas. Downers Grove: InterVarsity Press, 2000
BCE	Before Christian Era
BETL	Bibliotheca Ephemeridum Theologicarum Lovaniensium
CBQ	*Catholic Biblical Quarterly*
COS	*The Context of Scripture.* Edited by William W. Hallo. 3 vols. Leiden: Brill, 1997–2002
DOTHB	*Dictionary of the Old Testament: Historical Books.* Edited by Bill T. Arnold & H. G. M. Williamson. Downers Grove: InterVarsity Press, 2005
DOTT	*Documents from Old Testament Times.* Edited by D. Winton Thomas. New York: Harper, 1961
ESV	English Standard Version
JAOS	*Journal of the American Oriental Society*
JBL	*Journal of Biblical Literature*
J.W.	Josephus, *Jewish War*
KJV	King James Version
LHBOTS	The Library of Hebrew Bible/Old Testament Studies

LXX	The Septuagint (Greek Old Testament)
MT	Masoretic Text of the Hebrew Bible
NAC	New American Commentary
NASB	New American Standard Bible
NCBC	New Century Bible Commentary
NIV	New International Version
NIVAC	The NIV Application Commentary
NLT	New Living Translation
NRSV	New Revised Standard Version
OTL	Old Testament Library
OTM	Old Testament Message
RIMA	Royal Inscriptions of Mesopotamia, Assyrian Periods
RSV	Revised Standard Version
TOTC	Tyndale Old Testament Commentaries
UF	*Ugarit-Forschungen*
VT	*Vetus Testamentum*
WBC	Word Biblical Commentary
WSS	*Corpus of West Semitic Stamp Seals*. Edited by Hahman Avigad and Benjamin Sass. Jerusalem: The Israel Academy of Sciences and Humanities, 1997
ZIBBC	*Zondervan Illustrated Bible Backgrounds Commentary*. Edited by John H. Walton. Grand Rapids: Zondervan, 2009

Introduction to 1–2 Kings

Why Study Kings?

When I was a graduate student, one the most memorable classes I took examined corporate failures. Most business school classes study success stories (like Apple Computers); we studied companies that went bankrupt (like Osbourne Computers). Failure has become a hot topic the past few years,[1] but the Bible has been talking about failure for thousands of years. The book of Kings tells the story of many failures: how Solomon's sin led to the division of the monarchy, how Jeroboam's sin plagued the Northern Kingdom for centuries, and how persistent apostasy resulted in exile for both the kingdoms of Israel and Judah.

Why would anyone want to read such a depressing story? Great question. Because one can learn a lot from failure—ideally when other people are doing the failing. I still remember lessons from my graduate course on failure over thirty years later. Everyone experiences tragedies and failures in life, but not everyone learns from them. The book of Kings tells a tragic story that is meant to be instructive as it teaches lessons about God, idolatry, obedience, and spiritual leadership. A wise reader will listen well to its story.

Some readers might find the sections with little narrative and a lot of dates and formulaic information boring. There's not much poetry in Kings—for that, check out Psalms, Isaiah, or even Samuel. But there is something for everyone else. For animal lovers the book has bears, birds, dogs, horses, and lions. If you're into warfare, Kings includes arrows, battles, conquests, deportations, encampments, and fires. If miracles are your thing, you'll read about food deliveries by ravens, never-ending jugs and jars, lightning falling from heaven, salt purifying a poisoned spring, flour purifying a poisoned stew, a foreign general healed of leprosy, and a dead man's corpse being revived by the bones of Elisha (sounds like *The Walking Dead*). If you enjoy political intrigue, there are assassinations, rebellions, insurrections, and espionage. If prophets

1. See Scott Adams, *How to Fail at Almost Everything and Still Win Big* (Portfolio: New York, 2013); John C. Maxwell, *Failing Forward: Turning Mistakes into Stepping Stones for Success* (Nashville: Thomas Nelson, 2000).

are your heroes, you'll encounter them not only anointing, confronting, and deceiving kings but also predicting famines, reading minds, and resurrecting children.

The most fascinating part of Kings, however, is the main character, God himself, as he speaks, heals, judges, sends fiery chariots, and even talks trash. The kings of Kings, however, consistently fail to live up to God's standards, leaving readers longing for a future ruler, a descendant of David, who will bring the kingdom of heaven to earth (Matt 1:1; 4:17). An investment in the book of Kings will be richly rewarded. To introduce the book, we'll examine its canonicity, literary issues, historical background, and theological message.

Kings and the Canon

Name and Location

While many people speak about the books of 1–2 Kings, it is better to describe them as a single entity—the book of Kings—since the division into two parts came much later. Why was it divided? The book's forty-seven chapters couldn't fit into one scroll.[2] Therefore, in this commentary we will call it merely "Kings" or "the book of Kings." Surprisingly, the longest book in the Bible based on word count in the original languages isn't Psalms, Genesis, or Jeremiah, but the book of Kings (as one book).[3]

Kings is located in different places in the Greek and Hebrew Bible, and different traditions have a different name for the section of the canon where Kings is placed. Jewish tradition calls the book "Kings" (*malakim*) and situates it at the end of what is called the Former Prophets (Joshua, Judges, Samuel, and Kings), perhaps to emphasize the significant role prophets play (curiously few prophets appear in Joshua and Judges). In Kings, hundreds of prophets appear, playing the roles of both the heroes and the villains of the story.

Scholars call the books of Joshua, Judges, Samuel, and Kings the Deuteronomistic History since they use language and terminology reminiscent of Deuteronomy. Since Kings appears at the end of this history, it has been the focus of more research than the other three books regarding how Deuteronomistic redaction may have taken place.

The Greek Septuagint combines the books of 1–2 Samuel (also one book originally) and 1–2 Kings into a four-part history called A, B, C, D *Basileiōn*, or "Kingdoms," presumably because together they record the history of the

2. In the Jewish Talmud Kings is a single book (y. B. Bat. 14b–15a).
3. See https://overviewbible.com/longest-book-of-the-bible/.

monarchy. Many characters from 2 Samuel appear in the early chapters of 1 Kings (e.g., David, Joab, Solomon, Bathsheba, and Nathan). In the Christian tradition, the book of Kings is typically included among the Historical Books of the Old Testament, along with Joshua, Judges, Samuel, Chronicles, Ezra-Nehemiah, and sometimes Ruth and Esther.[4]

Connection to the Latter Prophets and Chronicles

As part of the Former Prophets, one might expect many explicit connections between Kings and prophetic literature. Ten of the prophets with books named after them may have ministered during the reigns of the rulers of Kings (Isaiah, Jeremiah, Ezekiel, Daniel, Hosea, Amos, Jonah, Micah, Zephaniah, Nahum, Habakkuk), but curiously only two of these individuals are mentioned in Kings: Jonah (2 Kgs 14:25) and Isaiah (2 Kgs 19:2, 5, 6).

However, a point of connection between the Former and Latter prophets are the long sections from 2 Kings that are repeated in prophetic books. This phenomenon occurs frequently in the Synoptic Gospels, as many stories are repeated across the three books. The narrative of King Hezekiah of Judah is repeated, largely verbatim, in Isaiah (2 Kgs 18:13–20:19; Isa 36–39), and parallel accounts of the destruction of Jerusalem and the temple conclude both Kings and Jeremiah (2 Kgs 24:18–25:30; Jer 52). Most scholars think the version of these stories from Kings predated those of Isaiah and Jeremiah. Just as the Gospel writers emphasized Jesus's feeding of the five thousand with repetition, so the Old Testament authors emphasized how Hezekiah's righteousness allowed Judah to be delivered from Assyria and how the nation's unfaithfulness allowed Judah to be destroyed by Babylon.

The book of Chronicles, however, includes the most overlap with the book of Kings, particularly in terms of the reigns of Solomon and the Southern Kingdom of Judah. Most scholars think that Kings came first.[5] This commentary will point out places where the Chronicler includes significant information omitted from Kings (e.g., Hezekiah's Passover: 2 Chr 30; Manasseh's repentance: 2 Chr 33:12–19).

Kings, Kingdoms, and Confusion

Kings is about kings, which sounds straightforward until you begin reading and discover it can be confusing. Unlike the book of Samuel, which covers

4. See also Mark A. Leuchter and David T. Lamb, *The Historical Writings: Introducing Israel's Historical Literature* (Minneapolis: Fortress, 2016).

5. See H. G. M. Williamson, *1 and 2 Chronicles*, NCBC (Grand Rapids: Eerdmans, 1982), 19.

only about a hundred years, the book of Kings spans more than four centuries. Samuel narrates the reigns of only two rulers (Saul and David), but Kings records the reigns of forty: two from the united monarchy (David and Solomon) and nineteen each from the Southern Kingdom of Judah and from the Northern Kingdom of Israel. Some of the names are familiar (David, Solomon, and Ahab), others less familiar (Abijam, Ahaziah, Azariah, Zimri, Zechariah, and Zedekiah). Five pairs of rulers have the same name (Jeroboam, Ahaziah, Jehoram, Jehoash, and Jehoahaz). Five sets of rulers have similar names (Amaziah and Azariah; Zimri and Omri; Pekahiah and Pekah; Jehoiakim and Jehoiachin; Ahab, Ahaz, and Ahaziah). The names of two rulers are changed (Eliakim to Jehoiakim; Mattaniah to Zedekiah; 2 Kgs 23:34; 24:17). Several rulers' names are shortened (Jehoash to Joash; Jehoahaz to Joahaz). In the prophetic narratives, the text often does not provide the ruler's name, merely calling him "the king of Israel" (e.g., 1 Kgs 20:28, 31, 32). It's confusing even for biblical scholars. The book begins with a single kingdom (under David and Solomon) that gets divided into two kingdoms (under Rehoboam and Jeroboam). Then the northern one gets exiled (under Hoshea), so there is one kingdom again, the southern one, which is then also exiled (under Jehoiachin and Zedekiah). During the divided monarchy the text switches back and forth from the Northern Kingdom to the Southern Kingdom.

While it may be tempting to ignore this confusing book, this commentary will help you understand it and profit from it since all Scripture is inspired. To make sense of this confusion, this commentary will refer to rulers by the names used by the NIV and will clarify rulers with similar or identical names by consistently including which kingdom they ruled over (Israel or Judah). The two Jeroboams of Israel will be distinguished by Roman numerals; the founder of the northern dynasty will be called Jeroboam I (1 Kgs 12–14), and the son of Joash will be called Jeroboam II (2 Kgs 14:25–29). The term "united monarchy" will refer to the kingdom that included all twelve tribes during the reigns of Saul, David, and Solomon. The term "divided monarchy" will refer to the period when Jeroboam I split off with the northern tribes to form the kingdom called Israel while Rehoboam held onto to the Southern Kingdom of Judah. This period continued until the Assyrian exile of the Northern Kingdom (2 Kgs 17:6), which began the period called "Judah alone" (2 Kgs 18–25), since the Northern Kingdom no longer existed. During this final section of the book, the name "Israel" can refer to the united monarchy of Solomon (2 Kgs 24:13), the Northern Kingdom (e.g., 2 Kgs 18:1; 21:3), or the people of God (2 Kgs 19:15, 20).

Literary Issues

Composition, Sources, and Royal Annals

According to the Talmud, Kings was written by Jeremiah,[6] but most scholars do not follow this conclusion. In terms of writing style, Kings has more in common with Deuteronomy than Jeremiah, and Kings itself mentions no author. The compositional process for Kings was probably complicated, with multiple authors, editors, scribes, and even possibly scribal schools. A variety of terms have been used for these individuals, many of whom may have been involved in various levels of Deuteronomistic redaction (Dtr, Dtr1, Dtr2, etc.; see "Deuteronomistic Redaction" below), but since these terms are confusing and scholarly opinion shifts over terms, I will merely speak of the "author" of the book.

An early step in the composition process must have involved the scribes who recorded the royal annals that are mentioned thirty-three times in the book. The consistent references to these royal annals serve to give authority to the historicity of Kings. Cogan observes that these sources "bear a certain similarity to the bibliographic footnotes one often finds in modern works."[7]

Three official historical sources are mentioned in Kings. First, the annals of Solomon are distinct since they are mentioned only once (1 Kgs 11:41) and focus on only one ruler. This Solomonic source must have contained extensive details about his reign since his narrative is far longer than that of any other ruler in the book (1 Kgs 1–11). Second, the annals of the kings of Israel are referenced seventeen times (e.g., 1 Kgs 14:19; 15:31; 16:5). The narratives of only two of the nineteen northern rulers have no reference to these annals (Jehoram and Hoshea). Third, the annals of the kings of Judah appear fifteen times in Kings (e.g., 1 Kgs 14:29; 15:23; 22:45). The narratives of only four southern rulers do not include a reference to these annals (Ahaziah, Jehoahaz, Jehoiachin and Zedekiah). We do not know who composed these annals, but we assume it was individuals like Shaphan, the royal secretary who played a key role in finding the book of the law (2 Kgs 22:3–12). These references are typically embedded in a rhetorical question: "As for the other events of Solomon's reign . . . are they not written in the book of the annals of Solomon?" (1 Kgs 11:41).

6. y. B. Bat. 14b–15a.

7. Mordechai Cogan, *I Kings*, AB 10 (New York: Doubleday, 2001), 90.

How were the annals of Kings used? Since the text mentions these annals so often, we can assume they were available to the author and, potentially, to readers. The author of Kings would have needed these royal records to write the book, particularly for the details of the regnal formulas (e.g., age at ascension, regnal years, synchronisms, names of parents) since the book narrates the over-four-hundred-year history of the monarchy, from the end of David's reign to the restoration of Jehoiachin.

The Persian annals of Ahasuerus included not merely regnal information but also narratives like the assassination plot against Ahasuerus uncovered by Mordecai (Esth 2:23; 6:1–2). The northern and southern annals may have included similar narrative material. The annals reference often lists other information, such as the might (*geburah*) of the king (1 Kgs 15:23; 16:5, 27; 22:45; 2 Kgs 10:34; 13:8, 12; 14:15, 28; 20:20), conspiracies committed (1 Kgs 16:20; 2 Kgs 15:15), sins committed (2 Kgs 21:17), wars fought (1 Kgs 14:19, 22:45; 2 Kgs 13:12), borders expanded (2 Kgs 14:28), an ivory house built (1 Kgs 22:39), cities built (1 Kgs 15:23; 22:39), and a pool and conduit built to bring water into the city (2 Kgs 20:20).

In addition to royal annals, scholars think other sources may have been used in the composition process of Kings. The so-called succession narrative is thought to be the source for 2 Samuel 9–20 and 1 Kings 1–2, since the material narrates how Solomon's older brothers (Amnon, Absalom, and Adonijah) proved unworthy to succeed David, their famous father, thus explaining why Solomon, the younger son, was chosen.[8] However, the theory of a Succession Narrative is undermined by several observations. The connections from 1 Kings 1–2 going forward to the rest of 1 and 2 Kings are much stronger than those going back to 2 Samuel. Solomon is barely mentioned in 2 Samuel (12:24–25), but he dominates the narrative of 1 Kings 1–11 (mentioned over 150 times).

Scholars also speculate that the author of Kings may have used a prophetic narrative source since prophets play a major role, particularly in the middle period of the divided monarchy (e.g., Elijah, Elisha; see also "Prophetic Narratives" below).[9] While it is difficult to be definitive, it is likely that the composition of the book of Kings was finished during the period of the exile, perhaps shortly after Jehoiachin's release from prison in Babylon (2 Kgs 25:27–30). Thus, Kings would answer the question of why God's people ended up in exile.

---

8. Leonard Rost wrote the classic work on the Succession Narrative, *The Succession to the Throne of David* (1926; repr. Sheffield: Almond, 1982).

9. See G. H. Jones, *1 and 2 Kings*, NCBC, 2 vols. (Grand Rapids: Eerdmans, 1984), 1:64–76.

Deuteronomistic Redaction

Much of the scholarly research on the book of Kings focuses on the question of how these and other sources were edited, or "redacted," into the form found in the book.

Language and themes from the book of Deuteronomy appear to have been added to the earlier source material, often in the contexts of speeches (e.g., 1 Kgs 2:1–4; 9:3–9). Scholars call this process Deuteronomistic redaction and the four books redacted (Joshua, Judges, Samuel, and Kings) the Deuteronomistic History.[10] These redactors highlighted crucial themes and important information to their perspective and omitted material from their sources they deemed less interesting, relevant, or supportive of their perspective.

The regnal formulas of the book of Kings will be discussed in the next two sections, but here we will look at their Deuteronomistic features and terminology. Two features of the regnal formula, the evaluation and the explanation, are commonly considered Deuteronomistic by scholars. Individuals in Deuteronomy are often described as doing evil or good in "the eyes of the Lord" (Deut 4:25; 12:25, 28; 17:2; 21:9; 24:4), and in Kings almost all Israelite and Judean rulers are evaluated as doing "evil" (*ra'*; e.g., 1 Kgs 15:26, 34; 22:52) or "good" (*yashar*; e.g., 1 Kgs 22:43; 2 Kgs 14:3) in the eyes of YHWH. The text provides a brief Deuteronomistic explanation for these evaluations. These explanations typically focus on crucial themes from the book of Deuteronomy, such as idolatry or devotion to YHWH (Deut 4:15–25; 5:8; 7:5; 9:12–16). Another common feature between Deuteronomy and Kings is a description of individuals pursuing YHWH with "all their heart" (e.g., Deut 4:29; 6:5; 10:12; 1 Kgs 2:4; 8:48; 9:4).

Scholars typically perceive that the redaction of these books may have occurred at different points in history with distinct layers of Deuteronomistic redaction, possibly focusing on specific rulers—Solomon, Hezekiah, or Josiah. Martin Noth, who was working in Germany during World War II, originally formulated the theory of one Deuteronomistic redactor writing during the period of the Babylonian exile.[11] The theory of a double redaction was theorized by Frank Cross and one of his students, Richard Nelson, who argued that the initial Deuteronomistic redactor (Dtr1) worked during Josiah's reign in the

10. For more on Deuteronomistic Redaction, see Lamb, *Righteous Jehu and his Evil Heirs: The Deuteronomists Negative Perspective on Dynastic Succession*, OTM (Oxford: Oxford University Press, 2007), 2–8.

11. Martin Noth, *The Deuteronomistic History* (1957; repr. Sheffield: Sheffield Academic Press, 1987).

late seventh century BC.[12] This redactor had a favorable view of the monarchy, but, according to Cross and Nelson, this redactor was followed by a second Deuteronomist (Dtr2) whose anti-monarchical view was shaped by the tragedy of the Babylonian exile. While the "double redaction" theory gained many scholarly supporters in the United States, in Europe the theory of a "triple redaction" developed by Rudolf Smend and two of his students (Timo Veijola and Walter Dietrich) was more popular.[13] According to the triple redaction theory, the first layer of Deuteronomistic redaction was primarily historical (DtrH), and this was followed by a nomistic (DtrN; *nomos* is Greek for law) redactor concerned with the law, and finally a prophetic redactor (DtrP). The tendency for layers of redaction to multiply has led to more alternative theories involving Deuteronomistic schools that may have worked before, during, and after the exile. The complexities of these theories and the rather subjective nature of attempting to discern multiple layers of Deuteronomistic redaction from source material has led to a lack of scholarly consensus on this issue. While the presence of Deuteronomistic language and themes in Kings (and Joshua, Judges, and Samuel) is undeniable, it is unlikely that agreement will be reached. In this commentary I will avoid speaking of Deuteronomistic redactors and merely talk about the author.

If thinking about how the books of Kings may have been composed or edited makes you nervous, that it somehow compromises the divine authority of Scripture, remember that God can inspire humans to write his word in a variety of ways, using scribes, authors, editors, and redactors. Anyone who teaches Scripture does something similar, ignoring or highlighting a verse, paragraph, or chapter depending upon how it fits or does not fit into the teacher's designated main point.

Israelite Regnal Formulas

The regnal formulas of Kings are one of the distinguishing features of the book.[14] While some readers may find them boring, regnal formulas provide

12. Frank Moore Cross, *Canaanite Myth and Hebrew Epic: Essays in the History of the Religion of Israel* (Cambridge: Harvard University Press, 1973), 274–89; Richard D. Nelson, *The Double Redaction of the Deuteronomistic History* (Sheffield: JSOT Press, 1981).

13. Rudolf Smend, "The Law and the Nations: A Contribution to Deuteronomistic Tradition History" in *Reconsidering Israel and Judah: Recent Studies on the Deuteronomistic History* (Winona Lake: Eisenbrauns, 2000), 95–110; Timo Veijola, *Die ewige Dynastie: David und die Entstehung seiner Dynastie nach der deuteronomistischen Darstellung* (Helsinki: Suomalainen Tiedeakatemia, 1975); Walter Dietrich, "Martin Noth and the Future of the Deuteronomistic History" in *The History of Israel's Traditions: The Heritage of Marth Noth*, edited by Steven L. McKenzie and M. Patrick Graham (Sheffield: Sheffield Academic Press, 1994), 153–75.

14. For a discussion of Northern regnal formulas, see Lamb, *Righteous Jehu*, 17–22.

invaluable information about the history of the monarchy. Detailed information regarding the rule and reign of each ruler is recorded in a formulaic manner, more typical of an article from an encyclopedia. The book of Kings contains thirty-eight regnal formulas, nineteen for the Northern Kingdom and nineteen for the Southern Kingdom. The formulas for northern and southern rulers are similar, but each has distinctive features. Table 1 displays the seven primary features of a regnal formula for a sample Israelite ruler, Jehoahaz, son of Jehu.

Table 1: An Israelite Regnal Formula Example[15]

#	**Elements**	**Jehoahaz of Israel (2 Kgs 13:1–2, 8–9)**
1	Judean synchronism	In the twenty-third year of Joash the son of Ahaziah, king of Judah,
2	Father's name	Jehoahaz the son of Jehu
3	Reign length	became king over Israel in Samaria, and he reigned seventeen years.
4	Evaluation	He did evil in the eyes of the LORD
5	Explanation	by following the sins of Jeroboam . . . he did not turn away from them.
	Narrative material	*Aram oppressed Israel, Jehoahaz cried out for help . . .* (2 Kgs 13:3–7)
6	Annals reference	As for the other events of the reign of Jehoahaz . . . are they not written in the book of the annals of the kings of Israel?
7	Death notice	Jehoahaz rested with his ancestors and was buried in Samaria. And Jehoash his son succeeded him as king.

Table 2 records the pattern of these seven elements for the nineteen Israelite rulers.[16]

15. A version of this table appeared in Lamb, *Righteous Jehu*, 18, and in Leuchter and Lamb, *Historical Books*, 266.

16. Two rulers who reigned in unusual circumstances and lack a regnal formula, Tibni of Israel (1 Kgs 16:21–22) and Athaliah of Judah (2 Kgs 11:1–20), are omitted from this table.

Table 2: Israelite Regnal Formulas[17]

#	Ruler	Reference[18]	Judean Synchronism	Father	Reign Length	Evaluation	Explan-ation	Annals Reference	Death Notice
1	Jeroboam I	1 Kgs 14:20		X	22 years	Evil	X	X	X
2	Nadab	1 Kgs 15:25	2nd year of Asa	X	2 years	Evil	X	X	
3	Baasha	1 Kgs15:33	3rd year of Asa	X	24 years	Evil	X	X	X
4	Elah	1 Kgs 16:8	26th year of Asa	X	2 years			X	
5	Zimri	1 Kgs 16:15	27th year of Asa		7 days	Evil	X	X	
6	Omri	1 Kgs 16:23	31st year of Asa		12 years	Evil	X	X	X
7	Ahab	1 Kgs 16:29	38th year of Asa	X	22 years	Evil	X	X	X
8	Ahaziah	1 Kgs 22:51	17th year of Jehoshaphat	X	2 years	Evil	X	X	X
9	Jehoram	2 Kgs 3:1	18th year of Jehoshaphat	X	12 years	Evil	X		
10	Jehu	2 Kgs 10:36		X	28 years	Right	X	X	X
11	Jehoahaz	2 Kgs 13:1	23rd year of Joash	X	17 years	Evil	X	X	X

#	Ruler	Reference[18]	Judean Synchronism	Father	Reign Length	Evaluation	Explan-ation	Annals Reference	Death Notice
12	Jehoash	2 Kgs 13:10	37th year of Joash	X	16 years	Evil	X	X	X
13	Jeroboam II	2 Kgs 14:23	15th year of Amaziah	X	41 years	Evil	X	X	X
14	Zechariah	2 Kgs 15:8	38th year of Azariah	X	6 months	Evil	X	X	
15	Shallum	2 Kgs 15:13	39th year of Azariah[19]	X	1 month			X	
16	Menahem	2 Kgs 15:17	39th year of Azariah	X	10 years	Evil	X	X	X
17	Pekahiah	2 Kgs 15:23	50th year of Azariah	X	2 years	Evil	X	X	
18	Pekah	2 Kgs 15:27	52nd year of Azariah	X	20 years	Evil	X	X	
19	Hoshea	2 Kgs 17:1	12th year of Ahaz	X	9 years	Evil			
	Totals		**17/19**	**17/19**	**19/19**	**17/19**	**16/19**	**17/19**	**10/19**

17. A version of this table appeared in Lamb, *Righteous Jehu*, 20, and in Leuchter and Lamb, *Historical Books*, 362–63.
18. This reference is to the king's regnal years, typically included at the beginning of the narrative.
19. The MT here has Uzziah, which is another name of Azariah.

The seven elements of a northern formula are typically divided into an initial section with five elements and a concluding section with two. The *Synchronism* usually begins the Israelite ruler's narrative, and it dates the beginning of the reign relative to the number of years that the Judean ruler has already been on the throne (e.g., "2nd Asa" means Nadab came to power in the second year of Asa's reign). All northern rulers except Jeroboam I and Jehu receive a synchronism. Next the text records the *Father's name*, which was used in ancient times to identify an individual, comparable to how a last or family name is used today. The fathers' names of only two rulers (Zimri and Omri) are absent from their regnal formulas. The *Reign length* is recorded for all Israelite kings: in years for sixteen, months for two (Zechariah and Shallum), and days for one (Zimri). Reign length is the only element to appear in all formulas, for both Israel and Judah. The *Evaluation* is then included, as either righteous or evil in the eyes of YHWH. Theologically speaking, the evaluation is the primary focus of the regnal formula. Unfortunately for Israel, sixteen of its rulers were evil. Two northern rulers have no evaluation (Elah and Shallum) and one, Jehu, is deemed as righteous. To justify the evaluation, the *Explanation* is given next, as seventeen Israelite rulers continue in the sins of Jeroboam I, specifically not removing the idolatrous golden calves he set up at Bethel in the south and Dan in the north (1 Kgs 12:25–33). Rulers are condemned for either walking in the sins of Jeroboam (e.g., 1 Kgs 15:26, 34) or not departing from his sins (e.g., 2 Kgs 3:3; 10:31). After the explanation, *Narrative material* is usually included concerning their reign, in a less formulaic manner. The final two elements of the regnal formula typically appear at the end of the ruler's narrative. The *Annals reference* suggests that information not recorded in the book of Kings is available in the northern annals. The final element, the *Death notice*, describes the king's burial and successor. The ten Israelite rulers who are succeeded by an heir all receive a death notice, but those who end their reigns in exile or by execution receive none.

Judean Regnal Formulas

Regnal formulas for Judah are similar to those of their northern neighbors with a few exceptions. Table 3 displays the pattern from one Judean ruler (Joash) listing the nine elements.

Table 4 shows the pattern of the regnal formulas for the nineteen Judean rulers.

Table 3: A Judean Regnal Formula Example[20]

#	Elements	Joash of Judah (2 Kgs 11:21–12:3, 19–21)
1	Synchronism	In the seventh year of Jehu, Joash became king,
2	Accession age	Joash was seven years old when he began to reign.
3	Reign length	and he reigned in Jerusalem forty years.
4	Mother's name	His mother's name was Zibiah; she was from Beersheba.
5	Evaluation	Joash did what was right in the eyes of the LORD
6	Explanation	All the years Jehoiada the priest instructed him.
7	High places	The high places, however, were not removed.
	Narrative material	*He repaired the temple . . .*
8	Annals reference	As for the other events of the reign of Joash . . . are they not written in the book of the annals of the kings of Judah?
9	Death notice	He died and was buried with his ancestors in the City of David. And Amaziah his son succeeded him as king.

Judean regnal formulas typically include nine elements, six of which appear in those of Israel: synchronism, reign length, evaluation, explanation, royal annals, and death notice. The *Synchronism* is from the Judean perspective, so southern rulers' reigns are dated from the current northern ruler ("18th Jeroboam" means Abijam came to power in the eighteenth year of the reign of Jeroboam). The eleven Judean rulers who come to power during the divided monarchy all have synchronisms, but none after Hezekiah need them since the Northern Kingdom has been exiled by Assyria. *Reign length* is recorded for all nineteen southern rulers, and they all receive an *Evaluation*. Eleven are deemed evil and eight deemed righteous. But only two of the righteous are evaluated as totally righteous, with no qualification (Hezekiah and Josiah). The text records an *Annals reference* and a *Death notice* for fifteen Judean rulers, the same group of four rulers are missing both (Ahaziah, Jehoahaz, Jehoiachin, and Zedekiah).

20. A version of this table appeared in Leuchter and Lamb, *Historical Books*, 269.

Table 4: Judean Regnal Formulas[21]

#	Ruler	Reference	Israelite Synchronism	Age	Reign Length	Mother	Evaluation	Explanation Comparison[22]	High Places	Annals Reference	Death Notice
1	Rehoboam	1 Kgs 14:21		41	17 years	X	Evil[23]		X	X	X
2	Abijam	1 Kgs 15:3	18th year of Jeroboam		3 years	X	Evil[24]	Not David		X	X
3	Asa	1 Kgs 15:10	20th year of Jeroboam		41 years	X	Right	David	X	X	X
4	Jehosh-aphat	1 Kgs 22:42	4th year of Ahab	25	25 years	X	Right	Asa	X	X	X
5	Jehoram	2 Kgs 8:16	5th year of Joram	32	8 years		Evil	Ahab		X	X
6	Ahaziah	2 Kgs 8:26	12th year of Joram[25]	22	1 year	X	Evil	Ahab			
7	Jehoash	2 Kgs 12:1	7th year of Jehu	7	40 years	X	Right	Priest	X	X	X
8	Amaziah	2 Kgs 14:2	2nd year of Joash	25	29 years	X	Right	Not David	X	X	X
9	Azariah	2 Kgs 15:2	27th year of Jeroboam	16	52 years	X	Right	Amaziah	X	X	X

10	Jotham	2 Kgs 15:33	2nd year of Pekah	25	16 years	X	Right	Uzziah	X	X	X
11	Ahaz	2 Kgs 16:2	17th year of Pekah	20	16 years		Evil	Not David	X	X	X
12	Hezekiah	2 Kgs 18:2	3rd year of Hoshea	25	29 years	X	Right	David		X	X
13	Manasseh	2 Kgs 21:1		12	55 years	X	Evil	Nations	X	X	X
14	Amon	2 Kgs 21:19		22	2 years	X	Evil	Manasseh		X	X
15	Josiah	2 Kgs 22:1		8	31 years	X	Right	David		X	X
16	Jehoahaz	2 Kgs 23:31		23	3 months	X	Evil	Fathers			
17	Jehoiakim	2 Kgs 23:36		25	11 years	X	Evil	Fathers		X	X
18	Jehoiachin	2 Kgs 24:8		18	3 months	X	Evil	Father			
19	Zedekiah	2 Kgs 24:18		21	11 years	X	Evil	Jehoiakim			
	Total		**11/19**	**17**	**19/19**	**17/19**	**19/19**	**19/19**	**9/19**	**15/19**	**15/19**

21. A version of this table appeared in Leuchter and Lamb, *Historical Books*, 364–65.
22. These comparisons vary greatly, so for simplicity only a name or a title is listed in this row.
23. Rehoboam is not evaluated as evil, but during his reign Judah did evil in the eyes of YHWH (1 Kgs 14:22).
24. Abijam is not evaluated as evil, but he committed all the sins of his father (1 Kgs 15:3).
25. Ahaziah of Judah has two synchronisms that don't agree (see 2 Kgs 8:25; 9:29).

Most of the shared elements are similar for the north and the south, but the explanations are different. Israelite rulers are compared to Jeroboam I, but Judean rulers are compared to a variety of people: thirteen to their father or fathers (Abijam, Asa, Jehoshaphat, Amaziah, Azariah, Jotham, Ahaz, Hezekiah, Amon, Josiah, Jehoahaz, Jehoiakim, and Jehoiachin), six to David (Abijam, Asa, Amaziah, Ahaz, Hezekiah, and Josiah), two to the kings of Israel (Jehoram and Ahaz), and six to other individuals, three good rulers (Asa, Amaziah, and Uzziah [= Azariah]) and three bad ones (Ahab, Manasseh, and Jehoiakim). Depending upon who is being referenced, the associations could be positive, but most are negative.

Southern regnal formulas include three distinct elements from the northern ones. The *Mother's name* is recorded instead of the father's, since all nineteen Judean rulers are descendants of David; their father was the previous ruler. The names of two Judean rulers' mothers are not recorded (Jehoram and Ahaz). The *Accession age* states when a ruler took the throne. This number is included for seventeen rulers (except Abijam and Asa). The most likely source for this number was the Judean royal annals. By adding the reign length and the accession age, one can easily calculate how old Judean rulers were at death (e.g., for Rehoboam, 41 + 17 = 58). Nine Judean rulers are associated with the *High places* (*bamot*), which may sound innocuous but were actually locations of idolatrous worship; they were viewed as negatively for Judah as Jeroboam's golden calves were for Israel. Of these nine rulers, three were evil (Rehoboam, Ahaz, and Manasseh), but shockingly six were righteous (Asa, Jehoshaphat, Jehoash, Amaziah, Azariah, and Jotham), explaining their qualified righteous evaluation. During his reign, Solomon added high places to the land, and his son Rehoboam added more (1 Kgs 3:3; 11:7; 14:23). These idolatrous worship locations survived for much of the divided monarchy until they were destroyed by Hezekiah (2 Kgs 18:4). Hezekiah's son Manasseh rebuilt them (2 Kgs 21:3), but then Manasseh's grandson Josiah destroyed them again (2 Kgs 23:8, 15); they were never rebuilt.

Why were regnal formulas included in Kings? We can't be sure, but they serve to give structure to a long narrative recording the reigns of forty rulers spanning over four hundred years. The regnal formulas are a source of basic information—not just for important rulers with long narratives (e.g., Solomon, Jehu, Hezekiah, and Josiah) but also for minor rulers with short narratives (e.g., Nadab, Amon, and Pekahiah).

Prophetic Narratives

The book of Kings is not merely about Kings, but, as the conclusion of the Former Prophets, it is, not surprisingly, also about prophets. Prophets appear rarely in Joshua and Judges (Josh 14:6; Judg 4:4; 6:8; 13:6, 8). In Samuel they begin to play a major role (e.g., Samuel and Nathan). In Kings, however, they dominate long sections of the text and serve as the heroes of the story. Most kings do evil in the eyes of YHWH, but most prophets speak and act for YHWH.

The book of Kings has more occurrences of terms associated with prophets than any other Old Testament book. Kings mentions forms of the word "prophet" (*nabi'*) eighty-four times (only the book of Jeremiah has more). The phrase "man of God" (*ish (ha)'elohim*) is used synonymously with prophets in the Hebrew Bible, and forms of this phrase appear over fifty-one times in Kings (far more than any other Old Testament book). The other prophetic term is "seer" (*hozeh*), which only appears once in Kings (2 Kgs 17:13).

Table 5 displays all prophetic individuals or groups in Kings, listing the reference, how they are identified, and which ruler they ministered under (personal names are bolded).

Table 5: Prophetic Figures in the Book of Kings[26]

Reference	Prophetic Individuals and Groups	Ruler
1 Kgs 11:29; 14:2, 18	**Ahijah**, prophet	Solomon, Jeroboam
1 Kgs 12:22	**Shemaiah**, man of God	Rehoboam
1 Kgs 13:1, 4; 2 Kgs 23:17, 18	Anonymous man of God from Judah	Jeroboam
1 Kgs 13:11, 18	Anonymous prophet from Bethel	Jeroboam
1 Kgs 16:1, 7, 12	**Jehu** son of Hanani, prophet	Baasha
1 Kgs 17:18; 18:22; 19:16; 2 Kgs 1:9	**Elijah**, prophet, man of God	Ahab, Ahaziah
1 Kgs 18:4, 13; 19:10,14; 2 Kgs 9:7	Prophets killed by Jezebel	Ahab
1 Kgs 18:4, 13	100 prophets saved by Obadiah	Ahab

(continued)

26. A version of this table appeared in Leuchter and Lamb, *Historical Books*, 273–75.

Reference	Prophetic Individuals and Groups	Ruler
1 Kgs 18:19, 20, 22, 40; 19:1	450 prophets of Baal	Ahab
1 Kgs 18:19, 20	400 prophets of Asherah	Ahab
1 Kgs 19:16; 2 Kgs 2:13; 3:11; 4:9; 5:3, 8, 13; 6:12; 8:7; 9:1; 13:19	**Elisha**, prophet, man of God	Ahab, Jehoshaphat, Jehu, Jehoash
1 Kgs 20:13, 22	Anonymous prophet	Ahab
1 Kgs 20:28	Anonymous man of God	Ahab
1 Kgs 20:35, 38, 41	Anonymous prophet	Ahab
1 Kgs 22:6, 10, 12, 22	400 prophets of YHWH	Ahab, Jehoshaphat
1 Kgs 22:7, 8	**Micaiah**, prophet	Ahab, Jehoshaphat
2 Kgs 2:3, 5, 7; 4:1, 38; 5:22; 6:1; 9:1	The company of the prophets	
2 Kgs 2:7	50 of the company of the prophets	
2 Kgs 3:13	Prophets of the king's parents	Jehoram
2 Kgs 9:1	Anonymous young prophet	Jehoram / Jehu
2 Kgs 10:19	Baal prophets killed by Jehu	Jehu
2 Kgs 14:25	**Jonah** ben Amittai	Jeroboam II
2 Kgs 17:13, 23	Prophets, seers warned Northern Kingdom, Southern Kingdom	
2 Kgs 19:2; 20:1, 11, 14	**Isaiah**	Hezekiah
2 Kgs 21:10 (cf. 24:2)	Prophets, servants of YHWH	Manasseh
2 Kgs 22:14	**Huldah**	Josiah
2 Kgs 23:2	Prophets	Josiah
2 Kgs 24:2 (cf. 21:10)	Prophets, servants of YHWH	Jehoiakim

The book of Kings mentions six anonymous prophets, and it includes names for ten individual prophets (Nathan, Ahijah, Shimaiah, Jehu son of Hanani, Elijah, Elisha, Micaiah, Jonah, Isaiah, and Huldah). Elisha has far more references in the text than any other prophet, including Elijah. After Solomon, Elisha is the most significant character in the book. His narrative dominates a major section of the text (1 Kgs 19:16–21; 2 Kgs 2:1–8:15; 9:1–3; 13:14–21), and his enduring ministry spans the reigns of six Israelite kings (Ahab, Ahaziah, Jehoram, Jehu, Jehoahaz, and Jehoash).

The book also refers to large groups of prophets: usually the good ones are connected with Elijah and Elisha and the bad ones with Ahab and Jezebel. Ahab's servant Obadiah saved a group of a hundred prophets (1 Kgs 18:4) from what was presumably a much larger group. On Mount Carmel the prophet Elijah confronted 400 prophets of Asherah and 450 prophets of Baal before slaughtering them (1 Kgs 18:19). Micaiah contradicted four hundred prophets of YHWH who had given false predictions of success, luring Ahab into battle against Aram where he died as Micaiah had predicted (1 Kgs 22:6). Elisha has several interactions with a prophetic company over the course of his ministry (2 Kgs 2:3, 5, 7; 4:1, 38; 5:22; 6:1; 9:1). At the end of his violent coup, Jehu slaughters a group of Baal prophets (2 Kgs 10:19, 25, 28). Anonymous groups of prophets both hear Josiah read the book of the covenant and speak judgment against the nation of Judah shortly before the exile (2 Kgs 21:10; 24:2). The numbers for these groups are probably estimates and may overlap, but if the numbers are merely added up, the book mentions over fourteen hundred prophets (1416 exactly, not counting generic prophetic groups: 2 Kgs 21:10, 23:2; 24:2).[27]

During the divided monarchy there is a surprising lack of prophetic activity in Judah. No prophets are recorded as ministering in Judah between the reigns of Rehoboam and Hezekiah. Jehoshaphat is the only southern ruler associated with prophets during this time, and his involvement is only in conjunction with northern rulers. However, the longest section of the book with no reference to prophets is in the Solomon narrative, which is almost ten chapters (1 Kgs 1:32–11:29). YHWH primarily speaks to rulers using prophetic mediators (e.g., 1 Kgs 13:2; 16:1; 17:1, but he speaks directly to Solomon on three occasions (1 Kgs 3:11; 6:11; 9:3).

Prophets are primarily spokespersons for YHWH in the book of Kings, delivering messages to rulers and to the people. The text uses two formulaic

27. Sixteen individuals (10 named + 6 anonymous) and 1400 in groups (= 100 + 450 + 400 + 400 + 50).

expressions to indicate the message comes from God. Forms of the phrase "this is what the LORD says" (*koh 'amar yhwh*) appear thirty-three times in Kings (e.g., 1 Kgs 11:31; 12:24; 13:2), far more than the occurrences in the other three books of the Former Prophets combined (11 total; Josh 7:13; 24:2; Judg 6:8; 1 Sam 2:27, 10:18; 15:2; 2 Sam 7:5, 8; 12:7; 11; 24:12). Forms of the phrase "the word of the LORD" (*debar yhwh*) appear forty-eight times in Kings (e.g., 1 Kgs 2:27; 12:24; 13:1), while in the rest of the Former Prophets the phrase only appears twelve times (Josh 8:8, 27; 1 Sam 3:1, 7, 21; 15:10, 23, 26; 2 Sam 7:4; 12:9; 22:31; 24:11). This phrase describes messages delivered directly to non-prophets (e.g., Solomon: 1 Kgs 6:11) and to prophets (1 Kgs 16:1, 7; 17:2, 8; 2 Kgs 20:4), but it appears most frequently in narratives describing a prophetic fulfillment (e.g., 1 Kgs 2:27; 13:5; 15:29; 16:12; 17:16; 2 Kgs 4:44). The recipients of these messages are most often rulers but also include an altar (1 Kgs 13:2), widows (1 Kgs 17:14; 2 Kgs 4:1–7), a foreign general (2 Kgs 5:10), a foreign emperor (2 Kgs 19:20–21), prophets (1 Kgs 13:18, 21; 20:36), and the people (1 Kgs 18:21–22; 2 Kgs 17:13).

Prophetic messages can be generally categorized into three types. First, prophets *give counsel* to kings during periods of crisis or warfare (e.g., 1 Kgs 12:24; 21:28–29). Second, prophets *make predictions* that involve the following: life and death (e.g., 2 Kgs 1:16; 7:2–20), drought and rain (1 Kgs 17:1; 18:41), defeat and victory (e.g., 1 Kgs 20:13, 28; 22:6, 17), and national deliverance or national destruction (e.g., 2 Kgs 17:23; 20:16–18; 21:10–16). Third, prophets *deliver judgments* targeting a variety of sins, including idolatry (e.g., 1 Kgs 11:33; 13:2; 14:9; 18:18), disobedience (1 Kgs 11:33; 18:18; 2 Kgs 17:13), injustice (1 Kgs 21:19–24), greed (2 Kgs 5:26–27), and bloodshed (2 Kgs 21:16; 24:4).

Kings are the individuals most directly affected by the divine messages delivered by prophets. Prophets often serve as catalysts both to remove and install new rulers on the throne, just as Samuel did with Saul and David. Nathan stopped Adonijah's rebellion and established David's son Solomon as his successor (1 Kgs 1:11–45). Ahijah split the united monarchy, taking the northern tribes from Rehoboam and giving them to Jeroboam I (1 Kgs 11:31–35; 14:7–14). The prophet Jehu replaced Nadab the son of Jeroboam with Baasha, then Elah the son of Baasha with Zimri (1 Kgs 16:1–4, 7). Elijah, Elisha, and Elisha's apprentice prophesy the fall of Ahab's dynasty and the establishment of Jehu's dynasty (1 Kgs 21:20–26; 2 Kgs 9:7–10; see also 10:30). Elisha contributes to both the downfall of King Ben-Hadad of Aram and the accession of the usurper Hazael (2 Kgs 8:13).

Two kings were anointed by prophets in Samuel (Saul in 1 Sam 10:1; David in 16:13), and two kings were anointed by prophets in Kings (Solomon in 1 Kgs 1:45; Jehu in 2 Kgs 9:6). Three rulers in Kings receive dynastic promises (Solomon, Jeroboam I, and Jehu). Only one of these three is delivered by a prophet, from Ahijah to Jeroboam I (1 Kgs 11:38); the promises to Solomon and Jehu are recorded without a prophetic mediator (1 Kgs 2:4; 6:12; 8:25; 9:4–5; 2 Kgs 10:30).

Prophets not only condemned and affirmed kings, but they impacted many others in various ways, bringing illness and death as well as healing and life, sometimes at the same time. Prophets wither and heal the hand of Jeroboam I (1 Kgs 13:4–6), heal Naaman the Aramean of leprosy and then pass Naaman's leprosy on to Gehazi (2 Kgs 5:10–14, 27), strike the Aramean army with blindness and then heal them (2 Kgs 6:18, 20), raise young boys from the dead (1 Kgs 17:17–24; 2 Kgs 4:8–37), and kill large numbers of people (1 Kgs 18:40; 2 Kgs 1:10, 12). Prophets also provide water for thirsty soldiers and residents of Jericho (2 Kgs 2:19–22; 3:16–17) and food for starving widows and prophets (1 Kgs 17:14–16; 2 Kgs 4:3–7, 41, 43). Prophets also controlled nature, calling down fire from heaven (1 Kgs 18:36–38; 2 Kgs 1:10, 12), siccing lions and bears on people (1 Kgs 13:21–24; 20:36; 2 Kgs 2:24), parting the Jordan River (2 Kgs 2:14), causing an ax head to float (2 Kgs 6:6–7), and causing the sun's shadow to move backwards (2 Kgs 20:11).

Some of the most popular and familiar sections of the book of Kings are the prophetic narratives that tell engaging stories of how YHWH dramatically works through his prophets. Three long prophetic narratives are distinct from the rest of Kings as they emphasize prophets and de-emphasize kings. These three narratives are set in the Northern Kingdom, focus primarily on one prophet (Ahijah, Elijah, and Elisha), and are set primarily during the reign of one northern ruler (Jeroboam I, Ahab, and Jehoram). The first prophetic narrative is divided into two sections (1 Kgs 11:26–39; 13:1–14:18), recording how Ahijah first supports Jeroboam, then how he and an anonymous man of God condemn Jeroboam and his dynasty. The second narrative records Elijah's clashes with kings (Ahab, Ahaziah) and prophets (Baal, Asherah), and Micaiah's deceptive prophecy (1 Kgs 17:1–2 Kings 2:12). The third records Elisha's dramatic ministry involving kings (Jehoram, Hazael, Jehu, and Jehoash), taunting boys, two women, fiery horses, prophetic groups, an Aramean general, and a reviving corpse (2 Kgs 2:13–8:15; 9:1–3; 13:14–21). Within these three sections, northern rulers are often not identified by name but merely as "the king of Israel" (e.g., 1 Kgs 20:4, 7; 22:2, 3; 2 Kgs 3:4, 9; 5:5, 6; 6:9, 10; 7:6). The context usually clarifies which king is being referred to, but when the prophets are named (Ahijah, Elijah and Elisha) and the kings are not, the role of the latter is diminished. Scholars speculate that the author of

Kings used prophetic sources for these narratives, but the text never mentions any prophetic records.[28]

Historical Background

The book of Kings is not "historical" as the word is frequently understood today. Historians study what they perceive took place in the past (e.g., alliances, battles, conquests, decrees). History in the modern sense is concerned with religious beliefs, not divine behavior. Historians relegate questions about what God did or said to the realm of theologians and ministers.

God, however, is the focus in the history of Kings. The main character of the book is YHWH, appearing over five hundred times throughout the book, from the beginning (1 Kgs 1:17) to the end (2 Kgs 25:16). The Hebrew word for "God" (*'elohim*) appears over two hundred times (e.g., 1 Kgs 1:17, 30; 2 Kgs 23:16, 17, 21). God may seem passive at times, particularly at the beginning (he is silent until 1 Kgs 3:5) and at the end while Jerusalem is destroyed (2 Kgs 25), but he is constantly working—speaking through prophets, empowering miracles, judging and blessing rulers, and controlling nations and emperors. Despite its theocentric orientation, the book of Kings still qualifies as a legitimate source for the history of ancient Israel and Judah.

The Three Surrounding Empires: Egypt, Assyria, and Babylon

To understand the historical context of the book, we will begin by examining how Israel and Judah relate to their neighboring nations during this period. We will discuss these nations in two categories, beginning with the three surrounding empires (Egypt, Assyria, and Babylon) and then the smaller neighboring countries (Ammon, Aram, Edom, Moab, Philistia, and Phoenicia).

Egypt plays a significant role in Kings, particularly at the beginning and end of the book, alternating between serving as an ally and an enemy for Israel or Judah. By marrying Pharaoh's daughter, Solomon cemented an alliance with Egypt (1 Kgs 3:1), and Pharaoh presented the Canaanite city of Gezer as a dowry to his daughter (1 Kgs 9:16). Despite the prohibition against royal equine acquisitions (Deut 17:16), Solomon imported many horses from Egypt (1 Kgs 10:28–29). King Shishak of Egypt offered sanctuary to Jeroboam I when he fled from Solomon (1 Kgs 11:40).[29] Shishak ended his alliance with Solomon by attacking his son, Rehoboam, and plundering the temple (1 Kgs

28. See Donald J. Wiseman, *1 & 2 Kings: An Introduction and Commentary*, TOTC (Downers Grove, IL: InterVarsity Press, 1993), 44–46; Cogan, *I Kings*, 92–94; Jones, *1 and 2 Kings*, 1:64–77.

29. In Egyptian sources he is called Shoshenq I.

14:25). During most of the period of the divided monarchy, Egypt ceased to play an active role as they were ruled by a series of weaker rulers. Shortly before Assyria conquered the Northern Kingdom, Hoshea asked for assistance from King So of Egypt (2 Kgs 17:4), but the text records no Egyptian response. Egypt finally reemerged as an active player when Pharaoh Necho of Egypt killed Josiah at Megiddo and then deposed Josiah's son, Jehoahaz, replacing him with his own brother, Eliakim, whom he renamed Jehoiakim (2 Kgs 23:29–35). In 605 BC at Carchemish, Nebuchadnezzar of Babylon defeated the combined forces of Egypt (led by Necho) and Assyria.

Assyria does not appear in the book of Kings until late in the history of the Northern Kingdom, during the reign of Menahem (2 Kgs 15:19). The Neo-Assyrian Empire was dominant in the region early in the divided monarchy (883–783 BC) and at the end of the Northern Kingdom (744–612 BC) and relatively weak in the middle of this period. At the battle of Qarqar (853 BC), Shalmaneser III of Assyria (858–824 BC) encountered a coalition of rulers that included Ahab of Israel. The Bible never mentions this battle, but one of Shalmaneser's inscriptions, the Kurkh Monolith, lists Shalmaneser's opponents, including Ahab.[30] The Black Obelisk, another royal inscription of Shalmaneser, not only mentions Jehu of Israel but also includes an image of him delivering his tribute to the ruler.[31] Ahab's reference on the Kurkh Monolith is the oldest inscription to mention an Israelite ruler (dated 852 BC), and Jehu's image on the Black Obelisk is the oldest pictorial representation of a biblical character (dated 841 BC).[32] Both of these inscriptions are currently located in the British Museum in London. After a period of Assyrian decline, Tiglath-Pileser III (745–727 BC) reasserted Assyrian dominance in the region. He extracted tribute from Menahem (2 Kgs 15:19), conquered most of Israel under Pekah, and took captives to Assyria (2 Kgs 15:29). Tiglath-Pileser's northern deportation was the first of five exiles of Israel and Judah. King Ahaz of Judah exchanged tribute for assistance from Tiglath-Pileser against Israel and Aram (2 Kgs 16:5–8). The son of Tiglath-Pileser, Shalmaneser V (726–722 BC), made Hoshea of Israel his vassal, but when Hoshea stopped giving tribute, the Assyrian besieged Samaria, the northern capital (2 Kgs 17:3–5). At some point during this campaign Shalmaneser died, perhaps killed by his brother Sargon II (721–705 BC; see also Isa 20:1), who was his successor and who completed the conquest of Israel and exiled the remainder of the nation (2 Kgs 17:6). Thus ended the Northern Kingdom (722 BC).

30. *COS* 2: 261–64.
31. *COS* 2: 269–70.
32. Four Assyrian inscriptions mention Jehu; see Lamb, *Righteous Jehu*, 124–28.

Sargon's son, Sennacherib (704–681 BC), invaded Judah in 701 BC, captured major cities, forced a tribute from Hezekiah, and besieged Jerusalem (2 Kgs 18:13–18). His messenger, the Rabshakeh, taunted Hezekiah, who refused to surrender, prayed, and sought out Isaiah the prophet (2 Kgs 19:1–19). YHWH retaliated in a trash talking poem and a slaughter of 185,000 Assyrian soldiers. Sennacherib then returned to Nineveh, his capital, where his sons performed regicidal patricide (2 Kgs 19:35–37). At this point the empire of Assyria disappears from the narrative, and the empire of Babylon emerges.

Babylon replaced Assyria as the dominant power in the region. A brief reference mentions some Babylonians (2 Kgs 17:24–30), but Babylon does not appear as a major player until Marduk-Baladan sent a delegation to Hezekiah (2 Kgs 20:12–13). After interrogating the Judean ruler about his naiveté for showing them all his treasures, the prophet Isaiah predicts Babylon will exile Hezekiah's descendants (2 Kgs 20:16–18). After his victory over Egypt and Assyria at Carchemish, Nebuchadnezzar of Babylon forced Jehoiakim of Judah to become his vassal, but Jehoiakim rebelled after three years (2 Kgs 24:1). Nebuchadnezzar then first conquered Jerusalem under Jehoiachin (597 BC), taking many of its citizens back to Babylon, including the king (2 Kgs 24:10–16). Jehoiachin's uncle Zedekiah succeeded him, but, in response to his rebellion, Nebuchadnezzar conquered Jerusalem again (587 BC), destroyed the city and the temple, and deported more residents, including the newly blinded Zedekiah (2 Kgs 24:10–25:21). Kings ends with Jehoiachin still in Babylon but allowed to eat at the table of Nebuchadnezzar's son, King Awel-Marduk (2 Kgs 25:27–30).

More than any other Old Testament book, Kings names many of the rulers of these three foreign empires. Elsewhere in Scripture the king of Egypt is typically anonymous, merely called "Pharaoh" (e.g., Gen 12:15; Exod 1:11; Deut 6:22; 1 Sam 2:27; 1 Chr 4:17; Neh 9:10; Ps 135:9; Isa 19:11; Jer 25:19; Ezek 17:17). With the exception of Nebuchadnezzar, most books of the Old Testament do not include personal names for the rulers of Assyria and Babylon (e.g., Isa 13:1–14:23; Jonah 3:6; Nah 3:18).

Fortunately for historians, Kings breaks this pattern in several instances, mentioning four Egyptian pharaohs by name (Shishak, So, Tirhakah, and Necho). Table 6 lists the five Egyptian rulers mentioned by name in the Old Testament.[33] Only one other pharaoh is named outside of Kings (Hophra in Jer 44:30). Almost half of these references are clustered in the book of Kings (8 of 18 = 44.4 percent).

33. In the Old Testament, the name "Rameses" refers to a location (Gen 47:11; Exod 1:11; 12:37; Num 33:3, 5), not the ruler.

Table 6: Rulers of Egypt Named in the Old Testament[34]

Egyptian Ruler	Ruler's dates (BC)	Kings references (8 total)	Non-Kings references (10 total)
Shishak (= Shoshenq I)	945–924	1 Kgs 11:40; 14:25	2 Chr 12:2, 5, 7, 9
So (= Osorkon IV?)	?	2 Kgs 17:4	
Tirhakah (= Taharqa)	690–664	2 Kgs 19:9	Isa 37:9
Necho	610–595	2 Kgs 23:29, 33, 34, 35	2 Chr 35:20, 22; 36:4; Jer 46:2
Hophra (= Apries)	588–569		Jer 44:30

Unlike much of the rest of Scripture, the book of Kings also provides personal names for rulers from Assyria and Babylon. Kings records the names of four Assyrian rulers (Tiglath-Pileser III, Shalmaneser V, Sennacherib, and Esarhaddon; see Table 7). Only one of the five Assyrian kings mentioned in the Old Testament is not named in Kings (Sargon II). Almost half of these references to named Assyrian rulers appear in Kings (12 of 27 = 44.4 percent).

Table 7: Rulers of Assyria Named in the Old Testament

Assyrian Ruler	Ruler's Dates (BC)	Kings References (12 total)	Non-Kings References (15 total)
Tiglath-Pileser III (also called "Pul")	745–727	2 Kgs 15:19, 20, 29; 16:7, 10	1 Chr 5:6, 26; 2 Chr 28:20
Shalmaneser V	727–721	2 Kgs 17:3; 18:9	
Sargon II	721–705		Isa 20:1
Sennacherib	690–664	2 Kgs 18:13; 19:16, 20, 36	2 Chr 32:1, 2, 9, 10, 22; Isa 36:1, 17, 21, 37.
Esarhaddon	610–595	2 Kgs 19:37	Ezra 4:2; Isa 37:38

34. A version of these next three tables (Rulers of Egypt, Babylon, and Assyria) appeared in Leuchter and Lamb, *Historical Books*, 297–98.

Kings records the names of three Babylonian rulers (Marduk-Baladan, Nebuchadnezzar, and Awel-Marduk; see Table 8). No other Babylonian king is named exclusively outside of Kings.

Table 8: Rulers of Babylon Named in the Old Testament

Babylonian Ruler	Ruler's Dates (BC)	Kings References (7 total)	Non-Kings References (87 total)
Marduk-Baladan (= Marduk-apla-iddina II)	721–710	2 Kgs 20:12	Isa 39:1
Nebuchadnezzar	605–562	2 Kgs 24:1, 10, 11; 25:1, 8, 22	85 non-Kings refs: Ezra 1:7; 2:1; Jer 21:2, 7; Dan 1–4
Awel-Marduk (= Amēl-Marduk)		2 Kgs 25:27	Jer 52:31

Kings is therefore unique among books of the Old Testament in recording personal names for ancient Near Eastern emperors. Many of the non-Kings references to foreign rulers (Shishak, Tirhakah, Necho, Tiglath-Pileser III, Sennacherib, Esarhaddon, Merodach-baladan, Evil-merodach) appear in parallels from Chronicles, Isaiah, and Jeremiah—books that probably used Kings as a source.

By providing names for these emperors, the book of Kings reveals a heightened interest in history, more so than other Old Testament books, and thus serves as an important ancient source for historians. For example, because the book of Exodus leaves the Pharaoh anonymous, biblical historians remain uncertain about the date of the exodus, and yet Depuydt observes that, for Pharaoh Shoshenq, "Egyptian chronology has been derived from biblical chronology, not the other way around."[35]

The Six Neighboring Nations (Ammon, Aram, Edom, Moab, Philistia, Phoenicia)

The six smaller neighboring nations (Ammon, Aram, Edom, Moab, Philistia, Phoenicia) each impacted Israel and Judah as allies, enemies, or vassals. While

35. See L. Depuydt, "Egypt, Egyptians" in *DOTHB*, 243. Chronicles mentions Shishak (2 Chr 12:2, 5, 7, 9) and Necho (2 Chr 35:20, 22; 36:4). Jeremiah mentions Necho (Jer 46:2).

Egypt, Assyria, and Babylon oppressed and required tribute from Israel and Judah, four of the six neighboring nations were controlled by Israel during at least a portion of the period of the united monarchy (Edom, Moab, Ammon, sections of Aram). David maintained control with his military, and his son, Solomon, used marriage alliances with wives from Ammon, Moab, Edom, and Phoenicia (1 Kgs 11:1). Table 9 lists these six nations, their key cities, rulers, gods, and references in Kings.

Table 9: The Six Nations Neighboring Israel and Judah in Kings[36]

Nation (cities)	Rulers	Gods	Kings References
Ammon (Rabbath)	Baalis (Jer 40:14)	Molech (or Milcom)	1 Kgs 11:1, 5, 7, 33; 14:21, 31; 2 Kgs 23:13; 24:2.
Aram (Damascus, Zobah)	Hadad-ezer, Hezion (Rezon), Tabrimmon, Ben-hadad I, II, III, Hazael, Rezin	Hadad	1 Kgs 11:25; 15:18; 19:15; 20:1, 20, 22, 23; 22:1, 3, 31; 2 Kgs 5:1, 5; 6:8, 11, 24; 8:7, 9, 13, 28, 29; 9:14, 15; 12:17, 18: 13:3, 4, 7, 17, 19, 22, 24; 15:37; 16:5, 6, 7.
Edom (Sela)	Hadad		1 Kgs 9:26; 11:14, 15, 16; 22:47; 2 Kgs 3:8, 9, 12, 20, 26; 8:20, 21, 22; 14:7, 10.
Moab	Mesha	Chemosh	1 Kgs 11:7, 33; 2 Kgs 1:1, 3:4, 5, 7, 10, 13, 18, 21, 22, 23, 24, 26; 13:20; 23:13; 24:2.
Philistia (Gath, Gaza, Ekron)	Achish	Dagon, Ashtoreth, Baal-Zebub	1 Kgs 2:39, 40, 41; 4:21, 24; 15:27; 16:15; 2 Kgs 1:2, 3, 6, 16; 8:2, 3; 12:17; 18:8.
Phoenicia (Tyre, Sidon)	Hiram, Ethbaal	Baal, Astarte	1 Kgs 5:1, 6; 7:13, 14; 9:11, 12; 11:5, 33; 16:31; 2 Kgs 23:13.

Ammon (located east of Israel, north of Moab) was the name of the descendants of Ben-Ammi, the son of Lot's incestuous relationship with his younger

36. A version of this table appeared in Leuchter and Lamb, *Historical Books*, 291.

daughter (Gen 19:38). At least one of Solomon's wives was from Ammon, and she (along with his other foreign wives) is blamed for leading the ruler into apostasy, specifically the worship of the Ammonite god Molech (1 Kgs 11:1–7, 33; 2 Kgs 23:13). His successor, Rehoboam, was the offspring of his marriage to an Ammonite wife (1 Kgs 14:21, 31).

Aram (northeast of Israel; also called Syria) was the nation that interacted most frequently with Israel in Kings. Throughout the monarchic period Aram and Israel flipped back and forth from allies to enemies. Solomon traded with Aram (1 Kgs 10:29), but Rezon, king of Damascus, raided Israel during the reign of Solomon (1 Kgs 11:23–25). Asa of Judah convinced Ben-Hadad of Aram to break his alliance with Baasha of Israel (1 Kgs 15:19–20). Ahab and Ben-Hadad II ended their conflict with a treaty that lasted three years but then restarted hostilities (1 Kgs 20:1–33, 34; 22:2–3). This pattern continues when Aram's king sent a gift to Israel's king; later, Aram attacked Israel, so Elisha convinced the northern ruler to show radical hospitality to Arameans, temporarily ending hostilities (2 Kgs 5:5; 6:8–9, 22–25). Ben-Hadad II later besieged Samaria (2 Kgs 6:24–25), but when he was ill he sent for Elisha the Israelite prophet (2 Kgs 8:7–8). During the reigns of three Jehuite rulers, Aram and Israel were at war (2 Kgs 10:32–33; 13:3–7, 17–24), but during the reign of Pekah, Aram and Israel were united (2 Kgs 15:37; 16:5).

Edom (southeast of Judah, south of Moab) means "red" and refers to the descendants of Esau, recalling the red porridge he traded for his birthright from his brother Jacob (Gen 25:30; 36:1). Solomon married at least one woman from Edom and was punished by YHWH with Hadad, an Edomite adversary (1 Kgs 11:1, 14). Solomon harbored his fleet of ships at the Edomite port city of Ezion Geber on the Red Sea, the same location where Jehoshaphat's fleet was wrecked (1 Kgs 9:26; 22:47–48). The king of Edom joined forces with Israel and Judah to attack Moab (2 Kgs 3:8–12). Under Jehoram of Judah, Edom finally gained independence (2 Kgs 8:20–22), but Amaziah of Judah later reconquered them (2 Kgs 14:7).

Moab (east of Judah, south of Ammon) was the name of the descendants of Lot's son Moab from his incestuous relationship with his older daughter (Gen 19:37). Solomon also married at least one woman from Moab, which led to his worship of the Moabite god, Chemosh (1 Kgs 11:7, 33). Moab was controlled by Israel under Omri and Ahab (according to the Mesha Stela[37]), but they rebelled after the death of Ahab (2 Kgs 1:1). Israel, Judah, and Edom formed

37. *COS* 2: 137–138.

an alliance to recapture Moab (2 Kgs 3:4–27). Bands of Moabite raiders invaded Israel under Jehoash and Judah under Jehoiakim (2 Kgs 13:20; 24:2).

Philistia (west of Judah along the Mediterranean Sea) was Israel's primary opponent in the book of Samuel (mentioned there over 180 times). But in Kings Philistia plays a minor role (mentioned only six times), appearing primarily in brief geographic references (1 Kgs 4:21; 15:27; 16:15; 2 Kgs 8:2, 3; 18:8). While Samuel includes many Israelite-Philistine conflicts (e.g., 1 Sam 4; 7; 13; 14; 17), Kings only includes two: when Hazael attacks Gath and when Hezekiah attacks Gaza (2 Kgs 12:17; 18:8).

Phoenicia (northwest of Israel), unlike these other neighbors, enjoyed a consistently amiable relationship with Israel. Hiram of Tyre had been an ally of David (1 Kgs 5:1), and he contributed lumber to Solomon for the temple (1 Kgs 5:8). However, the relationship between Israel and Phoenicia was too close for two Israelite rulers (Solomon and Ahab) who married Phoenicians and were led into worship of foreign gods (Ashtoreth and Baal; 1 Kgs 11:5; 16:31–32).

Rulers of Israel and Judah in Extrabiblical Sources

External validation for the historicity of Kings is found in nineteen extrabiblical inscriptions that mention rulers from Judah or Israel. Table 10 lists each inscription, the date, the ancient Near Eastern ruler who commissioned it, the ruler of Israel or Judah mentioned, and its reference (in either *COS* or *ANET*).

Table 10: References to Rulers of Israel and Judah in Extra-Biblical Sources[38]

Source (19 texts)	Date (BC)	ANE Ruler	Ruler of Israel, or Judah	Reference
Kurkh Monolith	852	Shalmaneser III	Ahab	*COS* 2:263d
Tel Dan Stele	820	Hazael of Aram[39]	David, [Jeho] ram? of Israel, [Ahaz]iah? of Judah	*COS* 2:161–62a

(continued)

38. A version of this table appeared in Leuchter and Lamb, *Historical Books*, 299.

39. While the Tel Dan Inscription does not clearly identify its author, most scholars believe it to be Hazael; see Lamb, *Righteous Jehu*, 102–10.

Source (19 texts)	**Date (BC)**	**ANE Ruler**	**Ruler of Israel, or Judah**	**Reference**
Moabite Stone	835	Mesha of Moab	Omri, Omri's son (= Ahab)	*COS* 2:137–38
Calah Bulls	841	Shalmaneser III	Omri, Jehu	*COS* 2:267c
Kurba'il Statue	838	Shalmaneser III	Omri, Jehu	*COS* 2:268d
Marble Slab	838	Shalmaneser III	Omri, Jehu	*COS* 2:268d
Black Obelisk	827	Shalmaneser III	Omri, Jehu	*COS* 2:270a
Tell al-Rimah	797	Adad-nirari III	Joash of Israel	*COS* 2:276a
Calah Annal 13	738	Tiglath-Pileser III	Menahem	*COS* 2:285c
Annals	734	Tiglath-Pileser III	Azriau = Azariah?	*ANET*, 282–83[40]
Iran Stele	733	Tiglath-Pileser III	Menahem	*COS* 2:287a
Summary 4	730	Tiglath-Pileser III	Pekah, Hoshea	*COS* 2:288a
Summary 7	730	Tiglath-Pileser III	Jehoahaz = Ahaz of Judah	*COS* 2:289c
Azekah Inscription	701	Sennacherib	Hezekiah	*COS* 2:304d
Taylor Prism Sennacherib Prism	701	Sennacherib	Hezekiah	*COS* 2:302–3
Prism B	674	Esarhaddon	Manasseh	*ANET*, 291b
Cylinder C		Ashurbanipal	Manasseh	*ANET*, 294b
Ration list	570	Nebuchadnezzar of Babylon	Jehoiachin	*ANET*, 308c–d

Along with the biblical references to foreign emperors, these external references to biblical rulers have profound significance for the historicity of the book of Kings. These ancient sources are dated roughly to the actual

40. See also *ZIBBC* 3:168–69.

reigns of these Israelite and Judean rulers, and they generally cohere with the biblical record chronologically. Sixteen of the nineteen are Assyrian, two are West Semitic (Moabite Stone and Tel Dan Stele), and one is Babylonian (Ration list). Fifteen Israelite and Judean rulers are named in these inscriptions: one from the united monarchy (David), eight from the Northern Kingdom (Omri, Ahab, Jehoram, Jehu, Joash, Menahem, Pekah and Hoshea), and six from the Southern Kingdom (Ahaziah, Azariah, Ahaz, Hezekiah, Manasseh and Jehoiachin). Over a third of the forty rulers from Israel and Judah are mentioned in extrabiblical sources (15 of 40 = 37.5 percent).

Additionally, the names of nine biblical rulers appear on seals and seal inscriptions: three from Israel (Jezebel, Jeroboam II, and Hoshea) and six from Judah (Azariah, Jotham, Ahaz, Hezekiah, Manasseh, and Jehoahaz).[41] While several problems make definite identifications of names from seal inscriptions difficult, it is still reasonable to assume that these inscriptions are referring to many biblical characters, including rulers.

Chronology

The book of Kings includes a lot of numbers—synchronisms, accession ages, regnal years, and other historical data—making it one of the most chronological books of the Bible. Most readers will not bother to add up the numbers of years, months, and days to see if they are internally consistent, but if one does, a number of problems emerge. Some are minor. Did Nadab of Israel reign for two years (1 Kgs 15:25) or only one (1 Kgs 15:28)? Others are more significant. The text states that Jehoram of Israel came to power in the second year of Jehoram of Judah and in the eighteenth year of Jehoshaphat of Judah, yielding a nine-year discrepancy (2 Kgs 1:17; 3:1). These two discrepancies are merely a sample of the chronological problems appearing in the text.[42]

The responses of scholars to these problems are generally three types. One, some scholars believe that according to ancient historical standards, Kings' chronology is relatively accurate.[43] Two, others conclude that these problems cannot be reconciled, and harmonization attempts are futile.[44] Three, still others (most notably, Thiele) attempt solutions using various dating conventions involving the calendar year, a ruler's accession year, and co-regencies.[45]

---

41. For an extended discussion of these seals, see Leuchter and Lamb, *Historical Books*, 301–5.

42. For other examples, see Edwin R. Thiele, *The Mysterious Numbers of the Hebrew Kings* (Grand Rapids: Zondervan, 1983), 7–11.

43. See Wiseman, *1 & 2 Kings*, 27.

44. See Thiele's discussion of these perspectives in *Mysterious Numbers*, 11–13.

45. See Thiele, *Mysterious Numbers*; K. A. Kitchen, *On the Reliability of the Old Testament* (Grand Rapids: Eerdmans, 2003), 26–32.

In the biblical world, the new year began either in the spring (Nisan = March/April) or the fall (Tishri = September/October), and the calendars of Israel and Judah may have started at different times, possibly explaining small discrepancies. Different conventions were also used for counting a ruler's incomplete accession year since rulers rarely die conveniently on New Year's Eve. In the ante-dating system, the first incomplete year was counted as a ruler's first year, but in the post-dating system, the ruler's first year starts after the following New Year's Day (so a ruler's initial incomplete year does not count). Egypt and the early Israelite monarchy (up to Jehoahaz) used the ante-dating system, but Mesopotamia, Judah, and the late Israelite monarchy (after Jehoahaz) used the post-dating system. (If you find this confusing, join the club.) These different accession year conventions could also explain minor problems, but to explain the more significant chronological problems, co-regencies are typically used, where a royal heir begins to share power with his father, creating a period of overlapping reigns. For example, Solomon began his reign while David still lived (1 Kgs 1:32–39), and Azariah allowed his son, Jotham, to govern when Azariah was struck with leprosy (2 Kgs 15:5). The nine-year discrepancy regarding Jehoram of Israel's accession year could easily be explained if Jehoshaphat and his son, Jehoram, had an extended period of co-regency. Thiele's solution for these problems has generally received wide support among conservative commentators, but none of the chronological solutions has received broad consensus, allowing the mathematically oriented the opportunity to continue this discussion.

Theological Message

While the book of Kings is interested in history, it is more concerned with theology, as it narrates the story of God's relationship with his people over the course of the monarchy. God is the primary character of the book, and the primary message of the book is that he judges his own people, even sending them into exile into Assyria and Babylon. While YHWH looked for worship and obedience, both his people and his leaders (prophets, priests, and kings) often responded with rebellion and idolatry. Lessons from these narratives continue to challenge today's readers to obedience and exclusive worship of God.

Worship and Idolatry

The text highly honors kings who worshiped YHWH properly (David, Jehu, Hezekiah, and Josiah) and harshly condemns the ones who did not

(Solomon, Jeroboam I, Ahab, and Manasseh). Proper worship in Kings focused on proper location, primarily the Jerusalem temple. Kings begins by narrating Solomon's fulfillment of YHWH's promise to David that his son would build a temple (2 Sam 7:13), including its preparation (1 Kgs 5), construction (1 Kgs 6), and dedication (1 Kgs 8). After Solomon, the temple is not mentioned in contexts of worship but only when a ruler decides it needs renovation, like Joash of Judah (2 Kgs 12) and Josiah of Judah (2 Kgs 22:2–7; 23:4–12), or when its treasuries are plundered. Three foreign rulers (Shishak of Egypt, Jehoash of Israel, and Nebuchadnezzar of Babylon) plunder the temple (1 Kgs 14:25–26; 2 Kgs 14:13–14; 24:13), but, surprisingly, four Judean rulers—even three righteous ones—give temple treasures to foreign powers (1 Kgs 15:18; 2 Kgs 12:17–18; 16:8; 18:15). The beginning of Kings narrates the temple's construction (1 Kgs 5–8), and the end of Kings narrates its destruction (2 Kgs 25).

Two types of improper worship practices are condemned frequently in Kings. All northern rulers (except Elah and Shallum) are criticized for continuing in the sins of Jeroboam and not removing the golden calves he set up in Dan and Bethel (e.g., 1 Kgs 15:26, 34; 16:19, 31). Rulers of both kingdoms (primarily southern ones) are condemned for worshiping at, or not removing, the high places (*bamot*) because they were associated with idolatrous worship practices (e.g., 1 Kgs 3:2–3; 12:31–32; 15:14; 22:43). Other less common improper practices condemned in Kings include witchcraft or divination (2 Kgs 17:17; 21:6), constructing and worshiping sacred poles called Asherah (e.g., 1 Kgs 15:13, 16:33; 18:19; see Deut 16:21), and child sacrifice, referred to euphemistically as making a child pass through fire (2 Kgs 16:3; 17:17; 21:6; 23:10; see also Deut 18:10).

While improper worship was common in Israel and Judah throughout the period of the monarchy, five rulers (Asa, Jehu, Joash, Hezekiah, and Josiah) instituted religious reforms. These rulers are praised for repairing the temple, removing idols, tearing down altars, and punishing Baal worship (1 Kgs 15:12–13; 2 Kgs 10:18–27; 12:4–16; 18:3–6; 23:1–20). The text records three extreme examples of religious slaughters: Elijah killing the prophets of Baal after the Mount Carmel conflict (1 Kgs 18:40), Jehu orchestrating the massacre of Baal worshipers after his violent coup (2 Kgs 10:18–27), and Josiah slaughtering the priests of the high places, thus fulfilling the man of God's prophecy to Jeroboam I (1 Kgs 13:2–3; 2 Kgs 23:15–20). The brutality of these events may be shocking to many readers, but YHWH had commanded his people to kill false prophets since they would lead Israel astray (Deut 13:1–5).

Obedience and Judgment

Idolatry is the primary form of disobedience condemned in Kings, but the book emphasizes obedience in other ways by showing how rulers who obey YHWH and his law are rewarded and how those who disobey him are judged. The numerous regnal formulas of the book evaluate rulers based on their obedience to the law. Ultimately, God condemns both nations to exile because of the disobedience of not just the kings but the entire nation (2 Kgs 17:7–23; 21:10–15; 24:2–4). The rest of this section will discuss how three areas of disobedience were punished: greed, intermarriage, and lack of respect for prophets.

Two examples of greed are judged harshly in the book. Ahab and Jezebel orchestrate the death of Naboth (their neighbor) to steal his vineyard, and Elijah prophesies a gruesome death involving canine consumption of these two royals (1 Kgs 21:1–24). After the generous gift from Naaman (the healed Aramean general) was refused by Elisha, the prophet's servant Gehazi chased him down, lied to him, and accepted a portion of it; he was therefore cursed with leprosy by Elisha for greed and deception (2 Kgs 5:19–27). Rulers were forbidden from acquiring massive quantities of horses, gold, and silver in Deuteronomy's law of the king (Deut 17:16–17). Solomon is the ruler who seems to break the law of the king's prohibition in the most flagrant manner as he stockpiled gold, silver, horses, and chariots (1 Kgs 10:14–29), but he curiously is never condemned for it. However, the text's record of his massive accumulations seems to imply a rebuke as it leads directly into his intermarriage and apostasy in the subsequent chapter.

Gold, silver, and horses were not the only things Solomon accumulated in great quantities; he also had seven hundred wives and three hundred concubines (1 Kgs 11:3). Deuteronomy's law of the king does not mention foreign wives, but it does prohibit rulers from acquiring many wives (Deut 17:17); thus intermarriage is another area where Solomon flouted the law. Foreign marriage is forbidden elsewhere in Deuteronomy (Deut 7:3–4), and both Solomon and Ahab were condemned for it (1 Kgs 11:4–8; 16:31–33) because their wives contributed to their apostasy and idolatry.

The people of Israel were commanded to respect the prophets of YHWH (Deut 18:15), so when an individual or a group in Kings disrespect prophets, not surprisingly the consequences are severe. Twice groups of fifty soldiers sent by Ahaziah of Israel to seize Elijah are consumed by fire from heaven (2 Kgs 1:1–16). A gang of teens that taunted Elisha by calling him "baldy" are attacked by bears (2 Kgs 2:23–25). In the midst of a famine, Elisha delivers an optimistic message of plummeting food prices, but when an Israelite captain doubts the prophetic word, Elisha pronounces a pessimistic prediction for the captain, and he is trampled to death at the gate of the city by starving Israelites (2 Kgs 7:1–3, 16–20).

Spiritual Leadership

The book of Kings offers many lessons regarding spiritual leadership. This section will therefore examine positive and negative examples of prophets, priests, kings, and key women exercising leadership gifts in the spiritual realm by speaking the words of God, calling people to obey, and confronting idolatry.

The primary spiritual leaders during the period of the monarchy were not kings but prophets. Three prophets play major roles over the course of multiple chapters (Elijah, Elisha, and Isaiah). A variety of named prophets serve in limited roles (Nathan, Ahijah, Shemaiah, Jehu, Micaiah, Jonah, and Huldah). Other minor prophetic individuals who minister remain anonymous (1 Kgs 13:1, 4, 11; 20:13, 22, 28, 35, 38, 41; 2 Kgs 9:1). While they also healed people and met people's physical needs, primarily prophets served as God's spokespersons. They delivered oracles of dynastic promise to righteous rulers (2 Sam 7:12–16; 1 Kgs 6:12; 2 Kgs 10:30) and oracles of dynastic judgment to evil rulers (1 Kgs 11:11–13, 31–35; 14:7–14; 16:1–4, 7; 21:20–26). They condemned rulers for disobedience and idolatry (1 Kgs 14:7–16; 16:1–7; 21:17–19). They encouraged rulers in the midst of political crisis (2 Kgs 19:20–34; 20:4–6; 22:18–20). Modern readers have a lot to learn from these prophets about confronting power, defaming idols, and calling for exclusive worship of God.

Priests such as Aaron, Eli, or Ahimelech play major roles in Israel's earlier story, but in the book of Kings priests fade into the background, at least in comparison to prophets. Two priests support opposite sides in the struggle to decide who will be David's successor, but neither play a determinative role as Solomon (supported by Zadok) emerges victorious over his older brother Adonijah (supported by Abiathar; 1 Kgs 1–2). For much of the divided monarchy priests are mentioned only briefly (1 Kgs 4:2, 4, 5; 8:3–11; 12:31–32), until Jehoiada the priest serves as kingmaker for the sole surviving son of Ahaziah, orchestrating the rebellion against Athaliah and restoring a Davidide to the throne of Judah (2 Kgs 11:1–21). Three priests are mentioned in passing (Uriah: 2 Kgs 16:10–16; Seraiah and Zephaniah: 2 Kgs 25:18), but two other priests serve as spiritual leaders at crucial times in the narrative. When lions terrorized the new residents of Samaria after the Israelite exile, the Assyrian king installs an anonymous priest to teach people to worship YHWH (2 Kgs 17:27–28). During Josiah's renovation of the temple, Hilkiah the priest finds the book of the law, which serves as the inspiration for Josiah's reforms (2 Kgs 22:3–20).

Despite not having much power in the context of their patriarchal culture, a series of women serve as spiritual leaders in the book of Kings. Many of these women lacked an official leadership role, but they were able to wield influence and even lead men who were around them. While Kings includes negative examples of queens (Solomon's wives, Jezebel, and Athaliah), it also includes positive examples of queens and a princess. Bathsheba helped convince David to make her son, Solomon, his successor (1 Kgs 1:15–31). The queen of Sheba not only praised the wisdom of Solomon but also blessed and praised Solomon's God (1 Kgs 10:1–13). When Athaliah took power after her son Ahaziah's death, she slaughtered the remainder of the royal family, but Jehosheba (Ahaziah's sister) risked her life to save her one-year-old nephew Joash until he could become king six years later (2 Kgs 11:1–12). This relatively unknown princess is one of the most significant heroes of the book as she not only rescued her nephew but also prevented the Davidic line of Jesus from being exterminated. After the priest Hilkiah found the book of the law, Josiah did not consult one of the famous prophets who ministered during his reign, such as Jeremiah (Jer 1:2) or Zephaniah (Zeph 1:1), but instead he sought direction from the prophetess Huldah to interpret it for him (2 Kgs 22:11–20).

The text records the narratives of four anonymous women with little status as positive examples of obedience, sacrifice, and faithfulness. The primary point of the story of the two prostitute mothers (1 Kgs 3:16–28) is that God gifted Solomon with great wisdom, but a secondary point is that a prostitute can serve as an example of a committed parent who is willing to make sacrifices for the sake of her son. In stark contrast to the series of disobedient rulers who reigned during the ministries of Elijah and Elisha, two widows faithfully obeyed the prophetic word (1 Kgs 17:8–15; 2 Kgs 4:1–7). Jesus must have been reading the book of Kings before he began his public ministry because, in his first public speech in Luke's Gospel, he recalled two stories from the book—Elijah and the widow of Zarephath and Elisha and Naaman the leper of Aram—to make the point that God shows compassion for non-Israelites (Luke 4:25–27). The story of how God worked through an unnamed Israelite servant girl to heal Naaman is one of the most dramatic examples of faithfulness and compassion in Scripture (2 Kgs 5:1–5). She was stolen from her family on a raid, which presumably was led by her future master Naaman, the Aramean general. She had many reasons to hate her foreign captors, but instead she tells Naaman's wife that her husband would be healed if he were to visit Elisha in

Israel. Her brief comment served as the catalyst for Naaman's healing. This Israelite servant girl not only displayed profound confidence in God's ability to heal foreign lepers, but she also demonstrated radical compassion by loving her foreign enemy. The stories of these women and girls of Kings provide powerful examples of faithfulness for women and men today.

Prophets, priests, and women all play supporting roles in the book, but Kings is primarily about kings. And while the political rulers of Israel and Judah should have provided spiritual leadership for their respective nations, in this capacity they utterly failed. All of the northern rulers except Jehu are judged as evil since they did not depart from the sins of Jeroboam I. Southern rulers fare slightly better than their northern counterparts, but only three receive unqualified righteous assessments (David, Hezekiah, and Josiah), and most of the Judean rulers are deemed evil (eleven of nineteen).

As national leaders, the idolatrous behavior of these evil rulers had a negative impact on the people. The text repeatedly emphasizes that Jeroboam's golden calf altars at Dan and Bethel caused the Northern Kingdom to sin (e.g., 1 Kgs 14:16; 15:26, 30, 34). The Southern Kingdom had a series of rulers who did not remove high places or engaged in other idolatrous practices that lead Judah into evil (e.g., 1 Kgs 14:22–24; 2 Kgs 8:18–19; 16:2–4, 15–16). However, the primary Judean ruler who was blamed for leading the nation into sin and exile was Manasseh (2 Kgs 21:11–16; 24:3–4).

In the midst of a preponderance of apostasy and idolatry, two positive examples of kings who exercise spiritual leadership for their nation stand out, one at the beginning of the book and one at the end. After the temple was finished, Solomon led the nation in a dedicatory prayer, sacrifice, and celebration (1 Kgs 8). As the culmination of his reformation in response to finding the book of the law, Josiah celebrated the Passover and commanded the nation to continue the practice (2 Kgs 23:21–23). But even the most righteous rulers of Kings (David, Jehu, Hezekiah, and Josiah) all had serious problems, leaving readers longing for a future truly righteous son of David, the ultimate King of kings and Lord of lords (Matt 1:1; Rev 19:16).

Resources for Teaching and Preaching

My hope is that readers will find all the resources listed in the footnotes of the commentary beneficial in understanding the books of 1–2 Kings. But here is a short list, compiled from literally hundreds of footnotes, of the resources I believe will be most helpful for teaching and preaching on the book of Kings.

Commentaries

Alter, Robert. *Ancient Israel, The Former Prophets: Joshua, Judges, Samuel, and Kings*. New York: Norton, 2013.

Barnes, William H. *1–2 Kings*. Cornerstone Biblical Commentary. Carol Stream, IL: Tyndale House, 2012.

Cogan, Mordechai. *1 Kings*. AB. New York: Doubleday, 2001.

Cogan, Mordechai, and Hayim Tadmor. *II Kings*. AB. New York: Doubleday, 1988.

Fretheim, T. E. *First and Second Kings*. Westminster Bible Companion. Louisville: Westminster John Knox, 1999.

Wiseman, D. J. *1 & 2 Kings: An Introduction and Commentary*. TOTC. Downers Grove, IL: InterVarsity Press, 1993.

Wray Beal, L. M. *1 & 2 Kings*. ApOTC. Downers Grove, IL: InterVarsity Press, 2014.

Other Resources

Arnold, Bill T., and H. G. M. Williamson, eds. *DOTHB*. Downers Grove, IL: InterVarsity Press, 2005.

Leuchter, Mark A., and David T. Lamb. *The Historical Writings: Introducing Israel's Historical Literature*. Minneapolis: Fortress, 2016.

Walton, John H., ed. *ZIBBC*. Grand Rapids: Zondervan, 2009.

Walton, John H., Victor H. Matthews, and Mark W. Chavalas, eds. *The IVP Bible Background Commentary*. Downers Grove, IL: InterVarsity Press, 2000.

CHAPTER 1

1 Kings 1:1–53

LISTEN to the Story

[1]When King David was very old, he could not keep warm even when they put covers over him. [2]So his attendants said to him, "Let us look for a young virgin to serve the king and take care of him. She can lie beside him so that our lord the king may keep warm."

[3]Then they searched throughout Israel for a beautiful young woman and found Abishag, a Shunammite, and brought her to the king. [4]The woman was very beautiful; she took care of the king and waited on him, but the king had no sexual relations with her.

[5]Now Adonijah, whose mother was Haggith, put himself forward and said, "I will be king." So he got chariots and horses ready, with fifty men to run ahead of him. [6](His father had never rebuked him by asking, "Why do you behave as you do?" He was also very handsome and was born next after Absalom.)

[7]Adonijah conferred with Joab son of Zeruiah and with Abiathar the priest, and they gave him their support. [8]But Zadok the priest, Benaiah son of Jehoiada, Nathan the prophet, Shimei and Rei and David's special guard did not join Adonijah.

[9]Adonijah then sacrificed sheep, cattle and fattened calves at the Stone of Zoheleth near En Rogel. He invited all his brothers, the king's sons, and all the royal officials of Judah, [10]but he did not invite Nathan the prophet or Benaiah or the special guard or his brother Solomon.

[11]Then Nathan asked Bathsheba, Solomon's mother, "Have you not heard that Adonijah, the son of Haggith, has become king, and our lord David knows nothing about it? [12]Now then, let me advise you how you can save your own life and the life of your son Solomon. [13]Go in to King David and say to him, 'My lord the king, did you not swear to me your servant: "Surely Solomon your son shall be king after me, and he will sit on my throne"? Why then has Adonijah become king?' [14]While you are

still there talking to the king, I will come in and add my word to what you have said."

[15]So Bathsheba went to see the aged king in his room, where Abishag the Shunammite was attending him. [16]Bathsheba bowed down, prostrating herself before the king.

"What is it you want?" the king asked.

[17]She said to him, "My lord, you yourself swore to me your servant by the LORD your God: 'Solomon your son shall be king after me, and he will sit on my throne.' [18]But now Adonijah has become king, and you, my lord the king, do not know about it. [19]He has sacrificed great numbers of cattle, fattened calves, and sheep, and has invited all the king's sons, Abiathar the priest and Joab the commander of the army, but he has not invited Solomon your servant. [20]My lord the king, the eyes of all Israel are on you, to learn from you who will sit on the throne of my lord the king after him. [21]Otherwise, as soon as my lord the king is laid to rest with his ancestors, I and my son Solomon will be treated as criminals."

[22]While she was still speaking with the king, Nathan the prophet arrived. [23]And the king was told, "Nathan the prophet is here." So he went before the king and bowed with his face to the ground.

[24]Nathan said, "Have you, my lord the king, declared that Adonijah shall be king after you, and that he will sit on your throne? [25]Today he has gone down and sacrificed great numbers of cattle, fattened calves, and sheep. He has invited all the king's sons, the commanders of the army and Abiathar the priest. Right now they are eating and drinking with him and saying, 'Long live King Adonijah!' [26]But me your servant, and Zadok the priest, and Benaiah son of Jehoiada, and your servant Solomon he did not invite. [27]Is this something my lord the king has done without letting his servants know who should sit on the throne of my lord the king after him?"

[28]Then King David said, "Call in Bathsheba." So she came into the king's presence and stood before him.

[29]The king then took an oath: "As surely as the LORD lives, who has delivered me out of every trouble, [30]I will surely carry out this very day what I swore to you by the LORD, the God of Israel: Solomon your son shall be king after me, and he will sit on my throne in my place."

[31]Then Bathsheba bowed down with her face to the ground, prostrating herself before the king, and said, "May my lord King David live forever!"

[32]King David said, "Call in Zadok the priest, Nathan the prophet and

Benaiah son of Jehoiada." When they came before the king, 33he said to
them: "Take your lord's servants with you and have Solomon my son
mount my own mule and take him down to Gihon. 34There have Zadok
the priest and Nathan the prophet anoint him king over Israel. Blow the
trumpet and shout, 'Long live King Solomon!' 35Then you are to go up
with him, and he is to come and sit on my throne and reign in my place.
I have appointed him ruler over Israel and Judah."

36Benaiah son of Jehoiada answered the king, "Amen! May the Lord,
the God of my lord the king, so declare it. 37As the Lord was with my
lord the king, so may he be with Solomon to make his throne even greater
than the throne of my lord King David!"

38So Zadok the priest, Nathan the prophet, Benaiah son of Jehoiada,
the Kerethites and the Pelethites went down and had Solomon mount
King David's mule, and they escorted him to Gihon. 39Zadok the priest
took the horn of oil from the sacred tent and anointed Solomon. Then
they sounded the trumpet and all the people shouted, "Long live King
Solomon!" 40And all the people went up after him, playing pipes and
rejoicing greatly, so that the ground shook with the sound.

41Adonijah and all the guests who were with him heard it as they were
finishing their feast. On hearing the sound of the trumpet, Joab asked,
"What's the meaning of all the noise in the city?"

42Even as he was speaking, Jonathan son of Abiathar the priest arrived.
Adonijah said, "Come in. A worthy man like you must be bringing
good news."

43"Not at all!" Jonathan answered. "Our lord King David has made
Solomon king. 44The king has sent with him Zadok the priest, Nathan
the prophet, Benaiah son of Jehoiada, the Kerethites and the Pelethites,
and they have put him on the king's mule, 45and Zadok the priest and
Nathan the prophet have anointed him king at Gihon. From there they
have gone up cheering, and the city resounds with it. That's the noise you
hear. 46Moreover, Solomon has taken his seat on the royal throne. 47Also,
the royal officials have come to congratulate our lord King David, saying,
'May your God make Solomon's name more famous than yours and his
throne greater than yours!' And the king bowed in worship on his bed
48and said, 'Praise be to the Lord, the God of Israel, who has allowed my
eyes to see a successor on my throne today.'"

49At this, all Adonijah's guests rose in alarm and dispersed. 50But

Adonijah, in fear of Solomon, went and took hold of the horns of the altar. [51]Then Solomon was told, "Adonijah is afraid of King Solomon and is clinging to the horns of the altar. He says, 'Let King Solomon swear to me today that he will not put his servant to death with the sword.'"

[52]Solomon replied, "If he shows himself to be worthy, not a hair of his head will fall to the ground; but if evil is found in him, he will die." [53]Then King Solomon sent men, and they brought him down from the altar. And Adonijah came and bowed down to King Solomon, and Solomon said, "Go to your home."

Listening to the Text in the Story: Biblical Texts: Judges; 1–2 Samuel (specifically Absalom's rebellion, 2 Samuel 13–18); Ancient Near Eastern Texts: The Kirta Epic; Esarhaddon's Fight for the Throne; Inscriptions of Panumuwa and Barrakab

After arriving in the promised land, Israel struggled during the time of the judges, cycling through periods of apostasy, oppression, and deliverance (e.g., Judg 2:11–23; 3:7–11, 12–30). YHWH then commissioned Israel's last judge, the prophet Samuel, to anoint Israel's first king, Saul (1 Sam 10:1). Unfortunately, Israel's leadership struggles continued under Saul's reign, prompting YHWH to replace Saul with a man after his own heart, David (13:14).

However, David the hero, warrior, lover, and emperor of 1–2 Samuel has at the beginning of Kings become pathetic: old and cold, impotent and ignorant. His weakened condition prompts a succession struggle between his oldest living son, Adonijah, and one of his younger sons, Solomon.

To help us listen to the story of Adonijah's failed attempt and Solomon's successful accession, it will be necessary to briefly discuss some of the parallel accounts found elsewhere in Scripture, as well as in ancient Near Eastern literature. A preliminary discussion of these parallels and their points of similarity and contrast will provide essential background to better understand the culture, values, and context behind Solomon's succession story.

Similar to David's situation, when King Kirta of Ugarit is old and infirm, his son Prince Yassubu thinks he is no longer worthy to rule. So he tells his father to yield the throne to him as his successor:

> Illness has become as it were (your) bedfellow,
> sickness (your) constant companion in bed.

> So descend from your kingship, I will reign,
> from your dominion, I, yes I, will sit (on your throne).
> (from "The Epic of Kirta")[1]

Not surprisingly, Kirta does not follow his son's suggestion but instead curses Yassubu for his impudence.

Several fascinating similarities can be seen between the succession stories of Esarhaddon of Assyria (681–669 BC) and Solomon of Israel (c. 970–930 BC). Both Esarhaddon and Solomon struggled with older brothers to gain the throne that their fathers had declared should be theirs. In the world of the ancient Near East, the principal of primogeniture typically dictated that the king's oldest son should rule after the king's death. Solomon was probably not David's youngest son, but he still was much younger than both Absalom, who attempted a coup earlier (2 Sam 13–18) and David's oldest surviving son, Adonijah, who attempts a coup in 1 Kings 1. In the narrative "The Fight for the Throne," Esarhaddon declares that, despite being the youngest among his brothers, his father Sennacherib (704–681 BC) selected him as the next ruler:

> I was indeed the youngest brother among my elder brothers, but my own father . . . has chosen me in due form and in the presence of all my brothers—saying: "This is the son to be elevated to the position of a successor of mine."[2]

Esarhaddon claims that his father's unusual choice of him as successor was confirmed by the Assyrian gods (Shamash and Adad). Sennacherib's decision that Esarhaddon was the heir was then declared publicly before all his brothers, who then swore an oath to Esarhaddon. Despite their oath, Esarhaddon's brothers hatched a plot against him and assassinated their father Sennacherib. Esarhaddon and his brothers then engaged in a civil war that he eventually won, and the Assyrian throne was secured. The story of Sennacherib's siege of Jerusalem during the reign of Hezekiah is told later (2 Kgs 18–19), and the biblical narrative supports the Assyrian version of these events (19:37)

While the books of Samuel and Kings do not include Solomon's divine election or a public declaration from his father, after Solomon's birth the text informs the reader, "The Lord loved him" (2 Sam 12:24); in the book of Chronicles, David, like Sennacherib, makes a public declaration that God has chosen his younger son, Solomon, to rule (1 Chr 28:5).

1. *COS* 1:342–43.
2. *ANET*, 289.

While a ruler's oldest son typically ruled after the father's death, exceptions to the primogeniture principle such as Esarhaddon and Solomon are found elsewhere in the Old Testament. One reason David may have selected Solomon over Adonijah was because David himself was the youngest son of Jesse (1 Sam 16:11). A prominent theme of Genesis is God choosing younger sons (Abel over Cain; Isaac over Ishmael; Jacob over Esau; Joseph over his older brothers).

The story of Adonijah's unsuccessful coup against his father David in 1 Kings 1 shares striking parallels with that of his older brother Absalom (2 Sam 13–18). Both took place while David was still alive. Both included a sacrifice (2 Sam 15:12; 1 Kgs 1:9), a festival where all the brothers (except Solomon) were invited (2 Sam 13:23; 1 Kgs 1:9–10), and the potential usurper gained power and popularity by riding around in a chariot with fifty men running alongside (2 Sam 15:1; 2 Kgs 1:5). The West Semitic vassal ruler, Bar-Rakib, performed a similar duty for his lord, Tiglath-Pileser III, "I ran at the wheel of my Lord, the king of Assyria."[3]

After discussing the relevant parallel biblical and extrabiblical texts, we can now turn to a more in-depth discussion of Solomon's succession. Adonijah's failed attempt to seize the throne is a highly structured narrative involving plans, reports, and promises. David is about to die, so Adonijah plans to make himself king (1 Kgs 1:1–10). Nathan's strategy to foil Adonijah's plan and inform the ignorant king involves three reports of Adonijah's activities: (1) Nathan to Bathsheba (vv. 11–14); (2) Bathsheba to David (vv. 15–21); and (3) Nathan to David (vv. 22–27). This information prompts the king to promise Bathsheba that her son, Solomon, would be king (vv. 28–31). David then unveils his own plan to make Solomon king, and his wishes are implemented by Zadok the priest, Nathan the prophet, and Benaiah the future general (vv. 32–40). The report of Solomon's successful succession is given to Adonijah by Jonathan, son of the priest Abiathar (vv. 41–48). Just as David's promise calmed Bathsheba's concerns, Solomon's promise to Adonijah calms his—temporarily (vv. 49–53).

David Is Decrepit and Adonijah Is Ambitious (1:1–10)

To address David's weakened situation, his advisors do not propose abdication like Yassubu (see Listen to the Story above) but suggest other options for

3. *COS* 2:161.

their ruler. In the spirit of the book of Ecclesiastes's advice ("If two lie down together, they will keep warm," Eccl 4:11), they suggest finding a young virgin to keep him warm. The search throughout the land for a young, beautiful girl parallels the situation at the beginning of Esther when the Persian royal officials were looking for a new queen for King Xerxes (Esth 2:2).

The text does not reveal what Bathsheba or any of his other wives thinks of this arrangement, but several biblical texts shed light on Bathsheba's complex roles both as wife to David and as queen mother to the nation. The role of queen mother in Israel and the ancient Near East could be a powerful one. During the period of the divided monarchy, the queen mother Athaliah seizes and manages to hold onto royal power for six years after her son, Ahaziah, was killed (2 Kgs 11). However, at least in Persia, it was also dangerous even for a wife to approach the king, as Queen Esther informs Mordecai (Esth 4:11). The beautiful Abishag's presence when the queen mother Bathsheba approaches her husband David adds yet another level of complexity to the potentially awkward dynamic.

In contrast to David, who is so old that even a beautiful young woman lying in bed with him does not arouse him sexually (1 Kgs 1:4), Adonijah is young and ambitious and declares, "I will be king" (v. 55). Adonijah, whose name means "YHWH is my lord," was likely the oldest surviving son of David after the deaths of Amnon and Absalom (2 Sam 13:28–29; 18:14–15).[4] All three were born in Hebron before David moved his capital to Jerusalem (3:2–4). Adonijah would have been much older than Solomon, who was not born until David had lived in Jerusalem for a while (12:24), so it is reasonable Adonijah expected to be David's successor.

Adonijah had witnessed Absalom's failed rebellion during David's healthy years, so he waited until David's health was gone to seize the throne. After describing how Adonijah was riding in a chariot with fifty runners, the narrator inserts an unusual comment that reflects negatively on David for not rebuking his son's inappropriate behavior (1 Kgs 1:6). The lack of a paternal rebuke is particularly surprising here, since the chariot-riding-with-fifty-runners phenomenon was one of the precursors to Absalom's failed coup (2 Sam 15:1). Two of David's key leaders who were loyal to him during Absalom's rebellion, Joab the general and Abiathar the priest, here support Adonijah while David still lives (1 Kgs 1:7). (Abiathar pays for his insubordination later; 2:26–27, 35.) With the support of these two and all his brothers (except Solomon),

4. David's second son, Kileab (2 Sam 3:3), disappears from the narrative, so most scholars assume he died earlier. See David G. Firth, *1 & 2 Samuel*, AOTC 8 (Downers Grove, IL: InterVarsity Press, 2009), 341.

Adonijah is well on his way to a successful succession. David is clueless; fortunately for Solomon, Nathan is not.

Nathan's Report to Bathsheba (1:11–14)

The prophet Nathan plays a crucial role in David's life, appearing earlier in two incidents, both of which have a direct impact on Solomon. First, Nathan delivered one of the most significant Old Testament prophesies from YHWH to David that both guaranteed a ruling Davidic heir on the throne "forever" and predicted that David's son (i.e., Solomon) would eventually build a temple for YHWH (2 Sam 7:12–16). Second, Nathan pronounced a judgment upon David after his power rape of Bathsheba and the murder of Uriah (12:1–15).[5]

Instead of going straight to David as he did to condemn him for the Bathsheba affair (12:1), Nathan goes to Bathsheba, who is now David's wife and Solomon's mother. Nathan informs her not only of Adonijah's plan but also of David's ignorance of it. Nathan begins his report to Bathsheba with a question, "Have you not heard . . . ?" (1 Kgs 1:11). The dialogue in this chapter and elsewhere in biblical narratives is often driven by questions, both genuine ones (vv. 16, 24, 27) and rhetorical ones (vv. 6, 11, 13 [2x]). Nathan's comments to Bathsheba do not focus on what Adonijah has done but on what they need to do now to save her life and that of her son. Nathan tells her to remind David of the oath he gave her (a quote in a quote in a quote: v. 13) guaranteeing that Solomon would succeed him. Interestingly, while Nathan, Bathsheba, and David each mention this promise regarding Solomon's succession (vv. 13, 17, 30), there is no record of it earlier in the narrative of 1–2 Samuel (but see 1 Chr 22:9–10). Nathan's strategy to interrupt her message with his own similar message to the king should provoke the passive king to take immediate action.

Bathsheba's Report to David (1:15–21)

Bathsheba follows Nathan's advice and goes to David ("the aged king," 1:15), which would have been awkward for her since he is with the young, beautiful Abishag. David's terse question, "What is it you want?" does not sound hospitable (v. 16). Bathsheba begins by reminding David of the promise given to

---

5. I argue that David's relationship with Bathsheba was a power rape, not consensual adultery; see David T. Lamb, *Prostitutes and Polygamists: A Look at Love, Old Testament Style* (Grand Rapids: Zondervan, 2015), 127–33. For a discussion of Davidic dynastic oracles, see David T. Lamb, "The Eternal Curse: Seven Deuteronomistic Judgment Oracles against the House of David" in *For and Against David: Story and History in the Books of Samuel*, ed. A. G. Auld and E. Eynikel, BETL 232 (Leuven: Peeters, 2010), 315–25.

her that Solomon would rule. While her language is deferential (repetitions of "my lord" and "your servant"), she has no qualms about boldly accusing the king of ignorance regarding Adonijah's recent usurpation of the throne. She gives David more details about Adonijah's uprising (the sacrifices, the support of Abiathar and Joab) than Nathan gave her, so she must have had additional sources of information. Bathsheba concludes with a dire prediction for herself and her son should Adonijah hold onto the throne (v. 21). Bathsheba's concern here is not simply paranoia, since newly installed rulers frequently begin their reign by eliminating potential rivals (see 1 Kgs 2:5–46; 2 Kgs 10:1–17)

Nathan's Report to David (1:22–27)

As planned, Nathan interrupts Bathsheba's report to give his own corroborating testimony to David concerning Adonijah's attempt to take the throne. Just as he did with Bathsheba, Nathan begins with a question (1:24). Then he details what Adonijah has done to make himself king, including the people's declaration, "Long live King Adonijah" (v. 25), which is surely meant to shock David, who knows he will not live much longer. Nathan, who knows how to use drama effectively with his king ("You are the man!," 2 Sam 12:7), concludes his address with a dramatic question, wondering whether David planned on Adonijah's succession all along without telling his servants (1 Kgs 1:27).

David's Promise to Bathsheba (1:28–31)

Nathan's two-stage plan works like a double-shot of adrenaline, and the aged king suddenly becomes invigorated and initiates his own two-stage plan. First, just as the prophet began with Bathsheba, the king calls her in and then reiterates the promise he said to her previously, swearing in the name of YHWH that he will make Solomon king that very day. She responds as someone whose royal request has been granted, wishing that he "live forever" (v. 31) in language similar to the people's declaration regarding the long life of "King Adonijah" (v. 25). Despite Bathsheba's wish, David will barely survive into the next chapter.

David's Plan to Zadok, Nathan, and Benaiah (1:32–40)

Second, David calls in Zadok the priest, Nathan the prophet, and Benaiah the future general to implement his plan publicly, ensuring that Solomon is installed as his successor. Solomon is to mount David's royal mule, to be anointed not just by a prophet as he and Saul were (1 Sam 10:1; 16:13) but also by a priest (Zadok) to establish his royal legitimacy with both prophetic and priestly authority. Just as David was anointed while Saul lived (16:1–2),

Solomon is to be anointed while David lives. The trumpet is to be blown, the proclamation "Long live King Solomon!" is to be shouted, and then he will sit on David's own throne. Unlike Kirta of Ugarit (see Listen to the Story above), who cursed his overly ambitious son Yassubu, David says nothing negative about Adonijah, never mentioning the older son by name in this narrative or even in his final deathbed curses (1 Kgs 2:5–9). David's plan pleases his servants, so Zadok, Nathan, and Benaiah faithfully execute the plan (1:38–40). The people of Israel are also apparently pleased since their rejoicing causes an earthquake (perhaps told hyperbolically). David has done everything in his power to guarantee that Solomon's throne is secure. David's decision to honor his son, Solomon, by having him ride on a royal steed (vv. 33, 38) is a practice that finds parallels in the story of Esther (6:8) as well as Jesus's entry into Jerusalem on Palm Sunday on a colt (Matt 21:5; Mark 11:2–7; see also Zech 9:9).

Jonathan's Report to Adonijah (1:41–48)

The tables are now turned for Adonijah. His brother has been proclaimed king, and he is ignorant. Adonijah and his guests hear the tumult, which prompts their curiosity. Adonijah inquires of Jonathan, the son of Abiathar the priest, who has just arrived. Adonijah's expectation of good news based on the messenger's character here (1:42) echoes David's statement to Ahimaaz, who was reporting the results of the battle against Absalom's forces (2 Sam 18:27). While Ahimaaz delivered good news, Jonathan's news is devastating to Adonijah.

While most English translations (including the NIV) either ignore it or translate it inconsistently, Jonathan thrice repeats a Hebrew expression (*wegam*; literally, "and also") at the beginning of verses 46, 47, and 48 to emphasize each of the things David has done to establish Solomon, rendered nicely each time by Alter as "And what's more . . ."[6] For a rebel, Jonathan's language sounds surprisingly deferential toward David as he twice speaks of "our lord King David" (vv. 43, 47), perhaps signaling that, despite his association with the rebellion, he is still loyal to the king. Jonathan's thorough report mentions all of David's important servants by name, the riding of the mule, the anointing, the cheering of the crowds, and David's final words of praise to YHWH ("Praise be to the LORD, the God of Israel," v. 48), which were not recorded earlier. Thus, Jonathan's inclusion of David's declaration of praise at the end

6. Robert Alter, *Ancient Israel, The Former Prophets: Joshua, Judges, Samuel, and Kings* (New York: Norton, 2013), 606.

of his speech sends a message to Adonijah that God is behind Solomon's succession, with an implicit warning to not continue in his rebellion. While Adonijah's rebellion got off to a strong start, David has quickly quashed it and effectively promoted Adonijah's younger brother instead.

Solomon's Conditional Promise to Adonijah (1:49–53)

Now that Solomon has the support of the people, David and his officials, and YHWH, Adonijah's followers realize that his campaign for the throne is a lost cause, so they flee. Just as Bathsheba earlier feared the consequences of Adonijah's succession for herself and her son, now Adonijah fears retribution from his younger brother who has successfully taken power. To avoid certain death, Adonijah goes to the altar where the sacrifices were presumably just made and grabs hold of the horns to claim sanctuary (as Joab will do also; see 1 Kgs 2:28). Adonijah's request here (v. 51) is similar to Bathsheba's earlier (vv. 16–21). In each case the supplicant asks from a precarious position for a promise of mercy from the sovereign ruler. The primary difference is that while Bathsheba has done no wrong, Adonijah is guilty of insurrection. Solomon grants his older brother's request (v. 52), provided that he behaves properly, a condition that Adonijah will fail to abide by (see 2:13–25).

Until he makes his conditional pronouncement of grace for Adonijah, Solomon is completely passive in the previous fifty-one verses of the narrative. Solomon's passivity stands out in stark contrast to Adonijah's initiative taking. Nathan, Bathsheba, David, Zadok, Benaiah, and others all take steps to ensure Solomon's successful accession to the throne, while he does nothing except go along for the ride, literally on a mule. And his first royal "act" is merely a decision to not act against his brother. However, after the death of David in the next chapter (2:10), Solomon's passivity ends.

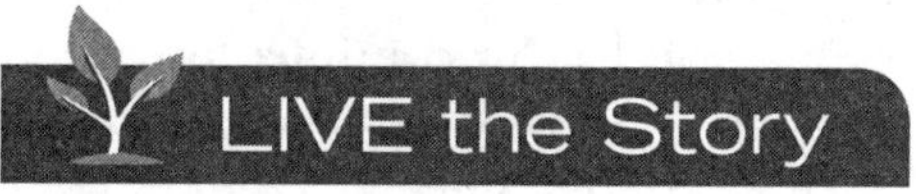

LIVE the Story

The Surprising Passivity of God

Not only is Solomon passive in the first chapter of 1 Kings, but God seems to be, also. YHWH is absent as an active character in the narrative of Adonijah's rebellion and Solomon's succession. He is mentioned in 1 Kings 1 only in the context of oaths and prayers (vv. 17, 29–30, 36–37, 47, 48). YHWH does not appear in parts of the story where one might expect him. While the text of 2 Kings later states that Jehu was anointed by YHWH three times (2 Kgs 9:3, 6, 12), there is no textual reference to YHWH as Solomon is anointed

(1 Kgs 1:34, 39). YHWH had clearly spoken about his choice of first Saul and then David as rulers over Israel (1 Sam 9:17; 16:12), so now during this crucial juncture in Israel's history, why is God silent?

God may be silent in 1 Kings 1, but he was not silent earlier in Solomon's life. God had actually spoken a word of blessing via the prophet Nathan upon the infant Solomon immediately after his birth.

> Then David comforted his wife Bathsheba, and he went to her and made love to her. She gave birth to a son, and they named him Solomon. The LORD loved him; and because the LORD loved him, he sent word through Nathan the prophet to name him Jedidiah. (2 Sam 12:24–25)

While the text is unclear about the message's recipients, it is reasonable to assume Nathan delivered it to his parents, David and Bathsheba. In the message, YHWH declares his love for Solomon and renames him "Jedidiah," meaning "beloved of YHWH." The text records nothing similar for any of David's other sons, suggesting that this initial word of divine blessing was sufficient guidance for David, Bathsheba, and Solomon to know God's will regarding the succession. The son that God uniquely loves should succeed David the man after God's own heart (1 Sam 13:14). Thus, David's praise to God for allowing him to see Solomon as his successor (1 Kgs 1:48) was founded in faith upon this earlier prophetic name that spoke of God's love for his son.

Just as David's family needed to remember God's earlier message during a period of divine silence, God's people today need to recall how he has spoken in the past. At several points in my doctoral studies program at Oxford I became discouraged and wanted to quit. I was struggling in my courses and Oxford did not seem to want me to continue. It was not worth the pain and anguish I was experiencing. My wife Shannon had to continue to remind me that God had spoken to us several years earlier, before I even began my program, that he had led me to obtain a doctorate in Old Testament. Because of her reminders of God's direction and the support of family and friends, I was able to persist and complete my program. If you are struggling in the midst of a time of crisis where God doesn't seem to be at work, spend time reflecting on ways he has spoken to you in the past that could encourage you.

Leadership Transition Lessons

Transitions are stressful. While 1–2 Samuel records only one royal transition (from Saul to David), Kings records dozens, although none perhaps as difficult and dramatic as the first (from David to Solomon). Several factors contributed to make Solomon's succession stressful. The earlier rebellions of Absalom and Sheba (2 Sam 15–18, 20) both led to civil wars between the forces of David and the rebels. The Israelite people would have been justifiably worried about another war between the two sons of David.

In a stressful social setting when there has been a tense interaction and a person finally makes a joke, those present tend to laugh too hard to relieve the stress. The people's ground-shaking response to Solomon's coronation has a similar feel. They were anxious about the succession, and at the point when there finally is an outlet, they release it in a vociferous celebration.

To make transitions less stressful, leaders in churches, ministries, and other organizations can learn three important lessons from the succession from David to Solomon. First, think about leadership transitions early. Many Christian leaders, a bit like David, put off thinking about leadership transitions. This often happens when a charismatic individual, again like David, has been in charge of an organization for an extended period of time. Nine years before his anticipated retirement, Jack Welch, the CEO of General Electric, said, "From now on, [choosing my successor] is the most important decision I'll make. It occupies a considerable amount of thought almost every day."[7] David did not seem to put much thought into who his successor would be. He was preoccupied with staying warm. David's delay was costly and almost resulted in another civil war. As key leaders get older, they can become resistant to change and often stay longer than they should. It is never too early to think about leadership succession. Jesus himself made the selection of leaders one of his first priorities, calling his disciples to follow him as soon as he began his public ministry (Mark 1:16–20; John 1:35–51).

Second, listen to key advisors during times of transition. Leaders of organizations can become insular and surrounded by people who are loyal but unwilling to challenge or confront people in power. Despite his faults, David still listened to the condemnation by Nathan regarding the murder of Uriah and the power rape of Bathsheba. Bathsheba, previously the object of David's lust (2 Sam 11:2–4), is now a bold advisor who, along with Nathan, challenges David to act on behalf of Solomon. Leaders need to surround themselves with people who are willing to exhort, challenge, and even rebuke. When these people speak, leaders should listen. Before selecting his twelve apostles, Jesus pulled an all-nighter in prayer listening to the advice of his Father about

7. From Robert Slater, *The New GE* (Homewood, IL: Irwin, 1993), 268, quoted from James C. Collins and Jerry I. Porras, *Built to Last: Successful Habits of Visionary Companies* (New York: HarperCollins, 1997), 169.

whom to choose (Luke 6:12–16). (Although some advice here should not be followed—when you are old and cold, it is not advisable to get a young virgin bed-warmer!)

Third, older leaders need to do everything possible to ensure the success of younger leaders. Like most new leaders, Solomon was in a precarious situation. It took David a while to get moving, but once he did, he held nothing back. He arranged the mobilization of leaders, the riding of the royal mule, the prophetic anointing, the blown trumpet, and the public proclamation. David wanted to give Solomon as much legitimacy as possible. Even younger leaders like Benaiah contributed by offering a prayer of blessing for the new king. Leaders young and old should pray for and bless new leaders to give them the best possibility of success. To bless his followers and ensure their successful ministry, Jesus prayed for them and gave them his own Spirit (John 15:26; 16:7–15; 17:6–26).

There is a temptation for leaders stepping out of significant leadership roles to sabotage the process, making their successors look bad in an attempt to make themselves look good. When US presidents leave office, they write a letter to their successor. After the difficult campaign of 1988, George H. W. Bush wrote to Bill Clinton, "You will be our President when you read this note . . . I am rooting for you."[8] Bush had plenty of reasons to harm the man who defeated him after only one term, yet even he worked to ensure the success of his successor. Christian leaders can thus learn from the examples of not only Jack Welch, George Bush, and King David, but most significantly our Lord Jesus.

Pointing to Jesus

While it is not always obvious to readers, 2 Kings is part of a much larger story that begins not just with the book of Joshua, as some scholars believe, but literally "in the beginning" of Genesis. After Kings, this long narrative is discontinued. Within the prophetic books and some of the other narrative books (e.g., Esther, Ezra-Nehemiah), aspects of Israel's exilic and postexilic story are told, but the extended narrative that encompasses the Pentateuch and the Historical Books has an ending of sorts at the conclusion of 2 Kings with the temple destroyed, Israel and Judah conquered, and no autonomous Israelite ruler on the throne. For Christians, however, the story does not end yet; the interruption in the story was just an extended intermission until the

8. Nancy Gibbs and Michael Duffy, *The Presidents Club: Inside the World's Most Exclusive Fraternity* (New York: Simon and Schuster, 2012), 1.

first book of the New Testament introduces the reader to Jesus, the son of David and Abraham (Matt 1:1).

Christians therefore read the narrative of Israel's and Judah's rulers in light of the story of the individual whom the New Testament authors portray as God's anointed ruler, Jesus. Just as the beginning of this discussion of 1 Kings 1 was set in the context of ancient Near Eastern literature, the end of each discussion will be set in the context of the New Testament, particularly the Gospels, as they contain the narrative of the birth, life, ministry, death, and resurrection of Jesus.

New Testament parallels related to Solomon's wisdom and the temple will be noted in the following chapters, but several striking ones between Solomon and Jesus from 1 Kings 1 should be mentioned here. The context for both Solomon and Jesus centered on a struggle for authority and power. For Solomon the conflict was primarily political, involving his brother Adonijah. For Jesus the conflict was primarily spiritual, involving the religious leaders (e.g., Mark 1:22; 2:7, 16, 24; 3:6). Both Solomon and Jesus needed legitimacy to validate their authority.

David gave legitimacy to both Solomon and Jesus. Solomon's father had received a dynastic promise from YHWH via the prophet Nathan: "Your house and your kingdom will endure forever before me; your throne will be established forever" (2 Sam 7:16). David's promise granted royal authority to his future heirs, and therefore both Solomon and Jesus are described as the son of David (1 Kgs 1:13; 2:12; Matt 1:1, 20; 9:27; cf. 1 Chr 29:22).

Royal rituals also contributed to their legitimacy. For Solomon, his mule ride gave him authority as the animal was previously ridden by the king; for Jesus, his donkey ride fulfilled the prophecy of a king's entrance to Jerusalem (1 Kgs 1:33, 38; Matt 21:2–7; see also Zech 9:9). Solomon was anointed by Zadok the priest and Nathan the prophet, and Jesus the Christ ("Christ" means "anointed one") was "anointed" by John the Baptist and God's Spirit at his baptism (Matt 3:13–16).

Finally, and perhaps most significantly, God gave legitimacy to both Solomon and Jesus in a declaration of love. At his birth, YHWH renames Solomon "Jedidiah," "beloved of YHWH" (2 Sam 12:24–25). At Jesus's baptism, God's voice speaks from heaven declaring to Jesus, "you are my son, whom I love" (Mark 1:11; Luke 3:22). In all these parallels we see a pattern of the father, both David and God, working to validate the reign of the son, both Solomon and Jesus.

CHAPTER 2

1 Kings 2:1–46

LISTEN to the Story

1When the time drew near for David to die, he gave a charge to Solomon his son.

2"I am about to go the way of all the earth," he said. "So be strong, act like a man, 3and observe what the Lord your God requires: Walk in obedience to him, and keep his decrees and commands, his laws and regulations, as written in the Law of Moses. Do this so that you may prosper in all you do and wherever you go 4and that the Lord may keep his promise to me: 'If your descendants watch how they live, and if they walk faithfully before me with all their heart and soul, you will never fail to have a successor on the throne of Israel.'

5"Now you yourself know what Joab son of Zeruiah did to me—what he did to the two commanders of Israel's armies, Abner son of Ner and Amasa son of Jether. He killed them, shedding their blood in peacetime as if in battle, and with that blood he stained the belt around his waist and the sandals on his feet. 6Deal with him according to your wisdom, but do not let his gray head go down to the grave in peace.

7"But show kindness to the sons of Barzillai of Gilead and let them be among those who eat at your table. They stood by me when I fled from your brother Absalom.

8"And remember, you have with you Shimei son of Gera, the Benjamite from Bahurim, who called down bitter curses on me the day I went to Mahanaim. When he came down to meet me at the Jordan, I swore to him by the Lord: 'I will not put you to death by the sword.' 9But now, do not consider him innocent. You are a man of wisdom; you will know what to do to him. Bring his gray head down to the grave in blood."

10Then David rested with his ancestors and was buried in the City of David. 11He had reigned forty years over Israel—seven years in Hebron

and thirty-three in Jerusalem. 12So Solomon sat on the throne of his father
David, and his rule was firmly established.

13Now Adonijah, the son of Haggith, went to Bathsheba, Solomon's
mother. Bathsheba asked him, "Do you come peacefully?"

He answered, "Yes, peacefully." 14Then he added, "I have something
to say to you."

"You may say it," she replied.

15"As you know," he said, "the kingdom was mine. All Israel looked to
me as their king. But things changed, and the kingdom has gone to my
brother; for it has come to him from the LORD. 16Now I have one request
to make of you. Do not refuse me."

"You may make it," she said.

17So he continued, "Please ask King Solomon—he will not refuse
you—to give me Abishag the Shunammite as my wife."

18"Very well," Bathsheba replied, "I will speak to the king for you."

19When Bathsheba went to King Solomon to speak to him for Adonijah,
the king stood up to meet her, bowed down to her and sat down on his
throne. He had a throne brought for the king's mother, and she sat down
at his right hand.

20"I have one small request to make of you," she said. "Do not
refuse me."

The king replied, "Make it, my mother; I will not refuse you."

21So she said, "Let Abishag the Shunammite be given in marriage to
your brother Adonijah."

22King Solomon answered his mother, "Why do you request Abishag
the Shunammite for Adonijah? You might as well request the kingdom for
him—after all, he is my older brother—yes, for him and for Abiathar the
priest and Joab son of Zeruiah!"

23Then King Solomon swore by the LORD: "May God deal with me, be
it ever so severely, if Adonijah does not pay with his life for this request!
24And now, as surely as the LORD lives—he who has established me securely
on the throne of my father David and has founded a dynasty for me as
he promised—Adonijah shall be put to death today!" 25So King Solomon
gave orders to Benaiah son of Jehoiada, and he struck down Adonijah
and he died.

26To Abiathar the priest the king said, "Go back to your fields in
Anathoth. You deserve to die, but I will not put you to death now, because

you carried the ark of the Sovereign LORD before my father David and
shared all my father's hardships." [27]So Solomon removed Abiathar from
the priesthood of the LORD, fulfilling the word the LORD had spoken at
Shiloh about the house of Eli.

[28]When the news reached Joab, who had conspired with Adonijah
though not with Absalom, he fled to the tent of the LORD and took hold
of the horns of the altar. [29]King Solomon was told that Joab had fled to the
tent of the LORD and was beside the altar. Then Solomon ordered Benaiah
son of Jehoiada, "Go, strike him down!"

[30]So Benaiah entered the tent of the LORD and said to Joab, "The king
says, 'Come out!'"

But he answered, "No, I will die here."

Benaiah reported to the king, "This is how Joab answered me."

[31]Then the king commanded Benaiah, "Do as he says. Strike him
down and bury him, and so clear me and my whole family of the guilt
of the innocent blood that Joab shed. [32]The LORD will repay him for the
blood he shed, because without my father David knowing it he attacked
two men and killed them with the sword. Both of them—Abner son of
Ner, commander of Israel's army, and Amasa son of Jether, commander
of Judah's army—were better men and more upright than he. [33]May the
guilt of their blood rest on the head of Joab and his descendants forever.
But on David and his descendants, his house and his throne, may there
be the LORD's peace forever."

[34]So Benaiah son of Jehoiada went up and struck down Joab and killed
him, and he was buried at his home out in the country. [35]The king put
Benaiah son of Jehoiada over the army in Joab's position and replaced
Abiathar with Zadok the priest.

[36]Then the king sent for Shimei and said to him, "Build yourself a
house in Jerusalem and live there, but do not go anywhere else. [37]The day
you leave and cross the Kidron Valley, you can be sure you will die; your
blood will be on your own head."

[38]Shimei answered the king, "What you say is good. Your servant will do
as my lord the king has said." And Shimei stayed in Jerusalem for a long time.

[39]But three years later, two of Shimei's slaves ran off to Achish son of
Maakah, king of Gath, and Shimei was told, "Your slaves are in Gath."
[40]At this, he saddled his donkey and went to Achish at Gath in search of
his slaves. So Shimei went away and brought the slaves back from Gath.

[41]When Solomon was told that Shimei had gone from Jerusalem to Gath and had returned, [42]the king summoned Shimei and said to him, "Did I not make you swear by the LORD and warn you, 'On the day you leave to go anywhere else, you can be sure you will die'? At that time you said to me, 'What you say is good. I will obey.' [43]Why then did you not keep your oath to the LORD and obey the command I gave you?"

[44]The king also said to Shimei, "You know in your heart all the wrong you did to my father David. Now the LORD will repay you for your wrongdoing. [45]But King Solomon will be blessed, and David's throne will remain secure before the LORD forever."

[46]Then the king gave the order to Benaiah son of Jehoiada, and he went out and struck Shimei down and he died.

The kingdom was now established in Solomon's hands.

Listening to the Text in the Story: Biblical Texts: 2 Samuel 2:23; 3:27; 16:5–13; 17:27–29; 19:16–23; 20:10; 1 Kings 1:1–4; Ancient Near Eastern Texts: The Ba'lu Myth; The Azatiwada Inscription

David, Israel's greatest king, the descendant of Judah and ancestor of Jesus, is about to die. But he knows Solomon's throne is not yet firmly established, so he gives some final words of advice to his son, which recall several incidents from his life. A brief review of these stories will provide important background to understand why David cares about the fates of Joab, Shimei, and Barzillai.

In the civil war between the Judean forces of David and the Israelite forces of Saul's son, Ishbaal (also called Ish-bosheth), Abner killed Joab's brother Asahel. Abner had warned Asahel to stop chasing him because he did not want to kill the brother of his friend, but Asahel had ignored the warning. When Abner later defected to David's side, Joab assassinated him while pretending to give a secret message (2 Sam 2:23; 3:27). David knew Joab's deed was dishonorable, so he cursed Joab's household. In a strikingly similar story, Amasa, who had been the commander of Absalom's rebel army, was pardoned by David and promoted to be his top general, replacing Joab, who, not surprisingly, then assassinated his rival while pretending to kiss him (20:9–10).

As David fled Jerusalem during the rebellion of his son, Absalom, he was cursed by a descendant of Saul named Shimei, but David refused to retaliate (16:5–13). Compared to Joab's violence, Shimei's insults could seem trivial, but Israel's culture valued honor far more than ours; therefore, his shaming taunts toward the king were a crime that warranted death (v. 9). Shortly after Shimei's curses, Barzillai came to bless David and his forces with generous provisions during their flight (17:27–29). David's curse on the "gray" heads of Joab and Shimei (1 Kgs 2:6, 9) is reminiscent of the Ba'lu Myth, which describes someone's "gray head" flowing with blood and the "gray hairs" of their beard flowing with gore.[1]

This chapter not only records Israel's first successful royal succession, but it also reveals many of the problems associated with these transitions. Bathsheba's earlier fear that her life was in danger (1 Kgs 1:21) was reasonable since rivals to the throne and their families are often eliminated to establish the new ruler's throne, as evidenced by Solomon's execution of Adonijah and Joab (2:24–25, 28–34). Perhaps the most extensive royal purge is performed by Jehu of Israel who, during the divided monarchy, wipes out not only the royal family of Israel but also the royal family of Judah (2 Kgs 9–10).

To bring stability, new leaders relied on the loyalty of officials. In the Phoenician Azatiwada Inscription, Azatiwada, a royal official in Cilicia, describes his loyal support offered to the son of his lord the king in a dynastic succession: "I caused him to reign upon the throne of his father."[2] Similarly, Barzillai, Zadok, and Benaiah are rewarded for their support of David and Solomon—and Joab and Abiathar are punished for their support of Adonijah.

The Charge of David to Solomon (2:1–12)

Death dominates the second chapter of 1 Kings, as David's looming death finally arrives and the executions of a brother of Solomon (Adonijah), a general of David (Joab), and a descendant of Saul (Shimei) are carried out. Solomon receives a final charge from David before his father "rested with his ancestors" (v. 10). Solomon then begins to firmly establish his kingdom by removing rivals and punishing disloyalty.

While obedience is emphasized in the first half of David's charge, in the rest of the chapter violence is emphasized. The noun "blood" (*dam*) appears seven times (vv. 5 [2x], 9, 31, 32, 33, 37), and the noun "sword" (*herev*) appears twice (vv. 8, 32). Forms of the verb "to die" (*mut*) appear thirteen times (vv. 1,

1. *COS* 1:254a.
2. *COS* 2:149b.

8, 24, 25, 26 [2x], 30, 34, 37 [2x], 42 [2x], 46), and forms of the verb "to strike down" (*paga'*) appear six times (vv. 25, 29, 31, 32, 34, 46). The beginning of Solomon's reign was characterized by bloodshed.

David's last speech to Solomon divides easily into two halves, the pious first section saying essentially "be a good boy" and the vicious second section saying essentially "kill the bastards." David begins by acknowledging his imminent death, then he commissions his son to "be strong," echoing YHWH's call to Joshua (Josh 1:6, 7, 9). We do not know Solomon's age at this point, but three factors suggest he was young.

1. David tells Solomon to "act like a man" (1 Kgs 2:2);
2. Solomon was born after David had already had numerous sons (2 Sam 3:2–5; 5:14–16);
3. Solomon tells YHWH later, "I am only a little child" (1 Kgs 3:7).

David exhorts his son to obey the Law (*torah*) of Moses in language reminiscent of Deuteronomy by walking in God's ways (Deut 8:6; 11:22) and keeping his decrees (6:2; 7:9) in order to prosper (6:24; 29:9). While David received from YHWH an unconditional dynastic promise (2 Sam 7:12–16), in the book of Kings Solomon's dynastic promise is consistently described as conditioned upon obedience, as it is here (1 Kgs 2:4; 6:12; 8:25; 9:4–5).[3] This language is unexpected since, as David's reigning heir, Solomon would be a benefactor of the same promise. Just as Solomon would later fail to walk in God's ways (1 Kgs 11), Adonijah would fail to fulfill the obligations placed upon him by his younger brother (1:52). While Solomon's punishment was delayed to the reign of his son, Rehoboam, Adonijah's was not.

As David shifts in his charge from obedience to vengeance, he introduces a major theme of Solomon's narrative—his son's wisdom (2:6, 9)—which will be necessary to execute the appropriate judgments, both in the short term and later in his reign. Solomon's primary accomplishment that his father could not achieve was the construction of the temple, but before he could get to any building projects, his father wanted him to eliminate a few individuals. Joab needed to die for killing his military rivals (Abner and Amasa) during times of peace, and Shimei's "gray head" needed to be sent "to the grave in blood" (v. 9) since he cursed David as he fled from Absalom (2 Sam 16:5–14). Alter describes David's language as "a last will and testament worthy of a dying

3. For a longer discussion of the conditional or unconditional nature of David's covenant, see T. E. Fretheim, *First and Second Kings*, Westminster Bible Companion (Louisville: Westminster John Knox, 1999), 28–29.

Mafia capo."[4] While Shimei is a minor character, Joab was David's right-hand man who often did his ruler's dirty work (leading the army while David raped Bathsheba [2 Sam 11–12]; killing the rebel Absalom [18:15]). Joab, along with Nathan, was part of a select group of people who were bold enough to confront King David (11:18–21; 14; 19:5–8). One of David's sons was named Nathan (5:14), but Joab's loyal and costly service to his king were not rewarded. The text is silent, but perhaps David was emphasizing to his son that individuals like Joab who kill royalty deserve death since Adonijah could still be punished by Solomon. David didn't kill Saul when he had the chance (1 Sam 24; 26), and he didn't want Absalom killed (2 Sam 18:5), so he certainly wouldn't want Adonijah killed, but curiously he doesn't mention Solomon's rebellious older brother at this point. Barzillai's sons, however, are to be rewarded for their faithful loyalty to David during his time of crisis.

The text gives a brief formulaic notice of David's death after a forty-year reign, but nothing is mentioned about anyone mourning the event. The absence of any grieving is particularly noticeable as many of Israel's key leaders were mourned by the entire nation: Jacob (Gen 50:1–3), Moses (Deut 34:8), Samuel (1 Sam 25:1), and Saul and Jonathan (2 Sam 1). The text then records that Solomon's "rule was firmly established" (1 Kgs 2:12) as if it were a done deal, but royal transitions are often times of great instability, as the narrative of chapter one reveals. Several other events still need to take place to solidify Solomon's power, and the text repeats similar phrases about Solomon's established rule each time (2:24, 45, 46; see also 3:28).

The Death of Adonijah (2:13–25)

David is gone, Solomon is king, but the power struggle continues. The failed rebel Adonijah approaches the queen mother Bathsheba. Adonijah clearly sees Bathsheba as a key figure during this transition, since she played an important role in bringing her son to the throne instead of him. Times are still tense, so Bathsheba asks if he is coming peacefully. He responds affirmatively, then proceeds to request Abishag, David's bed-warmer (1:3–4), as his wife. The request seems harmless to her, so she agrees to ask her son the king.

When Bathsheba approaches Solomon, she gets him to agree to her "small request" before she even asks it (always a bad idea; 2:20). After hearing of his brother's proposal of a marital union with his father's quasi-concubine, Abishag, Solomon erupts and, despite his earlier promise, refuses the request. Passive Solomon who barely spoke in 1 Kings 1 morphs into bloody Solomon

4. Alter, *The Former Prophets*, 608.

who declares that Adonijah would die that day. Solomon's only speech previously was to warn his brother to not act wickedly (1:52), and here he apparently decided that this small request was wicked.

What was so bad about this request? If Adonijah married Abishag, it would strengthen his claim to the throne, because he would appear to be favored by the legacy of father. Absalom had sex with David's concubines while he was attempting to seize his father's throne (2 Sam 16:21–22). Solomon is wise enough to know that his position is still precarious, as he acknowledges; Adonijah is older than Solomon, and Adonijah's supporters, Joab the general and Abiathar the priest, still control the military and the priesthood. Thus, a treasonous act, couched as a small favor, warranted a death sentence for Solomon's brother. Adonijah was quickly dispatched by Benaiah, Solomon's newly appointed executioner.

The Fates of Abiathar, Joab, and Shimei (2:26–46)

While it is difficult to be certain about the timing, Adonijah's scheme finally prompts Solomon to follow through on his father's commission and remove Adonijah's supporters from their positions of power. His message to Abiathar the priest stated that, even though he deserved death for endorsing Adonijah, because of his loyalty to David during Absalom's rebellion (2 Sam 15:24–35; see also 1 Sam 22:20–22; 23:6–9; 30:7; 2 Sam 8:17; 17:15; 19:11; 20:25), the new king would spare his life but remove him from the priesthood and exile him to Anathoth. Abiathar's demotion fulfilled a prophecy pronounced against the house of Eli before the establishment of the monarchy (1 Sam 2:31–33).

Joab discovers "the news," which presumably included both Adonijah's death and Abiathar's banishment. Seeing the writing on the wall, he attempts to claim sanctuary in the tabernacle by seizing the horns of the altar, prompting Benaiah to double-check with his boss. Solomon had shown mercy to Adonijah earlier when he seized the altar's horns (1 Kgs 1:50–53). The law of Moses, however, declared that sanctuary was only intended for people who killed accidentally, not intentionally (Exod 21:13–14) as Joab had done. Solomon does not spend much time deliberating about the Adonijah precedent or about Mosaic law but bluntly commands his executioner to do his job. When Joab resists the command to leave the tent, Benaiah tells Solomon that Joab said he would die where he was. At this point, the commander Benaiah is reluctant to kill the commander Joab in a time of peace to punish him for killing two commanders (Abner and Abasa) in times of peace. This incident is comparable to the anointed future king David not wanting to kill the anointed current king Saul (1 Sam 24; 26). The king tells the soldier to grant the general's request and kill him there, because he shed the innocent blood of his fellow commanders. In the ancient world, army commanders strengthened their reputation by killing other military heroes (e.g., David killing Goliath; 1 Sam 17). After Benaiah executes Joab, Solomon promotes him into Joab's old position as head of the army. Zadok is installed as priest in the place of Abiathar, perhaps because he had not supported Adonijah's royal claim earlier (1 Kgs 1:8).

The narrative curiously never mentions anything about Solomon following David's advice regarding the family of Barzillai but moves on to the fate of Shimei. While David told Solomon to kill Shimei for cursing the king as he fled from Absalom, Solomon initially shows him leniency, perhaps because he had not supported Adonijah earlier (1:8). Solomon tells Shimei to remain under house arrest in Jerusalem, where Solomon can keep a close watch on him. Solomon ominously vows that if Shimei crosses the Kidron Valley, he will die. Happy he did not suffer the same fate as Adonijah and Joab, he praises the sentence and promises to abide by it. However, three years later, his decision to retrieve two slaves who had run away to Gath constituted a breach of his agreement, so the king reminded him of his oath before telling Benaiah to strike him down. Thus, the "gray hairs" of both Joab and Shimei were finally sent to the grave as David had commanded.

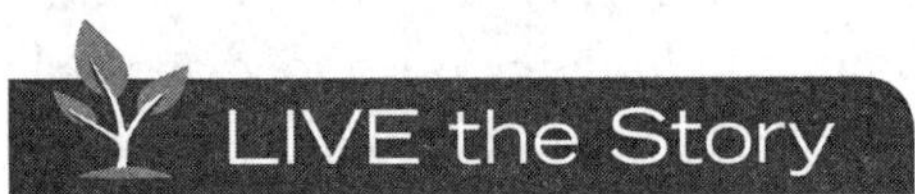

Walk in Obedience

Several of the major themes from the first chapter of 1 Kings continue into the book's second chapter as God remains absent in the midst of this crucial royal leadership transition. However, even though God does not act or speak, his words take center stage in David's final address to Solomon. The dying monarch tells his son to observe God's requirements, to walk in obedience to him, and to keep his decrees, commands, laws, and regulations as recorded in the law of Moses (2:3).

While some Christians think the Old Testament law is no longer valid for Christians, both Jesus and Paul seem to think otherwise (e.g., Mark 12:28–34; Rom 7:12–16). Certainly, some aspects of the law are no longer binding (particularly laws about diet and sacrifices), and one always needs to be careful to not think that obedience somehow allows a person to earn God's favor. There is too much to say on the relationship between faith and obedience, but Jesus's teaching on the subject needs to be remembered as a counter to those who simply say, "We're under grace, not law." Jesus taught that people who break even the most insignificant of the commandments and teach others to do the same will be called least in the kingdom of heaven, but people who practice and teach them will be called great in the kingdom (Matt 5:19). According to Jesus, David, despite his great sins, will be called great in heaven, because he taught his son to obey God.

We can therefore make two points regarding obedience here from David's example. First, leaders emphasize obedience. At the end of one's life, a person will want to focus on passing on the most important lessons. For David, and for Jesus, obedience was crucial. Immediately before Jesus left his disciples for the final time, he commissioned them to teach their disciples to obey everything Jesus had commanded them (28:20). David wasn't just a leader training his successor; he was also a parent training his child. Obedience to God's laws should be emphasized not only by older leaders to younger leaders but also by parents to children.

The second point is that obedience is meant to be a blessing, not a chore. David tells Solomon, "Do this so you may prosper" (1 Kgs 2:3). Before you say, "That sounds like the prosperity gospel"—that's not the type of prospering the Bible actually talks about. Although Solomon did prosper financially, as we'll see, many faithful people in Scripture did not (e.g., Jeremiah, Ezekiel, Peter, and Paul). Part of Solomon's prosperity will involve him simply remaining in power, but prospering as a result of obedience in Scripture is primarily focused on being connected to the God who issues the commands (e.g., Ps 1). Here David is pushing Solomon to pursue not just God's laws, but God himself. He exhorts his son to "walk in obedience" to God and to "walk faithfully" before God with all his heart and soul (1 Kgs 2:4). We need to remember that God's laws are meant to be a blessing. God's first command to the humans, "Be fruitful and increase in number" (Gen 1:28), was prefaced with "God blessed them and said to them." Just as the wise builder at the end of Jesus's Sermon on the Mount, who hears Jesus's words and does them, was protected from the storm (Matt 7:24–27), so will everyone who hears and obeys the commands of Scripture be protected from storms that everyone faces.

Mercy and Punishment

At first glance this chapter appears to be simply a brutal description of violence. How are Christians today supposed to apply vendettas and bloodshed? Before looking at what we might be able learn, a few comments need to be made about the nature of the violence in the context of this narrative. Life was violent in the world of the ancient Near East, where it was normal for new rulers to eliminate rivals. During the divided monarchy, after each came to the throne, Baasha wiped out the house of Jeroboam I (1 Kgs 15:29), Zimri wiped out the house of Baasha (16:11–12), and Jehu wiped out the royal houses of both Israel and Judah (2 Kgs 10:11–14).

But even in its context, the bloodshed in this chapter seems excessive. Alter describes Solomon's actions here as the "ruthless elimination of all potential enemies."[5] Is Alter's an accurate description of the events of this chapter? Is "ruth" completely absent here?

Jesus's behavior on the cross offers a stark contrast to Solomon's apparent vindictiveness here toward people who opposed him. After being betrayed by Judas, abandoned by his disciples, beaten by the guards, and sentenced to death by Pilate, Jesus prayed, "Father, forgive them, for they do not know what they are doing" (Luke 23:34). Jesus consistently modeled grace and mercy toward his enemies. And yet, as we keep looking at this chapter, we see some examples of mercy on Solomon's part.

While not as significant a theme as punishment, mercy permeates the chapter as well. Mercy was shown to all four of the characters punished in this chapter (Adonijah, Abiathar, Joab, and Shimei). Adonijah committed treason by attempting to seize the throne from his father and brother. Treason is typically a capital offense. Adonijah's older brother, Absalom, was killed for his rebellion (2 Sam 18:15). Adonijah deserved death for his rebellion but was initially spared by Solomon (1 Kgs 1:52). Only after Adonijah ignored his brother's warning was he killed.

Abiathar deserved death for supporting Adonijah's act of treason but was spared and merely demoted. Even though Joab showed no mercy to Abner and Amasa, his punishment was delayed for many years. In addition to his ruthless killings, he, like Abiathar, supported Adonijah's treason but was spared yet again. Shimei's punishment was delayed by first David, then later by Solomon, before punishment eventually came.

As one reflects upon the grace shown to these individuals, one sees a pattern that reveals a potential problem with mercy. When a person is shown mercy, it should lead them to repentance and to gratitude, but it can lead to license. Unfortunately, people can assume that, because there were no punishments for past crimes, there will be no negative consequences for future crimes. The three characters who were killed by Solomon in this narrative (Adonijah, Joab, and Shimei) were each given second or third chances, but they continued to make bad choices, apparently presuming upon the ruler's generosity. As we

5. Alter, *The Former Prophets*, 617.

see numerous examples of punishment and mercy as Solomon solidifies his reign, a question arises. How does one decide when to punish and when to show mercy? People in positions of authority (e.g., parents, leaders, pastors) often struggle with this question, particularly in contexts where experience is lacking. According to Scripture generally, and the book of Kings specifically, to discern when to enforce the law and when to extend grace, one will need divine wisdom—the subject of the next chapter.

CHAPTER 3

1 Kings 3:1–28

LISTEN to the Story

1Solomon made an alliance with Pharaoh king of Egypt and married his daughter. He brought her to the City of David until he finished
building his palace and the temple of the LORD, and the wall around
Jerusalem. 2The people, however, were still sacrificing at the high places,
because a temple had not yet been built for the Name of the LORD.
3Solomon showed his love for the LORD by walking according to the
instructions given him by his father David, except that he offered sacrifices and burned incense on the high places.

4The king went to Gibeon to offer sacrifices, for that was the most
important high place, and Solomon offered a thousand burnt offerings on that altar. 5At Gibeon the LORD appeared to Solomon during
the night in a dream, and God said, "Ask for whatever you want me to
give you."

6Solomon answered, "You have shown great kindness to your servant, my father David, because he was faithful to you and righteous and
upright in heart. You have continued this great kindness to him and
have given him a son to sit on his throne this very day.

7"Now, LORD my God, you have made your servant king in place of
my father David. But I am only a little child and do not know how to
carry out my duties. 8Your servant is here among the people you have
chosen, a great people, too numerous to count or number. 9So give
your servant a discerning heart to govern your people and to distinguish
between right and wrong. For who is able to govern this great people
of yours?"

10The Lord was pleased that Solomon had asked for this. 11So God
said to him, "Since you have asked for this and not for long life or
wealth for yourself, nor have asked for the death of your enemies but for
discernment in administering justice, 12I will do what you have asked.

I will give you a wise and discerning heart, so that there will never have been anyone like you, nor will there ever be. [13]Moreover, I will give you what you have not asked for—both wealth and honor—so that in your lifetime you will have no equal among kings. [14]And if you walk in obedience to me and keep my decrees and commands as David your father did, I will give you a long life." [15]Then Solomon awoke—and he realized it had been a dream.

He returned to Jerusalem, stood before the ark of the Lord's covenant and sacrificed burnt offerings and fellowship offerings. Then he gave a feast for all his court.

[16]Now two prostitutes came to the king and stood before him. [17]One of them said, "Pardon me, my lord. This woman and I live in the same house, and I had a baby while she was there with me. [18]The third day after my child was born, this woman also had a baby. We were alone; there was no one in the house but the two of us.

[19]"During the night this woman's son died because she lay on him. [20]So she got up in the middle of the night and took my son from my side while I your servant was asleep. She put him by her breast and put her dead son by my breast. [21]The next morning, I got up to nurse my son—and he was dead! But when I looked at him closely in the morning light, I saw that it wasn't the son I had borne."

[22]The other woman said, "No! The living one is my son; the dead one is yours."

But the first one insisted, "No! The dead one is yours; the living one is mine." And so they argued before the king.

[23]The king said, "This one says, 'My son is alive and your son is dead,' while that one says, 'No! Your son is dead and mine is alive.' "

[24]Then the king said, "Bring me a sword." So they brought a sword for the king. [25]He then gave an order: "Cut the living child in two and give half to one and half to the other."

[26]The woman whose son was alive was deeply moved out of love for her son and said to the king, "Please, my lord, give her the living baby! Don't kill him!"

But the other said, "Neither I nor you shall have him. Cut him in two!"

[27]Then the king gave his ruling: "Give the living baby to the first woman. Do not kill him; she is his mother."

[28]When all Israel heard the verdict the king had given, they held the

king in awe, because they saw that he had wisdom from God to administer justice.

Listening to the Text in the Story: Biblical Texts: Proverbs 2:6; Ancient Near Eastern Texts: The Shamash Hymn; The Code of Hammurabi; The Kirta Epic

After the succession struggles and brutal bloodshed of the first two chapters of 1 Kings, the third chapter shifts focus to divine wisdom, specifically how young Solomon will obtain and practice wisdom as he establishes his throne. God first asks Solomon in a dream what he desires, and he replies that he needs wisdom to rule. The king's actions after his interaction with God reveal that his wish was granted, as he displays great wisdom in determining which of the two prostitutes is the real mother of the living child.

Despite his young age and his self-assessment, one could argue that Solomon was wise already because of his decision to request wisdom from YHWH. Elsewhere in Scripture, God is often described as the source of true wisdom. The book of Proverbs, which is attributed to Solomon (Prov 1:1; 10:1), reiterates themes of divine wisdom found in 1 Kings 3, "For the Lord gives wisdom; from his mouth come knowledge and understanding" (Prov 2:6). While Solomon's eventual apostasy (1 Kgs 11) or his construction of the temple (chs. 5–8) could have defined him, wisdom characterized his legacy. The theme of wisdom dominates his narrative (3–10), and he is the primary figure associated with wisdom in the Old Testament (Ps 127:1; Prov 1:1; 10:1; 25:1; Eccl 1:1; Song 1:1; see also Matt 12:42).

Solomon's request was not unusual, as ancient Near Eastern rulers often sought wisdom from deities. A hymn addressed to Shamash, the Babylonian god of justice, declares, "You grant wisdom, O Shamash, to humankind, you grant those seeking you your raging fierce light."[1] In the epilogue to his law code, Hammurabi of Babylon speaks of "the wisdom which the god Ea allotted me."[2]

God's promise to grant wisdom to Solomon in a dream was unusual in two respects. First, God typically speaks to kings through prophets (e.g., 1 Kgs 11:31; 16:1; 17:1; 20:13). Second, Solomon is the only ruler of Israel

1. *COS* 1:419.
2. *COS* 2:351.

spoken to in a dream (3:5, 15). God often speaks through dreams in the Old Testament, but Solomon's dream is the only one in Kings (see also Live the Story below).

Many of the people God speaks to in these dreams are foreign rulers: Abimelech, Pharaoh, Solomon, and Nebuchadnezzar. The Ugaritic Kirta Epic (or "Legend of Keret") includes a story with several striking parallels to Solomon.[3] Kirta is a king who receives a dream where his god speaks to him, asking a question about why he is crying; Kirta replies that he does not want silver or gold but sons, so he can have descendants to follow him on the throne. Thus, both rulers have divine dreams, and both do not request wealth: Kirta asks for heirs, while Solomon requests wisdom.

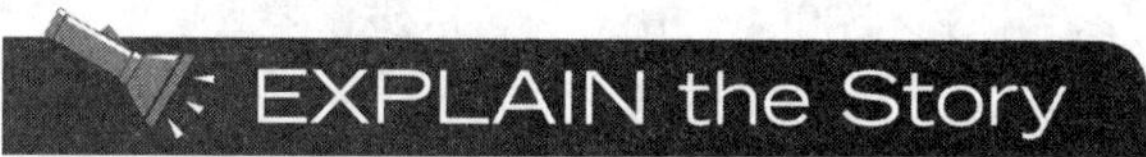

EXPLAIN the Story

Problematic Marriages and Sacrifices (3:1–3)

Young Solomon next does two things many ancient rulers did to bring stability to their reigns, both of which are problematic. First, Solomon makes a marriage alliance, in this case with Egypt, as he marries the daughter of Pharaoh. The anonymous Pharaoh is probably either Siamun (978–959 BC) or his successor Psusennes II (959–945 BC).[4] While marital unions like these were common to unify nations or to ratify a new treaty (see 1 Kgs 16:31), this marriage was not a match made in heaven. God had told Israel not to marry foreigners (Deut 7:3), and he had warned rulers to limit their connections to Egypt (17:16).[5] God also had said not to marry many wives (17:17), which is exactly what Solomon eventually does (1 Kgs 11:1–3) and was thus subsequently led into apostasy. This particular wife was special among his harem, since Solomon would build her a separate palace (7:8).

Second, Solomon offers sacrifices to his God on the high places. Superficially, this action could seem to be a positive step, but, like his marriage to Pharaoh's daughter, this practice also was problematic, as the rest of the book reveals. Solomon loved YHWH and obeyed God's commands, but his sacrifices at the high places were viewed negatively (see "High Places" below).

3. *COS* 1:333–34.

4. See Wiseman, *1 & 2 Kings*, 82.

5. While it is difficult to be certain how much of the law of Moses Solomon or the authors of Kings were aware of, most scholars perceive a connection between Deuteronomy and the Deuteronomistic History (see discussion in "Deuteronomistic Redaction" in the Introduction). See also Lissa M. Wray Beal, *1 & 2 Kings*, AOTC 9 (Downers Grove, IL: InterVarsity Press, 2014), 46–48.

Excursus: High Places

The book of Kings refers over forty times to "high places" (*bamot*), which were places of worship located usually on hills but also sometimes in valleys. They typically consisted of altars, sacred poles, and simple sanctuaries. While some of these locations were associated with YHWH worship (as in the case of Solomon; 1 Kgs 3:3–4), they were frequently associated with worship of foreign gods, which is why Kings viewed them so negatively. They contributed to the syncretism and apostasy of the nation, and many rulers were evaluated primarily based on what they did in relationship to the high places. During the period of the divided monarchy, most of the references to high places are focused on the Southern Kingdom since the Northern Kingdom had its own version—the golden calves in Dan and Bethel.

Thirteen rulers in the book of Kings (mostly Southern ones) are mentioned in relationship to the high places, and most of these references are negative. These rulers can be put in four categories, along a spectrum of worst to best. Three rulers built or rebuilt the high places: Jeroboam I (12:31), Rehoboam (14:23), and Manasseh (2 Kgs 21:3). Two rulers sacrificed at high places: Solomon (1 Kgs 3:3) and Ahaz (2 Kgs 16:4). Six rulers did not remove high places: Asa (1 Kgs 15:14), Jehoshaphat (22:43), Jehoash (2 Kgs 12:3), Amaziah (14:4), Azariah (15:4), and Jotham (15:35). Two rulers removed high places: Hezekiah and Josiah (18:4; 23:8, 13, 19).

Thus, the text views the builders/rebuilders most negatively as actively contributing to the apostasy of the nation, while the two rulers who tore the high places down are viewed highly positively and declared as righteous in the eyes of YHWH. The six rulers who merely allowed them to continue are all evaluated as righteous, but their assessments are qualified because they did not remove them.

The Dream at Gibeon: Solomon Asks for Wisdom (3:4–15)

While the rest of the book views high-place worship negatively, God has no problem interacting with Solomon very positively here at Gibeon, perhaps because the temple had not been built yet or because the king now offers an impressive array of sacrifices. We should not necessarily interpret the phrase "a thousand burnt offerings" here literally;[6] regardless of our interpretation, the king's sacrifice was clearly dramatic, significant, and costly.

---

6. See Wiseman, *1 & 2 Kings*, 84.

God has been silent and passive for the first two chapters of Kings, but he finally makes an appearance. Just as he did with young Samuel (1 Sam 3), God appeared to young Solomon at night, this time in a dream. Instead of bringing a word of judgment as he did to Samuel, YHWH's short message (only four words in Hebrew) is shockingly positive, essentially, "Ask for whatever you want." While reminiscent of Jesus's words in the Sermon on the Mount, "Ask and it will be given to you" (Matt 7:7), it is still a strange command, comparable to the proverbial story of a genie coming out of a bottle granting a wish. (If I were Solomon, I would have asked for more wishes.)

Solomon's extensive reply can be divided into three parts: God's kindness in the past, Solomon's situation in the present, and Solomon's request for the future. Solomon recalls YHWH's great "kindness" (*hesed*) to his father David because of his faithfulness and righteousness. If you are wondering how appropriate it is to describe David as righteous in light of what he did to Bathsheba and Uriah (2 Sam 11–12), see "The Righteous Portrayal of David in Kings" (below).

Excursus: The Righteous Portrayal of David in Kings

After his death in the second chapter of 1 Kings, David is mentioned frequently in the rest of the book. He is often described as doing what was right in the eyes of YHWH, and in many of these contexts he is used as the positive benchmark to which many later kings are compared (1 Kgs 11:33, 38; 14:8; 15:5, 11; 2 Kgs 14:3; 16:2; 18:3; 22:2). But how could a man who committed murder and probably rape[7] (2 Sam 11–12) be considered righteous? The book of Kings never mentions what David did to Bathsheba and only briefly alludes to his orchestrating the death of her husband, when it describes him as righteous "except in the case of Uriah the Hittite" (1 Kgs 15:5). How does the book justify praising David for his piety while ignoring what he did to Bathsheba and glossing over what he did to Uriah? Unfortunately, many commentaries do not even address this issue.

Three possible explanations come to mind for this glaring discrepancy between the portrayals of David in Samuel and in Kings. First, we could conclude that Kings is simply biased in favor of David. It is hard not to perceive at least an element of bias in this portrayal of Israel's most famous

7. See my discussion of David's power rape of Bathsheba in *Prostitutes and Polygamists*, 127–33.

ruler. But against this conclusion we must remember that the only reason we know what happened with Bathsheba and Uriah is because the book of Samuel informed us. And Kings is clearly connected to Samuel; they are part of one long, continuous narrative about Israel's monarchy. The reference to Uriah, while brief, still reminds readers that David was flawed. Second, David was righteous and obedient for much of his life, even impressively so. He killed the Philistine giant; he rescued the city of Keilah; he did not kill Saul on two separate occasions; he sought out YHWH; he brought the ark to Jerusalem, praising God along the way. He was literally a "man after [God's] own heart" (1 Sam 13:14). Third, David repented for his heinous sins and was therefore considered righteous (2 Sam 12:13; Ps 51). After David's confession, the prophet Nathan informs him that YHWH "has taken away your sin" (2 Sam 12:13), which is consistent with his surprisingly positive portrayal in Kings. Like the women Jesus interacts with in Luke 7, his sins, which were many, were forgiven (Luke 7:47).

After reviewing YHWH's faithfulness in the past, Solomon speaks of his own current situation in humble language. His humility goes beyond normal deferential language of subject to their lord ("your servant" is repeated four times in four verses) as he emphasizes his own unworthiness to rule such a great and numerous people, as he is still just a "little child" (1 Kgs 3:7). When Solomon describes God's chosen people as too numerous to count (v. 8), it hearkens back to the patriarchs, as God repeatedly promised to bless Abraham, Isaac, and Jacob with descendants as numerous as the dust of the ground, the sand of the sea, and the stars of the sky (Gen 13:16; 15:5; 22:17; 26:4; 28:14; 32:12).

Solomon's request flows naturally from what God has done previously and what Solomon needs currently. God's great people need a leader with wisdom, but Solomon is young and lacks experience. But he is wise enough already to know he needs help, and God is the one to help him. He does not technically ask for "wisdom," merely a "discerning heart" (literally, a "listening," *shomea'*, heart), but wisdom is clearly the implication, and that is how YHWH interprets it in his response to the request (1 Kgs 3:12). The heart of discernment Solomon desires will help him govern and distinguish between right and wrong.

The narrator of Kings does not usually tell the readers what YHWH is feeling, so it is worth noting that here we are informed that YHWH was pleased with Solomon's request (v. 10), so pleased that YHWH decides not just to grant his request but to bless him in other ways. YHWH appears almost surprised that Solomon did not ask for wealth, a long life for himself, or a short life for his enemies. One could ask, "Weren't all of Solomon's enemies taken care of in chapters 1 and 2?" But rulers and leaders always have rivals, and YHWH himself will raise up adversaries for Solomon later in his reign (11:14, 23).

God tells Solomon that his wish will be granted, and no other person will ever be as wise as he. The theme of the uniqueness of particular rulers reappears at several points in Kings. Six rulers are described as being unique among their peers, three positively (Solomon, Hezekiah, and Josiah) and three negatively (Omri, Ahab, and Manasseh). Rulers are often compared to David, but the text does not describe him as unique or superlative in any respect. Among this special group of rulers, Solomon is unique as the only one whose characteristics are explicitly given by God and as the only one with more than one unique characteristic. YHWH promises three for Solomon: wisdom, wealth, and honor. Solomon will not just be wiser than other rulers but wiser than anyone who has ever lived (3:12). Because he did not ask for the selfish things other rulers would have asked for, God will give him those things—wealth and honor—but not at the same level as the wisdom grant, only more so than any other contemporary ruler (which still sounds pretty good).

God mentions one final gift, another one that Solomon did not ask for—long life—but it will be conditioned upon obedience to God's commands (v. 14). The law of the king in Deuteronomy makes a similar promise of a long life to future kings who observe the words of God's law (Deut 17:19–20). While Solomon's reign was long (forty years; 1 Kgs 11:42), we do not know how old he was when he died because we do not know how old he was when he came to power. Solomon's eventual apostasy (11:6) should have shortened his life in light of this promise.

Solomon wakes up and realizes his interaction with God was a dream (3:5, 15). While many contemporary readers of the Bible after a similar realization might be tempted to simply ignore it ("It was just a dream"), in Solomon's world dreams were taken seriously. Solomon's is the only dream mentioned in Kings (see Listen to the Story above). But during the time of the judges God encourages Gideon before battle as he overhears the dream of a Midianite soldier (Judg 7:13–15), and, early in the monarchy, Saul turned to a medium when he was looking for divine guidance because

YHWH did not speak to him through the normal channels of prophets or dreams (1 Sam 28:6, 15).

Because Solomon believed his dream would come true, he immediately returned to Jerusalem, stood before the ark of the covenant, and did what he did at the beginning of the story: offered sacrifices to his God. Then to celebrate he threw a feast for his court, and suddenly two unexpected guests arrive.

The Two Prostitutes: Solomon Displays Wisdom (3:16–28)

During his court festival, Solomon had an opportunity to display his newly acquired divine wisdom as two prostitutes appeared on the scene with a dilemma. We assume these prostitutes were not part of his court, so the question arises: how did two prostitutes get an audience with the king? Unfortunately, the text does not address this question.

One of the two prostitutes (we'll call her A) begins by telling her side of the story (3:17–21). She and her housemate (we'll call her B) each had a newborn son, born only a few days apart, and no one else lives with them to attest to their version of events (there is no C). According to A, B's son died because she slept on top of him, suffocating him in the night. B then switched A's living child with her own dead one. When A woke up in the morning, she noticed the child next to her was dead, but it was not the child she gave birth to. At this point B, who has been listening to A's rendition, interrupts and says A's story is false, her son is the living one, and A's son is actually the dead one (v. 22). A then contradicts B's account, and they continue bickering before the king. Any parent of more than one child will recognize a version of this dialogue.

Solomon then summarizes the problem (A says hers is living; B says hers is living), essentially a "she said" / "she said" story with no other witnesses. Perhaps the most common parallel situation today involves an accusation of rape, which often occurs in a private setting, like a dorm room, in the middle of the night, with no other witnesses, and the participants tell contradictory stories ("It was consensual" / "I was coerced"). College administrators struggle to administer justice in these contexts. They need the wisdom of Solomon.

The whole court has heard the witnesses and the judge's brief recital of the arguments, so they wait for his decision. Shockingly, he declares, "Bring me a sword!" The courtroom watches as someone finds a sword and brings it to the king. He orders the living child cut in two, giving half to each mother. While we might think Solomon's audience should have known his threat to butcher a newborn baby was merely a bluff, in Solomon's context kings and their henchmen often did comparable acts; anyone familiar with recent events would know that Solomon was not adverse to shedding blood, as he had just ordered the execution of his rivals (Adonijah, Shimei, and Joab).

One of the women, whom the text identifies as the mother of the living boy, clearly thinks the slaughter will happen, as she cries out to save the child and give him to the other mother. Because of her deep love for her son, she is willing to give up her right to raise him; she does not want him killed. In stark contrast, the other mother affirms the king's ruling, "Cut him in two" (v. 26). At this point in the narrative, it no longer takes the wisdom of Solomon to decide which of these two women is, or at least should be, the mother of the living child. When Solomon declares that the compassionate one, not the violent one, is the true mother, not just his court but all Israel hears about his wisdom, holds him in awe, and acknowledges that his wisdom came from God.

We need to make three final observations about Solomon's judgment here. First, we do not know which mother, A or B, was the true mother. While most English translations (NIV, ESV, NRSV, NASB) clarify who Solomon gives the child to by adding "the first woman" (therefore, A), the Hebrew text merely says, "Give to her the living child."[8] Most scholars believe the first (A) is the one who wanted to save the child and was the genuine mother, but there is sufficient textual ambiguity to read it either way.

Second, we should not be too harsh in our condemnation of what appears to be heartless behavior by one of these mothers (assuming it was B). She had just lost a son and probably felt guilty over what happened to the child. It was not her idea to kill the child. In the midst of intense grief that only a mother who has lost a newborn can understand, she merely consented to the king's ruling. A compassionate interpretation of her behavior is also supported by the fact that the text does not record that she was punished for lying to the king.

Third, Solomon had a listening heart. His request for a "discerning" heart (v. 9) could be literally translated as a "listening" (*shomea'*) heart. Before speaking to the women, he merely listens to both sides of the story in silence for six verses. After pronouncing the judgment of dividing the child, it is by listening to the responses of the two mothers that he knows which one is the real mother. Two proverbs are particularly relevant here.

8. See the discussion in Wray Beal, *1 & 2 Kings*, 88, and in Fretheim, *Kings*, 34.

To answer before listening—
that is folly and shame. (Prov 18:13)

Solomon answers after listening, and it is his wisdom and honor.

If a king judges the poor with fairness,
his throne will be established forever. (Prov 29:14)

Solomon judged these two poor prostitutes with fairness, and it established his kingdom as the whole nation realized God's wisdom was with him to administer justice (1 Kgs 3:28).

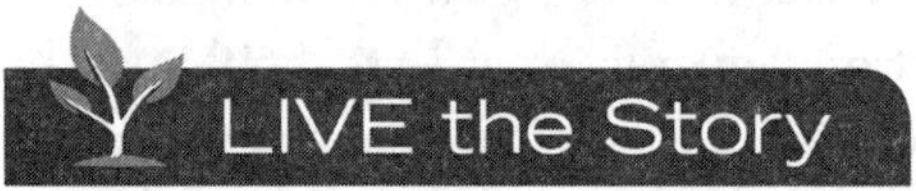

Listening to God's Voice in Dreams

God primarily speaks to his people through Scripture, but the Bible itself reveals a variety of other methods of divine communication, including people, creation, illness, and, most relevant for this story, dreams. Throughout the Bible God often communicates through dreams. He spoke not only to Israelites (Jacob, Daniel, Joseph the son of Jacob, and Joseph the father of Jesus) but also to foreigners (Abimelech, Pharaoh and his cupbearer and baker, a Midianite soldier, Nebuchadnezzar, the wise men, and Pilate's wife). Most of the dreams in Scripture appear in three biblical books: Genesis (20:3–6; 28:12; 31:10–11; 31:24; 37:6–10; 40:5–19; 41:1–32), Daniel (2:1–45; 4:5–19; 7:1), and Matthew (1:20, 2:12, 13, 19, 22; 27:19). Perhaps the highest concentration of dreams in Scripture surround the birth of Jesus in Matthew's gospel, as God guided Joseph and the wise men to protect the infant Jesus (see also 27:19). Clearly, God used dreams to guide his people throughout Scripture generally, and they play a crucial role in Jesus's birth narrative. Solomon's dream shaped the way he ruled as a wise king.

An unusual element here is that Solomon is an active participant in the dream interaction with God as he makes his request for wisdom. The books of Joel and Acts tell us that God speaking through dreams is in fact a sign of the presence of God's Spirit in the midst of his people (Joel 2:28; Acts 2:17). As we are attentive to God's voice in the diverse ways he speaks, let's not forget to listen to his voice in dreams. Ask God to speak to you in dreams as you pray before going to sleep.

Not all dreams are from God; sometimes they may be more a function of what we ate or watched the night before. But many of us have had dreams which felt more vivid, more spiritual, or more relevant than usual. We need to reflect on and share these dreams with wise friends to help us understand them. Many of the dreams in Scripture were shared with others who interpreted them for the dreamer.

While I was working on this section, my wife shared with me over breakfast one morning her dream from the previous night. It was fascinating to think about what, if anything, God might have been trying to communicate to her. To be honest, I'd had a dream, too, but I decided not to share it because it was embarrassing. Later I went to my office and wrote the chapter you just read (about God speaking to someone through a dream), and I thought about my reluctance to share my own dream with my wife earlier that day. I was convicted. At lunch I shared my dream with her, and we discussed what God might be saying to us through it. It wasn't life altering, but it was a remarkably helpful practice to assume that God is speaking, if I only have ears to hear (or a "listening heart").

Asking for a Listening Heart

In light of the facts that Solomon asked for a "listening heart," that God was pleased with his request, and that God granted his request, it makes sense that we would make similar requests in our prayers. God apparently expected Solomon to request wealth or health (good for himself and bad for his enemies), and many of my own prayers (as well as ones I've listened to) seem focused on comparable versions of these things. God listens to a lot of prayers, so he knows that many of them, both then and now, focus on blessing the one praying with things like health and wealth, but Solomon's focus was blessing others by listening to them and administering justice (1 Kgs 3:11, 28).

Listening doesn't come naturally. Most of us would rather talk than listen. But of course, we like it when people listen to us. Listening takes work. It takes humility, which Solomon also modeled for us in this story (vv. 7–9). We need help to listen, and God seems eager to grant us the kind of heart that listens well to him and to others. God himself modeled it at the beginning of this story when he told Solomon to ask for whatever he wanted. Then God listened to Solomon ask for a listening heart.

Like Solomon, Jesus displayed great wisdom, even at a young age, as he was filled with wisdom and God's favor was upon him (Luke 2:40, 52). In his interactions with teachers in the temple, Jesus listened and asked questions, prompting those around to be amazed at his understanding (2:46–47). And as he began his adult ministry, everyone who listened to his teaching was amazed at his wisdom (Matt 13:54). Just as Solomon exercised great wisdom to discern who the true mother was, Jesus exercised wisdom in his use of questions and parables, often frustrating the religious leaders who attempted to trap him (e.g., Mark 11:27–12:40).

The New Testament book of James, which resonates with many wisdom themes, exhorts its readers, "if any of you lacks wisdom, you should ask God, who gives generously to all without finding fault, and it will be given to you" (Jas 1:5). While Solomon didn't ask for wisdom, listening is connected to wisdom both by God in this passage (1 Kgs 3:11–12) and elsewhere in books like Proverbs (1:5; 4:1; 5:1; 8:33; 13:1; 19:20). Wise people know they need to listen to others, to learn and gain more wisdom. Solomon didn't just want to grow wiser for the sake of acquiring knowledge but to govern and serve his people. Like Solomon, we can ask God for a listening heart as we pray, we can listen to God speak to us through Scripture and dreams, and we can listen to people around us who seek out our wisdom to discern between right and wrong.

All this reminds me of a story that took place in a family I'm quite familiar with. Once upon a time, there were two sons, each of whom wanted to read a book (*Brisingr* by Christopher Paolini—it's about dragons) that had just come out and had arrived in the mail that day. They fought over the book, as they both wanted to start reading it right away and didn't want to wait until their brother was finished. So their wise father, who was in the kitchen in the middle of this dispute, grabbed a butcher knife and declared, "Chop the book in half! Give half to each!" One son said, "Yeah, chop it in half!" while the other son said, "No, let my brother have it." Their wise father declared, "The book will go to the son who was willing to forgo the book to preserve its unity. He is the true owner." And they all lived happily ever after.

CHAPTER 4

1 Kings 4:1–34

LISTEN to the Story

[1]So King Solomon ruled over all Israel. [2]And these were his chief officials:

Azariah son of Zadok—the priest;
[3]Elihoreph and Ahijah, sons of Shisha—secretaries;
Jehoshaphat son of Ahilud—recorder;
[4]Benaiah son of Jehoiada—commander in chief;
Zadok and Abiathar—priests;
[5]Azariah son of Nathan—in charge of the district governors;
Zabud son of Nathan—a priest and adviser to the king;
[6]Ahishar—palace administrator;
Adoniram son of Abda—in charge of forced labor.

[7]Solomon had twelve district governors over all Israel, who supplied provisions for the king and the royal household. Each one had to provide supplies for one month in the year. [8]These are their names:

Ben-Hur—in the hill country of Ephraim;
[9]Ben-Deker—in Makaz, Shaalbim, Beth Shemesh and Elon Bethhanan;
[10]Ben-Hesed—in Arubboth (Sokoh and all the land of Hepher were his);
[11]Ben-Abinadab—in Naphoth Dor (he was married to Taphath daughter of Solomon);
[12]Baana son of Ahilud—in Taanach and Megiddo, and in all of Beth Shan next to Zarethan below Jezreel, from Beth Shan to Abel Meholah across to Jokmeam;
[13]Ben-Geber—in Ramoth Gilead (the settlements of Jair son of Manasseh in Gilead were his, as well as the region of Argob in Bashan and its sixty large walled cities with bronze gate bars);

[14]Ahinadab son of Iddo—in Mahanaim;
[15]Ahimaaz—in Naphtali (he had married Basemath daughter of
Solomon);
[16]Baana son of Hushai—in Asher and in Aloth;
[17]Jehoshaphat son of Paruah—in Issachar;
[18]Shimei son of Ela—in Benjamin;
[19]Geber son of Uri—in Gilead (the country of Sihon king of the
Amorites and the country of Og king of Bashan). He was the
only governor over the district.

[20]The people of Judah and Israel were as numerous as the sand on
the seashore; they ate, they drank and they were happy. [21]And Solomon
ruled over all the kingdoms from the Euphrates River to the land of the
Philistines, as far as the border of Egypt. These countries brought tribute
and were Solomon's subjects all his life.

[22]Solomon's daily provisions were thirty cors of the finest flour and sixty
cors of meal, [23]ten head of stall-fed cattle, twenty of pasture-fed cattle and
a hundred sheep and goats, as well as deer, gazelles, roebucks and choice
fowl. [24]For he ruled over all the kingdoms west of the Euphrates River,
from Tiphsah to Gaza, and had peace on all sides. [25]During Solomon's
lifetime Judah and Israel, from Dan to Beersheba, lived in safety, everyone
under their own vine and under their own fig tree.

[26]Solomon had four thousand stalls for chariot horses, and twelve
thousand horses.

[27]The district governors, each in his month, supplied provisions for
King Solomon and all who came to the king's table. They saw to it that
nothing was lacking. [28]They also brought to the proper place their quotas
of barley and straw for the chariot horses and the other horses.

[29]God gave Solomon wisdom and very great insight, and a breadth
of understanding as measureless as the sand on the seashore. [30]Solomon's
wisdom was greater than the wisdom of all the people of the East, and
greater than all the wisdom of Egypt. [31]He was wiser than anyone else,
including Ethan the Ezrahite—wiser than Heman, Kalkol and Darda, the
sons of Mahol. And his fame spread to all the surrounding nations. [32]He
spoke three thousand proverbs and his songs numbered a thousand and
five. [33]He spoke about plant life, from the cedar of Lebanon to the hyssop
that grows out of walls. He also spoke about animals and birds, reptiles

and fish. [34]From all nations people came to listen to Solomon's wisdom, sent by all the kings of the world, who had heard of his wisdom.

Listening to the Text in the Story: Biblical Texts: 1 Kings 1:7–8; 2:26–27, 35; Psalms 88:1; 89:1; Proverbs 1:1; 10:1; 25:1; Ancient Near Eastern Text: The Code of Hammurabi

In the last chapter, Solomon's wisdom in judgment was displayed for the entire nation as he has discerned the true mother of the living child (1 Kgs 3:23–28). In this chapter his wisdom in administration, speech, and literature is the subject. The first half of 1 Kings 4 consists primarily of lists of royal officials and district governors. The vast majority of the names are minor characters who do not appear elsewhere in Kings. However, four names stand out: Zadok, Abiathar, Benaiah, and Nathan (4:2, 4, 5). Abiathar was the priest who supported Adonijah and was demoted (2:26–27), and Zadok was the priest who supported Solomon and took Abiathar's place (2:35). Benaiah the general is here called "commander in chief" (4:4). The Nathan mentioned here could refer to an individual not mentioned previously, but most likely it refers to either Nathan the prophet (2 Sam 7:2) or Nathan the son of David (1 Chr 3:5). If the Nathan here is the prophet, then all four of these names are mentioned during the succession struggle between Adonijah and Solomon (1 Kgs 1:7–8).

The end of 2 Kings 4 lists Solomon's literary achievements related to his wisdom—composing three thousand proverbs and over a thousand songs—a description consistent with his portrayal as the sage behind the book of Proverbs (1:1; 10:1; 25:1). In the context of the description of his proverb-writing prowess, Solomon is compared favorably to two poets who are mentioned in the headings of two psalms, Heman (Ps 88:1) and Ethan the Ezrahite (89:1).

Solomon's wisdom is praised as greater than all the wisdom of Egypt and the people of the East (i.e., Mesopotamia). Perhaps the greatest Egyptian associated with wisdom was Imhotep, who lived in the twenty-seventh century BC and was an architect, engineer, philosopher, poet, and, like Solomon, had numerous wise sayings attributed to him by later Egyptian scholars. The greatest wise ruler from the East would presumably be Hammurabi of Babylon, who reigned during the eighteenth-century BC and is the eponymous individual behind the Code of Hammurabi. In the epilogue to the code, Hammurabi describes how the gods gave him wisdom to rule and to achieve his accomplishments.

> With the mighty weapon which the gods Zababa and Ishtar bestowed upon me, with the wisdom which the god Ea allotted to me, with the ability which the god Marduk gave me, I annihilated enemies everywhere, I put an end to wars, I enhanced the well-being of the land, I made the people of all settlements lie in safe pastures, I did not tolerate anyone intimidating them.[1]

Hammurabi's accomplishments were more militaristic than Solomon's, but in both cases their divinely granted wisdom allowed them to rule effectively and bless their nation.

Solomon's Officials and Governors (4:1–19)

Readers of 1 Kings 4 may find much of the chapter rather boring, but this material provides important background to understand how Solomon used wisdom to organize his kingdom and delegate responsibility. It consists mainly of lists of names of Solomon's officials, which can be sorted into five categories: priests, secretaries, military commanders, administrators, and district governors. The first four types are initially listed together in a random fashion, then the governors are listed in order geographically. Most of these individuals (eight of eleven in vv. 1–6) are identified by a patronymic (A son of B), which served then like a surname does today to distinguish people who have the same first name. For example, Azariah the son of Zadok is a priest and Azariah the son of Nathan supervises the governors (vv. 2, 5).

There are four priests (Azariah, Zadok, Abiathar, and Zabud), three secretaries or recorders (Elihoreph, Ahijah, and Jehoshaphat), one military commander (Benaiah), four administrators (Azariah, Zabud, Ahishar, and Adoniram), and twelve district governors (Ben-Hur, Ben-Deker, Ben-Hesed, Ben-Abinadab, Baana son of Ahilud, Ben-Geber, Ahinadab, Ahimaaz, Baana son of Hushai, Jehoshaphat, Shimei, and Geber). Priests came from the tribe of Levi and were religious leaders who typically offered sacrifices. Secretaries could serve in a wide variety of positions ranging from a "humble writer to a Secretary of State."[2] Benaiah served in his military capacity as he performed executions for the king in chapter 2, but his role also included being in

1. *COS* 2:351.
2. See Wiseman, *1 & 2 Kings*, 89.

charge of the army (v. 4). I use the term administrators to encompass a variety of roles that could involve supervising the governors (Azariah son of Nathan) or advising the king (Zabud son of Nathan). Twelve district governors were in charge of supplying the royal provisions to the palace, one district per month.

Several observations can be made about these individuals listed here and the offices they held. Following the order of the text, we will first focus on the four initial types of officials, then discuss the twelve governors. There are several familial relationships mentioned. There is a father-son pair, Zadok and Azariah, both of whom are called priests. There are two sets of brothers: the sons of Shisha, Elihoreph and Ahijah, are both secretaries, while one son of Nathan, Azariah, supervises the governors and another son of Nathan, Zabud, is both a priest and royal advisor. Surprisingly, Abiathar is still listed as a priest, despite his earlier demotion (2:35), which could suggest that these lists of royal officials were not generated from a particular moment in time but included the names of anyone who served in these offices over the course of Solomon's reign.

As we move to the district governors, another factor suggests that the lists were not limited to a narrow time period. Two of the district governors (Ben-Abinadab and Ahimaaz) both married a daughter of Solomon (4:11, 15). Since he described himself in the previous chapter as a "little child" (3:7), he must have grown up a lot between these two events in order to father multiple daughters of marriageable age. These marriages would deepen trust between the king and the governors, comparable to Solomon's own treaty marriages to foreign princesses (3:1; 11:1).

A curious pattern appears as one inspects the names of these twelve governors. Five of the first six governors are listed only by their patronymic (e.g., Ben-Hur, literally "the son of Hur," 4:8; Ben-Deker, literally "the son of Deker," v. 9). Then six governors are listed by their name and their patronymic (e.g., "Baana son of Ahilud," v. 12; "Ahinadab son of Iddo," v. 14). Only one is just listed by his name with no patronymic, Ahimaaz (v. 15). Ahimaaz's father's name may have been unnecessary since he married a royal princess and played an important role supporting David during the rebellion of Absalom (2 Sam 15:27; 17:17–21; 18:19–29).

While one might expect that the boundaries of the twelve districts who support the royal court monthly would be drawn based on the twelve tribal divisions, these traditional boundaries were not followed strictly. Only five tribes are mentioned by name in this section (Ephraim, v. 8; Naphtali, v. 15; Asher, v. 16; Issachar, v. 17; and Benjamin, v. 18). There is, however, a loose pattern: the first five districts are located in the center of the nation (vv. 8–12), the next two are east of the Jordan (vv. 13–14), the next three in the north (vv. 15–17), and the final two in the south (vv. 18–19).

Solomon's Daily Provisions (4:20–28)

The next section focuses on descriptions of the enormity of the population (4:20), the happiness of the people (vv. 20, 25), the extensiveness of the national borders (v. 21), and the abundance of the royal provisions and stables (vv. 22–24, 26–28).[3]

The language used to describe the size of the population of Israel and Judah, "as numerous as the sand on the seashore," is used elsewhere to describe an enormous enemy army (Josh 11:4; Judg 7:12), but it also recalls YHWH's promise to Abraham that his descendants would be as numerous as the "sand of the sea" (Gen 22:17; 32:12; see also 2 Sam 17:11; Isa 10:22; Jer 33:22; Hos 1:10). Thus, the Abrahamic promise, given centuries earlier, is now clearly fulfilled.

The borders of the kingdom, from the Euphrates to the border of Egypt, also recall the promise of YHWH to Abraham (Gen 15:18); a second Abrahamic fulfillment under Solomon is thus recorded. Scholars often interpret these boundary descriptions to be somewhat hyperbolic, since they lack geographic precision and seem intended to honor the ruler by describing his dominion in grandiose language.[4]

The people were not merely numerous, but the narrator also tells us that they ate, drank, and were happy (1 Kgs 4:20; see also Eccl 2:24; 3:13; 5:18; 8:15; 9:7). The description of the people's festive condition here is strikingly similar to that of the people during Solomon's temple dedication feast later (1 Kgs 8:65–66).

The daily provisions for the royal court, given here in detail, were significant. Thirty cors of fine flour was probably over five tons, and sixty cors of meal were about eleven tons. Animals included both stall-fed and pasture fed cattle, sheep, goats, deer, gazelles, roebuck, and choice fowl. While these provisions may seem like an inordinate amount for a single day, the massive size suggests that Solomon's court was huge, presumably necessary to oversee his extensive empire.

---

3. The section of verses numbered 4:21–34 in English Bibles is numbered 5:1–14 in the Hebrew Bible. Several verses present here in the Hebrew (20–21, 25–26) are absent in the Septuagint version of 2 Kgs 4, and similar versions of much of this material are added to the end of chapter 2, at verse 46, although they are shifted around there; see Simon J. DeVries, *1 Kings* (Waco: Word, 1985), 66.

4. See Wray Beal, *1 & 2 Kings*, 97.

The people of Israel and Judah appear happy now, as they experience rest from their enemies and enjoy harvesting their own wine and fruit (4:20, 25), but they will complain about Solomon's oppressive tax burdens shortly after his son, Rehoboam, came to power (12:4).

In addition to providing for Solomon's court, the district governors were responsible to supply barley and straw for his horses (4:28), quantities that would have also needed to be massive given that Solomon had four thousand stalls for chariot horses and twelve thousand horses (v. 26). The number of horse stalls in the Hebrew is forty thousand, which is followed by many English translations (ESV, NASB, NRSV), but the NIV here follows the Septuagint with four thousand, which is the number that appears in Chronicles (2 Chr 9:25). Either forty or four thousand chariot stalls might seem excessively hyperbolic, but according to the Kurkh Monolith of Shalmaneser III of Assyria, King Ahab of Israel had two thousand chariots,[5] so the lower number is certainly historically viable.

While the description of Solomon's grandiose stables could seem positive, one wonders if the narrator intended these comments to be interpreted negatively, since Deuteronomy's law of the king explicitly prohibited rulers from acquiring many horses (Deut 17:16). No precise limitation is mentioned in Deuteronomy, but presumably twelve thousand horses would have exceeded his quota.

Solomon's Great Wisdom (4:29–34)

After being absent from the narrative since the dream interaction, God is mentioned briefly here (4:29). In the dream, God said he would give the king wisdom, then he displayed wisdom in his interaction with the two prostitutes; now the narrator explicitly states that God gave Solomon wisdom. The breadth of Solomon's divine understanding is appropriately described "as measureless as the sand of the seashore," since the population of the nation was described using the same phrase (vv. 20, 29).

The superlative descriptions of Solomon's wisdom dominate this final section of 1 Kings 4. He was wiser than everyone in the East, which would have included the kingdoms of Assyria and Babylon; everyone in Egypt, which was to the west of Israel; and everyone within Israel's wisdom tradition (Ethan, Heman, Kalkol, and Darda; see 1 Chr 2:6). His fame was spreading, and people begin to come to listen to his wisdom (1 Kgs 4:34). Ancient sages often collected their wisdom, and Solomon was no exception. The text emphasizes

---

5. *COS* 2:263d.

his speaking (vv. 32, 33), but his wise sayings would have been written down, perhaps by the secretaries or recorders mentioned at the beginning of the chapter, in order to count them. Thus, his wisdom manifested itself in his extensive literary projects: three thousand proverbs and a thousand and five songs (v. 32). Wiseman states that the book of Proverbs contains 582 proverbs of Solomon.[6] The subjects of his proverbs and songs often came from the realm of creation: plants and trees, as well as diverse types of animals, birds, reptiles, and fish (v. 33). Similarly, when Jesus speaks about how to avoid anxiety in the Sermon on the Mount, a section of the Gospels permeated with wisdom themes (e.g., Matt 7:24), he tells his follows to look to creation, the birds, the lilies, and the grass because God meets their needs, arraying the flowers even more impressively than King Solomon (Matt 6:25–30).

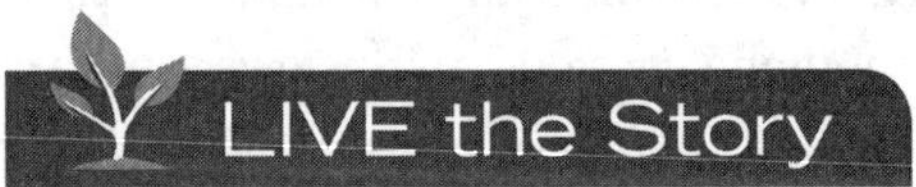

Solomon's Wise Delegation

Solomon's empire was enormous, both in terms of population and geography; his people were numerous and his borders expansive. For most of the chapter, the only action Solomon performs is to rule (1 Kgs 4:1, 21, 24), and he merely appears in the background. But what allowed him to rule such a vast empire was his ability to delegate responsibility to leaders he could trust, and this chapter lists at least twenty-three of them. While the text here doesn't go into detail describing the selection of these leaders, the fact that most of the chapter is devoted to listing the names and positions of these leaders (vv. 1–19) in the context of describing his supernatural wisdom suggests not only that these individuals were important to Solomon but also that the task of delegation was a practical manifestation of his wisdom. Solomon delegated responsibility to these individuals in various realms: religious, military, literary, administrative, and economic. Because he didn't micromanage his empire, he had time to share his wisdom by speaking and composing songs and proverbs (v. 32).

Delegation is a difficult lesson for people in ministry to learn. Most of us have a hard time trusting people to do things since our perception is that they won't perform the task as well as we would. While Solomon had far more responsibility than most of us ever will, he still was able to share these responsibilities with these leaders.

It is always difficult to delegate, and yet Scripture is full of examples of

6. Wiseman, *1 & 2 Kings*, 96.

delegation, beginning in Eden, as God handed over his precious garden to the first human (Gen 2:15), and as God called leaders like Noah, Abraham, Moses, and Deborah to perform tasks that we assume he could have performed better by himself. Jesus also valued delegation, even in shocking ways. He sent out his disciples on numerous occasions to do what they had seen him do (Matt 10:5–15; Mark 3:14; 6:7–13; Luke 9:1–6; 10:1–16); after only a few years of training, he delegated the responsibility of establishing his church to his followers (Matt 16:18–19; 28:16–20), who hadn't proven themselves to be particularly trustworthy (Mark 8:32; 9:28, 33–37; 10:13, 35–45; 14:37–41). While we might be tempted to question the wisdom of Jesus delegating so much responsibility to a group that did not seem ready, in the context of speaking of the visit of the queen of Sheba (see the discussion in Chapter 8, "The Queen of Sheba Visits"), Jesus declared that his wisdom was greater than that of Solomon.

One of the ways I motivate myself to delegate is to recall times when people delegated responsibility to me, often when I had done nothing to deserve their trust. I remember over thirty years ago, the first time I spoke to a large group of people about Scripture, to my fellow students in the InterVarsity group I was involved with at Stanford. It felt great to be honored to be given such a significant responsibility. I didn't want to blow it, so I worked hard and asked for a lot of help from my staff worker, Greg. Even so, I was still terribly anxious, not having had a lot of public speaking experience. Fortunately, the passage was from the Sermon on the Mount: "Do not be anxious" (Matt 6:25–34; ESV). Jesus's words to not worry spoke powerfully throughout the process to me, and presumably to the leaders who had asked me to speak since they had ample reasons to worry about how I would do. Despite my inadequacies, it went well. I told the audience to remember the lilies because even Solomon in his glory was not arrayed like one of them. As I look back on that experience, one of the most significant events leading me to think that God was calling me into Christian ministry, the only reason it happened is that the leaders in charge were willing to delegate like King Solomon.

Where in your life have you grown because someone delegated responsibility to you? How could you delegate responsibility to help someone else grow?

CHAPTER 5

1 Kings 5:1–7:51

LISTEN to the Story

[1]When Hiram king of Tyre heard that Solomon had been anointed king to succeed his father David, he sent his envoys to Solomon, because he had always been on friendly terms with David. [2]Solomon sent back this message to Hiram:

> [3]"You know that because of the wars waged against my father David from all sides, he could not build a temple for the Name of the LORD his God until the LORD put his enemies under his feet. [4]But now the LORD my God has given me rest on every side, and there is no adversary or disaster. [5]I intend, therefore, to build a temple for the Name of the LORD my God, as the LORD told my father David, when he said, 'Your son whom I will put on the throne in your place will build the temple for my Name.'
>
> [6]"So give orders that cedars of Lebanon be cut for me. My men will work with yours, and I will pay you for your men whatever wages you set. You know that we have no one so skilled in felling timber as the Sidonians."

[7]When Hiram heard Solomon's message, he was greatly pleased and said, "Praise be to the LORD today, for he has given David a wise son to rule over this great nation."

[8]So Hiram sent word to Solomon:

> "I have received the message you sent me and will do all you want in providing the cedar and juniper logs. [9]My men will haul them down from Lebanon to the Mediterranean Sea, and I will float them as rafts by sea to the place you specify. There I will separate them and you can

take them away. And you are to grant my wish by providing food for
my royal household."

[10]In this way Hiram kept Solomon supplied with all the cedar and
juniper logs he wanted, [11]and Solomon gave Hiram twenty thousand cors
of wheat as food for his household, in addition to twenty thousand baths
of pressed olive oil. Solomon continued to do this for Hiram year after
year. [12]The LORD gave Solomon wisdom, just as he had promised him.
There were peaceful relations between Hiram and Solomon, and the two
of them made a treaty.

[13]King Solomon conscripted laborers from all Israel—thirty thousand
men. [14]He sent them off to Lebanon in shifts of ten thousand a month,
so that they spent one month in Lebanon and two months at home.
Adoniram was in charge of the forced labor. [15]Solomon had seventy thousand carriers and eighty thousand stonecutters in the hills, [16]as well as
thirty-three hundred foremen who supervised the project and directed
the workers. [17]At the king's command they removed from the quarry large
blocks of high-grade stone to provide a foundation of dressed stone for the
temple. [18]The craftsmen of Solomon and Hiram and workers from Byblos
cut and prepared the timber and stone for the building of the temple.

[6:1]In the four hundred and eightieth year after the Israelites came out
of Egypt, in the fourth year of Solomon's reign over Israel, in the month
of Ziv, the second month, he began to build the temple of the LORD.

[2]The temple that King Solomon built for the LORD was sixty cubits
long, twenty wide and thirty high. [3]The portico at the front of the main
hall of the temple extended the width of the temple, that is twenty cubits,
and projected ten cubits from the front of the temple. [4]He made narrow
windows high up in the temple walls. [5]Against the walls of the main hall
and inner sanctuary he built a structure around the building, in which
there were side rooms. [6]The lowest floor was five cubits wide, the middle
floor six cubits and the third floor seven. He made offset ledges around
the outside of the temple so that nothing would be inserted into the
temple walls.

[7]In building the temple, only blocks dressed at the quarry were used,
and no hammer, chisel or any other iron tool was heard at the temple site
while it was being built.

[8]The entrance to the lowest floor was on the south side of the temple; a stairway led up to the middle level and from there to the third. [9]So he built the temple and completed it, roofing it with beams and cedar planks. [10]And he built the side rooms all along the temple. The height of each was five cubits, and they were attached to the temple by beams of cedar.

[11]The word of the LORD came to Solomon: [12]"As for this temple you are building, if you follow my decrees, observe my laws and keep all my commands and obey them, I will fulfill through you the promise I gave to David your father. [13]And I will live among the Israelites and will not abandon my people Israel."

[14]So Solomon built the temple and completed it. [15]He lined its interior walls with cedar boards, paneling them from the floor of the temple to the ceiling, and covered the floor of the temple with planks of juniper. [16]He partitioned off twenty cubits at the rear of the temple with cedar boards from floor to ceiling to form within the temple an inner sanctuary, the Most Holy Place. [17]The main hall in front of this room was forty cubits long. [18]The inside of the temple was cedar, carved with gourds and open flowers. Everything was cedar; no stone was to be seen.

[19]He prepared the inner sanctuary within the temple to set the ark of the covenant of the LORD there. [20]The inner sanctuary was twenty cubits long, twenty wide and twenty high. He overlaid the inside with pure gold, and he also overlaid the altar of cedar. [21]Solomon covered the inside of the temple with pure gold, and he extended gold chains across the front of the inner sanctuary, which was overlaid with gold. [22]So he overlaid the whole interior with gold. He also overlaid with gold the altar that belonged to the inner sanctuary.

[23]For the inner sanctuary he made a pair of cherubim out of olive wood, each ten cubits high. [24]One wing of the first cherub was five cubits long, and the other wing five cubits—ten cubits from wing tip to wing tip. [25]The second cherub also measured ten cubits, for the two cherubim were identical in size and shape. [26]The height of each cherub was ten cubits. [27]He placed the cherubim inside the innermost room of the temple, with their wings spread out. The wing of one cherub touched one wall, while the wing of the other touched the other wall, and their wings touched each other in the middle of the room. [28]He overlaid the cherubim with gold.

[29]On the walls all around the temple, in both the inner and outer

rooms, he carved cherubim, palm trees and open flowers. [30]He also covered
the floors of both the inner and outer rooms of the temple with gold.

[31]For the entrance to the inner sanctuary he made doors out of olive
wood that were one fifth of the width of the sanctuary. [32]And on the two
olive-wood doors he carved cherubim, palm trees and open flowers, and
overlaid the cherubim and palm trees with hammered gold. [33]In the same
way, for the entrance to the main hall he made doorframes out of olive
wood that were one fourth of the width of the hall. [34]He also made two
doors out of juniper wood, each having two leaves that turned in sockets.
[35]He carved cherubim, palm trees and open flowers on them and overlaid
them with gold hammered evenly over the carvings.

[36]And he built the inner courtyard of three courses of dressed stone and
one course of trimmed cedar beams.

[37]The foundation of the temple of the LORD was laid in the fourth
year, in the month of Ziv. [38]In the eleventh year in the month of Bul, the
eighth month, the temple was finished in all its details according to its
specifications. He had spent seven years building it.

[7:1]It took Solomon thirteen years, however, to complete the construction of his palace. [2]He built the Palace of the Forest of Lebanon a hundred
cubits long, fifty wide and thirty high, with four rows of cedar columns
supporting trimmed cedar beams. [3]It was roofed with cedar above the
beams that rested on the columns—forty-five beams, fifteen to a row.
[4]Its windows were placed high in sets of three, facing each other. [5]All the
doorways had rectangular frames; they were in the front part in sets of
three, facing each other.

[6]He made a colonnade fifty cubits long and thirty wide. In front of it
was a portico, and in front of that were pillars and an overhanging roof.

[7]He built the throne hall, the Hall of Justice, where he was to judge,
and he covered it with cedar from floor to ceiling. [8]And the palace in which
he was to live, set farther back, was similar in design. Solomon also made
a palace like this hall for Pharaoh's daughter, whom he had married.

[9]All these structures, from the outside to the great courtyard and from
foundation to eaves, were made of blocks of high-grade stone cut to size
and smoothed on their inner and outer faces. [10]The foundations were laid
with large stones of good quality, some measuring ten cubits and some
eight. [11]Above were high-grade stones, cut to size, and cedar beams. [12]The
great courtyard was surrounded by a wall of three courses of dressed stone

and one course of trimmed cedar beams, as was the inner courtyard of the temple of the LORD with its portico.

[13]King Solomon sent to Tyre and brought Huram, [14]whose mother was a widow from the tribe of Naphtali and whose father was from Tyre and a skilled craftsman in bronze. Huram was filled with wisdom, with understanding and with knowledge to do all kinds of bronze work. He came to King Solomon and did all the work assigned to him.

[15]He cast two bronze pillars, each eighteen cubits high and twelve cubits in circumference. [16]He also made two capitals of cast bronze to set on the tops of the pillars; each capital was five cubits high. [17]A network of interwoven chains adorned the capitals on top of the pillars, seven for each capital. [18]He made pomegranates in two rows encircling each network to decorate the capitals on top of the pillars. He did the same for each capital. [19]The capitals on top of the pillars in the portico were in the shape of lilies, four cubits high. [20]On the capitals of both pillars, above the bowl-shaped part next to the network, were the two hundred pomegranates in rows all around. [21]He erected the pillars at the portico of the temple. The pillar to the south he named Jakin and the one to the north Boaz. [22]The capitals on top were in the shape of lilies. And so the work on the pillars was completed.

[23]He made the Sea of cast metal, circular in shape, measuring ten cubits from rim to rim and five cubits high. It took a line of thirty cubits to measure around it. [24]Below the rim, gourds encircled it—ten to a cubit. The gourds were cast in two rows in one piece with the Sea.

[25]The Sea stood on twelve bulls, three facing north, three facing west, three facing south and three facing east. The Sea rested on top of them, and their hindquarters were toward the center. [26]It was a handbreadth in thickness, and its rim was like the rim of a cup, like a lily blossom. It held two thousand baths.

[27]He also made ten movable stands of bronze; each was four cubits long, four wide and three high. [28]This is how the stands were made: They had side panels attached to uprights. [29]On the panels between the uprights were lions, bulls and cherubim—and on the uprights as well. Above and below the lions and bulls were wreaths of hammered work. [30]Each stand had four bronze wheels with bronze axles, and each had a basin resting on four supports, cast with wreaths on each side. [31]On the inside of the stand there was an opening that had a circular frame one cubit deep.

This opening was round, and with its basework it measured a cubit and
a half. Around its opening there was engraving. The panels of the stands
were square, not round. [32]The four wheels were under the panels, and
the axles of the wheels were attached to the stand. The diameter of each
wheel was a cubit and a half. [33]The wheels were made like chariot wheels;
the axles, rims, spokes and hubs were all of cast metal.

[34]Each stand had four handles, one on each corner, projecting from
the stand. [35]At the top of the stand there was a circular band half a cubit
deep. The supports and panels were attached to the top of the stand. [36]He
engraved cherubim, lions and palm trees on the surfaces of the supports
and on the panels, in every available space, with wreaths all around. [37]This
is the way he made the ten stands. They were all cast in the same molds
and were identical in size and shape.

[38]He then made ten bronze basins, each holding forty baths and measuring four cubits across, one basin to go on each of the ten stands. [39]He
placed five of the stands on the south side of the temple and five on the
north. He placed the Sea on the south side, at the southeast corner of the
temple. [40]He also made the pots and shovels and sprinkling bowls.

So Huram finished all the work he had undertaken for King Solomon
in the temple of the Lord:

[41]the two pillars;
the two bowl-shaped capitals on top of the pillars;
the two sets of network decorating the two bowl-shaped capitals on top of the pillars;
[42]the four hundred pomegranates for the two sets of network (two rows of pomegranates for each network decorating the bowl-shaped capitals on top of the pillars);
[43]the ten stands with their ten basins;
[44]the Sea and the twelve bulls under it;
[45]the pots, shovels and sprinkling bowls.

All these objects that Huram made for King Solomon for the temple
of the Lord were of burnished bronze. [46]The king had them cast in
clay molds in the plain of the Jordan between Sukkoth and Zarethan.
[47]Solomon left all these things unweighed, because there were so many;
the weight of the bronze was not determined.

[48]Solomon also made all the furnishings that were in the LORD's temple:

the golden altar;
the golden table on which was the bread of the Presence;
[49]the lampstands of pure gold (five on the right and five on the left, in front of the inner sanctuary);
the gold floral work and lamps and tongs;
[50]the pure gold basins, wick trimmers, sprinkling bowls, dishes and censers;
and the gold sockets for the doors of the innermost room, the Most Holy Place, and also for the doors of the main hall of the temple.

[51]When all the work King Solomon had done for the temple of the LORD was finished, he brought in the things his father David had dedicated —the silver and gold and the furnishings—and he placed them in the treasuries of the LORD's temple.

Listening to the Text in the Story: Biblical Texts: Exodus 25–31; 35–40; 2 Samuel 5:11; 7:1–17; Ancient Near Eastern Texts: The Azatiwada Inscription; The Report of Wenamum; The Baal Myth

Solomon was famous for his wisdom, but his greatest achievement was the construction of the temple. David asked to build YHWH a house; YHWH said he could not do it, but his son could (2 Sam 7:1–17). YHWH instead promised that he would build David a house, a royal dynasty that would endure. YHWH also said that he would eventually allow David's heir to build a temple (7:13). Now it is time for Solomon to fulfill this prophecy to build a permanent house, a temple for YHWH. Thus begins an extended section in Solomon's narrative of his building projects that, in addition to the temple (1 Kgs 5–6), included the Palace of the Forest of Lebanon, a colonnade (the Hall of Pillars), the Hall of Justice, his personal dwelling, and a house for the daughter of Pharaoh (ch. 7). Solomon's construction narrative concludes with a temple dedication ceremony and prayer (ch. 8), the subject of the next chapter.

Shortly after leaving Egypt and receiving the Ten Commandments, YHWH told Israel to construct a tabernacle, which was the symbolic presence of God in their midst (Exod 40:34). YHWH gave them detailed instructions for how to make the tabernacle, the ark of the covenant, and other tabernacle furnishings (chs. 25–31), which they then followed strictly in their construction (chs. 35–40). The tabernacle continued to be used as a sanctuary through the wilderness wanderings, the period of the judges, and the early monarchy (Josh 18:1; 1 Sam 2:22; 2 Sam 7:6; 1 Kgs 2:28–30; 8:4). It made sense for YHWH to "live" in a tent amongst his people, particularly while Israel lived in tents, since he is a God who dwells incarnationally with his people (2 Sam 7:6–7). Now that they lived in permanent homes, it is time for YHWH to have a permanent dwelling.

In order to provide some historical context for these chapters, we will briefly mention several parallels between Solomon's construction of the temple and the situations of other ancient Near Eastern rulers. Solomon tells Hiram of Tyre that he can start the construction project since YHWH has crushed the enemies of David under his feet (1 Kgs 5:3). Similarly, an inscription of the Phoenician ruler Azatiwada speaks of his enemies being crushed under his feet.[1] Solomon goes to Phoenicia for cedar for YHWH's temple; in a report dated about a century before Solomon, an Egyptian official named Wenamun from the temple of Amon at Karnak traveled to the Phoenician city of Byblos to obtain lumber for the ceremonial barge for his god.[2] In the Baal Myth, the god Baal complains that he does not have his own sanctuary but has to live in the temple of the god El;[3] then the gods decree that a house should be built for Baal, a house of cedar, and then gold, silver, and gems are gathered to prepare for the construction project.[4]

EXPLAIN the Story

Hiram and Solomon Trade Cedar for Food (5:1–12)[5]

The kingdom of Phoenicia, north of Israel along the Mediterranean Sea, was one of David's few allies. Early in David's reign, King Hiram of Tyre sent cedar trees, carpenters, and masons to David to help him build a palace (2 Sam 5:11). When Hiram heard that Solomon had succeeded his father, he took

1. *COS* 2:149; *ANET*, 654; see also Josh 10:24; Ps 110:1.
2. *COS* 1:89–93; *ANET*, 25–29.
3. *COS* 1:253; *ANET*, 131.
4. *COS* 1:259–260; *ANET*, 133.
5. The section of verses is numbered 5:1–18 in English Bibles, is numbered 5:15–32 in the Hebrew Bible.

the initiative and sent messengers, presumably to make sure he was viewed favorably by the new king. Royal transitions were times of uncertainty for neighboring nations, and Solomon's succession would be particularly stressful for Phoenicia. Israel was a larger kingdom that had been militaristic under David, fighting against the Philistines, the Moabites, the Arameans, and the Ammonites (5:17–25; 8; 10), but not against Phoenicia—presumably because of Hiram's gift of timber and labor.

In his reply, Solomon first reminded Hiram of David's wars that had prevented him from building a temple. Now that Israel's borders are at rest, Solomon informs Hiram he is planning to construct a temple for YHWH. Solomon says the temple is actually for the name of YHWH his God, a phrase repeated twice in three verses (1 Kgs 5:3–5) and recalling YHWH's own language spoken to David (2 Sam 7:13). While Solomon's borders may be at rest now, at some point YHWH will raise up adversaries against Solomon because of his apostasy (1 Kgs 11:14–25). Solomon finally gets to the heart of his message to Hiram. He asks for the same thing that was given to David: lumber and labor. Hiram agrees to Solomon's request for cedar wood and lumberjacks. In the mountains of Lebanon, cedar trees typically thrive at altitudes between three thousand and six thousand feet and can grow to a height of over one hundred feet with trunks up to eight feet in diameter. Because of their length, they were often used by Egyptian, Assyrian, and Babylonian rulers in temples to span large ceilings.[6] Solomon's "request" could appear to be a demand, "Give orders that cedars of Lebanon be cut for me" (5:6), particularly given Israel's position of prominence in the region, but Solomon's offer of labor payment makes it seem mutual. Solomon says essentially to Hiram, "We'll hire 'em."

It is good news for Hiram: Solomon wants wood, not war, so he was greatly pleased and praised YHWH for giving David a wise successor. While it might seem strange for a foreigner to bless YHWH like this, several other non-Israelites honored YHWH in a similar manner (e.g., Jethro: Exod 18:10; Naaman: 2 Kgs 5:15; Nebuchadnezzar: Dan 3:28); in their context, it would not be uncommon for polytheists to praise deities of other nations.

Hiram's reply to Solomon appears to comply with the king's request (cedar and juniper logs) except Hiram does not want Israelite workers in his land, since he says his men will deliver them in rafts by sea to Israel's port of choice, without mentioning any Israelite labor helping. Presumably, he wanted to avoid a large foreign incursion. Solomon, however, insisted that he would send in large numbers to help, in groups of ten thousand as he had initially

6. Wiseman, *1 & 2 Kings*, 100.

suggested, despite Hiram's offer of a purely Sidonian delivery. Hiram agrees to work for food. To give some perspective on the magnitude of this transaction, if one were to translate the court of Solomon's daily non-meat provisions from the previous chapter (1 Kgs 4:24) into annual amounts, the total would be over thirty thousand cors of flour and meal, about a quarter less than the forty thousand cors of wheat and oil promised to Hiram annually while this transaction continues (5:11). While the goods being provided are different in the two chapters, the amounts are roughly comparable. As a result of this transaction, Solomon, whose name means "peace," had peaceful relations with Hiram, and they established a treaty making it official.[7]

At this point, we can review the development of Solomon's wisdom in Kings. David had told his son to act according to his wisdom (2:6). Solomon had asked for a listening heart (3:9), so God promised him a wise heart (3:12). Both the people and Hiram perceived God's wisdom was in Solomon (3:28; 5:7). God gave him wisdom in the context of his domestic policies (4:29), and now God gives him wisdom in the context of his foreign policies (5:11).

Solomon's Conscripted Labor Force (5:13–18)

To complete Solomon's ambitious building projects, he needs a huge labor force, so he conscripts almost two hundred thousand men from the nation as laborers. Thirty thousand lumberjacks worked in Lebanon alongside Hiram's lumberjacks in three shifts, one month in Lebanon and two months in Israel, so only ten thousand were away at a time (5:14). Solomon had eighty thousand stonecutters quarrying the large stone blocks in the hills, and to transport the loads of wood and stone there were seventy thousand burden carriers (v. 15). Three thousand, five hundred foremen supervised all the work. When Solomon died, Jeroboam and the Israelite people complained to Solomon's successor Rehoboam about the hard service they performed under Solomon (1 Kgs 12:1–4).[8]

The Temple Dating (6:1, 37–38)

The chapter begins with a date for the beginning of the construction of Solomon's Temple four hundred and eighty years after the exodus from Egypt. Three features make this date distinctive. First, this date includes not only the year (Solomon's fourth) but also the month (Ziv, the second month of that year; 6:1, 37). The date of the completion of the temple also includes the year

7. Solomon's name in Hebrew is *Shelomoh*, probably derived from the Hebrew word *shalom*.
8. To paraphrase Monty Python, "they were lumberjacks, but they were not okay."

(Solomon's eleventh) and the month (Bul, the eighth), meaning the entire project took seven years and six months (v. 38). Kings often dates events, usually royal ascensions, but typically no months are mentioned. More precise dating is a chronological feature more common at the end of the book (e.g., 2 Kgs 25:1, 3, 8, 25, 27). Many of these precise dates are connected to the destruction of Jerusalem and the temple. It is difficult to know why the month is included for Solomon's temple construction, but presumably significant events in Israel's history warranted precise dating. The fact that a more precise date is given for the beginning and the completion of the temple, as well as for the final destruction of the temple, is not surprising, since the temple played a significant role in Israel's history for the nearly four hundred years that it endured.

Second, it is unusual to date events relative to events in Israel's premonarchic history. Most of the dates in Kings are given relative to other events within the monarchy; most royal ascension years are dated relative to the ascension year of another king (e.g., 1 Kgs 15:1, 9, 25, 33). This date is actually the first reference to the exodus in Kings, although the exodus becomes a prominent theme later in the book (8:9, 16, 21, 51, 53; 9:9; 12:28; 2 Kgs 17:7, 36; 21:15).

Third, the date appears to be particularly symbolic. The total—four hundred and eighty—is the product of two numbers that have particular significance for Israel: twelve and forty. Jacob had twelve sons, and therefore Israel had twelve tribes (Gen 35:22; 49:28); Moses was on the mountain for forty days, and Israel was in the wilderness for forty years (Exod 24:18; Num 14:33–34). Some scholars interpret this number literally and therefore situate the exodus in the fifteenth century BC (about 1440), since Solomon's fourth year is typically dated between 968 and 957 BC.[9] However, other scholars think the number should be understood figuratively as the passing of twelve generations and thus situate the exodus in the thirteenth century during the reign of Ramesses II (see Exod 1:11).

The Temple Exterior (6:2–10, 14)

Outside of 1 Kings 6, YHWH interacted directly with Solomon three times (1 Kgs 3:5–14; 9:3–9; 11:11–13). YHWH speaks directly to Solomon once here in the context of temple construction (6:11–13), but curiously he never gives instructions about the temple or its furnishings. In stark contrast,

9. For discussions of the dating of the exodus relevant to this date in 1 Kgs 6:1, see Wiseman, *1 & 2 Kings*, 104; DeVries, *1 Kings*, 93–94.

YHWH gave Moses detailed instructions for the tabernacle and its furnishings, spanning almost seven chapters (Exod 25–31).

While YHWH apparently granted freedom to Solomon to design the temple, YHWH's design of the tabernacle appeared to inspire Solomon's plans since the general floorplan was similar, although the dimensions of Solomon's Temple here are about twice the size of the tabernacle (Exod 26:15–25). The measurements in the text are given in cubits; while cubit size varied, for purposes of this commentary, we will assume an eighteen-inch cubit and therefore will multiply the cubit measurements by 1.5 to calculate measurements in feet.[10]

The structure of the temple was approximately ninety feet long, thirty feet wide, and forty-five feet high. The details are difficult to discern, but general comments can be made about the main features. There was a portico or porch at the entrance to the temple that was thirty feet wide (the width of the temple), and it extended out from the inner sections of the sanctuary by fifteen feet (1 Kgs 6:3). Along the side of the temple there appeared to be high, narrow windows (v. 4). Also along the outer wall were three levels of side rooms that would be used for storage of priestly garments or other valuables. Even though these storage rooms had three levels, they only went up half the height of the temple (15 cubits = 22.5 feet; v. 10), so they did not block the high windows. Stairways were constructed to give access to the upper two levels of storage rooms (v. 8). The stone used in construction needed to be shaped at the quarry so no iron tools would be used at the site of the temple (v. 7). The text here does not explain the lack of iron tools on the temple site, but Mosaic laws mandated that altars be made from uncut stones, since iron tools would profane them (Exod 20:25; Deut 27:5–6). Cedar planks were used to cover the roof and to attach the side rooms to the temple structure (1 Kgs 6:10).

YHWH's Address (6:11–13)

In the midst of the detailed description of Solomon's construction project, YHWH spoke to the ruler a second time. YHWH's address is prefaced with, "the word of the Lord came to" (6:11), a phrase that appears eleven times elsewhere in the book (13:20; 16:1; 17:2, 8; 18:1, 31; 19:9; 21:17, 28; 2 Kgs 20:4). What makes the usage of this phrase unique in Solomon's case is that,

10. The cubit was defined as the distance from the elbow to the end of the middle finger, typically eighteen inches, but since arm-lengths were not standardized then (or now), the standard cubit size varied between seventeen and twenty-two inches. My "cubit" is 18.5 inches. How long is your cubit?

in these other references, the divine message always comes directly to a prophet and never a king.[11]

YHWH's speech here is often described as Deuteronomistic since it focuses on obedience, with repetitive language reminiscent of Deuteronomy. Solomon is to follow, observe, keep, and obey YHWH's decrees, laws, and commands (1 Kgs 6:12). Three blessings are promised: (1) YHWH fulfilling David's covenant; (2) YHWH living among the Israelites; and (3) YHWH not abandoning his people (6:12–13). But these blessings are conditioned upon Solomon's obedience, which is consistent with the conditional nature of previous messages from David to Solomon (2:3–4) and from YHWH to Solomon (3:14). The promise to dwell with his people in his house is a theme that Solomon will revisit in his temple dedication (8:12, 13, 27).

The Temple Interior (6:15–30)

The interior of the ninety-foot-long temple was divided into two parts. The Most Holy Place (literally, "the holy of holies") was a thirty-by-thirty-by-thirty-foot cube, and it made up a third of the sanctuary space. While later in Solomon's narrative this space is called the Most Holy Place (7:50; 8:6, 8, 10), it is more frequently referred to in this section as "the inner sanctuary" (6:16, 19, 20, 21, 22, 23, 31). The outer sanctuary, between the Most Holy Place and the portico, is called both "the main hall" (6:3, 5, 17, 33; 7:50) and "the Holy Place" (8:8, 10). In this section I will use the terms most frequently used here: the inner sanctuary and the main hall.

The main hall, which is between the inner sanctuary and the portico, was twice as big as the inner sanctuary, a sixty-foot-long and thirty-foot-wide rectangular box making up two-thirds of the sanctuary space. Cedar boards lined the interior walls and planks of juniper covered the floor, so no stone was uncovered (6:15, 18). The inner sanctuary was then prepared to house the ark of the covenant (v. 19). Gold was used to cover the entire interior, both the inner sanctuary and the main hall, as well as the cedar altar and the inner sanctuary altar; gold chains were extended across the entrance of the inner sanctuary (vv. 20–22, 30).

The interior of the inner sanctuary would have been dominated by two large identical cherubim (the plural of cherub) made out of olive wood. It is impossible to say what cherubim looked like, but they probably would not have been baby-faced children with puffy cheeks, as they are often portrayed.

11. Although several prophets are supposed to relay their message to a ruler (e.g., 1 Kgs 16:1; 18:1; 2 Kgs 20:4–5).

Cherubim first appear in the Bible as guards with flaming swords to prevent the first man and woman from returning to the garden of Eden (Gen 3:24). They probably appeared more like warriors than children. The cover of the ark of the covenant (also called the mercy seat) also had two cherubim, above which YHWH's presence was meant to dwell (Exod 25:18–22). In the book of Ezekiel, cherubim take a more human form than they do in 1 Kings and are often associated with chariot imagery (Ezek 1:5–14; 9:3; 10:1–20; 28:14, 16).

We do know two things about the appearance of the two cherubim in the inner sanctuary: they were big and had wings. They were fifteen feet tall and had fifteen-foot wingspans (1 Kgs 6:23–26). The tip of each cherub's wing touched opposite walls, and their other wings touched each other in the middle of the inner sanctuary (v. 27), literally spanning the room. They were also covered in gold (v. 28). These cherubim were not to be taken lightly. Carved cherubim also decorated the walls, along with palm trees and flowers (v. 29).

The Temple Entrance and Courtyard (6:31–36)

Two sets of doors were made of wood: olive for the inner sanctuary and juniper for the main hall (6:31, 34). The doorframes for the main hall were made from olive wood (v. 33). Since one can never have enough cherubim, both sets of doors were decorated with carved cherubim, along with palm trees and flowers. Finally, all the doors were covered with hammered gold (vv. 32, 35).

The text describes an inner courtyard surrounding the temple, which suggests that, even though the text does not mention it, there was an outer courtyard as well. The description of the inner courtyard lacks detail about the dimensions, except that it notes that for every three layers of stone a layer of cedar was inserted (v. 36), which would have strengthened the wall and added stability in the event of an earthquake.[12]

The temple furnishings were not yet finished (7:13–50), and the divine presence had not yet filled the temple (8:10–11), but after seven years the construction project was completed (6:38). The text includes no concluding textual comment describing the glory of the temple, but it would have been an impressive structure of stone, gold, cedar, olive, juniper, palm, flowers, and magnificent cherubim. Solomon's Temple was so glorious that anyone old enough to still remember it after it was destroyed would have thought that the Second Temple constructed during the time of Haggai was nothing in comparison (Hag 2:3).

---

12. See Cogan, *I Kings*, 247.

Solomon's Palace Complex (7:1–12)

The narrative shifts from the construction of Solomon's Temple to the construction of his palace by noting that the temple project took seven years to finish but his palace took thirteen (1 Kgs 7:1). The fact that his personal palace complex took almost twice as long as the temple and that, at least as it is narrated, it appears to interrupt the work on the temple (completed in 7:13–51) could suggest that Solomon's palace building projects are meant to be viewed negatively.[13] It is difficult to say whether work on the temple stopped while Solomon completed his palace complex; even if they took place concurrently, his personal construction project would have taken resources away from the temple project and therefore would have delayed its completion.

Solomon's palace complex includes five buildings. The largest, the Palace of the Forest of Lebanon (vv. 2–5), was enormous (one hundred and fifty feet long, seventy-five feet wide, and forty-five feet high). Its roof was the same height as the temple, but its sides were much larger, making its square footage over four times that of the temple, yet another factor that could lead one to view Solomon's work here negatively.[14] The structure would have been impressive with its four rows of cedar columns, giving it the appearance of a forest and thus inspiring the name. Like the temple, it had a cedar roof and high windows.

The second building was a colonnade, also called a "Hall of Pillars" (ESV, NRSV, NAS), which was seventy-five feet high and forty-five feet wide (no height is given) with a porch and overhanging roof (v. 6). The third building, Solomon's throne hall (also called "the Hall of Justice"), was covered in cedar and served as the location for his judgments (v. 7). The fourth and fifth buildings, the personal dwellings of Solomon and his wife, the daughter of Pharaoh, were similar in design to the Hall of Justice (v. 8). No dimensions are recorded for these final three buildings. This section concludes with comments about the construction materials (high-quality stone and cedar) and how a courtyard encompassed the palace complex (v. 9–12).

The Temple's Furnishings (7:13–51)

The focus of the construction shifts back to the temple, specifically the furnishings that will be placed inside. Solomon brings a skilled craftsman named

13. See Wray Beal, *1 & 2 Kings*, 121–22.

14. Both structures were forty-five feet high, so comparing their floor plans, the Palace of the Forest of Lebanon was 150' by 75' (so 11,250 square feet) and the temple was 90' by 30' (so 2700 square feet).

Huram from Tyre to make the bronze objects that will fill the sanctuary.[15] His father was from Tyre, and his mother was from the tribe of Naphtali, one of the northern tribes near Tyre. Huram is described in similar language to Bezalel and Oholiab, the skilled artisans who did comparable work for the furnishings of the tabernacle (Exod 31:1–10; 35:30–36:2). The descriptions of Huram's bronze creations divides easily into three sections: (1) two pillars and two capitals (1 Kgs 7:15–22); (2) the Sea (vv. 23–26); and (3) ten stands and ten basins (vv. 27–39).

The two bronze pillars were twenty-seven feet high and eighteen feet in circumference (about a six-foot diameter), and each was topped with a bronze seven-and-a-half-foot-high capital shaped like a lily (vv. 15–22). They were adorned with networks of woven chains and pomegranates. They were positioned on the east side of the temple at the portico, and they were given names. The one on the right or south was called "Jakin" ("he establishes"), and the one on the left or north was called "Boaz" ("in him is strength").

The Sea was comparable to an above-ground bronze swimming pool (vv. 23–26).[16] It was fifteen feet in diameter and seven and a half feet high. Under the Sea were twelve bulls to support it, three facing each direction, with their hindquarters facing the center of the Sea. The Sea held two thousand baths (about twelve thousand gallons of water, the capacity of a typical above-ground pool).

Huram also made ten identical bronze stands (vv. 27–39) that held the ten bronze basins, which would have been filled from the Sea. The stands were six feet tall, six feet wide, and four and half feet high and were portable with four wheels. They were decorated with lions, bulls, cherubim, wreaths, and palm trees. The wheels were comparable to chariot wheels with axles, rims, spokes, and hubs all made of metal. The ten bronze basins that rested on the stands were six feet in diameter and each held forty baths (about two hundred and forty gallons). The Sea was positioned in the southeast corner of the temple. Five of the stand basins were positioned on the south side of the temple and five on the north side. The text includes a summary of Huram's bronze workmanship (pillars, capitals, stands, basins, the Sea and bulls, pots, shovels, and bowls; vv. 40–45). Many of these items would have been used in the sacrifice rituals (see Exod 27:3).

---

15. The name in the Hebrew is "Hiram" (but distinct from the king of Tyre; 1 Kgs 5:1). Many English translations render the name as "Hiram" (e.g., ESV, NRSV, NAS), but several render it as "Huram," along with the NIV, presumably based on 2 Chr 2:13, which gives his name as "Huram-abi."

16. The text here says the Sea was made of cast metal, but when it was destroyed, the text states it was bronze (2 Kgs 25:13).

The description of the furnishings' construction concludes with the gold work (1 Kgs 7:48–50). The text says Solomon made it, but we assume he merely delegated the task to the people skilled in goldwork. Objects of gold included the altar, the table for the bread of the presence, the ten lampstands, floral work, more lamps, tongs, basins, trimmers, bowls, dishes, censers, door sockets, and doors. Finally, the precious objects of gold and silver that David had already dedicated (2 Sam 8:10–12) were placed in the temple treasury (1 Kgs 7:51).

Solomon's Temple survived almost four hundred years, but it was eventually destroyed by Nebuchadnezzar of Babylon in 587 BC at the end of the book of Kings (2 Kgs 25:8–17). Several parallels can be seen between the construction of Solomon's Temple in 1 Kings 5–6 and the construction of the Second Temple under Haggai and Zechariah. First, in each case YHWH commissions a ruler to start the process (for the Second Temple the one commissioned was the Persian king, Cyrus; 2 Chr 36:22–23; Ezra 1:1–4). Second, for both temples the Israelite people use lumber from the neighboring hills as material to build the house (1 Kgs 5:6; Hag. 1:8). Third, the text narrates in detail the actual construction of both temples (1 Kgs 6; Ezra 3–6; Hag 1–2).

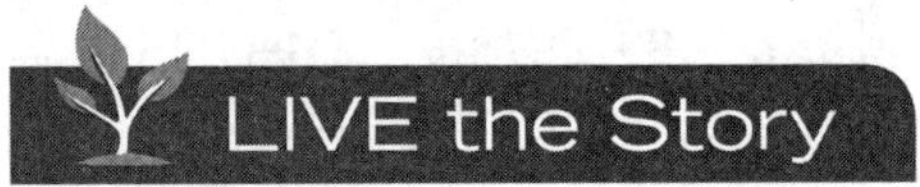

Why Narrate Solomon's Detailed Construction Projects?

The only time YHWH is active in these three chapters, he is emphasizing obedience, but the rest of the narrative merely describes Solomon's various construction projects. Why spend 106 verses describing the details of Solomon's Temple and his palace complex? What can we learn from this section? I see two lessons that come through clearly.

First, working together unifies God's people. David came to power after a tumultuous civil war (2 Sam 2–4), and during his reign warfare unified the nation, fighting against common enemies: the Philistines, the Ammonites, and the Arameans (2 Sam 8; 10). Solomon came to power after a series of three rebellions, two of which were led by his older brothers (2 Sam 15–21; 1 Kgs 1). He didn't use warfare to bring the country together, but construction. It is hard not to think negatively about Solomon's work projects based on Jeroboam's complaint about Solomon's conscripted labor force, but I will wait until 1 Kings 12 to address that issue. Here I will focus on positive aspects of working together.

According to the text, Solomon engaged hundreds of thousands of people in his projects, which would have been a significant proportion of the total population. The people mentioned in the text include Solomon, Hiram, Huram, lumberjacks, load carriers, stonecutters, and foremen. We assume many others were involved, including people who worked under Huram to make the bronze objects and everyone who worked on the royal palace complex.

While most Christian communities don't experience crises as severe as a civil war or a rebellion, a major group project can bring a team, a church, or a ministry together after a difficult time. The obvious application to this idea might be a church building program, but, unfortunately, many of these programs limit people's involvement to giving money. Service projects, outreach events, or other types of programs often provide wider arrays of opportunities for people to get involved, to use their gifts, and to give them a common focus. The best aspect of these programs is often not the completed project but the process of working together and creating something together, which leads to the next point.

Second, a creative project connects people to the Creator. Tragically, in the context of Christian ministry, creative people are often undervalued, and artists are even sometimes viewed with suspicion. But this was not the case in the world in the Bible. The first act God performed in the Bible was to create (Gen 1:1), and verbs of creation dominate these chapters: "make" (*'asah*) appears twenty-six times (e.g., 1 Kgs 5:22, 23; 6:4, 12; 7:6, 7), "build" (*banah*) appears twenty-two times (e.g., 5:17, 19 [20x]; 6:1, 2; 7:1, 2), "overlaid" or "covered" (piel of *tsaphah*) appears twelve times (6:15 [2x], 20 [2x], 21 [2x], 22 [2x], 28, 30, 32, 35), "carved" (*qala'*) appears six times (6:29, 32, 34, 35), and "cast" (*yatsaq*) appears five times (7:23, 24, 30, 33, 46). Not only were beautiful objects from creation used, including minerals (stone and gold) and trees (cedar, juniper, and olive), but also beautiful images from creation adorned both the walls of the temple and the furnishings in the temple: trees, flowers, pomegranates, lilies, gourds, lions, and bulls. By first building the structure of the temple and then filling it with beautiful furnishings, Solomon follows God's pattern from creation: to first build the containers in days one through three (Gen 1:3–13), then to fill them with things and with life in days four through six (1:14–31).[17]

The process of constructing a temple gave the people an opportunity to create. While Solomon's design was based on God's design from the tabernacle, there was plenty of room for Solomon, Huram, and other artists to be creative along the way. The text doesn't detail all the other ways creativity was expressed,

---

17. See Gordon J. Wenham, *Genesis 1–15* (Waco: Word Books, 1987), 6–7; Tremper Longman III, *Genesis* (Grand Rapids: Zondervan, 2016), 35.

but when the text says "Solomon did something," we can be confident that he delegated many creative tasks to people he could trust, as he did in 1 Kings 4. These people created, among other things, beautiful pomegranates, bulls, and cherubim to adorn the temple. And everyone involved, even the lumberjacks and laborers, were part of the creation of something significant, something that would remind them of their Creator who created them in his image (Gen 1:26–27). The temple was designed to help God's people experience God visually, artistically, and creatively. God's people therefore need to make spaces for those of us who are creative (and those of us who aren't) to use our gifts artistically, which will help us connect to our Creator.

Obedience and Divine Abandonment

Throughout these three chapters YHWH is mainly passive and silent. The only time God speaks is in the middle of chapter 6, to remind Solomon to obey God's laws (1 Kgs 6:11–13). Curiously, YHWH doesn't seem to be particularly impressed thus far with Solomon's building project. He mentions it ("as for this temple you are building," v. 12) merely as a preamble to his reminder to keep the commands. God is more interested in Solomon's obedience than in his construction projects. While the tabernacle was God's idea (Exod 25:1–9), the temple was David's; God didn't seem particularly eager to have it built. God did allow David's son to build it (2 Sam 7:13), but, even when YHWH and Solomon interacted earlier in the context of the dream, no mention was made of YHWH wanting a temple. However, the theme of obedience was emphasized previously in both the words of David to Solomon and those of YHWH to Solomon (1 Kgs 2:2–4; 3:14). Throughout the Old Testament, God prioritized obedience over the rituals that took place at the temple: offerings and sacrifices (e.g., 1 Sam 15:22; Ps 40:6; Isa 1:11–15; Jer 7:22–23). Jesus also said obeying the commands to love God and love one's neighbor was better than offering sacrifices (Mark 12:33).

In this divine message, which interrupts the narrative of the construction, YHWH makes his point clearly to Solomon. YHWH will not abandon his people and will continue to live with them, not merely because a temple was built for him but because Solomon obeys. God's conditional word to Solomon here should have served as a warning not only to Solomon but also to other rulers and to the Israelite people. The nation and its leaders, however, did not obey, so God eventually abandoned them (2 Kgs 24:20) and his temple, allowing the Babylonians to swoop in and destroy Solomon's impressive structure and its furnishings (25:8–17). From Israel's tragic mistakes, we learn that God takes obedience seriously.

Divine Presence and the Word Made Flesh

The idea of God dwelling with his people (1 Kgs 8:10–13) is found throughout the Old Testament. Prior to the construction of the tabernacle, YHWH was with Jacob (Gen 28:15), with Joseph (39:2, 3, 23), and with Moses (Exod 3:12). During the period of the monarchy YHWH was with rulers: Saul (1 Sam 10:7), David (18:12, 14, 28), Solomon (1 Chr 28:20), Jehoshaphat (2 Chr 17:3), and Hezekiah (2 Kgs 18:7). God walks with his people (Gen 3:8; 5:22–23; 6:9), he speaks to his people (e.g., Gen 1:28; Mal 4:5–6), and, most relevantly for these chapters, he dwells with his people (Exod 29:45; 1 Kgs 6:13).

This Old Testament language of divine presence powerfully points forward to Jesus's incarnation, as he is the Word who became flesh and dwelt among his people (John 1:14). Just as YHWH in the Old Testament walked with, spoke to, and dwelt with his people, Jesus himself was incarnate among his people, calling his disciples to follow him (Mark 1:17; 2:14; 8:34) and to simply be with him (3:14). Jesus was the physical manifestation of the temple in human form. Paul expresses this profound truth as he states, "For in Christ all the fullness of the Deity lives in bodily form" (Col 2:9). It was difficult for the people of Jesus's day to comprehend how a human could incarnate God's presence in their midst, but for people who were familiar with the Old Testament, it shouldn't have been a shock. From the beginning of Genesis God was manifesting his love for his people by moving toward them, being with them, and desiring to be present in their midst.

Just as the temple of Solomon was destroyed, so was the temple of Jesus's body destroyed (John 2:19), providing the ultimate sacrifice to deliver us from the consequences of disobedience (Heb 10:12–14). As the great high priest, Jesus is able to enter the heavenly temple, appearing upon our behalf (4:14; 9:24). And because of this, he will be exalted as every knee will bow and every tongue confess that Jesus Christ is Lord (Phil 2:8–11).

CHAPTER 6

1 Kings 8:1–66

LISTEN to the Story

[1]Then King Solomon summoned into his presence at Jerusalem the
elders of Israel, all the heads of the tribes and the chiefs of the Israelite
families, to bring up the ark of the LORD's covenant from Zion, the City
of David. [2]All the Israelites came together to King Solomon at the time of
the festival in the month of Ethanim, the seventh month.

[3]When all the elders of Israel had arrived, the priests took up the ark,
[4]and they brought up the ark of the LORD and the tent of meeting and all
the sacred furnishings in it. The priests and Levites carried them up, [5]and
King Solomon and the entire assembly of Israel that had gathered about
him were before the ark, sacrificing so many sheep and cattle that they
could not be recorded or counted.

[6]The priests then brought the ark of the LORD's covenant to its place in
the inner sanctuary of the temple, the Most Holy Place, and put it beneath
the wings of the cherubim. [7]The cherubim spread their wings over the
place of the ark and overshadowed the ark and its carrying poles. [8]These
poles were so long that their ends could be seen from the Holy Place in
front of the inner sanctuary, but not from outside the Holy Place; and
they are still there today. [9]There was nothing in the ark except the two
stone tablets that Moses had placed in it at Horeb, where the LORD made
a covenant with the Israelites after they came out of Egypt.

[10]When the priests withdrew from the Holy Place, the cloud filled
the temple of the LORD. [11]And the priests could not perform their service
because of the cloud, for the glory of the LORD filled his temple.

[12]Then Solomon said, "The LORD has said that he would dwell in a
dark cloud; [13]I have indeed built a magnificent temple for you, a place for
you to dwell forever."

[14]While the whole assembly of Israel was standing there, the king
turned around and blessed them. [15]Then he said:

"Praise be to the LORD, the God of Israel, who with his own hand has fulfilled what he promised with his own mouth to my father David. For he said, [16]'Since the day I brought my people Israel out of Egypt, I have not chosen a city in any tribe of Israel to have a temple built so that my Name might be there, but I have chosen David to rule my people Israel.'

[17]"My father David had it in his heart to build a temple for the Name of the LORD, the God of Israel. [18]But the LORD said to my father David, 'You did well to have it in your heart to build a temple for my Name. [19]Nevertheless, you are not the one to build the temple, but your son, your own flesh and blood—he is the one who will build the temple for my Name.'

[20]"The LORD has kept the promise he made: I have succeeded David my father and now I sit on the throne of Israel, just as the LORD promised, and I have built the temple for the Name of the LORD, the God of Israel. [21]I have provided a place there for the ark, in which is the covenant of the LORD that he made with our ancestors when he brought them out of Egypt."

[22]Then Solomon stood before the altar of the LORD in front of the whole assembly of Israel, spread out his hands toward heaven [23]and said:

"LORD, the God of Israel, there is no God like you in heaven above or on earth below—you who keep your covenant of love with your servants who continue wholeheartedly in your way. [24]You have kept your promise to your servant David my father; with your mouth you have promised and with your hand you have fulfilled it—as it is today.

[25]"Now LORD, the God of Israel, keep for your servant David my father the promises you made to him when you said, 'You shall never fail to have a successor to sit before me on the throne of Israel, if only your descendants are careful in all they do to walk before me faithfully as you have done.' [26]And now, God of Israel, let your word that you promised your servant David my father come true.

[27]"But will God really dwell on earth? The heavens, even the highest heaven, cannot contain you. How much less this temple I have built! [28]Yet give attention to your servant's prayer and his plea for mercy, LORD my God. Hear the cry and the prayer that your servant is praying in

your presence this day. [29]May your eyes be open toward this temple night and day, this place of which you said, 'My Name shall be there,' so that you will hear the prayer your servant prays toward this place. [30]Hear the supplication of your servant and of your people Israel when they pray toward this place. Hear from heaven, your dwelling place, and when you hear, forgive.

[31]"When anyone wrongs their neighbor and is required to take an oath and they come and swear the oath before your altar in this temple, [32]then hear from heaven and act. Judge between your servants, condemning the guilty by bringing down on their heads what they have done, and vindicating the innocent by treating them in accordance with their innocence.

[33]"When your people Israel have been defeated by an enemy because they have sinned against you, and when they turn back to you and give praise to your name, praying and making supplication to you in this temple, [34]then hear from heaven and forgive the sin of your people Israel and bring them back to the land you gave to their ancestors.

[35]"When the heavens are shut up and there is no rain because your people have sinned against you, and when they pray toward this place and give praise to your name and turn from their sin because you have afflicted them, [36]then hear from heaven and forgive the sin of your servants, your people Israel. Teach them the right way to live, and send rain on the land you gave your people for an inheritance.

[37]"When famine or plague comes to the land, or blight or mildew, locusts or grasshoppers, or when an enemy besieges them in any of their cities, whatever disaster or disease may come, [38]and when a prayer or plea is made by anyone among your people Israel—being aware of the afflictions of their own hearts, and spreading out their hands toward this temple—[39]then hear from heaven, your dwelling place. Forgive and act; deal with everyone according to all they do, since you know their hearts (for you alone know every human heart), [40]so that they will fear you all the time they live in the land you gave our ancestors.

[41]"As for the foreigner who does not belong to your people Israel but has come from a distant land because of your name—[42]for they will hear of your great name and your mighty hand and your outstretched arm—when they come and pray toward this temple, [43]then hear from heaven, your dwelling place. Do whatever the foreigner asks of you,

so that all the peoples of the earth may know your name and fear you,
as do your own people Israel, and may know that this house I have
built bears your Name.

44“When your people go to war against their enemies, wherever you
send them, and when they pray to the Lord toward the city you have
chosen and the temple I have built for your Name, 45then hear from
heaven their prayer and their plea, and uphold their cause.

46“When they sin against you—for there is no one who does not
sin—and you become angry with them and give them over to their enemies, who take them captive to their own lands, far away or near; 47and
if they have a change of heart in the land where they are held captive,
and repent and plead with you in the land of their captors and say, ‘We
have sinned, we have done wrong, we have acted wickedly’; 48and if
they turn back to you with all their heart and soul in the land of their
enemies who took them captive, and pray to you toward the land you
gave their ancestors, toward the city you have chosen and the temple I
have built for your Name; 49then from heaven, your dwelling place, hear
their prayer and their plea, and uphold their cause. 50And forgive your
people, who have sinned against you; forgive all the offenses they have
committed against you, and cause their captors to show them mercy;
51for they are your people and your inheritance, whom you brought
out of Egypt, out of that iron-smelting furnace.

52“May your eyes be open to your servant’s plea and to the plea of
your people Israel, and may you listen to them whenever they cry out
to you. 53For you singled them out from all the nations of the world
to be your own inheritance, just as you declared through your servant
Moses when you, Sovereign Lord, brought our ancestors out of Egypt.”

54When Solomon had finished all these prayers and supplications to
the Lord, he rose from before the altar of the Lord, where he had been
kneeling with his hands spread out toward heaven. 55He stood and blessed
the whole assembly of Israel in a loud voice, saying:

56“Praise be to the Lord, who has given rest to his people Israel
just as he promised. Not one word has failed of all the good promises
he gave through his servant Moses. 57May the Lord our God be with
us as he was with our ancestors; may he never leave us nor forsake us.

[58]May he turn our hearts to him, to walk in obedience to him and keep
the commands, decrees and laws he gave our ancestors. [59]And may
these words of mine, which I have prayed before the LORD, be near to
the LORD our God day and night, that he may uphold the cause of his
servant and the cause of his people Israel according to each day's need,
[60]so that all the peoples of the earth may know that the LORD is God
and that there is no other. [61]And may your hearts be fully committed
to the LORD our God, to live by his decrees and obey his commands,
as at this time."

[62]Then the king and all Israel with him offered sacrifices before the
LORD. [63]Solomon offered a sacrifice of fellowship offerings to the LORD:
twenty-two thousand cattle and a hundred and twenty thousand sheep and
goats. So the king and all the Israelites dedicated the temple of the LORD.
[64]On that same day the king consecrated the middle part of the
courtyard in front of the temple of the LORD, and there he offered burnt
offerings, grain offerings and the fat of the fellowship offerings, because
the bronze altar that stood before the LORD was too small to hold the
burnt offerings, the grain offerings and the fat of the fellowship offerings.
[65]So Solomon observed the festival at that time, and all Israel with
him—a vast assembly, people from Lebo Hamath to the Wadi of Egypt.
They celebrated it before the LORD our God for seven days and seven
days more, fourteen days in all. [66]On the following day he sent the people
away. They blessed the king and then went home, joyful and glad in heart
for all the good things the LORD had done for his servant David and his
people Israel.

Listening to the Text in the Story: Biblical Texts: 1 Samuel 4–6; 2 Samuel 2–7; Ancient Near Eastern Texts: The Inscribed Cylinders of Gudea of Lagash; The Qadesh Battle Poem of Ramesses II of Egypt; The Funerary Inscription of Thebariya Velinas of Phoenicia

After seven years of construction, the temple is finally finished. All that remains is to dedicate the temple, which Solomon does by bringing in the ark, blessing the people, praying through seven future scenarios, blessing the people again, offering abundant sacrifices, and hosting an extravagant feast.

Israel had serious problems with the ark previously, so moving it into the

Most Holy Place could have been a stressful task. The ark had been captured by the Philistines during the priesthood of Eli, but the ark caused problems for the Philistines, so they returned it on a cart; it remained at Kiriath-jearim, nine miles west of Jerusalem, for twenty years (1 Sam 4–6). While David attempted to transport the ark to Jerusalem, Uzzah tried to stabilize the ark when the oxen pulling the cart stumbled; God struck him dead (2 Sam 6). The story of Uzzah's death is troubling, but the Israelites were not transporting the ark in the manner YHWH had mandated.[1] God told the Israelites to move the ark using poles (Exod 25:10–15; Num 7:7–9; Deut 10:8), not a cart, and had warned them that if they touched the ark they would die (Num 4:15). David's first attempt to bring the ark stalled for three months at the house of Obed-edom the Gittite, but when David discovered Obed-edom was blessed by the ark's presence, he had it carried successfully by priests using the poles to the city of David (2 Sam 6:12–19). This chapter completes the story of the ark's final resting place in the temple.

Solomon's prayer is the longest in the book of Kings (thirty-one verses; 1 Kgs 8:23–53) and one of the longest (outside of the Psalms) in the Old Testament. The prayers of several other Old Testament characters share certain features with that of Solomon's. Nathan's oracle (2 Sam 7:1–16), promising a dynasty and a temple completed by his descendant (referenced several times in 1 Kgs 8), prompts a long prayer from David in which he praises God for the promise and requests God's blessing (2 Sam 7:18–29).

Several ancient Near Eastern texts include parallels to 1 Kings 8—blessing the people, praying over and dedicating a new temple, and praying toward a temple from a remote location. On a Sumerian inscribed cylinder, Gudea (2144–2124 BC), ruler of Lagash in southern Mesopotamia, pronounces a blessing and tells his god, Nirgirsu, "I have built a temple for you, may you enter it with joy" (see also 1 Kgs 8:12); like Solomon, he prepares a temple dedication banquet.[2] In a list of achievements he performed for Amun, Ramesses II (1279–1213 BC) states, "I built for you my Memorial Temple . . . I caused to be offered myriads of cattle."[3] Later in this inscription, Ramesses speaks of praying from a distant land: "I made petition from the back of beyond, my voice echoing in Thebes."[4] A Phoenician inscription on a sheet of

1. For a longer discussion of Uzzah and the ark, see David T. Lamb, *God Behaving Badly: Is the God of the Old Testament Angry, Sexist and Racist?* (Downers Grove, IL: InterVarsity Press, 2011), 27–33.

2. *COS* 2:428, 430, 432; *ANET*, 268–69.

3. *COS* 2:34; see 1 Kgs 8:20, 62–64.

4. *COS* 2:35; see 1 Kgs 8:29–30, 42, 44.

gold leaf (dated about 500 BC) describes the construction and dedication of a shrine by King Thebariye Velinas: "To the Lady 'Ashtart: This holy place which Thebariye Velinas, king over Kaysriye, made and dedicated in the month of the Sacrifice of the Sun as a gift (and) as a temple. I built it because 'Ashtart requested it from me in the third year of my reign in the month of Kirar on the day of the burial of the god."[5]

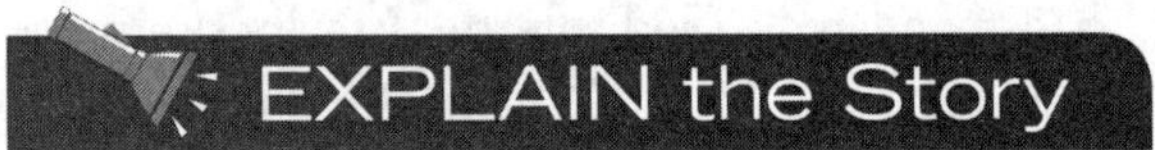

The Structure of Solomon's Dedication Narrative

The narrative of Solomon's Temple dedication is structured as a chiasm (a literary device where a pattern is repeated in reverse order). The first element of the pattern is paired with the last, the second with the second to last, and so on. Though scholarly arguments for chiasms in biblical texts often seem forced, the chiastic pattern in 1 Kings 8 is clear. The pattern is highlighted below as each linked pair (A and A', B and B') is indented at the same level.

A: Solomon summons the nation (v. 1).
  B: Israel celebrates the festival (v. 2).
    C: Solomon offers abundant sacrifices to YHWH (v. 5).
      D: Solomon blesses the people (vv. 14–21).
        E: Solomon prays, mentioning seven scenarios (vv. 22–53).
      D': Solomon blesses the people (vv. 55–61).
    C': Solomon offers abundant sacrifices to YHWH (vv. 62–63).
  B': Israel celebrates the festival (v. 65).
A': Solomon dismisses the nation (v. 66).

At the beginning of the narrative Solomon summons the nation (A), and at the end he dismisses the nation (A'). They celebrate (B and B'), Solomon sacrifices (C and C'), Solomon blesses (D and D'), and Solomon prays (E). In a chiasm the center is usually emphasized, which fits here as the central element and the focus on the whole passage is Solomon's long prayer, which features seven future scenarios that should prompt God's people to pray.

5. *COS* 2:184.

The Ark Arrives in the Temple (8:1–13)

Solomon gathers the whole nation to Jerusalem to celebrate the dedication of the new temple (1 Kgs 8:1). Several types of leaders are mentioned: elders, heads of tribes, and chiefs of families. These leaders play significant roles during important transitions in Israel's history. At the end of his life, Joshua twice summoned the nation together, and two types of national leaders listed here are mentioned there (elders and heads of tribes; Josh 23:2; 24:1). When Samuel made his corrupt sons judges in his place, the elders of the nation gathered and requested a king instead (1 Sam 8:1–5).

The festival celebrated here was the Feast of Tabernacles (1 Kgs 8:2), held in the seventh month of the year. This was a convenient time for Solomon's national assembly to dedicate the temple since the nation was already gathered for the festival (Lev 23:34–36). The text mentions only the month for this dedication, so it is possible it took place a month before the temple was finished, in the eighth month of Solomon's eleventh year (1 Kgs 6:38). But it is more likely they delayed eleven months to Solomon's twelfth year, as the narrative chronology suggests. The delay would also give Huram time to finish up all the bronze items (ch. 7). Since the temple would replace the tabernacle as the dwelling of YHWH in their midst, the Festival of Tabernacles would be the perfect time to dedicate the new structure.

The ark of the covenant makes one final dramatic appearance in this chapter (8:1, 3, 4, 5, 6, 7 [2x], 9, 21) before disappearing from Israel's history (until its rediscovery by Indiana Jones?), as it is never mentioned again in the book of Kings.[6] The text clarifies that this time the ark is properly transported by priests using poles. The offering of countless sacrifices accompanies the occasion, as the ark is carefully situated in its designed location inside the Most Holy Place (or "inner sanctuary") beneath the wings of the cherubim (vv. 3–7). The poles were so long they stuck out and were visible from the Holy Place (also called the "the main hall"). The curious notice that the poles were "still there today" (v. 8) suggests that this narrative was written before the destruction of the temple in 587 BC, despite the fact that the book must not have been completed until after the fall of Jerusalem and the temple (2 Kgs 25). While the ark had contained the tablets with the Ten Commandments, a jar of manna, and Aaron's rod (Exod 16:33; Num 17:10; Heb 9:4), at this point it only contained the two tablets (1 Kgs 8:9). The ongoing presence of the tablets was yet another way the text emphasizes the priority of God's law,

6. Chronicles mentions the ark in the context of Josiah's Passover (2 Chr 35:3).

inside the ark, in the Most Holy Place, within the temple—at the very center of the most sacred spot on earth.

Though God does not speak here, he makes his presence known. After the priests depart from the Most Holy Place, he blesses the new temple with manifestations of his presence by filling the temple with a cloud and with his glory (vv. 10–11), preventing the priests from doing their jobs. Similarly, after the tabernacle was completed, God covered the tent of meeting with a cloud, and the glory of YHWH filled the tabernacle (Exod 40:34). In response to these divine manifestations, Solomon utters a cryptic poetic fragment, which begins speaking about YHWH and his cloud in third-person language, "The Lord has said that he would dwell in a dark cloud," but then shifts to second-person language to describe his own creation, "I have indeed built a magnificent temple for you, a place for you to dwell forever" (1 Kgs 8:12–13).

Solomon's First Blessing (8:14–21)

At the completion of creation, God blessed the humans (Gen 1:28). At the completion of the tabernacle, Moses blessed the nation (Exod 39:43). Thus, it is fitting that at the completion of the temple, Solomon blesses the nation (1 Kgs 8:14). Blessing follows creation and completion.

The phrase at the beginning of Solomon's two blessings, rendered in the NIV as "Praise be to the Lord" (vv. 15, 56), is more literally "Bless the Lord" (*baruk yhwh*). Thus, before and after his prayer, Solomon blesses both his people and his God. However, in his blessing of YHWH and the people, Solomon never addresses either of them directly, only speaking of them in third person.

Besides blessing, four other themes are emphasized by Solomon here. First, Solomon emphasizes divine deliverance as he references God bringing his people out of Egypt, at the beginning and the end (vv. 16, 21). Second, Solomon stresses YHWH's faithfulness to his promises in this blessing, in his prayer, and in the second blessing (vv. 15, 20, 24 [2x], 25, 26, 56 [2x]) as he paraphrases YHWH's address to David in 2 Samuel 7, where he had promised David's son would succeed him. Third, Solomon repeatedly refers to a temple that is built for the Name of YHWH (1 Kgs 8:16, 17, 18, 19, 20), which echoes language YHWH himself used when speaking to David through Nathan (2 Sam 7:13). YHWH said David's descendant would complete it, but Solomon's paraphrase of 2 Samuel 7 is rather loose, since YHWH never said it was good that David wanted to build a temple. Fourth, Solomon emphasizes his connection to David. In his blessing and in his prayer, Solomon highlights that David is his father, mentioning him by name eight times (1 Kgs 8:15, 16, 17, 18, 20, 24,

25, 26). Solomon's emphasis on David, the hero who united Israel and Judah and defeated their enemies, is logical since a greater public awareness of the dynastic connection would add legitimacy to Solomon's own reign.

Solomon's Prayer of Dedication (8:22–53)

After his blessing, Solomon lifts his hands to heaven and starts his extended prayer of dedication. The language of Solomon's dedication prayer is similar to Nehemiah's prayer when he heard about the condition of Jerusalem and its wall: "let your ear be attentive and your eyes open to hear the prayer of your servant" (Neh 1:6).

Solomon's words here are a prayer about prayer. He emphasizes both his own prayer and the future prayers of anonymous individuals by using a variety of prayer synonyms (twenty-six repetitions of six different words). Solomon repeats two nouns throughout his prayer: "prayer" (*tepillah*) six times (1 Kgs 8:28, 29, 38, 45, 49, 54) and "plea" or "supplication" (*tehinnah*) eight times (vv. 28, 30, 38, 45, 49, 52(2), 54). The verb "pray" (hithpael of *palal*) appears nine times (vv. 28, 29, 30, 33, 35, 42, 44, 48, 54). Three verbs each appear once: "make supplication" (hithpael of *hanan*; v. 33), "cry" (*rinah*; v. 28), and "cry" (*qara'*; v. 52).

Solomon begins by speaking of God's uniqueness, specifically in regards to his loyalty to his servants (vv. 23–24). He reiterates that YHWH was faithful to keep the promise that David's heir would succeed him; he then requests that the Davidic line would continue, acknowledging that the blessing would be conditioned upon obedience of his royal descendants (vv. 25–26).

Solomon next asks a profound theological question, "[W]ill God really dwell on earth?" (v. 27). His answer highlights the paradox of divine anthropomorphisms (depictions of God in human terms): the transcendence of the divine cannot be fully captured in the realm of the human. Solomon declares, "The heavens, even the highest heaven, cannot contain you" (v. 27), an idea that finds a striking parallel in the Hymn to Shamash, the Babylonian god of justice.

> The heavens are too puny to be the glass of your gazing,
> The world is too puny to be (your) seer's bowl.[7]

Solomon's words here provide an apt reminder that, even though YHWH now has a temple, his people must never forget that God cannot be contained

7. *COS* 1:419.

in a box, whether a small one like the ark or a grandiose one like the temple. His willingness to accommodate them by manifesting his presence in a cloud filling the temple should not lead them to think that he can be controlled or limited.

Throughout the prayer Solomon spoke of people praying toward the temple or Jerusalem (1 Kgs 8:29, 30, 35, 38, 42); when Darius's advisors convinced the Persian ruler to declare an edict that no one could pray to anyone except Darius, Daniel faced Jerusalem and prayed on his knees (Dan 6:10). Solomon prayed on his knees here (v. 54).

Most of the rest of Solomon's prayer consists of seven scenarios that should prompt someone to pray:

1. Wronging a neighbor (vv. 31–32);
2. Being defeated by an enemy (vv. 33–34);
3. A lack of rain (vv. 35–36);
4. Famine, plague, blight, locust, or disease (vv. 37–40);
5. Curious foreigners (vv. 41–43);
6. Warfare against enemies (vv. 44–45);
7. Captivity in a distant land (vv. 46–51).

Before he goes through the seven scenarios, Solomon gives an overview where he introduces the pattern (vv. 28–30). The pattern has four steps, most of which are introduced in the overview then repeated in each scenario.

First, some type of crisis occurs. These crises can be classified into three categories (several fit in multiple categories). Five involve some type of sin: wronging a neighbor (#1), losing in battle due to sin (#2), no rain due to sin (#3), famines and plagues due to "afflictions of the heart" (#4; v. 38), and captivity due to sin (#7). Two crises involve natural disasters: no rain (#3) and famine and plagues (#4). Three involve warfare: defeat (#2), battle (#6), and captivity (#7).

Second, in response to the crisis, God's people (or the foreigner in #5) pray in, or toward, the temple. In the first two scenarios, people are praying in (the Hebrew preposition *b-*) the temple (vv. 31, 33), presumably because they are nearby and therefore have access to it. In the final five scenarios, people pray toward (the Hebrew preposition *'el-*) the temple (vv. 29, 30, 35, 38, 42, 44), presumably because present circumstances limit their movements, as in the case of the exile (#7).

Third, Solomon implores YHWH to hear their prayers from heaven. In his prayer, he mentions "heaven" twelve times (vv. 23, 27 [2x], 30, 32, 34,

35, 36, 39, 43, 45, 49) and "hearing" thirteen (vv. 28, 29, 30 [3x], 32, 34, 36, 39, 42, 43, 45, 49, 52). While it may seem strange to ask God to hear a prayer ("Doesn't he hear all prayers?"), the language is common in the Psalms (Ps 4:1; 17:6; 39:12; 54:2; 84:8; 86:6; 102:1; 143:1) and, in the context of prayer, "hearing" is not merely listening. A divine response is expected, which leads to the next step.[8]

Fourth, Solomon asks YHWH to respond to their prayer by acting in their favor. In five of the scenarios, forgiveness is requested (1 Kgs 8:30, 34, 36, 39, 50). Other actions requested by Solomon include judging right and wrong (v. 32), acting generally (vv. 32, 39), restoring their land (v. 34), sending rain (v. 36), doing what was requested (v. 43), and upholding their cause (vv. 45, 49).

The final scenario, describing a period of future captivity, shares connections to three other significant events in Israel's history: the exodus, the time of the judges, and the exile. Similar to the first blessing, Solomon mentions Egypt twice in this scenario (vv. 51, 53), but in this context it is particularly relevant because he is speaking of a future time of exile, when a reminder of the Egyptian deliverance would be a source of great hope. The language of this scenario is comparable to the cycles in Judges: Israel sins, God hands them over to their enemies, they repent, and God sends a deliverer (Judg 2:11–23). For the exile of the kingdom of Judah by the Babylonians 587 BC (2 Kgs 25), the temple would no longer have been standing, which explains why the text for this scenario adds praying not just toward the temple but also toward the land of Israel and the city of Jerusalem (1 Kgs 8:48).

Solomon's Second Blessing (8:54–61)

In the transition between Solomon's prayer and his second blessing, the text includes observations about his posture, hands, and voice. Solomon had been standing at the beginning of his prayer (8:22), but by the end he is kneeling (v. 54). His position has changed, but his hands are still stretched toward heaven (vv. 22, 54). As anyone who has tried to hold their hands up for a long time knows, this is difficult to do. Moses needed help from Aaron and Hur to support his outstretched hands (Exod 17:11–12). While we assume Solomon spoke loud enough for the nation to hear him during his first blessing and prayer, the text makes it explicit here that his blessing on the whole assembly was proclaimed with a loud voice (1 Kgs 8:55).

8. For example, in the Sermon on the Mount, Jesus stresses how hearing his words must be connected to responding in obedience (Matt 7:24–27).

In addition to the theme of blessing, Solomon reiterates one other theme from the first blessing: God is faithful to his promises (vv. 56). He mentions several other themes in this second benediction. Instead of David, he emphasizes Moses and his law (vv. 56, 58, 61). Solomon knows how much trouble Israel has had with obedience, so he now requests divine assistance to keep the commands, decrees, and laws given to their ancestors (vv. 58, 61). If God's people obey and God responds positively to their prayers, Solomon envisions a future where "all peoples of the earth may know that the LORD is God and that there is no other" (v. 60).

Solomon Dedicates the Temple with Sacrifices (8:62–66)

The text proceeds to describe Solomon's third major sacrifice. At Gibeon, before the dream theophany, he offered a thousand burnt offerings (1 Kgs 3:4). At the beginning of this narrative, the sheep and goats were so numerous they could not be counted (8:5). This time they can be counted, but just barely; Solomon and all Israel offer twenty-two thousand cattle and a hundred thousand sheep and goats, so much that they had to consecrate a larger area in a section of the temple courtyard (vv. 62–64). It is important to note this enormous sacrifice consisted of fellowship offerings (literally, "peace offerings," *zebah hashelamim*; Lev 3:9–17; 22:18–30), which were the only type of sacrifice when the common worshipers (non-priests) were able to eat the meat from the sacrificed animals (7:11–36). While many of us today eat meat multiple times a day, that would not have been the case for the common Israelite, who typically would only consume meat during festivals. This extravagant provision of sheep and goats surely contributed to the festive mood, which lasted a total of fourteen days (1 Kgs 8:65). Finally, Solomon sent the people away and, after being blessed twice by their king (vv. 14, 55), they return the favor, blessing him and departing in good spirits, "glad and joyful in heart" (v. 66; see also 4:20).

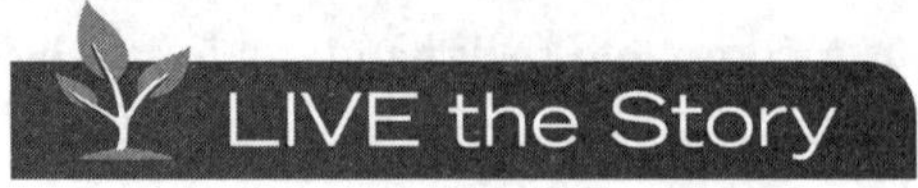

Following Solomon's Example of Blessing

The two primary things Solomon does in this chapter are to pray and to bless, so now we will discuss how to follow his example. Blessing is a major theme in Scripture, as the Bible begins and ends with blessing. The first thing God does to the freshly created humans is to bless them (Gen 1:28), a few chapters later God tells Abraham he will bless him and all the families of the earth (12:1–3), and Genesis concludes with Jacob's blessing on his sons (chs. 48–49). The book of Revelation opens and closes with blessings on those who read, hear, and keep what is written in the book (Rev 1:3; 22:7, 14).

We know blessing is important, but it can be difficult to define. What is blessing? Biblically, it's not just something you do when someone sneezes. When a person blesses God in Scripture it usually implies praising and honoring him, which is what Solomon does here (1 Kgs 8:15, 56). When people bless other people, it may involve praising them but more often involves granting good things to them (e.g., land, animals, gifts) or wishing good things for them (e.g., land, descendants, health).

While wishing something positive may seem strange to us, almost like magic, spoken words have power. Most people can remember words spoken to them by a parent that were either highly positive (essentially blessings) or highly negative (essentially curses). In a way that we may never fully understand, words of power affect us for good or ill.

Blessings are also comparable to prayers and are sometimes indistinguishable from prayers. Blessings typically do not address God (in second-person language), but he is still a witness and is often mentioned (in third-person language). In Solomon's second blessing, he addresses the people but expresses various wishes that God would show favor to his people. These desires are rendered here in the NIV (often jussives in the Hebrew) with a phrase that begins with "may . . ." (8:57 [2x], 58, 59, 61). Solomon is essentially praying in his blessing for God's presence, for help to obey, for God to uphold their cause, and for people to know YHWH is God.

There are at least three lessons we can learn from Solomon about blessing here. First, bless people with Scripture. In his first blessing, Solomon reminds the people of God's promise to David; in his second blessing, he reminds the people to obey God's word. As our blessings are based on God's faithfulness and promises, we can be confident that they will be powerful and effective.

Second, when in positions of authority, bless those in your care. Solomon had more power than anyone in the nation, and, at this point, he uses all his power and authority to serve and bless the people. Tragically, his son, Rehoboam, did not bless those under him and, as a result, he lost the northern tribes (ch. 12). Many of us are in positions of authority as parents, supervisors, teachers, or pastors. Use the power you have to bless your children, your employees, your students, or your congregation.

Third, bless people during celebrations. Celebration and blessing go together. The nation of Israel had worked hard for over seven years to finish the temple. In the midst of their two-week-long celebration, they are twice blessed by their king. Find times when you can celebrate and bless the people God has put around you.

My wife loves to throw crazy birthday parties for my sons. One year it was a *Star Wars* theme with real pod-racing (don't try that at home). Another year the theme was *Harry Potter*, and we played Quidditch (before it was a game on college campuses). When the theme was *Lord of the Rings*, she made a Shelob (the giant spider) piñata that the boys and their friends attacked with their "daggers." In the midst of these crazy celebrations, surrounded by their friends, Shannon and I would pronounce a blessing on them, that God would look out for them and that he would be with them throughout their whole lives. Celebration and blessing go together.

Following Solomon's Model of Praying

Most Christians have encountered books on prayer that offer a biblical model of prayer. And while many of these models are helpful, we should be suspicious of any model that claims to be *the* biblical model (particularly if it forms a catchy acronym) since Scripture includes so many types of prayers. As we read through the book of Psalms, we encounter prayers of lament, thanksgiving, confession, imprecation (cursing), wisdom, praise, and other types as well. From Solomon's life we find several types of prayers.

If we go back and reflect on Solomon's dream interaction with YHWH at Gibeon (1 Kgs 3:5–14), we find another model of prayer. Solomon begins by reviewing God's deeds in the past (vv. 6–7), then he humbles himself by listing the ways he isn't qualified for the task before him (vv. 7–8), and finally he requests wisdom, not as an end in itself but to rule well and to bless the nation (v. 9). As we pray, following Solomon's example from earlier, we can review and remember God's faithfulness, then humbly express our own inadequacies before we boldly request divine assistance to bless the people God has put around us.

In Solomon's dedication prayer, we see another example to follow.

Solomon prays with his posture. During most prayer meetings I've attended people are seated in comfortable chairs, but that's not how people in Scripture typically pray. Solomon starts out standing, with hands extended to heaven, and by the end he's kneeling, with his hands still extended to heaven (1 Kgs 8:22, 54). Other individuals in the book of Kings manifest even more unusual behavior than Solomon while praying. Elijah laid three times on the dead body of a boy while praying (17:21). One time Hezekiah covered himself with sackcloth, another time he spread his enemy's letter before God, and another time he wept bitterly (2 Kgs 19:1, 14; 20:3). Josiah tore his clothes and wept (22:19). Christians can also learn from Muslims who pray on their knees and bow toward Mecca. While we may want to refrain from laying on a corpse while praying, most of us can still learn from the examples of Solomon, Elijah, Hezekiah, and Josiah to pray more passionately, expressively, and emotionally.

Solomon prays about prayer. It may seem strange to pray about prayer, but that's what Solomon does. He repeats the idea of praying at least twenty-six times in his prayer. Why does he pray about prayer? We can't be sure, but as we look at the seven prayer scenarios, we see the types of situations Solomon envisions that should prompt people to pray: sin, natural disasters, and warfare. Presumably, as the people who heard his prayer (or their descendants who heard about the prayer) find themselves in these types of situations, they will hopefully remember Solomon's prayer, turn to Solomon's Temple, and intercede knowing that Solomon has already mediated on their behalf. We may not pray facing the temple, but we can still pray that when the people we know and love find themselves in situations of crisis they will turn in prayer to God, who will hear and act according to their request.

Solomon prays publicly. When Jesus tells his followers to pray in secret, he is addressing the problem of hypocrisy in prayer. Jesus himself prayed in public (Matt 27:46; Mark 8:6; Luke 9:28; John 17:1), as did many other people in Scripture (Num 21:7; Ezra 9:6; Neh 4:9; Acts 1:24; 4:31; 6:6; 7:59). Paul frequently tells people he's praying for them (e.g., Rom 1:10; Eph 1:16; Col 1:3; 2 Thess 1:11). As Solomon prays publicly, he would know that he is modeling prayer for the entire nation. He uses this public opportunity to teach about God and prayer. Solomon's question, "Will God really dwell on earth?" (1 Kgs 8:27), teaches a profound truth about God's transcendence that needed to be emphasized after a seven-year building program, which could lead one to think that God could be contained in a human-made structure. From the perspective of the Gospels, we realize that God can really dwell in a specific location on earth, not primarily in a building made by humans but as a human, who takes on flesh to tabernacle among us, who is full of grace and truth, and who makes God known (John 1:1, 14–17).

Just as Solomon prayed for the nation here, Jesus prayed for his disciples in his "High Priestly Prayer" at the end of his earthly ministry (17:1–26). These two extended prayers, by far the longest recorded prayers for either, begin with a focus on heaven (1 Kgs 8:23; John 17:1) and emphasize themes of protection, unity, divine blessing (both material and spiritual), and the glorification of God's name. Solomon was dedicating the temple, and Jesus was dedicating his disciples for their ministry that would change the world.

Both Davidic rulers realized that the most powerful way to bless the people God has placed in their care is to pray for them. Jesus specifically mentioned not just his current followers but all future ones (John 17:20). As we have been blessed by this High Priestly Prayer, let us follow the example of our Lord and pray for the dedication, protection, and blessing of those whom God has placed around us.

CHAPTER 7

1 Kings 9:1–28

LISTEN to the Story

[1]When Solomon had finished building the temple of the LORD and the royal palace, and had achieved all he had desired to do, [2]the LORD appeared to him a second time, as he had appeared to him at Gibeon. [3]The LORD said to him:

"I have heard the prayer and plea you have made before me; I have consecrated this temple, which you have built, by putting my Name there forever. My eyes and my heart will always be there.

[4]"As for you, if you walk before me faithfully with integrity of heart and uprightness, as David your father did, and do all I command and observe my decrees and laws, [5]I will establish your royal throne over Israel forever, as I promised David your father when I said, 'You shall never fail to have a successor on the throne of Israel.'

[6]"But if you or your descendants turn away from me and do not observe the commands and decrees I have given you and go off to serve other gods and worship them, [7]then I will cut off Israel from the land I have given them and will reject this temple I have consecrated for my Name. Israel will then become a byword and an object of ridicule among all peoples. [8]This temple will become a heap of rubble. All who pass by will be appalled and will scoff and say, 'Why has the LORD done such a thing to this land and to this temple?' [9]People will answer, 'Because they have forsaken the LORD their God, who brought their ancestors out of Egypt, and have embraced other gods, worshiping and serving them—that is why the LORD brought all this disaster on them.'"

[10]At the end of twenty years, during which Solomon built these two buildings—the temple of the LORD and the royal palace—[11]King Solomon

gave twenty towns in Galilee to Hiram king of Tyre, because Hiram had supplied him with all the cedar and juniper and gold he wanted. [12]But when Hiram went from Tyre to see the towns that Solomon had given him, he was not pleased with them. [13]"What kind of towns are these you have given me, my brother?" he asked. And he called them the Land of Kabul, a name they have to this day. [14]Now Hiram had sent to the king 120 talents of gold.

[15]Here is the account of the forced labor King Solomon conscripted to build the LORD's temple, his own palace, the terraces, the wall of Jerusalem, and Hazor, Megiddo and Gezer. [16](Pharaoh king of Egypt had attacked and captured Gezer. He had set it on fire. He killed its Canaanite inhabitants and then gave it as a wedding gift to his daughter, Solomon's wife. [17]And Solomon rebuilt Gezer.) He built up Lower Beth Horon, [18]Baalath, and Tadmor in the desert, within his land, [19]as well as all his store cities and the towns for his chariots and for his horses—whatever he desired to build in Jerusalem, in Lebanon and throughout all the territory he ruled.

[20]There were still people left from the Amorites, Hittites, Perizzites, Hivites and Jebusites (these peoples were not Israelites). [21]Solomon conscripted the descendants of all these peoples remaining in the land—whom the Israelites could not exterminate—to serve as slave labor, as it is to this day. [22]But Solomon did not make slaves of any of the Israelites; they were his fighting men, his government officials, his officers, his captains, and the commanders of his chariots and charioteers. [23]They were also the chief officials in charge of Solomon's projects—550 officials supervising those who did the work.

[24]After Pharaoh's daughter had come up from the City of David to the palace Solomon had built for her, he constructed the terraces.

[25]Three times a year Solomon sacrificed burnt offerings and fellowship offerings on the altar he had built for the LORD, burning incense before the LORD along with them, and so fulfilled the temple obligations.

[26]King Solomon also built ships at Ezion Geber, which is near Elath in Edom, on the shore of the Red Sea. [27]And Hiram sent his men—sailors who knew the sea—to serve in the fleet with Solomon's men. [28]They sailed to Ophir and brought back 420 talents of gold, which they delivered to King Solomon.

Listening to the Text in the Story: Biblical Texts: Deuteronomy 29:24–28; Judges 1:29; 1 Kings 3:1, 14; 6:12–13; Ancient Near Eastern Texts: Abbael's Gift of Alalakh Treaty; Letter from Hattusili III of Hatti to Kadasman-Enlil II of Babylon; The Merneptah Stele; Letter from the King of Tyre to the King of Ugarit in the Matter of Storm-Damaged Ships

Even while his presence filled the recently dedicated temple in the previous chapter, YHWH was silent. However, he begins this chapter with his longest direct address to Solomon. He has already reminded Solomon twice that he will need to obey if he wants to hold onto the throne of Israel (1 Kgs 3:14; 6:12–13), but the tone of this third warning is more stern and the consequences more severe, not just for his heirs but also for the nation and even the recently completed temple. The chapter also narrates details concerning Solomon's other building projects, both inside Jerusalem (temple, palace, wall) and outside Jerusalem (other cities, ships).

In YHWH's speech to Solomon, the language is highly Deuteronomistic as YHWH focuses on obedience to the commands, decrees, and laws. Toward the end (9:8–9), YHWH envisions a hypothetical question and answer that is strikingly similar to a passage in Deuteronomy:

> All the nations will ask: "Why has the Lord done this to this land? Why this fierce, burning anger?"
>
> And the answer will be: "It is because this people abandoned the covenant of the Lord, the God of their ancestors, the covenant he made with them when he brought them out of Egypt. They went off and worshiped other gods and bowed down to them, gods they did not know, gods he had not given them." (Deut 29:24–26)

In both Deuteronomy 29 and 1 Kings 9, the severity of the disaster prompts the question, "Why did this happen?" In both instances the responder states that Israel broke the covenant and worshiped other gods, so YHWH their God brought the punishment. We will discuss YHWH's entire address in detail below, but at this point we can note from these two texts that YHWH views question-and-answer discussions as a valuable teaching methodology.

After YHWH's address, the focus shifts to Solomon's other building projects and his dealings with Hiram of Tyre and with Pharaoh of Egypt. Two gifts of cities are described in this chapter: Solomon gives twenty cities to Hiram (1 Kgs 9:11), and Pharaoh gives a wedding gift of a city (listed on her registry?) to his daughter, Solomon's wife (3:1; 9:16). We encounter a similar civic grant in an Old Babylonian treaty that describes Abbael's gift of the city of Alalakh as a reward to an ally for military assistance.

> He [conquered?] Irride and captured his [ene]my. At that time Abbael, according to his gracious heart, gave Alalakh in exchange for Irride, which his father gave.[1]

The city Pharaoh gave to his daughter was Gezer, which he had recently conquered (9:16). Gezer was an important Canaanite city, located on a ridge overlooking the Aijalon Valley and guarding the road from Jerusalem down to the Mediterranean port city of Joppa. Shortly after the time of the conquest, the Egyptian pharaoh Merneptah also speaks of an Egyptian conquest of Gezer very briefly: "Gezer is captured" (The Merneptah Stele).[2] In 1 Kings 9 Solomon rebuilds and fortifies Gezer. A palace dated to the tenth century BC has recently been excavated in Gezer, led by Steven Ortiz.[3] While we do not know who owned this building, since Solomon rebuilt Gezer after Pharaoh's destruction, the excavation team referred to it as "Solomon's Palace."

Two letters between ancient Near Eastern rulers provide important contextual background for events in 1 Kings 9. To communicate his displeasure regarding the low quality of the towns, King Hiram of Tyre sends a message to his treaty partner Solomon, addressing him as "my brother" (9:13; see also 5:12). A letter from the Hittite ruler Hattusili III to his treaty partner, the Babylonian ruler Kadashman-Enlil II (dated about 1200 BC), uses similar language:

> When your father and I made peace and became "brothers" we did not do so for just a single day. Was it not for eternity that we became brothers and concluded peace?[4]

Apparently, kings of Tyre often called their royal allies "my brother" and gave naval assistance to kings other than Solomon (9:26–28), as we see in this

1. *COS* 2:329; see also *COS* 2:370.
2. *COS* 2:41b; see also Josh 12:12; 16:10.
3. Philippe Bohstrom, "King Solomon-era Palace Found in Biblical Gezer" *Haaretz*, August 31, 2016, http://www.haaretz.com/jewish/archaeology/1.739358.
4. *COS* 3:52.

letter from a king of Tyre (not Hiram) to his Ugaritic "brother" that explains how the Ugaritic navy was damaged by a storm:

> To the king of Ugarit, my brother, say: Message of the king of Tyre, your brother. . . . Your ships that you dispatched to Egypt were wrecked near Tyre when they found themselves caught in a bad storm.[5]

EXPLAIN the Story

Scholars do not agree how to divide up the material in this chapter. Some commentators discuss Solomon's interaction with YHWH (1 Kings 9:1–9) with Solomon's dedication ceremony in 1 Kings 8 (e.g., Wiseman, DeVries[6]). Others add the comments about Solomon's navy (9:26–28) to Solomon's international affairs in 1 Kings 10 (e.g., Wray Beal[7]). Still others discuss most of 1 Kings 9 and 10 together (e.g., Fretheim[8]). However, I will discuss 1 Kings 9 and 10 each as separate chapters, since they are good sized portions (twenty-eight verses and twenty-nine verses respectively) and they hold together as chapters thematically. Chapter 9 brings closure to Solomon's building projects: his temple, his palace, his wall, his construction of cities around Israel, and his navy. Chapter 10 focuses on Solomon's wealth and his foreign affairs.

YHWH's Warning (9:1–9)

The temple was thoroughly planned (1 Kgs 5), externally completed (ch. 6), internally completed (ch. 7), and eventually dedicated (ch. 9), but it continues to be a focus here with eight references scattered throughout the chapter (9:1, 3, 7, 8 [2x], 10, 15, 25).[9] While the text has already recorded numerous times that the work on the temple was finished (6:9, 14, 38; 7:22, 40, 51), this chapter begins by reiterating its completion as well as the completion of Solomon's palace (9:1). Then YHWH appeared a second time to Solomon (v. 2), as he had done at Gibeon (3:5–14).

YHWH's comments to Solomon here include three sections: an initial promise and two conditional statements, each beginning with "if" (*'im*). The message starts highly positively: God promises his perpetual presence in the

5. *COS* 3:93–94.
6. Wiseman, *1 & 2 Kings*, 124–25; DeVries, *1 Kings*, 127.
7. Wray Beal, *1 & 2 Kings*, 147–49.
8. Fretheim, *Kings*, 57–61.
9. The Hebrew word translated as "temple" in the NIV is *bayit,* literally "house."

temple (9:3). The first conditional describes a good scenario characterized by obedience and the subsequent blessing (vv. 4–5). The second conditional is a bad scenario characterized by disobedience and the subsequent punishment (vv. 6–9). While the message begins positively, the overall emphasis is rather negative, since each section is not only less optimistic than the previous one but also longer (1 verse, 2 verses, 4 verses), ending with a dark description of divine abandonment and temple destruction.

In his temple dedication prayer, Solomon repeatedly asked YHWH to hear his prayers and those of others, and here YHWH begins by informing Solomon that his prayer was heard and the temple was consecrated (v. 3). When YHWH speaks about the blessings of obedience in the first conditional (vv. 4–5), he does not mention the temple but merely Solomon's royal dynasty being established. When YHWH speaks about the consequences of disobedience in the second conditional (vv. 6–9), he does not mention Solomon's dynasty, but merely the temple's rejection and destruction. But taken together, we infer that the temple will remain if they are obedient, and Solomon's dynasty will be cut off if he is disobedient.

Within YHWH's message, we find two textual tensions. First, the text describes Solomon's father David as walking faithfully, with integrity and uprightness, despite the fact that he was guilty of adultery or rape and murder (2 Sam 11–12).[10] For a discussion of David's righteous portrayal in Kings, see the excursus "The Righteous Portrayal of David In Kings," Chapter 3). Second, YHWH promised that his name and his heart will remain at Solomon's Temple forever (9:3), but just a few verses later YHWH makes it clear that if Solomon, his descendants, and the Israelites do not obey, then YHWH's temple will be rejected and destroyed (vv. 6–8). How is YHWH's promise of eternal presence to be reconciled with his warning of potential rejection?

As we saw from the two conditionals, the fate of Solomon's dynasty and that of the temple are intertwined. One may assume the Hebrew terms translated here as "forever" (vv. 3, 5) and "always" (v. 3) must literally mean eternity, but in other narrative contexts they are used to describe events that merely endure a long time.[11] The lifetimes of Samuel, David, and Jonathan are described as enduring "forever" (1 Sam 1:22; 20:15, 23). The priestly promise granted to Eli's house and a royal promise to Saul are described as lasting "forever," yet both were revoked due to disobedience (2:30; 13:13).

10. For an argument that David power raped Bathsheba, see Lamb, *Prostitutes and Polygamists*, 127–33.

11. The expressions used here are *ʿad-ʿolam* ("forever," 9:3), *kol-hayamim* ("always," 9:3) and *leʿolam* ("forever," 9:5).

Neither were permanent, but both the Davidic dynasty in Judah and the Solomonic temple in Jerusalem endured almost four centuries, far longer than ancient Near Eastern temples and dynasties typically lasted.[12] If we understand these expressions as they are used elsewhere, the textual tension is diminished. God's presence in the temple and Solomon's dynasty both lasted for centuries, but, as we will see—both in the short term for Solomon and in the long term for Israel—disobedience will be punished.

Solomon's Cities and Ships (9:10–28)

Solomon completed his two main building projects over the course of twenty years (1 Kgs 9:10), which might suggest that the thirteen years for the palace (7:1) did not begin until the seven years for the temple were finished (6:38). At this point, Solomon gives twenty Galilean towns to Hiram king of Tyre.[13] Solomon and Hiram had established a trade treaty twenty years earlier (5:12). The details are not clear, but here is what we know about the obligations of each party. Solomon provided food earlier (5:11) and cities now (9:11). Hiram supplied lumber (5:10; 9:11) and gold (9:11, 14) for Solomon's building projects. Three questions come to mind as we examine this passage.

Why is Solomon giving cities now instead of food? Wiseman thinks Solomon's building program led him into debt, so trading the cities for gold moves him from red to black.[14] DeVries thinks the exchanged territory may have been in dispute between Israel and Tyre, so it would not have been a costly exchange for Solomon.[15] Both of these views are possible, but since the text does not provide a reason, we will avoid speculation. Where are the twenty cities from? The text does not give details, but Galilee was a reasonable area to exchange, since it was in the north between Tyre and Israel. The three northwestern tribes were Zebulun, Ashur, and Naphtali, but the twenty cities probably came from one of the latter two since, in the book of Joshua, Galilee was connected to Naphtali (Josh 12:23; 20:7; 21:32) and the city of Kabul was in the territory of Asher (19:27). Hiram had called them the "Land of Kabul" to show his displeasure over the quality of the cities.

Why does the text conclude with the note that Hiram sent one hundred and twenty talents of gold to Solomon (1 Kgs 9:14)? English translations are divided whether to say Hiram "had sent" (NIV, ESV, NRSV) or merely that he "sent" (NASB, KJV, JPS) the gold to Solomon. The Hebrew could be

---

12. On the subject of ancient royal dynasties, see Lamb, *Righteous Jehu*, 206–9.
13. Chronicles has Hiram giving Solomon cities at the end of twenty years (2 Chr 8:1–2).
14. Wiseman, *1 & 2 Kings*, 126.
15. DeVries, *1 Kings*, 132.

translated either way.[16] While the gift may have taken place earlier ("had sent"), the placement at the end of this section suggests that it is happening now as payment for the twenty cities. In any case, it was a massive amount of gold, about four tons.[17] Later, the queen of Sheba also makes a gift to Solomon of one hundred and twenty talents of gold (10:10).

The text then describes Solomon's use of forced labor to build in Jerusalem (the temple, the palace, terraces, and the wall) as well as various Israelite cities, listed generally from north to south: Hazor, Megiddo, Gezer, Lower Beth Horon, Baalath, and Tadmor (9:15–18). The cities he chose to rebuild were all in strategic locations, guarding the primary approaches to the nation. Solomon also fortified other locations used for storing his horses and chariots. Solomon is thinking about military strategy, but his narrative has yet to mention any military engagements.

Solomon benefitted from his trade treaty with Hiram (5:12) and from his marriage treaty with Pharaoh (3:1). In addition to receiving his daughter as a wife earlier, Pharaoh now gives her an important city, Gezer, which Solomon then rebuilt because Pharaoh had destroyed it by fire (9:16). After Solomon finished her house, she moved from her dwelling in the City of David (v. 24).

To accomplish all these building projects, Solomon used both Israelites (v. 15) and non-Israelites (v. 21). Israelites were not supposed to make their countrymen permanent slaves (Lev 25:39–46), and the text here notes that Solomon did not do that (1 Kgs 9:22). But he did use forced labor (also called the corvée), a form of temporary slavery, to accomplish his ambitious goals. Early in Solomon's narrative, the text informs us that he put Adoniram in charge of forced labor (4:6). Solomon drafted thirty thousand Israelite men as forced laborers to work in Lebanon to help Hiram with the lumber (5:13–14). Later Jeroboam, who would become the first ruler of divided Israel, would be in charge of forced labor of the house of Joseph (11:28). Solomon's son continued the practice, as Rehoboam assigned Adoram to be the taskmaster of forced labor (12:18). In each of these contexts, the laborers are clearly coming from the nation of Israel. Solomon also gave his fellow countrymen leadership positions in construction, in government, and in the military (9:22–23).

YHWH had allowed Israelites to buy slaves from the surrounding nations (Lev 25:44), and here Solomon conscripted slaves from the surrounding non-Israelite peoples (Amorite, Hittite, Perizzite, Hivite, and Jebusite). The foreign

---

16. The form is a *vav* consecutive imperfect (*shalah*)—normally just translated as "sent," but both renderings are possible.

17. See Wiseman, *1 & 2 Kings*, 126.

slaves were clearly permanent, since the narrator adds that they remained slaves "to this day" (1 Kgs 9:21; see also 8:8; 9:13).

The text next includes a comment that seems out of place, regarding Solomon's annual worship practices. He sacrificed three times a year, presumably during the three primary festivals: Passover, Pentecost, and Tabernacles (Exod 23:14–17; Deut 16:1–17). While YHWH repeatedly exhorted Solomon to obey his law (1 Kgs 3:14; 6:12; 9:4), the narrative has not mentioned any specific ways the king did that thus far—except in the realm of offerings and sacrifices (3:3–4, 15; 8:5, 63–64).

After building temples, palaces, walls, cities, and forts, Solomon decides he needs a fleet of ships. His fleet makes its port at Ezion Geber, which was probably on the northern tip of the Gulf of Aqaba, the northeast arm of the Red Sea. Just as he received help on his northern border with lumberjacks from Hiram, on his southern border he receives help with sailors from Hiram (9:27). Together the combined Tyrian-Israelite fleet sailed to Ophir to bring back 420 talents of gold (three and half times what Hiram gave; vv. 14, 28). Scholars are not sure where Ophir is located, but possible locations include Africa, Arabia, or India, since Solomon's fleet could access them through the Gulf of Aqaba and the Rea Sea. The one thing we know about Ophir from elsewhere in the Old Testament is that it was a frequent source of gold (10:11; 22:48; Job 22:24; 28:16; Ps 45:9; Isa 13:12).

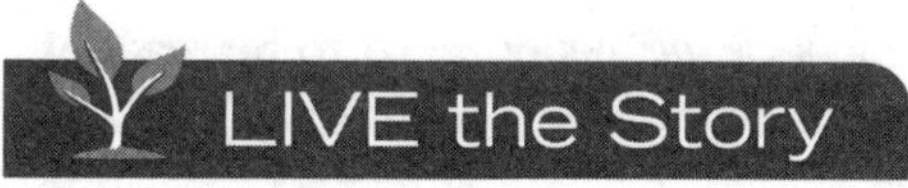

Solomon: The Anti-Moses and Anti-Joshua

Solomon offers more sacrifices here, but two of his other actions involve behaviors viewed highly negatively elsewhere in the Old Testament. Curiously, in neither instance does the text here condemn him. Solomon gives away a significant portion of the promised land that Joshua had fought hard to obtain. In his temple dedication prayer, Solomon acknowledged that YHWH had given them the land (8:34, 40). YHWH just reminded Solomon that being cut off from the land would be a punishment for disobedience (9:7). Despite these reminders from YHWH and from Solomon himself that their land was a gift from God, he "regifts" these twenty cities to Hiram. In this regard, Solomon is a type of anti-Joshua as he hands over large portions of Israel's precious land.

Solomon makes thousands of slaves, temporary ones from among the Israelites and permanent ones from among the non-Israelites. While the law allowed for both of these practices (Lev 25:39–46), it never advocated for them, and elsewhere in Scripture practices associated with slavery are condemned (e.g., Jer 34:9–16; Amos 1:6, 9; 2:6). Generally, laws that legislated slavery do not need to be interpreted as favoring the practice but could merely be acknowledging the reality of it and protecting the rights of slaves in the midst of it.[18] Both the slave wife law (Exod 21:7–11) and the prisoner-of-war wife law (Deut 21:10–14) were not primarily encouraging these practices but were protecting vulnerable women against abusive situations. The clearest way we see God's opposition to slavery is his call to Moses to bring the Israelite people out of oppression in Egypt (Exod 3–4). This act of national deliverance is mentioned literally hundreds of times in the Old Testament, making it the defining action of YHWH.[19]

In our text we see two tragic ironies. First, Solomon is now allied with Egypt, the nation responsible for enslaving them for centuries. Pharaoh is no longer an oppressor but a friend. Second, immediately after describing Solomon's enslavement policies (1 Kgs 9:15, 21), the text describes him offering sacrifices for the three festivals, one of which was Passover, the national celebration of deliverance from slavery in Egypt (Exod 12). Thus, Solomon is portrayed here as a type of anti-Moses, ironically celebrating deliverance as he delivers people, even his own, into slavery.[20]

It is easy when reading narrative texts to think that behavior that isn't explicitly condemned is acceptable to the author or to God. But an absence of condemnation does not constitute an affirmation. In order to understand the attitude of the text toward certain behaviors, we always need to be reading a particular narrative in light of its broader context—of the whole book, of other similar books (Historical Books for Kings), of the rest of the Old Testament, and in light of Jesus and the New Testament. While the final judgment condemning Solomon doesn't get pronounced until 1 Kings 11, the text includes plenty of clues along the way that the verdict will not be good. There are more clues found in 1 Kings 10.

---

18. For discussions of these laws in the context of polygamy, see Lamb, *Prostitutes and Polygamists*, 63–67; in the context of slavery, see Christopher J. H. Wright, *Old Testament Ethics for the People of God* (Downers Grove, IL: InterVarsity Press, 2004), 333–37; and in the context of ancient Near Eastern parallels, see David L. Baker, *Tight Fists or Open Hands: Wealth and Poverty in Old Testament Law* (Grand Rapids: Eerdmans, 2009), 111–74.

19. It is mentioned eleven times in Kings (1 Kgs 6:1; 8:9, 16, 21, 51, 53; 9:9; 12:28; 2 Kgs 17:7, 36; 21:15).

20. On Solomon and Moses, see Marvin Sweeney, *I & II Kings*, OTL (Louisville: Westminster John Knox, 2007), 143.

CHAPTER 8

1 Kings 10:1–29

 LISTEN to the Story

1When the queen of Sheba heard about the fame of Solomon and his relationship to the LORD, she came to test Solomon with hard questions. 2Arriving at Jerusalem with a very great caravan—with camels carrying spices, large quantities of gold, and precious stones—she came to Solomon and talked with him about all that she had on her mind. 3Solomon answered all her questions; nothing was too hard for the king to explain to her. 4When the queen of Sheba saw all the wisdom of Solomon and the palace he had built, 5the food on his table, the seating of his officials, the attending servants in their robes, his cupbearers, and the burnt offerings he made at the temple of the LORD, she was overwhelmed.

6She said to the king, "The report I heard in my own country about your achievements and your wisdom is true. 7But I did not believe these things until I came and saw with my own eyes. Indeed, not even half was told me; in wisdom and wealth you have far exceeded the report I heard. 8How happy your people must be! How happy your officials, who continually stand before you and hear your wisdom! 9Praise be to the LORD your God, who has delighted in you and placed you on the throne of Israel. Because of the LORD's eternal love for Israel, he has made you king to maintain justice and righteousness."

10And she gave the king 120 talents of gold, large quantities of spices, and precious stones. Never again were so many spices brought in as those the queen of Sheba gave to King Solomon.

11(Hiram's ships brought gold from Ophir; and from there they brought great cargoes of almugwood and precious stones. 12The king used the almugwood to make supports for the temple of the LORD and for the royal palace, and to make harps and lyres for the musicians. So much almugwood has never been imported or seen since that day.)

13King Solomon gave the queen of Sheba all she desired and asked for,

besides what he had given her out of his royal bounty. Then she left and
returned with her retinue to her own country.
[14]The weight of the gold that Solomon received yearly was 666 talents,
[15]not including the revenues from merchants and traders and from all the
Arabian kings and the governors of the territories.
[16]King Solomon made two hundred large shields of hammered gold;
six hundred shekels of gold went into each shield. [17]He also made three
hundred small shields of hammered gold, with three minas of gold in each
shield. The king put them in the Palace of the Forest of Lebanon.
[18]Then the king made a great throne covered with ivory and overlaid
with fine gold. [19]The throne had six steps, and its back had a rounded top.
On both sides of the seat were armrests, with a lion standing beside each
of them. [20]Twelve lions stood on the six steps, one at either end of each
step. Nothing like it had ever been made for any other kingdom. [21]All King
Solomon's goblets were gold, and all the household articles in the Palace of
the Forest of Lebanon were pure gold. Nothing was made of silver, because
silver was considered of little value in Solomon's days. [22]The king had a
fleet of trading ships at sea along with the ships of Hiram. Once every three
years it returned, carrying gold, silver and ivory, and apes and baboons.
[23]King Solomon was greater in riches and wisdom than all the other
kings of the earth. [24]The whole world sought audience with Solomon to
hear the wisdom God had put in his heart. [25]Year after year, everyone who
came brought a gift—articles of silver and gold, robes, weapons and spices,
and horses and mules.
[26]Solomon accumulated chariots and horses; he had fourteen hundred
chariots and twelve thousand horses, which he kept in the chariot cities and
also with him in Jerusalem. [27]The king made silver as common in Jerusalem as
stones, and cedar as plentiful as sycamore-fig trees in the foothills. [28]Solomon's
horses were imported from Egypt and from Kue—the royal merchants purchased them from Kue at the current price. [29]They imported a chariot from
Egypt for six hundred shekels of silver, and a horse for a hundred and fifty.
They also exported them to all the kings of the Hittites and of the Arameans.

Listening to the Text in the Story: Biblical Texts: Deuteronomy 17:16–17; Judges 14:12–18; 1 Kings 3:13; 9:14; Ancient Near Eastern Texts: The Inscriptions of Tiglath-Pileser III; The Inscribed Ivories from Nimrud; An Ugaritic letter from the King to the Queen-mother; The Azatiwada Inscription

The focus of Solomon's narrative thus far has been on his domestic policies and accomplishments: his administration, temple, palace, and rebuilding of cities. This chapter's focus is international: on his trading, shipping, and relationship with other rulers. The other rulers include one we have seen before, Hiram, and one we have not, the mysterious queen of Sheba who brings a massive tribute to Solomon. To get background for these events, we will look at relevant biblical texts and extrabiblical sources.

Most scholars think this queen's home, the land of Sheba, was located in southwestern Arabia, modern-day Yemen.[1] One queen of Arabia, a certain Zabibe, is mentioned only a few centuries after Solomon in inscriptions of the Assyrian ruler Tiglath-Pileser III (745–727 BC), in his list of tributaries who offered gold and other precious goods, including ivory.[2] Ivory was one of the items Solomon's ships brought back to Israel (1 Kgs 10:22), and he made his throne out of ivory and gold (1 Kgs 10:18). In 1961 a British excavation at the Assyrian capital of Nimrud uncovered inscribed ivory fragments written in Hebrew that appear to mention YHWH the God of Israel:

> May Ya[hweh] shatter [. . . who come af]ter me, from great king [to . . .
> if they should co]me and efface th[is ivory].[3]

McCarter thinks these ivories may have been part of the plunder when Shalmaneser V (727–722 BC) of Assyria sacked the city of Samaria in 722 (2 Kgs 17:3).[4] The message seems to be a curse on anyone who damages the inscription.

> The goal of the queen's visit was to test Solomon's wisdom. The judge Samson engaged in a riddle competition with thirty Philistines (Judg 14:12–18), but the competition between Sheba's queen and Israel's king was probably more elaborate than Samson's. Similarly, the Assyria ruler, Assurbanipal (668–627 BC), bragged about his great wisdom and his success in debates with other wise men.[5]

---

1. See Wiseman, *1 & 2 Kings*, 129.
2. *COS* 2:286a; 287a; *ANET*, 283b.
3. *COS* 2:224.
4. McCarter dates the writing on these ivories to the middle of the eighth century BC (*COS* 2:224). Ahab of Israel had a house of ivory (1 Kgs 22:39).
5. See *BBCOT*, 430a.

The queen's tribute of 120 talents of gold was curiously the same amount of gold that Solomon appeared to trade for the twenty Galilean cites (1 Kgs 9:14). An Ugaritic letter written from the king to the Queen-mother describes a much smaller but similar gift of gold to a foreign ruler:

> Now Yabninu has left for the court of Amurru and he has taken with him one hundred (shekels of) gold . . . for the king of Amurru.[6]

The queen of Sheba's gift included not only gold but silver and spices, and, several centuries later, King Hezekiah of Judah showed the envoys from Babylon his treasures of gold, silver, and spices (2 Kgs 20:13).

The end of this chapter describes Solomon's great wealth, which included his golden shields and his massive stables. We find parallel accomplishments listed in the Inscription of Azatiwada who served under Awariku, the king of the Danunians (modern Turkey). Azatiwada describes how he increased the number of his horses and shields and how he, like Solomon in the previous chapter (1 Kgs 9:15, 17, 19), built fortifications in various strategic locations.[7]

The Queen of Sheba Visits (10:1–13)

After YHWH's long address to Solomon in the previous chapter, YHWH again goes silent as the text describes first Solomon's dealings with the queen of Sheba and Hiram and then his wealth. YHWH is spoken about in this chapter exclusively in third-person language (1 Kgs 10:1, 5, 9, 12, 24).

The text does not clarify how the queen of Sheba heard about Solomon's fame, but the context suggests it resulted from his burgeoning sea trade (9:26–28; 10:11, 22). Curiously, she is interested not only in his wisdom but also his relationship with YHWH. She asks hard questions, but Solomon has great answers. After hearing his answers, seeing his accomplishments, and experiencing his wisdom (10:3–5), she was clearly impressed. The Hebrew phrase translated in the NIV as "was overwhelmed" (v. 5) is literally "there was no more spirit in her" (*lo'-hayah bah 'od ruah*).

6. *COS* 3:91.
7. *COS* 2:149.

As a result of her fact-finding excursion, she exclaims that the claims about Solomon, which she thought were hyperbolic, were in fact true and "not even half" (v .7) were told to her. She declares that Solomon's people and his officials were happy to have him as their ruler (vv. 6–9; see 4:20). The Hebrew word translated as "happy" here (*'ashre*; twice in 10:8) could be translated as "blessed," and the word translated as "Praise be to" here (*barak*; v. 9) could also be translated as "bless"—she blessed not only Solomon's people, but also his God.

The queen then presents the Israelite ruler with all the gold, spices, and precious stones that she transported in her camel caravan to Jerusalem (vv. 2, 10). Two of the gifts are highlighted for their extraordinary nature: a record amount of spices and 120 talents of gold (see also 9:14).

A parenthetical comment is then included about the imports of almugwood and precious stones brought in from Hiram's ships (10:11; see also 9:26–28; 10:22). Scholars are not sure what almugwood is, but its resonant quality was apparently good for making musical instruments like harps and lyres (10:12).

Solomon reciprocates with gifts, and the lack of details here has led to some interesting speculations. Did Solomon and the queen of Sheba have sex, as some have speculated based on the statement that he gave her "all that she desired" (v. 13)? It is possible, since Solomon had a strong sexual appetite, as the next chapter informs us (11:3). But similar forms of the expression are used in the context of Solomon's narrative to describe how Hiram and Solomon satisfied their partner in their timber trade (5:8; 9:11) and in their food exchange (5:9). The same Hebrew verb translated as "desired" (*haphets*) here is translated as "delighted" a few verses earlier to describe YHWH's attitude toward Solomon.[8] When the text wants to imply sexual relations, it has many ways to make it clear, but this passage lacks any of them. It is unlikely that this passage is implying anything sexual took place. Thus, Solomon here models how an Israelite ruler should interact with foreign women, in contrast to what we see in the following chapter (see Jesus's interactions non-Jewish women in Mark 7:24–30 and John 4:1–28).

The King of Israel Acquires Gold and Horses (10:14–29)

One of the results of Solomon's interactions with the queen of Sheba, Hiram, and other trading partners is that he became extraordinarily wealthy, as this

8. See the discussion of speculations of what took place between these two rulers in Cogan, *I Kings*, 315.

next section reveals. Solomon's yearly revenue of gold was a beastly amount, 666 talents, about twenty-five tons, and this figure did not include revenue from merchants and traders (10:14–15).

The passage explains how some of the gold was fashioned into shields, a throne, goblets, and other objects. When the text says "Solomon made" something we assume this means he delegated the task to others—goldsmiths in this instance. They made two hundred large golden shields weighing six hundred shekels (about fifteen pounds each) and three hundred smaller golden shields weighing three minas (between four and seven pounds each). Since gold is soft and heavy, these shields would not be useful on the field of battle, except perhaps to intimidate a foe, so they were probably merely ceremonial and left on display in the Palace of the Forest of Lebanon (vv. 16–17; see also 7:2–5). Solomon made many shields, but ironically, unlike his famous warrior father, he never led the Israelites into battle. These gold shields were captured by the Pharaoh Shishak of Egypt during the reign of Solomon's son, Rehoboam (14:25–27).

The king's throne was covered with ivory and fine gold (10:18). It had six steps decorated with twelve lions, two on each step (vv. 19–20). There were two more lions on the side of the armrests. King Ahiram of Byblos (a Phoenician city north of Tyre) had a comparable throne depicted on his sarcophagus with winged lions on the side.[9] All the goblets and the household articles from the Palace of the Forest of Lebanon were made of gold (10:21).

The text makes two negative comments about silver: it was of little value (v. 21), and it was as common as stone (v. 27). While these comments make the point clearly that the enormity of Solomon's gold reserves depressed the relative price of silver, the immediate context reveals them to be hyperbolic. Silver was considered a valuable trading commodity, listed with gold, ivory, apes, and baboons brought back from exotic ports by ship (v. 22). Silver was valued as a gift from foreign visitors, along with gold, robes, weapons and spices, horses, and mules (v. 25). And silver allowed one to purchase valuable chariots and horses from Egypt (v. 29). As we understand the literary device used here, in this case hyperbole, the tension is resolved. For clarity, the text could have said silver was still valuable, but it was less valuable because there was so much more gold—but that would be more boring and less dramatic than "silver had become worthless."

Gold was not the only thing in abundance, as the final section of this chapter reveals. Solomon was greater in riches and wisdom than any other king

9. For an image, see *ANEP*, 157–58; #456, 458.

on the earth (v. 23). The whole world wanted to meet with him and hear his wisdom, and they would bring him valuable gifts (vv. 24–25). Just as wealthy celebrities today may collect automobiles, so Solomon collected chariots (fourteen hundred) and horses (twelve thousand). Previously, we found out that Solomon had forty thousand horse stalls (and twelve thousand horses; 4:26). Horses and chariots were extremely valuable in military contexts, so one would assume these would have been used for warfare, but the text never records Solomon fighting battles. He did not just stockpile these equine weapons, but he was also a trader. He imported horses and chariots from Egypt and Kue (eastern Cilicia in Asia Minor) and exported them to the kings of the Hittites and the Arameans (10:28–29).

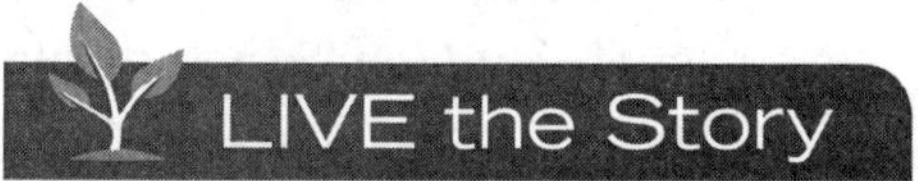

Words of Wisdom about Wealth

Scripture has a lot to say about money and wealth, and passages like 1 Kings 10 can easily be misinterpreted with respect to these issues. It takes wisdom to discern what lessons about wealth we can get from this chapter and its broader biblical context. We discussed the textual tension regarding silver, but a more problematic tension arises as we examine this section in light of two other texts in their attitudes toward wealth.

The first text is God's dream interaction where wealth is clearly a good thing, a blessing from God as he promises to give Solomon great wealth, wisdom, and honor (1 Kgs 3:12–13). First Kings 10 makes it clear that YHWH's promise is now fulfilled. The text has mentioned ways that this promise has already been realized in Solomon's reign in terms of his wisdom (3:28; 4:30–31), his wealth (7:1–8; 9:14, 28), and his honor (3:28; 4:34). While wealth was mentioned in these earlier passages, 1 Kings 10 emphasizes his outrageous wealth. We learned about his buildings and palaces earlier, but here we get details of all his precious possessions. And among his possessions, the chariots and horses receive even greater emphasis. While this passage doesn't explicitly refer back to YHWH's promise, the point is still made that YHWH was faithful to Solomon in uniquely blessing him in the areas of wisdom, wealth, and honor.

The second text is Deuteronomy's law of the king (= LOK; Deut 17:14–20), which gave guidance to Israel about how a ruler should govern, specifically in terms of limiting his possessions. All the restrictions that the LOK places on a ruler appear to be not merely broken by Solomon but literally shattered by him. The LOK says a king should not have excessive gold and silver, but Solomon's annual income was well over twenty-five tons of gold and he made silver as common as stone. The LOK limits how many horses Israel's ruler should obtain; Solomon has twelve thousand. The LOK expressively forbids importing horses from Egypt since YHWH doesn't want them to return there, but Egypt is Solomon's primary source for his stables. The LOK limits how many wives a ruler should have, but Solomon's wives are the subject of 1 Kings 11, so we'll wait until the next chapter to discuss it. While the LOK doesn't specify numerical limits of gold, silver, wives, or horses, we can be pretty sure that Solomon "bagged" his in each of these areas.[10]

The passage in 1 Kings 3 views Solomon's extravagant wealth positively as a divine blessing, while Deuteronomy 17 views it negatively, presumably because wealth can easily become an idol that one worships before God. So how should Solomon's wealth be interpreted in light of Deuteronomy 17 and 1 Kings 3?

On the one hand, one could argue that Solomon's excessive wealth should be viewed positively. YHWH's dream promise should take precedence as it comes not only in the book of Kings but also in the context of Solomon's narrative. Generally, it is preferable to use texts in closer proximity to interpret an unclear text.

On the other hand, one could argue it should be viewed negatively. Deuteronomy 17 comes from not only a legal context, but it is specifically a law addressing the monarchy (written from the perspective of several centuries beforehand). Generally, it is easier to apply legal texts than narrative ones, since they are prescriptive ("Do this") instead of descriptive ("This happened").

YHWH will tell Solomon what he thinks about the king's many wives in the next chapter, but he is silent in this chapter about the king's wealth. But we do have three comments from YHWH earlier in Solomon's narrative. In each of his major addresses to the Israelite ruler, YHWH strictly emphasized obedience. Solomon was to walk in YHWH's ways, keeping his statutes (3:14). Solomon was to walk in YHWH's statutes, obey his rules, and keep all his commandments (6:12). Solomon was to walk before YHWH with integrity, doing all that he commanded, and keeping his statutes and his rules (9:4). YHWH may be silent here, but elsewhere he's not silent about whether or not Solomon should obey his commands, which include Deuteronomy's law of the king. The final condemnation against this ruler is delayed for a few more verses, but as we read the description of Solomon's extravagant wealth

10. It seems wrong today to consider wives as possessions, but that was the ancient patriarchal mindset.

in 1 Kings 10 in light of Deuteronomy 17 and 1 Kings 3, 6, and 9, it is clear that he was blatantly disobedient. Solomon's example is not to be emulated but avoided. From the narrative of Solomon's possessions, we can offer three words of wisdom about wealth.

First, wealth is a blessing from God. God promised wealth to Solomon early in his reign, but God's blessing in this area goes back much further, as he blessed the first humans materially in the garden of Eden, providing gold and many other material blessings. The first reference to gold in the Bible appears in Genesis 2, in the context of God's abundant provisions of food ("you are free to eat from any tree"), water (four rivers), and precious stones (bdellium and onyx; Gen 2:8–16). God blessed Abraham also with abundant silver and gold (13:2). The absence of wealth is, however, not necessarily a sign of divine displeasure, since Jesus himself had little in the way of possessions (Luke 9:58), but generally Scripture views wealth as a gift from God, which leads to the next point.

Second, wealth should remind us of God's goodness. God is the source of wealth, so when one is blessed by it, one should express gratitude to God as the giver of all good gifts. The extravagance of his gifts reveals his goodness, which should lead us to give thanks and praise for the ways he has blessed us materially. Unfortunately, it is easy to focus on the gift, not the giver. While it is tempting, wealth is not be worshiped. It can't buy us love, security, or happiness. Tragically, money and possessions may be the biggest idols of our age, even amongst Christians. The best way to avoid idolizing something is to defame it. How do we defame wealth as an idol? Great question, which leads to the final point.

Third, wealth should be used to bless others. God gives his people wealth so they can share it with others. The reason God was initially so pleased with Solomon's request for wisdom in 1 Kings 3 was that he wanted it in order to be a good ruler over God's people. God blessed Solomon with wealth, but the only one who was blessed by it appears to have been Solomon. The church in the West has been blessed by God in extraordinary ways, and sometimes we generously share our wealth with others. But often it gets used, like in Solomon's case, to create impressive buildings that, like the temple, will eventually crumble. People, however, are eternal and therefore are more worthwhile "investments" for our assets. It's hard to know exactly what Jesus meant when he said, "store up treasures in heaven" (Matt 6:20), but we know people will be there. As we share our material blessings with others, we will be acting like God who shared his blessings with us. Wealth should help us better love our God and our neighbor.

The "Solomon" of the Middle Ages was named Mansa Musa (c. AD 1280–1337), also probably the richest person in history.[11] He was the ruler of the empire of Mali in West Africa. His inflation adjusted fortune was about $400 billion. He was not just famous for his wealth, like Solomon, but also for his generosity. Like Solomon, he was a builder, but Solomon's most impressive structure was his multiple-building palace complex for himself and his wives (1 Kgs 7:1–12), while Mansa Musa's were for others as he constructed numerous mausoleums, libraries, and mosques, many of which have endured until today. And on his extravagant pilgrimage to Mecca (AD 1324–1325), he gave so much gold to the poor it had a devastating effect on the local economies, which he attempted to rectify on his return to Mali. The fact that he would use his position and power to help the oppressed is appropriate, since his name Musa is Arabic for Moses.

For the past twenty years, the title of wealthiest person in the world has usually been held by Bill Gates, one of the co-founders of Microsoft. Gates is the King Solomon of our day. Many people have criticized his anti-competitive business tactics, but it would be difficult to critique his philanthropy. In 2000 he and his wife created the Bill and Melinda Gates Foundation (BMGF), which recently was deemed the world's wealthiest charitable foundation with assets over $30 billion. Their plan is to give 95 percent of their wealth to charitable organizations. By 2007, they had given over $20 billion to charity, making them the second-most generous philanthropists in the US. In 2006 a grant for $5 million was announced for the International Justice Mission, an organization founded by Christians to combat sex trafficking and slavery. Even with Bill Gates's incredible giving, he still has incredible wealth, but what makes his example most impressive is that he transitioned out of his position at Microsoft in 2008, so he could devote his energy full-time to his foundation. The Gates family attends a Catholic church, but Bill appears to be an agnostic; and yet his example is still one for Christians to emulate.[12] King Solomon chose to acquire great wealth; Bill Gates did the same for much of his life, but now he's choosing to share his wealth to bless others. As we chose to share our wealth, according to Jesus, we are laying up treasures in heaven (Matt 6:19–20).

The Queen of the South and the Wisdom of Jesus

Jesus refers to the visit of "the queen of the South" to Solomon in the context of his interrogation and testing by the religious leaders (Matt 12:42;

---

11. For more on Mansa Musa, see https://www.businessinsider.com/mansa-musa-the-richest-person-in-history-2016-2.

12. See Gate's *Rolling Stone* interview by Jeff Goodell, https://www.rollingstone.com/culture/news/bill-gates-the-rolling-stone-interview-20140313, March 27, 2014.

Luke 11:31). While Jesus doesn't mention Sheba, it was probably located in southwest Arabia, hence the title "queen of the South." As was his style, he speaks of himself indirectly, essentially claiming that his wisdom is greater than that of Solomon ("now something greater than Solomon is here"; Matt 12:42; Luke 11:31). Beyond Solomon's obvious foolishness with wives and idols (recorded in 1 Kgs 11), Jesus displayed his superior wisdom in a variety of ways. Jesus is arguably the best, and wisest, storyteller in history. Over a third of Jesus's spoken teaching comes in the form of parables, many of which are the best-loved stories not only in Scripture but in all literature (e.g., the prodigal son, the good Samaritan). Jesus's wise questions frequently confounded and silenced his critics (e.g., Matt 12:11, 26, 27, 29, 34, 48; 21:25). Jesus's most famous sermon (delivered "On the Mount," 5:1) concludes with a story of two builders (7:24–27). The wise builder built on the rock so that his house stood firm during the storm, like Jesus's wise followers who hear and obey his words. The foolish builder built on sand, like Jesus's foolish listeners who merely hear but do not obey his teaching. Jesus evoked the "queen of the South" to warn his listeners to repent, to listen, and to respond to his words. The foolish behavior of Jesus's opponents in Matthew 12, of Jesus's sand builder in Matthew 7, and Jesus's ancestor (Solomon) in 1 Kings 11 provide ominous warnings to those with ears to hear.

CHAPTER 9

1 Kings 11:1–43

LISTEN to the Story

1King Solomon, however, loved many foreign women besides Pharaoh's daughter—Moabites, Ammonites, Edomites, Sidonians and Hittites. 2They were from nations about which the LORD had told the Israelites, "You must not intermarry with them, because they will surely turn your hearts after their gods." Nevertheless, Solomon held fast to them in love. 3He had seven hundred wives of royal birth and three hundred concubines, and his wives led him astray. 4As Solomon grew old, his wives turned his heart after other gods, and his heart was not fully devoted to the LORD his God, as the heart of David his father had been. 5He followed Ashtoreth the goddess of the Sidonians, and Molek the detestable god of the Ammonites. 6So Solomon did evil in the eyes of the LORD; he did not follow the LORD completely, as David his father had done.

7On a hill east of Jerusalem, Solomon built a high place for Chemosh the detestable god of Moab, and for Molek the detestable god of the Ammonites. 8He did the same for all his foreign wives, who burned incense and offered sacrifices to their gods.

9The LORD became angry with Solomon because his heart had turned away from the LORD, the God of Israel, who had appeared to him twice. 10Although he had forbidden Solomon to follow other gods, Solomon did not keep the LORD's command. 11So the LORD said to Solomon, "Since this is your attitude and you have not kept my covenant and my decrees, which I commanded you, I will most certainly tear the kingdom away from you and give it to one of your subordinates. 12Nevertheless, for the sake of David your father, I will not do it during your lifetime. I will tear it out of the hand of your son. 13Yet I will not tear the whole kingdom from him, but will give him one tribe for the sake of David my servant and for the sake of Jerusalem, which I have chosen."

14Then the LORD raised up against Solomon an adversary, Hadad the

Edomite, from the royal line of Edom. [15]Earlier when David was fighting with Edom, Joab the commander of the army, who had gone up to
bury the dead, had struck down all the men in Edom. [16]Joab and all the
Israelites stayed there for six months, until they had destroyed all the men
in Edom. [17]But Hadad, still only a boy, fled to Egypt with some Edomite
officials who had served his father. [18]They set out from Midian and went
to Paran. Then taking people from Paran with them, they went to Egypt,
to Pharaoh king of Egypt, who gave Hadad a house and land and provided
him with food.

[19]Pharaoh was so pleased with Hadad that he gave him a sister of his
own wife, Queen Tahpenes, in marriage. [20]The sister of Tahpenes bore him
a son named Genubath, whom Tahpenes brought up in the royal palace.
There Genubath lived with Pharaoh's own children.

[21]While he was in Egypt, Hadad heard that David rested with his
ancestors and that Joab the commander of the army was also dead. Then
Hadad said to Pharaoh, "Let me go, that I may return to my own country."

[22]"What have you lacked here that you want to go back to your own
country?" Pharaoh asked.

"Nothing," Hadad replied, "but do let me go!"

[23]And God raised up against Solomon another adversary, Rezon son of
Eliada, who had fled from his master, Hadadezer king of Zobah. [24]When
David destroyed Zobah's army, Rezon gathered a band of men around
him and became their leader; they went to Damascus, where they settled
and took control. [25]Rezon was Israel's adversary as long as Solomon lived,
adding to the trouble caused by Hadad. So Rezon ruled in Aram and was
hostile toward Israel.

[26]Also, Jeroboam son of Nebat rebelled against the king. He was one
of Solomon's officials, an Ephraimite from Zeredah, and his mother was
a widow named Zeruah.

[27]Here is the account of how he rebelled against the king: Solomon had
built the terraces and had filled in the gap in the wall of the city of David
his father. [28]Now Jeroboam was a man of standing, and when Solomon
saw how well the young man did his work, he put him in charge of the
whole labor force of the tribes of Joseph.

[29]About that time Jeroboam was going out of Jerusalem, and Ahijah
the prophet of Shiloh met him on the way, wearing a new cloak. The
two of them were alone out in the country, [30]and Ahijah took hold of the

new cloak he was wearing and tore it into twelve pieces. [31]Then he said
to Jeroboam, "Take ten pieces for yourself, for this is what the LORD, the
God of Israel, says: 'See, I am going to tear the kingdom out of Solomon's
hand and give you ten tribes. [32]But for the sake of my servant David and
the city of Jerusalem, which I have chosen out of all the tribes of Israel,
he will have one tribe. [33]I will do this because they have forsaken me and
worshiped Ashtoreth the goddess of the Sidonians, Chemosh the god of
the Moabites, and Molek the god of the Ammonites, and have not walked
in obedience to me, nor done what is right in my eyes, nor kept my decrees
and laws as David, Solomon's father, did.

[34]"'But I will not take the whole kingdom out of Solomon's hand;
I have made him ruler all the days of his life for the sake of David my
servant, whom I chose and who obeyed my commands and decrees. [35]I will
take the kingdom from his son's hands and give you ten tribes. [36]I will give
one tribe to his son so that David my servant may always have a lamp
before me in Jerusalem, the city where I chose to put my Name. [37]However,
as for you, I will take you, and you will rule over all that your heart desires;
you will be king over Israel. [38]If you do whatever I command you and walk
in obedience to me and do what is right in my eyes by obeying my decrees
and commands, as David my servant did, I will be with you. I will build
you a dynasty as enduring as the one I built for David and will give Israel to
you. [39]I will humble David's descendants because of this, but not forever.'"

[40]Solomon tried to kill Jeroboam, but Jeroboam fled to Egypt, to
Shishak the king, and stayed there until Solomon's death.

[41]As for the other events of Solomon's reign—all he did and the wisdom
he displayed—are they not written in the book of the annals of Solomon?
[42]Solomon reigned in Jerusalem over all Israel forty years. [43]Then he rested
with his ancestors and was buried in the city of David his father. And
Rehoboam his son succeeded him as king.

Listening to the Text in the Story: Biblical Texts: Genesis 2:18–25; Exodus 21:7–11; Deuteronomy 7:3–4; 17:16–17; 21:10–14; 25:5–6; 2 Samuel 7:12–16; Ancient Near Eastern Texts: The Mesha Stele; The Marriage Stela of Ramesses II

We have seen hints along the way that Solomon was not walking in the ways of his father David (1 Kgs 3:1, 3; 10:14–29) and that he was disobeying the law, particularly the law of the king (Deut 17:16–17), but no criticism of his behavior has been made explicit—until now. Judgment falls hard on Solomon and his house in this chapter, which narrates not only his apostasy and his divine condemnation but also the divinely appointed adversaries, two foreign (Hadad and Rezon) and two domestic (Ahijah and Jeroboam). The chapter concludes with the death of Solomon. Before working through this chapter, we will examine relevant biblical texts and ancient Near Eastern parallels that provide background for the events surrounding Solomon's downfall and demise.

Arguably the most important passage outside of 1 Kings for the whole Solomon narrative is David's dynastic promise delivered for YHWH by his prophet, Nathan. David's promise mentions three themes that are relevant to Solomon's story, two of which have been dominant themes thus far in 1 Kings—a royal eternal dynasty and an heir building the temple (2 Sam 7:12–16). A third theme appears in this chapter—punishment. YHWH declares, "When he does wrong, I will punish him with a rod wielded by men, with floggings inflicted by human hands" (7:14).

Solomon is condemned for idolatry, which presumably had many causes, but the text here focuses on his many marriages to foreign wives (see excursus below, "Polygamy in the Old Testament"). YHWH declared in Deuteronomy that he would clear out the Canaanites living in the land and then explicitly commanded, "Do not intermarry with them. Do not give your daughters to their sons or take their daughters for your sons, for they will turn your children away from following me to serve other gods, and the Lord's anger will burn against you and will quickly destroy you" (Deut 7:3–4). One of the idolatrous practices Solomon engaged in was constructing a high place (see excursus "High Places" in Chapter 3) for Chemosh, the god of Moab. King Mesha of Moab, in his inscription on the Moabite Stone, similarly states that he "made this high-place for Kemosh in Karchoh."[1]

Solomon's polygamy was not ideal, but that was not his primary problem. His biggest problem was his wives' foreignness and their worship of foreign deities. We assume many of Solomon's foreign marriages took place to cement a treaty, like his alliance with Egypt through his marriage to pharaoh's daughter (1 Kgs 3:1). These types of arrangements were common in the ancient Near East. Rulers would be reluctant to attack nations where family or in-laws lived. Zimri-Lim of Mari often established treaties with surrounding nations by marrying off his daughters to other rulers.[2] The Hittite ruler Hattusili III

1. *COS* 2:137b.
2. See *BBCOT*, 364.

offered his eldest daughter to the Egyptian pharaoh Ramesses III to successfully end a period of warfare between their two nations.

Excursus: Polygamy in the Old Testament

While the intention of the law was not to encourage polygamy, several texts allowed it (e.g., Exod 21:7–11; Deut 21:10–14; 25:5–6), leaving some to think that God validated the practice. But Genesis makes it clear that lifelong monogamy between a man and a woman was the ideal (Gen 2:18–25). The point of these polygamy laws was not to promote it but, in a non-ideal world where polygamy was common, to legislate how it should take place in order to ensure the rights of all parties involved: wives, husbands, sisters, kings, slaves, widows, concubines, and prisoners of war.[3]

Polygamy in Scripture is generally viewed negatively. The first polygamist, Lamech, was a violent, verbally abusive braggart (4:19–24). The polygamous situations in the families of Abraham and Jacob caused severe tensions among the wives and children. Among royal polygamists, most are evaluated as doing evil in the eyes of YHWH (eight of ten). David had fifteen wives (1 Chr 3:1–9), and at least one of them was the daughter of a foreign ruler (2 Sam 3:3); curiously, he was not condemned for it. Joash of Judah (also called Jehoash) was the only other righteously evaluated polygamist ruler (2 Chr 24:3). Evil royal polygamists included Saul (1 Sam 14:50; 2 Sam 3:7; 12:8), Solomon, Rehoboam (2 Chr 11:21), Ahab (1 Kgs 20:3, 7), Abijah (2 Chr 13:21), Jehoram of Judah (2 Chr 21:6, 17), Jehoiachin (2 Kgs 24:15), and Zedekiah (Jer 38:23). While polygamy is never condemned as a sin, the fact that polygamists and polygamous families are generally viewed negatively suggests that it was not good.

Solomon's Wives and Idolatry (11:1–13)

Thus far in his narrative Solomon has displayed wisdom and constructed impressive structures, but here his foolishness and disobedience are revealed and condemned. The text already recorded Solomon's marriage to Pharaoh's

3. For more on this topic, see the discussion of polygamy in the Bible in Lamb, *Prostitutes and Polygamists*, 59–86.

daughter (1 Kgs 3:1); now we discover he had a total of seven hundred wives and three hundred concubines. While David conquered the surrounding kingdoms, Solomon married them. The number of Solomon's wives may be hyperbolic and, since both numbers are multiples of a hundred, they are probably round.

While it seems wrong or even sexist to consider wives as possessions of the king (like gold, silver, and horses), I argue elsewhere that we need to read texts like these in light of their ancient and biblical contexts.[4] As we take these contexts seriously, the problems do not disappear, but we can make more sense of them. For example, the Bible begins by portraying women in shockingly favorable ways, particularly as God creates both the man and the woman in his own image (Gen 1:26–27) and sets up the marriage ideal as a mutual partnership (2:18–25). Man ruling over woman in marriage resulted from their eating the forbidden fruit (3:16).

The chapter begins by mentioning Solomon's marriages to women from at least six peoples: the Moabites, Ammonites, Edomites, Sidonians, Hittites, and Egyptians. Of these nations, only the Hittites appear in the Pentateuch in the repeated lists of Canaanite peoples that Israel was to destroy and therefore not marry (e.g., Exod 3:8; Num 13:29; Deut 7:1). But the principle still applies to Solomon's wives, since any kind of engagement with other nations exposes the Israelites to their culture and, most relevantly here, to their gods.

It will be helpful to briefly give some background on each of these peoples, their gods, and their locations. While the general locations of these nations were stable, their borders shifted as they lost or gained territory in battles with neighbors. The Hittites of Canaan were located along the central ridge of Judah south of Jerusalem, near Hebron (it is difficult to say whether or not they were associated with the Hittite Empire of Asia Minor, 1800–1200 BC). The Sidonians were a Phoenician people, to the north of Israel along the Mediterranean Sea. The Phoenicians were a loose confederation of city-states that, in addition to Sidon, included the cities of Tyre (home of Hiram), Byblos, and Zarephath. The goddess of Sidon was Ashtoreth, also called Astarte (Greek), Attarat (Canaanite), and Ishtar (Babylonian). She was the goddess of love and fertility.

According to Genesis, the Edomites, the Moabites, and the Ammonites all trace their genealogy back to Abraham's family. The Edomites were the descendants of Esau, Jacob's oldest son (Gen 25:30; 32:3). They lived south of Judah and Moab. David conquered Edom (2 Sam 8:13–14), and the

4. For more on sexism in the Old Testament, see Lamb, *God Behaving Badly*, 47–70.

Edomites provided Solomon with a port on the Red Sea (1 Kgs 9:26). Moab and Ammon were the descendants of the incestuous relationship between Abraham's nephew Lot and his two daughters (Gen 19:30–37). Moab and Ammon were both located east of Judah and north of Edom, on the far side of the Dead Sea. The national god of Moab was Chemosh, and the national god of Ammon was Molek (also called Milcom); both these gods were associated with child sacrifice (2 Kgs 3:26–27; 23:10).[5]

While the narrator's perspective on Solomon and his actions has been favorable or neutral thus far, as we move into Solomon's decline into apostasy in his later years, it becomes highly polemical by referring to the deities of Sidon, Ammon, and Moab as "detestable" (*shiqquts,* repeated three times in 1 Kgs 11:5, 7). Solomon, the builder of God's temple, also built high places (see excursus "High Places" in chapter 3) for the gods of all his foreign wives. Several centuries later, King Josiah of Judah destroyed the high places constructed by Solomon for Ashtoreth, Chemosh, and Molech as a part of his religious reform (2 Kgs 23:13).

The language of Solomon's condemnation is Deuteronomistic, as his heart was "not fully devoted" to YHWH (1 Kgs 11:4; cf. Deut 6:5) and he "did evil in the eyes of the Lord" (1 Kgs 11:6; cf. Deut 4:25; 17:2). In stark contrast to Solomon, David's heart is described as fully devoted to his God, and the text emphasizes this assessment twice (1 Kgs 11:4, 6; see also "The Righteous Portrayal of David in Kings" in chapter 3).

YHWH is often described as being "slow to anger" (e.g., Exod 34:6; Num 14:18; Neh 9:17; Ps 86:15; Joel 2:13; Jonah 4:2), but Solomon's apostasy provokes his anger here (1 Kgs 11:9). While Solomon's divine condemnation was delayed until 1 Kings 11, we have repeatedly seen problems with his extravagant acquisition of horses, gold, silver, and now wives, which were clearly forbidden by Deuteronomy's law of the king. In the midst of his excessive behavior, YHWH had been silent until now. The text's lack of criticism for his behavior is consistent with God's patient character. YHWH gets angry, but he gets there slowly.[6]

Solomon turned his heart from YHWH, the God of Israel, despite the fact he had appeared twice to the king (1 Kgs 3:5; 9:2). YHWH had already spoken three times directly to Solomon (3:5–14; 6:11–13; 9:3–9), but only in two of them does the text note that YHWH appeared. For most other Israelite rulers, YHWH uses prophets to mediate his message (e.g., 1 Sam

5. For an examination of these deities, see John Day, *Yahweh and the Gods and Goddesses of Canaan*, LHBOTS 265 (Sheffield: Sheffield Academic, 2000).

6. See Lamb, "Angry or Loving?" in *God Behaving Badly*, 25–46.

22:5; 2 Sam 7:17; 1 Kgs 16:7; 17:1; 2 Kgs 1:16; 20:15). With four direct divine interactions, Solomon had a unique relationship with his God. Yet he still fell hard into idolatry.

In the announcement of his judgment against Solomon, YHWH does not specifically mention idolatry to the ruler (even though the context does), but he focuses on disobedience to the commands (1 Kgs 11:10). The consequences will be severe—"The kingdom" will be torn from him. The theme of tearing reappears in a few verses as Ahijah describes the details of how the tearing will take place. However, because of the promise to Solomon's father David, grace will be shown in two ways. First, the loss of the kingdom will be delayed to Solomon's son (11:12), whom we meet in the following chapter (Rehoboam). Other royal dynastic judgments are also delayed a generation in the book of Kings: the sons of Jeroboam (Nadab and others: 1 Kgs 15:25–29), the sons of Baasha (Elah and others: 1 Kgs 16:7–11), and the sons of Ahab (Ahaziah, Jehoram, and others: 1 Kgs 21:29; 2 Kgs 9:9). Second, one tribe will remain under Solomon's son's control (1 Kgs 11:13). We will discuss the tribal breakdowns and the identity of the "one tribe" in the interaction between Ahijah and Jeroboam in a few verses and in the interaction between Rehoboam and Solomon in the next chapter.

Solomon's Adversaries: Hadad and Rezon (11:14–25)

The text does not delay its description of how the punishment against Solomon will be meted out. YHWH raises up adversaries against Solomon: two foreign, Hadad and Rezon, and two domestic, Ahijah and Jeroboam. Even with divine, foreign, and domestic adversaries, Solomon has no one to blame but himself, since his troubles resulted from his own disobedience.

The word "adversary" (1 Kgs 11:14, 23, 25) is *satan* in Hebrew, a term that has different connotations in the Old Testament than in the New Testament (the Greek is *Satanas*). In the Old Testament it can refer either to supernatural beings (Num 22:22, 32; 1 Chr 21:1; Job 1:6, 9, 12) or merely to humans who oppose someone, often in military contexts comparable to this chapter (1 Sam 29:4; 2 Sam 19:22). Earlier Solomon boasted to Hiram he had no "adversary" (*satan*), and the context suggests he means no human adversary (1 Kgs 5:3–4). Despite Solomon's claim to Hiram, this text describes Rezon as the adversary of Israel "as long as Solomon lived" (11:25).

The first adversary, Hadad, was from Edom, the land that David had conquered, brutally killing "all the men of Edom" (11:15; see also 2 Sam 8:13–14). The second adversary, Rezon, was from Aram, located to the north of Israel. Aram was one of Israel's main rivals during the period of the divided monarchy (e.g., 1 Kgs 20, 22; 2 Kgs 6–7; 8:12, 28; 9:14–15).

The narratives of Solomon's two foreign adversaries share the same plot line. Both involve a flashback to the time of David, when his army inflicted heavy casualties against their nation's army (1 Kgs 11:15, 24). Both adversaries flee to avoid slaughter (for Hadad, to Egypt; for Rezon, to Damascus). Eventually both come to the throne and then harass Solomon, although the text provides few details about what their adversarial relationship with Israel involved.

The text goes into more detail about Hadad's story, but in the stories of both adversaries we see several interesting parallels with other familiar biblical characters.[7] While Hadad was in the land of Egypt, he gains favor with Pharaoh (like Joseph; Gen 41:37–45), he marries Pharaoh's daughter (like Solomon; 1 Kgs 3:1), he has a child, and he has a debate with Pharaoh, even saying, "Let me go" (like Moses; Exod 5:1). Rezon gathers a band of men around him, becomes their leader, and then eventually becomes king (like David; 1 Sam 22:1–2).

The nation of Egypt hosts not only Hadad but also another adversary of Solomon, Jeroboam, as he fled when the Israelite king tried to kill him (1 Kgs 11:40). By harboring Solomon's enemies, Egypt acts more like an enemy to Israel than an ally. Solomon's adversaries ironically come from nations he had established alliances with by marriage (Egypt [3:1] and Edom [11:1]) or by trade (Aram and Egypt; 10:29). YHWH wanted his rulers to depend exclusively on him, not on other nations. When Solomon sought security with marriages and trade agreements, YHWH exposed the foolishness of this approach.

Solomon's Adversaries: Ahijah and Jeroboam (11:26–40)

Solomon's first domestic adversary is a rebel from the tribe of Ephraim,who was in charge of forced labor over the tribes of Ephraim and Manasseh and would be the first king of divided Israel—Jeroboam (11:26–28). While Jeroboam will be vilified throughout the book of Kings as the ruler who set up altars in Dan and Bethel, he makes a good first impression here as a hard worker who gets promoted. As the one administering the labor force, he would have firsthand knowledge of how oppressive Solomon's workload was, the nature of which was the catalyst for the rebellion of the northern tribes (12:4).

Instead of jumping straight into the narration of Jeroboam's rebellion, the text provides an unusual prefatory comment: "Here is the account of how he rebelled against the king" (11:27). The prophet Ahijah, Solomon's second domestic adversary, meets Jeroboam on the road leaving Jerusalem

---

7. See also Sweeney, *I & II Kings*, 157.

(v. 29). The longest portion of Kings with no reference to a prophet (almost ten chapters) occurs between the reference to Nathan at the beginning of Solomon's narrative (1:32) and this reference to Ahijah at the end (11:29). This absence is shocking, since Solomon desperately needed someone to confront him for his excesses and idolatry. As Ahijah speaks to Jeroboam, he invokes a version of the prophetic messenger formula, "this is what the LORD, the God of Israel, says" (v. 31), the first of over thirty of these formulas to appear in the book of Kings, typically as a prophet begins his oracle (e.g., 12:24; 13:2; 14:7). When Ahijah and Jeroboam meet, a new coat is worn by one of them (11:29). Even though English translations may clarify the issue, based on the Hebrew it is difficult to determine who is wearing the coat (Cogan argues for Jeroboam[8]). Whoever the wearer was, the cloak will not do him much good as Ahijah ripped it into twelve pieces, symbolizing the division of the twelve tribes of Israel (v. 30). The prophet next tells Jeroboam to take ten for himself, since YHWH is tearing the kingdom away from Solomon and giving ten tribes to him, with one tribe for Solomon (vv. 31–32, 34–36). The prophet explains why—because of Solomon's idolatry and disobedience (v. 33)—which should have served as an effective warning (but does not) for the founder of the Northern Kingdom.

In times of judgment or mourning, many other characters rend their garments throughout the book of Kings. Ahab tears his clothes in response to Elijah's judgment (21:27). Elisha tears his garment in mourning over Elijah's death (2 Kgs 2:12). The king of Israel does it several times (2 Kgs 5:7–8; 6:30). Athaliah tears her robes when faced with rebellion (2 Kgs 11:14). Both Hezekiah and his officials tear their clothes in response to the Assyrian threat (18:37; 19:1). In response to the reading of the law, Josiah tears his clothes (22:11). For Ahab and Josiah, their acts of clothes rending prompt YHWH to delay judgments (1 Kgs 21:29; 2 Kgs 22:19). If you are thinking, "There are twelve tribes, but ten plus one only equals eleven"—well done. Typically, three explanations are given for this discrepancy. First, the tribe of Levi has no tribal inheritance but was scattered throughout the nation (Josh 21), so, not counting Levi, the total is eleven. Second, the tribal allotment of Simeon was encompassed by that of Judah (19:1–9), so removing Simeon would again reduce the number of tribes by one. Third, Benjamin is considered part of Judah, which is perhaps the most likely explanation since they remain united with Judah in the next chapter (1 Kgs 12:21). None of these explanations achieves consensus among scholars, and if we become preoccupied with

8. See Cogan, *I Kings*, 339.

figuring how to make ten plus one equal twelve, we miss the point of this passage. Solomon's punishment is catastrophic not only for his heirs but also for the nation of Israel, as the monarchy becomes divided and never recovers.

The prophet reiterates from YHWH's earlier message to Solomon the ways that grace will be shown to Solomon: judgment will be delayed, and one tribe will remain. The remaining tribe means that the Davidic dynasty will always have a "lamp" (*nir*; 11:36) in Jerusalem. In two other places in the book of Kings, similar expressions are used to refer to an ongoing lamp for David (15:4; 2 Kgs 8:19). All three of these "lamp oracles" can be connected to David's dynastic promise (2 Sam 7), as they speak of Davidic heirs continuing to reign and refer to David as the servant of YHWH (2 Sam 7:5, 8; 1 Kgs 11:36, 2 Kgs 8:19).[9] In each of these contexts, the lamp oracle explains why an evil ruler (Rehoboam, Abijam, and Jehoram) is allowed to remain in power in Jerusalem.

As Ahijah winds down his message, he promises not only that Jeroboam will rule over all that his "heart desires" but also that, if he remains obedient, his dynasty will endure like David's (1 Kgs 11:37–38; see also excursus "Dynastic Promises in Kings" below).

Jeroboam gives no recorded response to this auspicious oracle, but Solomon finds out about it and tries to kill his former labor administrator. In this regard, Solomon is like the first king of Israel, Saul, as he hunted down Solomon's father, David, whom YHWH had selected to succeed him (1 Sam 18:10–11; 19:9–10). Jeroboam flees to Egypt (like Hadad), where he finds hospitality with Shishak until Solomon dies. The Egyptian ruler Shishak is well known in Egyptian records as Shoshenq I (943–922 BC), the founder of the twenty-second dynasty of Egypt. This reference is the first time the Bible mentions an Egyptian pharaoh by name. Frustratingly for historians, the ruler of Egypt has been previously referred to merely as "Pharaoh" (e.g., Gen 12:15; 39:1; Exod 1:11, 19; Deut 6:22; 1 Kgs 3:1; 9:16).

Excursus: Dynastic Promises in Kings

Dynastic promises from YHWH are given at key moments in the history of the monarchy to reward obedient rulers and provide stability for the nation of Israel. However, only four of the forty-one kings of Israel and Judah receive dynastic promises from YHWH that their heirs will continue to rule: David (2 Sam 7:13, 16), Solomon (1 Kgs 2:4; 6:12;

9. For a discussion of these "lamp oracles," see Lamb, *Righteous Jehu*, 228–30.

8:25; 9:4–5), Jeroboam (1 Kgs 11:38), and Jehu (2 Kgs 10:30). Two of these rulers receive conditional promises (Solomon and Jeroboam), and two receive unconditional promises (David and Jehu). The unconditional ones appear to be granted based on past obedience, while the conditional ones are based on future obedience.

While one might not think that Solomon would need a dynastic promise since he was David's son, versions of his promise are repeated four times in the text (1 Kgs 2:4; 6:12; 8:25; 9:4–5; the promises of David, Jeroboam, and Jehu are each mentioned once). Solomon's promise, however, differs slightly from David's in that it makes explicit its conditional nature and his rule over Israel. Two of these promises are given directly to the ruler (or future ruler) by YHWH (Solomon's and Jehu's), and two of them are mediated by prophets (David's by Nathan and Jeroboam's by Ahijah). Three of these promises are intended to last "forever" (David, Solomon, and Jeroboam), while Jehu's is limited to four generations.[10] In terms of the outcomes, both rulers who receive conditional promises fail to obey; thus the promise is revoked in the second generation, as Solomon's son, Rehoboam, loses the northern tribes and Jeroboam's son, Nadab, loses the throne to Baasha (12:19; 15:28). However, both rulers with unconditional promises have dynasties that survive, David's over Judah for four centuries and Jehu's over Israel for four generations.

Solomon's Death (11:41–43)

The text next records the death of Solomon after his forty-year reign (11:42–43), just like his father (2:11). While David's narrative was longer (roughly from 1 Sam 16 to 2 Kgs 2), Solomon's is far longer than any other ruler in the book of Kings (1 Kgs 1–11). His name is mentioned over 160 times in Kings, far more than any other human in the book. Solomon's death notice follows the formulaic pattern of most rulers, describing other deeds being recorded in a book of royal annals, how they euphemistically "rested with their ancestors" and were buried, and how they were succeeded by their son (unless followed by a usurper). Two features make Solomon's death notice unique. First, while there are over thirty references to the annals of the kings of Israel or Judah, this is the only reference to the "annals of Solomon" (11:41; see discussion

10. See also Lamb, "The Non-Eternal Dynastic Promises of Jehu of Israel and Esarhaddon of Assyria," *VT* (2010): 337–44.

of "Composition, Sources, and Royal Annals" in the Introduction). Second, his notice mentions "the wisdom he displayed," which only characterized the earlier years of his reign. Perhaps it is appropriate in this eulogistic final remark to focus on the positive and not the foolishness of his later years.

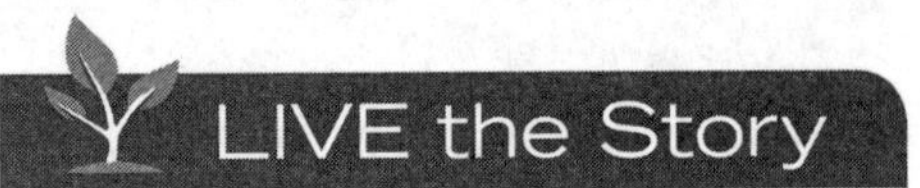

Making Messages Memorable

Ahijah's tearing of the new cloak and handing it to Jeroboam is called a "sign-act," a provocative action that dramatically communicates a specific message. Sign-acts were often performed by prophets; perhaps the most notable examples were performed by Isaiah, Jeremiah, and Ezekiel. Isaiah walked around naked for three years to show how Egypt will be led away to captivity by Assyria (Isa 20:2–5). Jeremiah buried his linen loincloth to symbolize how Israel's pride will be ruined (Jer 13:1–11). He wore a yoke on his neck to predict how Israel will serve Babylon (27:1–22). He piled up large stones at pharaoh's palace in Egypt before the Judeans to show how Nebuchadnezzar of Babylon will build his throne over these stones (43:8–13). Ezekiel laid on his left side for 390 days for the punishment of Israel and on his right side for forty days for the punishment of Judah (Ezek 4:4–8).

While much teaching in the church may be entertaining, engaging, and even enlightening, the reality is that most of it gets forgotten within a day or two. When audiences only listen to spoken words, the message is not as memorable as when it is accompanied by actions. The Old Testament prophets realized that, to communicate their message in provocative and therefore memorable ways, they needed to be dramatic.

In their best-selling book, *Made to Stick*, brothers Chip and Dan Heath discuss how marketers, teachers, and parents can make their messages more "sticky" or memorable to their intended audiences.[11] If pastors and teachers want to make their sermons and lessons have a more dramatic impact, I can't recommend this book highly enough. While their book primarily targets businesspeople and teachers (and therefore includes many examples from those realms), in their chapter on storytelling (stories are sticky!) they mention perhaps two of the best-known stories ever, both from Scripture: David and Goliath and the good Samaritan. As they discuss how shocking people in

11. Chip and Dan Heath, *Made to Stick: Why Some Ideas Survive and Others Die* (New York: Random House, 2007).

unexpected ways captures people's attention, they could have mentioned many examples of biblical prophets, like Ahijah who, three thousand years before Heath and Heath, knew that a provocative sign-act of tearing a new garment into twelve pieces would make the message stick for Jeroboam.

One time, as I was teaching on 1 Kings 11 to my students, in the middle of my lecture I started ripping the dark red button-down shirt I was wearing into many pieces (I was wearing an undershirt). The shirt wasn't new, but it had been one of my favorite shirts. In fact, it was still in good enough condition that I had trouble tearing across the seams, and, slightly embarrassed, I had to resort to scissors; eventually I "tore" it into about fifty pieces. I then handed a small piece of the shirt to every student in the class. I challenged them to keep the torn rag and display it near their desk or workspace so it would remind them to teach, not in a boring way but provocatively like the prophets, thus making their messages memorable.

Few Leaders Finish Well

"Few leaders finish well." This refrain was repeated in several of my leadership classes with J. Robert Clinton.[12] This truth is sobering. Solomon provides perhaps the prototypical example of a person who started well but ended tragically. His reign got off to a great start. He didn't seize the throne of Israel but was placed there by people around him, primarily his father who, shortly before his death, challenged his son to remain faithful (1 Kgs 2:1–4). When YHWH gave him an opportunity to request anything he wanted, he wisely chose wisdom, which he then went on to display in a variety of ways before the nation (chs. 3–4). He channeled much of his energy into building a temple for YHWH (chs. 5–8).

But along the way his wisdom became foolishness, as he fell prey to three of the most deadly idols: money, sex, and power. While Deuteronomy's law of the king mandated limits for rulers on gold, silver, horses, and wives, Solomon acquired all of them in massive quantities. YHWH wanted rulers to rely on him alone, but Solomon looked for security from other sources as he made political alliances with the surrounding nations, and his treaty marriages led him further into idolatry as he established altars to the gods of these other nations. As he was building his temple and other military projects, he oppressed his workers, which ultimately contributed to the division of the monarchy. At the end of his reign he, like Saul, attempted to kill the man God had ordained to rule over the northern tribes.

12. See also J. Robert Clinton, *The Making of a Leader* (Colorado Springs: NavPress, 2012).

Solomon's tragic example should be instructive for any of us who want to "buck the trend" and finish well. To avoid following Solomon into idolatry and apostasy, we can follow the example of another "son of David," Jesus (Matt 1:1; Mark 10:47; Luke 3:31). Jesus's exhortation to be last of all and servant of all (Mark 9:35; 10:43–44) will help us avoid worshiping the idol of power. To defame the idol of wealth, we can follow Jesus's call to de-accumulate and to give our money away generously (Matt 6:19–21; Mark 10:21; 12:43–44). While Jesus was never married, he spoke powerfully against idolizing sex by taking drastic measures to avoid lust (Matt 5:27–30). Many of us who've struggled with sexual sin and lust have found great support in accountability partners to whom we can confess our sins on a regular basis (Jas 5:16; 1 John 1:9). As we follow the example of our Lord Jesus Christ and defame the idols of money, sex, and power, we can be confident that he will help us finish well.

Jesus, the Son of David

Just as David, the man after God's own heart, fell into serious sin, so did his son, Solomon, the man who asked God for wisdom. As the narrative of Kings continues recording rulers of both Israel and Judah, the vast majority of them will prove to be bad kings, doing evil in the eyes of YHWH. David was given a dynastic promise that his sons would continue to reign (2 Sam 7:12–16), but so many of them proved to be unworthy. Because of the sins of the rulers and the people, both Israel and Judah would be destroyed and exiled. The experiment of human kingship in the book of Kings appears to be a failure.

But the New Testament begins by telling the story of another royal son of David, Jesus the Christ (Matt 1:1), who would restore the monarchy. David and Solomon were anointed, and Jesus would be called the Christ, "the anointed one." One of Jesus's most common titles was "son of David" (Matt 1:1, 20; 9:27; 12:23; 15:22; 20:30, 31; 21:9, 15; 22:42), which clearly had royal connotations. King Jesus, who was both fully human and fully divine, would prove worthy to rule in a way his ancestors could not. Unlike David and Solomon, Jesus would consistently do what was right in the eyes of God (3:17). Even the Romans would testify that Jesus was a righteous man (27:19; Luke 23:47). Jesus would begin his ministry declaring that the kingdom of God was at hand (Mark 1:15) and would tell parables describing what his righteous kingdom and his righteous reign would look like (e.g., Matt 13:11–52). Jesus would not only be greater than Solomon (12:42) but also greater even than David (Mark 12:35–37). The ultimate act of his sacrificial kingship was to endure the suffering of the cross, which made him worthy to take his seat at the right hand of the throne of God (Heb 12:2).

CHAPTER 10

1 Kings 12:1-33

LISTEN to the Story

[1]Rehoboam went to Shechem, for all Israel had gone there to make him king. [2]When Jeroboam son of Nebat heard this (he was still in Egypt, where he had fled from King Solomon), he returned from Egypt. [3]So they sent for Jeroboam, and he and the whole assembly of Israel went to Rehoboam and said to him: [4]"Your father put a heavy yoke on us, but now lighten the harsh labor and the heavy yoke he put on us, and we will serve you."

[5]Rehoboam answered, "Go away for three days and then come back to me." So the people went away.

[6]Then King Rehoboam consulted the elders who had served his father Solomon during his lifetime. "How would you advise me to answer these people?" he asked.

[7]They replied, "If today you will be a servant to these people and serve them and give them a favorable answer, they will always be your servants."

[8]But Rehoboam rejected the advice the elders gave him and consulted the young men who had grown up with him and were serving him. [9]He asked them, "What is your advice? How should we answer these people who say to me, 'Lighten the yoke your father put on us'?"

[10]The young men who had grown up with him replied, "These people have said to you, 'Your father put a heavy yoke on us, but make our yoke lighter.' Now tell them, 'My little finger is thicker than my father's waist. [11]My father laid on you a heavy yoke; I will make it even heavier. My father scourged you with whips; I will scourge you with scorpions.'"

[12]Three days later Jeroboam and all the people returned to Rehoboam, as the king had said, "Come back to me in three days." [13]The king answered the people harshly. Rejecting the advice given him by the elders, [14]he followed the advice of the young men and said, "My father made your yoke heavy; I will make it even heavier. My father scourged you with

whips; I will scourge you with scorpions."15So the king did not listen to the people, for this turn of events was from the LORD, to fulfill the word the LORD had spoken to Jeroboam son of Nebat through Ahijah the Shilonite.

16When all Israel saw that the king refused to listen to them, they answered the king:

> "What share do we have in David,
> what part in Jesse's son?
> To your tents, Israel!
> Look after your own house, David!"

So the Israelites went home. 17But as for the Israelites who were living in the towns of Judah, Rehoboam still ruled over them.

18King Rehoboam sent out Adoniram, who was in charge of forced labor, but all Israel stoned him to death. King Rehoboam, however, managed to get into his chariot and escape to Jerusalem. 19So Israel has been in rebellion against the house of David to this day.

20When all the Israelites heard that Jeroboam had returned, they sent and called him to the assembly and made him king over all Israel. Only the tribe of Judah remained loyal to the house of David.

21When Rehoboam arrived in Jerusalem, he mustered all Judah and the tribe of Benjamin—a hundred and eighty thousand able young men—to go to war against Israel and to regain the kingdom for Rehoboam son of Solomon.

22But this word of God came to Shemaiah the man of God: 23"Say to Rehoboam son of Solomon king of Judah, to all Judah and Benjamin, and to the rest of the people, 24'This is what the LORD says: Do not go up to fight against your brothers, the Israelites. Go home, every one of you, for this is my doing.'" So they obeyed the word of the LORD and went home again, as the LORD had ordered.

25Then Jeroboam fortified Shechem in the hill country of Ephraim and lived there. From there he went out and built up Peniel.

26Jeroboam thought to himself, "The kingdom will now likely revert to the house of David. 27If these people go up to offer sacrifices at the temple of the LORD in Jerusalem, they will again give their allegiance to their lord, Rehoboam king of Judah. They will kill me and return to King Rehoboam."

[28]After seeking advice, the king made two golden calves. He said to the people, "It is too much for you to go up to Jerusalem. Here are your gods, Israel, who brought you up out of Egypt." [29]One he set up in Bethel, and the other in Dan. [30]And this thing became a sin; the people came to worship the one at Bethel and went as far as Dan to worship the other.

[31]Jeroboam built shrines on high places and appointed priests from all sorts of people, even though they were not Levites. [32]He instituted a festival on the fifteenth day of the eighth month, like the festival held in Judah, and offered sacrifices on the altar. This he did in Bethel, sacrificing to the calves he had made. And at Bethel he also installed priests at the high places he had made. [33]On the fifteenth day of the eighth month, a month of his own choosing, he offered sacrifices on the altar he had built at Bethel. So he instituted the festival for the Israelites and went up to the altar to make offerings.

Listening to the Text in the Story: Biblical Texts: Exodus 32; Leviticus 20:2; Deuteronomy 13:6–10; 17:2–5; 21:18–21; 22:13–21; Joshua 7:25; 2 Samuel 16:15–17:14; Ancient Near Eastern Texts: The Cyrus Cylinder; Gilgamesh and Akka

This chapter narrates the tragic division of the united monarchy into two kingdoms, as predicted by the prophet Ahijah, because of Solomon's idolatry and apostasy (1 Kgs 11:31–38). Solomon's heir, Rehoboam, and Solomon's labor administrator, Jeroboam, were both briefly mentioned at the end of the last chapter as passive characters. However, in this chapter they accuse and insult each other and nearly start a civil war. Rehoboam and Jeroboam share several interesting similarities (beyond their oddly rhyming names). They both are the first rulers of their respective divided nation, Rehoboam over the Southern Kingdom of Judah and Jeroboam over the Northern Kingdom of Israel. They both seek out advisors when faced with a difficult decision, they both unfortunately listen to the wrong advisors, and as a result they both follow foolish advice.

To help us listen to the story better, we will look at parallel texts from both the biblical and ancient context. Most ancient rulers had teams of counselors they would pursue for guidance. But the advisors often did not agree, which was the case for Rehoboam. When Solomon's older brother

Absalom tried to seize the throne from his father David, he sought counsel from two wise men (2 Sam 16:15–17:14). Ahithophel told Absalom to pursue David quickly with a small force, while Hushai said wait and gather the nation and then pursue David with the whole army. Fortunately for David, Absalom listened to the voice of Hushai, who was secretly working for David. The delay allowed David time to escape and regroup. The text notes that YHWH had ordained Ahithophel's wise counsel to be defeated (2 Sam 17:14), just as he caused Rehoboam to not listen to the complaints of the Israelites (1 Kgs 12:15).

A short Sumerian text (Gilgamesh and Akka) relates a story where, comparable to Rehoboam's situation, the advice of the elders conflicts with that of the younger men. In a conflict between Gilgamesh of Uruk and Akka of Kish, Akka demanded that the residents of Uruk dig wells. Gilgamesh first spoke to both the city elders who advised digging the wells and to the young men who advocated rebellion.

> [Gilgamesh] did not take to heart the words of his city's elders again. Gilgamesh before the able-bodied men of his city again laid the matter, seeking for words.[1]

Gilgamesh, like Rehoboam, followed the advice of the young men.

The complaint of Jeroboam against Solomon for oppressing the Israelites is similar to the accusation of Cyrus of Persia against Nabonidus (the Cyrus Cylinder) for enslaving the Babylonians.

> [Nabonidus] continually did evil against his (Marduk's) city. Daily he [imposed] the corvée upon its inhabitants unrelentingly, ruining them all.[2]

Cyrus delivered the oppressed Babylonians, just as Jeroboam delivers the oppressed Israelites.

Adoniram, Rehoboam's representative to the rebellious northern tribes, was stoned by the people. The law spoke of stoning a person for a variety of sins, including child sacrifice (Lev 20:2), breaking the Sabbath (Num 15:35–36), idolatry (Deut 13:6–10; 17:2–5), a rebellious son (21:18–21), and a bride who was not a virgin (22:13–21). While Adoniram was apparently not guilty of those crimes, he was presumably responsible for much of the oppressive

1. *COS* 1:550.
2. *COS* 2:315.

labor conditions and therefore deserving of his fate, from the perspective of the people. Two other people were stoned earlier in Israel's history: an anonymous man for breaking the Sabbath (Num 15:32–36) and Achan for taking devoted things from the city of Jericho (Josh 7:25). Later in Kings Naboth is framed and stoned unjustly, essentially for refusing to sell his tribal inheritance to Ahab (1 Kgs 21:1–14). When the religious leaders tested Jesus by bringing to him a woman caught in adultery, whom the law says should be stoned, he famously declared, "Let any one of you who is without sin be the first to throw a stone at her" (John 8:7).

The most significant biblical parallel is the story of Aaron and Israel making a golden calf in the wilderness (Exod 32). Jeroboam makes not one but two golden calves and has the audacity to make essentially the same declaration that Aaron made, "Here are your gods, who brought you up out of Egypt" (32:4; 1 Kgs 12:28). It is shocking that, at such a crucial point in Israel's history, Jeroboam decided to repeat arguably Israel's gravest sin (see excursus below, "What Was so Bad about Jeroboam's altars?")

EXPLAIN the Story

Rehoboam Listens to the Wrong Advisors (12:1–15)

Royal successions are often times of instability, and even though Israel's monarchy was relatively young, each of the previous royal successions was characterized by turmoil. After the death of Saul, his son, Ish-Bosheth, ruled over the tribes of Israel, but David reigned over the tribe of Judah (2 Sam 2:8–11), leading to a seven-year civil war between the north and south. After Ish-Bosheth was assassinated, the northern tribes made David their king and the monarchy was reunited under one ruler (5:1–5). David fought off two rebellions led by his own sons, as first Absalom attempted to seize his father's throne (chs. 15–18) and then Adonijah declared himself king despite David's wish that Solomon succeed him (1 Kgs 1). Solomon's early reign was characterized by bloodshed as he killed several of his rivals, including David's general Joab and his own brother Adonijah (ch. 2).

Thus, Rehoboam may have gone to Shechem with trepidation, fearing another civil war or, perhaps, a rebellion. Shechem was a reasonable location for all Israel to acknowledge Rehoboam as king, since it was centrally located in the hill country of Ephraim and was the site of important events in Israel's history. At Shechem YHWH appeared to Abram (Gen 12:6–7), Joshua renewed the covenant, and Joseph's bones were buried (Josh 24:1, 32). Generally, after this point in the text, the term "Israel" no longer refers to the united monarchy but to the northern tribes.

Jeroboam had fled to Egypt when Solomon tried to kill him (1 Kgs 11:40). When he heard about the king's death, he returns and is selected as a spokesperson for the northern tribes, who are unwilling to pledge allegiance until they get the new ruler to lighten the workload (12:3–4). To describe the onerous nature of their labor, the image of a "yoke" (*'ol*) is used (vv. 4 [2x], 10 [2x], 11, 14). A yoke was wooden frame attached to pairs of draught animals, often oxen, so they could work together, but it represented servitude (i.e., Lev 26:13; Deut 28:48; Isa 9:4; Jer 28:14; Hos 11:4).

Solomon had constructed numerous ambitious projects, using forced labor to build an elaborate temple, a grandiose palace complex, and multiple military fortifications (1 Kgs 5:13–18; 9:15–23), so their complaint was reasonable. Since Jeroboam had been in charge of forced labor in Ephraim (11:28), he could speak to the problem with authority. While Ahijah had said that Jeroboam would be king (v. 31), he does not start a rebellion yet; he simply makes a request for a lighter workload. If Rehoboam agrees, then the northern tribes promise to serve him faithfully (12:4). Rehoboam later follows the foolish advice of his friends, but here his decision to request three days to consider their request was wise (v. 5).

Rehoboam first consults the elders who counseled his father. During Israel's monarchy, elders play a crucial role in establishing a ruler's authority. Israel's elders initially requested a king (1 Sam 8:4–5), they anointed David as ruler over Israel (2 Sam 5:3), and they advised rulers in wartime (17:4; 1 Kgs 20:7–8). Their advice to young Rehoboam here was wise, as they recommend agreeing to the Israelite request to lighten the workload. Rehoboam rejects their recommendation and turns to his friends (1 Kgs 12:7–9). While the text calls the king's second group of counselors "young men," it is likely they were middle-aged since they grew up with him, and he was forty-one when he came to the throne (14:21). The word translated as "young men" (*yeladim*) has a broad range of meaning, but it often refers to "children" or even "infants"—it was used recently for the infant sons of the two prostitutes (3:25–27). Alter thinks its usage here "underscores their puerile behavior."[3]

In contrast to the elders' message to serve the people, Rehoboam's friends suggest insulting them (12:10–11). While their language was base and demeaning, it was also creative and poetic, which is typical of both ancient

3. Alter, *The Former Prophets*, 669.

and modern trash talking.[4] The response they advise has three parts, each line claiming that Rehoboam was stronger, more virile, and more severe of a taskmaster than his father. The first line is the crudest—more appropriate for a locker room than a palace. They suggest that Rehoboam boast that his "little finger" is thicker than his father's loins. Most commentators (i.e., Cogan, Alter, Barnes, Sweeney, Wray Beal) think "little finger" is a euphemism for penis (boys will be boys). The second line is the least clever, that he would make the yoke even harder. The third line contrasts Solomon's wimpy whips to Rehoboam's stinging scorpions, nail-barbed whips that could inflict brutal damage to the skin in a scourging.[5]

When the people return to hear Rehoboam's response, he wisely omitted the little finger comment but foolishly repeated the two other comments about intensifying the work and scourging with scorpions (12:12–14). The text repeats that Rehoboam rejected the counsel of the elders (vv. 8, 13) and observes that he did not listen to the people. While Solomon asked YHWH for literally "a listening heart" (3:9; NIV has "a discerning heart"), Rehoboam refuses to listen to the reasonable request of the people or to the sage advice of the elders. The passage concludes with a remark that YHWH was sovereignly guiding the process to fulfill Ahijah's prophecy to Jeroboam (11:31–39).

Israel Rebels against Rehoboam (12:16–24)

The poetic taunt from Rehoboam elicits a poetic response from the people of Israel (12:16). Rehoboam spoke of his father Solomon; the Israelites speak of his grandfather David, also called "Jesse's son" (v. 16; 1 Sam 17:12). In their poem "David" represents Judah, the tribe of David. The Israelites who were willing to swear fealty to Rehoboam reject him for insulting them and declare they have no part in David. They will return to their homes, and Judah can take care of its own house, implying both they will not serve Rehoboam and that they want nothing to do with David's dynasty. Rehoboam is not their king; they will select their own king soon (1 Kgs 12:20).

It is not clear what Rehoboam was thinking when he sent Adoniram, the man who had been in charge of forced labor, to them, presumably to whip them into shape and get them to submit. Despite the massive nature of Rehoboam's little finger, the only whipping was done by the Israelites, who

4. For a discussion of biblical trash talking, see David T. Lamb, "'I Will Strike You Down and Cut off Your Head' (1 Sam 17:46): Trash Talking, Derogatory Rhetoric, and Psychological Warfare in Ancient Israel" in *Warfare, Ritual, and Symbol in Biblical and Modern Contexts*, ed. Brad E. Kelle, Frank Ritchel Ames, and Jacob Wright, AIL 18 (Atlanta: Society of Biblical Literature, 2014), 111–30.

5. See Wiseman, *1 & 2 Kings*, 141.

stoned Adoniram and chased Rehoboam away, barely escaping on his chariot to Jerusalem (v. 18).

The text includes a comment that Israel was independent "to this day" (v. 19), suggesting this material was composed before the fall of the Northern Kingdom in 722 BC.[6] They then select Jeroboam as their king. Once he becomes ruler, scholars often call him Jeroboam I to distinguish him from Jeroboam II, who ruled over Israel about one hundred and fifty years later (2 Kgs 14:23–29). As Ahijah had predicted, Jeroboam "tore" the ten northern tribes from Rehoboam, leaving him only Judah and Benjamin (1 Kgs 12:20–21).

Upon his arrival in Jerusalem, Rehoboam musters a force of one hundred and eighty thousand men, a number that is problematically large. The Septuagint only has one hundred and twenty thousand, but that number is still problematic for the combined tribes of Judah and Benjamin. Some scholars perceive it to be schematic,[7] while others think that the Hebrew word translated as "thousand" (*'eleph*) is here referring to a "company" or "division," which could be much less than a thousand.[8]

But before their forces engage in battle, Shemaiah the man of God intervenes (vv. 22–24). In narrative books and particularly in the book of Kings, the term "man of God" is often used for prophets: Samuel (1 Sam 9:10–14), Elijah (1 Kgs 17:24), and Elisha (2 Kgs 5:8). Forms of the phrase "man of God" appear over seventy times in the Old Testament, but the vast majority of these occur in Kings (fifty-one times). This usage of the term "man of God" for Shemaiah is the first of many in the book. While there was a dearth of prophets during the reign of Solomon, we now encounter a second prophet shortly after Ahijah's appearance. Shemaiah prohibits Rehoboam from starting another civil war, informing him that YHWH was behind these events. Rehoboam had failed to listen to the wise counsel of the elders, but this time he wisely listens to the prophet and returns home (1 Kgs 12:24). While the God of the Old Testament is often accused of being overly belligerent, there are many biblical texts like this one where he prevents war and promotes peace (2 Kgs 6:20–23; Isa 2:4; 19:24–25; Jer 29:7).

Jeroboam Constructs Golden Calves (12:25–33)

Jeroboam rebuilt the city of Shechem, the location of Rehoboam's rejection, and made it the first capital of the Northern Kingdom (1 Kgs 12:25). He also

6. See Wiseman, *1 & 2 Kings*, 142.
7. See DeVries, *1 Kings*, 158.
8. See *BBCOT*, 432–33.

built up Peniel (also spelled "Penuel"), which was where Jacob wrestled the God-man (Gen 32:22–32). Both of these cities would have had not only historical significance but also strategic importance. Shechem was a central location in Ephraim and oversaw key east-west trade routes. Peniel was located on the east side of the Jordan along the Jabbok River and had hosted a tower until it was destroyed by Gideon to punish the local residents for not providing food for his army (Judg 8:8–9, 17).

At the beginnings of their reigns, both Rehoboam and Jeroboam were concerned about the stability of their kingdom (1 Kgs 12:26). Jeroboam was worried that the Israelite tribes that had just made him king might return to Rehoboam as they traveled to Jerusalem on a regular basis to make sacrifices at the temple there. Jeroboam had just seen Rehoboam almost get killed by angry subjects, and he thought the same could happen to him (vv. 18, 27). Like his southern counterpart, Jeroboam wisely sought advice, and, like his southern counterpart, the advice he listened to was foolish (v. 28). To provide northerners with alternative places of worship, he constructed two altars, one in the far north at the city of Dan near the border of Aram and one in the far south at the city of Bethel, near the border of Judah. After they were unable to establish their tribal inheritance along the coastal plain, the Danites moved far north, conquered Laish, and renamed it Dan (Judg 18). Bethel, which means "house of God," was where Abraham set up an altar and where Jacob dreamed of a ladder to heaven (Gen 12:8; 28:19). Jeroboam's logic may make sense to modern readers who make location a key criterion in their selection of a church to attend. It is conceivable that Jeroboam intended these altars to be places for people to worship YHWH, but the text speaks of them in highly negative terms. For more on this subject, see excursus "What Was so Bad about Jeroboam's altars?" below.

Excursus: What Was So Bad about Jeroboam's Altars?

The text states that Jeroboam's construction of the golden calves at Bethel and Dan was one of the gravest sins in Israel's history and condemned dozens of times throughout the book of Kings (e.g., 1 Kgs 15:30, 34; 16:2, 19, 26, 31). All the northern rulers except for two (Elah: 16:8; Shallum: 2 Kgs 15:13) were condemned for either walking in the sins of Jeroboam (e.g., 1 Kgs 15:26, 34; 16:19, 26, 31) or not departing from the sins of Jeroboam (e.g., 2 Kgs 3:3; 10:31; 14:24; 15:9, 18). The former expression ("walking") is more often associated with earlier northern rulers (e.g., Nadab, Baasha, Zimri, Omri, Ahab), while the latter expression ("not departing") is associated with later rulers (e.g., Jehoram, Jehu, Jeroboam II, Zechariah, Menahem). What these rulers actually did in association with these altars is not clear, but they should have torn them down. Both of these sites survived for the duration of the Northern Kingdom. We do not know what happened to the altar at Dan, but the city of Dan was conquered with other northern cities when Tiglath-Pileser III of Assyria took control of the northern regions (2 Kgs 15:29). The altar at Bethel and its high place was destroyed by King Josiah of Judah approximately three hundred years after Jeroboam I (23:15). Presumably because of its remote location in the far north, the Dan altar was not mentioned as often as the one at Bethel. In prophetic literature, worship at Bethel is repeatedly condemned (Jer 48:13; Hos 10:15; Amos 3:14; 4:4; 5:5–6).

What was so bad about Jeroboam's altars? Four factors about these sites would be problematic for the biblical authors. First, Jeroboam's act revealed that he does not trust the prophetic word from Ahijah that God would give him ten tribes and that, if he obeyed, his dynasty would be secure (1 Kgs 11:38). Second, Jeroboam's choice of these locations conflicted with Deuteronomy's emphasis that YHWH would choose one central place of worship (Deut 12:5, 11, 14, 18, 21, 26). Third, Jeroboam's altars were associated with non-orthodox religious practices like high places, non-Levitical priests, and an alternative religious festival. Fourth, and most shockingly, the construction of golden calves is the same sin that their ancestors committed in the wilderness. Amazingly, Jeroboam even uses the same language that Aaron did when he presented his golden calf to the people (Exod 32:4). The story of Jeroboam's persistent sin reminds us that God desires pure worship. Peripheral aspects of worship, such as buildings, locations, or types of music, can quickly take our focus off God and become idolatrous.

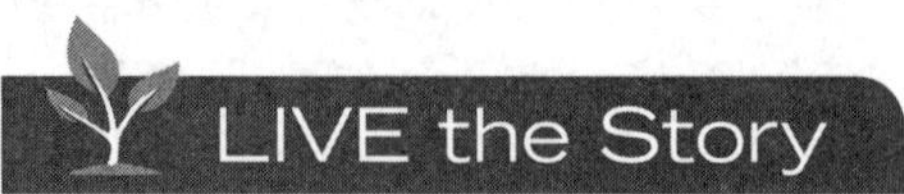

Advice Advice

When the nation of Israel asked the prophet Samuel to appoint for them a king like other nations, he warned them about the costs of being royal subjects and concluded by telling them "you yourselves will become his slaves" (1 Sam 8:17). They rejected the prophet's advice and persisted in their request.

After the reigns of Saul, David, and Solomon, the people of Israel are tired of serving as slaves under a monarch, but when they ask for a reprieve, Rehoboam refuses their request. Early in his reign Solomon asked for a listening heart, then he wisely heard the case of the two prostitutes. Early in the reign of Rehoboam, he hardens his heart and does not listen to the people. It takes wisdom to know when and how to listen to advice.

Based on this passage, we will offer three words of advice about obtaining advice. First, ask for advice. Sometimes counsel will be offered without it being requested (Shemaiah), but most "underlings" will be hesitant to offer their thoughts to people in positions of power (bosses, parents, pastors, or ministry leaders) until it is requested. When we are in positions where we lack knowledge or confidence, we are more likely to seek guidance, but the reality for most of us is that we need wisdom even in areas of our expertise. Most people feel like it is an honor to be asked for their perspective. As I was working on this chapter, I sent an email to an Old Testament scholar friend (Fred Putnam), whom I see on a regular basis but rarely ask for input. He graciously replied within a few hours with great insights on the passage. Asking for advice on a regular basis makes us not only humble but also wise.

Second, discern good advice. To their credit, both Rehoboam and Jeroboam ask for advice. Their problem is they listened to the wrong advice. This chapter is full of people offering requests, suggestions, and counsel to these two rulers: the people, the elders, Rehoboam's friends, Shemaiah the prophet, and Jeroboam's royal advisors. It takes wisdom to discern which advice to follow and which to ignore. Good advice was given in this chapter. The elder's counsel to listen and serve the people would have brought stability to Rehoboam's throne. The prophet's advice to not start a war prevented massive bloodshed. But foolish advice (insult the people, build golden calves) was not only given, it was also heeded. Wise advice will often tell us things we don't want to hear (submit to the people), and it will be consistent with important biblical themes, which relates to the next point.

Third, seek advice from God. None of these rulers sought God for advice. Sometimes God sends prophets like Shemaiah, who share God's perspective when it's not asked for, but all leaders need to consistently be pursuing God for guidance in our decisions, both big and small. Perhaps the best example of a ruler who pursued YHWH's advice is David in regard to the city of Keilah (1 Sam 23:1–14). When David discovered that Keilah was being attacked by the Philistines, he asked YHWH twice if he should go rescue them, and YHWH said both times, "Go save them." When he heard that Saul was approaching Keilah, he asked YHWH if Saul would come to Keilah;

YHWH said Saul was coming. Finally, David asked if Keilah would surrender him to Saul even though he had just delivered them; YHWH said they would. David models for us a persistent and committed pursuit of God in decision making. Leaders and anyone who needs counsel can get wisdom from God through Scripture, prayer, and from the community of God's people.

Oppression and Servanthood

Rehoboam here provides negative leadership lessons for us. While his father Solomon successfully constructed the temple of YHWH, his many building projects involved oppressive labor practices that Rehoboam foolishly decided to continue (1 Kgs 11:28; 12:4, 11). He was given a choice to listen to a reasonable request presented by Jeroboam, one of his loyal managers. Rehoboam chose not only to continue to exploit his workers but also to insult them as he threatened them with torture if they chose insubordination. His brutal style of leadership is, tragically, not uncommon. Not surprisingly, Jeroboam and the northern tribes rebelled at this blatant abuse of power. Leaders of churches, businesses, schools, or other organizations do well to listen to those under their authority and to make sure that people are given meaningful work, reasonable workloads, and sufficient rest. The longest of the Ten Commandments is the one to remember the Sabbath and to rest; YHWH mandated that the rest included not just one's family but also male and female servants, even the animals (Exod 20:8–11). God wants his people—as well as their servants—to rest and not be exploited for their labor.

The elders' advice here to Rehoboam to serve the people was some of the wisest advice given to a ruler in Scripture, as it is consistent with what Jesus taught: that servanthood is the basis for true, legitimate authority. Jesus repeatedly told his followers that greatness comes through service (Mark 9:35; 10:42–45; John 13:14–15). Jesus specifically tells his followers that their leadership was not to be characterized by the oppressive, tyrannical style so typical among the Gentiles (Mark 10:42–45) that Rehoboam illustrates in this chapter. Leaders must serve the people around them by making sure they have reasonable workloads, by listening to their reasonable requests, by not insulting them but honoring them. When followers, employees, or students don't sense that their leaders are interested in their welfare, it often leads to burnout, a condition that is endemic to churches and Christian ministries. Ministry is hard, but ultimately we should remember that Jesus came primarily not to be served but to serve and to give his life as a ransom for many (10:45). Solomon's yoke was heavy and Rehoboam threatened to make it heavier, but Jesus says, "my yoke is easy and my burden is light" (Matt 11:30).

CHAPTER 11

1 Kings 13:1–14:20

 LISTEN to the Story

1By the word of the LORD a man of God came from Judah to Bethel, as
Jeroboam was standing by the altar to make an offering. 2By the word of
the LORD he cried out against the altar: "Altar, altar! This is what the LORD
says: 'A son named Josiah will be born to the house of David. On you he
will sacrifice the priests of the high places who make offerings here, and
human bones will be burned on you.'" 3That same day the man of God
gave a sign: "This is the sign the LORD has declared: The altar will be split
apart and the ashes on it will be poured out."

4When King Jeroboam heard what the man of God cried out against
the altar at Bethel, he stretched out his hand from the altar and said,
"Seize him!" But the hand he stretched out toward the man shriveled up,
so that he could not pull it back. 5Also, the altar was split apart and its
ashes poured out according to the sign given by the man of God by the
word of the LORD.

6Then the king said to the man of God, "Intercede with the LORD your
God and pray for me that my hand may be restored." So the man of God
interceded with the LORD, and the king's hand was restored and became
as it was before.

7The king said to the man of God, "Come home with me for a meal,
and I will give you a gift."

8But the man of God answered the king, "Even if you were to give me
half your possessions, I would not go with you, nor would I eat bread or
drink water here. 9For I was commanded by the word of the LORD: 'You
must not eat bread or drink water or return by the way you came.'" 10So he
took another road and did not return by the way he had come to Bethel.

11Now there was a certain old prophet living in Bethel, whose sons
came and told him all that the man of God had done there that day. They
also told their father what he had said to the king. 12Their father asked

them, "Which way did he go?" And his sons showed him which road the man of God from Judah had taken. [13]So he said to his sons, "Saddle the donkey for me." And when they had saddled the donkey for him, he mounted it [14]and rode after the man of God. He found him sitting under an oak tree and asked, "Are you the man of God who came from Judah?"

"I am," he replied.

[15]So the prophet said to him, "Come home with me and eat."

[16]The man of God said, "I cannot turn back and go with you, nor can I eat bread or drink water with you in this place. [17]I have been told by the word of the LORD: 'You must not eat bread or drink water there or return by the way you came.'"

[18]The old prophet answered, "I too am a prophet, as you are. And an angel said to me by the word of the LORD: 'Bring him back with you to your house so that he may eat bread and drink water.'" (But he was lying to him.) [19]So the man of God returned with him and ate and drank in his house.

[20]While they were sitting at the table, the word of the LORD came to the old prophet who had brought him back. [21]He cried out to the man of God who had come from Judah, "This is what the LORD says: 'You have defied the word of the LORD and have not kept the command the LORD your God gave you. [22]You came back and ate bread and drank water in the place where he told you not to eat or drink. Therefore your body will not be buried in the tomb of your ancestors.'"

[23]When the man of God had finished eating and drinking, the prophet who had brought him back saddled his donkey for him. [24]As he went on his way, a lion met him on the road and killed him, and his body was left lying on the road, with both the donkey and the lion standing beside it. [25]Some people who passed by saw the body lying there, with the lion standing beside the body, and they went and reported it in the city where the old prophet lived.

[26]When the prophet who had brought him back from his journey heard of it, he said, "It is the man of God who defied the word of the LORD. The LORD has given him over to the lion, which has mauled him and killed him, as the word of the LORD had warned him."

[27]The prophet said to his sons, "Saddle the donkey for me," and they did so. [28]Then he went out and found the body lying on the road, with the donkey and the lion standing beside it. The lion had neither eaten the

body nor mauled the donkey. [29]So the prophet picked up the body of the man of God, laid it on the donkey, and brought it back to his own city to mourn for him and bury him. [30]Then he laid the body in his own tomb, and they mourned over him and said, "Alas, my brother!"

[31]After burying him, he said to his sons, "When I die, bury me in the grave where the man of God is buried; lay my bones beside his bones. [32]For the message he declared by the word of the LORD against the altar in Bethel and against all the shrines on the high places in the towns of Samaria will certainly come true."

[33]Even after this, Jeroboam did not change his evil ways, but once more appointed priests for the high places from all sorts of people. Anyone who wanted to become a priest he consecrated for the high places. [34]This was the sin of the house of Jeroboam that led to its downfall and to its destruction from the face of the earth.

[14:1]At that time Abijah son of Jeroboam became ill, [2]and Jeroboam said to his wife, "Go, disguise yourself, so you won't be recognized as the wife of Jeroboam. Then go to Shiloh. Ahijah the prophet is there—the one who told me I would be king over this people. [3]Take ten loaves of bread with you, some cakes and a jar of honey, and go to him. He will tell you what will happen to the boy." [4]So Jeroboam's wife did what he said and went to Ahijah's house in Shiloh.

Now Ahijah could not see; his sight was gone because of his age. [5]But the LORD had told Ahijah, "Jeroboam's wife is coming to ask you about her son, for he is ill, and you are to give her such and such an answer. When she arrives, she will pretend to be someone else."

[6]So when Ahijah heard the sound of her footsteps at the door, he said, "Come in, wife of Jeroboam. Why this pretense? I have been sent to you with bad news. [7]Go, tell Jeroboam that this is what the LORD, the God of Israel, says: 'I raised you up from among the people and appointed you ruler over my people Israel. [8]I tore the kingdom away from the house of David and gave it to you, but you have not been like my servant David, who kept my commands and followed me with all his heart, doing only what was right in my eyes. [9]You have done more evil than all who lived before you. You have made for yourself other gods, idols made of metal; you have aroused my anger and turned your back on me.

[10]"'Because of this, I am going to bring disaster on the house of Jeroboam. I will cut off from Jeroboam every last male in Israel—slave or

free. I will burn up the house of Jeroboam as one burns dung, until it is all gone. [11]Dogs will eat those belonging to Jeroboam who die in the city, and the birds will feed on those who die in the country. The LORD has spoken!'

[12]"As for you, go back home. When you set foot in your city, the boy will die. [13]All Israel will mourn for him and bury him. He is the only one belonging to Jeroboam who will be buried, because he is the only one in the house of Jeroboam in whom the LORD, the God of Israel, has found anything good.

[14]"The LORD will raise up for himself a king over Israel who will cut off the family of Jeroboam. Even now this is beginning to happen. [15]And the LORD will strike Israel, so that it will be like a reed swaying in the water. He will uproot Israel from this good land that he gave to their ancestors and scatter them beyond the Euphrates River, because they aroused the LORD's anger by making Asherah poles. [16]And he will give Israel up because of the sins Jeroboam has committed and has caused Israel to commit."

[17]Then Jeroboam's wife got up and left and went to Tirzah. As soon as she stepped over the threshold of the house, the boy died. [18]They buried him, and all Israel mourned for him, as the LORD had said through his servant the prophet Ahijah.

[19]The other events of Jeroboam's reign, his wars and how he ruled, are written in the book of the annals of the kings of Israel. [20]He reigned for twenty-two years and then rested with his ancestors. And Nadab his son succeeded him as king.

Listening to the Text in the Story: Biblical Texts: 1 Samuel 13:13–14; 15:26–28; 2 Samuel 12:1–15; 1 Kings 11:11–13, 31–39

The story thus far in 1 Kings has been about Israel's rulers, David and Solomon, and, more recently, Rehoboam and Jeroboam. Prophets have only made a few cameos. But as we move into this section of judgments against Jeroboam and his altar, prophetic individuals dominate the narrative: one we have seen before, Ahijah, and two new, anonymous ones (see excursus below, "Prophetic Narratives"). In this passage prophets are primarily speaking words of condemnation against King Jeroboam and his altar.

To better understand these oracles, we will look back to earlier royal judgments pronounced by prophets, as well as forward to how these prophecies are later fulfilled. For his premature sacrifice and incomplete slaughter, Saul, Israel's first ruler, was condemned by Samuel (1 Sam 13:13–14; 15:26–28), the prophet who had initially anointed him (10:1). In the second of these messages, Samuel uses language comparable to Ahijah's first oracle as he speaks of tearing the kingdom away from Saul and giving it to another (2 Sam 15:28; 1 Kgs 11:11; 31). For sleeping with Bathsheba then killing her husband Uriah to cover it up, Nathan declares that the sword will never leave David's house and the child would die (2 Sam 12:1–15). Judgments were also spoken against Solomon, but the message that was addressed to him was delivered directly by YHWH (1 Kgs 11:11–13); the one delivered by a prophet was addressed to Jeroboam (vv. 31–39). Beyond merely being delivered by a prophet to a ruler, these oracles share other similarities. Kings are evaluated negatively because of their disobedience, and the consequences are delayed as they mainly target future generations. Comparable to Ahijah's initial and final messages for Jeroboam, several of these prophets pronounced positive and negative oracles for the same ruler (Samuel for Saul; Nathan for David).

Excursus: Prophetic Narratives

In this section the focus shifts from kings to prophets. Because of this shift and the distinctive nature of the writing, this passage is often considered one of three prophetic narratives in the book (1 Kgs 13:1–14:18; 17:1–2 Kgs 2:12; 2 Kgs 2:13–8:15). Each of these three narratives is set during the reign of one primary northern ruler (Jeroboam I, Ahab, and Jehoram), who interacts with one primary prophet (Ahijah, Elijah, and Elisha) as well as other anonymous prophets. Prophetic narratives in Kings have at least four characteristics that distinguish them from the other material in the book.

First, prophetic narratives tell engaging stories of dramatic events and supernatural signs performed by prophets. For many readers of Kings, the prophetic narratives are their favorite parts of the book. Because the heroic exploits of Elijah and Elisha are entertaining (making great Sunday school lessons), it is likely these narratives were derived from oral and not written sources. In contrast, the royal annals appear to be the written sources for the information in the rather mundane regnal formulas.

Second, the primary characters in prophetic narratives are often anonymous; rulers may be simply called "the king of Israel," and prophets may be called a "man of God." For example, the two prophets in 1 Kings 13 are simply called "the man of God" and "the old prophet." The context usually allows readers to identify the king and sometimes the prophet.

Third, prophetic narratives are set in the Northern Kingdom involving northern rulers and northern prophets. Since the end of 1 Kings and the beginning of 2 Kings primarily consist of prophetic narratives, these sections of the book have a decidedly northern flavor, although the perspective on Israel and its rulers in this material is highly negative.

Fourth, prophetic narratives focus on the word of God. While their signs and wonders may get our attention, the text emphasizes their divine message. In this section of fifty-four verses, the word and speech of God is referenced at least eighteen times: the expression "the word of the LORD" appears eleven times (1 Kgs 13:1, 2, 5, 9, 17, 18, 20, 21, 26, 32; 14:18), the expression "this is what the LORD says" appears twice (13:2, 21), and other similar expressions describing divine speech are mentioned five times (13:3, 18, 21; 14:5, 7). The primary purpose of a prophet is to speak for God.

The Man of God and Jeroboam (13:1–10)

As Jeroboam is standing next to his altar at Bethel, a man of God from Judah appears and speaks a word of condemnation against the altar by addressing the altar directly. The term "man of God" refers to a prophetic individual and will distinguish for readers this anonymous prophet from Judah with the "old prophet" who later appears in this story. The terms "prophet" and "man of God" appear to be interchangeable, seen in the later dialogue where the old prophet says to the man of God, "I too am a prophet, as you are" (13:18). The man of God declares that a Davidic descendant named Josiah will destroy this altar, killing its priests and burning their bones (v. 2). While the man does not explain why the altar is to be desecrated, presumably the narrative from the previous chapter gives sufficient warrant (see also excursus "What Was So Bad about Jeroboam's Altars?" in Chapter 10 above). But to provide a sign for Jeroboam that his prophecy, which will not be fulfilled for hundreds of years, was true, the prophet declares that the altar would be broken in two and the ashes poured out, which happens as he described (vv. 3, 5).

Jeroboam knows what to do with this upstart who dared to condemn his new sanctuary, but as he gives the order for the prophet's seizure, his outstretched hand shrivels. The text does not say that God shriveled Jeroboam's hand, but the context suggests he was responsible since the man was acting as God's messenger. The hand shriveling and altar splitting are the first supernatural signs (apart from divine appearances) in the book of Kings. While one might hope that the king would repent here, like Saul and David did after their prophetic condemnations (1 Sam 15:25; 2 Sam 12:13), Jeroboam is simply concerned with his damaged hand. He then pleads with the man of God to intercede on his behalf for a healing. After damaging Jeroboam's altar and hand, the man of God, perhaps surprisingly, agrees to pray for the king, and God listened to his prayer and healed him. This healing is the first of several in Kings, most of which are performed in the contexts of prophetic narratives by Elijah and Elisha (e.g., 1 Kgs 17:17–24; 2 Kgs 2:19–22; 4:8–37; 5:1–19; 13:21).

With his fully functioning hand, Jeroboam is in a good mood, so he invites the man of God to his palace for a meal and gift (1 Kgs 13:7). The prophet turns down the king, since he was forbidden from eating there, drinking there, or returning by the same road (v. 8). We assume this message was given by YHWH earlier and was part of the "word of the Lord" mentioned at the beginning of this story (v. 1), but at several points in this prophetic narrative it is not clear which of the prophetic messages truly were generated from YHWH. Here, the restriction on remaining in Bethel is reasonable from God's perspective. In a context where hospitality was important, if the man of God were to share a meal with Jeroboam, it could communicate that he was somehow endorsing, not denouncing, the king and the altar. The man of God headed home after obediently fulfilling his commission to Bethel, but problems appear from an unexpected source on his way.

The Man of God and the Old Prophet (13:11–34)

Prophets are portrayed highly favorably during the period of the monarchy (see the narratives of Samuel, Nathan, Ahijah, Shemaiah, Elijah, Micaiah, Elisha, Isaiah, and Huldah). While most kings were doing evil in the eyes of YHWH, prophets were speaking and acting for YHWH. The main exceptions to this rule are the groups of royal prophets associated with Ahab and Jezebel (1 Kgs 18:19–40; 19:1; 22:6–22). We meet the other possible exception in this passage, the old prophet who essentially tricks the man of God to his death. It is a confusing story, so let's try to make sense of it.

While many aspects about this prophet's background are a mystery, we know he is old, he lives in Bethel, and he had sons. His association with Bethel should probably be interpreted negatively. Even if he did not actively support Jeroboam's altar, there is no record of him condemning it in the text. Since Bethel was his home, if he were truly a prophet of YHWH, he should have already spoken against the altar. The fact that the man of God had to travel all the way from Judah to Bethel to judge the altar was an indirect indictment against him.

The narrative slows down here, giving readers more details than normal about the interactions between the old man and his sons, about donkeys being saddled and the direction the man of God traveled (13:11–13). The old prophet's dinner invitation to the man of God is similar to that of Jeroboam (vv. 7, 15). The man of God's rejection this time is similar, but not as strong as before. To the old prophet he omits the line that he could not be bribed with half of the host's possessions, presumably because a prophet's possessions would be much less than a king's (v. 8, 16). To Jeroboam he said he was "commanded" by the word of YHWH, now to the old prophet he said he was merely "told" by the word of YHWH (vv. 9, 17).

At this point the old prophet reveals to the man of God that he is also a prophet, and an angel spoke to him, telling him that the man of God should join him for food and drink. As a reader, we could be confused by two contradictory messages from YHWH, but the text informs us that the old prophet was lying (v. 18). Unfortunately, the man of God did not know this, so he believed his new prophetic colleague and agreed to join him for a meal (v. 19).

We might assume the old prophet's deception in 1 Kings 13 would disqualify him from being considered a genuine prophet, but the story of Micaiah might lead to the opposite conclusion (Micaiah lied at first, and God sometimes sends lying spirits; 1 Kgs 22). His association with Bethel and his deception reflects negatively upon him. However, as the story continues, the old prophet seems to be both a man of honor and an authentic prophet, which suggests that God may have been using him all along to trick the man of God. Often the Bible portrays characters in shades of gray; it takes wisdom to determine what lessons are to be learned.

While eating together, the lying prophet delivers what appears to be a genuine word from YHWH, condemning the man of God for defying the word of YHWH and disobeying his command not to eat and drink at Bethel (13:21–22). The judgment does not speak to the timing or manner of the man of God's death, merely that his body would not be buried with his ancestors. The word translated as "body" (v. 22) here is *nevelah,* and it can mean "carcass" or "corpse." It is often used in contexts where a person has been killed in a grisly or violent manner (e.g., Josh 8:29; 2 Kgs 9:37; Jer 26:23). In this passage, it is repeated ten times in just nine verses (1 Kgs 13:22, 24 [2x], 25 [2x], 28 [3x], 29, 30), perhaps to emphasize the gruesome nature of his death.

The old prophet's prediction is fulfilled instantly as a lion kills him on the road (v. 24). Lions were common in Palestine until the thirteenth century,[1] so an attack does not necessarily need to be interpreted as supernatural, but the timing of it and the fact that the lion stood guard over the dead man's body (vv. 24–28) suggests God caused it.

After initially condemning the man of God, the old prophet begins an extended series of actions to honor the man whom he tricked to his death. As the man of God is departing, he saddles his donkey. After the lion attack, he finds the man's dead body, brings it home, mourns over him, buries him in his own tomb, expresses his wish to be buried next to him, and declares that his message against Jeroboam's altar was true (vv. 27–32). It is difficult to know what motivated the old prophet's actions. It may have been guilt over his own deception, a desire to be associated with a genuine prophet, or perhaps even divine guidance.

We find parallels to this strange incident in the stories of two other prophets, Balaam and Micaiah. King Balak of Moab tried to hire Balaam to curse the Israelites on the Moabite plains (Num 22–24). YHWH initially told Balaam to refuse, so he said no; after they persisted, YHWH told him he could go with them. But on the road Balaam had donkey problems, because he should have obeyed the first message and not listened to the deceptive second message (comparable to the man of God here). Like Balaam, the man of God twice turned down the invitation to go before he was tricked into agreeing. When asked by Ahab of Israel if he and Jehoshaphat of Judah should attack Aram, the prophet Micaiah initially agreed (deceptively) with Ahab's prophets, who said God would grant victory. Ahab prods Micaiah to tell the truth (1 Kgs 22:1–40), so he declares Ahab's prophets had received a deceptive spirit from YHWH. Ahab ignored Micaiah's words and died in battle. The stories of Balaam, Micaiah, and the man of God here make the point that discerning genuine messages from God can sometimes be complicated, particularly when "prophets" appear to disagree. This issue will be discussed in the Live the Story section below.

The narrative ends with a comment that "even after this, Jeroboam did not change his evil ways" (13:33), suggesting that the actions of these prophets should have prompted his repentance. Upon reflection, we see similarities between Jeroboam and the prophet killed by a lion. Both initially obeyed,

---

1. Wiseman, *1 & 2 Kings*, 147.

but both listened to the wrong advice (building golden calves, eating a meal in Bethel), and then they suffered the consequences—death by lion for the prophet and the end of a dynasty for the king.

Ahijah Condemns Jeroboam's House (14:1–20)

When Prince Abijah becomes sick, his father Jeroboam comes up with a not-very-clever plan to trick another prophet (it worked for the old prophet from Bethel, why not for the king?). He tells his wife to put on a disguise and go to the home of Ahijah (the names of the prophet and the prince rhyme) in Shiloh (14:1–3). Shiloh had important religious associations, since it housed the ark before the reign of David (e.g., 1 Sam 1:3; 2:14; 3:21; 4:3; 14:3). He tells her to bring bread, cakes, and honey, then ask about her son's sickness. Jeroboam curiously assumes the prophet will supernaturally know about her son's fate but not about her own identity. Despite Ahijah's blindness, Jeroboam's wife's disguise does not fool the prophet. Jacob tricked his blind father Isaac (Gen 27), and Tamar tricked her amorous father-in-law Judah (Gen 38). Perhaps patriarchs were easier to deceive than prophets?

Ahijah knew she was coming and what she would ask, since he had been tipped off by YHWH (1 Kgs 14:5). YHWH tells the prophet what to say ("give her such and such an answer"), but the reader has to wait to find out the content of the message until he actually delivers it to Jeroboam's wife. As she approaches, Ahijah wastes no time revealing that he knows her identity—"Come in, wife of Jeroboam"—then lays out for her the bad news (v. 6). He gives her a message from God for her husband. While multiple layers of communication can distort a message, and this one has four (God to Ahijah to Jeroboam's wife to Jeroboam), presumably it reached its intended target intact. Ahijah invokes divine authority by using the prophetic messenger formula ("This is what the Lord, the God of Israel, says . . . ," v. 7a). YHWH's reminder of Jeroboam's call ("I raised you up . . . and appointed you ruler over my people Israel," vv. 7b–8) is reminiscent of Nathan's judgment against David ("I anointed you king over Israel . . . I delivered you from the hand of Saul," 2 Sam 12:7–8). Despite these parallels to David's judgment, David here is described as obediently following God with all his heart (1 Kgs 14:8; see also "The Righteous Portrayal of David in Kings" in Chapter 3).

The indictment against Jeroboam, that he has done more evil than all who were before him (v. 9), will be repeated in some form for three later northern rulers: Omri (16:25), Ahab (16:30), and Manasseh (2 Kgs 21:9, 11). Solomon's idolatry made YHWH angry (1 Kgs 11:9), and the altars at Bethel and Dan are mentioned ("other gods, idols made of metal") as the catalysts for YHWH's anger here (14:9). Whereas the condemnation of the man of God primarily targeted the Bethel altar (13:2–3), Ahijah here primarily targets Jeroboam and his family (14:10–14). The judgment against Jeroboam's house will involve the death of all his male descendants.

The language used here for the condemnation against Jeroboam is graphic and dramatic, bordering on trash talking. The Hebrew behind the translation "male" here (*mashtin beqir*) literally means "the ones who urinate against the wall" (v. 10; rendered elegantly in the KJV as "him that pisseth against the wall"). This idiomatic expression for males is used elsewhere in Kings in similar contexts of graphic dynastic judgments (1 Kgs 16:11; 21:21; 2 Kgs 9:8). If this is your favorite genre (which probably means you're a teenage boy), there is good news since more scatological language is coming, as Jeroboam's house will get burned like dung (1 Kgs 14:10). Among his descendants, city dwellers will get eaten by dogs, and rural ones will be eaten by birds. The former curse is the first of an extended series of canine consummation condemnations (14:11; 16:4; 21:19, 23, 24; 22:38; 2 Kgs 9:10, 36).

Why do God and the prophet use such severe language? Presumably, the intense language was meant to provoke Jeroboam to repent. After Ahab heard a comparably severe dynastic judgment from Elijah, his repentance led to a revised, more lenient punishment from YHWH (1 Kgs 21:17–29).

Ahijah finally details the fate of the prince to Jeroboam's wife—as she sets foot in the city, he will die (14:12). The nation will mourn him, and he will be buried. But he will be the only descendant of Jeroboam buried, because he was the only one YHWH found good in (v. 13). At this point, one might ask, "If good was found in him, why was he killed?" This is a difficult question that this text does not address, but the consistent message of Scripture is that a person's sin often negatively affected other people—including family members.

The prophet next lays out a series of predictions and consequences. YHWH will raise up a new king, who will wipe out Jeroboam's house (i.e., Baasha; v. 14), and he will kill Jeroboam's heir, Nadab, as well as the rest of Jeroboam's descendants (15:27–30). Ahijah shifts to the distant future as he predicts the fall of the Northern Kingdom, which will not occur for about two hundred years, when the Assyrians conquer the land (2 Kings 15:29; 17:5–6). He ominously concludes by attributing this future catastrophe to Jeroboam's sins of idolatry.

After hearing her son would die as soon as she entered the city, many mothers would be tempted to never return, but she does anyway. Technically, he was supposed to die when she entered the city, but the text says it happened as she entered the house (1 Kgs 14:12, 17). Throughout this passage, Jeroboam's wife never speaks. The boy died, was buried, and was mourned, just as the prophet predicted (vv. 17–18).

Jeroboam's regnal formula concludes his narrative (vv. 19–20). Like most formulas, it mentions the northern annals (see "Composition, Sources, and the Royal Annals" in the Introduction), the length of his reign (twenty-two years), and his other activities. The regnal formula also curiously mentions Jeroboam's wars, but there is no narrative material recording any battles for the northern ruler. The concluding regnal formulas for Rehoboam and Abijah speak of each of their ongoing wars with Jeroboam (14:30; 15:7), but again no details are provided.

The second of the two prophecies of this section (14:10–16) is fulfilled first, as the usurper Baasha kills Nadab, the son of Jeroboam I (15:27–30), as predicted by Ahijah to the wife of Jeroboam. The first prophecy of this section, from the anonymous man of God against Jeroboam's altar (13:2–3), is not fulfilled for several centuries, after the fall of the Northern Kingdom during the reign of Josiah. Josiah destroys Jeroboam's altar, slaughters the priests, and burns their bones (2 Kgs 23:15–20). He desecrates the graves at the site of the altar, but he allows the bones of the two prophets to remain there (23:17–18). While some scholars consider this an *ex eventu* prophecy (one written after the event had already taken place) because it mentions Josiah by name,[2] people who believe that YHWH had the power to first damage and then heal Jeroboam's hand (1 Kgs 13:4–6) should be able to envision God being able to reveal the name of the ruler who would eventually destroy Jeroboam's altar.

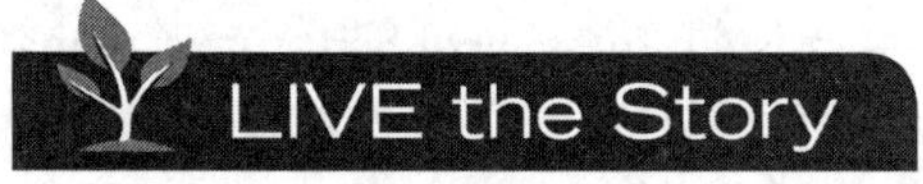

Questioning the Text

While many Old Testament stories are difficult to understand, this story about these prophets is particularly bewildering. As we attempt to make sense of it, various questions arise. Was the old prophet really from God? If so, why did he trick the man of God into eating with him? What was so bad about eating a meal with someone? Should the penalty for eating in Bethel really be death? Speaking of death, why does a good boy need to die for the sin of his father? God's Word can be confusing.

Bewildering texts like this one are often avoided by preachers and teachers.

2. See, for example, Jones, *1 and 2 Kings*, 1:263; Alter, *The Former Prophets*, 674.

If we ignore this story, assuming all Scripture (not just our favorite texts) is inspired and profitable for teaching (2 Tim 3:16), we aren't profiting from this highly prophetic text. Difficult texts teach profound lessons about God and God's word. And we will profit from studying, teaching, and preaching about these tricky prophets. Questions will arise, but that's a good thing.

The church doesn't always encourage questions. In a *Non Sequitur* comic strip from 2011 titled "The Invention of Religion,"[3] three people are standing around wearing Flintstone-esque garb (primitive fur coats). The man in charge is standing in front of a big statue of a head that looks similar to his own. He's talking to a couple who are listening attentively. He begins, "OK, here's how it works . . . First you never question anything I tell you . . ." It's funny and tragic because it's true. The popular perception of religion, and sometimes the church in general, is that we don't always encourage people to ask difficult questions. Questions are perceived as threatening.

Jesus valued good questions, often posing important questions to his disciples at key points in his ministry (Mark 8:29; Luke 10:36; John 1:38; 21:23). While the religious leaders of his day used questions to trap or interrogate Jesus (Mark 2:18; 6:2–3; 11:28; 12:23; 14:60–61), he welcomed genuine questions from his disciples and others (Matt 3:14; Mark 7:17; 9:11; 10:17, 26; 13:3–4; 14:12).

Confusing stories like this one invite us to question the text, to wrestle with it as we discuss it and try to make sense of it. That's not something to avoid or discourage but something to embrace. Discuss problematic texts like this with friends and family, with people at church and with people at work. Some of our questions will get answered, others perhaps not. But we will hopefully be content with some level of tension or ambiguity. And perhaps the process will humble us, which is a good thing. As Jesus says, humility is the path to exaltation (Luke 18:14). In our humility we can take our questions to God, seeking to find answers from him in prayer.

The Word of the Lord

While this prophetic narrative tells a strange story that raises difficult questions about the Bible and how to discern authentic prophecy, we need to move beyond merely asking questions into making applications from this text. Three points stand out from this passage about the word of God.

God's people focus on God's word. The narrator and the three prophets who speak here make at least eighteen references to the word of God in these

3. Dated January 1, 2011.

verses. They refer to it frequently, and it gives their message authority and power. Just as these prophets were guided and directed by God's word, it needs to be central in our lives and ministries. We need to be studying it both on our own and with others, not ignoring difficult texts like this one, because we believe all Scripture is inspired and profitable for teaching. Knowledge of God's word should make it harder for us to be deceived by people who may be claiming divine authority but, in reality, are teaching something that contradicts Scripture. Ultimately, a focus on the word of God is a focus on God.

God's word will come true. When God says something will happen, we can be confident that it will come to pass. In this passage, we see events that are fulfilled right away (the splitting of the altar and the deaths of the man of God and Jeroboam's son), ones that took place within a generation (the death of Jeroboam's heirs), and others in the distant future (the destruction of the Bethel altar, the exile of the Northern Kingdom). It is difficult to predict events in the immediate future because you will know right away whether you were right or wrong. Because they knew God's word comes true, each of these three prophets made a short-term prediction based on what they had heard from God, and each was instantly fulfilled.

God's word is powerful. God's word gives these prophets the power both to wound and to heal. It gives them power to confront kings and prophets about disobedience and idolatry. It gives them confidence to predict events that will happen right away and ones that are centuries in the future. Because of the power of Scripture, there are tragic implications for people who choose to disobey it. As we focus on God's word in our ministries, we will see the power of God at work, prompting people to repent, to reach out to people around them in service, and to reconcile with others and with God.

John's Gospel begins by boldly claiming not only that the Word (*logos*) was God, the Word was with God in the beginning, and all was created through the Word, but also that this divine Word became flesh and dwelt among humans (John 1:1–2, 14). Jesus, as the incarnate Word of God, lived a life focused on God's word as he constantly referred to Scripture (e.g., Matt 4:4, 7, 10; 11:10; 21:13; 26:24). He revealed how God's word was true and would be fulfilled (e.g., Luke 4:21; 21:22; 24:44). And finally, he demonstrated that the word of God is powerful (e.g., Mark 5:30; 6:2; 12:24; 13:26; 14:62).

CHAPTER 12

1 Kings 14:21–15:24

LISTEN to the Story

21Rehoboam son of Solomon was king in Judah. He was forty-one years old when he became king, and he reigned seventeen years in Jerusalem, the city the LORD had chosen out of all the tribes of Israel in which to put his Name. His mother's name was Naamah; she was an Ammonite.

22Judah did evil in the eyes of the LORD. By the sins they committed they stirred up his jealous anger more than those who were before them had done. 23They also set up for themselves high places, sacred stones and Asherah poles on every high hill and under every spreading tree. 24There were even male shrine prostitutes in the land; the people engaged in all the detestable practices of the nations the LORD had driven out before the Israelites.

25In the fifth year of King Rehoboam, Shishak king of Egypt attacked Jerusalem. 26He carried off the treasures of the temple of the LORD and the treasures of the royal palace. He took everything, including all the gold shields Solomon had made. 27So King Rehoboam made bronze shields to replace them and assigned these to the commanders of the guard on duty at the entrance to the royal palace. 28Whenever the king went to the LORD's temple, the guards bore the shields, and afterward they returned them to the guardroom.

29As for the other events of Rehoboam's reign, and all he did, are they not written in the book of the annals of the kings of Judah? 30There was continual warfare between Rehoboam and Jeroboam. 31And Rehoboam rested with his ancestors and was buried with them in the City of David. His mother's name was Naamah; she was an Ammonite. And Abijah his son succeeded him as king.

15:1In the eighteenth year of the reign of Jeroboam son of Nebat, Abijah became king of Judah, 2and he reigned in Jerusalem three years. His mother's name was Maakah daughter of Abishalom.

3He committed all the sins his father had done before him; his heart was not fully devoted to the LORD his God, as the heart of David his forefather had been. 4Nevertheless, for David's sake the LORD his God gave him a lamp in Jerusalem by raising up a son to succeed him and by making Jerusalem strong. 5For David had done what was right in the eyes of the LORD and had not failed to keep any of the LORD's commands all the days of his life—except in the case of Uriah the Hittite.

6There was war between Abijah and Jeroboam throughout Abijah's lifetime. 7As for the other events of Abijah's reign, and all he did, are they not written in the book of the annals of the kings of Judah? There was war between Abijah and Jeroboam. 8And Abijah rested with his ancestors and was buried in the City of David. And Asa his son succeeded him as king.

9In the twentieth year of Jeroboam king of Israel, Asa became king of Judah, 10and he reigned in Jerusalem forty-one years. His grandmother's name was Maakah daughter of Abishalom.

11Asa did what was right in the eyes of the LORD, as his father David had done. 12He expelled the male shrine prostitutes from the land and got rid of all the idols his ancestors had made. 13He even deposed his grandmother Maakah from her position as queen mother, because she had made a repulsive image for the worship of Asherah. Asa cut it down and burned it in the Kidron Valley. 14Although he did not remove the high places, Asa's heart was fully committed to the LORD all his life. 15He brought into the temple of the LORD the silver and gold and the articles that he and his father had dedicated.

16There was war between Asa and Baasha king of Israel throughout their reigns. 17Baasha king of Israel went up against Judah and fortified Ramah to prevent anyone from leaving or entering the territory of Asa king of Judah.

18Asa then took all the silver and gold that was left in the treasuries of the LORD's temple and of his own palace. He entrusted it to his officials and sent them to Ben-Hadad son of Tabrimmon, the son of Hezion, the king of Aram, who was ruling in Damascus. 19"Let there be a treaty between me and you," he said, "as there was between my father and your father. See, I am sending you a gift of silver and gold. Now break your treaty with Baasha king of Israel so he will withdraw from me."

20Ben-Hadad agreed with King Asa and sent the commanders of his forces against the towns of Israel. He conquered Ijon, Dan, Abel Beth

Maakah and all Kinnereth in addition to Naphtali. [21]When Baasha heard
this, he stopped building Ramah and withdrew to Tirzah. [22]Then King
Asa issued an order to all Judah—no one was exempt—and they carried
away from Ramah the stones and timber Baasha had been using there.
With them King Asa built up Geba in Benjamin, and also Mizpah.
[23]As for all the other events of Asa's reign, all his achievements, all he
did and the cities he built, are they not written in the book of the annals
of the kings of Judah? In his old age, however, his feet became diseased.
[24]Then Asa rested with his ancestors and was buried with them in the city
of his father David. And Jehoshaphat his son succeeded him as king.

Listening to the Text in the Story: Biblical Texts: 1 Kings 11:1–13; 12:22–24; Ancient Near Eastern Texts: Inscription from Kuntillet 'Ajrud; Amon Temple at Karnak List of Cities Captured by Shoshenq I; Ramesses II's Record of the Battle of Kadesh; The Kulamuwa Inscription

Terence Fretheim says, "Read 1 Kings 15–16 or 2 Kings 15 when you are having trouble getting to sleep!"[1] Many readers of Scripture may share Fretheim's sentiments about these next few chapters, which have a high density of detailed information about kings and very little engaging narrative material. Solomon's story is told over eleven chapters, so we get to know him well. The stories of nine rulers are told in just over two chapters (1 Kgs 14:21–16:34), so not surprisingly, only a few of them are familiar names. But anyone who agrees with Paul that all Scripture is inspired and profitable for teaching (2 Tim 3:16) should be able to find important lessons and applicable insights from these verses.

The focus of the text now shifts from Jeroboam in the north to Rehoboam and two of his successors in the south. Jeroboam has died, so the text backs up and looks at the reigns of the three southern rulers who overlapped with him: Rehoboam, Abijah, and Asa. (Throughout the divided monarchy, the Southern Kingdom is called Judah and the Northern Kingdom is called Israel.)

Solomon had a thousand wives and concubines, so there could have been a lot of tension between his sons to succeed him. Before Solomon came to power, his older brothers committed rape, fratricide, and rebellion (2 Sam 13; 15); after the deaths of Amnon, Absalom, and Adonijah, Solomon was the last

1. Fretheim, *First and Second Kings*, 2.

man standing. In the ancient Near East, royal power struggles were common (see for example, 2 Kgs 19:36–37). Rebellion and usurpation also dominated the northern throne throughout the history of the divided monarchy. But the text records no power struggle among Solomon's heirs. Rehoboam was somehow selected to succeed Solomon, perhaps because he was the oldest. The text informs us that Rehoboam's mother was an Ammonite woman named Naamah, one of Solomon's many foreign wives mentioned earlier (1 Kgs 11:1).

During the reign of Rehoboam, the nation of Judah continued in the idolatry that characterized Solomon's reign (11:2–13), and one of the objects they set up were Asherah poles. In the biblical text, "Asherah" can refer to a Canaanite goddess or to the sacred pole that represents the goddess; the latter is referred to in this passage (14:23). Throughout the history of the monarchy, Israel and Judah both set up and worshiped these cultic objects (e.g., 1 Kgs 14:15; 16:33; 18:19; 2 Kgs 13:6; 17:10; 21:3). Three righteous rulers, Asa in this section and Hezekiah and Josiah much later, enacted religious reforms, cutting down these sacred poles (1 Kgs 15:13; 2 Kgs 18:4; 23:4). Despite the efforts of these three reforming rulers, Asherah worship persisted during the monarchy. It is therefore not surprising that there are archaeological records of idolatrous worship practices, combining worship of YHWH and Asherah, as seen in this inscription on a pithos (a large ceramic jar) from Kuntillet 'Ajrud in northeastern Sinai: "I bless you by Yahweh of Samaria and his Asherah."[2] Thus, the syncretistic activities of the people of Israel and Judah recorded in Kings are thus supported by this and other comparable inscriptions.[3]

The end of the last section mentioned Jeroboam's wars but not his foes (1 Kgs 14:19); here we discover that two of them were Judean rulers (14:30; 15:7). Despite the exhortation to avoid civil war pronounced by Shemaiah the prophet (12:22–24), each of these three Judean rulers fought against their Israelite counterparts (14:30; 15:7, 16). During the reign of Rehoboam, the conflict was described as "continual warfare" (14:30).

To strengthen his position against Baasha of Israel, Asa of Judah paid Ben-Hadad the king of Aram with silver and gold to break his agreement with Israel and join him. Ben-Hadad switched sides and then attacked Israelite cities in the far north. The hiring of foreign armies to assist in battle was not uncommon in the ancient world. In his poetic account of the battle of Qadesh, Ramesses II of Egypt describes the desperate measures that his opponent, Muwatallis II of Hatti, took as he hired mercenary forces.

2. *COS* 2:171.

3. See also *COS* 2:172, 179.

He left no money in his land,
he had stripped himself of all his property;
He gave it to all the(se) countries,
to bring them with him, to fight.[4]

Similarly, a Phoenician ruler, Kulamuwa, speaks of his battle against a far stronger Danunian army that prompted him to hire help from the king of Assyria.[5]

Apparently Shishak, ruler of Egypt, needed no help in his campaign against Judah. Our passage records the attack of Shishak in Rehoboam's fifth year. Somehow, Egypt has gone from being an ally and trading partner (1 Kgs 3:1; 10:28) to playing host to enemies and being a military adversary against Israel (11:17–19, 40; 14:25).

In Egyptian sources this pharaoh is known as Sheshonq I or Shoshenk (943–922 BC). The south wall of the temple of Amon at Karnak lists cities from Palestine and Syria that were conquered by Sheshonq I, presumably on this campaign, including Beth-horon, Gibeon, Mahaniam, Rehob, Beth-shean, Megiddo, Penuel, and Succoth.[6] Since the Egyptian sources are unclear, we only know about the date of Sheshonq's invasion (923 BC) from this text (14:25), the fifth year of Rehoboam's reign.[7]

Rehoboam of Judah (14:21–31)

While Rehoboam's accession to the throne and the story of how his response to Jeroboam's request led to the division of the monarchy has already been recorded (1 Kgs 12), the text rewinds to the beginning of Rehoboam's reign, informing us that he was forty-one when he became king; then it fast-forwards to the end, stating that he ruled for seventeen years in Jerusalem. Typically, the length of reign is given for both northern and southern rulers, but only southern regnal formulas include accession age. Similarly, only the names of the mothers of Judean rulers are recorded in regnal formulas.

4. *COS* 2:34.

5. *COS* 2:147.

6. For the list of cities, see *ANET*, 242–43; for an image of the wall, see *ANEP*, 118, 290 (image #349).

7. See the discussion in Cogan, *I Kings*, 388, 390.

Rehoboam's mother was Naamah the Ammonite, presumably one of Solomon's foreign wives mentioned earlier (11:1). While the text does not make the connection explicit, the fact that her name and nationality are mentioned twice suggests it was important (14:21, 31). The first reference to his mother comes immediately before the text itemizes Rehoboam's idolatry. For his father, the text made it clear that Solomon's foreign wives contributed to his apostasy. Molech, the god of the Ammonites, was one of the idols Solomon worshiped (11:5).

Typically, regnal formulas for both kingdoms next record an evaluation of the king, how they either did good or, more often, did evil "in the eyes of the LORD." Instead of evaluating Rehoboam, here the text evaluates the entire nation of Judah. The Septuagint here and the parallel in Chronicles both speak of Rehoboam doing evil (2 Chr 12:14).[8] Rehoboam's son, Abijah, will be judged for committing "all the sins his father had done" (1 Kgs 15:3). To support this negative assessment, the text lists all the idolatrous behavior that had provoked YHWH to jealous anger (14:22–24). They had set up places of worship associated with other gods: high places (see "High Places," Chapter 3), sacred stones, and Asherah poles. The sacred stones (*massebot*) and sacred poles, called Asherah, were used in worship practices at sacred locations to signify devotion to a deity.

Additionally, in the land there were literally "those set apart as holy" (*qedeshim*, masculine plural) which is often translated "male shrine prostitutes" (14:24). Wray Beal translates the term as "male cult personnel," since she thinks the traditional view that they were prostitutes is no longer valid.[9] We are not sure who these people were or what they did, but despite possible positive connotations with the root Hebrew word ("sacred"), these people clearly are not holy.

Several points can be made about these *qedeshim*. They are viewed highly negatively, spoken about here in the contexts of idolatry and detestable practices (14:22–24). Elsewhere in the book, reforming rulers such as Asa, Jehoshaphat, and Josiah expelled them from the land (15:12; 22:46; 2 Kgs 23:7). While it is difficult to say from the context what these *qedeshim* were doing in Kings, other biblical texts connect the word explicitly to prostitution. Tamar pretended to be a prostitute to trick her father-in-law Judah into impregnating her, in order to propagate heirs for her deceased husband's line, and the feminine singular form of the term is used to describe her behavior

8. See Wiseman, *1 & 2 Kings*, 151.
9. See Wray Beal, *1 & 2 Kings*, 204–5.

(Gen 38:21 [2x], 22). The book of Deuteronomy forbade the sons and daughters of Israel from becoming *qedeshim* in the context of other laws concerning prostitutes (Deut 23:17–18).[10] Hosea condemns Israel for playing the harlot, committing adultery, and sacrificing with "shrine prostitutes" (using the feminine plural form *qedeshot*; 4:14). The evidence of other texts supports the idea that they were cult prostitutes.

While 1 Kings 14 does not make it explicit, in Chronicles the prophet Shemaiah explains to Rehoboam that the invasion of Shishak, the ruler of Egypt who earlier hosted the fugitive Jeroboam (11:40), took place because they abandoned YHWH (2 Chr 12:2–5). However, the Chronicler records that when the leaders and the king humbled themselves, God prevented Shishak from destroying them (12:6–9). Here Shishak carried off treasures from the temple and the palace, including all the five hundred gold shields (two hundred large, three hundred small) from the Palace of the Forest of Lebanon that his father made (1 Kgs 10:16–17). While some commentators think this action was an "attempt to buy off Shishak" by Rehoboam,[11] it was probably a premeditated plundering by the Egyptian ruler and not a voluntary gift from the Judean ruler (14:26). The bronze shields made by Rehoboam to replace his father's gold ones (v. 27) would have been much less valuable, signifying how far Jerusalem had fallen economically since the prosperous days of the Solomonic empire.

Rehoboam's concluding regnal formula provides no new information except that he experienced "continual warfare" with Jeroboam (v. 30). To reconcile this comment about perpetual war with the statement that Rehoboam heeded the word of Shemaiah to not engage in civil war (12:24), one must interpret this one as hyperbole—after an initial period of peace, warfare was constant between north and south.

Abijah of Judah (15:1–8)

The narrative of Abijah of Judah is one of the shortest for a southern king, only eight verses, with little narrative details included about his life and relatively short three-year reign. Most English translations call this Judean ruler "Abijam" based on the majority of Hebrew manuscripts, but the NIV follows the Septuagint and 2 Chronicles (12:16; 13:1, 2), which call him "Abijah." The name "Abijah" means "my father is YHWH," and his portrayal in Chronicles is more favorable. In Kings he follows in the evil deeds of his

10. For a discussion of biblical laws about prostitutes, see Lamb, *Prostitutes and Polygamists*, 89–90.

11. For example, see William H. Barnes, *1–2 Kings* (Carol Stream: Tyndale House, 2012), 132.

father Rehoboam, and his name is also less pious ("Abijam" means "my father is the sea"). Curiously, both Rehoboam and Jeroboam have sons named Abijah (1 Kgs 14:1), an ironic name for the sons of idolaters.

After Rehoboam's death, Abijah comes to power in the eighteenth year of Jeroboam (14:31–15:1). These chronological comments dating each king's reign from the perspective of their counterparts are called synchronisms, and this is the first of many in the book (see excursus "Northern and Southern Synchronisms" below). Since Rehoboam reigned for seventeen years (14:21), Jeroboam must have become ruler in the first year of Rehoboam's reign. For most southern rulers (seventeen of nineteen), their age of accession is recorded; the only rulers lacking this bit of information are Abijah and his son Asa.

Abijah's mother was Maakah, daughter of Abishalom, which is another form of Absalom. Because David's son Absalom only had one daughter and her name was Tamar (2 Sam 14:27), some scholars are hesitant to identify Abijah's grandfather with the long-haired usurper who got caught hanging in a tree during his failed rebellion (2 Sam 15–18),[12] but there is still sufficient reason to suggest he is intended here. The word translated as "mother" here could mean "ancestor" or "grandmother," which is what it means at the beginning of the Asa narrative in a few verses (1 Kgs 15:10). Abijah's mother's name is Maakah, which was also the name of Absalom's mother (2 Sam 3:3); it is reasonable to assume a daughter would be named after one of her female ancestors. The tandem Maakah and Abishalom appears to be important since, instead of stating who Asa's mother was at the beginning of his narrative, it states who his grandmother was (1 Kgs 15:10). Finally, in 2 Chronicles 11:20–22 the name is spelled "Absalom," and the only other Absalom mentioned in Chronicles is the son of David (1 Chr 3:2).

While we cannot speak definitively about Abijah's maternal ancestry, on his paternal side his great-grandfather David is mentioned four times in this short narrative (1 Kgs 15:3, 4, 5, 8). The text reports that Abijah followed in the sins of his father and that his heart was not like David's, fully devoted to YHWH (v. 3), but because YHWH wanted to give David a lamp in Jerusalem, he would allow him to stay on the throne. This is the second of three so-called lamp oracles (11:36; 15:4; 2 Kgs 8:19; see also "Dynastic Promises in Kings" in Chapter 9), allowing David's heirs to remain in power despite their evil behavior. This verse is the only time the book of Kings alludes to David's affair with Bathsheba. The text here records how he kept YHWH's commands

12. For example, see Alter, *Former Prophets*, 686; Wiseman, *1 & 2 Kings*, 154; Wray Beal, *1 & 2 Kings*, 210.

all his life, "except in the matter of Uriah the Hittite" (1 Kgs 15:5; see "The Righteous portrayal of David in Kings" in Chapter 3), but the attitude toward David is far from harsh as the language used is vague with no mention of adultery, rape, murder, or the name of Bathsheba.

Over the course of the next few chapters we will see a high density of regnal formulas (e.g., 15:9–11, 23–26, 31–34; 16:5–6, 8, 14, 20, 25–28), so they will become familiar. Abijah's concluding regnal formula is standard (15:6–8; his other activities, the royal annals reference, resting with ancestors, his successor), except for two statements about warfare. In the NIV the first statement reads, "There was war between Abijah and Jeroboam throughout Abijah's lifetime" (15:6), and the second one reads, "There was war between Abijah and Jeroboam" (v. 7). Both statements agree, but when virtually identical statements like this appear in the text, scholars often assume that they can be explained by dittography, an accidental repetition by a scribe or copyist.[13] In the Septuagint, the first statement (v. 6) is entirely absent, which would support the idea of dittography. The other problem appears when we look at other English translations of 15:6 as they speak of war between Jeroboam and Rehoboam, not Abijah (e.g., ESV, NAS, NRS, KJV). The translation of Rehoboam receives the support of the majority of the Hebrew manuscripts, but the NIV probably reflects what was intended, since that is what 15:7 states and the context of this comment is Abijah's narrative. Alter reasonably assumes "Rehoboam" here refers to his house, which would therefore include Abijah.[14]

Excursus: Northern and Southern Synchronisms

As the story of the divided monarchy is told (1 Kings 13 to 2 Kings 17), the focus of the narrative shifts between north and south. To allow the text to record the complete story of a ruler, the narration is not strictly chronological, since kings from the different kingdoms rarely died at the same time. For example, after the death of Jeroboam is recorded (1 Kgs 14:19–20), the text backs up and finishes reporting on the three Judean rulers who overlapped with him (Rehoboam, Abijah, and Asa). After recording the death of Asa (1 Kgs 15:24), the text goes back and reports on the six Israelite rulers who overlapped with him (Nadab, Baasha, Elah, Zimri, Omri, and Ahab). Asa overlapped with six northern rulers because he reigned a long time (forty-one years), and three of these Israelite rulers

13. See Cogan, *I Kings*, 393; Barnes, *1–2 Kings*, 134.
14. Alter, *Former Prophets*, 686.

had exceptionally short reigns (Nadab: two years; Zimri: seven days; Elah: two years).

In order to date when each ruler came to power, a synchronism with the other kingdom is provided for most of these rulers. There are twenty-eight synchronisms in Kings. The synchronism dates the beginning of one king's reign relative to the other ruler who is already on the throne. The first synchronism is southern (15:1), focused on King Abijah of Judah, and his synchronism informs us that he came to power during the eighteenth year of Jeroboam of Israel. Seventeen of the nineteen northern rulers have synchronisms; only Jeroboam I and Jehu lack one. All eleven of the southern rulers of the divided monarchy (after Rehoboam) have a synchronism.

Asa of Judah (15:9–24)

Asa, son of Abijah, came to power in the twentieth year of Jeroboam, and he reigned forty-one years, longer than any previous ruler of Israel or Judah. The only king after him with a longer reign was Manasseh of Judah, who reigned fifty-five years (2 Kgs 21:1). Jeroboam II of Israel also reigned forty-one years (14:23), while David and Solomon both reigned only forty years (1 Kgs 2:11; 11:42). Deuteronomy's law of the king states that rulers who read and keep the law will live a long time (Deut 17:19–20), thus Asa's long reign is consistent with Deuteronomy since he was evaluated as righteous (1 Kgs 15:11). However, the long reigns of evil Manasseh and Jeroboam II are problematic from the perspective of Deuteronomy (2 Kgs 14:24; 21:2).

Asa is the first ruler of the divided monarchy to receive a righteous evaluation: "he did what was right in the eyes of the Lord" (1 Kgs 15:11). He is first praised as being like David (v. 11), the yardstick that many other rulers, particularly Judean, are measured by, either positively like Asa (e.g., 2 Kgs 18:3; 22:2) or, more often, negatively like Abijah (e.g., 1 Kgs 14:8; 15:3; 2 Kgs 14:3; 16:2). The text calls David his father, but the word "father" (*'av*) can mean ancestor; David was his great-great-grandfather.

Asa's actions as a reformer are what earned him his favorable assessment. He expelled the male prostitutes that his grandfather Rehoboam had allowed in the land (1 Kgs 14:24; 15:12). He got rid of idols his ancestors made (15:12), which presumably included the sacred stones and Asherah that were prevalent in Judah during the reigns of Rehoboam and Abijah (14:23; 15:3). He removed Maakah, his grandmother, from being queen mother (*gebirah*) and cut down and burned the Asherah pole she had constructed. While the position of *gebirah* is only mentioned a few times in the book (11:19; 15:13; 2 Kgs 5:3; 10:13), the fact that the mothers of the Judean king are mentioned in their introductory regnal formulas suggests that this was a constant position throughout the period of the southern monarchy, providing an element of additional stability during royal transitions.

The tone of the language here is highly polemical, which is not unusual in contexts describing judgments for idolatry (e.g., 1 Kgs 14:7–14; 21:20–24). The word translated as "idols" (15:12) is *gillulim,* which comes from root for "dung." The word translated as "repulsive" (v. 13), modifying the Asherah, is *mipletset.* Since *mipletset* appears rarely in the Old Testament (only here and in the parallel text in 2 Chr 15:16), we are not sure what it means; most commentators assume it connotes an object of horror.[15] The word is actually repeated twice in 15:13, but unfortunately most English translations only render it once (except the NASB).

While Asa performed many acts to help the nation focus their worship on YHWH, the text also records other behaviors that reflect negatively upon him. Asa was one of six southern rulers who received qualified righteous evaluations; the others were Jehoshaphat, Jehoash, Amaziah, Azariah, and Jotham (1 Kgs 22:43; 2 Kgs 12:2; 14:3; 15:3; 15:34). For each of these six rulers, the qualification is based on the fact that they, like Asa in this passage (1 Kgs 15:14), didn't remove the high places (22:43; 2 Kgs 12:3; 14:4; 15:4, 35; see "High Places" in Chapter 3).

While the text only condemns Asa's not removing the high places, other actions of his can be viewed negatively in light of other texts. He engaged in a civil war with Baasha of Israel (1 Kgs 15:16), even though Shemaiah had told Rehoboam to avoid it (12:24). He also sent tribute to Ben-Hadad of Aram (15:18–19), which would have been viewed negatively for two reasons. First, the silver and gold for the tribute were taken from the temple (he also took from his own palace), so valuables that had been dedicated to YHWH were now handed over to foreigners. Second, dependence on foreign nations like Aram was often condemned, since YHWH wanted his people to rely exclusively on him. In the parallel passage in Chronicles, the seer Hanani condemns Asa for trusting in Aram and not in YHWH (2 Chr 16:7–9).

There are several Aramean rulers named Ben-Hadad mentioned in Kings (1 Kgs 15:18; 20:1–34; 2 Kgs 13:3). The name Ben-Hadad in Hebrew literally means "son of the god Hadad" (equivalent to "Bar-Hadad" in Aramaic) and appears to be merely a generic throne name for the king of Aram, analogous

15. See Barnes, *1–2 Kings*, 136; Wray Beal, *1 & 2 Kings*, 212.

to "Pharaoh" as the king of Egypt. Asa's generous gift convinces Ben-Hadad to help him, and, as he attacked cities in the far north, Baasha had to stop building his fortifications in the far south at Ramah, a city only about five miles north of Jerusalem. If Baasha had completed his fort at Ramah, it would have been a major threat to Judah. But Baasha needed to return to Tirzah, the first capital of Israel (1 Kgs 14:17). After Baasha left, Asa conscripted "all Judah—no one was exempt" (15:22) to remove the stones and timber, thus destroying Baasha's work. He then used the materials to build up his own fortifications at Geba (two miles east of Ramah) and Mizpah (three miles north of Ramah), cities along his northern border, thus preventing Baasha or other northern rulers from refortifying Ramah in the future.

Unique aspects of Asa's concluding regnal formula include a reference to the cities he built (Geba, Mitzah, and perhaps others) and his foot disease that came in his old age (v. 23). While scholars speculate about the type of disease (Wiseman suggests gangrene; Talmudic sources thought gout)[16] or about how it contributed to his death (see Cogan, DeVries),[17] the text yields few clues regarding any of these theories. His son, Jehoshaphat, succeeded him, but the text backs up historically to cover the reigns of six northern rulers, so he will not reappear in the narrative until the end of the book (1 Kgs 22:41).

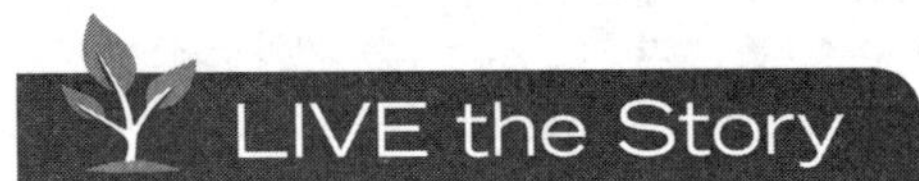

The Eyes of the Lord

As one reads the entire history of the monarchies of Israel and Judah, one can easily get discouraged by the prevalence of evil. Most rulers were evil—all the northern kings (except Jehu) and the majority of the southern kings, including the first two (Rehoboam and Abijah). If you are looking for positive role models in the Old Testament, you won't find many among these rulers.

Just as we ask today when evil surrounds us and it seems like no one is doing good, we might ask about the period of the monarchy, "Where is God here?"[18] God's anger is stirred up over Judah's sins (1 Kgs 14:22), but other than that he appears here to be passive. He doesn't seem to care that the temple treasury was plundered by both Shishak of Egypt and Asa of Judah. Judah is practicing idolatry in a wide variety of creative ways, and he sends no prophet to condemn them, nor does he confront any rulers directly like

16. See Wiseman, *1 & 2 Kings*, 157.
17. Cogan, *I Kings*, 402; DeVries, *1 Kings*, 191.
18. We will revisit the question "Where is God?" in Chapters 31 and 40.

he did with Solomon (11:11–13). While we don't know many details, Israel and Judah are engaged in a decades-long civil war (15:6–7, 16, 32), and God does nothing to stop it. The authors of this section of Kings seem more concerned about recording information regarding the details of how long kings reigned, where they were buried, and who succeeded them than how God was responding to the preponderance of sin.

We look for God here in Kings and can't seem to find him. When God seems to be absent, people are more likely to act in an evil manner, so things just get worse. Where there is no accountability, sin increases.

Anyone who has been a victim of an internet troll knows why this happens. Joel Stein recently wrote about anonymous evil in a cover story for *Time* magazine titled, "Why We're Losing the Internet to the Culture of Hate."[19] One of the reasons trolls freely spout forth vicious and violent speech on the internet is that they are anonymous. Stein states, "Psychologists call this the online disinhibition effect, in which factors like anonymity, invisibility, a lack of authority and not communicating in real time strip away the mores society spent millennia building." Trolls think their actions are invisible, no one sees what they are doing. The hatred and violence they spew rarely gets expressed in public settings.

Trolls on the internet and rulers in Judah and Israel may think their actions are anonymous, but God always sees what we do, and he is looking on at these kings. Even though he doesn't do much in this passage, he sees what is going on. The phrase "the eyes of the LORD" appears three times in this section (14:22; 15:5, 11) and forty-two times in the entire book (e.g., 11:6; 15:26, 34; 16:7, 19, 25, 30). God sees everything done by the evil kings of Kings. The text could have simply said a ruler was evil, full stop, but the text emphasizes that their behavior, whether good or bad, was always witnessed by YHWH. Four kings are evaluated in this passage: two do evil (Rehoboam, Abijah), and two do good (David, Asa). Asa's father Abijah, his grandfather Rehoboam, and great-grandfather Solomon were idolaters, but he was able to follow the example of his great-great-grandfather, David. Their status as ruler may have given these kings a false impression of immunity, but God still witnessed all they did.

It is essential that we are constantly reminded that God is a witness to everything we do today. The anonymity of the internet has given rise not just to trolls but also to an epidemic of pornography. One way many Christians have overcome porn addictions is through services like Covenant Eyes, which

19. Joel Stein, "Why We're Losing the Internet to the Culture of Hate," *Time*, August 29, 2016.

provides protection from harmful internet sites. But there are still many ways to sin away from the internet. We all need to be reminded that all we do is seen by God.

God is looking for righteous rulers, and while a few are highly praised in the text (David, Hezekiah, Josiah), even they have serious sins. When the story of the monarchy ends, God still hasn't found what he's looking for. The search for a truly righteous ruler continues until we get to the New Testament, where we finally encounter Jesus. Coincidentally, as we are introduced to Jesus through his family tree, we also find the only passage in the New Testament where we see Rehoboam, Abijah, and Asa, the three kings featured in our passage (Matt 1:7–8). Jesus is introduced as the only righteous son of David, the Messiah, who, despite his evil ancestors, will die for the evil committed by all of us in the eyes of God. Part of how he revealed his righteousness was to be willing to be baptized (3:15). And as he emerged from the water he saw God's Spirit descend upon him like a dove, and he heard God's voice declare that he was the beloved son of God in whom God was well pleased (3:16–17).

Jesus also reminded his followers that all we do is seen by God in the Sermon on the Mount (chs. 5–7). When he spoke to his disciples about practicing their acts of piety—giving alms, praying, and fasting—he reminds them three times that their Father who sees in secret will reward them (6:4, 6, 18). God sees both the good and the bad we do. As we remember that our Father in heaven is watching our behavior, hopefully we will be motivated to act righteously. Fortunately, even when we don't act as we should, we know we have a God who is also looking to show mercy to repentant sinners (Luke 15:3–10).

"Christmas Bells"

In the middle of another civil war, over twenty-seven centuries after the one between Israel and Judah, eighteen-year-old Charles Appleton Longfellow left his home in Cambridge, Massachusetts, and got on a train headed to Washington, D.C. He told no one in his family what he was up to. He wanted to fight for the army of President Lincoln in the American Civil War.

On November 27, 1863, Charles was severely wounded in the Battle of New Hope Church (Virginia). He was shot in his left shoulder. His father, Henry David Longfellow, received a telegram a few days later. Longfellow, who had recently lost his beloved wife Frances in a fire, was inspired on December 25, 1863, to write about his despair and his hope in the poem "Christmas Bells," which starts out rather hopefully.

I heard the bells on Christmas Day
Their old familiar carols play.
And wild and sweet
The words repeat
Of peace on earth, good will to men!

But the tone changes in stanzas four and five as he speaks of how "the cannon thundered in the south" and "an earthquake rent the hearth-stones of a continent." Unfortunately, stanzas four and five are omitted in "I Heard the Bells on Christmas Day," the carol based on Longfellow's poem.[20] But his anguished cry of stanza six is included.

And in despair I bowed my head;
"There is no peace on earth," I said;
"For hate is strong
And mocks the song
Of peace on earth, good-will to men!"

The nation is ravaged by war; its sons are dying by the thousands. Where is God? Is he watching? In the midst of Longfellow's despair, the bells deliver a final message.

Then pealed the bells more loud and deep:
"God is not dead; nor doth he sleep!
The Wrong shall fail,
The Right prevail,
With peace on earth, good-will to men."

Peace does come with the arrival to earth of the descendant of Rehoboam, Abijah, and Asa, the only righteous son of David, the Prince of Peace, Jesus the Christ. And after his birth, the angels declared to the shepherds, "On earth peace, good will toward men" (Luke 2:14 KJV).

20. Music by John Baptiste Calkin.

CHAPTER 13

1 Kings 15:25–16:34

LISTEN to the Story

25Nadab son of Jeroboam became king of Israel in the second year of
Asa king of Judah, and he reigned over Israel two years. 26He did evil in
the eyes of the LORD, following the ways of his father and committing the
same sin his father had caused Israel to commit.
27Baasha son of Ahijah from the tribe of Issachar plotted against him,
and he struck him down at Gibbethon, a Philistine town, while Nadab
and all Israel were besieging it. 28Baasha killed Nadab in the third year of
Asa king of Judah and succeeded him as king.
29As soon as he began to reign, he killed Jeroboam's whole family. He
did not leave Jeroboam anyone that breathed, but destroyed them all,
according to the word of the LORD given through his servant Ahijah the
Shilonite. 30This happened because of the sins Jeroboam had committed
and had caused Israel to commit, and because he aroused the anger of the
LORD, the God of Israel.
31As for the other events of Nadab's reign, and all he did, are they not
written in the book of the annals of the kings of Israel? 32There was war
between Asa and Baasha king of Israel throughout their reigns.
33In the third year of Asa king of Judah, Baasha son of Ahijah became
king of all Israel in Tirzah, and he reigned twenty-four years. 34He did evil
in the eyes of the LORD, following the ways of Jeroboam and committing
the same sin Jeroboam had caused Israel to commit.
16:1Then the word of the LORD came to Jehu son of Hanani concerning Baasha: 2"I lifted you up from the dust and appointed you ruler over
my people Israel, but you followed the ways of Jeroboam and caused my
people Israel to sin and to arouse my anger by their sins. 3So I am about
to wipe out Baasha and his house, and I will make your house like that of
Jeroboam son of Nebat. 4Dogs will eat those belonging to Baasha who die
in the city, and birds will feed on those who die in the country."

5As for the other events of Baasha's reign, what he did and his achievements, are they not written in the book of the annals of the kings of Israel?
6Baasha rested with his ancestors and was buried in Tirzah. And Elah his
son succeeded him as king.

7Moreover, the word of the LORD came through the prophet Jehu son
of Hanani to Baasha and his house, because of all the evil he had done in
the eyes of the LORD, arousing his anger by the things he did, becoming
like the house of Jeroboam—and also because he destroyed it.

8In the twenty-sixth year of Asa king of Judah, Elah son of Baasha
became king of Israel, and he reigned in Tirzah two years.

9Zimri, one of his officials, who had command of half his chariots,
plotted against him. Elah was in Tirzah at the time, getting drunk in the
home of Arza, the palace administrator at Tirzah. 10Zimri came in, struck
him down and killed him in the twenty-seventh year of Asa king of Judah.
Then he succeeded him as king.

11As soon as he began to reign and was seated on the throne, he
killed off Baasha's whole family. He did not spare a single male, whether
relative or friend. 12So Zimri destroyed the whole family of Baasha, in
accordance with the word of the LORD spoken against Baasha through
the prophet Jehu—13because of all the sins Baasha and his son Elah had
committed and had caused Israel to commit, so that they aroused the anger
of the LORD, the God of Israel, by their worthless idols.

14As for the other events of Elah's reign, and all he did, are they not
written in the book of the annals of the kings of Israel?

15In the twenty-seventh year of Asa king of Judah, Zimri reigned in
Tirzah seven days. The army was encamped near Gibbethon, a Philistine
town. 16When the Israelites in the camp heard that Zimri had plotted
against the king and murdered him, they proclaimed Omri, the commander of the army, king over Israel that very day there in the camp. 17Then
Omri and all the Israelites with him withdrew from Gibbethon and laid
siege to Tirzah. 18When Zimri saw that the city was taken, he went into
the citadel of the royal palace and set the palace on fire around him. So he
died, 19because of the sins he had committed, doing evil in the eyes of the
LORD and following the ways of Jeroboam and committing the same sin
Jeroboam had caused Israel to commit.

20As for the other events of Zimri's reign, and the rebellion he carried
out, are they not written in the book of the annals of the kings of Israel?

[21]Then the people of Israel were split into two factions; half supported Tibni son of Ginath for king, and the other half supported Omri. [22]But Omri's followers proved stronger than those of Tibni son of Ginath. So Tibni died and Omri became king.

[23]In the thirty-first year of Asa king of Judah, Omri became king of Israel, and he reigned twelve years, six of them in Tirzah. [24]He bought the hill of Samaria from Shemer for two talents of silver and built a city on the hill, calling it Samaria, after Shemer, the name of the former owner of the hill.

[25]But Omri did evil in the eyes of the LORD and sinned more than all those before him. [26]He followed completely the ways of Jeroboam son of Nebat, committing the same sin Jeroboam had caused Israel to commit, so that they aroused the anger of the LORD, the God of Israel, by their worthless idols.

[27]As for the other events of Omri's reign, what he did and the things he achieved, are they not written in the book of the annals of the kings of Israel? [28]Omri rested with his ancestors and was buried in Samaria. And Ahab his son succeeded him as king.

[29]In the thirty-eighth year of Asa king of Judah, Ahab son of Omri became king of Israel, and he reigned in Samaria over Israel twenty-two years. [30]Ahab son of Omri did more evil in the eyes of the LORD than any of those before him. [31]He not only considered it trivial to commit the sins of Jeroboam son of Nebat, but he also married Jezebel daughter of Ethbaal king of the Sidonians, and began to serve Baal and worship him. [32]He set up an altar for Baal in the temple of Baal that he built in Samaria. [33]Ahab also made an Asherah pole and did more to arouse the anger of the LORD, the God of Israel, than did all the kings of Israel before him.

[34]In Ahab's time, Hiel of Bethel rebuilt Jericho. He laid its foundations at the cost of his firstborn son Abiram, and he set up its gates at the cost of his youngest son Segub, in accordance with the word of the LORD spoken by Joshua son of Nun.

Listening to the Text in the Story: Biblical Text: Joshua 6:26; Ancient Near Eastern Texts: The Mesha Stele; The Black Obelisk of Shalmaneser III; The Annals of Shalmaneser III; The Annals of Tiglath-Pileser III; The Annals of Sargon II; The Jezebel Seal

While readers with a devotional interest may not appreciate 1 Kings 15 and 16, readers with a historical interest should be excited as we begin to meet Israelite rulers that are mentioned in important ancient Near Eastern inscriptions: Omri and his son Ahab. The narrative of Omri is limited to eight verses (16:21–28), and he is only mentioned by name thirteen times in the Old Testament (all in Kings), suggesting he was a relatively minor king. However, Omri is mentioned at least fourteen times in extrabiblical texts, far more than any other ruler of Israel or Judah, which could suggest he was more significant than any other, perhaps more so even than David or Solomon.

The most significant reference to Omri appears in the Mesha Stele (also called the Moabite Stone). In 1868 a local Bedouin named Zattam, in what is now Jordan, showed a German missionary named Frederick Augustus Klein a black basalt stone. Unfortunately, in a dispute over the ownership among the Germans, the French, and the Turks, the stele was badly damaged by local Arab tribesmen. Fortunately, a "squeeze" (a paper-mache impression) was made before it was damaged. The stele was reconstructed based on the squeeze, and it is now located in the Louvre.

> I am Mesha, the son of Kemosh, the king of Moab, the Dibonite . . .
>
> **Omri** was the king of ***Israel***, and he oppressed Moab for many days, for Kemosh was angry with his land. And his son succeeded him, and he said—he too—"I will oppress Moab!"
>
> In my days did he say [so] but I looked down on him and on his house, and ***Israel*** has gone to ruin, yes, it has gone to ruin for ever! And **Omri** had taken possession of the whole la[n]d of Medeba, and he lived there (in) his days and half the days of his son, forty years, but Kemosh [resto] red it in my days . . .
>
> The king of ***Israel*** built Ataroth for himself, and I fought against the city, and I captured it, and I killed all the people [from] the city as a sacrifice(?) for Kemosh and for Moab . . .
>
> And Kemosh said to me: "Go take Nebo from ***Israel***!" And I went in the night, and I fought against it from the break of dawn until noon, and I took it, and I killed [its] whole population, 7000 male citizens and aliens, and servant girls; for I had put it to the ban for Ashtar Kemosh. And from there, I took th[e ves]sels of YHWH, and I hauled them before the face of Kemosh.
>
> And the king of ***Israel*** had built Jahaz, and he stayed there during his campaigns against me, and Kemosh drove him away before my face.[1]

1. *COS* 2:137.

The discovery of the Mesha Stele is one of the most significant archaeological finds in the region, particularly for biblical studies. It is dated to about 835 BC, and it contains the earliest certain ancient reference to YHWH, the God of Israel. It is the longest Iron Age inscription found in the region. While three other ancient inscriptions each mention Israel once (the Kurkh Monolith, the Tel Dan Stele, and the Merneptah Stele), the Mesha inscription refers to Israel by name five times and to Omri twice. While the account of Omri's reign in Kings is brief and includes no details of wars or battles, the Mesha Stele provides crucial background regarding his conquest of and rule over Moab.

Just as the Israelites had provoked the anger of YHWH under Omri (and Nadab, Baasha, Elah, and Ahab), so had the Moabites, according to this inscription, provoked the anger of Kemosh, their god. The inscription also speaks of Omri's son continuing the oppressive policies of his father. The son of Omri who succeeded him was Ahab, but based on the events described, the son referenced here may be his grandson Jehoram,[2] since he and Mesha waged a war that is recorded in 2 Kings 3.

While the inscription speaks of Israel's ruin, this hyperbolic language is typical for stelae like this, which was an ancient form of political spin. Mesha begins his reign with Israel oppressing Moab, and, because of Mesha's amazingness, now the cursed Israelites are in ruin. It is possible this period of weakening may refer to Israel's losses suffered under Jehu (2 Kgs 10:32–33).[3]

Omri is also mentioned briefly in twelve Neo-Assyrian inscriptions (see Table 10 in the Introduction), four associated with Shalmaneser III, one with Adad-nirari III, three with Tiglath-Pileser III, and four with Sargon II.[4] All of these inscriptions mentioning Omri are dated after his death. Four of them call Jehu, the ruler who killed Omri's grandson Jehoram and wiped out his family (2 Kgs 9–10), a "son of Omri."[5] Six of them mention Omri in the context of describing Israel as "the land of the house of Omri." For reasons we cannot be certain of, in Assyrian inscriptions the land and royal dynasty of Israel are associated with Omri, even long after he and his descendants had lost power. Curiously, it is not David, Solomon, or Jeroboam who becomes the ruler most famously associated with Israel outside their borders, but Omri the father of Ahab.

2. See *COS* 2:137, n. 7.

3. See also *COS* 2:137, n. 8.

4. For a discussion of the twenty Assyrian inscriptions mentioning Israelite rulers, see Lamb, *Righteous Jehu*, 29–40.

5. E.g., *ANET*, 280, 281.

The Kurkh Monolith of Shalmaneser III mentions King Ahab of Israel among a coalition of twelve states from Syria-Palestine that opposed Shalmaneser at the battle of Qarqar (853 BC). This reference to Ahab is important, since it is probably the oldest extant reference to a ruler of Israel or Judah. The Tel Dan inscription mentions "the house of David," but it is typically dated at least a decade after the Kurkh inscription.[6] The Mesha Stele mentions Ahab's father Omri, but it is written after Omri's death and is typically dated about fifteen years after the Kurkh inscription.

The Kurkh inscription does not provide much information about Ahab, Israel, or any of their allies—except the size of each army. According to the inscription, Ahab had a sizable force that included two thousand chariots and ten thousand soldiers.[7] The two main partners in the coalition opposing Shalmaneser were Ahab of Israel and Hadad-ezer of Aram. Hadad-ezer had more soldiers than Ahab (twenty thousand vs. ten thousand), but Ahab had more chariots (two thousand vs. one thousand, two hundred). The Hadad-ezer mentioned in the Kurkh Inscription is not the Hadad-ezer from the time of Solomon (1 Kgs 11:23), but he may be Ben-hadad II, Ahab's rival (ch. 20).[8]

The name of Ahab's wife Jezebel appears on an ancient stamp seal now located in the Israel Museum in Jerusalem. Seals were often used as official authorizations when signing ancient documents.[9] Jezebel uses Ahab's seal to forge letters to frame and essentially murder Naboth so her husband could take possession of his vineyard (ch. 21). While it is difficult to make definitive determinations about the identity of a name from a seal, because of its large size and elaborate decoration, Korpel argues that this seal that appears to have her name on it was "fit for a queen," specifically Jezebel of Israel.[10]

The identifications of Omri, Ahab, and Jezebel from these inscriptions are not without issues, but there is a general consensus among scholars, at least about the two northern kings, that they are indeed the individuals being referred to. While a small minority of scholars persist in arguing that ancient Israel was a fictional creation of ancient scribes, these numerous references to Omri, Ahab, and Mesha (as well as many others to be discussed in subsequent chapters) provide significant external validation for the historicity of the book of Kings.

---

6. For a discussion of the Tel Dan Inscription and the relevant historical issues, see Lamb, *Righteous Jehu*, 102–10.

7. *COS* 2:263d.

8. See *COS* 2:263, n. 23.

9. See also my discussion of seals in Leuchter and Lamb, *Historical Writings*, 301–5.

10. Marjo C. A. Korpel, "Fit for a Queen: Jezebel's Royal Seal," *BAR* 34.2 (2008): 32–37, 80.

EXPLAIN the Story

Perhaps one of the reasons Fretheim considers this section a cure for insomnia (see last chapter) is because it is highly formulaic, with language repeated both within this passage and in other regnal narratives in the book. To work through the narratives of these six northern rulers, we will begin with a brief discussion of each of their reigns: Nadab, Baasha, Elah, Zimri, Omri, and Ahab. This will be followed by examinations of unique aspects of their regnal formulas, rebellions, and prophetic judgments, comparing each of these to similar phenomena elsewhere in the book of Kings. A consistent theme permeating this passage is the evilness of these six northern rulers.

This passage narrates the reigns of three of Israel's shortest reigning rulers: Nadab, Elah, and Zimri. Nadab and Elah are members of a distinguished club among the northern rulers with four members, each of whom reign for only two years, the other two being Ahaziah and Pekahiah. Zimri holds the dubious record of being the shortest-reigning Israelite king at just seven days (1 Kgs 16:15). Despite his brief, week-long reign, Zimri is still condemned for following in the ways of evil Jeroboam (16:19).

Nadab Son of Jeroboam (15:25–32)

Most of the narrative of Nadab, son of Jeroboam, is dominated by Baasha the usurper, who slew Nadab during his siege of the Philistine city of Gibbethon. Gibbethon was three miles west of Gezer, near the Israel-Philistia border. Baasha's father is Ahijah, but the text informs us he is from the tribe of Issachar to distinguish him from the similarly named prophet from Shiloh who prophesied twice to Jeroboam (11:29–39; 14:6–14). Since Nadab only reigned for two years, there is not much to say except that as he and his family were slaughtered by Baasha. The first dynasty of divided Israel, that of Jeroboam, was extinguished.

Baasha Son of Ahijah (15:33–16:7)

Baasha's brief narrative is surprising, since he was the third-longest-reigning northern ruler (twenty-four years). One could expect more details about his conquests or construction projects. Baasha was the first of eight northern usurpers of the throne. His narrative mainly consists of the prophecy from Jehu condemning him for following in the sins of Jeroboam. Jehu is not called a prophet—merely the son of Hanani—which distinguishes him from King Jehu, the son of Jehoshaphat (2 Kgs 9:2). This is the only time Jehu, son of

Hanani, appears in Kings, but in Chronicles he speaks to, and chronicles the life of, King Jehoshaphat (2 Chr 19:2–3; 20:34).

Elah Son of Baasha (16:8–14)

Baasha was succeeded by his son, Elah. While many similarities between Elah and his successors can be observed, what distinguishes him from most other northern rulers was his lack of an evil evaluation. Only two rulers, he and Shallum (2 Kgs 15:13), are not condemned for doing "evil in the eyes of the Lord." The text, however, does say that Elah committed all the sins has father Baasha did (1 Kgs 16:13), so he continues the pattern of evil northern rulers.

As we examine Elah's reign in light of the previous three rulers, we are struck by the many parallels between the dynasty of his father Baasha and that of Jeroboam. The first two northern dynasties both barely qualify to be considered dynasties, with only one successful succession. Both founders were usurpers with long reigns; Jeroboam reigned twenty-two years and Baasha twenty-four. Both successors had short, two-year reigns and were assassinated in a coup (Nadab by Baasha and Elah by Zimri). Both dynasties were cut short when all male descendants were wiped out by usurpers. Both founders were condemned by prophets (Jeroboam by Ahijah and Baasha by Jehu), and, after both houses were destroyed, the text records a notice of the fulfillment of the prophecy. As we move forward in the narrative of northern rulers, we will see many of these features repeated.

Zimri (16:15–20)

Zimri was a commander of half of Israel's chariot force (16:9). Chariots were a major component of Israel's military. According to the Kurkh Monolith, only a few decades later, Ahab had two thousand chariots at his disposal to use against Shalmaneser III of Assyria. Zimri's name could be Aramean; Zimri-Lim was a famous ruler of ancient Mari.[11]

Zimri's seven-day reign, while short, was certainly long on drama. While Elah was drunk at the home of Arza, one of his officials, Zimri assassinated the king, declared himself the new ruler, and then slaughtered Baasha's family (vv. 9–11). Meanwhile, the army remains in what appears to be a long siege of the Philistine city of Gibbethon (15:27; 16:15). When they discover that Zimri (who was in charge of only half of the chariots), staged a coup, the army stages their own counter-coup and declares Omri, Zimri's supervisor as commander of the entire army, to be king (16:16). The military siege by Israel's

11. See Wiseman, *1 & 2 Kings*, 159.

army shifted from Gibbethon to Tirzah, Israel's capital. Zimri realizes his attempt to hold onto the throne is futile, so he sets the palace aflame and dies in a blaze of glory. Cogan sees a parallel between Zimri's actions here and those of Sin-shar-ishkun, the final Assyrian ruler who, according to tradition, when he saw that Nineveh was to be overthrown, flung himself into the burning palace—a tragic yet heroic death.[12]

The only other time Zimri is mentioned in Kings is when Jezebel the wife of Ahab engages in trash talk with Jehu by calling him "Zimri" (2 Kgs 9:31). Presumably she connects Jehu with Zimri since both are military commanders who overthrow their commander-in-chief. She essentially predicts Jehu will also have a short reign like Zimri, who was killed by her father-in-law, Omri. Her curse on Jehu was ineffectual; he reigned twenty-eight years (2 Kgs 10:36).

Omri (16:21–28)

The first and third rulers of divided Israel (Jeroboam I and Baasha) only have one dynastic successor, and the fifth has none (Zimri). But beginning with Omri, the dynastic chaos that has characterized the Northern Kingdom calms down a bit. Omri establishes a dynasty with three successors (Ahab, Ahaziah, and Jehoram), and then Jehu establishes a dynasty with four (Jehoahaz, Jehoash, Jeroboam II, and Zechariah). After this period of relative stability, the reigns of Israel's final five rulers (Shallum, Menahem, Pekahiah, Pekah, and Hoshea) are even more chaotic than the first five.

As we compared the synchronisms of Zimri and Omri, a chronological problem emerges. Zimri came to power in the twenty-seventh year of Asa and reigned seven days (16:15). Then Omri came to power in the thirty-first year of Asa (v. 23). We are missing four years. Most scholars think that the civil war between Tibni and Omri endured for four years. The synchronism refers to the point in time that had no more rivals (the third year of Asa), then he had eight more years for his twelve-year total.

Just as David established Jerusalem as his new capital (2 Sam 5:6–10), Omri established Samaria as his new capital (1 Kgs 16:24). Omri reigned in the old capital, Tirzah, for six years, despite the fact that Zimri had burned the royal palace there. If Omri had not moved the capital from Tirzah to Samaria, perhaps Jesus would have told the parable of the Good Tirzarian (Luke 10:25–37).

12. Cogan, *I Kings*, 413.

Ahab Son of Omri (16:29–34)

Omri's son, Ahab, succeeds him. Most of what we learn about Ahab comes in the context of the prophetic narrative of Elijah. His father Omri was mentioned more than any other ruler in extrabiblical texts, but even with all the references to Jeroboam's sin for most northern kings, Ahab is mentioned more often in the book of Kings than any other northern ruler.[13] Ahab reigned for twenty-two years, the Northern Kingdom's fifth-longest reign, but his notoriety is primarily due to the fact that he is the foil for the prophet Elijah over the course of six chapters (1 Kgs 17–22).

In his introductory regnal formula, we learn that he was uniquely evil (see excursus "Regnal Formulas" below). We will learn more about his sins in the subsequent chapters, but here we discover that he followed not only Jeroboam I's sins but also Solomon's sins by marrying a foreign princess, Jezebel, daughter of Ethbaal the king of Sidon (16:31). Baal worship had occasionally been practiced by Israelites earlier (Num 25:3–5; Judg 6:25–32), but apparently it disappeared during the early monarchy, as the text does not mention Baal in the book of Samuel or previously in Kings. But just as Solomon's wives imported their religious practices, so Jezebel brought in Baal worship, and Ahab set up an altar and a temple for Baal in the capital Samaria.

After the Israelites captured Jericho during the period of the Canaanite conquest, Joshua pronounced a curse upon whoever would attempt to rebuild the city.

> At the cost of his firstborn son
>   he will lay its foundations;
> at the cost of his youngest
>   he will set up its gates. (Josh 6:26)

During the reign of Ahab, a man who only appears here, Hiel of Bethel, rebuilt Jericho "at the cost" of his oldest son, Abiram, and his youngest son, Segub (1 Kgs 16:34), thus fulfilling the curse of Joshua. DeVries thinks what is being described is a foundation sacrifice to appease the gods and guarantee the stability of the construction.[14] While the language could suggest a sacrifice, what seems to be implied is that YHWH somehow punished the family, since the text explicitly links the judgment to the word of YHWH (v. 34).

---

13. The name "Jeroboam" appears a few more times than "Ahab" (seventy-nine to seventy-six), but eight of these occurrences of "Jeroboam" refer to the son of Jehoash, Jeroboam II, not Jeroboam I.

14. DeVries, *1 Kings*, 204–5.

Excursus: Regnal Formulas

Regnal formulas dominate the accounts of these six northern rulers, with little narrative, in stark contrast to what immediately follows with the prophetic narrative of Elijah. Several observations about the patterns of these regnal formulas can be observed. We find six synchronisms for these six northern rulers, all of whom come to power during the long forty-one-year reign of Asa of Judah (1 Kgs 15:25, 33; 16:8, 15, 23, 29). Three of the rulers have very short reigns (Nadab, Elah, Zimri), and three have relatively long reigns (Baasha, Omri, Ahab).

Five of the six rulers did evil in the eyes of YHWH (Nadab, Baasha, Zimri, Omri, and Ahab), but the one exception, Elah, committed all the sins his father Baasha had committed (16:13). Both Omri and Ahab are described as having done more evil than all who were before them (vv. 25, 30). Presumably the "all" here refers to all rulers of Israel and Judah, eleven for Omri and twelve for Ahab. Several other rulers are described using superlative language. Solomon was uniquely wise and wealthy (3:12, 13), Hezekiah uniquely trusting in YHWH (2 Kgs 18:5), and Josiah uniquely devoted to YHWH (23:25). Manasseh was, like Omri and Ahab, more evil than all who were before him (21:11). While the positive superlatives for Solomon, Hezekiah, and Josiah describe distinct favorable characteristics, the three negative ones could overlap. Although Manasseh is described as more evil than the Amorites before him (2 Kgs 21:11), Ahab would just need to exceed his father in evilness. But before we spend too much time trying to harmonize these statements, we should remember the tone is hyperbolic, which is meant to make a dramatic point and not to be taken too literally. One can hardly evaluate a ruler's evilness quotient objectively.

At the end of each narrative, the text comments generically about other events not included in this narrative from a king's reign that were recorded in the royal annals. This section includes this formulaic comment for the first five rulers, but for Ahab's we will have to wait until the end of 1 Kings when he dies (22:39). For Nadab and Elah, there is nothing unique mentioned. The text records for Baasha "his achievements" (16:5) and for Omri "the things he achieved" (v. 27). The least generic comment in these concluding remarks is Zimri's, which speaks of "the rebellion he carried out" (v. 20), which is curious since Baasha and Omri both also rebel but no reference is included for them.

Excursus: Rebellions

While there is not much narrative recorded for these six rulers, what little there is focuses on rebellions. The Northern Kingdom experienced eight rebellions that were instigated by Baasha (1 Kgs 15:27), Zimri (16:9), Omri (16:16), Jehu (2 Kgs 9:14), Shallum (15:10), Menahem (15:14), Pekah (15:25), and Hoshea (15:30). The beginning and the end of the Northern Kingdom were characterized by dynastic chaos when most of these coups took place. In the middle period of the Northern Kingdom, relative stability ensues as four Omrides (Omri, Ahab, Ahaziah, and Jehoram) and five Jehuites rule (Jehu, Jehoahaz, Jehoash, Jeroboam II, and Zechariah).

Each of the rebellions follows a basic pattern, which can be extended to those of later Israelite usurpers. There is plot or conspiracy against the ruler, often led by military figures (e.g., Zimri, Omri, and Jehu). The usurper kills the king, then the royal family, particularly the males (1 Kgs 15:29: 16:12; 2 Kgs 10:1–11). This practice may seem brutal, but it was typical after a coup in ancient times. A dynastic purge prevented reprisals or lost heirs (like Jehoash, 2 Kgs 11) returning to power. It also makes a statement; the new king now has the power to completely crush all his rivals, sending a clear message not to attempt a counter-coup.

Why were there so many rebellions in the north? It is likely that a number of factors contributed to the northern dynastic instability, but the primary explanation given in the text is theological. They were judged by God for their idolatry, particularly the golden calves set up by Jeroboam, which endured at least in Bethel until after the northern exile (2 Kgs 23:15). The text frequently speaks of Jeroboam's sins but curiously only mentions the actual calves at the beginning of the Northern Kingdom (1 Kgs 12:28, 32), once in the middle (2 Kgs 10:29), and once at the end (2 Kgs 17:16).

The other theological factor contributing to the lack of northern dynastic continuity is that they were not Davidides. When southern rulers were evil, the text records that YHWH wanted David to have a lamp in Jerusalem (1 Kgs 11:36; 15:4; 2 Kgs 8:19). The mercy shown to David's heirs for his model of obedience was not extended to northern rulers.

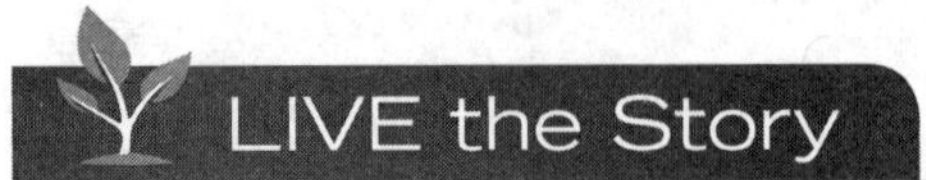

Prophetic Judgments and Fulfillments

The theological explanations against northern rulers are framed in prophetic judgments, and while only one is pronounced in this section (1 Kgs 16:1–4, 7), three prophecies are fulfilled here (15:29; 16:12, 34). The judgment recorded here is from Jehu to Baasha (16:1–4, 7), and the two earlier prophecies fulfilled here are from Ahijah to Jeroboam (14:7–14; 15:29) and by Joshua about the city of Jericho (16:34; Josh 6:26). For the first three northern dynasties (Jeroboam I, Baasha, and Omri; Zimri didn't have a successor), the prophetic judgment includes a canine consummation curse: the dogs will eat the city dwellers and the birds will eat the rural folk (1 Kgs 14:11; 16:4; 21:24). Throughout this section we see how the ruler's idolatry arouses the anger of YHWH, which is mentioned by the prophet in their pronouncement of the judgment or by the narrator as the reason for the judgment.

Divine Anger

The text mentions the anger of YHWH more frequently in 1 Kings 14–16 than anywhere else in the book. Three Hebrew words are used. The verb "to provoke to anger" (hiphil of *ka'as*) appears eight times (14:9, 15; 15:30; 16:2, 7, 13, 26, 33), and the related noun (also *ka'as*, but the Hebrew vowels are different) appears once (15:30). The verb "to be jealous" (piel of *qana'*) also appears once (14:22). The actions of the Israelites, specifically their kings, makes God angry, and during this period of the monarchy that was happening a lot.

No one wants to be around someone who is angry. When a member of one's household starts yelling or slamming doors, others scurry to hide, making sure they are not the next victim of a tantrum or tirade. But when God gets angry, where does one go to hide? During the reign of David, YHWH's anger burst forth against Uzzah as he reached out and touched the ark of the covenant, and he was instantly killed (2 Sam 6:1–11). None of us want to be the next Uzzah who gets smitten by an angry God. There are, however, three pieces of good news when it comes to divine anger.

First, God is slow to anger. The description of God as slow to anger appears in a wide variety of Old Testament genres to describe God: in historical contexts (Exod 34:6; Num 14:18; Neh 9:17), in prophetic contexts (Joel 2:13; Jonah 4:2; Nah 1:3), and in poetic contexts (Ps 86:15; 103:8; 145:8). Slowness to anger is so much of part of his character that YHWH even includes it in his name (Exod 34:6). Sometimes it may be difficult to see how God's slowness to anger affects his punishments upon his people, but we see it here in several ways. Condemnations against dynastic founders are delayed until their successors. Presumably, if their heirs repented, God would show mercy, but that doesn't happen in this section. Also, God delayed the ultimate judgment against the Northern Kingdom for several hundred years, until the Assyrian destruction in 722 BC (2 Kgs 17). Just as God was slow to anger with his people in the times of the monarchy, the good news for us today is that he continues to be slow to anger, giving us opportunities to repent and not just to delay but to avoid judgment completely.

Second, God's anger reveals he cares about his relationship with his people. People get angry about things that are really important to them. In these chapters in Kings, God gets angry about idolatry. He had established several covenants with their ancestors (Gen 8–9; 12; 15; 17; Exod 24; Josh 24), essentially agreeing that he would be their God and they would be his people. As they worshiped other gods like Baal or Asherah (1 Kgs 14:15, 23; 15:13; 16:31–33), the covenant was broken. In a marriage analogy, the Israelites had committed adultery. The fact that God was angry about this infidelity tells us that he values the relationship with his people. It is good God was angry. You want him to want his people to be in an exclusive relationship with him. If the wife of a man who slept with another woman wasn't angry with her husband, we would say something was wrong with her. God wants his people to focus on him, to love him with their whole heart, soul, mind, and strength (Deut 6:5; Matt 22:37; Mark 12:30; Luke 10:27) and when they don't, he gets mad, but he does it slowly, giving them opportunities to repent. It would be difficult not to conclude that Jesus was angry in the temple as he drove out the livestock sellers with a whip and overturned the tables of the moneychangers (Matt 21:12–13; Mark 11:15–17; Luke 19:45–46; John 2:14–16). These animal traders and moneychangers were doing business in the court of the Gentiles; Jesus's anger was motivated by the fact that foreigners were being prevented from being able to pray and worship God. Jesus desperately wanted all people and nations to connect to God. That's a good thing to get angry about. I should be more angry, like Jesus, when I see people being prevented from connecting to God.

Third, Jesus's death spares us from God's anger. John prepared the way for Jesus by warning people to repent to avoid the upcoming wrath (Matt 3:7–8) and by declaring that Jesus was the Lamb of God who would take away the sins of the world (John 1:29). Paul reminds us of the ultimate bit of good news: that God showed his love for us in sending Christ to die, which therefore saves us from the wrath of God (Rom 5:8–9). God's anger should get our attention, because we can be sure from the examples of these kings and many other people in Scripture that he does punish sinful behavior. Fortunately, God is slow to anger, so we have plenty of time to repent, and God himself becomes the means to allow us to avoid his wrath. We would be fools to worship other gods.

CHAPTER 14

1 Kings 17:1–18:15

LISTEN to the Story

1Now Elijah the Tishbite, from Tishbe in Gilead, said to Ahab, "As the
Lord, the God of Israel, lives, whom I serve, there will be neither dew nor
rain in the next few years except at my word."
2Then the word of the Lord came to Elijah: 3"Leave here, turn eastward
and hide in the Kerith Ravine, east of the Jordan. 4You will drink from
the brook, and I have directed the ravens to supply you with food there."
5So he did what the Lord had told him. He went to the Kerith Ravine,
east of the Jordan, and stayed there. 6The ravens brought him bread and
meat in the morning and bread and meat in the evening, and he drank
from the brook.

7Some time later the brook dried up because there had been no rain
in the land. 8Then the word of the Lord came to him: 9"Go at once to
Zarephath in the region of Sidon and stay there. I have directed a widow
there to supply you with food." 10So he went to Zarephath. When he
came to the town gate, a widow was there gathering sticks. He called to
her and asked, "Would you bring me a little water in a jar so I may have
a drink?" 11As she was going to get it, he called, "And bring me, please,
a piece of bread."
12"As surely as the Lord your God lives," she replied, "I don't have any
bread—only a handful of flour in a jar and a little olive oil in a jug. I am
gathering a few sticks to take home and make a meal for myself and my
son, that we may eat it—and die."
13Elijah said to her, "Don't be afraid. Go home and do as you have
said. But first make a small loaf of bread for me from what you have and
bring it to me, and then make something for yourself and your son. 14For
this is what the Lord, the God of Israel, says: 'The jar of flour will not be
used up and the jug of oil will not run dry until the day the Lord sends
rain on the land.'"

[15]She went away and did as Elijah had told her. So there was food every day for Elijah and for the woman and her family. [16]For the jar of flour was not used up and the jug of oil did not run dry, in keeping with the word of the LORD spoken by Elijah.

[17]Some time later the son of the woman who owned the house became ill. He grew worse and worse, and finally stopped breathing. [18]She said to Elijah, "What do you have against me, man of God? Did you come to remind me of my sin and kill my son?"

[19]"Give me your son," Elijah replied. He took him from her arms, carried him to the upper room where he was staying, and laid him on his bed. [20]Then he cried out to the LORD, "LORD my God, have you brought tragedy even on this widow I am staying with, by causing her son to die?" [21]Then he stretched himself out on the boy three times and cried out to the LORD, "LORD my God, let this boy's life return to him!"

[22]The LORD heard Elijah's cry, and the boy's life returned to him, and he lived. [23]Elijah picked up the child and carried him down from the room into the house. He gave him to his mother and said, "Look, your son is alive!"

[24]Then the woman said to Elijah, "Now I know that you are a man of God and that the word of the LORD from your mouth is the truth."

[18:1]After a long time, in the third year, the word of the LORD came to Elijah: "Go and present yourself to Ahab, and I will send rain on the land." [2]So Elijah went to present himself to Ahab.

Now the famine was severe in Samaria, [3]and Ahab had summoned Obadiah, his palace administrator. (Obadiah was a devout believer in the LORD. [4]While Jezebel was killing off the LORD's prophets, Obadiah had taken a hundred prophets and hidden them in two caves, fifty in each, and had supplied them with food and water.) [5]Ahab had said to Obadiah, "Go through the land to all the springs and valleys. Maybe we can find some grass to keep the horses and mules alive so we will not have to kill any of our animals." [6]So they divided the land they were to cover, Ahab going in one direction and Obadiah in another.

[7]As Obadiah was walking along, Elijah met him. Obadiah recognized him, bowed down to the ground, and said, "Is it really you, my lord Elijah?"

[8]"Yes," he replied. "Go tell your master, 'Elijah is here.'"

[9]"What have I done wrong," asked Obadiah, "that you are handing

your servant over to Ahab to be put to death? [10]As surely as the Lord your
God lives, there is not a nation or kingdom where my master has not sent
someone to look for you. And whenever a nation or kingdom claimed
you were not there, he made them swear they could not find you. [11]But
now you tell me to go to my master and say, 'Elijah is here.' [12]I don't know
where the Spirit of the Lord may carry you when I leave you. If I go and
tell Ahab and he doesn't find you, he will kill me. Yet I your servant have
worshiped the Lord since my youth. [13]Haven't you heard, my lord, what
I did while Jezebel was killing the prophets of the Lord? I hid a hundred
of the Lord's prophets in two caves, fifty in each, and supplied them with
food and water. [14]And now you tell me to go to my master and say, 'Elijah
is here.' He will kill me!"

[15]Elijah said, "As the Lord Almighty lives, whom I serve, I will surely
present myself to Ahab today."

Listening to the Text in the Story: Ancient Near Eastern Texts: The Ba'lu Myth, The Atrahasis Epic, The Instruction of Amenemope, The Kirta Epic, The Aramaic Text in Demotic Script

Introduction

After wandering through the wilderness of regnal formulas, we finally arrive at the promised land, the stories of Elijah the prophet. One of the longest continuous narratives in the book of Kings (divided into two chapters in this commentary) recounts Elijah's ministry during the extended drought, his conflict with the prophets of Baal on Mount Carmel, his flight from Jezebel, and his subsequent depression (1 Kgs 17–19).

God and Gods as Providers of Rain

Elijah suddenly appears on the scene and announces to King Ahab of Israel that there will be no rain. If King Ahab did any praying during the drought, it presumably would have been to Baal, the god that he and his wife Queen Jezebel worshiped (1 Kgs 16:31–32). Baal was the god of storms and fertility, so, according to Ahab's worldview, a drought would have fallen under his jurisdiction. Elijah's proclamation of "neither dew nor rain" (17:1) would have been a direct confrontation to both Ahab and his god, round one of an epic heavyweight battle.

The image of Baal as storm god is depicted dramatically in a stele called

"Baal with Thunderbolt" found in 1932 by Claude Schaeffer in northwestern Syria in the temple of Baal in the acropolis of ancient Ugarit.[1] Baal is displayed striding powerfully forward on the mountains, and his left hand holds a thunderbolt in the shape of a spear. The portrayal of Baal as provider of rain is seen in another source from ancient Ugarit, the Baal Cycle, as Anat, the consort of Baal, petitions him to provide rain:

> May Ba'lu place his watering devices in [the heavens]
> May [Haddu] bring the [rain of] his X.[2]

In his comments about Elijah's conflict with the prophets of Baal, Monson states, "By stopping the rain and dew the prophet effectively rendered impotent both Baal and his priesthood."[3]

In a similar manner, in the ancient Akkadian Epic of Atrahasis, the gods withhold rain because they are disturbed by the uproar the humans are making. The humans are keeping the gods awake, so the god Enlil said to the other gods:

> Oppressive has become the clamor of mankind.
> By their uproar they prevent sleep . . .
> Let Adad make scarce his [rain] . . .
> Let the clouds be blown up
> [That rain from heaven] pour not forth.
> [Let] the land [with]draw its yield.[4]

Ancient deities were perceived as responsible for the blessing of rain as well as the curse of drought, so Elijah's announcement of an extended period with no rain would lead not only to a famine but also to a loss of perceived power for Baal and for rulers like Ahab who worshiped him. Ahab could have lost his throne in the midst of the crisis.

Several ancient Near Eastern texts describe times of famine that involved comparable circumstances to those experienced by the Israelites during the reign of Ahab. The Ugaritic Epic of Kirta describes a period when the earth had failed to produce bread, wine, and oil:

---

1. For an image see *ANEP*, 168, 307; #490.
2. *COS* 1:253; see also 260.
3. *ZIBBC* 3:74.
4. *ANET*, 104.

The ploughman lifted (their) heads,
on high those who work the grain,
(For) the bread was depleted from their bins,
the wine was depleted from their skins,
the oil was depleted from [their jars].[5]

While Israel struggled to find food during the famine, YHWH provided for Elijah during his wanderings with ravens, a widow, and an angel. Elijah convinced the widow of Zarephath to share the contents of her jar of oil and her flour (1 Kgs 17:8–16). The Egyptian Instruction of Amenemope addresses a similar situation of hospitality:

Do not refuse your oil jar to a stranger,
Double it before your brothers.
God prefers him who honors the poor
To him who worships the wealthy.[6]

As we examine Elijah's narrative, we will see the surprising ways God kept the prophet alive during Israel's three-and-a-half-year famine.

Elijah Is Fed by Ravens (17:1–6)

The reference to Elijah in 1 Kings 17:1 is the first of about a hundred in the Bible. His name, meaning "YHWH is my God," is appropriate for a prophet who modeled and called for exclusive devotion to YHWH. The text emphasizes his home by stating redundantly that he was both a Tishbite and from Tishbe in Gilead (v. 1).

After recording Elijah's announcement of drought to Ahab, Kings mentions no prophetic prayer or the exact duration of the drought; however, these details are provided in the New Testament. When Jesus was experiencing a hostile reception in his hometown of Nazareth as he began his ministry, he spoke of how a widow from the Gentile town of Zarephath fed the prophet Elijah during the three-and-a-half-year famine (Luke 4:25–26). The book of James

5. *COS* 1:341; see also 1 Kgs 17:14.
6. *COS* 1:121.

states that Elijah prayed that it would not rain and that the drought lasted three and a half years (Jas 5:17).

YHWH sends Elijah to the Kerith Ravine (1 Kgs 17:1–3). Both Tishbe and the Kerith Ravine have uncertain locations but are on the eastern side of the Jordan River, perhaps near each other. The Kerith Ravine must have been sufficiently remote to prevent Ahab from finding Elijah during his pre-Zarephath wanderings.

While this passage includes many references to the word of YHWH (vv. 2, 5, 8, 14, 16, 24; 18:1), Elijah's first, and perhaps his most important, message to Ahab curiously lacks a reference to divine authorization, which would have marked him as a prophet and would have given his message greater legitimacy. Instead of mentioning the word of YHWH, Elijah includes an oath, "As the Lord, the God of Israel lives" (1 Kgs 17:1). Forms of this oath are repeated three other places in this passage, spoken by the widow, by Obadiah, and by Elijah again (v. 12; 18:10, 15). In each of these instances, the oath serves to accentuate the seriousness of the corresponding message, as it does here with Elijah's dire prediction to Ahab that there will be no dew or rain for the next few years.

While Egypt and the nations of Mesopotamia had access to the constant flows of their major rivers (the Nile, the Tigris, and the Euphrates) to irrigate their lands, Israel and its neighboring nations depended heavily upon rain and dew for the welfare of their crops and harvest. Because the land of Canaan was arid, when famine came people were often forced to move to more fertile lands. During periods of famine, Abraham and his family traveled to Egypt (Gen 12:10; 26:1; 42:3–5; 47:3–4), and Ruth and her family traveled to Moab (Ruth 1:1). Elijah's initial message to Ahab was not only a prediction of catastrophe but also, as noted above, a direct challenge to Ahab's god, Baal, who was thought to be responsible for storms and fertility.

Immediately after Elijah delivers his ominous message to the king, the word of YHWH comes to him, sending him to Kerith Ravine, where Elijah would get water from the brook and food from ravens (1 Kgs 17:3). YHWH's command to Elijah here is unexpected on several levels—being fed by birds would be strange enough, but ravens were unclean animals according to the law (Lev 11:15; Deut 14:14). Ravens ate fruit such as dates, but they also ate carrion. Contact with dead animals makes an object unclean (Lev 11:24–25, 39), and presumably some of the carrion ravens ate would have come from unclean animals. We do not know what type of meat the ravens brought to Elijah (beware of food simply labeled "meat"), but it is not unreasonable to assume it would have been consistent with their normal diet, that is, carrion. While Elijah has yet to be identified as a prophet (see 1 Kgs 18:36), if he were a man of God who was concerned with dietary laws, we might expect him to respond negatively, like Peter, to the call to eat unclean animals in his dream (Acts 10:14). Despite the craziness of the divine command, Elijah obeys (1 Kgs 17:5). The ravens fed him bread and meat in the morning and evening (v. 6), reminiscent of the manna and quail God provided for the Israelites in the wilderness (Exod 16:12).

Elijah Is Fed by the Widow of Zarephath (17:7–16)

While we do not know chronological details, sufficient time has elapsed for Elijah's precious brook to dry up, so it was time to move on. God's guidance this second time follows a strikingly similar pattern to the first time, when God told him to go to the Kerith. The "word of the Lord came" to him again, telling him to leave and move to a new place (17:2–3, 8–9). YHWH says, "I have directed" a provider (a widow this time, ravens last time) "to supply you with food" (17:4, 9). Despite the bizarre nature of these two divine commands, Elijah does not hesitate but instantly obeys in both instances (17:5, 10). But, unlike the ravens, the widow offers some resistance.

In the world of the Bible, widows were vulnerable because they had no way to earn a living or support themselves. In Israel's ancient patriarchal culture, men owned the land and provided food and clothing for their family. This widow of Zarephath also had to feed her young son. The Hebrew word often translated as "orphan" (*yatom*) literally means "fatherless child" because, when it came to material provision for children, fathers had all the resources. To be fatherless in Elijah's day would be roughly equivalent to being an orphan today. Widows and fatherless children were always needy, but during times of famine they would have been particularly vulnerable.

Many Old Testament texts group three classes of marginalized people together: widows, the fatherless, and sojourners. Because each of these groups were so easily exploited, many commands exhort the Israelites to care for them (e.g., Exod 22:21–22; Lev 22:13; Deut 14:28–29; 24:17–22). As Elijah was sent by God to a family consisting of a widow and a fatherless child, one might expect him to provide for them, but that did not appear to be the case initially.

Curiously, God sends Elijah north along the Phoenician coast, to Zarephath in the land of Sidon (1 Kgs 17:8–9). Jezebel, the woman who tried to kill Elijah (1 Kgs 18:4; 19:2), is also from Sidon (16:31). He is hunted by one Sidonian woman and fed by another.

When Elijah meets the widow, he asks for water, precious during a famine, and as she is getting it for him, he asks for some bread as well (17:10–11). ("If you give a prophet some water, he's going to ask for a piece of bread . . .") While she did not hesitate to obtain water for a foreign prophet, at this point she balks, informing him she has just enough flour and oil for one last supper for her and her son before they die (v. 12), implying she does not have enough to share with a freeloading Israelite.

Now the story gets even stranger. Elijah's response includes good news and bad news for the widow. He promises that YHWH, the God of Israel, is going to provide for her, but he also tells her to first take her precious flour and oil and make him a loaf of bread, and then afterwards she can feed herself and her son (vv. 13–14). (He must have been hungry.) None of the Old Testament commands concerning widows hinted that prophets should take advantage of a foreign widow's hospitality during times of famine. In the Covenant Code, God warns the Israelites to not wrong or oppress widows or the fatherless, otherwise his wrath will burn and he will kill them (Exod 22:21–24). It could appear that Elijah was risking incurring the wrath of God.

But YHWH had commanded Elijah to go there, and he told Elijah that the widow would provide for him (1 Kgs 17:9). The other thing to remember is that, as an Israelite in the land of Sidon, Elijah himself is a sojourner, and thus as he joins her family, the trifecta of marginalization is now complete—a widow, a fatherless child, and a sojourner.

God may have told the widow to feed him, but she does not seem to be aware of this fact yet, or at least she is not acknowledging it. If you thought getting fed by ravens was wild, asking a starving widow to feed you from her scarce resources before she starves was at least as bizarre.

While Elijah's "me first" behavior here appears to be selfish, we should remember that he has been risking his life as he was following YHWH's direction, trusting his God as he confronted a king, and obeyed commands to travel to remote locations where he would mysteriously be provided for by ravens and a widow.

Elijah was also giving this foreign woman an opportunity to trust God, like he has been doing, and to watch God come through, but it would involve a serious risk, not just for herself but also for her son. She does it, and just as Elijah predicted, the jar of flour and the jug of oil were never used up (vv. 15–16). Her behavior is comparable to that of Rebekah, who, in response to the request of Abraham's servant for water, provided water for his camels as well (Gen 24:15–20). Obedience is a prominent theme in the book of Kings, and particularly in the narrative of Elijah. The kings of Israel do not obey God, but the ravens, the widow, and the prophet do, and they experience his blessing and provision along the way (17:5–6, 10, 15). YHWH provides for his obedient servants, while Baal the god of storms does nothing—a pattern that will be repeated on Mount Carmel.

Elijah Raises the Widow's Son (17:17–24)

After staying with the widow for an extended period of time, the widow's son dies (17:17). The narrative of his miraculous healing by Elijah shares many striking similarities with that of Elisha raising the Shunammite woman's son (see 2 Kgs 4:18–37). The text states that the boy stopped breathing, but some commentators think he may not be actually dead,[7] which would make his healing still miraculous but not nearly as dramatic as a resurrection. However, since the two eyewitnesses present, the mother and Elijah, both state that the boy is dead (1 Kgs 17:18, 20), it is more reasonable to assume that he was not merely "mostly dead" (to quote Miracle Max from *The Princess Bride*),[8] but that he was in fact "all dead."

The narrator provides no window into her thoughts or feelings apart from what she says to Elijah. And she makes no direct statements, merely asking him two questions (v. 18), but her questions are loaded with meaning as she grieves the loss of her final remaining family member and vents her pain at the prophet who has been living with her but did nothing to prevent it. She partly blames herself for his death as she assumes her son's death is somehow caused by her own sin. Her view is not surprising, since the perception that death or illness was the result of personal sin was common in their context (e.g., the perspective of Job's three friends). She also blames Elijah, whose presence reminds her of her sin and somehow contributed to the death of her son. Despite her accusation of murder against him, he gives no defense but merely requests her son's lifeless body (v. 19). The boy was presumably small enough to be easily carried upstairs by the prophet, who was staying in an upper room in her house.

Elijah proceeds to shift the blame from himself to his God, asking a similar question in his lament, even using the same expression that the widow used in reference to him. Elijah accuses YHWH of "causing her son to die" (v. 20), which is a good literal translation of the Hebrew here (hiphil of the infinitive

7. See Alter, *Former Prophets*, 697; Fretheim, *Kings*, 98; Sweeney, *I & II Kings*, 215.

8. Max reminds us, "There's a big difference between mostly dead and all dead. Mostly dead is slightly alive."

construct of *mut*). Unfortunately, the NIV translates the identical form she used earlier (hiphil of the infinitive construct of *mut*) as "kill him" (v. 18), which essentially means the same thing but makes it harder to see how Elijah's language clearly mimics that of the widow.

Then Elijah stretched himself out on top of the boy's corpse three times, a behavior that may seem bizarre, but Elisha does something similar as he heals the Shunammite woman's son (2 Kgs 4:34). Contact with a corpse made a person temporarily unclean (Lev 21:1, 11; 22:4), but that is not a problem for a prophet who was fed by unclean ravens for an extended period of time. Similarly, when Jesus touched a leper, he did not become unclean but passed his cleanness into the leper (Mark 1:40–44). Elijah's desperate prayer may not seem unusual to readers of Scripture who could take resurrections for granted (e.g., 2 Kgs 4:35; 13:21; Luke 7:15; John 11:44), but this was the first healing of a dead person recorded in Scripture. Elijah was a pioneer in the realm of resurrection.

YHWH heard Elijah's plea, the boy came back to life, and he was immediately reunited with his mother as the prophet exclaimed, "Look, your son is alive!" (1 Kgs 17:22–23). Prayer was the difference between life and death—if that does not motivate you to pray, I don't know what would. Even though her food has been miraculously provided via the ministry of Elijah, it is when the widow receives her son back that she declares that she knows he is a man of God and his words are true (v. 24).

Obadiah Meets Elijah (18:1–15)

YHWH speaks to Elijah once again (18:1; see also 17:2, 8), directing him to go visit Ahab, the man who has been looking for him and probably wants to kill him. But just as he has done so faithfully in the past, Elijah obeys (18:2). But this time the message to the king will be good news, for at last YHWH is going to show mercy and send rain.

During Elijah's travels, Queen Jezebel of Israel has been killing prophets of YHWH, presumably because Elijah was the prophet who announced the drought. Perhaps Jezebel thought that killing them would get Elijah's attention, but he was apparently too far away to find out.

One of Ahab's administrators, Obadiah, was harboring a hundred prophets of YHWH, hiding them in caves and somehow feeding them during the famine (v. 4). He was a servant of Ahab, but his name means "servant of YHWH." Despite his position, his name was still appropriate, given the risk he was taking to protect and sustain YHWH's prophets. The narrator informs us that Obadiah feared YHWH greatly (v. 3), and Obadiah makes a similar statement about himself to Elijah as he declares that he has feared YHWH from his youth (v. 12).[9]

While one might be tempted to condemn Obadiah for serving an apostate king like Ahab, it was his unique position that allowed him to rescue these prophets. Numerous other biblical characters are viewed positively even though they served pagan rulers: Joseph (Gen 41:46), Daniel (Dan 2:48), Mordecai (Esth 2:21), and Nehemiah (Neh 1:11).[10]

The story is comical, as a sovereign ruler (Ahab) and his palace administrator (Obadiah) wander throughout the land, desperately searching for grass to feed their horses and mules (1 Kgs 18:5–6), a bit like young Saul searching for his missing donkey (1 Sam 9). As a result of the drought that he sent upon the land, YHWH has humbled the mighty Ahab. Presumably, Ahab and Obadiah each had an entourage assisting them in their quest for grass.

As Ahab and Obadiah part ways, Elijah appears to Obadiah, who is incredulous: "Is it really you, my lord Elijah?" (1 Kgs 18:7). As they interact, the text paints a contrast between Elijah's exclusive devotion to YHWH and Obadiah's divided loyalties. Elijah, whose name means "my God is YHWH," is serving YHWH exclusively and confronting King Ahab. Obadiah, whose names means "servant of YHWH," who fears YHWH, and who is working hard to serve God as he risks his life saving prophets, repeatedly calls Elijah "my lord" (vv. 7, 13) and Ahab "my master" (vv. 10, 11, 14), and he speaks of YHWH as Elijah's God (v. 10).

In response to Elijah's message to inform the king that he has found the prophet (v. 8), Obadiah explodes in a series of questions and dramatic exclamations. While most recently Ahab has been looking for grass, for the past few years he has searched in every nation and kingdom for the missing prophet responsible for the drought and famine (v. 10). Obadiah assumes that, after he relays his message, the prophet will magically disappear once again as the spirit of YHWH carries him to a new destination (vv. 11–12). In the beginning, the middle, and the end of his reply to Elijah, he reiterates that Ahab will kill him when Elijah does not actually appear (vv. 9, 12, 14). In case he has not already heard, Obadiah informs Elijah that Jezebel has been killing prophets, but he has been saving them (v. 13). To calm poor Obadiah, Elijah vows on the life of YHWH, whom he serves, that he will present himself to Ahab that day (v. 15). Elijah went on to fulfill that vow as he appeared to Ahab, where

9. While it is not clear from the NIV, the same Hebrew word, "fear" (*yare'*) is used in both 18:3 and 18:12 to describe Obadiah's service of YHWH.

10. See also Barnes, *1–2 Kings*, 155.

he issued another challenge to the king and his god to decide once and for all who was the true God of Israel.

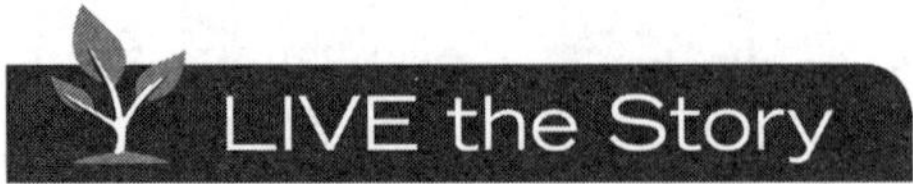

Elijah, Moses, Elisha, John, and Jesus

The prophet Elijah appears alongside Moses with Jesus on the Mount of Transfiguration, representing Old Testament prophets (Matt 17:3–4; Mark 9:4–5; Luke 9:30–33).[11] One could argue that other prophets were more deserving of that role. His successor Elisha does more miracles and has a longer narrative (Elijah appears in six chapters, Elisha appears in ten). Isaiah, Jeremiah, and Ezekiel have long books named after them.

Why does Elijah take preeminence over these other worthy candidates? As we examine the life and ministry of Elijah in these chapters, we will revisit this question, reflecting on the connections between Elijah and John the Baptist, Elijah and Moses, and on the reasons why Elijah assumes the mantle of the prototypical prophet.

Divine Provision

The theme of God's provision dominates the narrative of Israel's famine. God withholds rain but still provides water, food, and direction for his prophet Elijah in his associations with ravens, a widow, and Obadiah. Elijah is unique in his understanding that God is the only one who can meet his needs, and, during a dark time in Israel's history, he is the one the text focuses on. After suddenly appearing on the scene out of nowhere, Elijah instantly becomes the hero of the story, while King Ahab, the son of mighty King Omri, is passive and remains in the background. Elijah and Ahab provide a great contrast in their attitude toward God, as Elijah totally depends on YHWH and Ahab totally forsakes YHWH for Baal. The response that God desires from his people is dependence upon his provision, and he is willing to take extreme measures to make that happen.

Why did God send a drought? We don't know that God withheld rain because Ahab worshiped Baal, but the text suggests this conclusion because the drought prediction (1 Kgs 17:1) comes just a few verses after the indictment against Ahab and Jezebel for idolatry (16:31–33). God clearly wanted his people to depend upon him exclusively, not on foreign gods like Baal, and he

11. For a list of parallels between Elijah and Moses, see Table 12 in Chapter 19 of this commentary.

was willing to teach them that lesson in midst of hardship, even by sending a famine. God often does the same to us, allowing negative experiences to get our attention and drive us back to a position of exclusive dependence upon him. Elijah's underlying message to the widow, to Obadiah, to Ahab, and later to the people is, "You can trust God to provide. He alone is God."

For the widow, to put herself in a place to see God provide involved a serious risk for herself and her son as she shared her sparse provisions with a foreign prophet. And it might have seemed cruel for Elijah to ask that of her. But he knew God would provide, and it would be a blessing to watch God do it in a miraculous manner.

We don't know what Elijah was thinking when he told the widow to feed him first, but many people who raise money for their ministry (missionaries, parachurch workers, etc.) feel uncomfortable asking others to give to their support. I know I often did while I was on staff with InterVarsity Christian Fellowship and had to ask friends and family to give to fund my ministry. It felt like begging. God forced Elijah to beg for his food, first from ravens and then from a foreign widow, but God blessed Elijah in the process. Elijah knew it was good to depend upon God, even in risky ways, so he invited the widow and Obadiah to join him and trust God with their lives. In a similar way, we should view it as a privilege to call other people to trust God as they meet our needs. By inviting people to share their possessions, we are encouraging them, like Elijah and the widow, to be blessed by God and see him come through in dramatic ways.

When I was doing campus ministry in Los Angeles, I experienced God providing for me in a dramatic way as I did evangelistic hitchhiking with students. We had been studying Luke 10, where Jesus sends out the seventy in pairs and tells them to take nothing. I was reflecting on how to apply that text, particularly how to put myself in a place to see God provide as I depended upon the hospitality of strangers (like Elijah and the widow), and it felt like God said, "evangelistic hitchhiking." In response to my invitation, an international student from Korea named Jin agreed to join me on the trip from Los Angeles to our evangelism project in Berkeley, about four hundred miles north. I told him to check with his parents; his father responded, "It's about time you started hitchhiking."

Our first ride was a guy who was in the middle of a messy divorce, and we had a moving prayer time for him in his pickup truck beneath an underpass on the 10 Freeway. Because we spent an extra couple of hours with our first ride, we made slow progress, and, to make things worse, we said yes to a ride that took us off the main freeway. We had planned to do it in a day, but now it was after dinner, and our last ride dropped us off up in the mountains, near a town called Tehachapi.

It was getting dark, there were no motels for miles around, and we were at about four thousand feet elevation (this was before cell phones). It was summer, but it gets cold in the mountains even in summer, and I was wearing shorts. We did have sleeping bags, but they weren't going to help much. Some sleeping bags have names like "Arctic Tundra" or "Siberian Winter" because they will keep campers warm in those conditions. My bag was called, "Living Room Couch"; it was rated to 70 degrees Fahrenheit. I was going to freeze.

I'm sure Tehachapi has many wonderful things to offer, but, unfortunately for Jin and me, the town had a maximum-security prison. Who is going to try to hitchhike near a prison? On roads near prisons, signs are often posted saying, "Don't pick up hitchhikers." Like Elijah, the widow, and Obadiah in the midst of a severe famine, Jin and I needed divine intervention.

As it got darker and colder, Jin and I tried futilely to get a ride, and we were becoming hopeless. We finally started yelling up at heaven, "God help us" (a bit like Elijah on Mount Carmel; see 1 Kgs 18:36–37). Instantly, a truck drives by and slams on the brakes. We run up. The driver blurts out, "Hi, my name is Jonny Martin. I saw you guys out here. I felt sorry for you. It's cold. It's dark. You're right next to a prison. No one is going to pick you up here. Get in."

Just as God provided for Jin and me that night, and as he provided for Elijah, the widow, and Obadiah, he can be trusted to provide for us in dramatic and mundane ways. We can therefore agree with the widow's declaration that God's word is the truth (17:24).

CHAPTER 15

1 Kings 18:16–19:21

LISTEN to the Story

16So Obadiah went to meet Ahab and told him, and Ahab went to meet
Elijah. 17When he saw Elijah, he said to him, "Is that you, you troubler
of Israel?"

18"I have not made trouble for Israel," Elijah replied. "But you and your
father's family have. You have abandoned the LORD's commands and have
followed the Baals. 19Now summon the people from all over Israel to meet
me on Mount Carmel. And bring the four hundred and fifty prophets of
Baal and the four hundred prophets of Asherah, who eat at Jezebel's table."

20So Ahab sent word throughout all Israel and assembled the prophets
on Mount Carmel. 21Elijah went before the people and said, "How long
will you waver between two opinions? If the LORD is God, follow him;
but if Baal is God, follow him."

But the people said nothing.

22Then Elijah said to them, "I am the only one of the LORD's prophets
left, but Baal has four hundred and fifty prophets. 23Get two bulls for us.
Let Baal's prophets choose one for themselves, and let them cut it into
pieces and put it on the wood but not set fire to it. I will prepare the other
bull and put it on the wood but not set fire to it. 24Then you call on the
name of your god, and I will call on the name of the LORD. The god who
answers by fire—he is God."

Then all the people said, "What you say is good."

25Elijah said to the prophets of Baal, "Choose one of the bulls and prepare it first, since there are so many of you. Call on the name of your god,
but do not light the fire." 26So they took the bull given them and prepared it.

Then they called on the name of Baal from morning till noon. "Baal, answer us!" they shouted. But there was no response; no one answered. And they danced around the altar they had made.

27At noon Elijah began to taunt them. "Shout louder!" he said. "Surely

he is a god! Perhaps he is deep in thought, or busy, or traveling. Maybe he
is sleeping and must be awakened." [28]So they shouted louder and slashed
themselves with swords and spears, as was their custom, until their blood
flowed. [29]Midday passed, and they continued their frantic prophesying
until the time for the evening sacrifice. But there was no response, no one
answered, no one paid attention.

[30]Then Elijah said to all the people, "Come here to me." They came to
him, and he repaired the altar of the LORD, which had been torn down.
[31]Elijah took twelve stones, one for each of the tribes descended from
Jacob, to whom the word of the LORD had come, saying, "Your name shall
be Israel." [32]With the stones he built an altar in the name of the LORD, and
he dug a trench around it large enough to hold two seahs of seed. [33]He
arranged the wood, cut the bull into pieces and laid it on the wood. Then
he said to them, "Fill four large jars with water and pour it on the offering
and on the wood."

[34]"Do it again," he said, and they did it again.

"Do it a third time," he ordered, and they did it the third time. [35]The
water ran down around the altar and even filled the trench.

[36]At the time of sacrifice, the prophet Elijah stepped forward and
prayed: "LORD, the God of Abraham, Isaac and Israel, let it be known
today that you are God in Israel and that I am your servant and have done
all these things at your command. [37]Answer me, LORD, answer me, so these
people will know that you, LORD, are God, and that you are turning their
hearts back again."

[38]Then the fire of the LORD fell and burned up the sacrifice, the wood,
the stones and the soil, and also licked up the water in the trench.

[39]When all the people saw this, they fell prostrate and cried, "The
LORD—he is God! The LORD—he is God!"

[40]Then Elijah commanded them, "Seize the prophets of Baal. Don't let
anyone get away!" They seized them, and Elijah had them brought down
to the Kishon Valley and slaughtered there.

[41]And Elijah said to Ahab, "Go, eat and drink, for there is the sound
of a heavy rain." [42]So Ahab went off to eat and drink, but Elijah climbed
to the top of Carmel, bent down to the ground and put his face between
his knees.

[43]"Go and look toward the sea," he told his servant. And he went up
and looked.

"There is nothing there," he said.

Seven times Elijah said, "Go back."

44The seventh time the servant reported, "A cloud as small as a man's hand is rising from the sea."

So Elijah said, "Go and tell Ahab, 'Hitch up your chariot and go down before the rain stops you.'"

45Meanwhile, the sky grew black with clouds, the wind rose, a heavy rain started falling and Ahab rode off to Jezreel. 46The power of the LORD came on Elijah and, tucking his cloak into his belt, he ran ahead of Ahab all the way to Jezreel.

19:1Now Ahab told Jezebel everything Elijah had done and how he had killed all the prophets with the sword. 2So Jezebel sent a messenger to Elijah to say, "May the gods deal with me, be it ever so severely, if by this time tomorrow I do not make your life like that of one of them."

3Elijah was afraid and ran for his life. When he came to Beersheba in Judah, he left his servant there, 4while he himself went a day's journey into the wilderness. He came to a broom bush, sat down under it and prayed that he might die. "I have had enough, LORD," he said. "Take my life; I am no better than my ancestors." 5Then he lay down under the bush and fell asleep.

All at once an angel touched him and said, "Get up and eat." 6He looked around, and there by his head was some bread baked over hot coals, and a jar of water. He ate and drank and then lay down again.

7The angel of the LORD came back a second time and touched him and said, "Get up and eat, for the journey is too much for you." 8So he got up and ate and drank. Strengthened by that food, he traveled forty days and forty nights until he reached Horeb, the mountain of God. 9There he went into a cave and spent the night.

And the word of the LORD came to him: "What are you doing here, Elijah?"

10He replied, "I have been very zealous for the LORD God Almighty. The Israelites have rejected your covenant, torn down your altars, and put your prophets to death with the sword. I am the only one left, and now they are trying to kill me too."

11The LORD said, "Go out and stand on the mountain in the presence of the LORD, for the LORD is about to pass by."

Then a great and powerful wind tore the mountains apart and shattered

the rocks before the LORD, but the LORD was not in the wind. After the
wind there was an earthquake, but the LORD was not in the earthquake.
12After the earthquake came a fire, but the LORD was not in the fire. And
after the fire came a gentle whisper. 13When Elijah heard it, he pulled his
cloak over his face and went out and stood at the mouth of the cave.

Then a voice said to him, "What are you doing here, Elijah?"

14He replied, "I have been very zealous for the LORD God Almighty.
The Israelites have rejected your covenant, torn down your altars, and put
your prophets to death with the sword. I am the only one left, and now
they are trying to kill me too."

15The LORD said to him, "Go back the way you came, and go to the
Desert of Damascus. When you get there, anoint Hazael king over Aram.
16Also, anoint Jehu son of Nimshi king over Israel, and anoint Elisha son
of Shaphat from Abel Meholah to succeed you as prophet. 17Jehu will
put to death any who escape the sword of Hazael, and Elisha will put to
death any who escape the sword of Jehu. 18Yet I reserve seven thousand in
Israel—all whose knees have not bowed down to Baal and whose mouths
have not kissed him."

19So Elijah went from there and found Elisha son of Shaphat. He was
plowing with twelve yoke of oxen, and he himself was driving the twelfth
pair. Elijah went up to him and threw his cloak around him. 20Elisha
then left his oxen and ran after Elijah. "Let me kiss my father and mother
goodbye," he said, "and then I will come with you."

"Go back," Elijah replied. "What have I done to you?"

21So Elisha left him and went back. He took his yoke of oxen and
slaughtered them. He burned the plowing equipment to cook the meat
and gave it to the people, and they ate. Then he set out to follow Elijah
and became his servant.

Listening to the Text in the Story: Biblical Texts: Exodus 14; Deuteronomy 13:1–11; Judges 7; 1 Samuel 17; Ancient Near Eastern Texts: The Kirta Epic; The Admonitions of Ipuwer; The Royal Inscriptions of Thutmose III, Ramesses II, Sargon II, and Sennacherib

The World Series, the Super Bowl, the final match of the World Cup—all epic competitions with huge audiences, often with exciting finishes culminating with one side experiencing the thrill of victory while the other, the agony of defeat. Alongside the most dramatic victories of YHWH over Israel's enemies—Moses's defeat of the Egyptians at the Red Sea (Exod 14), Gideon's defeat of the Midianites in the Valley of Jezreel (Judg 7), David's defeat of Goliath and the Philistines in the Valley of Elah (1 Sam 17)—stands Elijah's defeat of the prophets of Baal on Mount Carmel. The story has all the elements of a classic underdog tale, a righteous man who has been hunted by a powerful leader, daring to confront hundreds of his competitors in an epic competition before a large crowd.

Before looking at this amazing narrative in detail, an examination of the various relevant parallel texts within Scripture, as well as within the literature of the ancient Near East, will provide helpful background, allowing us to better understand the story. We will look at three topics: prophetic conflict, divine silence, and taunt speech.

Prophetic Conflict

Elijah's opponents here, the prophets of Baal and Asherah, are the only biblical examples of actual prophets who serve non-Israelite gods.[1] However, prophetic conflicts are still mentioned or alluded to in several other Old Testament contexts. The book of Deuteronomy speaks of YHWH testing his people with prophets who lead them into worship of other gods; but it makes it clear that they are not to listen to them but should put those false prophets to death (Deut 13:1–11). The fact that Israel's rulers, King Ahab and Queen Jezebel, not only listened to these prophets of Baal and Asherah, but they also fed them (1 Kgs 18:19), is a further indictment against them.

Divine Silence

As the prophets of Baal call, dance, yell, and slash themselves to get the attention of their god, the text five times repeats there was no divine response or answer (18:26, 29). Ancient peoples during times of crisis often wondered why their deities appeared distant, passive, or absent. Several ancient parallel texts describe situations where the gods of Israel's neighbors are silent. In the Kirta Epic, the great god El asks for one of the gods to heal Kirta, but "none of the gods responded to him," a line that is repeated four times in a short section.[2] In "The Admonitions of Ipuwer," the speaker Ipuwer critiques the Sun-God Re for his lack of response to fix the problems of their day, "Where is he today? Is he asleep? Behold his power is not seen . . ."[3]

1. See Cogan, *I Kings*, 439.
2. *COS* 1:341c; *ANET*, 148c.
3. *COS* 1:97.

Taunt Speech

Taunt speech appears frequently in both biblical and extrabiblical texts, uttered by Israel's enemies, their prophets, their kings, and even their God.[4] The satirical questioning tone of Ipuwer's complaint in his "Admonitions" is comparable to Elijah's trash talking taunt against the prophets of Baal (1 Kgs 18:27). A brief overview of ancient literature will show that these biblical examples are not unique in their context. In Egyptian sources, Thutmose III repeatedly calls his opponents a "feeble enemy",[5] and Ramesses II refers to the Hittites as "effeminate weaklings," bragging that he will pounce like a falcon, "killing, slaughtering, felling to the ground."[6] In Assyrian sources, Sargon II describes how the noise of his weapons and the sound of his approaching army causes his enemies to flee in fear,[7] and Sennacherib boasts that his siege of Jerusalem overwhelmed Hezekiah "by the awesome splendor of [Sennacherib's] lordship" and made him "like a bird in a cage."[8]

Elijah and Ahab (18:16–20)

When Elijah and Ahab finally meet, they accuse each other of being the troubler of Israel (18:17–18). Ahab does not give a reason for the troubling, but Elijah attributes it to Ahab's practice of abandoning YHWH and following Baal. Elijah goes on to tell the king his plan for a battle of the gods. According to the text, YHWH does not tell Elijah to issue a challenge, so it appears to be the prophet's idea, like the drought (17:1).

Elijah wants the entire nation present, to make a dramatic statement. He selects a location where it would be widely visible, Mount Carmel. Mount Carmel is a twenty-five-mile ridge approximately 1700 feet in elevation on the border between Israel and Phoenicia. The northwestern end of the ridge overlooks the Mediterranean Sea, and the southeastern end overlooks the Jezreel Valley.[9]

Elijah and the People I (18:21–24)

After Ahab sends messengers to gather the nation (18:20), Elijah has his first of three interactions with the people. Over the course of these exchanges the

4. See also Lamb, "Trash Talking," 111–30.
5. *COS* 2:9, 11, 12, 16.
6. *COS* 2:36.
7. *COS* 2:296–97, 300.
8. *COS* 2:303.
9. See *BBCOT*, 378.

people undergo a gradual yet dramatic transformation. In his initial remarks Elijah rebukes the people for their fickle wavering between following YHWH and following Baal (v. 21). He tells the people to pick a side, either YHWH or Baal. His curious tactic is reminiscent of the approach taken by Joshua in his final speech to the nation at Shechem, where he tells the people to "choose for yourselves this day whom you will serve" (Josh 24:15). Moses also asks a comparable question to the Israelites after the golden calf incident, "Who is on the Lord's side?" (Exod 32:26 NRSV). The Israelites at Mount Carmel have not decided whose side they are on yet, since their response to Elijah's exhortation is silence (1 Kgs 18:21). Moses, Joshua, and Elijah all want the people to choose YHWH, but in each instance they know it is important for the people to own their decision.

Elijah informs the people that he is the only prophet of YHWH left (v. 22), a complaint he makes two more times to YHWH himself (19:10, 14). However, the prophet's count is off by at least ninety-nine, which he should have been aware of, since Ahab's servant Obadiah just told him that a hundred of YHWH's prophets were rescued from Jezebel (18:4). Perhaps we can excuse Elijah for his dramatic exaggeration since he felt alone and isolated over the past few years, as Israel's rulers have been trying to kill him while he was fed by ravens and a widow.

Finally, Elijah gives the people instructions for how to set up the divine competition: each side will get a bull, cut it up, and place it on the altar, but not light the fire (vv. 23–24). The prophets are then to call out to their respective gods, and whoever responds with fire is the true God (v. 24). The people were silent before (v. 21), but in response to his idea for a divine competition, they finally speak, declaring it good (v. 24).

Elijah and the Prophets of Baal (18:25–29)

After his interactions with Ahab and the people, Elijah now turns to the prophets of Baal, allowing them to select their bull and go first (18:25). To use a football analogy, Elijah allowed his opponents to skip the coin toss and just elect to receive the ball and select the direction of play. He also voluntarily gives up homefield advantage, since there were other mountains more centrally located in Israel (e.g., Ebal, Gerizim, and Tabor), but Elijah's choice for the location of Mount Carmel is on the border of Phoenicia (the land of Baal and Jezebel).[10] Elijah was confident that his side would prevail.

10. Wray Beal uses similar language of Baal having "home-court advantage" (*1 & 2 Kings*, 243–44).

Elijah also gives his opponents plenty of time. From morning until noon they cry to Baal, getting no response, dancing around their altar (v. 26). The same verb (*pasah*) is used to describe Israel's wavering (v. 21) and the prophets' dancing here (v. 26). Baal may be silent, but Elijah can keep silent no more as he begins to taunt them. His initial words, "Shout louder" (v. 27), rhyme in Hebrew (*beqol gadol*); a looser paraphrase in English that captures both the rhyme and taunting flavor of Elijah's words might be "yell like hell!"

Then Elijah's taunting shifts to a series of questions that address possible reasons for the lack of Baal's response: perhaps he is *deep in thought*? We all know people who seem impossible to distract when they are thinking about something fascinating (for me, my father and older brother). Perhaps he is *traveling*? Baal could be like the small shop owner who needs to shut down the business for a two-week summer holiday. Perhaps he is *sleeping*? This idea apparently really got their attention since the Baal prophets start shouting louder.

Perhaps he is *busy*?[11] The translations display a great variety of options here (NIV: "busy"; KJV: "pursuing"; NRSV: "wandered away"; NAS: "gone aside"), which is not surprising because the Hebrew verb (*sig*) is rare. But Rendsburg effectively argues for a scatological translation here, and some recent translations have rendered it accordingly (NLT and ESV: "relieving himself").[12] Rendsburg suggests a translation for the Hebrew as "he may be defecating/urinating," which seems accurate but too academic for a taunt. If one wanted to render the phrase in a manner that would be more appropriate for this specific context, one should utilize vernacular verbal forms more consistent with the genre of trash talking ("peeing" and "pooping" would be appropriate for a children's Bible; I will refrain from making suggestions for adult versions).

Elijah's taunts and the lack of response from Baal prompts the prophets to cut themselves with swords and spears until "their blood flowed" (v. 28) in an attempt to get Baal's attention. The specific practice of self-mutilation to provoke a divine response is attested in Ugaritic sources ("My brothers bathed in their own blood like [an] ecstatic [prophet]"), and the general practice of ecstatic prophesy is attested in Egyptian sources.[13] Another Ugaritic source, the Baal Epic, describes how the god El mourns the death of the god Baal by cutting his own skin, similar to the Baal prophets here.[14] Despite the prophets'

11. I discuss Elijah's second question ("Busy?") last because it requires the most explanation.

12. Gary A. Rendsburg, "The Mock of Baal in 1 Kings 18:27," *CBQ* 50 (1988): 414–17.

13. For self-mutilation and the source of the quotation, see J. J. M. Roberts, "A New Parallel to 1 Kings 18:28–29," *JBL* 89 (1970): 76–77; for ecstatic prophecy in the Report of Wenamun, see *COS* 1:90.

14. *COS* 1:268.

desperate attempts to elicit a divine response, Baal, not surprisingly, makes none. Just as he was powerless to bring water during the drought, now Baal is powerless to bring fire upon the altar. Baal had the homefield advantage but failed to show up to play. The text is suggesting that there is no god but YHWH (see Isa 44:6; 45:5).

Another prophetic clash like this occurs later in Ahab's reign between prophets who all supposedly serve YHWH, as Micaiah's prediction that Ahab's forces would be destroyed conflicts with Ahab's four hundred prophets who predicted a victory for the northern ruler (1 Kgs 22:1–28). Shortly before the Babylonian exile, the prophet Hananiah contradicted the prophet Jeremiah's pessimistic message about judgment, but Jeremiah declared that Hananiah was a false prophet and would soon die (Jer 28).

Elijah's words and actions against the royal prophets are the catalyst for a war of trash talking that continues for decades. After the slaughter of her prophets, Jezebel retaliates by issuing a threat against Elijah's life (1 Kgs 19:2). Her messages initially send Elijah into a suicidal depression, but he eventually recovers and delivers a prediction that dogs and birds will devour the corpses of Jezebel and Ahab (21:19–24), and Elisha's prophetic apprentice repeats a version of this curse as he anoints Jehu as king (2 Kgs 9:10). Jehu elevates the trash talking when he essentially calls Jezebel, the mother of the King Jehoram, a witch and a whore (9:22). When Jehu arrives outside her window, Jezebel calls him "Zimri" (v. 31), which may not seem like an insult until one realizes that Zimri was not only killed by Jezebel's father-in-law Omri, but he was also the shortest-reigning ruler of Israel and Judah (only seven days; 1 Kgs 16:15). Jezebel got the last word in the taunt battle, but the words of Elijah and others were fulfilled immediately after she issued her taunt (2 Kgs 9:33–37).

Elijah and the People II (18:30–35)

Much of 1 Kings 18:30–35 focuses on Elijah's interaction with the people, but he first prepares the altar and the surrounding area. The text describes Elijah repairing an altar of YHWH that had been torn down (v. 30) and also building an altar (v. 32), which is not a separate altar but merely an expansion of the repaired one. For his building materials Elijah uses twelve stones, symbolic of the twelve tribes and following the pattern set by Moses when he constructed an altar with twelve stones before establishing a covenant between YHWH and the people (Exod 24:4). Around the altar Elijah constructs a ditch capable of holding two seahs of seed (1 Kgs 18:32), an uncertain volume that commentators think to be either fifteen liters (e.g., Wiseman, Cogan) or thirty liters (e.g., Barnes, Wray Beal).[15] Just as Elijah used twelve stones, now he uses twelve jarfuls of water (four jars filled three times) to dose the altar and the trench.

The act of dumping twelve jars of water serves three purposes for Elijah. First, a drenched altar would be harder to ignite (but not for YHWH), thus making the miracle more dramatic and more glorious when the fire eventually arrives. Second, Elijah's actions show that he did not cheat by secretly hiding fire or hot ashes somewhere in the newly constructed altar. Third, it gave the people an opportunity to display great faith as they "wasted" precious water during the time of a drought. While some commentators think the water could have come from the Mediterranean,[16] the sea would have been many miles away anywhere along the Carmel ridge, so it makes more sense to view this act as a sacrifice, a costly water libation.[17]

In Elijah's first interaction with the people of Israel (18:21–24), they were passive, but in this second interaction (vv. 30–35), the prophet involves them in what he is doing, gradually shifting them from spectators to participants in the competition. Elijah tells the people to come, to fill and pour, to fill and pour again, to fill and pour a third time. Surprisingly, each time they obey. While previously they had been following Baal and abandoning the commands of YHWH (18:18, 21), now they follow the commands of YHWH and his prophet (see also "Elijah Mentors the People" in Live the Story below).

Elijah and YHWH (18:36–38)

In stark contrast to the frenetic raving, yelling, and slashing of the Baal prophets, Elijah's preparation appears calm and purposeful as he elaborately prepares the altar, the stones, the trench, the wood, the bull, and the jarfuls of water. He has yet to call out to his God, but now that the time of the sacrifice has come, he finally prays, addressing YHWH as the God of the patriarchs: Abraham, Isaac, and Israel.

We can assume, based upon their response, that Elijah's prayer must have been sufficiently audible for many of the Israelites present to hear and comprehend it. Curiously, he never explicitly asks for fire to come down and ignite the altar, but this action seems implied by each of the three things he does emphasize (18:36–37). First, he requests that the people would know that YHWH is God and that Elijah is his servant (see Jesus's prayer at Lazarus's tomb; John 11:42). Second, he requests an answer, repeated twice in the middle of his

---

15. Wiseman, *1 & 2 Kings*, 170; Cogan, *I Kings*, 442; Barnes, *1–2 Kings*, 157; Wray Beal *1 & 2 Kings*, 244–45.

16. *BBCOT*, 379.

17. See also Wray Beal, *1 & 2 Kings*, 244.

short prayer. Third, he requests that the hearts of the people are turned back to YHWH. While the prophets of Baal prayed all day to no avail, as soon as Elijah finishes his petition, the fire of YHWH comes down from heaven and consumes the sacrifice, the wood, the stones, and the soil, and literally "licked up" (*lahak*) all the water in the trench (1 Kgs 18:38). YHWH must have been thirsty. Later in his ministry we see that "fire from heaven" becomes Elijah's go-to miracle (2 Kgs 1:10, 12; see also Rev 13:13; 20:9).

Elijah and the People III (18:39–46)

In response to this dramatic sign, Elijah's prayer for the people is instantly answered as they are overwhelmed, fall down, and twice cry out that YHWH is indeed God (18:39). Elijah boldly seizes the moment and issues a series of commands to the people, to the king, and to his servant. He tells the people to seize the prophets, and they are brought to the Kishon Valley and killed (v. 40). While this severe action may be morally troubling to modern readers, YHWH had commanded that idolatrous prophets should be put to death (Deut 13:1–18), and it could also be viewed as divine judgment for the slaughtering of the prophets of YHWH (1 Kgs 18:4, 13). Similar slaughters of idolaters are performed by the tribe of Levi against those who worshiped the golden calf (Exod 32:25–29) and by Jehu against those who worshiped Baal (2 Kgs 10:18–28).

At the beginning of this story Ahab accused Elijah of troubling Israel (1 Kgs 18:17), but now he dutifully obeys Elijah's command to go, eat, and drink since the rains are coming (vv. 41–42). After Ahab leaves, Elijah climbs to the top of the mountain, bows down, and prays for rain. Thus far Elijah seemed to be traveling alone, but the text now mentions that he has a servant (only mentioned in 18:43 and 19:3), whom Elijah asks to serve as a lookout. Earlier Elijah asked the Israelites to fill the jars three times, and now he asks his servant to look to the sea seven times. Just as the Israelites obeyed, so now his servant dutifully obeys his request (18:44). He sees nothing the first six times he looks, but the seventh time he notices a cloud, a sign of a coming storm, a sufficient omen to prompt Elijah to warn Ahab to get moving before his chariot wheels get stuck in the mud. YHWH empowered his prophet to race down the mountain, arriving at Jezreel before Ahab (v. 46). Elijah will get more opportunities in the next chapter to display supernatural feats of running endurance (19:3, 20). In the Baal Myth, Baal is described as sending rain, driving showers, and lightning bolts,[18] but on Mount Carmel YHWH

18. *COS* 1:260.

is the one who proves victorious over Baal, as he sends fire from heaven and ends the drought with a downpour (18:41–45).

Elijah, Jezebel, and the Angel (19:1–9a)

Upon his arrival in Jezreel, Ahab informs Jezebel that Elijah slaughtered her prophets just as she had done to YHWH's prophets earlier (18:4, 13; 19:1). The only response from Jezebel recorded in the text is her threat in the form of a vow to kill the prophet within twenty-four hours. While Elijah was not afraid of pronouncing a multi-year famine, of being fed by ravens and a foreign widow, of meeting a king who wanted to kill him, or of confronting and slaughtering hundreds of prophets of Baal before the entire nation, Jezebel's threat provokes sufficient fear to lead him into a suicidal depression (19:3).[19] He flees to Beersheba, the southernmost city in the Southern Kingdom of Judah, far from the domain of Ahab and Jezebel (v. 3). After the incident on Mount Carmel, Elijah undertakes three increasingly long journeys (see Table 11, "Elijah's Journeys").

Table 11: Elijah's Journeys (1 Kings 18–19)

Reference	Starting Point	Ending Point	Distance (as the crow flies)	Comment
1 Kgs 18:46	Mount Carmel	Jezreel	20 miles	Racing Ahab to Jezreel
1 Kgs 19:3	Jezreel	Beersheba	100 miles	Fleeing Jezebel's death threat
1 Kgs 19:8	Beersheba	Mount Horeb	200 miles[20]	Traveling to meet with YHWH

Elijah leaves his servant behind (not a good idea when depressed), travels into the wilderness, sits under a broom bush, and asks God to let him die (vv. 3–4). It may be shocking that Elijah would get depressed like this (see discussion of "Ministry Depression" below), but other biblical characters experienced similar emotions. In the midst of the incessant complaining of the people in the wilderness, Moses asked God to let him die ("If this is how you are going to treat me, please go ahead and kill me"; Num 11:15). And Jonah

19. Most English translations follow the LXX and the Syriac, which have Elijah being "afraid," while the Masoretic Text has "Elijah saw."

20. Assuming the location is Jebel Musa near the southern tip of the Sinai Peninsula.

also pleaded with God to kill him after the hated Ninevites repented ("Now, Lord, take away my life, for it is better for me to die than to live"; Jonah 4:3).

Fortunately, YHWH did not grant his request but instead sent him an angel who twice woke him up and twice fed him a meal of water and fresh bread (1 Kgs 19:5–7), similar to Elijah's previous supernatural feedings from the ravens and the widow of Zarephath (17:6, 15–16).

After Elijah's second post-nap meal, the angel explains he will need sustenance, because the journey will be long. The text does not record YHWH telling Elijah where to go, but somehow he knows to head to Mount Horeb. Horeb, identified here as the mountain of God, was another name for Mount Sinai, where Moses received his call and the Ten Commandments (Exod 3:1; 17:6; 19:23; 24:16). The exact location of Sinai/Horeb is uncertain, but the commonly held view associates it with Jebel Musa (literally, "Mount Moses") near the southern tip of the Sinai Peninsula, a distance of several hundred miles from Beersheba. His journey lasted forty days and nights, establishing another connection with Moses, who spent forty days and forty nights on the mountain (Exod 24:18).[21] Upon his arrival at Horeb, Elijah spent the night in a cave (1 Kgs 19:9).

Elijah and YHWH II (19:9b–18)

The interaction between YHWH and Elijah at Horeb is unusually formulaic for a prophetic narrative in Kings. YHWH speaks to Elijah four (or perhaps five) times in this section (19:9, 11, 12?, 13, 15). YHWH asks Elijah the same question twice (vv. 9, 13), and Elijah gives YHWH the same answer twice (vv. 10, 14). After each of Elijah's responses, YHWH commands him to go and do something (vv. 11, 15). The first time, Elijah goes and experiences three natural elements (wind, earthquake, and fire) in a highly formulaic manner. The second time, Elijah is called to go and anoint three new leaders of Aram and Israel (Hazael, Jehu, and Elisha).

YHWH's question, "What are you doing here, Elijah?" is interpreted in various ways by commentators: as a rhetorical question by Cogan,[22] as a challenge or rebuke by Alter and DeVries,[23] or as a call to reflection by Wiseman,[24] but the role the question serves in this narrative is simply to provide space for the depressed prophet to speak to his divine counselor, expressing his raw emotions upon finding that his zeal for God has been responded to with

21. See Table 12 on the parallels between Elijah and Moses (2 Kings 1:1–2:18), p. 294.

22. Cogan, *I Kings*, 452.

23. Alter, *Former Prophets*, 707; DeVries, *1 Kings*, 236.

24. Wiseman, *1 & 2 Kings*, 172.

abandonment, both by his people and by his God. There is no explicit rebuke in the interaction, not even to Elijah's grossly underestimated accounting of the number of prophets and worshipers of YHWH (18:22; 19:10, 14). Elijah thinks he is unique, but we know that there were at least a hundred prophets loyal to YHWH (18:4, 13), and YHWH will later inform Elijah there are seven thousand YHWH worshipers (19:18; see also Paul's discussion, Rom 11:1–5). However, a divine numerical correction ("Actually . . .") is not the first step YHWH takes to bring Elijah out of his depression.

Instead, YHWH merely asks Elijah to step outside to experience the power of God in nature, first in a wind, then an earthquake, and finally a fire. While God is clearly revealing his power to Elijah through these phenomena, in each of these three instances the divine presence is somehow "not in" them, paradoxically labeled "non-theophanies" by Barnes.[25] Moses experienced God's power and presence via wind as YHWH used it to part the Red Sea (Exod 14:21; 15:10), via an earthquake as Mount Sinai "trembled violently" while he was there (Exod 19:18), and via fire as YHWH called him at the burning bush (Exod 3:2). But for Elijah, he experiences God here through "a gentle whisper" (1 Kgs 19:12), which could literally be translated as "a whisper-thin voice" (*qol demamah daqah*).[26] Although the text does not state that YHWH was speaking through the voice, the lack of a negative comment and the fact that the "voice" of 19:13 (using the same Hebrew word, *qol*, that appeared in v. 12 to describe the still, small *voice*) is clearly God's, suggests that the soft voice came from God as well.

Why does God use a gentle voice and not these powerful natural manifestations to communicate to his prophet here? It appears to be a subtle way that YHWH is attempting to bring peace to Elijah. Like a good therapist during a counseling session, he uses questions, nature, and now a silent whisper to soothe his troubled prophet.

YHWH asks the same question he asked before (vv. 9, 13; "What are you doing here?"), and Elijah gives the same response (vv. 10, 14; "I have been very zealous. . . ."). While last time YHWH told him to step outside, this time YHWH tells him to return and anoint Hazael king over Aram, Jehu king over Israel, and Elisha as prophet instead of him.[27]

---

25. Barnes, *1–2 Kings*, 163.

26. English translations offer a wide variety of options for this phrase: "the sound of a low whisper" (ESV); "a sound of a gentle blowing" (NASB); "a sound of sheer silence" (NRSV); "a gentle whisper" (NIV), but the familiar "a still small voice" (KJV) is perhaps best. For an alternative perspective on this sound, see Jeffrey Niehaus, *God at Sinai: Covenant and Theophany in the Bible and Ancient Near East* (Grand Rapids: Zondervan, 1995), 247–48.

27. See also David T. Lamb, "'A Prophet Instead of You' (1 Kings 19.16): Elijah, Elisha and Prophetic Succession" in *Prophecy and the Prophets in Ancient Israel*, ed. J. Day, LHBOTS 531 (New York: T&T Clark, 2010), 172–87.

There are three unusual aspects to YHWH's commission to Elijah here. First, Elijah anoints none of these people. He throws his cloak over Elisha (v. 19), his successor Elisha serves as a catalyst for Hazael's coup (2 Kgs 8:7–15), and Elisha's apprentice anoints Jehu (9:1–6). Even if one were to argue that these interactions constituted a type of "anointing," only the first was performed by Elijah. And yet each of these leadership transitions took place as YHWH predicted, and Elijah was somehow involved in the process.

Second, foreign rulers are not typically anointed by Israelite prophets. The text records Israelite prophets anointing three Israelite rulers (Saul: 1 Sam 9:16; David: 1 Sam 16:13; Solomon: 1 Kgs 1:34–45), but there are no recordings of foreign rulers being anointed, particularly by Israelites.

Third, prophets are not typically anointed by a predecessor. Typically, prophets are raised up by a divine call (e.g., 1 Sam 3; Isa 6; Jer 1:4–10), not by the prophet they are meant to replace. The Elijah-Elisha prophetic transition is unique.

YHWH also informs Elijah that these new leaders will wield swords that will continue the slaughter that he began against the prophets of Baal. And while Elijah may have felt alone and isolated in his devotion, there were at least seven thousand who had not corrupted themselves by worshiping Baal (1 Kgs 19:18).

Elijah and Elisha (1 Kgs 19:19–21)

With his depression lifted, Elijah finds Elisha right away; presumably the patronymic ("son of Shaphat") and the geographic designation ("from Abel Meholah") was sufficient information to locate him quickly. Elisha was a wealthy man, as he appears to own twelve yoke of oxen (19:19).

Both individuals display reluctance to move into a mentor-apprentice relationship during this encounter. Elijah does not anoint Elisha or even speak a word to him initially but merely throws his cloak over his successor, who will "take up the mantle" of Elijah after his dramatic departure (2 Kgs 2:13). Elisha wants to delay, to kiss his parents goodbye (1 Kgs 19:20), a response comparable to several would-be disciples that Jesus interacts with (Luke 9:59–62). The call to discipleship is always costly (Luke 14:25–33), which explains why it is not popular and is often ignored.

Elijah's cryptic response ("What have I done to you?," 1 Kgs 19:20) could be interpreted either as a rebuke or merely as a reminder that Elisha will need to return after his farewell.[28] By burning his yoke and slaughtering his oxen, Elisha made a dramatic statement that he had indeed counted the cost, that he

28. See Wiseman, *1 & 2 Kings*, 174–75.

would become Elijah's disciple, and that he would celebrate this decision with a feast with family and friends (v. 21). At this point Elijah disappears from the narrative for a chapter and half (21:17), and Elisha does not reappear until immediately prior to Elijah's departure (2 Kgs 2:1).

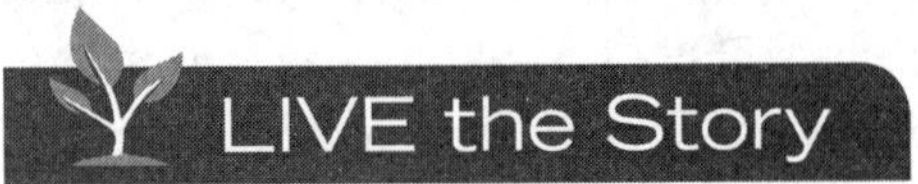

LIVE the Story

Divine Silence

YHWH will speak clearly and dramatically by the end of the story, and we aren't surprised by Baal's silence. But divine silence, even for YHWH, is a theme reappearing in many biblical texts, particularly in the Psalms, as God is accused of not responding to the psalmist's plight, "For if you remain silent, I will be like those who go down to the pit" (Ps 28:1; see also Pss 83:1; 109:1).

The prophet Habakkuk expresses a similar idea as he asks YHWH, "Why are you silent while the wicked swallow up those more righteous than themselves?" (Hab 1:13). Many people of faith have asked God similar questions during times of spiritual drought and testing, and, just as Elijah had to wait in hiding for several years before he experienced the power and deliverance of God, Christians who wonder about God's silence can look to the examples of people like Elijah for hope. Even Jesus on the cross, when he asked God why he was forsaken, seemed to receive no answer (Mark 15:34), but we know that because of his obedience unto death he was ultimately exalted by God (Phil 2:9–11; Heb 12:2).

Elijah Mentors the People

Before he begins to disciple Elisha, Elijah mentors the people of Israel, moving them away from Baal and toward YHWH. The people go from silence (1 Kgs 18:21), to "good idea" (v. 24), to coming when he calls (v. 30), to filling and pouring three loads of precious water (vv. 33–34), to declaring YHWH is God (v. 39), and finally to attacking the prophets of Baal (v. 40). How did Elijah take people who weren't even willing to declare a side and make them zealous YHWH worshipers?

While it would be tempting to merely focus on the dramatic divine display of power as the fire came down from heaven, we would be remiss if we skipped the many other ways Elijah was influencing the people toward YHWH along the way. Some of Elijah's actions are not applicable for us today (calling people to kill false prophets), but much of what he does we can emulate. Elijah asks the people a question (v. 21), explains his plan to them (vv. 23–24), calls them near (v. 30), models preparation for worship by constructing the altar (vv. 32–33), asks them to do something costly (vv. 33–34), prays for them to see God (vv. 36–37), and, after the fire fell down, he commands them to seize the Baal prophets (v. 40). Jesus mentors his disciples in a variety of similar ways: by asking questions (Mark 6:38; 7:18), by explaining what was going to happen (8:31; 11:2–3), by calling them to take dramatic steps (8:34–38; 10:43–44), and by praying for them (6:46; 14:32; John 17:6–19).

We can therefore learn from the examples of Elijah and Jesus as we think about mentoring family and friends, moving them closer to God. While we may desperately desire dramatic decisions (a conversion, a recommitment, a decision to go on a summer mission trip) in the people we are trying to mentor, getting them to that place often involves many small steps. We ask them a question about where they are with God. We tell them what God is doing in our lives. We invite them to go to a small group or to church with us. We ask them to help us in one of our acts of servanthood (working at a soup kitchen). We pray for them like Elijah. After they have begun to take these types of small steps, then it may be time to ask them to take the next step, a bigger step of commitment. For both the Israelites in the time of Elijah and our friends and family today, conversion and commitment is often a process.

YHWH Counsels the Prophet

Elijah's behavior in this passage is shocking. What prompted the courageous prophet who confronted hundreds of prophets of Baal to flee in fear and ask God to kill him as he sat under the broom tree? The prophet's actions here, however, are not as surprising to anyone who has been in ministry for a while. Many of us are familiar with the valley that immediately follows a mountaintop experience—the Monday after a weekend retreat, the week at home after returning from a summer mission. Elijah's competition with and victory over the prophets of Baal on Mount Carmel would qualify on both a figurative and literal level.

Just as we can learn from Elijah's mentoring of the people in 1 Kings 18, we can learn from YHWH's counseling of Elijah in chapter 19. YHWH serves as the prophet's counselor as he cared for his physical needs as well as his emotional and spiritual needs. YHWH's angel gives him time to sleep, makes sure he has plenty of food, and gives him a task that will involve a long journey (vv. 5–8). For people who are experiencing discouragement or depression, simply eating, sleeping, and exercise can work wonders to lift one's spirits. They don't fix everything, but a nap, a snack, and walk will make most people feel better.

Like a good counselor, YHWH also asks questions and gives Elijah a chance to talk, even to repeat himself. And knowing the therapeutic power of nature, YHWH allows him to experience the power of creation with wind, an earthquake, and fire. As their therapy session is ending, YHWH gives him a task (homework, essentially): to anoint three new leaders (Hazael, Jehu, and Elisha). One may question YHWH's approach here, "If you want to die, I can replace you with Elisha," but it apparently proved effective at lifting the prophet's depression, since he obeys and immediately goes to find Elisha. Wise leaders should be able both to anticipate these types of broom-tree experiences and to learn from YHWH's example here as he cares for both the physical and spiritual needs of his prophet as he begins to mentor his own successor.

Just as YHWH counseled the prophet, so Jesus served as a counselor to the people he interacted with. We don't learn the details of their counseling session, but, after healing the woman with a flow of blood, Jesus listened to her whole story while Jairus, the ruler of the synagogue, was left waiting (Mark 5:33). In John's Gospel, Jesus has long interactions with Nicodemus at night (John 3:1–21) and with a Samaritan woman at a well, the latter conversation breaking down barriers of race and gender (John 4:7–28). Even as he was about to leave, Jesus promised to send a counselor, the Holy Spirit, to be with his disciples, to teach them and to bear witness about himself (John 14:16, 26; 15:26).

God Reveals His Power in Kazakhstan

While I have never called down fire from heaven, the closest I've come to experiencing a similar "power encounter" happened during the summer of 1994 when my wife Shannon and I directing a team of eight InterVarsity students on a project to Kazakhstan in Central Asia. We were teaching English and learning Kazakh. Each of the Americans had a Kazakh roommate, all of whom were Muslim.

Ten days before we were supposed to leave, I went on an errand with our Kazakh friend Zhanar to buy tickets to fly back to Moscow. To purchase our tickets, I needed to carry with me all our cash ($2400) and our ten passports. En route, the bus Zhanar and I were traveling on broke down, so the passengers from two crowded buses were shoved into one extraordinarily crowded bus. In the confusion I became separated from Zhanar. I noticed the zipper to my backpack was open. I reached in to make sure that the passports and money were still there. They weren't.

In the chaos a thief reached into my backpack that was tucked under my arm, unzipped it, and grabbed the passports and money. I was devastated—all our money and all our passports were gone. It was the worst day of my life. I had to go back and tell the team what happened. While doing this, I wept.

The next week was filled with ups and downs, attempting to get the passports and money replaced. We were supposed to leave Saturday morning, but by Wednesday morning we had made no progress. The US embassy was having problems issuing passports, so we weren't going to be able to get new passports until Thursday afternoon at the earliest. But to leave the country we needed exit visas, and visas normally take one to two weeks. The money that was wired from the US had arrived, but the Kazakh banks didn't have enough dollars and might not be able to pay us for another week. And I just found out earlier that our ten flight tickets were going to cost us $2000, instead of the $800 they had promised us earlier.

We needed cash to get passports; passports to get visas; and cash, passports, and visas to get tickets. We were supposed to leave in less than three days; we had nothing. The Kazakhs were saying "God is punishing you for not being Muslim."

Wednesday afternoon I complained to God in my anger, "Why are you doing this?" Then I started to laugh. This situation was too horrible, like something that would happen in the Bible. God must be behind it. We needed to display our dependence on him in a dramatic way. We decided to pray like Elijah on Mount Carmel (1 Kgs 18:36–37). That night we held an all-night prayer vigil, praying in shifts that God would get us home, reveal himself to our Kazakh friends, and make it clear that he alone was God.

Thursday afternoon the Kazakh bank finally had enough cash to pay us, so we rushed to the US embassy at 2:30, and after being disappointed for the past four days, they finally had our passports, which we could finally pay for. We arrived at the visa agency at 3:30. The woman said she could give us our visas Friday morning (which was breaking several rules). Our Kazakh friend and translator said that isn't good enough. She called the vice president of our university, who called an administrator at the visa agency. Ten minutes later, this administrator came down and said, "Give them their visas now." We left the agency at 4:30 with ten visas.

The airline ticketing office closed at 5:00. Shannon, Yernar, one of the Kazakh students, and I sprinted to catch a taxi. I didn't want to take public transportation this time. We met Zhanar there. We arrived at 4:45 and waited in several lines. We were hoping to pay $800 for the ten tickets but were expecting to pay $2000. When we finally got to the front of the line, I asked Zhanar, "Which rate will we pay?" She replied, "You will pay the cheaper rate." We celebrated.

I turned to Zhanar, "You know we prayed all night."

"Yes, I know, Yernar told me. It seemed to work." You bet it worked.

That night we worshiped God with our Kazakh friends, and Saturday morning we left as scheduled. God revealed both to us and to our Muslim friends that he alone is God (1 Kgs 18:39).

CHAPTER 16

1 Kings 20:1–43

LISTEN to the Story

1Now Ben-Hadad king of Aram mustered his entire army. Accompanied by thirty-two kings with their horses and chariots, he went up and besieged Samaria and attacked it. 2He sent messengers into the city to Ahab king of Israel, saying, "This is what Ben-Hadad says: 3'Your silver and gold are mine, and the best of your wives and children are mine.'"

4The king of Israel answered, "Just as you say, my lord the king. I and all I have are yours."

5The messengers came again and said, "This is what Ben-Hadad says: 'I sent to demand your silver and gold, your wives and your children. 6But about this time tomorrow I am going to send my officials to search your palace and the houses of your officials. They will seize everything you value and carry it away.'"

7The king of Israel summoned all the elders of the land and said to them, "See how this man is looking for trouble! When he sent for my wives and my children, my silver and my gold, I did not refuse him."

8The elders and the people all answered, "Don't listen to him or agree to his demands."

9So he replied to Ben-Hadad's messengers, "Tell my lord the king, 'Your servant will do all you demanded the first time, but this demand I cannot meet.'" They left and took the answer back to Ben-Hadad.

10Then Ben-Hadad sent another message to Ahab: "May the gods deal with me, be it ever so severely, if enough dust remains in Samaria to give each of my men a handful."

11The king of Israel answered, "Tell him: 'One who puts on his armor should not boast like one who takes it off.'"

12Ben-Hadad heard this message while he and the kings were drinking in their tents, and he ordered his men: "Prepare to attack." So they prepared to attack the city.

[13]Meanwhile a prophet came to Ahab king of Israel and announced, "This is what the LORD says: 'Do you see this vast army? I will give it into your hand today, and then you will know that I am the LORD.'"

[14]"But who will do this?" asked Ahab.

The prophet replied, "This is what the LORD says: 'The junior officers under the provincial commanders will do it.'"

"And who will start the battle?" he asked.

The prophet answered, "You will."

[15]So Ahab summoned the 232 junior officers under the provincial commanders. Then he assembled the rest of the Israelites, 7,000 in all.
[16]They set out at noon while Ben-Hadad and the 32 kings allied with him
were in their tents getting drunk. [17]The junior officers under the provincial
commanders went out first.

Now Ben-Hadad had dispatched scouts, who reported, "Men are advancing from Samaria."

[18]He said, "If they have come out for peace, take them alive; if they have come out for war, take them alive."

[19]The junior officers under the provincial commanders marched
out of the city with the army behind them [20]and each one struck down
his opponent. At that, the Arameans fled, with the Israelites in pursuit. But Ben-Hadad king of Aram escaped on horseback with some of his
horsemen. [21]The king of Israel advanced and overpowered the horses and
chariots and inflicted heavy losses on the Arameans.

[22]Afterward, the prophet came to the king of Israel and said, "Strengthen your position and see what must be done, because next spring the king of Aram will attack you again."

[23]Meanwhile, the officials of the king of Aram advised him, "Their
gods are gods of the hills. That is why they were too strong for us. But if
we fight them on the plains, surely we will be stronger than they. [24]Do
this: Remove all the kings from their commands and replace them with
other officers. [25]You must also raise an army like the one you lost—horse
for horse and chariot for chariot—so we can fight Israel on the plains. Then surely we will be stronger than they." He agreed with them and acted accordingly.

[26]The next spring Ben-Hadad mustered the Arameans and went up to
Aphek to fight against Israel. [27]When the Israelites were also mustered and
given provisions, they marched out to meet them. The Israelites camped

opposite them like two small flocks of goats, while the Arameans covered
the countryside.
[28]The man of God came up and told the king of Israel, "This is what
the LORD says: 'Because the Arameans think the LORD is a god of the hills
and not a god of the valleys, I will deliver this vast army into your hands,
and you will know that I am the LORD.'"
[29]For seven days they camped opposite each other, and on the seventh
day the battle was joined. The Israelites inflicted a hundred thousand casualties on the Aramean foot soldiers in one day. [30]The rest of them escaped
to the city of Aphek, where the wall collapsed on twenty-seven thousand
of them. And Ben-Hadad fled to the city and hid in an inner room.
[31]His officials said to him, "Look, we have heard that the kings of
Israel are merciful. Let us go to the king of Israel with sackcloth around
our waists and ropes around our heads. Perhaps he will spare your life."
[32]Wearing sackcloth around their waists and ropes around their heads,
they went to the king of Israel and said, "Your servant Ben-Hadad says:
'Please let me live.'"

The king answered, "Is he still alive? He is my brother."
[33]The men took this as a good sign and were quick to pick up his word.
"Yes, your brother Ben-Hadad!" they said.

"Go and get him," the king said. When Ben-Hadad came out, Ahab had him come up into his chariot.

[34]"I will return the cities my father took from your father," Ben-Hadad
offered. "You may set up your own market areas in Damascus, as my father
did in Samaria."

Ahab said, "On the basis of a treaty I will set you free." So he made a treaty with him, and let him go.

[35]By the word of the LORD one of the company of the prophets said to
his companion, "Strike me with your weapon," but he refused.
[36]So the prophet said, "Because you have not obeyed the LORD, as soon
as you leave me a lion will kill you." And after the man went away, a lion
found him and killed him.
[37]The prophet found another man and said, "Strike me, please." So the
man struck him and wounded him. [38]Then the prophet went and stood
by the road waiting for the king. He disguised himself with his headband
down over his eyes. [39]As the king passed by, the prophet called out to him,
"Your servant went into the thick of the battle, and someone came to me

with a captive and said, 'Guard this man. If he is missing, it will be your life for his life, or you must pay a talent of silver.' [40]While your servant was busy here and there, the man disappeared."

"That is your sentence," the king of Israel said. "You have pronounced it yourself."

[41]Then the prophet quickly removed the headband from his eyes, and the king of Israel recognized him as one of the prophets. [42]He said to the king, "This is what the LORD says: 'You have set free a man I had determined should die. Therefore it is your life for his life, your people for his people.'" [43]Sullen and angry, the king of Israel went to his palace in Samaria.

Listening to the Text in the Story: Biblical Texts: 2 Samuel 12:1–7; 14:1–20; 1 Kings 15:18; Ancient Near Eastern Texts: The Inscription of Zakkur; A Letter from Hattusili III; The Kurkh Monolith

Biblical Parallels

At this point in the narrative the prophet Elijah disappears, until he reappears at the end of the next chapter to condemn Ahab for killing Naboth and stealing his vineyard (1 Kgs 21:17–29). Because of this disappearance, some scholars think the Septuagint's ordering of these chapters, where the account of Naboth's vineyard immediately follows the commissioning of Elisha (19:19–21), is more reasonable than the MT's ordering, which is followed by English translations.[1]

This chapter tells the story of the Aramean threat against Israel, as Ben-Hadad besieged and attacked Samaria and made severe demands of tribute to Ahab of Israel. Despite Ahab's status as an evil idolater, YHWH twice delivers him in battle from Aram, sending a constant stream of anonymous prophets, with the final one condemning the king for not killing Ben-Hadad. The prophetic condemnation takes the form of an enacted drama that prompts Ahab to essentially pronounce judgment on himself (20:39–40), comparable to the stories told to David by Nathan (2 Sam 12:1–7; "You are the man!") and by the wise woman of Tekoa (2 Sam 14:1–20; "does he not convict himself?").

The name Ben-Hadad means "son of the god Hadad," and it appears to be a throne name borne by at least three rulers of Aram (1 Kgs 15:18,

1. See for example, Barnes, *1–2 Kings*, 168.

20; 20:1–34; 2 Kgs 6:24; 8:7, 9; 13:3, 24, 25), analogous to how Egyptian rulers were called simply "Pharaoh."[2] To distinguish him from Ben-Hadad I, who overlapped with Asa (1 Kgs 15:18), or Ben-Hadad III, who overlapped with Jehoahaz of Israel (2 Kgs 13:3), this Aramean ruler is typically called Ben-Hadad II.

Ancient Near Eastern Parallels

Several ancient Near Eastern references provide important background to the events in this chapter, particularly as they focus on the nature of conflict between Israel and Aram. The engagement here begins as the text records Ben-Hadad bringing thirty-two kings as allies with him to battle (1 Kgs 20:1). In his inscription, Zakkar king of Hamath speaks of Bar-Hadad of Aram, son of Hazael, bringing seventeen kings with him to battle.[3]

The Kurkh Monolith of Shalmaneser III also speaks of Aram in a twelve-king coalition against Assyria,[4] apparently led by Hadad-ezer of Aram, who is probably Ben-Hadad II.[5] Problematically, the Kurkh Monolith includes Ahab as one of Aram's primary allies in this encounter. However, as we see in 1 Kings 20, the relationship between Israel and Aram can quickly shift from adversarial to collegial. By the end of this chapter they establish a treaty and become allies (20:34). This quick shift is not surprising since Israel and Aram were constantly changing from adversaries to allies throughout the monarchy. As he greets Ben-Hadad and establishes a treaty, Ahab calls his new friend "brother" (vv. 32–34), using language similar to that used by Hattusili III of Hatti as he mentions their treaty in his letter to Kadasman-Enlil II of Babylon: "Was it not for eternity that we became 'brothers' and concluded peace?"[6]

Ben-Hadad Threatens Ahab (20:1–12)

Aram and Israel experienced military tensions earlier in Kings (1 Kgs 11:25; 15:18–20), but here the text devotes an entire chapter to detailing a series of

2. See Mordechai Cogan and Hayim Tadmor, *II Kings*, AB 11 (New York: Doubleday, 1988), 78–79.

3. *COS* 2:155. Bar-Hadad is the Aramaic equivalent of Ben-Hadad; *bar* is "son" in Aramaic and *ben* is "son" in Hebrew. The Aramean ruler mentioned here is presumably Ben-Hadad III (2 Kgs 13:3, 24, 25).

4. *COS* 2:263–64.

5. See Cogan, *1 Kings*, 462, 473–74; Wiseman, *1 & 2 Kings*, 175.

6. *COS* 3:52.

campaigns between the two nations. Ben-Hadad lays siege to Israel's capital city Samaria with thirty kings plus horses and chariots. In the Kurkh Monolith, the Aramean ruler (Hadad-ezer = Ben-Hadad II) has twelve hundred chariots, twelve hundred cavalry, and twenty thousand troops, while Ahab has more chariots (two thousand) but half as many troops (ten thousand).[7]

This passage is framed by three rounds of messages between the kings of Aram and Israel. In his first message, Ben-Hadad lays claim to Ahab's gold, silver, wives, and children (20:2–3), and Ahab shockingly consents immediately to handing over his wealth and family to the man he calls "my lord," presumably because he viewed himself as a vassal of Aram (v. 4).[8] Wiseman assumes that Ben-Hadad's heightened threat (round two) to return the next day to ransack the palace and seize everything (vv. 5–6) was meant to "instigate war" and was not because he was somehow dissatisfied with Ahab's initial response.[9]

While Ahab merely offered tribute to Ben-Hadad II here (vv. 4, 9), fourteen rulers of Israel and Judah actually gave tribute or were plundered by foreign powers (Rehoboam, Asa, Jehu, Jehoash of Judah, Jehoash of Israel, Amaziah, Menahem, Ahaz, Hezekiah, Jehoahaz of Judah, Jehoiakim, Jehoiachin, and Zedekiah).[10] But the two most relevant examples are Asa of Judah's gift of silver and gold from the temple and his royal treasury to Ben-Hadad I of Aram (1 Kgs 15:18), and Jehoash of Judah's gift to Hazael of Aram (2 Kgs 12:18).

To get counsel in the midst of the crisis, Ahab hastily summons all the elders of the land, who either were already in Samaria or somehow managed to get past the Aramean siege of the city. After he tells them Ben-Hadad's latest demand, they advise him to refuse to comply. By doing so, these leaders are essentially agreeing to support him in war against their northern neighbors. Ahab then informs his "lord" that he can only agree to the first demand, not the second, more severe one. Even the craven Ahab has limits.

While Ahab cowardly offers his treasures, wives, and children in his initial interaction with Ben-Hadad, eventually he responds more courageously, as he taunts the Aramean ruler with a proverb (vv. 10–12). We see a similar bold use of a wise saying from an evil Israelite ruler in a military context when Jehoash of Israel responds to the invitation to fight from Amaziah of Judah with a parable (2 Kgs 13:11; 14:9–10). The third and final message of Ben-Hadad to Ahab, essentially swearing to obliterate Samaria (1 Kgs 20:10), is framed in

7. *COS* 2:263.

8. See Wray Beal, *1 & 2 Kings*, 264.

9. Wiseman, *1 & 2 Kings*, 176.

10. See my discussion of tribute in the ancient Near East and in biblical sources in *Righteous Jehu*, 119–29.

language ("May the gods deal with me . . .") that is strikingly reminiscent of Jezebel's earlier threat to Elijah (19:2). While the faithful prophet of YHWH was so severely intimidated by the queen's words that he spiraled into a suicidal depression (vv. 3–4), the idolatrous ruler of Israel loses his fear at this point and acts courageously. Ahab reciprocates with an aphorism cautioning soldiers to refrain from boasting until after the victory (20:11). If Ben-Hadad desired a confrontation, Ahab's response was exactly what he was looking for, so he orders his men to get ready for battle. The narrator slips in two comments that the Aramean generals were drinking (v. 12) and getting drunk right before the battle (v. 16; see also 16:9), which Barnes perceives to be a "folkloristic theme for incompetence and overconfidence."[11] Ben-Hadad, despite his superior military force, illustrates the truth of the proverb, "Pride goes before destruction, a haughty spirit before a fall" (Prov 16:18). And as we will soon see, YHWH also plays a role in Aram's defeat.

YHWH Defeats Ben-Hadad for Ahab: Round 1 (20:13–22)

YHWH has been silent thus far in the narrative, but at this point he begins speaking through a series of prophetic messages that, unlike Ahab's encounters with Elijah, are cordial, as the king defers to the prophet. While the text is not clear, Cogan reasonably assumes the first three references to anonymous prophetic individuals (20:13, 22, 28) all refer to the same person.[12] In the first interaction, which involves questions from both sides, the prophet informs Ahab that (1) YHWH will provide victory; (2) the junior officers will lead the battle; (3) and Ahab will start the battle (vv. 13–14). The prophet emphasizes to the king that God wants him to know that the victory came from YHWH ("then you will know that I am the Lord"; v. 13), a message that will be repeated in the context of the subsequent victory over Aram (v. 28) and is reminiscent of the message that God sent through the prophet Elijah on Mount Carmel (18:37).

The text goes into more detail than normal for a battle narrative (20:15–16), listing the exact number of junior officers (232), as well as the number of total soldiers (7000). The decision to attack at noon caught the Arameans unaware and drunk (v. 16). In response to the warning that Israel is advancing, Ben-Hadad confidently commands his troops to "take them alive" whether they are coming for peace or war (vv. 17–18). Once the battle is finally engaged, victory comes quickly for Israel as the fleeing Arameans are pursued, overpowered, and defeated decisively (vv. 19–21). The text recorded multiple rounds of messages

11. Barnes, *1–2 Kings*, 169.

12. Cogan, *I Kings*, 465, 467.

to Ahab, both from Ben-Hadad and from YHWH, but the Aramean demands, threats, and boasts come to nothing, and the prophetic prediction is fulfilled. The prophet returns with one final message for Ahab—to get ready for round two, next spring when the king of Aram attacks again (v. 22).

YHWH Defeats Ben-Hadad for Ahab: Round 2 (20:23–34)

Ahab has been receiving counsel from the elders and a prophet, and now Ben-Hadad listens to the advice of his officials, who suggest that they attack again after replacing their officers, horses, and chariots (20:23–25). Their confidence is based on their perception that Israel's gods have authority over hills not plains, so they predict success in a different location. The last battle took place in the mountainous terrain around the city of Samaria, making the Aramean chariots ineffective. The Israelites should have known that YHWH was sovereign over all of his creation (1 Kgs 8:43, 60; 2 Kgs 19:15, 19), but the common understanding in the ancient Near Eastern context was that gods had limited domains of authority.[13]

Just as the man of God had predicted (1 Kgs 20:22), Aram musters its forces for an attack the following spring (v. 26). Compared to the vastness of the Aramean army that "covered the countryside," Israel's forces appear insignificant, "like two small flocks of goats" (v. 27). This hyperbolic language is typical of military narratives, as Gideon's opponents the Midianites were described as numerous as locusts and their camels were like the sand of the sea (Judg 7:12). No reason is given for the seven-day delay; Wiseman speculates that it may have been due to the Arameans waiting for a favorable omen.[14] When the battle is finally joined, few details are provided, except that Israel won and inflicted heavy losses on the Arameans. The casualty levels sound hyperbolic, one hundred thousand soldiers in the field of battle and another twenty-seven thousand in the city of Aphek, signifying a severe defeat. Wiseman notes that with a slight change to the Hebrew pointing (from *'elep* to *'allup* with no change to the consonants) the word "thousand" becomes "officer"; thus the defeats could have involved one hundred officers in the field or twenty-seven officers at Aphek.[15] The deadly wall collapse at Aphek is reminiscent of Joshua's victory over Jericho (Josh 6), particularly since it came on the seventh day (1 Kgs 20:29–30).

The boastful Ben-Hadad now becomes like the fearful Ahab at the beginning of the chapter, hiding from the forces of the Israelite ruler in an inner room that

13. See Barnes, *1–2 Kings*, 171.
14. Wiseman, *1 & 2 Kings*, 178.
15. Wiseman, *1 & 2 Kings*, 178.

apparently was far enough from the city wall to not be destroyed (v. 30; see also 22:25; 2 Kgs 9:2). Somehow the Aramean officials have heard that Israel's rulers are merciful (*hesed*), so they put sackcloth on their bodies and ropes around their necks as signs of humility and submission and send one final message to Ahab begging for mercy. After the king of Aram besieged, attacked, threatened, and insulted him, Ahab essentially loves his enemy, calling Ben-Hadad "my brother." They agree to a treaty, which involved setting up market areas to promote trade and the return of Israelite cities captured in the past. While the narrative of Omri, Ahab's father, is short (1 Kgs 16:21–28), no mention is made of any losses to Aram, so presumably this treaty restores territory captured by Ben-Hadad I of Aram from Baasha of Israel (15:20). At every step of the conflict thus far, Ahab has received guidance from both the elders and YHWH via a prophet (20:7–8, 13–14, 22, 28), but at this critical juncture, as he decides the fate of Israel's enemy, he foolishly consults neither his leaders nor his God.

Lions, and Prophets, and Kings (20:35–43)

The scene shifts from an interaction between kings to one between prophets. The prophetic guild, mentioned here for the first time in Kings (20:35), was active during the reign of Saul (1 Sam 19:20) but more frequently during the ministry of Elisha (2 Kgs 2:3, 5, 7, 15; 4:1, 38; 5:22; 6:1; 9:1). While comparisons can be made between the prophet's enacted parable here to Ahab and the stories both of Nathan and of the wise woman of Tekoa to David (2 Sam 12:1–7; 14:4–11), in those scenarios the reader has a clue about the intended message to David; here we, like Ahab, are in the dark until the final reveal.

This incident has several parallels to the bizarre incident of the prophet-killing lion in 1 Kings 13. The expression "by the word of the LORD" appears seven times there (13:1, 2, 5, 9, 17, 18, 32); likewise here it is used to inform us that this prophet's unusual behavior had divine sanction (20:35). The first prophet tells a second prophet to use his weapon to strike (hiphil of *nakah*) the first, but he refuses, so the first informs the second that he will be struck down (hiphil of *nakah*) by a lion, a word that was immediately fulfilled (v. 36). Within prophetic narratives, lions are the predator of choice to bring judgment on disobedient prophets (13:24; 20:36; bears are used for children: 2 Kgs 2:23–25; dogs and birds for royal corpses: 1 Kgs 14:11; 16:4; 21:19, 23, 24; 2 Kgs 9:10, 36). The eventual intended recipient of the message will be Ahab, but the sudden death of one of his prophetic colleagues communicated clearly to a third prophet the importance of obedience, so when the first prophet asked him to strike him (hiphil of *nakah*), he quickly complies (1 Kgs 20:37), giving the first a wound to make him look like he had just been fighting.

While we wonder what this masochistic prophet is planning next, he dons a disguise before speaking to Ahab (v. 38). The freshly wounded prophet tells the story of a captive soldier that he was charged to guard, having been warned that if he lost the captive then he would forfeit either a talent of silver or his own life (vv. 39–40). A fine of a talent of silver (three thousand shekels) would have been impossible for most soldiers to pay, an amount a hundred times the cost of a slave (Exod 21:32). The disguised prophet never asks, but the circumstances clearly imply that he is looking for a judgment from the ruler who, immediately after showing mercy to his enemy Ben-Hadad, shows none now to his own soldier as he declares the penalty for losing his charge is a talent or death (v. 40). At this point the prophet makes his dramatic reveal, removing his disguise and declaring that just as Ahab had pronounced essentially death for the disguised prophet, so YHWH declares death for Ahab, since he released Ben-Hadad, whom YHWH had determined should die (vv. 41–42).

The ancient Jewish historian Josephus (*Ant.* viii. 14.5) identifies the unnamed member of the company of the prophets as Micaiah, a reasonable assumption because Ahab later declares that he hates Micaiah because he "never prophesies good" for the king, and Micaiah also repeats a death sentence for Ahab (22:17–23). The prophet speaks confidently that Ahab should have known he needed to kill Ben-Hadad, but where does YHWH tell Ahab to kill Ben-Hadad? This incident is not as clear as when Samuel commanded Saul to wipe out the Amalekites and the king disobeys (1 Sam 15). However, YHWH had said he would deliver the whole army into Ahab's hands (1 Kgs 20:13, 28), which could imply utter destruction, and Ahab was certainly guilty of not seeking divine guidance when the Aramean ruler pleaded for mercy. One could argue that the reason Ahab had not heard this command was because he had not asked. Ignorance of the expectations of the law is no excuse. While the judgment on Ahab may seem severe, Ahab's death sentence is not carried out immediately and will be delayed by YHWH himself (21:29) and revived by Micaiah (22:20) before his eventual death in battle (22:34–38). Ahab leaves depressed and angry, and his emotional state continues into the next chapter (21:4).

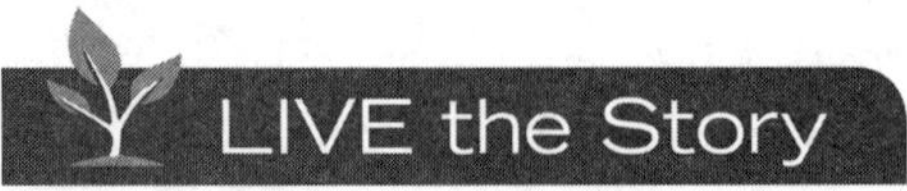

Learning Life Lessons from a Flawed Figure

King Ahab of Israel is one of the most intriguing characters in Scripture, and in this passage, we encounter him at his best and his worst. Previously in his narrative he was condemned as an idolater, and at the beginning of the conflict with Aram he is fearful and submissive, even to demands that he hand over his wives and children. Ahab's despicable behavior here is reminiscent of the patriarchs Abraham and Isaac, who both risked the honor (and perhaps lives) of their wives to save themselves (Gen 12:10–20; 20; 26:1–11).

While Ahab behaves foolishly at the end of this passage, in the middle he displays wisdom in a variety of unexpected ways. He seeks the advice of his elders in the midst of a crisis. He not only follows their advice, but by involving them in the process he has also gained partners as he goes off to battle. He speaks wisely as he confronts a more powerful ruler. It is difficult to know how he transformed from being a cowering king to a courageous leader, but his words were not only sage advice, they also prompted the Aramean attack. He listened to YHWH's prophets several times in this narrative, risking his life as he followed the advice that he would lead the battle. Ahab's last encounter with a prophet of YHWH ended badly for him, as his Baal prophets were first humiliated and then slaughtered. However, in this conflict Ahab unexpectedly follows YHWH's prophets and their guidance.

But perhaps the most shocking lesson to reflect on from this story is how God was willing to work with, to speak to, and ultimately to deliver in battle an evil, fearful, and idolatrous ruler like Ahab. Perhaps however, this lesson shouldn't surprise us since God is consistently using people who don't honor him to accomplish his purposes (e.g., Nebuchadnezzar of Babylon and Cyrus of Persia). Just as God showed mercy to Ahab here, we all can be thankful to God for all the many ways he shows mercy to us, flawed figures that we are.

CHAPTER 17

1 Kings 21:1–29

LISTEN to the Story

[1]Some time later there was an incident involving a vineyard belonging to Naboth the Jezreelite. The vineyard was in Jezreel, close to the palace of Ahab king of Samaria. [2]Ahab said to Naboth, "Let me have your vineyard to use for a vegetable garden, since it is close to my palace. In exchange I will give you a better vineyard or, if you prefer, I will pay you whatever it is worth."

[3]But Naboth replied, "The LORD forbid that I should give you the inheritance of my ancestors."

[4]So Ahab went home, sullen and angry because Naboth the Jezreelite had said, "I will not give you the inheritance of my ancestors." He lay on his bed sulking and refused to eat.

[5]His wife Jezebel came in and asked him, "Why are you so sullen? Why won't you eat?"

[6]He answered her, "Because I said to Naboth the Jezreelite, 'Sell me your vineyard; or if you prefer, I will give you another vineyard in its place.' But he said, 'I will not give you my vineyard.'"

[7]Jezebel his wife said, "Is this how you act as king over Israel? Get up and eat! Cheer up. I'll get you the vineyard of Naboth the Jezreelite."

[8]So she wrote letters in Ahab's name, placed his seal on them, and sent them to the elders and nobles who lived in Naboth's city with him. [9]In those letters she wrote:

> "Proclaim a day of fasting and seat Naboth in a prominent place among the people. [10]But seat two scoundrels opposite him and have them bring charges that he has cursed both God and the king. Then take him out and stone him to death."

11So the elders and nobles who lived in Naboth's city did as Jezebel directed in the letters she had written to them. 12They proclaimed a fast and seated Naboth in a prominent place among the people. 13Then two scoundrels came and sat opposite him and brought charges against Naboth before the people, saying, "Naboth has cursed both God and the king." So they took him outside the city and stoned him to death. 14Then they sent word to Jezebel: "Naboth has been stoned to death."

15As soon as Jezebel heard that Naboth had been stoned to death, she said to Ahab, "Get up and take possession of the vineyard of Naboth the Jezreelite that he refused to sell you. He is no longer alive, but dead." 16When Ahab heard that Naboth was dead, he got up and went down to take possession of Naboth's vineyard.

17Then the word of the LORD came to Elijah the Tishbite: 18"Go down to meet Ahab king of Israel, who rules in Samaria. He is now in Naboth's vineyard, where he has gone to take possession of it. 19Say to him, 'This is what the LORD says: Have you not murdered a man and seized his property?' Then say to him, 'This is what the LORD says: In the place where dogs licked up Naboth's blood, dogs will lick up your blood—yes, yours!'"

20Ahab said to Elijah, "So you have found me, my enemy!"

"I have found you," he answered, "because you have sold yourself to do evil in the eyes of the LORD. 21He says, 'I am going to bring disaster on you. I will wipe out your descendants and cut off from Ahab every last male in Israel—slave or free. 22I will make your house like that of Jeroboam son of Nebat and that of Baasha son of Ahijah, because you have aroused my anger and have caused Israel to sin.'

23"And also concerning Jezebel the LORD says: 'Dogs will devour Jezebel by the wall of Jezreel.'

24"Dogs will eat those belonging to Ahab who die in the city, and the birds will feed on those who die in the country."

25(There was never anyone like Ahab, who sold himself to do evil in the eyes of the LORD, urged on by Jezebel his wife. 26He behaved in the vilest manner by going after idols, like the Amorites the LORD drove out before Israel.)

27When Ahab heard these words, he tore his clothes, put on sackcloth and fasted. He lay in sackcloth and went around meekly.

28Then the word of the LORD came to Elijah the Tishbite: 29"Have you noticed how Ahab has humbled himself before me? Because he has humbled himself, I will not bring this disaster in his day, but I will bring it on his house in the days of his son."

Listening to the Text in the Story: Biblical Texts: Judges 6:33; 1 Samuel 8:14; Ancient Near Eastern Texts: The Eloquent Peasant; The Jezebel Seal; An Akkadian Marriage Agreement; Ashurbanipal's Royal Annals; The Ahiram Sarcophagus

King Ahab of Israel has many evil deeds on his royal resume, but standing passively on the sidelines while his wife Jezebel orchestrated the death of his neighbor Naboth so he could possess his vineyard is perhaps the most heinous. YHWH thought so, as is evident from the shocking condemnation pronounced by Elijah at the end of the chapter. But before working through this tragic and twisted tale, a brief survey of relevant biblical and ancient Near Eastern parallels will help us understand its culture and context.

The setting is Ahab's palace in the city of Jezreel, about fifty miles north of Jerusalem and about twenty miles north of Samaria, on the edge of the Jezreel Valley. During the time of the judges, the Midianites and their allies gathered in the Jezreel Valley to attack the forces of Gideon (Judg 6:33). Ahab's son, Jehoram, was killed in Jezreel by Jehu, and his body was thrown onto the plot of ground that had belonged to Naboth the Jezreelite. Jehu construed his own actions as a fulfillment of the prophecy pronounced against Ahab (2 Kgs 9:25–26; see also 1 Kgs 21:19).

In order to force the elders and nobles of Naboth's city to do her bidding, Jezebel used her husband Ahab's seal on her letter (21:8). In their context, individuals in positions of power, often used seals to authorize important documents to ensure the compliance of their subordinates.[1] In 1964 a beautiful seal was found with distinctive Phoenician symbols bearing the name "Jezebel" and dated to the ninth century. Many scholars believe this seal actually belonged to Queen Jezebel.[2]

Ahab takes possession of Naboth's vineyard after having accused him (falsely) of treason (v. 16). Similarly, an Akkadian marriage agreement speaks of a criminal who was executed for a crime and then his estate was confiscated

1. See images in *ANEP*, 75, 82, 85; #239, 265, 276–78.

2. See *ZIBBC* 3.71. For images of the seal and an argument that it belonged to Queen Jezebel of Israel, see Marjo C. A. Korpel, *BAR* 34.2 (2008): 32–37, 80.

by the palace.[3] The Egyptian story of "The Eloquent Peasant" narrates how a certain noble man attempted unsuccessfully to steal the possessions of a poor farmer, who was sufficiently articulate to gain the ear of the pharaoh who, unlike Ahab, gave him justice.[4] Before Saul became king, the prophet Samuel warned the people of Israel that if they were to choose a king, he would confiscate their property, specifically their best fields and vineyards (1 Sam 8:14), a task that Ahab seemed unwilling to undertake here without his wife's initiative.

At the end of the previous chapter, King Ahab received a prophetic condemnation (1 Kgs 20:42); at the end of this chapter, Elijah pronounces a gruesome judgment upon him, his wife, and his descendants. Elijah's curse predicted that the bodies of Ahab and Jezebel would be consumed by dogs and birds. Ahab's blood was in fact licked up by dogs (22:38), and Jezebel was trampled by horses before her carcass was consumed by dogs (2 Kgs 9:33–37). In the annals of King Ashurbanipal of Assyria, similar fates befall people who blaspheme against the god Ashur, "I fed their corpses to dogs, pigs, *zibu*-birds, vultures."[5]

The canine consummation curse got Ahab's attention, so, just as the Arameans did earlier (1 Kgs 20:32), he puts on sackcloth in response to the word of judgment from Elijah (21:27); for an image of similar practices associated with mourning, see the Ahiram sarcophagus from Phoenicia.[6]

EXPLAIN the Story

Naboth's Refusal (21:1–4)

YHWH is silent for much of the story, only speaking through the voice of the prophet Elijah at the end (21:17). The setting is Jezreel, probably the winter home of King Ahab since it was at a lower altitude (about 380' above sea level), and therefore milder, than his main capital in Samaria (about 1350' feet above sea level) in the hill country.[7]

Ahab covets his neighbor's Naboth's vineyard (see Deut 5:21) to make his own vegetable garden (1 Kgs 21:1–2). While it is easy to vilify Ahab here, his initial request to Naboth is reasonable—a fair payment or a better vineyard

3. *COS* 3:251; for other examples of royal confiscation, see *COS* 3:256–57.
4. *COS* 1:99; *ANET*, 407.
5. *ANET*, 288.
6. *ANEP*, #459.
7. See Wiseman, *1 & 2 Kings*, 183.

in exchange for a vineyard. There are certainly precedents for these types of transactions. The patriarch Abraham had paid his neighbor Ephron for a field in Machpelah (Gen 23). Since Ahab's father Omri had successfully purchased a hill from Shemar to use as his new capital Samaria (named after its previous owner; 1 Kgs 16:24), Ahab reasonably assumed he would succeed in his attempt to purchase land from Naboth (21:2). To his credit, Ahab's first response was not royal confiscation, as Samuel had predicted (1 Sam 8:14).

Naboth's response could appear self-righteous as he invokes a curse upon himself should he decide to sell his tribal inheritance. But his response is reasonable in light of laws concerning the sale of property. While Leviticus did not completely restrict sales of property, it forbade the permanent sale of land, since all the land belonged to YHWH (Lev 25:23); any temporary land sales were to revert to the original tribal owner at the year of Jubilee (Lev 25:28), preventing the rich from getting richer while the poor get poorer. Unfortunately, it is possible, perhaps even likely, that the Jubilee principle was never put into practice.[8]

After hearing Naboth's refusal to sell or trade, Ahab becomes "sullen and angry" (1 Kgs 21:4), which is how he was described at the end of the previous chapter after being condemned by the anonymous prophet (20:43). Scholars typically describe Ahab's emotional response here as highly negatively. Barnes speaks of the "immaturity of the pouting king"; Alter calls him "a petulant adolescent"; Freedman describes him as manipulative.[9] However, there is little evidence supporting the idea that Ahab's emotional response should be viewed negatively (see also the discussion in Chapter 36 of Hezekiah's prayer in 2 Kgs 20:1–6). Two words are used to describe Ahab's emotions here. The first, *sar*, "sullen," only appears three times in Scripture, always describing Ahab (1 Kgs 20:43; 21:4, 5), so there is not sufficient usage of the word to form a definitive opinion about its connotations. The second, *za'ep*, "angry," is used elsewhere to describe both negative and positive behavior, even three times to describe YHWH ("the LORD . . . with *raging* anger": Isa 30:30; the *rage* of the sea was caused by YHWH: Jonah 1:15; "the LORD's *wrath*": Mic 7:9). The fact that Ahab responded emotionally, with the text using a term elsewhere used for YHWH, should not be used as *prima facie* evidence to suggest that the ruler is being condemned for expressing emotions. In his final judgment, YHWH expresses condemnation not for Ahab's emotional outburst but for the actions

8. See Gordon J. Wenham, *The Book of Leviticus*, NICOT (Grand Rapids: Eerdmans, 1979), 318.

9. Barnes, *1 and 2 Kings*, 177; Alter, *Former Prophets*, 718; Freedman in Cogan, *I Kings*, 485.

that Jezebel, with his approval, carried out. YHWH is pleased with Ahab's emotional repentance at the end of the narrative. We should be careful not to quickly condemn emotional responses that do not seem appropriate to us.

Jezebel's Plot (21:5–16)

Jezebel notices her husband's behavior, specifically that he was not eating, and asks him why he is feeling blue. He relates to his wife what happened with Naboth (21:6). She tells him to cheer up and eat—she will take care of the problem (v. 7). To her credit, Jezebel knew how to get things done, and, ultimately, she solves her husband's dilemma. But her means and her end were diabolical. Her wicked scheme involved deception, blasphemy, murder, and theft. Jezebel knew how other rulers, as predicted by Samuel, treated their subjects.

To implement her evil plot, she writes letters to the elders and nobles of Naboth's city, authorizing them with her husband's seal (v. 8), forcing these leaders to obey or be accused of disobeying a royal edict. Ahab must have given consent to use his seal. The leaders of Naboth's town were to proclaim a fast day (v. 9)—ironic, after she had just told Ahab to end his fast—which would signal a national crisis (2 Chr 20:3; Esth 4:16; Jer 36:9), making everyone involved eager to quickly resolve the situation (even to kill an innocent man) so they could get back to eating normally. She wanted to kill Naboth, but since the death penalty required two witnesses (Num 35:30; Deut 17:6; 19:15), her plot required two "scoundrels" (1 Kgs 21:10, 13), individuals willing to perjure themselves to besmirch Naboth's reputation by accusing him of blasphemy. The word "scoundrel" (literally "son of worthlessness," *bene-beliyya'al*) is a strong term of derision, not used elsewhere in Kings but used in Samuel for the priest Eli's corrupt sons (1 Sam 2:12); Abigail's first husband, the fool Nabal (1 Sam 25:17, 25); and the rebel Sheba (2 Sam 20:1). After the false accusation of these scoundrels—who would face the death penalty if discovered (Deut 19:16–19)—Naboth would then be stoned (1 Kgs 21:10).

Naboth's noble neighbors do not behave nobly as they unhesitatingly cooperate with Jezebel's diabolical scheme, starting with the fast, then the accusation, and finally the stoning of Naboth (vv. 11–13). The city leaders eagerly send word back to the queen, who then orders the king to get up and take possession of the vineyard he covets (vv. 14–15). The text records no comment from Ahab, merely his obedience to his wife's directives (v. 16).

Deuteronomy's law of the king mandated that Israel's rulers read and obey the law every day of their lives (Deut 17:18–20). Shockingly, the behavior of Israel's king and queen in this story involve breaking at least four of the

Ten Commandments (coveting, bearing false witness, murder, and theft; Exod 20; Deut 5).

YHWH's Judgment (21:17–29)

After an absence of fifty-nine verses (since 19:21), Elijah finally reappears in the narrative;[10] and after being silent thus far in this story, YHWH finally speaks, to pronounce judgment upon Ahab, his wife, and his family. The divine judgment section divides into five distinct sections:

YHWH's commission to Elijah (21:17–19),
Elijah's judgment against Ahab (21:20–22),
Elijah's judgment against Jezebel (21:23–24),
the narrator's condemnation of Ahab (21:25–26), and
the responses of Ahab and YHWH (21:27–29).

In the first section the text makes it clear that YHWH is the source of Ahab's condemnation. It states, "the word of the LORD came to Elijah" (v. 17), a formula that was last used when YHWH spoke to Elijah at Horeb (19:9). The Hebrew verb "to say" (*'amar*) is a common one, but rarely does it appear four times in one verse as it does in 21:19 (twice as "say" and twice as "says" in the NIV), in each case emphasizing that the prophet was speaking as the voice of YHWH.

YHWH begins by giving Elijah information regarding Ahab's location (Naboth's vineyard; v. 18). Then YHWH tells him to ask Ahab an accusatory rhetorical question regarding whether he committed crimes of murder and theft of property. Curiously, YHWH does not refer to Jezebel or her actions (v. 19a). Finally, YHWH informs his prophet of the sentence for Ahab's crimes. In the spirit of *lex talionis* (the law of retaliation: "an eye for an eye," Exod 21:24), in the same location that dogs licked up Naboth's blood, dogs will lick up Ahab's blood (1 Kgs 21:19b).

Rather abruptly, the narration shifts from an interaction between God and prophet (vv. 17–19) to one between king and prophet (vv. 20–24). Readers fill this ellipsis by assuming Elijah obeyed YHWH's command to "Go down to meet Ahab" (v. 18). Ahab's chilly reception of Elijah here, "So you have found me, my enemy" (v. 20), is consistent with how he views prophets elsewhere: "you troubler of Israel" (to Elijah earlier, 18:17) and "I hate him" (about Micaiah later, 22:8).

10. The Septuagint places the story of Naboth's vineyard at the end of 1 Kgs 19.

Elijah's speech was a loose paraphrase of YHWH's words, as he quickly goes off script. YHWH focused on Ahab exclusively (21:17–19), while Elijah targets not only Ahab but also his descendants (vv. 21–22) and his queen (vv. 23–24). For YHWH the crime was murder and theft (v. 19); for Elijah it was doing "evil in the eyes of the Lord" (v. 20). YHWH makes no mention of Ahab's dynasty, but Elijah declares the king's dynasty will be cut off, just as the two previous northern dynasties were (Jeroboam's and Baasha's). YHWH speaks of dogs licking Ahab's blood (v. 19), but Elijah mentions no dogs for Ahab, just dogs (and birds!) for Ahab's wife and children (vv. 23–24).

Elsewhere during the monarchy, we see great variety in how the text records messages traveling from YHWH to a prophet to a ruler, but not as wide a gap between what YHWH tells the prophet and what the prophet tells the king. The narration of the interaction between YHWH and the prophet could be terse with no details, while the details emerge when the prophet speaks to the ruler (see 1 Kgs 14:5). The narration of interaction between YHWH and the prophet could be extended with all the details, then the interaction between the prophet and the ruler is terse, lacking details (see 2 Sam 7:17). There could be no record of YHWH speaking to the prophet beforehand, just that of the prophet's interaction with the ruler (see 1 Kgs 20:42). One can resolve these tensions by assuming that Elijah, as a man of God, had the freedom to improvise as he delivered the gist of YHWH's message to the king.

The formulaic language of this canine consummation curse (see comments in Chapter 11 on 1 Kgs 14:11 earlier) is not only gruesome, it is also typical of prophetic dynastic judgments in Kings: males are described vividly as those who "pisseth against the wall" (21:21 in the KJV; see also 1 Sam 25:22, 34; 1 Kgs 14:10; 16:11; 2 Kgs 9:8), and dogs consume the urban carcasses while birds consume the rural ones (1 Kgs 21:23–24; see also 14:11; 16:4; 21:19; 22:38; 2 Kgs 9:10, 36).

After the condemnations of YHWH and Elijah, the narrator piles on his own condemnations against King Ahab (1 Kgs 21:25–26). This parenthetical judgment not only builds upon Elijah's version by using the same description of Ahab (selling himself "to do evil in the eyes of the Lord," 21:20, 25), it also accuses him of gross idolatry, thus breaking another of the Ten Commandments (see Exod 20:3–6). The conclusion that Ahab was uniquely evil is consistent with the assessment given about him earlier in Kings (1 Kgs 16:30) but somewhat in tension with similar hyperbolic conclusions about the evilness of two other rulers: Omri and Manasseh (1 Kgs 16:25; 2 Kgs 21:11).

Shockingly, after hearing Elijah's words, Ahab appears to repent. While the text never states that he confessed or repented, his actions suggest contrition.

He tore his clothes, wore sackcloth, fasted, and went about in a dejected manner (1 Kgs 21:27).[11] Perhaps the gruesomeness of the judgment got his attention and prompted his repentance? Perhaps he was genuinely sorry that he granted so much freedom to Jezebel and was shocked to discover what she had done? In any case, YHWH was moved by his penitential behavior to show compassion and changed his mind about the consequences. He informed Elijah that he had delayed the dynastic disaster for a generation (v. 29). We will see a similar divine change take place in response to Hezekiah's prayer later in the narrative (2 Kgs 20:1–6).

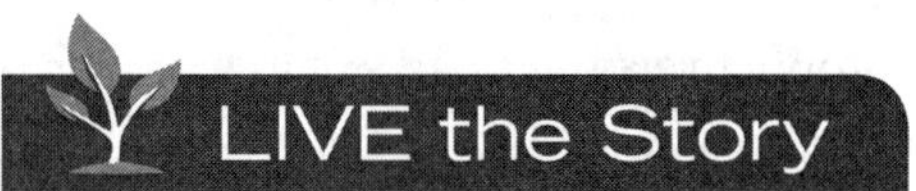

Power, Service, and Love

The story of Naboth's vineyard begins innocently with the possibility of a simple business transaction that didn't go the way the king had hoped. The text doesn't condemn Ahab for his emotional expression or for informing his wife of the reason for his disappointment. The problems began for Ahab when Jezebel said she'd resolve the situation and he didn't ask her how. And it got much worse when he handed over his seal, giving her carte blanche to do whatever she deemed necessary. While Naboth was wealthy enough to own an attractive vineyard near the palace, Jezebel and Ahab had more power, and they were willing to use it to get what they wanted. The law commanded the Israelites to love their neighbor (Lev 19:18), but the king and queen of Israel hated their neighbor Naboth enough to have him killed because he got in the way of what they coveted.

Jesus tells us that the rulers of the Gentiles use their power to exploit and take advantage of those underneath them (Mark 10:42), as Ahab and Jezebel did here. While most readers of this story have much less power than these two sovereigns, all of us have spheres of power in our families, at our schools, with our friends, at our jobs—places where we can use our power to get what we want, what we covet. As we get older and our power expands with more education, professional promotions, and greater wealth, it is tempting to use power to benefit ourselves, just as Ahab and Jezebel did. Many of us are aware of businesspeople or political leaders who are corrupted by power and use power to exploit people underneath them. But we also need to ask how we do

11. The word translated in the NIV as "meekly" (*'aṭ*) in 21:27 is also translated as "dejectedly" (ESV, NRSV, RSV), "despondently" (NASB), or "deep mourning" (NLT).

similar things within our own spheres, using our power (albeit limited) to force neighbors, children, spouses, employees, or friends to serve us or benefit us.

Jesus shows us a radically different way to use power. Jesus didn't have a problem with people wanting greatness; he just wanted people to pursue it like he did—through servanthood (10:43–44). In great contrast to how Ahab and Jezebel treated their neighbor Naboth, Jesus also tells a story illustrating how one can serve one's neighbor, one often called "the good Samaritan" (Luke 10:25–37). Ahab was from Samaria (1 Kgs 21:18); ironically, the hero of Jesus's parable is another resident of Samaria,[12] the one who showed compassion on the half-dead man on the side of the road. He's the one who proved to be a neighbor to the man. In the spirit of Jesus's words to the lawyer in Luke ("Go and do likewise," Luke 10:37), take a practical step this week to love your neighbor (mow their lawn, shovel their snow, pluck their weeds, or give them fruit from your garden).

Sin and Repentance

In this story Ahab and Jezebel seem to be attempting to break as many of the Ten Commandments as possible. In some instances they are doing the breaking, in others they are forcing others to, but at some point in this chapter they are ultimately responsible for coveting (#10 in the Ten Commandments), false witness (#9), theft (#8), murder (#6), and idolatry (#1, #2).[13] Part of what made Ahab and Jezebel so evil here, worthy of being consumed as carrion, is that they not only broke so many of these major sins themselves, but they also forced other people to be complicit in their wickedness.

Ahab had power, certainly more power than Naboth; fortunately, the one who has ultimate power saw the ruler's sins and sent his prophet to confront him. And to his credit, Ahab, one of Israel's most evil rulers, repented. Ahab's repentance wasn't perfect, not Psalm 51 worthy, but God was so eager to show mercy that—a bit like the father figure in another parable of Jesus, "the prodigal son" (Luke 15:11–32)—he was willing to show mercy to wicked Ahab, which should give great hope to all of us sinners.

12. In Kings, Samaria is a city; in the New Testament, it is a region.

13. My numbering of the Ten Commandments is based on the classic Reformed system.

CHAPTER 18

1 Kings 22:1–53

LISTEN to the Story

1For three years there was no war between Aram and Israel. 2But in the
third year Jehoshaphat king of Judah went down to see the king of Israel.
3The king of Israel had said to his officials, "Don't you know that Ramoth
Gilead belongs to us and yet we are doing nothing to retake it from the
king of Aram?"
4So he asked Jehoshaphat, "Will you go with me to fight against
Ramoth Gilead?"
Jehoshaphat replied to the king of Israel, "I am as you are, my people
as your people, my horses as your horses." 5But Jehoshaphat also said to
the king of Israel, "First seek the counsel of the LORD."
6So the king of Israel brought together the prophets—about four hundred men—and asked them, "Shall I go to war against Ramoth Gilead,
or shall I refrain?"
"Go," they answered, "for the Lord will give it into the king's hand."
7But Jehoshaphat asked, "Is there no longer a prophet of the LORD here
whom we can inquire of?"
8The king of Israel answered Jehoshaphat, "There is still one prophet
through whom we can inquire of the LORD, but I hate him because he
never prophesies anything good about me, but always bad. He is Micaiah
son of Imlah."
"The king should not say such a thing," Jehoshaphat replied.
9So the king of Israel called one of his officials and said, "Bring Micaiah
son of Imlah at once."
10Dressed in their royal robes, the king of Israel and Jehoshaphat king
of Judah were sitting on their thrones at the threshing floor by the entrance
of the gate of Samaria, with all the prophets prophesying before them.
11Now Zedekiah son of Kenaanah had made iron horns and he declared,

"This is what the LORD says: 'With these you will gore the Arameans until they are destroyed.'"

12All the other prophets were prophesying the same thing. "Attack Ramoth Gilead and be victorious," they said, "for the LORD will give it into the king's hand."

13The messenger who had gone to summon Micaiah said to him, "Look, the other prophets without exception are predicting success for the king. Let your word agree with theirs, and speak favorably."

14But Micaiah said, "As surely as the LORD lives, I can tell him only what the LORD tells me."

15When he arrived, the king asked him, "Micaiah, shall we go to war against Ramoth Gilead, or not?"

"Attack and be victorious," he answered, "for the LORD will give it into the king's hand."

16The king said to him, "How many times must I make you swear to tell me nothing but the truth in the name of the LORD?"

17Then Micaiah answered, "I saw all Israel scattered on the hills like sheep without a shepherd, and the LORD said, 'These people have no master. Let each one go home in peace.'"

18The king of Israel said to Jehoshaphat, "Didn't I tell you that he never prophesies anything good about me, but only bad?"

19Micaiah continued, "Therefore hear the word of the LORD: I saw the LORD sitting on his throne with all the multitudes of heaven standing
around him on his right and on his left. 20And the LORD said, 'Who will
entice Ahab into attacking Ramoth Gilead and going to his death there?'

"One suggested this, and another that. 21Finally, a spirit came forward,
stood before the LORD and said, 'I will entice him.'

22"'By what means?' the LORD asked.

"'I will go out and be a deceiving spirit in the mouths of all his prophets,' he said.

"'You will succeed in enticing him,' said the LORD. 'Go and do it.'

23"So now the LORD has put a deceiving spirit in the mouths of all these prophets of yours. The LORD has decreed disaster for you."

24Then Zedekiah son of Kenaanah went up and slapped Micaiah in the face. "Which way did the spirit from the LORD go when he went from me to speak to you?" he asked.

[25]Micaiah replied, "You will find out on the day you go to hide in an inner room."

[26]The king of Israel then ordered, "Take Micaiah and send him back to Amon the ruler of the city and to Joash the king's son [27]and say, 'This is what the king says: Put this fellow in prison and give him nothing but bread and water until I return safely.'"

[28]Micaiah declared, "If you ever return safely, the LORD has not spoken through me." Then he added, "Mark my words, all you people!"

[29]So the king of Israel and Jehoshaphat king of Judah went up to Ramoth Gilead. [30]The king of Israel said to Jehoshaphat, "I will enter the battle in disguise, but you wear your royal robes." So the king of Israel disguised himself and went into battle.

[31]Now the king of Aram had ordered his thirty-two chariot commanders, "Do not fight with anyone, small or great, except the king of Israel." [32]When the chariot commanders saw Jehoshaphat, they thought, "Surely this is the king of Israel." So they turned to attack him, but when Jehoshaphat cried out, [33]the chariot commanders saw that he was not the king of Israel and stopped pursuing him.

[34]But someone drew his bow at random and hit the king of Israel between the sections of his armor. The king told his chariot driver, "Wheel around and get me out of the fighting. I've been wounded." [35]All day long the battle raged, and the king was propped up in his chariot facing the Arameans. The blood from his wound ran onto the floor of the chariot, and that evening he died. [36]As the sun was setting, a cry spread through the army: "Every man to his town. Every man to his land!"

[37]So the king died and was brought to Samaria, and they buried him there. [38]They washed the chariot at a pool in Samaria (where the prostitutes bathed), and the dogs licked up his blood, as the word of the LORD had declared.

[39]As for the other events of Ahab's reign, including all he did, the palace he built and adorned with ivory, and the cities he fortified, are they not written in the book of the annals of the kings of Israel? [40]Ahab rested with his ancestors. And Ahaziah his son succeeded him as king.

[41]Jehoshaphat son of Asa became king of Judah in the fourth year of Ahab king of Israel. [42]Jehoshaphat was thirty-five years old when he became king, and he reigned in Jerusalem twenty-five years. His mother's name was Azubah daughter of Shilhi. [43]In everything he followed the ways

of his father Asa and did not stray from them; he did what was right in the eyes of the LORD. The high places, however, were not removed, and the people continued to offer sacrifices and burn incense there. [44]Jehoshaphat was also at peace with the king of Israel.

[45]As for the other events of Jehoshaphat's reign, the things he achieved and his military exploits, are they not written in the book of the annals of the kings of Judah? [46]He rid the land of the rest of the male shrine prostitutes who remained there even after the reign of his father Asa. [47]There was then no king in Edom; a provincial governor ruled.

[48]Now Jehoshaphat built a fleet of trading ships to go to Ophir for gold, but they never set sail—they were wrecked at Ezion Geber. [49]At that time Ahaziah son of Ahab said to Jehoshaphat, "Let my men sail with yours," but Jehoshaphat refused.

[50]Then Jehoshaphat rested with his ancestors and was buried with them in the city of David his father. And Jehoram his son succeeded him as king.

[51]Ahaziah son of Ahab became king of Israel in Samaria in the seventeenth year of Jehoshaphat king of Judah, and he reigned over Israel two years. [52]He did evil in the eyes of the LORD, because he followed the ways of his father and mother and of Jeroboam son of Nebat, who caused Israel to sin. [53]He served and worshiped Baal and aroused the anger of the LORD, the God of Israel, just as his father had done.

Listening to the Text in the Story: Biblical Texts: 1 Samuel 23:2–4; Ancient Near Eastern Texts: Kurkh Monolith; The Mari Letters of Zimri-Lim; Zakkur Stele; The Epic of Aqhat; Assyrian Royal Annals; The Code of Hammurabi; The Aramaic Text with Demotic Script

It may seem strange to end the book of 1 Kings in the middle of King Ahaziah of Israel's reign, but that is not the strangest part of this wild chapter, which includes battles between kings and battles between prophets, heavenly counsels and lying spirits, and blood being bathed in by prostitutes and being licked up by dogs. The other significant event recorded in 1 Kings 22 is the death of evil Ahab of Israel. While he is not always the primary focus of the text, Ahab's reign spans seven chapters (1 Kgs 16–22), more than any other ruler of Israel or Judah except Solomon.

The chapter begins with a notice about a three-year truce between Israel and Aram, presumably going back to the treaty established between Ahab and Ben-Hadad (20:34). This time of peace may have been when Ahab and his Aramean allies went against the Assyrian forces led by Shalmaneser III in the Battle of Qarqar (853 BC) as recorded on the Kurkh Monolith (see Chapter 13).[1]

Before attacking Aram, Ahab and Jehoshaphat sought divine direction (22:5, 15), a common practice for ancient rulers going to war. David inquired of YHWH before he delivered the city of Keilah from the Philistines (1 Sam 23:2, 4), although his method of divination probably involved an ephod, not a prophet. From extrabiblical divine oracles, we see that many prophetic messengers seem merely to be telling rulers what they want to hear, as Ahab's prophets do in this chapter.

According to the Mari Letters,[2] a servant of the Mari ruler Zimri-Lim assembled his royal prophets together, just as Ahab does here (1 Kgs 22:6), and then the Mari prophets delivered an oracle of well-being for Zimri-Lim and his health.[3] In another letter to Zimri-Lim, a different prophet makes a prediction that Zimri-Lim would eventually defeat Hammurabi of Babylon:

> Concerning Babylon I inquired about the matter by giving signs to drink. This man (Hammurabi) unsuccessfully tried to determine many things against that country. My lord will see what God will do to this man: You will capture him and stand over him. His days are running short, he will not live long. My lord should know this.[4]

Just as Ahab's prophets gave him an optimistic message and were proved wrong when Ahab died, Zimri-Lim's hopeful prophets were proved wrong when the city of Mari was destroyed by Hammurabi about 1760 BC, at which point in time Zimri-Lim probably died. The Zakkur Stele records a time when King Zakkur of Hamath was fighting against Aram (like Ahab) and received an encouraging message from his god Baal Shamayim, "Do not be afraid! Since I made you king I will stand beside you."[5]

The shepherd-ruler metaphor used here by Micaiah (1 Kgs 22:17) is found in other ancient Near Eastern parallels. Many Assyrian rulers (Ashurnasirpal II, Adad-nirari III, Esarhaddon, and Ashurbanipal) are described as

---

1. *COS* 2:261-64.

2. The Mari Letters were early second century BC Akkadian tablets that provide background about the city of Mari (located in what is now Syria, on the banks of the Euphrates River).

3. Recorded in the Mari Letters; see Martti Nissinen, *Prophets and Prophecy in the Ancient Near East*, Writings from the Ancient World 12 (Atlanta: SBL Press, 2003), 50–51.

4. Nissinen, *Prophets and Prophecy*, 46.

5. *COS* 2:155.

great shepherd-rulers of their people[6] and in the preface to his famous law code, Hammurabi describes himself as "the shepherd, selected by the god Enlil."[7] Micaiah's prison rations were bread and water (1 Kgs 22:27), and the Aramaic Text with Demotic Script describes a similar situation where foreign emissaries are imprisoned by a ruler and given bread and water as provisions.[8]

EXPLAIN the Story

Ahab and Jehoshaphat Consult with Prophets (22:1–6)

Earlier in history of the divided monarchy, King Asa of Judah, the father of Jehoshaphat, had asked the king of Aram to break his alliance with Israel and form a new one with Judah against Israel (1 Kgs 15:19–20). Now, the king of Israel asks Jehoshaphat, the king of Judah, to join him in an alliance against Aram, breaking the Northern Kingdom's three-year-old treaty (22:1; see also 22:44). The northern ruler is Ahab, but the text does not call him "Ahab" until Micaiah's second message (v. 20). This north-south agreement was probably established by a marriage alliance between Ahab's daughter Athaliah and Jehoshaphat's son, Jehoram (2 Kgs 8:18). We will encounter Athaliah again after the death of her husband (2 Kgs 11).

Ahab intends to retake Ramoth Gilead, a goal that Ahab makes clear when he says to his officials, "Don't you know that Ramoth Gilead belongs to us . . . ?" (1 Kgs 22:3). The city was located in the tribal allotment of Gad and was one of three cities of refuge on the east side of the Jordan River (Deut 4:43; Josh 20:8), and it had been one of Solomon's administrative centers (1 Kgs 4:13).

After commenting to his officials that nothing was being done to retake the city, Ahab asks his southern neighbor to help him in this endeavor (22:4). Jehoshaphat seems more than willing. His eager response to Ahab here (v. 4) is identical to his response to a similar request from Ahab's son, Jehoram (2 Kgs 3:7). But Jehoshaphat wants to make sure their campaign receives divine support (1 Kgs 22:5). Not wanting to offend his guest and military partner, Ahab complies by summoning a horde of prophets (about four hundred), who provide a hearty divine endorsement for the campaign (v. 6). Ahab must have been pleased by their optimistic message. In the book of Jeremiah, YHWH

6. *ANET*, 281, 289, 298, 558.
7. *COS* 2:336.
8. *COS* 1:323.

warns the people of Israel about listening to optimistic prophets who give them false hope (Jer 23:16).

The text does not clarify which god these prophets serve, but several lines of evidence suggest they did not support YHWH. First, we have only seen prophetic quantities of this magnitude with the four hundred and fifty prophets of Baal and the four hundred prophets of Asherah who opposed Elijah at Mount Carmel (1 Kgs 18:19). Second, they speak of "the Lord" (*'adonay*; 22:6), which does not necessarily imply YHWH—it could be referring to Baal or some other deity.[9] Third, Jehoshaphat's comment—"Is there no longer a prophet of the LORD (=YHWH) here"—suggests they were not associated with YHWH (v. 7). Finally, their prophecy of total success was totally wrong.

Micaiah Prophesies Success (22:7–16)

Despite the quantity of prophets and the clarity of message, Jehoshaphat is not convinced, so he wonders if a prophet of YHWH is not available (22:7). Jehoshaphat's question is comparable to the one asked by the prophet Samuel to Jesse about whether or not he had any other sons (1 Sam 16:11). Just as Jesse was able to produce his son David, so Ahab is able to produce his prophet Micaiah. Although Ahab clearly does so reluctantly, since he hates this particular prophet who only declares disaster for the king (1 Kgs 22:8). Micaiah is not mentioned by name elsewhere in Scripture (except in the 2 Chronicles 18:7–27 parallel), but if he were the anonymous prophet who predicted Ahab's death earlier (see discussion of 1 Kgs 20:42 in "Lions, Prophets, and Kings" in Chapter 16 above), it would make sense of Ahab's statement here. Jehoshaphat wisely rebukes Ahab for his remarks, so the king sends for Micaiah (22:8–9). Curiously, there is no mention of Elijah in this narrative. His absence may be explained by the fact that Ahab hates him, too (18:17; 21:20).

While waiting for Micaiah to arrive, Ahab and Jehoshaphat are dressed in royal robes (which Ahab will soon change as part of his disguise; 22:30) and are seated on thrones at the threshing floor, at the entrance to the gate of the city (v. 10). A strikingly ancient Near Eastern parallel to their situation is found in the Ugaritic Epic of Aqhat as King Dan'el is "upright, sitting before the gate . . . on the threshing floor, judging the cause of the widow."[10]

Zedekiah, presumably the leader of the prophetic gang of four hundred, made a visual aid to help bring his point home, declaring that with the horns of iron he had constructed, Ahab would gore the Arameans (v. 11), alluding

9. Although later these prophets speak of YHWH (22:12).
10. *ANET*, 151.

to Moses's final blessing on the descendants of Joseph, who would gore the nations (Deut 33:17). Jeremiah and Ezekiel performed many of these symbolic acts to provide a visual aid to accompany their messages and make them more memorable (e.g., Jer 13:1–11; 18:1–11; 19:1–15; 27:1–22; Ezek 4:1–17; 5:1–12; 12:1–12). Zedekiah proved to be a false prophet (1 Kgs 22:37), but he gets points for creativity.

While the kings are waiting for Micaiah to arrive, the prophetic horde keeps repeating their victory prediction (v. 12). The messenger sent to summon Micaiah pressures Micaiah to fall in line with the other optimistic prophets (v. 13). Micaiah's declaration that he will only speak what YHWH tells him (v. 14) is reminiscent of Balaam's words to King Balak of Moab (Num 22:38). Unlike Balaam, who was called to curse Israel but blessed them instead, Micaiah is called to predict success, but eventually prophesies disaster instead.

Micaiah swore that he would only speak what YHWH had told him, but his first message, "Attack and be victorious" (1 Kgs 22:15), does not appear to have been from YHWH.[11] Micaiah must have spoken with a sarcastic tone, since Ahab immediately rebukes him for not speaking the truth (v. 16).[12] Ahab is a complex character; he hates his pessimistic prophet, but when he receives uncharacteristically good news from this source, he gets frustrated and demands the truth.

Micaiah Prophesies Disaster (22:17–28)

In stark contrast to the optimistic first message, the tone of Micaiah's second and third messages is dire. Micaiah envisions Israel scattered on the hills like sheep without a shepherd, implying that their shepherd, Ahab, would be killed in battle. Ahab, even though he got the truth he demanded, is never pleased; he now turns and complains to Jehoshaphat about Micaiah's message by saying essentially, "I told you it would be like this."

Ahab may have wished Micaiah was finished, but the prophet continues with a third message, and it gets more bizarre. He describes a heavenly council where YHWH is seated on a throne with the council members on his right and left (22:19), a similar scenario to other heavenly visions (Job 1:6; Isa 6:1) as well as to Ahab's earthly court as he and Jehoshaphat sat on thrones on the threshing floor (1 Kgs 22:10). YHWH's prophets had twice declared death for Ahab (20:42; 22:19), so now YHWH requests proposals from his council members how to achieve his regicidal goal (22:20).

11. We discover later that the four hundred prophets were speaking a message generated from a deceptive spirit from YHWH (22:22–23).

12. See Barnes, *1–2 Kings*, 186.

While the text does not state who YHWH's council members are, we know at least three things about them: they were in YHWH's presence (v. 19), YHWH asked them for suggestions (v. 20), and one of them is called a "spirit" (*ruah*; vv. 21, 22, 23). It sounds like they were angelic beings. After several ideas that apparently were not worthy of being recorded, the proposal that carries the day comes from one who offers to be a spirit of deception (*sheqer*) who will trick Ahab by speaking through his prophetic horde (v. 22). Thus, we learn that the source of Ahab's prophet's message was none other than YHWH himself, in order to entice Ahab to fight and die.

Micaiah mentioned YHWH briefly in his first message (v. 16) but never stated that the source of his information was YHWH. In stark contrast, in his second and third messages Micaiah emphasizes six times that his words are YHWH's words (vv. 17, 19, 20, 22 [2x], 23). These later messages have both the ring of truth and divine endorsement.

Zedekiah was not pleased by the accusation of possession by a spirit of deception, so he struck Micaiah on the chin. The NIV says he was "slapped" because the blow was to his face, but the Hebrew verb (*nakah*) often connotes violence resulting in death (e.g., 15:29; 16:7, 10; 20:20, 21, 29; 22:34), so it could be rendered as "punched him in the face." The last person to be "struck" (*nakah*) by a prophet was wounded by the blow (20:37). It is hard to envision a horn-wielding prophet who had moments earlier boasted about goring nations giving Micaiah a light slap on the face.

As is typical of people whose first reaction is violence, Zedekiah's verbal response was not particularly clever but just a rhetorical question for Micaiah about how he received YHWH's spirit (22:24). Micaiah's rejoinder, however, was cryptic and threatening: Zedekiah would discover the answer to his question while hiding in a closet, a bit like Ben-Hadad had done when the Arameans were fleeing from the Israelites (20:30). Ahab had summoned Micaiah, exhorted him to speak the truth, and now, instead of listening to the prophet, he throws him in jail on a diet of bread and water (22:26–27). The prophet Jeremiah was also imprisoned and thrown into a cistern for delivering unpopular messages (Jer 37:15–16; 38:6). Micaiah's fourth message acknowledges that if Ahab returns, then his messages were not from YHWH (1 Kgs 22:28), but of course the inverse would also be true. If Ahab does not return, the words from Zedekiah's prophetic horde would not be from YHWH, meaning they were false prophets (or were from a lying spirit). Micaiah concludes with an ominous warning: "Mark my words, all you people!" (v. 28). Many people died because his words were unmarked.

Ahab Dies in Battle (22:29–40)

The kings of Israel and Judah ignore Micaiah's warning and head toward Ramoth Gilead, but Ahab hopes to avoid the prophesied disaster using a disguise (22:30). A disguise was used successfully against Ahab by a prophet (20:38), but Ahijah the prophet was not fooled by the disguise of Jeroboam's wife (14:2–6), and Micaiah's dire prediction will not be averted. While Ahab is in disguise, he tells his partner Jehoshaphat to wear his royal robes and Jehoshaphat agrees, not having a problem with being the only royal target on the battlefield. His agreement to Ahab's scheme could suggest that Ahab had more power in the relationship or that Jehoshaphat was not particularly intelligent.

The king of Aram focuses his attack on the king of Israel (22:31). The primary reason for his fixation on Ahab was probably because he knew that the Israelite king was responsible for breaking their treaty. If Aram succeeded at taking down Israel's leader, then, like "sheep without a shepherd," the Israelite troops will likely be scattered. When the Aramean commanders see an opponent in royal robes, they assume Jehoshaphat was the king of Israel and surround him (v. 32). Jehoshaphat identifies himself to them with a cry, which stops their pursuit (v. 33). In Chronicles his cry is a prayer that YHWH immediately responds to, drawing the Arameans away (2 Chr 18:31).

In the midst of the fray, an unnamed Aramean archer shoots a random arrow that happened to slice through a slit in Ahab's armor (1 Kgs 22:34). Ahab is removed from the fighting but is still propped up facing the Arameans, perhaps to give hope to his forces (v. 35). Over the course of the day, Ahab slowly bleeds to death, and his blood covers the floor of his chariot.[13] As their shepherd was no more, the Israelites returned home as prophesied (vv. 17, 36). What seemed like random events was the work of God, who was not fooled by a disguise.

Ahab's body was returned to Samaria, his capital, where it was buried. The blood from his chariot was washed in a pool, and then it appears that prostitutes may have bathed in his blood, perhaps superstitiously for fertility.[14] The story of the defeat of Israel at Ramoth Gilead fulfills numerous prophetic predictions from the life of Ahab: his death (20:42; 21:19; 22:17–23, 35, 37), his "sheep" being scattered (22:17, 36), and dogs licking his blood (21:19, 38).

13. Chronicles' version of Josiah's death includes striking parallels to Ahab's. Both kings ignore a warning from God, both are shot in their chariot in the field of battle by a random arrow, both ask to be removed from the battle because of a severe wound, then both die and are returned to their capital for burial (1 Kgs 22:17–35; 2 Chr 35:21–24).

14. See discussion of this pool in Jones, *1 and 2 Kings*, 2:371–71.

Problematically, the location of the canine blood licking was supposed to be in Naboth's vineyard (21:19), not a pool in Samaria. However, the spirit of this last prophecy is fulfilled when Ahab's son, Jehoram, was shot by an arrow (like his father) and died in the plot that had belonged to Naboth (2 Kgs 9:25–26).[15] The sovereign fulfillment of the word of God is often actualized over an extended period of time, in stages. Two of the three prophetic anointings commissioned by YHWH at Mount Horeb (1 Kgs 19:15–16) have yet to be fulfilled, and we are still waiting for the prophesied death of Queen Jezebel (21:23). However, all of these prophecies will be fulfilled within the next generation of leadership (2 Kgs 8:7–15; 9:1–13, 30–37).

Ahab's final regnal formula (1 Kgs 22:39–40) mentions his construction projects, his accomplishments, and his successor—Ahaziah. One unique aspect of this final comment is the reference to his ivory palace (v. 39). While ivory adornments are viewed highly negatively later by the prophet Amos (3:15; 6:4), ivory palaces are depicted positively in the book of Psalms (Ps 45:8). Ahab is condemned for many sins, but there is no condemnation here for his ivory palace (see also 1 Kgs 10:18, 22).

The Reign of Jehoshaphat of Judah (22:41–50)

The focus of the narrative for the past seven chapters (since 15:24) has been the Northern Kingdom, mainly involving the prophetic narratives of Elijah and the royal narratives of Ahab. Finally, a southern ruler, Jehoshaphat, moves into the center spotlight. However, he does not get much unique coverage, and his actual narrative is rather short (22:41–50). Most of what we learn about Jehoshaphat comes via his associations with northern rulers in military campaigns (vv. 2–32; 2 Kgs 3:1–14).

Jehoshaphat was a righteous ruler, praised for following the ways of his father Asa and for removing the male prostitutes (1 Kgs 22:43, 46; see also 14:24; 15:12; 2 Kgs 23:7) but critiqued for not removing the high places and for associating with Ahab (1 Kgs 22:43–44). Jehoshaphat built a fleet of trading ships to acquire gold (like Solomon; 9:26; 10:22), but they were wrecked at Ezion Geber, the port at the northern end of the Gulf of ʻAqabah (the northeast extension of the Red Sea). Ahaziah of Israel attempted to partner with Jehoshaphat in his naval endeavors, but after the failed military campaign with Ahaziah's father (Ahab), Jehoshaphat said no (22:49). After his death and burial in the city of David, Jehoshaphat was succeeded by his son, Jehoram (v. 50).

---

15. See also Barnes's resolution of this discrepancy, *1–2 Kings*, 178.

The Reign of Ahaziah of Israel (22:51–53)

After a short southern interruption, the narrative refocuses on the Northern Kingdom for eight chapters (until 2 Kgs 8:16), which will focus mainly on the ministry and exploits of Elisha. But before winding down 1 Kings, we are introduced briefly to Ahab's son, Ahaziah, who was a chip off the old block in that he was evil and followed in the ways of his father, his mother Jezebel, and Jeroboam I. Ahaziah did not remove Jeroboam's altars, he served and worshiped Baal, and he aroused the anger of YHWH. While several other rulers walked in the ways of their fathers (1 Kgs 15:3, 26; 22:43; 2 Kgs 21:21; 22:2), only Ahaziah is compared like this to his mother, presumably because of the extreme nature of Jezebel's wickedness. The story of Ahaziah's wickedness continues in 2 Kings.

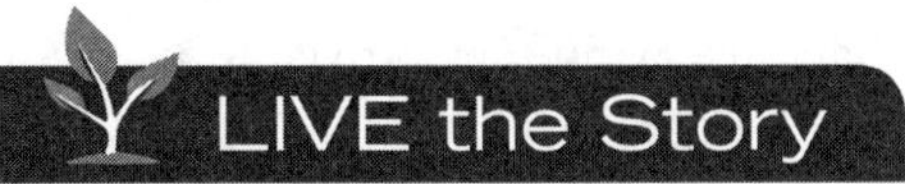

Sheep without Shepherds, Sheep with the Good Shepherd

In the vision he shares with Ahab, Micaiah describes the Israelites scattered over the hills as "sheep without a shepherd," essentially informing Ahab that, as Israel's leader, he was going to die (1 Kgs 22:17). Throughout Israel's history their leaders are often depicted as shepherds. Joshua is appointed as Moses's successor so YHWH's people are not "like sheep without a shepherd" (Num 27:17). YHWH selected David to be king while he was just a shepherd (1 Sam 16:11; 2 Sam 7:8; see also Ps 23). Ezekiel describes the tragic consequences of having evil shepherds for the people, and then YHWH speaks of how he would shepherd his scattered sheep (Ezek 34). The book of Zechariah also describes situations where sheep are oppressed or scattered because of the absence of a shepherd (Zech 10:2; 13:7). And perhaps the most important parallel text is where the people are described as "sheep without a shepherd" (Mark 6:34) before Jesus feeds the five thousand. In this context the hungry people's lack of a shepherd prompts Jesus to have compassion for them and culminates in his feeding this large "herd." Jesus's ministry, like the shepherd in his parable of the hundred sheep, often involved his pursuit of people who had "strayed from the fold" (Luke 15:1–7). In John's Gospel Jesus describes in depth what it means for him to be "the good shepherd," culminating in his prediction of his laying down his life for the sheep (John 10:1–18), foreshadowing his death on the cross.

Deception

Deception dominates this chapter. Prophets lie, a king disguises himself to deceive the enemy, an angelic spirit lies, and YHWH himself authorizes the sending of this spirit of deception. It seems like no one can be trusted, not even God. While we've seen prophets and kings act like this before, the image of a deceptive God is highly problematic. While many texts could be cited to support the truthful nature of God's character, perhaps the words of Samuel to Saul are clearest, "He who is the Glory of Israel does not lie" (1 Sam 15:29; see also John 14:6; Heb 6:18).

How are we to understand the idea of divine deception here? We could conclude that honesty is usually, but not always, the best policy. After all, Scripture includes many stories of good people acting in a deceptive manner. God tested Abraham when he didn't really want the patriarch to kill his son, Isaac (Gen 22). Joseph tricked his brothers, making it appear that Benjamin had stolen his special cup of divination (Gen 44). The Hebrew midwives allowed the Hebrew children to live and lied to Pharaoh, saying they arrived too late for the birth; YHWH rewarded them for their behavior (Exod 1:15–21). Rahab the prostitute told the men of Jericho who were looking for the two Israelite spies that they had already left, even though she was hiding the spies on her roof (Josh 2). David told the priest Ahimelech that he was on a mission from Saul when he was really being chased by Saul (1 Sam 21:2). Earlier in Kings we saw an anonymous prophet trick another prophet, so that the other prophet was killed by a lion (1 Kgs 13:11–31). Later in Kings we will see Elisha deceive the king of Aram so that he and his army march into Samaria, Israel's capital, where they could have been slaughtered (2 Kgs 6:19–23). Perhaps most problematically, in John's Gospel Jesus tells his brothers that he wasn't going to the festival (John 7:8), but then he immediately traveled to the festival in secret (John 7:10). While there are extenuating circumstances in all of these instances, in several of these situations it appears that the ends do justify the means.

Or we could argue that God is more concerned about bearing false witness than the occasional deception. God clearly condemns bearing false witness (Exod 20:16; Deut 5:20), but none of the incidents cited in the previous paragraph involve testifying falsely. However, in the previous chapter Ahab and Jezebel coerced the two scoundrels to commit perjury by falsely accusing Naboth of blasphemy (1 Kgs 21:9–13). We could say YHWH was merely using deception against a deceiver. What goes around, comes around.

Or we could focus on what motivated the deception. The deception of two scoundrels against Naboth was motivated by the greed and coveting of Ahab and Jezebel (21:9–13), and similarly, the deception of Elisha's servant Gehazi was motivated by his greed, and he was therefore condemned (2 Kgs 5:20–27). If, however, a person's deception is motivated by a good thing—a desire to not allow someone to prematurely learn about their own surprise birthday party—they shouldn't be condemned. The motivation for the deception in this chapter is a desire to fulfill the just punishment against Ahab for his breaking of all those commandments, including false witness.

But what helps me the most to make sense of YHWH's apparently deceptive behavior is when I realize that God is, ironically, honest about the deception. God was so honest that he tells Ahab to his face that he was lying to him earlier. That's not how deceptive people behave. Most lies involve a cover-up and more lies to make sure the truth is never discovered, but YHWH sends Micaiah to Ahab to tell him that he had sent the deceptive spirit. Righteous Job never got to hear what went on in the heavenly council meeting between YHWH and the Satan (Job 1:6–12; 2:1–6), but evil Ahab heard all of what went on in the heavenly council meeting between YHWH and the deceptive spirit. This story would be far more problematic if YHWH had never informed Ahab about the deceptive spirit.

Ultimately, God sent to Ahab both deceptive prophets and an honest prophet who told the king the previous message was wrong. God presented Ahab with a choice. He could believe the four hundred prophets whose unanimous optimistic message smelled fishy, or he could believe the one prophet whose shocking pessimistic message had the ring of truth. Ahab chose . . . poorly.

Truth

Like Ahab, we are often faced with a choice of who to believe when we hear contradictory messages, whether it be from a friend, a pastor, or a politician. And like the prophets of 1 Kings 22, we are often in positions where we can choose to speak truth. While it would be nice if it were always easy, speaking the truth is often painful.

The truth can be painful to hear because everyone wants to hear optimistic messages (like Ahab). But if you look at the messages of the prophets of Scripture, many of them were pessimistic. Barnes captures the prophetic perspective well: "The default position, if you will, is pessimism; optimists must prove the divine inspiration of their words!"[16] Before they give good news, biblical prophets often give bad news, which should make us suspicious of people who only tell us what we want to hear. We can be like Ahab, listening to advice from multiple sources, then only following the message we want to hear because it seems less painful. But as we see in this story, that approach

---

16. Barnes, *1–2 Kings*, 184.

is foolish. The painful truth in the short run would have saved Ahab's life in the long run.

The truth can be painful to deliver because people often punish the bearer of bad news, like Ahab did to Micaiah. However, people who speak God's words will need to give people messages they don't want to hear. If we tell people to be more honest, more generous, more hospitable, more gracious, it could get us in trouble. As we speak truth, we should expect pushback or even persecution. Telling people the truth can get you in trouble—it can get you killed. It did for Jesus.

More than any other person in history, Jesus spoke the truth. Like an Old Testament prophet, he was always telling people things they didn't want to hear. Jesus rebuked the disciples for keeping children from him (Mark 10:13–16). Jesus called the rich man to give all his money to the poor (10:21). Jesus told his followers they needed to become servants and slaves (10:43–44).

Jesus tells a parable that summarizes the story of how poorly Israel listened to truth from God's prophets, in the context of a vineyard owner and his tenants (12:1–12). Jesus's parable makes the point that not only does Israel refuse to listen to prophets, but they also persecute and punish prophets for delivering messages they don't want to hear (like Ahab). As Jesus speaks of the brutal killing of the vineyard owner's son by the tenants, he is prophesying his own death. When the religious leaders realize that Jesus told the parable against them, they begin plotting how to arrest and kill him, ironically moving Jesus's death prediction a step closer to fulfillment. People wanted to kill Jesus because his words were painfully true. Just as it was for Micaiah and Jesus, it will be costly for Jesus's followers to speak the truth. But we can be confident that God will be at work in these situations of prophetic honesty, building a glorious work of God that is, in the words of Jesus, "marvelous in our eyes" (12:11).

CHAPTER 19

2 Kings 1:1–2:18

LISTEN to the Story

1After Ahab's death, Moab rebelled against Israel. 2Now Ahaziah had fallen through the lattice of his upper room in Samaria and injured himself. So he sent messengers, saying to them, “Go and consult Baal-Zebub, the god of Ekron, to see if I will recover from this injury.”

3But the angel of the LORD said to Elijah the Tishbite, “Go up and meet the messengers of the king of Samaria and ask them, ‘Is it because there is no God in Israel that you are going off to consult Baal-Zebub, the god of Ekron?’ 4Therefore this is what the LORD says: ‘You will not leave the bed you are lying on. You will certainly die!’” So Elijah went.

5When the messengers returned to the king, he asked them, “Why have you come back?”

6“A man came to meet us,” they replied. “And he said to us, ‘Go back to the king who sent you and tell him, “This is what the LORD says: Is it because there is no God in Israel that you are sending messengers to consult Baal-Zebub, the god of Ekron? Therefore you will not leave the bed you are lying on. You will certainly die!”‘“

7The king asked them, “What kind of man was it who came to meet you and told you this?”

8They replied, “He had a garment of hair and had a leather belt around his waist.”

The king said, “That was Elijah the Tishbite.”

9Then he sent to Elijah a captain with his company of fifty men. The captain went up to Elijah, who was sitting on the top of a hill, and said to him, “Man of God, the king says, ‘Come down!’”

10Elijah answered the captain, “If I am a man of God, may fire come down from heaven and consume you and your fifty men!” Then fire fell from heaven and consumed the captain and his men.

11At this the king sent to Elijah another captain with his fifty men.

The captain said to him, "Man of God, this is what the king says, 'Come down at once!'"

[12]"If I am a man of God," Elijah replied, "may fire come down from heaven and consume you and your fifty men!" Then the fire of God fell from heaven and consumed him and his fifty men.

[13]So the king sent a third captain with his fifty men. This third captain went up and fell on his knees before Elijah. "Man of God," he begged, "please have respect for my life and the lives of these fifty men, your servants! [14]See, fire has fallen from heaven and consumed the first two captains and all their men. But now have respect for my life!"

[15]The angel of the LORD said to Elijah, "Go down with him; do not be afraid of him." So Elijah got up and went down with him to the king.

[16]He told the king, "This is what the LORD says: Is it because there is no God in Israel for you to consult that you have sent messengers to consult Baal-Zebub, the god of Ekron? Because you have done this, you will never leave the bed you are lying on. You will certainly die!" [17]So he died, according to the word of the LORD that Elijah had spoken.

Because Ahaziah had no son, Joram succeeded him as king in the second year of Jehoram son of Jehoshaphat king of Judah. [18]As for all the other events of Ahaziah's reign, and what he did, are they not written in the book of the annals of the kings of Israel?

[2:1]When the LORD was about to take Elijah up to heaven in a whirlwind, Elijah and Elisha were on their way from Gilgal. [2]Elijah said to Elisha, "Stay here; the LORD has sent me to Bethel."

But Elisha said, "As surely as the LORD lives and as you live, I will not leave you." So they went down to Bethel.

[3]The company of the prophets at Bethel came out to Elisha and asked, "Do you know that the LORD is going to take your master from you today?"

"Yes, I know," Elisha replied, "so be quiet."

[4]Then Elijah said to him, "Stay here, Elisha; the LORD has sent me to Jericho."

And he replied, "As surely as the LORD lives and as you live, I will not leave you." So they went to Jericho.

[5]The company of the prophets at Jericho went up to Elisha and asked

him, "Do you know that the Lord is going to take your master from you
today?"

"Yes, I know," he replied, "so be quiet."

[6]Then Elijah said to him, "Stay here; the Lord has sent me to the
Jordan."

And he replied, "As surely as the Lord lives and as you live, I will not
leave you." So the two of them walked on.

[7]Fifty men from the company of the prophets went and stood at a distance, facing the place where Elijah and Elisha had stopped at the Jordan.
[8]Elijah took his cloak, rolled it up and struck the water with it. The water
divided to the right and to the left, and the two of them crossed over on
dry ground.

[9]When they had crossed, Elijah said to Elisha, "Tell me, what can I do
for you before I am taken from you?"

"Let me inherit a double portion of your spirit," Elisha replied.

[10]"You have asked a difficult thing," Elijah said, "yet if you see me when
I am taken from you, it will be yours—otherwise, it will not."

[11]As they were walking along and talking together, suddenly a chariot of fire and horses of fire appeared and separated the two of them,
and Elijah went up to heaven in a whirlwind. [12]Elisha saw this and cried
out, "My father! My father! The chariots and horsemen of Israel!" And
Elisha saw him no more. Then he took hold of his garment and tore it
in two.

[13]Elisha then picked up Elijah's cloak that had fallen from him and
went back and stood on the bank of the Jordan. [14]He took the cloak that
had fallen from Elijah and struck the water with it. "Where now is the
Lord, the God of Elijah?" he asked. When he struck the water, it divided
to the right and to the left, and he crossed over.

[15]The company of the prophets from Jericho, who were watching, said,
"The spirit of Elijah is resting on Elisha." And they went to meet him and
bowed to the ground before him. [16]"Look," they said, "we your servants
have fifty able men. Let them go and look for your master. Perhaps the
Spirit of the Lord has picked him up and set him down on some mountain
or in some valley."

"No," Elisha replied, "do not send them."

[17]But they persisted until he was too embarrassed to refuse. So he said,
"Send them." And they sent fifty men, who searched for three days but did

not find him. [18]When they returned to Elisha, who was staying in Jericho, he said to them, "Didn't I tell you not to go?"

Listening to the Text in the Story: Biblical Texts: Genesis 2–3; 5:24; 19:24; 37:34; Exodus 9:23–24; 14; 16; 19; 24:4; 32–34; Numbers 11:1–3, 15; Joshua 3:17; 2 Samuel 13:31; 1 Kings 17–19; Ancient Near Eastern Texts: Mesopotamian Epic of Adapa; Ugaritic Letter from 'Abniya; The Etana Legend

Fire and Heaven

The king is dead (Ahab), but the new king does not live long (Ahaziah). The book of 2 Kings begins by telling the story of how Ahab's son, Ahaziah, is cursed by Elijah, his father's old nemesis. After recording Ahaziah's subsequent death, the text narrates the story of the final interaction between Elijah and Elisha, which concluded just before the older prophet is swooped up to heaven by a whirlwind in a chariot of fire.

A fiery departure was appropriate for a prophet whose go-to supernatural wonder was fire. Elijah called down fire from heaven onto the altar at Mount Carmel (1 Kgs 18:36–38) and on two different groups of fifty soldiers sent by King Ahaziah to get him (2 Kgs 1:10–14). Previously in Israel's story, fiery judgments were also sent by God against Sodom and Gomorrah (Gen 19:24), against the Egyptians in the midst of the plagues (Exod 9:23–24), and against Israelite complainers in the wilderness (Num 11:1–3).

Elijah was not the only biblical character to ascend to heaven (although his was the coolest—a whirlwind and a chariot of fire; 2 Kgs 2:1, 11). We are not sure of the details, but Enoch the ancestor of Noah was taken directly by God, presumably to heaven (Gen 5:24). Apart from these two references, it is difficult to find support for the idea of an afterlife in the Old Testament since elsewhere Sheol, the land of the dead, is one's final destination (e.g., Gen 37:35; Num 16:33; 1 Sam 2:6; 1 Kgs 2:6, 9; Job 7:9; Ps 6:5).

The Mesopotamian Epic of Adapa narrates the eponymous character's trip to heaven.[1] Adapa was an ancient Mesopotamian wise man with a divine ancestry who cursed and damaged the south wind for blowing over his fishing boat, so he was summoned to heaven to account for his actions. Unlike Elijah, the reason for Adapa's trip was clearly not a reward. Because he refused to eat

1. *COS* 1:449.

food that may have given him immortality, Adapa's story is often compared to the story of Adam and Eve in the garden of Eden (Gen 2–3). Another Akkadian legend tells the tale of Etana, a ruler of Kish, who rode, not in a whirlwind, but on the back of an eagle to heaven on his quest for an heir.[2]

Vow Swearing and Clothes Tearing

During their final interaction, Elisha three times swears to his mentor Elijah, "As surely as the LORD lives and as you live, I will not leave you" (2:2, 4, 6). An Ugaritic letter from an official named ʿAbniya includes a similar vow to the recipient of his letter, ʿUrtenu: "As you live, and as do I."[3]

After Elijah departs, Elisha tears his clothes, a practice that was common in times of loss or crisis. Jacob does it after being told Joseph was dead (Gen 37:34). David and his officials do it after hearing Absalom killed the king's sons (2 Sam 13:31). Hezekiah and his officials do it after Sennacherib's threat (2 Kgs 18:37–19:1; Isa 36:22–37:1).

Elijah and Moses

Many of the parallels between the lives of Elijah and Moses have already been noted, but as Elijah's ministry winds down it will be helpful to review them. Table 12 summarizes the parallels between these two great figures, listed chronologically in the order of Elijah's life as recorded in Kings. Both Elijah and Moses were involved with feeding miracles: Elijah provided meal and oil for the widow of Zarephath, and Moses provided manna and quail for the Israelites in the wilderness (1 Kgs 17:8–16; Exod 16). Elijah achieved a victory of Baal on Mount Carmel, and Moses defeated Egypt at the Red Sea (1 Kgs 18; Exod 14). Each challenged the people at a point of crisis to decide whether they are on God's side (1 Kgs 18:21; Exod 32:26). Both constructed a twelve-stone altar (1 Kgs 18:31; Exod 24:4). Both instigated a slaughter of idolaters (1 Kgs 18:40; Exod 32:26–28). Elijah traveled for forty days, while Moses met with YHWH for forty days (1 Kgs 19:8; Exod 24:18). Elijah's travel took him to Mount Horeb, where YHWH had met with Moses earlier (1 Kgs 19:8; Exod 19:3). Before traveling to Horeb, Elijah asked God to kill him; Moses made a similar request in response to the complaints of the people (1 Kgs 19:4; Num 11:15). After their Horeb interaction, YHWH passed by Elijah, as he had done with Moses at Horeb (1 Kgs 19:11; Exod 33:19–34:6). Both parted a body of water and crossed on dry ground, for Elijah the Jordan

2. *COS* 1:453–57.
3. *COS* 3:113.

River and for Moses the Red Sea (2 Kgs 2:8; Exod 14). Both mentored their successors (Elisha for Elijah and Joshua for Moses), which involved two of the most successful leadership transitions in Israel's history (1 Kgs 19:16, 19–21; 2 Kgs 2:1–12; Exod 24:13; 33:11; Deut 31:7–8; 34:9). Their successors both parted the Jordan (2 Kgs 2:14; Josh 3:17). Finally, and most dramatically, both made a New Testament appearance on the Mount of Transfiguration (Matt 17:3–4; Mark 9:4–5; Luke 9:30–33)—Moses the lawgiver and Elijah the prototypical prophet, standing alongside Jesus. The significance of their parallel lives and ministry is thus given a divine endorsement.

Table 12: Parallels between Elijah and Moses

Parallel	**Elijah**	**Moses**
Feeding miracles	1 Kgs 17:8–16	Exod 16
Dramatic victories over . . .	**Baal** @ Mt. Carmel (1 Kgs 18)	**Egypt** @ Red Sea (Exod 14)
Telling Israel to choose a side	1 Kgs 18:21	Exod 32:26
Building a twelve stone altar	1 Kgs 18:31	Exod 24:4
Slaughtering idolaters	1 Kgs 18:40	Exod 32:26–28
Asking God to kill them	1 Kgs 19:4	Num 11:15
Forty days of . . .	**Traveling**: 1 Kgs 19:8	**Meeting**: Exod 24:18
Meeting YHWH at Mt Horeb	1 Kgs 19:8	Exod 19:3
God passing by them	1 Kgs 19:11	Exod 33:19–34:6
Parting a body of water	2 Kgs 2:8	Exod 14
Crossing on dry ground	2 Kgs 2:7–8	Exod 14:16
Mentoring their successors	**Elisha**: 1 Kgs 19:16, 19–21; 2 Kgs 2:1–12	**Joshua**: Exod 24:13; 33:11; Deut 31:7–8; 34:9
Their successors part the Jordan	2 Kgs 2:14	Josh 3:17
Transfiguration appearance	Matt 17:3–4; Mark 9:4–5; Luke 9:30–33	Matt 17:3–4; Mark 9:4–5; Luke 9:30–33

EXPLAIN the Story

Ahaziah's Injury and Inquiry (2 Kings 1:1–8)

The book of 2 Kings begins with a comment that Moab rebelled against Israel (1:1). Because 2 Kings 3 focuses on the conflict between Moab and Israel, a longer discussion of the Moabite conflict will be delayed to Chapter 20.

We learn little information about the life of Ahaziah, except that he was clumsy enough to fall through a lattice and seriously injure himself (1:2). His injury was significant enough to cause him to wonder if he would die. His concern for his health and longevity may be due in part to the fact that northern dynasties did not last long. With his succession, the relatively short-reigning Omride dynasty now becomes Israel's longest with three rulers (Omri, Ahab, and Ahaziah).

Ahaziah sends messengers to consult Baal-Zebub, the god of the Philistine city of Ekron, whose name literally means "lord of the flies." Many scholars think the text here has intentionally been changed from Baal-Zebul, "Baal the Prince," to insult the deity by changing his primary association from royalty to insects.[4] In the New Testament, Beelzebul was considered the prince of demons (Matt 12:24; Mark 3:22; Luke 11:15).

As Ahaziah's messengers (*mal'akim*) are en route, an angelic messenger (*mal'ak*) from YHWH commissions Elijah to intercept them (2 Kgs 1:3–4). Elijah is commissioned to ask why Ahaziah is consulting with a foreign god instead of Israel's God. Then he is to inform the king that he would not survive; he will not even get out of bed again. Like his father Ahab, Ahaziah is to receive a death prediction from the prophet Elijah (1 Kgs 21:21; see also 20:42; 22:19–23). When Ahaziah asks about their quick return (a roundtrip to Ekron was about fifty miles and should have taken several days), they relay the message from the strange man, which prompts the king to ask them to describe the individual (2 Kgs 1:5–7). Their description of his attire, a hairy garment and leather belt, was sufficiently distinctive for him to determine that it was his father's nemesis, Elijah (v. 8).

Consuming Fire Fell from Heaven (2 Kings 1:9–15)

Just as Ahab attempted to circumvent Micaiah's dire prediction (1 Kgs 22), Ahaziah attempts to get around Elijah's. Ahaziah sends a group of fifty soldiers to capture or perhaps kill the prophet (2 Kgs 1:9). Elijah fled from Jezebel's

---

4. Day, *Yahweh and the Gods and Goddesses*, 77–81.

threat (1 Kgs 19:2–3), but there is no running this time. In response to the captain's command, "Come down!," Elijah offers a conditional threat of fire from heaven if he truly is a man of God (2 Kgs 1:9–10). As the soldiers are consumed by fire, Elijah's prophetic status is thus confirmed.

The incident is repeated with a second captain and fifty soldiers, but this time the message to Elijah is longer and more severe ("Come down at once!" v. 11). Elijah's threat is identical this second time, as is the result (v. 12).[5] Somehow the message of the fiery consumption of the two previous groups of soldiers got back to Ahaziah's soldiers, so the third captain approaches the prophet deferentially, begging for mercy on his knees (vv. 13–14).[6] At this point an angelic messenger (*mal'ak*) appears and commissions Elijah to go with this third group of soldiers.

Some readers might wonder if the punishment of being consumed by fire fits the crime in this incident (a similar issue comes up in the next chapter with Elisha, the boys, and the bears; 2:23–25). When Jesus's disciples want to call down fire from heaven upon a Samaritan village that did not welcome them (it worked for Elijah—why not them?), Jesus rebukes them (Luke 9:52–55). One could argue this incident is another example of the mean God of the Old Testament that contrasts the loving God of the New Testament.[7]

The text does not seem interested in providing a rationale for these deaths, but there are several points that could be made to help us understand why they were necessary. Ahaziah's parents were killing prophets en masse (1 Kgs 18:4), so it is reasonable to assume that Ahaziah's soldiers were planning to kill Elijah. Ahaziah had sent only messengers to Baal-Zebub (2 Kgs 1:2), but now he's sending soldiers to Elijah, suggesting a hostile intent (vv. 9, 11). Also, if Ahaziah were merely hoping to arrange a personal consultation between prophet and king, a much smaller entourage than fifty would have been sufficient. That the angel tells Elijah "[D]o not be afraid" (vv. 15) suggests that Ahaziah intended violence.

Ahaziah's Death (2 Kings 1:16–18)

When Elijah finally meets with Ahaziah, the message is identical to the one given to the messengers earlier—Ahaziah will certainly die (1:6, 16). The text then immediately informs us that, just as Elijah prophesied, the king died (v. 17). Ahaziah only reigned for just over a year, which explains why his regnal

---

5. The NIV moves the word order around, but other English translations (e.g., ESV, NRSV, NASB) more literally reflect the word order of the Hebrew in 1:10 and 1:12.

6. For a discussion of the "folklore" elements in this story, see Barnes, *1–2 Kings*, 198.

7. See the discussion of this supposed divine contradiction in Lamb, *God Behaving Badly*, 9–24.

formula is unusually terse.[8] Because he had no son, Ahaziah was succeeded by his brother Jehoram, Israel's first sibling succession (Jehoahaz was succeeded by his brother, Jehoiakim; 23:34). Omri's dynasty now has four successive northern rulers (Omri, Ahab, Ahaziah, and Joram[9]), a record that will soon be passed by the five rulers of Jehu's dynasty.

Elisha Stays with Elijah (2 Kings 2:1–6)

Before narrating Elijah's final farewell tour, the text informs us that YHWH would take him to heaven in a whirlwind (2:1). The narration of Elijah's four-stop tour (Gilgal, Bethel, Jericho, and the Jordan) is highly formulaic. Three times Elijah tells Elisha, "Stay" (but not "Sit") "the Lord has sent me to Bethel / Jericho / the Jordan" (2:2, 4, 6). Like the loyal, but not always obedient, dog that refuses to stay, Elisha is determined to follow, and he replies three times, "As surely as YHWH and you live, I won't leave you" (2:2, 4, 6; author's translation). They then travel together to the next stop (2:2, 4, 6). The formulaic nature of the story here emphasizes Elisha's deep commitment to his mentor.

While the text does not state how the knowledge became public, the prophetic companies already knew about Elijah's fate. These prophetic groups reappear at various points in Elisha's narrative (2 Kgs 4:1, 38–41; 6:1–7). At Bethel and Jericho the resident company of prophets poses an identical and annoying question to Elisha: "Do you know that the Lord is going to take your master from you today?" (2:3, 5). Clearly perturbed by their question, Elisha informs both sets of prophets that he already knows about Elijah's fate, so they should shut up (vv. 3, 5). Elisha is understandably upset about losing his master. It is difficult to know why these prophets keep reminding Elisha that his mentor will soon leave, but perhaps they were simply jealous of Elisha, a phenomenon that is unfortunately too common in Christian ministry, particularly after a promotion.

Chariots of Fire (2 Kings 2:7–14)

The tone of the narrative becomes less formulaic and more emotional as Elijah and Elisha arrive at the Jordan River. Just as Moses used a prop (his staff; Exod 14:16) to divide the sea, Elijah uses one (his cloak) to part the waters of the

8. While his regnal formula states that Ahaziah reigned for two years (1 Kgs 22:51), Wray Beal explains it was probably closer to one (*1 & 2 Kings*, 293–94).

9. Both Israel and Judah have rulers named "Jehoram" who are also called "Joram" (which is confusing even to biblical scholars). Here I follow the NIV, which refers to the northern ruler as "Joram" and the southern ruler as "Jehoram."

Jordan to cross on dry ground (2 Kgs 2:8). Elijah asks Elisha, the man who has served him since he threw his cloak over him (1 Kgs 19:19–21), a question servants typically ask their master, "What can I do for you?" (2 Kgs 2:9).

It is difficult to be certain what Elisha was requesting when he asked for a "double portion" of Elijah's spirit (v. 9). He seems to be referring to the double portion passed down as an inheritance from a father to the oldest son (Deut 21:17). But several questions still arise. Who are the other, younger sons—the company of prophets? What does Elijah "own" that could be passed on? Is Elisha proposing a shift from charismatic succession to hereditary succession for prophets?[10] While it is not clear to us, Elijah understands what Elisha was asking and acknowledges that, even though it was a bold request, it would be granted if he sees Elijah's departure (2 Kgs 2:10). As the two are walking and talking, a fiery chariot and fiery horses separate them before Elijah is taken up to heaven in a whirlwind (v. 11). Post-resurrection, Jesus also ascended into heaven (Mark 16:19; Luke 24:51; Acts 1:9).

It is hard to know all that it implies, but there are five observations to make about Elijah's double-portion request. First, Elisha's request appears to be granted, because the text states he saw Elijah's departure (2 Kgs 2:12). During Elijah's ascension, Elisha declares, "My father! My father! The chariots and horsemen of Israel!" (v. 12); King Jehoash of Israel makes a strikingly similar declaration at the point of Elisha's death (13:14). Elisha's servant sees a similar fiery-horse-chariot image when he and Elisha are surrounded by the Aramean forces (17). Second, YHWH had already commissioned Elijah to anoint Elisha as his successor (1 Kgs 19:16), so Elisha's request presumably was not identical to YHWH's commission. Third, Elisha picked up the cloak of Elijah (2 Kgs 2:13), which would distinguish him as the heir of Elijah to anyone who recognized the cloak. Fourth, Elisha performed several of the same miracles as Elijah. After picking up Elijah's cloak and asking, "Where now is the Lord, the God of Elijah?" Elisha repeated the last miracle performed by Elijah when he re-parted the Jordan (vv. 13–14). Elisha's other miraculous "repeats" from his mentor include miraculous feedings (1 Kgs 17:8–16; 2 Kgs 4:1–7, 42–44) and resurrecting a woman's only son (1 Kgs 17:17–24; 2 Kgs 4:8–37). Fifth, the company of the prophets see that Elijah's spirit rests on Elisha (2:15). Thus, the proof of the request being granted is seen as Elisha wears his predecessor's cloak, continues his predecessor's ministry, and manifests his predecessor's spirit.

10. For an extended discussion of prophetic succession generally, and the Elijah-Elisha succession specifically, see Lamb, "Prophetic Succession," 172–87.

Search for Elijah's Body (2 Kings 2:15–18)

As they watched him part the Jordan, the prophetic company had enough evidence to be convinced that he had his master's spirit, so they quickly bow before their new master (2:15). But their subservience to their new master does not last long as they immediately begin to argue with Elisha that they should search for Elijah's body, presumably to avoid the fate predicted for Ahab and his descendants—carnivorous carrion consumption (1 Kgs 21:19, 23–24). Elisha thinks a search is a bad idea but eventually relents, which allows him to basically say "I told you so" after the three-day search party returns unsuccessful (2:16–18).

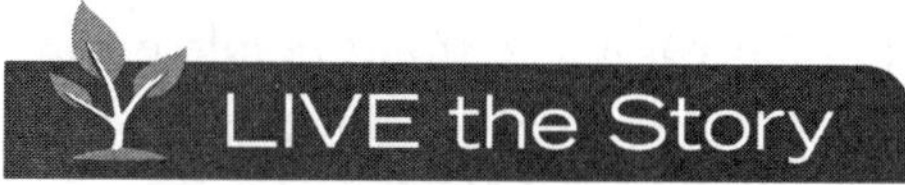

Elijah's Legacy: Why Was He So Important?

One could argue that, since only few chapters focus on him (1 Kgs 17–19; 21:17–29; 2 Kgs 1–2), Elijah was a relatively minor character in the Bible. Three of the patriarchs (Abraham, Jacob, and Joseph) are the focus of far more narrative material than Elijah. Even in the book of Kings, David, Solomon, and Jeroboam are mentioned by name more frequently.[11] Among the prophets, Isaiah, Jeremiah, and Ezekiel have long books named after each of them; Elijah does not even get his own book. Based on the number of his miracles, Elijah's disciple Elisha appears to be greater than his master (2 Kgs 2–8).

And yet, English versions of the Old Testament end with an ominous prophecy of Elijah's return before the great and terrible day of the Lord (Mal 4:5–6).[12] The Gospels begin with a character, John the Baptist, who is a type of Elijah reborn (Matt 11:14; 17:10–12; Mark 1:6; 9:11–13; Luke 1:17).[13] With no other physical description, Elijah's clothes were sufficiently distinctive for Ahaziah to identify the unknown messenger here (2 Kgs 1:8), and John the Baptist had a similar prophetic uniform (Matt 3:4; Mark 1:6). The first Old Testament character mentioned by Jesus in his inaugural address in Luke is Elijah (Luke 4:25–26). Only two Old Testament individuals appeared next to Jesus during his transfiguration (Matt 17:3–4; Mark 9:4–5; Luke 9:30–33): to represent the law, Moses, and to represent the prophets, not Isaiah, Jeremiah, or Ezekiel, but Elijah.

---

11. David is mentioned 96 times, Solomon 162 times, Jeroboam I 71 times, and Elijah 62 times.
12. The Hebrew Bible ends with the book of Chronicles, not Malachi.
13. In John's Gospel, John the Baptist denies the connection to Elijah (John 1:21).

Why was Elijah so important? As we look back on the life and ministry of the prophet Elijah, we see many reasons why he assumed the mantle of becoming the prototypical prophet. He trusted God to provide for his needs in dramatic ways (via ravens and a foreign widow). He boldly challenged idolatry and called people back to God. He prayed risky prayers that displayed total dependence on God. He was honest with God about his pain, disappointment, and disillusionment. He risked his life confronting evil rulers (Ahab and Ahaziah). But that's not all the Elijah did.

Mentoring, Discipling, Training

Perhaps Elijah's most significant accomplishment, and the one that he shares most dramatically with the two other men whom he stood beside during the transfiguration, was that he focused on mentoring and discipling. Moses trained Joshua, Elijah trained Elisha, and Jesus trained the twelve disciples. Granted, Elijah seemed to be a reluctant mentor of Elisha (see "Elijah and Elisha" in Chapter 15 for a discussion of 1 Kgs 19:19–21), and we don't have a lot of information about the middle of their relationship, but we are able to gain a lot from the beginning and the end of their relationship (1 Kgs 19:16–21; 2 Kgs 2:1–14). Based on their relationship, we can draw four principles about discipling and mentoring.

Mentors hear from God about whom they should disciple. Elijah wasn't searching for a disciple when God spoke to him about Elisha; he was complaining to God about feeling alone (1 Kgs 19:10, 14). In the midst of this interaction, God told Elijah that Elisha should be his successor. The decision was made by God, not Elijah. Likewise, before selecting the twelve disciples, Jesus prayed all night in order to hear clearly from God whom he should focus on (Luke 6:12–16). We need to spend time in prayer listening to God as we think about selecting our mentees.

Mentors make discipling a priority. YHWH told Elijah to anoint three people, Jehu, Hazael, and Elisha, and while neither he nor his disciples seemed to be in a particular hurry to promote the first two into their new roles, the first thing Elijah does after hearing YHWH's commission is to search and find Elisha and throw his cloak over his new disciple (1 Kgs 19:19–20). Elijah made the training of Elisha his first priority. Jesus not only prioritized making disciples during his ministry, but he also commissioned his disciples to do the same with his final words before being taken up to heaven (Matt 28:16–20). Many people in ministry spend too much time honing sermons, preparing Sunday school lessons, and planning programs (and writing commentaries?) and not nearly enough time training the next generation of leaders. All of these ministry-preparation activities can and should be done alongside less experienced people, whenever possible, to train and empower them.

Mentors spend time with their disciples. We don't know all the details of their relationship after Elisha became Elijah's disciple, but we know Elisha was called Elijah's servant (1 Kgs 19:21), Elijah is repeatedly called Elisha's master by the two prophetic companies (2 Kgs 2:3, 5, 16), and Jehoram's officer later describes Elisha as Elijah's servant (3:11). The two of them must have spent significant time together for their mentoring relationship to become public knowledge. Thus it appears that while Elijah was confronting Ahab, Jezebel, and Ahaziah, Elisha was with him. Clearly, Elisha values their time together, because he is unwilling to leave his master during his final moments on earth. When Jesus called his disciples, the first priority, before preaching, casting out demons, or healing, was simply to "be with him" (Mark 3:14). Jesus knew disciples and their mentors need to spend time together. Make time to eat, walk, relax, and serve alongside the people you are mentoring.

Mentors serve their disciples. We don't see Elijah doing a lot for Elisha, but right before he departs, he asks his disciple, "What can I do for you?" (2 Kgs 2:9)—a servant's question. He wanted to serve his servant one more time. In the kingdom of God, masters serve servants. Jesus asked James and John a similar question ("What do you want me to do for you?," Mark 10:36) before telling them that they must become servants of all (vv. 43–44). Somehow Elijah's cloak gets left behind as Elijah and the rest of his clothes get swooped up to heaven. Perhaps Elijah left it intentionally for his disciple, as a final gift of servanthood. Thus the same cloak that was used to commission Elisha into ministry is used to posthumously empower him into a new realm of responsibility, to literally take up the mantle of God's prophet. Jesus didn't just tell his disciples they needed to serve, he modeled it for them shortly before he died by washing each of his disciples' feet (John 13:1–20). Followers of Jesus need to serve the people they are training and discipling.

CHAPTER 20

2 Kings 2:19–3:27

LISTEN to the Story

[19]The people of the city said to Elisha, "Look, our lord, this town is well situated, as you can see, but the water is bad and the land is unproductive."

[20]"Bring me a new bowl," he said, "and put salt in it." So they brought it to him.

[21]Then he went out to the spring and threw the salt into it, saying, "This is what the LORD says: 'I have healed this water. Never again will it cause death or make the land unproductive.'" [22]And the water has remained pure to this day, according to the word Elisha had spoken.

[23]From there Elisha went up to Bethel. As he was walking along the road, some boys came out of the town and jeered at him. "Get out of here, baldy!" they said. "Get out of here, baldy!" [24]He turned around, looked at them and called down a curse on them in the name of the LORD. Then two bears came out of the woods and mauled forty-two of the boys. [25]And he went on to Mount Carmel and from there returned to Samaria.

[3:1]Joram son of Ahab became king of Israel in Samaria in the eighteenth year of Jehoshaphat king of Judah, and he reigned twelve years. [2]He did evil in the eyes of the LORD, but not as his father and mother had done. He got rid of the sacred stone of Baal that his father had made. [3]Nevertheless he clung to the sins of Jeroboam son of Nebat, which he had caused Israel to commit; he did not turn away from them.

[4]Now Mesha king of Moab raised sheep, and he had to pay the king of Israel a tribute of a hundred thousand lambs and the wool of a hundred thousand rams. [5]But after Ahab died, the king of Moab rebelled against the king of Israel. [6]So at that time King Joram set out from Samaria and mobilized all Israel. [7]He also sent this message to Jehoshaphat king of Judah: "The king of Moab has rebelled against me. Will you go with me to fight against Moab?"

"I will go with you," he replied. "I am as you are, my people as your
people, my horses as your horses."

[8]"By what route shall we attack?" he asked.

"Through the Desert of Edom," he answered.

[9]So the king of Israel set out with the king of Judah and the king of
Edom. After a roundabout march of seven days, the army had no more
water for themselves or for the animals with them.

[10]"What!" exclaimed the king of Israel. "Has the LORD called us three
kings together only to deliver us into the hands of Moab?"

[11]But Jehoshaphat asked, "Is there no prophet of the LORD here,
through whom we may inquire of the LORD?"

An officer of the king of Israel answered, "Elisha son of Shaphat is here.
He used to pour water on the hands of Elijah."

[12]Jehoshaphat said, "The word of the LORD is with him." So the king
of Israel and Jehoshaphat and the king of Edom went down to him.

[13]Elisha said to the king of Israel, "Why do you want to involve me? Go
to the prophets of your father and the prophets of your mother."

"No," the king of Israel answered, "because it was the LORD who called
us three kings together to deliver us into the hands of Moab."

[14]Elisha said, "As surely as the LORD Almighty lives, whom I serve, if I
did not have respect for the presence of Jehoshaphat king of Judah, I would
not pay any attention to you. [15]But now bring me a harpist."

While the harpist was playing, the hand of the LORD came on Elisha
[16]and he said, "This is what the LORD says: I will fill this valley with pools
of water. [17]For this is what the LORD says: You will see neither wind nor
rain, yet this valley will be filled with water, and you, your cattle and your
other animals will drink. [18]This is an easy thing in the eyes of the LORD; he
will also deliver Moab into your hands. [19]You will overthrow every fortified
city and every major town. You will cut down every good tree, stop up all
the springs, and ruin every good field with stones."

[20]The next morning, about the time for offering the sacrifice, there it
was—water flowing from the direction of Edom! And the land was filled
with water.

[21]Now all the Moabites had heard that the kings had come to fight
against them; so every man, young and old, who could bear arms was
called up and stationed on the border. [22]When they got up early in the
morning, the sun was shining on the water. To the Moabites across the way,

the water looked red—like blood. [23]"That's blood!" they said. "Those kings must have fought and slaughtered each other. Now to the plunder, Moab!"

[24]But when the Moabites came to the camp of Israel, the Israelites rose up and fought them until they fled. And the Israelites invaded the land and slaughtered the Moabites. [25]They destroyed the towns, and each man threw a stone on every good field until it was covered. They stopped up all the springs and cut down every good tree. Only Kir Hareseth was left with its stones in place, but men armed with slings surrounded it and attacked it.

[26]When the king of Moab saw that the battle had gone against him, he took with him seven hundred swordsmen to break through to the king of Edom, but they failed. [27]Then he took his firstborn son, who was to succeed him as king, and offered him as a sacrifice on the city wall. The fury against Israel was great; they withdrew and returned to their own land.

Listening to the Text in the Story: Biblical Texts: Leviticus 18:21; Joshua 6:26; Judges 11:34–40; 1 Kings 13–16; 21–22; 2 Kings 1:10, 12; 5:27; 9–10; Ancient Near Eastern Text: The Mesha Stele

Elisha is on his own. His master is gone, and the narrative proceeds to record the miracles of his early ministry: healing a polluted spring, siccing bears on boys, and providing water in the wilderness of Edom for the armies of Israel and Judah in their campaign against Moab. We will wait to discuss the ethical problems associated with a man of God calling down bears on boys for taunting him; at this point, we will merely acknowledge that many prophetic judgments in Kings involve animal attacks. Elsewhere we see lions (1 Kgs 13:22–26; 20:36; 2 Kgs 17:25–26), dogs (1 Kgs 14:11; 15:29; 16:4, 12; 21:19–24; 22:38; 2 Kgs 9:10, 36), and birds (1 Kgs 14:11; 15:29; 16:4, 12; 1 Kgs 21:24; 2 Kgs 10:10, 17), but this chapter includes the only episode of a judgment involving bears (2:24). Prophets use other means to punish, including fire (2 Kgs 1:10, 12) and illness (1 Kgs 13:4; 2 Kgs 5:27), but these grisly animal judgments get one's attention and would have been a stark warning to take prophets (and their words) seriously.

A useful source of background for the conflict here between Moab and Israel is the Mesha Stele, or Moabite Stone. The inscription was discussed in the context of 1 Kings 16, since it refers to Jehoram's grandfather Omri.[1]

1. *COS* 2:137–38.

The stele's inscription describes how Omri and his son (Ahab or Joram) oppressed Moab, but then Mesha, mentioned only once by name in this text (2 Kgs 3:4), regained autonomy for Moab (see 1:1; 3:5).

A bizarre incident occurs toward the end of 2 Kings 3 as King Mesha sacrifices his son to garner divine assistance and change the fortunes of the battle against Israel. The textual issues surrounding this troubling incident will be discussed in the Explain the Story section, but here we will mention other biblical examples of human sacrifice.[2] While the law prohibited human sacrifice (Lev 18:21), God tested Abraham by asking him to offer Isaac (Gen 22:1–15), and the judge Jephthah appeared to offer his unnamed daughter to fulfill a rashly taken vow (Judg 11:34–40). Hiel of Bethel's rebuilding of Jericho invoked the curse that Joshua had placed on the ruined city involving the death of his oldest and youngest sons (Josh 6:26; 1 Kgs 16:34). Two later Judean rulers, the father and son of Hezekiah, Ahaz and Manasseh, both made their sons "pass through the fire" (2 Kgs 16:2–3; 21:1, 6), a euphemism for child sacrifice.

Elisha Heals Jericho's Water (2 Kings 2:19–22)

In terms of longevity and the number of miracles, Elisha's ministry surpasses that of his mentor. But like many of Elijah's miracles (see Chapter 19 above), Elisha's first miracles—parting and purifying bodies of water—are reminiscent of Moses (2:14, 20–21; Exod 14; 15:23–25).

Elisha remained near Jericho after Elijah's departure, so the elders of the city inform the prophet that the spring providing water for their city and the surrounding fields was contaminated. Their humble request for help is viewed favorably by the newly commissioned prophet of God. The Hebrew term *meshakkaleth,* translated as "unproductive" in the NIV (2 Kgs 2:19, 21), more literally means "bereft of children," so other versions translate it as "miscarriage" in 2:21 (NSRV, ESV; see also Gen 27:45; 31:38; 42:36; 43:14), where it is mentioned along with death. It is reasonable to assume that both the crops and the birth rate would have been severely affected by a contaminated spring.[3]

2. For ancient Near Eastern examples of human sacrifice, see Cogan and Tadmor, *II Kings*, 47, and M. Weinfeld, "The Worship of Molech and the Queen of Heaven and Its Background," *UF* 4 (1972): 133–40.

3. See also Barnes, *1–2 Kings*, 205.

A spring called "Elisha's Spring" near the modern city of Jericho (in 'Ain es-Sultan) produces about a thousand gallons of water per minute.

Wiseman offers two possible reasons that the spring may have led to sterility: contamination by some type of radioactive mineral or a parasitic infection.[4] Moses healed the waters at Marah by tossing in a stick (Exod 15:25), and Elisha heals Jericho's spring by tossing in salt from a bowl and making a pronouncement (2 Kgs 2:20–22). The writer adds a comment that the spring has remained pure "to this day"—which prompts scholars to ask, "what day is being referred to?" But the purpose of the comment is not to make a vague allusion to the timing of the final composition but merely to attest that the miraculous purification was not merely a temporary reprieve.

Elisha, the Boys, and the Bears (2:23–25)

After healing their water, Elisha leaves Jericho to travel to Bethel. Jericho is located in the Jordan Valley (also called the Jordan Rift), 825 feet below sea level, far deeper than Death Valley, the lowest spot in North America (282 feet below sea level). Modern Jericho is the lowest city in the world.[5] Bethel is about 2800 feet above sea level, meaning his twelve-mile hike there involved a steep climb (over 3600 feet). On his way, he meets a group of boys. While some commentators think the boys are from Bethel (e.g., House, Fretheim), the perspective of Jones that they were from Jericho is more reasonable.[6] The boys' taunt of Elisha could be translated literally as "Go up, go up!" (2:23; rendered in the NIV as "Get out of here"), which only makes sense from the perspective of the lower altitude Jericho. Also, Elisha's harsh reaction to the boys makes more sense if they were from Jericho, since he just purified their water.

After the boys jeer at him, Elisha curses them in the name of YHWH. While Elisha's curse did not specify what was to happen, the immediate appearance of two attacking she-bears suggests that YHWH was the cause.[7] While bears are no longer found in Palestine (the last record of a bear in Palestine was in the 1930s), they were not uncommon in biblical times. When David was a young shepherd, YHWH delivered him from bears and lions (1 Sam 17:34–37). Other texts speak of how notoriously vicious she-bears were (2 Sam 17:8; Prov 17:12; Hos 13:8). Elisha's she-bears mauled forty-two of these boys (2 Kgs 2:24).

---

4. Wiseman, *1 & 2 Kings*, 197.

5. See Barnes, *1–2 Kings*, 201.

6. Paul House, *1, 2 Kings*, NAC 8 (Nashville: B & H Publishing, 1995), 260; Fretheim, *Kings*, 139; Jones, *1 and 2 Kings*, 2:389.

7. The verb used here for "came out" is feminine, and most English translations make it clear that the bears are female (ESV, KJV, NRSV, NASB).

Since Elisha curses the boys "in the name of the LORD" (v. 24) and the bears seem to be divinely sent, this incident could be cited as another example of God behaving badly. Why would God ordain the slaughter of children who are merely engaged in taunting? I discuss this problem at length elsewhere,[8] so here it will suffice to make the following three points.

First, the boys were not a group of young children but were essentially a teenage gang. There are three words used to describe Elisha's taunters, and each of them are used elsewhere for young adults. Two of them (*ne'arim qetannim*) are translated by the NIV as "boys" in 2:23, and the other one (*yeladim*) is also translated as "boys" by the NIV in 2:24. Singular forms of both *yeladim* and *qetannim* are used to describe Joseph's brother Benjamin when he was in his twenties (Gen 44:20). Likewise, young king Solomon uses singular forms of both *ne'arim* and *qetannim* to describe himself (1 Kgs 3:7). Since these three words have a broad range of meaning, we must look to the context to decide what they mean here. A large group of youth with no parental supervision is harassing a solitary older man—behavior we would expect from a gang of teenagers, not a preschool.

Second, the teens here were not killed but merely injured. For other animal attacks in Kings, the text states explicitly that death was the result (1 Kgs 13:24; 20:36). Logistically, it is hard to imagine how only two bears would have been able to kill forty-two teenagers, unless the boys waited in line to be slaughtered. The text does not provide details regarding the extent of their injuries, but we assume they were taught a lesson.

Third, prophets were being slaughtered by Ahaziah's parents (1 Kgs 18:4), so it is very likely Elisha's life once again was in danger here, as was Elijah's in the previous chapter (1 Kgs 1:9–15). Elisha was acting in self-defense. It is impossible to say why God allowed so many of his prophets to be killed previously, but now Elisha is delivered, and he goes on to heal the sick, to feed the hungry, to pray for a barren woman who then gives birth, to raise the dead, and to prevent a war (2 Kgs 4–6, 8, 13). Many people in Israel were glad that he survived this threat, since the remainder of his ministry was characterized by acts of mercy worthy of Jesus or Mother Theresa.

If these boys were from Jericho, then this incident adds another stage to the tumultuous story of the city. Jericho was destroyed by Israel and cursed by Joshua (Josh 6:26), but the family of the prostitute from Jericho, Rahab, was delivered, and her descendants are among Jesus's ancestors (Matt 1:5). The city was rebuilt by Hiel, who lost two of his sons in the process (1 Kgs 16:34).

8. See Lamb, *God Behaving Badly*, 95–99.

Jericho's water was purified, but then a large number of its youth are attacked for taunting a man of God (2 Kgs 2:19–24). Throughout its dramatic history, God has punished and blessed the residents of Jericho.

Joram Becomes King (2 Kings 3:1–3)

Because Ahaziah has no heirs, his brother Joram (son of Ahab and Jezebel) becomes the next northern ruler (3:1). Both Israel and Judah had rulers named Jehoram whose reigns overlapped (1:17), and, to make it more confusing, both rulers' names are occasionally shortened to Joram (8:16, 21). In this commentary I will follow the NIV translation that solves this problem by consistently referring to the ruler of Israel as "Joram" and the ruler of Judah as "Jehoram." Both versions of the name mean "YHWH is exalted." Joram is evaluated as evil (he did not remove Jeroboam's altars), but he was an improvement over his parents Ahab and Jezebel, since he removed the sacred stone (*matsebah*) that his father had installed to worship Baal (3:2). Worship associated with similar stones or pillars appears earlier in the Southern Kingdom (1 Kgs 14:23) and later in the Northern Kingdom (2 Kgs 10:26–27).

Moab Rebels, Israel Mobilizes (2 Kings 3:4–8)

The only biblical reference to King Mesha of Moab appears here (3:4), but he is well known from the Mesha Stele or Moabite Stone. Like David, Mesha raised sheep, although presumably as ruler he did not do the actual shepherding. Under the reigns of Saul and David, Moab was controlled by Israel (1 Sam 14:47; 2 Sam 8:2, 11–12), and Solomon established a marriage alliance with Moab (1 Kgs 11:1). Moab remained an Israelite vassal and gave a massive annual tribute in the form of a hundred thousand goats and a hundred thousand rams, numbers that Barnes describes as "folkloristic,"[9] emphasizing Moab's complete submission. The text repeats the comment of 2 Kings 1:1—after the death of Ahab, Moab rebelled against Israel (3:5). As he mobilized his forces for war, Joram sent a message to his father's old ally, Jehoshaphat of Judah, asking for assistance (v. 7; see also 1 Kgs 22:4). For the remainder of the narrative, the text does not use Joram's name, merely calling him "the king of Israel" (e.g., 2 Kgs 3:9, 10, 11, 12, 13), while consistently using the southern ruler's name in contrast. Jehoshaphat's positive response is identical to the one he gave Ahab when he asked for assistance against Aram (1 Kgs 22:4; 2 Kgs 3:7). The text does not state when, but Jehoshaphat's son, Jehoram of Judah, marries Joram of Israel's sister, Athaliah, to cement this alliance (8:18).

9. Barnes, *1–2 Kings*, 209; see also Cogan and Tadmor, *II Kings*, 43.

Moab was located along the east bank of the Dead Sea, so to reach it from Samaria or Jerusalem their armies could go the direct route over the northern part of the sea or the longer route around the southern tip of the sea through the land of Edom. The two rulers decide to take the longer route through Edom, presumably to avoid the main fortifications along Moab's northern border (3:8).

Water Shortage Solved (2 Kings 3:9–20)

The southern route should give Israel and Judah the element of surprise against Moab, and it also allows them to add another ally, Judah's vassal, the king of Edom (Edom later rebelled against Judah; 8:20–22). But the long journey through an arid region caused these combined forces to run out of water (3:9), prompting Joram to panic and wonder if YHWH led them to be defeated by Moab (v. 10), despite the fact that YHWH was not consulted beforehand. Joram may be an evil ruler, but he was wise to choose Jehoshaphat, a ruler who depended upon God as his primary ally. Using language almost identical to what he said to Ahab before the Aram conflict (1 Kgs 22:5, 7), Jehoshaphat advises the consultation of a prophet of YHWH (2 Kgs 3:11). When an anonymous officer suggests Elisha, the servant of Elijah, Jehoshaphat is sufficiently familiar with him to attest that God is with him (vv. 11–12). No explanation is given for Elisha's presence on this campaign far from Samaria; Elijah never traveled with Ahab. Typically, rulers summon subjects (e.g., 1 Kgs 2:36; 22:9; 2 Kgs 12:7), but in their desperation these three kings visit the prophet (3:12). Grumpy Elisha is not impressed by their effort to see him, so he tells them to seek guidance from Ahab's parents' prophets (v. 13), which is what Ahab did before the Aram campaign (1 Kgs 22:5–6). Joram persists and claims, with no textual support, that YHWH was the one who commissioned them for this task (2 Kgs 3:13). Elisha begrudgingly agrees to help, but only because the faithful Jehoshaphat is there (v. 14).

Elisha's request for a harpist may seem strange, but elsewhere prophecy is linked to music, specifically harp playing, both during the time of Saul and that of David (1 Sam 10:5–11; 1 Chr 25:1–3). The music calms the beast in the prophet, as he is empowered by the hand of YHWH and predicts an abundance of water. Elijah prophesied rain (1 Kgs 18:41), but Elisha's miraculous water source is not visible rain (2 Kgs 3:16–17). (Perhaps it was a distant downfall flowing into the Zered River along the border of Edom and Moab?) The rain will provide for all three armies and all their animals. Elisha predicts a complete destruction of not only the Moabite army but also their cities, land, and forests (vv. 18–19). Elisha's prediction is shocking in its magnitude and seems to violate the Torah's prohibition against harming foreign forests during warfare (Deut 20:19–20). By the next morning, the word of YHWH as pronounced by Elisha is fulfilled, and the land is full of water (2 Kgs 3:20). Jehoshaphat and Joram are not mentioned again by name until Jehoram of Judah's regnal formula (8:16).

The Battle and the Sacrifice (2 Kings 3:21–27)

At this point the narrative shifts to the Moabite camp. A three-nation army does not move surreptitiously, so in response to the looming threat, the Moabites issue a total call to arms (3:21). When the Moabites see the flowing liquid, they assume that it is blood, not water, and that their opponents have been fighting each other (v. 22). This conclusion may seem ridiculous, but the location where this conflict probably took place, the Zered Canyon, was known for its red sandstone, which could give water flowing over it a blood-like appearance. Since they had seen no rain, the Moabites conclude it must have been foreign blood, so they decide to strike quickly and seize the plunder (v. 23). Unfortunately for the Moabites, the three-nation army was at full strength, and they utterly destroy the Moabites, their towns, and their lands, as Elisha predicted (vv. 24–25).

When Mesha realizes he is losing, he tries to use an elite division to break through against Edom, perhaps because, as the vassal of Judah, he assumes Edom was the weak spot (v. 26). When that attempt fails, Mesha sacrifices his own heir on the city wall, presumably in the sight of his enemies (v. 27). The conclusion to the conflict is briefly recorded: because of great "fury against Israel," the coalition forces withdraw and return home.

While the final result may seem unresolved, even with Israel's hasty withdrawal, the land and people of Moab clearly suffered a mighty defeat, and Elisha's prophecy was essentially fulfilled. Who was the source of the great fury (*qetsep gadol*) against Israel? There are at least three options. First, the Moabites were angry at their ruler, so they fought ferociously against Israel, driving them back. Second, the Israelites were appalled that their enemy would do something so atrocious, making them fearful and leading to their withdrawal. Third, YHWH was angry at the alliance for Joram's idolatry and lack of faith, so he caused their retreat. In cases where the text is unclear, there is often a reason for the ambiguity, and that perhaps is the case here: Moab was empowered, Israel was shocked, and God was angry at the unfaithful house of Ahab. Sources for the fury against Israel may be fascinating to examine, but the text here provides few clues.[10]

---

10. See discussions in Barnes (*1–2 Kings*, 211–213), Wray Beal (*1 & 2 Kings*, 315–316), and Cogan and Tadmor (*II Kings*, 47–48).

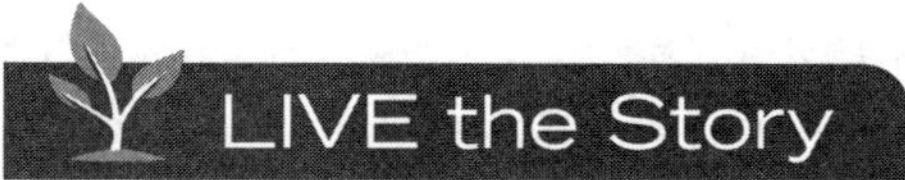

How Do We Handle Problematic Passages?

Several ethical problems emerge from the stories of Elijah calling down fire on the soldiers in 2 Kings 1 and Elisha calling down bears on the taunting boys here. The Old Testament includes many problematic passages like these: the conquest of Canaan (Josh 10–11), the smiting of Uzzah (1 Sam 6:1–11), the destruction of the Amalekites (15:1–9). What should we do with problematic texts like these?

A few years ago I was leading a seminar on my book *God Behaving Badly* for a group of pastors. As we discussed what to do with these difficult texts, a pastor shared, "When I was growing up in the church, we never studied the difficult texts of the Old Testament."

I asked, "When did you first encounter them?"

He replied, "At college, in my religion classes, which were taught by atheists. They loved to 'enlighten' us naïve freshmen about all the problems in the Bible."

"How did you feel about that?"

"At first I was embarrassed. It was humbling to realize I didn't know my Bible very well. But then I was angry. I was mad at my home church. I felt betrayed and unprepared. Why didn't we ever talk about these stories?"

I've had many similar conversations. Here are six steps to help churches and ministries address these troubling texts.

Don't avoid them. If teachers of the Bible avoid these difficult texts, people will only encounter them in contexts where they are less likely to get help understanding them: when reading the Bible on their own, when confronted by a coworker, or when sitting in a college religion class. If we truly believe that all Scripture is inspired and profitable for teaching (2 Tim 3:16), we need to teach all Scripture, including the difficult passages like Elisha, the boys, and the bears.

State the problem as problematically as possible. While problematic passages aren't taught often, when they are, the problem is typically downplayed or discounted, implying that anyone who wonders about them is either not intelligent or not faithful. Downplaying the problem can infuriate people who have genuine questions about these texts, but emphasizing the problem will allow them to feel taken seriously. For this passage, I would state the problem thus: "A prophet of God appears to call down judgment to slaughter innocent infants." I don't think that's what actually happened (see "Elisha, the Boys, and the Bears" above), but that's how I would begin framing a discussion of this text. I have been in contexts speaking to atheists on college campuses where I've stated the problem as problematically as possible, and they have said, "Actually, it's not that bad." Then they proceed to explain how I have overstated the problem. This step can transform a "devil's advocate" into a "God's advocate."

Examine the language. After stating the problem, examine the language that makes the passage difficult to understand. If one has access to the Hebrew (or Greek for the New Testament), look up the relevant words. Most readers of the Old Testament won't know Hebrew, but they can still use online resources like Bible Gateway to see how other translations render a crucial word or phrase. An examination of the words used in 2 Kings 2:23–24 for "boys" revealed that the victims were probably not small children but teenagers.

Understand the context. Modern assumptions regarding cultural values and norms can make these problematic texts more difficult to understand, so we need to work to understand what was going on in both the biblical context and in the ancient context. Elisha's ursine curse makes more sense when we realize that many prophets were being killed and that Elisha later went on to perform many acts of supernatural service to the Israelite community.

Discuss with others. Over the thirty-five years I've been teaching the Bible, I've gained much wisdom from literally thousands of discussions with students, friends, and family about the Bible. (If you have questions about my current state of wisdom, you should have seen where I was thirty-five years ago.) Interactions over stories like Elisha, the boys, and the bears not only help us understand Scripture better, they draw us into deeper relationships with our conversation partners. At the end of the discussion, humbly acknowledge points of uncertainty, graciously summarize the main conclusions, and faithfully pray for more understanding moving forward.

Point people to Jesus. The primary need of people who struggle to understand the troubling texts of Scripture is a relationship with Jesus. We need to both listen to people who ask about these difficult passages and also to tell them to take their questions to Jesus in prayer. During his ministry, Jesus welcomed people who asked him difficult questions (e.g., Mark 4:10; 12:34). Jesus himself asked his father a brutal question as he hung dying on a cross, "My God, My God, why have you forsaken me?" (Mark 15:34). If we are troubled by the curse pronounced by Elisha on these boys, we should be amazed by, and grateful for, Jesus's willingness to become accursed by dying on a cross in order to share God's blessings with all peoples (Gal 3:13–14).

CHAPTER 21

2 Kings 4:1–44

LISTEN to the Story

1The wife of a man from the company of the prophets cried out to
Elisha, "Your servant my husband is dead, and you know that he revered
the LORD. But now his creditor is coming to take my two boys as his slaves."
2Elisha replied to her, "How can I help you? Tell me, what do you have
in your house?"
"Your servant has nothing there at all," she said, "except a small jar of
olive oil."
3Elisha said, "Go around and ask all your neighbors for empty jars.
Don't ask for just a few. 4Then go inside and shut the door behind you and
your sons. Pour oil into all the jars, and as each is filled, put it to one side."
5She left him and shut the door behind her and her sons. They brought
the jars to her and she kept pouring. 6When all the jars were full, she said
to her son, "Bring me another one."
But he replied, "There is not a jar left." Then the oil stopped flowing.
7She went and told the man of God, and he said, "Go, sell the oil and
pay your debts. You and your sons can live on what is left."
8One day Elisha went to Shunem. And a well-to-do woman was there,
who urged him to stay for a meal. So whenever he came by, he stopped
there to eat. 9She said to her husband, "I know that this man who often
comes our way is a holy man of God. 10Let's make a small room on the
roof and put in it a bed and a table, a chair and a lamp for him. Then he
can stay there whenever he comes to us."
11One day when Elisha came, he went up to his room and lay down
there. 12He said to his servant Gehazi, "Call the Shunammite." So he called
her, and she stood before him. 13Elisha said to him, "Tell her, 'You have
gone to all this trouble for us. Now what can be done for you? Can we
speak on your behalf to the king or the commander of the army?'"
She replied, "I have a home among my own people."
14"What can be done for her?" Elisha asked.

Gehazi said, "She has no son, and her husband is old."

[15]Then Elisha said, "Call her." So he called her, and she stood in the doorway. [16]"About this time next year," Elisha said, "you will hold a son in your arms."

"No, my lord!" she objected. "Please, man of God, don't mislead your servant!"

[17]But the woman became pregnant, and the next year about that same time she gave birth to a son, just as Elisha had told her.

[18]The child grew, and one day he went out to his father, who was with the reapers. [19]He said to his father, "My head! My head!"

His father told a servant, "Carry him to his mother." [20]After the servant had lifted him up and carried him to his mother, the boy sat on her lap until noon, and then he died. [21]She went up and laid him on the bed of the man of God, then shut the door and went out.

[22]She called her husband and said, "Please send me one of the servants and a donkey so I can go to the man of God quickly and return."

[23]"Why go to him today?" he asked. "It's not the New Moon or the Sabbath."

"That's all right," she said.

[24]She saddled the donkey and said to her servant, "Lead on; don't slow down for me unless I tell you." [25]So she set out and came to the man of God at Mount Carmel.

When he saw her in the distance, the man of God said to his servant Gehazi, "Look! There's the Shunammite! [26]Run to meet her and ask her, 'Are you all right? Is your husband all right? Is your child all right?'"

"Everything is all right," she said.

[27]When she reached the man of God at the mountain, she took hold of his feet. Gehazi came over to push her away, but the man of God said, "Leave her alone! She is in bitter distress, but the LORD has hidden it from me and has not told me why."

[28]"Did I ask you for a son, my lord?" she said. "Didn't I tell you, 'Don't raise my hopes'?"

[29]Elisha said to Gehazi, "Tuck your cloak into your belt, take my staff in your hand and run. Don't greet anyone you meet, and if anyone greets you, do not answer. Lay my staff on the boy's face."

[30]But the child's mother said, "As surely as the LORD lives and as you live, I will not leave you." So he got up and followed her.

[31]Gehazi went on ahead and laid the staff on the boy's face, but there was no sound or response. So Gehazi went back to meet Elisha and told him, "The boy has not awakened."

[32]When Elisha reached the house, there was the boy lying dead on his couch. [33]He went in, shut the door on the two of them and prayed to the Lord. [34]Then he got on the bed and lay on the boy, mouth to mouth, eyes to eyes, hands to hands. As he stretched himself out on him, the boy's body grew warm. [35]Elisha turned away and walked back and forth in the room and then got on the bed and stretched out on him once more. The boy sneezed seven times and opened his eyes.

[36]Elisha summoned Gehazi and said, "Call the Shunammite." And he did. When she came, he said, "Take your son." [37]She came in, fell at his feet and bowed to the ground. Then she took her son and went out.

[38]Elisha returned to Gilgal and there was a famine in that region. While the company of the prophets was meeting with him, he said to his servant, "Put on the large pot and cook some stew for these prophets."

[39]One of them went out into the fields to gather herbs and found a wild vine and picked as many of its gourds as his garment could hold. When he returned, he cut them up into the pot of stew, though no one knew what they were. [40]The stew was poured out for the men, but as they began to eat it, they cried out, "Man of God, there is death in the pot!" And they could not eat it.

[41]Elisha said, "Get some flour." He put it into the pot and said, "Serve it to the people to eat." And there was nothing harmful in the pot.

[42]A man came from Baal Shalishah, bringing the man of God twenty loaves of barley bread baked from the first ripe grain, along with some heads of new grain. "Give it to the people to eat," Elisha said.

[43]"How can I set this before a hundred men?" his servant asked.

But Elisha answered, "Give it to the people to eat. For this is what the Lord says: 'They will eat and have some left over.'" [44]Then he set it before them, and they ate and had some left over, according to the word of the Lord.

Listening to the Text in the Story: Biblical Texts: Exodus 21:2; Deuteronomy 15:12; Ancient Near Eastern Texts: The Code of Hammurabi; The Widow's Plea

In 2 Kings 4 Elisha performs a series of five miracles of compassion: providing oil for a widow, prophesying the birth of a son for a barren woman, resurrecting the same woman's dead son, purifying a pot of deadly stew, and multiplying bread during a famine. The provision for the widow centered around the practice of debt slavery, since her sons were to be sold as slaves to their father's creditor. Debt slavery was a common way for ancient people to pay off debts. The law of Moses allowed it but limited the years of servitude to six (Exod 21:2; Deut 15:12). The Code of Hammurabi mandated that a debt slave was to be released after three years.

> If an obligation is outstanding against a man and he sells or gives into debt service his wife, his son, or his daughter, they shall perform service in the house of their buyer or of the one who holds them in debt service for three years; their release shall be secured in the fourth year.[1]

Ancient widows had many things to be concerned about (on the vulnerability of ancient widows, see the discussion of 1 Kgs 17:8–24 in Chapter 14). An ancient Hebrew ostraca (an inscribed potsherd) includes a request for help, from a widow to a certain official, similar to that of the widow in this text.

> And now, may my lord the official listen to your maidservant. My husband has died leaving no sons. I request politely that the following happen: let your hand be with me and entrust to your maidservant the inheritance about which you spoke to 'Amasyahu.[2]

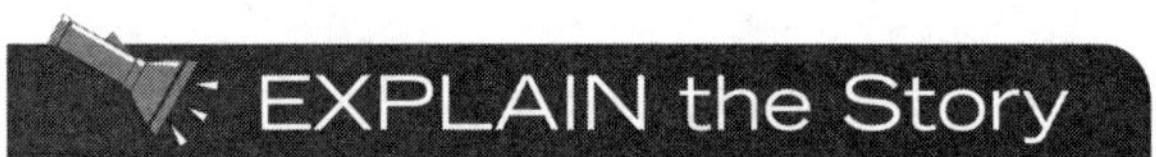

Elisha Provides Oil for a Widow (2 Kings 4:1–7)

Elisha was last reported providing water for the combined forces of Israel, Judah, and Edom (2 Kgs 3:16–20), but it is possible these stories are not arranged chronologically. In any case, there is a break at the beginning of this chapter, as the focus shifts from conflicts between nations to a series of personal crises.

A widow whose husband was a member of the prophetic company approaches Elisha with news that her two sons are about to become debt slaves (4:1).

1. *COS* 2:343.
2. *COS* 3:86; for an image, see *ZIBBC* 3:131.

While the law allowed for debt slavery (see Listen to the Story above), abuses of this practice were common, and the prophet Amos later railed against these: "They sell the innocent for silver, and the needy for a pair of sandals" (Amos 2:6; see also 8:6). To make the prophet more sympathetic to her cause, she reminds Elisha that her husband "revered the LORD" (2 Kgs 4:1). Elisha's two questions suggest that he is willing but uncertain how to assist her (v. 2). Just as Elijah did with the widow of Zarephath (1 Kgs 17:8–16), Elisha here uses what she has available, in this case a "small jar of olive oil" (*'asuk*[3] *shemen*). Elisha tells her to collect jars (*kelim*) from her neighbors, and as she pours her limited oil, it will be multiplied, filling up all the jars. Israelite jars were not clear glass like they are today but were made of red or brown clay, often with decorations. Some of these jars could have held over ten gallons,[4] so Elisha's miraculous provision of an abundant supply of jars of olive oil could easily erase her debts and give her a nest egg. Even though the dead prophet's creditors were not extending mercy to this woman and her sons, the prophet of God generously met her need and averted the crisis.

A Shunammite Woman Gives Birth (2 Kings 4:8–17)

Elisha traveled next to Shunem, a city located about five miles north of Jezreel in the tribal region of Issachar (Josh 19:18). In his journeys the prophet passed through that region often enough for a wealthy woman from Shunem to provide him regular meals and a guest room (bed, table, chair, and a lamp; 2 Kgs 4:10).[5] Elsewhere in Scripture we see similar examples of hospitality: during the famine Elijah was provided for by the poor widow of Zarephath (1 Kgs 17:8–16), and during his ministry Jesus was supported by a group of wealthy women (Luke 8:3).

Perhaps because he did not feel comfortable being in debt to this Shunammite woman, Elisha asks her if there is anything he can do to help. She has learned the secret of being content (see Phil 4:12), so merely replies, "I have a home among my own people" (2 Kgs 4:13). Elisha was not content to let the issue go, so he persists, seeking advice from his servant Gehazi,

3. The word translated as "jar" (*'asuk*) here is a *hapax legomenon* (the only occurrence in the Hebrew Bible), but from the context it must have been a small oil container.

4. See Barnes, *1–2 Kings*, 214.

5. A potsherd with the name "Elisha" discovered at a home at Tel Rehov has led scholars to speculate if this house was the prophet's home; see Noah Wiener, "Tel Rehov House Associated with the Biblical Prophet Elisha," *Bible History Daily*, July 23, 2013, https://www.biblicalarchaeology.org/daily/biblical-sites-places/biblical-archaeology-sites/tel-rehov-house-associated-with-the-biblical-prophet-elisha/.

mentioned here for the first time. Since Elisha was Elijah's servant before becoming his successor, one might expect the same promotion for Gehazi, and he does play a role later in restoring this woman's land (8:4–5). But his greed and deception after the healing of Naaman prompt a condemnation and a sentence of leprosy from Elisha (5:20–27). In this respect, training a successor, Elisha does not follow in the steps of his master.

Gehazi points out that the woman is barren, and her husband is old (4:14), which could put her in a more dire predicament than the widow at the beginning of the chapter. Elisha makes a prediction reminiscent of the one given to Abraham and Sarah (Gen 18:10, 14), that in a year she would hold a son in her arms (2 Kgs 4:16). Sarah's doubt was expressed in laughter (Gen 18:12); this woman's was expressed in an objection that she does not want to be misled. Within a year she gave birth, just as Elisha had said (2 Kgs 4:17).

Elisha Raises the Shunammite's Son (2 Kings 4:18–37)

The narrative jumps ahead at least five years, from the prediction about the boy (4:16), to his birth (v. 17), to his speaking and running around (v. 18). One day, the boy ran out to his father in the field crying "My head! My head!" (v. 19). Scholars speculate his headache may have been caused by sunstroke, cerebral malaria, or meningitis.[6] The mother, who holds her son in her lap as he dies, presumably has a plan involving Elisha, since she lays her son's body on the prophet's bed and shuts the door (vv. 20–21). Perhaps she had heard that Elijah revived the son of the widow of Zarephath (1 Kgs 17:17–24)? In any case, she does not give up hope but requests a donkey to visit Elisha. Her clueless husband wonders why she is looking for a prophet when it is not a holiday (2 Kgs 4:23). Her curious response rendered, as "That's all right" in the NIV (v. 23), is literally "peace," in Hebrew, *shalom*—her one-word response reveals she does not have time to explain. Her urgency is also seen in her command to the servant to not slow down (v. 24), as they begin a long journey to Mount Carmel (forty–fifty miles roundtrip).

When Elisha sees her, he sends Gehazi to ask if she, her husband, and her boy are all right (vv. 25–26). Elisha uses the word *shalom* three times in his query, each with the interrogative particle (thus, *hashalom*), which could be translated literally as "Is it peace?" Her terse response is the same she gave to her husband, *shalom* (here rendered as "Everything is all right," v. 26). Thus, the word *shalom* is repeated here five times, twice by the woman at the point in her life where one might expect her to be the least peaceful, when her young

6. See Wiseman, *1 & 2 Kings*, 204.

miracle boy has just died in her own arms. She had amazing faith that, even after an extended period of time, Elisha could do something dramatic for her. She had a peace that "passeth all understanding" (Phil 4:7 KJV).

Gehazi attempts to extract her after she grabbed the prophet's feet, but Elisha has enough sense to know she is in serious distress, so he allows her to continue (2 Kgs 4:27). She never states what happened, but her two rhetorical questions make it clear her son is dead (v. 28). Her lament to Elisha that she did not want to be disappointed suggests that she was already acquainted with grief.

Elisha eventually resurrects the boy, but it occurs in three stages, like Jesus's two-part healing of the blind man from Bethsaida (Mark 8:22–26). First, Elisha sends Gehazi on ahead to lay his staff on the boy's face, while the mother and Elisha return to Shunem at a slower pace (2 Kgs 4:29–30). Second, Elisha lays his body on the boy's corpse, similar to Elijah (1 Kgs 17:21), but here the text adds more details: mouth to mouth, eyes to eyes, hands to hands (2 Kgs 4:34). It took faith for the mother to speak "peace" while her son was dead, but it also took great faith for the prophet to have such intimate contact with a corpse that must have been dead for several days. The staff on the face had no effect, but the prophet's body caused the boy's body to warm up. Third, Elisha stretches out on him again, which prompts a series of seven sneezes and open eyes (v. 35). Upon seeing her son alive, the mother falls at Elisha's feet again (vv. 27, 37), before finally departing with her son. The Shunammite woman will reappear in the narrative later (8:1–2).

Elisha's Feeding Miracles (2 Kings 4:38–44)

After leaving Shunem in the north, Elisha returns to Gilgal (see 2:1) to minister during a time of famine (4:38).[7] Famines were common in ancient Israel (e.g., Gen 12:10; Ruth 1:1; 2 Sam 21:1; 24:13); the most recent was a source of conflict between Elijah and Ahab (1 Kgs 17:1; 18:2).

Thus far, individuals associated with prophetic companies have initiated with Elisha (2 Kgs 2:3, 5, 16; 4:1), but now he invites himself to join them for a meal (4:38), perhaps to honor his visit. While searching for ingredients for the stew, a difficult undertaking during a famine, one of the cooks found a significant quantity of a mysterious gourd and decided to add it to the concoction (reminiscent of famous last words—"Hey, these mushrooms look edible!"). During a time of normal harvests, the cooks would have been

7. Some commentators think this Gilgal is near Jericho (Wray Beal, *1 & 2 Kings*, 302, 325), others north of Bethel (Wiseman, *1 & 2 Kings*, 205; Barnes, *1–2 Kings*, 220).

more selective. Shortly after tasting it, they blurt out one of the best lines of Scripture, "[D]eath in the pot!" (v. 40). The mystery gourd ruined the whole meal, disastrous for poor prophets during a famine. Just as he added salt to purify the spring at Jericho (2:21), Elisha adds flour to the stew, miraculously making it safe for human consumption (4:41).

Next a barley bread baker arrives, offering twenty loaves and new grain. Wiseman notes that the first fruits of the harvest are meant to be devoted to YHWH as a gift to the priests (Lev 23:10), so he thinks this offering designates Elisha as YHWH's representative.[8] Even though wheat is more desirable, the barley harvest is typically earlier (March–April) than the wheat harvest (May–June),[9] so this incident probably occurred in early spring. In John's Gospel the bread boy brings barley loaves for Jesus's multiplication miracle (John 6:9, 13). Just as Jesus's disciples questioned Jesus's command to share the barley loaves with the crowd (John 6:9), Elisha's servant (Gehazi?) wonders how twenty loaves could feed a hundred (2 Kgs 4:43). These loaves were much smaller than a modern loaf with many slices. Elisha compels his servant by invoking the word of YHWH, promising not just a sufficient amount, but leftovers (v. 43). The story concludes with the only reference in this chapter to the word of YHWH as the prophet's prediction is fulfilled (v. 44). Just as Elijah and Jesus met people's physical needs, Elisha provides abundantly, once again modeling the abundant extravagance of God.

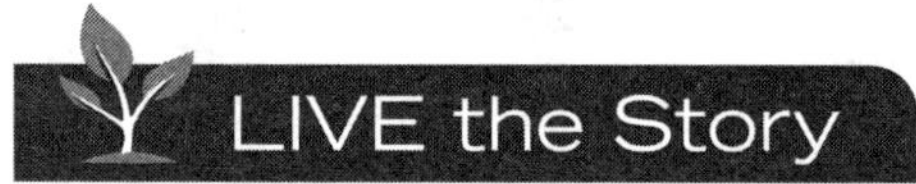

Compassion

The theme of compassion unites the five miracle stories of this chapter. The primary person showing compassion throughout this passage is Elisha, but we also see at least two others displaying compassion. Three points can be made about how compassion manifests itself here.

First, compassion asks questions. Elisha here takes the initiative by asking questions to see how he might be able to serve others. He asks eight questions, two to the widow at the beginning (2 Kgs 4:2), three about how to serve the Shunammite in the middle (vv. 13–14), and three more to the Shunammite about how she is doing (v. 26). Elisha asked questions about practical needs (vv. 2, 13–14) as well as emotional needs (v. 26). In each case his questions

8. Wiseman, *1 & 2 Kings*, 205–6.

9. See Barnes, *1–2 Kings*, 220.

preceded his next miracle. Questions model humility, show interest in another person, and communicate care and compassion. If we are to follow Elisha's compassionate example, we will need to be continually asking people what they need and how they want to be served.

Second, compassion meets needs. Our compassionate questions should lead to acts of compassion. There are a lot of needy people in this passage: the worried widow, the barren Shunammite, the bereft Shunammite, the prophetic company, the hungry people, and even Elisha who needs a bed, a table, a chair, and a lamp (v. 10). Elisha meets the needs of the widow, the Shunammite woman, the prophetic company, and the people. The miraculous acts of compassion done by Elisha may get our attention (the unending oil, the barren birth, the boy's resurrection, the purified stew, and the multiplied bread), but we shouldn't forget the less dramatic but equally significant acts of hospitality not performed by Elisha. The Shunammite shows hospitality toward Elisha, and the barley bread baker generously shares his precious provision with the people during a famine.

However, there are a lot of obstacles that can prevent us from showing compassion. While working on this chapter, a *Washington Post* article came out revealing that Christians, relative to the rest of the population, are more than twice as likely to blame poverty on lack of effort.[10] While I wasn't surprised, the findings were deeply troubling. If we think people are poor because they aren't working hard, we are less likely to show compassion. There are passages that make it clear that lack of effort can be a cause of poverty (Prov 24:30–34; 2 Thess 3:10), but throughout Scripture we see poverty far more frequently caused by natural disasters, injustice, and oppression. Why are people poor in this chapter? There is no hint here that poverty is caused by lack of effort. We see three reasons: death (2 Kgs 4:1, 20), famine (v. 38), and choosing ministry as a profession (vv. 1, 38). Elisha encountered a variety of people who were somehow impoverished, but he never wavered in his commitment to meet their needs. One could argue that Elisha himself was poor, since he needed help from the Shunammite widow to establish a ministry base in this region. Like Elisha, Jesus consistently helped people who were poor (Mark 6:30–44; 8:1–9) and was helped by others in his own poverty (Luke 8:3). Presumably, Christians don't think Elisha and Jesus were poor because of lack of effort.

Third, compassion takes risks. As we ask and act compassionately, it will involve taking risks, doing things we haven't done as we step out in faith.

10. Julie Zauzmer, "Christians Are More Than Twice as Likely to Blame a Person's Poverty on Lack of Effort," *Washington Post*, August 3, 2017.

When we read these stories, it's easy to assume Elisha's miracles came easily to the prophet, but each of them involved a risk and a step of faith on the prophet's part. He had never raised someone from the dead. Notice what he did to the dead's boy's cold corpse. After praying, he laid down on it, putting his hands on the boy's hands, his mouth on the boy's mouth, and his eyes on the boy's eyes. I'm not sure how he did the eye thing, but almost three thousand years later it still feels creepy. And holy people weren't supposed to have contact with a dead body (Lev 22:4).

Elijah, Elisha, and Jesus

Each of the ways Elisha displayed compassion were evidenced in the life and ministry of Jesus. Jesus's compassion moved him to ask questions (e.g., Mark 5:9, 30), to meet needs (e.g., Mark 6:34; 8:2), and to take risks (John 2:1–11; 4:7–26). While we aren't sure what a double portion of Elijah's spirit entailed (see "Chariots of Fire" in Chapter 19 for a discussion of 2 Kings 2:9–10), the ministry of Elisha certainly included miracles comparable not only to that of his predecessor but also to that of Jesus. Like Elijah, Elisha provided extra oil for a widow to avert a crisis (1 Kgs 17:14–16; 2 Kgs 4:3–6). Like Elijah and Jesus, Elisha resurrected the dead son of a woman (1 Kgs 17:21; 2 Kgs 4:34–35; Luke 7:11–17). Like Jesus, Elisha healed a foreign leper (2 Kgs 5:8–14; Luke 4:27; 17:11–19) and provided left over loaves of bread for a crowd (2 Kgs 4:44; Mark 8:8; Luke 9:17). The dramatic ministries of these two prophets foreshadowed the even more powerful ministry of Jesus, and their resurrections foreshadowed Jesus's own resurrection, God's ultimate act of risky compassion, giving hope to a spiritually impoverished world.

CHAPTER 22

2 Kings 5:1–27

LISTEN to the Story

[1]Now Naaman was commander of the army of the king of Aram. He was a great man in the sight of his master and highly regarded, because through him the LORD had given victory to Aram. He was a valiant soldier, but he had leprosy.

[2]Now bands of raiders from Aram had gone out and had taken captive a young girl from Israel, and she served Naaman's wife. [3]She said to her mistress, "If only my master would see the prophet who is in Samaria! He would cure him of his leprosy."

[4]Naaman went to his master and told him what the girl from Israel had said. [5]"By all means, go," the king of Aram replied. "I will send a letter to the king of Israel." So Naaman left, taking with him ten talents of silver, six thousand shekels of gold and ten sets of clothing. [6]The letter that he took to the king of Israel read: "With this letter I am sending my servant Naaman to you so that you may cure him of his leprosy."

[7]As soon as the king of Israel read the letter, he tore his robes and said, "Am I God? Can I kill and bring back to life? Why does this fellow send someone to me to be cured of his leprosy? See how he is trying to pick a quarrel with me!"

[8]When Elisha the man of God heard that the king of Israel had torn his robes, he sent him this message: "Why have you torn your robes? Have the man come to me and he will know that there is a prophet in Israel." [9]So Naaman went with his horses and chariots and stopped at the door of Elisha's house. [10]Elisha sent a messenger to say to him, "Go, wash yourself seven times in the Jordan, and your flesh will be restored and you will be cleansed."

[11]But Naaman went away angry and said, "I thought that he would surely come out to me and stand and call on the name of the LORD his God, wave his hand over the spot and cure me of my leprosy. [12]Are not Abana and Pharpar, the rivers of Damascus, better than all the waters of

Israel? Couldn't I wash in them and be cleansed?" So he turned and went off in a rage.

[13]Naaman's servants went to him and said, "My father, if the prophet had told you to do some great thing, would you not have done it? How much more, then, when he tells you, 'Wash and be cleansed'!" [14]So he went down and dipped himself in the Jordan seven times, as the man of God had told him, and his flesh was restored and became clean like that of a young boy.

[15]Then Naaman and all his attendants went back to the man of God. He stood before him and said, "Now I know that there is no God in all the world except in Israel. So please accept a gift from your servant."

[16]The prophet answered, "As surely as the LORD lives, whom I serve, I will not accept a thing." And even though Naaman urged him, he refused.

[17]"If you will not," said Naaman, "please let me, your servant, be given as much earth as a pair of mules can carry, for your servant will never again make burnt offerings and sacrifices to any other god but the LORD. [18]But may the LORD forgive your servant for this one thing: When my master enters the temple of Rimmon to bow down and he is leaning on my arm and I have to bow there also—when I bow down in the temple of Rimmon, may the LORD forgive your servant for this."

[19]"Go in peace," Elisha said.

After Naaman had traveled some distance, [20]Gehazi, the servant of Elisha the man of God, said to himself, "My master was too easy on Naaman, this Aramean, by not accepting from him what he brought. As surely as the LORD lives, I will run after him and get something from him."

[21]So Gehazi hurried after Naaman. When Naaman saw him running toward him, he got down from the chariot to meet him. "Is everything all right?" he asked.

[22]"Everything is all right," Gehazi answered. "My master sent me to say, 'Two young men from the company of the prophets have just come to me from the hill country of Ephraim. Please give them a talent of silver and two sets of clothing.'"

[23]"By all means, take two talents," said Naaman. He urged Gehazi to accept them, and then tied up the two talents of silver in two bags, with two sets of clothing. He gave them to two of his servants, and they carried them ahead of Gehazi. [24]When Gehazi came to the hill, he took the things from the servants and put them away in the house. He sent the men away and they left.

[25]When he went in and stood before his master, Elisha asked him, "Where have you been, Gehazi?"

"Your servant didn't go anywhere," Gehazi answered.

[26]But Elisha said to him, "Was not my spirit with you when the man got down from his chariot to meet you? Is this the time to take money or to accept clothes—or olive groves and vineyards, or flocks and herds, or male and female slaves? [27]Naaman's leprosy will cling to you and to your descendants forever." Then Gehazi went from Elisha's presence and his skin was leprous—it had become as white as snow.

Listening to the Text in the Story: Biblical Texts: Leviticus 13–14; Numbers 31:9; Deuteronomy 20:14; 21:10–14; Joshua 2:9–11; Judges 5:30; 1 Samuel 4:9; Ancient Near Eastern Texts: The Inscription of Zakkur, King of Hamath

The narrative of the healing of Naaman the Aramean general is one of the greatest stories, not only in Kings but in all of the Old Testament, which is perhaps why it is mentioned by Jesus at the beginning of his ministry (see Live the Story below). Naaman's leprosy is the first time the illness is mentioned in the book of Kings. Leviticus gives extensive guidance about how people suffering from leprosy were to be kept separate from the broader Israelite community to limit spreading (Lev 13–14; see also 2 Kgs 7:3–8). When the Bible speaks of leprosy, it is not describing what we would call leprosy today (Hansen's disease) but some form of less severe disease like psoriasis, eczema, or vitiligo,[1] perhaps explaining why Naaman could continue to serve as commander of the Aramean army.

The text states that YHWH gave Naaman victory in battle. Many ancient inscriptions speak of divine assistance in warfare, but the one most relevant is the inscription of King Zakkur of Hamath.[2] Zakkur describes how his god Baʿalshamayn gave him assistance against a coalition of kings including "Bar-Hadad" of Aram (Ben-Hadad in Hebrew).

The process by which Naaman obtained his Israelite girl, capturing and enslaving a prisoner of war, was common in ancient times (e.g., Num 31:9; Judg 5:30; 1 Sam 4:9). Even though it was allowed in the law of Moses

1. See Wray Beal, *1 & 2 Kings*, 332; Barnes, *1–2 Kings*, 222.
2. *COS* 2:155; for an image see *ZIBBC* 3:133.

(Deut 20:14), restrictions were supposed to prevent abuses (Deut 21:10–14). After his healing, Naaman makes a dramatic monotheistic declaration (2 Kgs 5:15) comparable to that of Rahab when she is speaking to the Israelite spies: "I know that the LORD has given you this land . . . for the LORD YOUR GOD is God in heaven above and on the earth below" (Josh 2:9, 11).

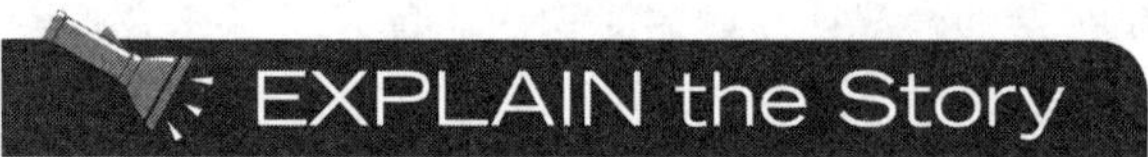

EXPLAIN the Story

Naaman, the Servant Girl, and the King of Aram (2 Kings 5:1–7)

Few characters are introduced as positively in Scripture as Naaman. The textual introductions of Elijah and Elisha mention nothing praiseworthy (1 Kgs 17:1; 19:16), but here we have a list of four impressive qualifications about Naaman: commander of Aram's army, a great man in the eyes of his master (Aram's king), highly regarded, and a valiant soldier (2 Kgs 5:1).[3] In the midst of this impressive resume, we find two surprising pieces of information.

First, not only his king and his people respected him, but even YHWH favored Naaman by giving him victory in battle. We do not know what nation Naaman was victorious over, but since Israel and Aram fought constantly (1 Kgs 11:25; 15:18–20; 20:1–21, 26–33; 22:2–38; 2 Kgs 6:8–21, 24; 8:28–29; 10:32–33; 13:17–24) and he had an Israelite slave girl, Israel was probably one of his conquests. God gave victory to Israel's enemies earlier, during the time of the judges (e.g., Judg 2:14; 3:8, 13), and later in the monarchy (e.g., 2 Kgs 17:6–7; 24:2–3), but it is unusual to include a note like this, describing the successes of a foreign general, with no explanation for why.

Second, at the end of this list of commendations we discover that Naaman was a leper (5:1). In the Hebrew the effect is more dramatic, with twenty-two words detailing his impressiveness, ending abruptly with the one-word conclusion: "leper" (*metsora'*). This powerful man, loved by king and country, needs healing, which sets up the story perfectly.

The next character could not be more different from Naaman. She is a young female. We never learn her name, but Naaman's name, which probably means "gracious," is mentioned eleven times (5:1, 2, 6, 9, 11, 17, 20, 21 [2x], 23, 27).[4] She is an Israelite slave; he is an Aramean general. He has all the power; she has none. But knowledge is power, and she knows something he does not.

3. Josephus identifies the unnamed archer who shot the arrow that killed Ahab (1 Kgs 22:34–37) as Naaman (*Ant.* 8.15.5).

4. In the Hebrew, Naaman's name appears eleven times in these verses. The NIV adds "Naaman" in 5:4, when the Hebrew has an implied "he."

We are not sure who actually captured her, but since Naaman was the army's commander, he was ultimately responsible for her enslavement. Also, since she ended up serving Naaman's wife, it is reasonable to assume Naaman was behind her kidnapping. Female slaves were routinely mistreated by their mistress. Even Sarah mistreated her slave, Hagar, and threw her out twice (Gen 16:1–6; 21:8–14). There are many reasons this slave girl might not want to help her master. And yet she is the catalyst for his healing, as her one line in Scripture (delivered only to Naaman's wife; 2 Kgs 5:3) starts a chain of events affecting not only her master but also two kings and the prophet Elisha. On her own she may have no power, but she realizes that God is ultimately sovereign and that the man of God has power over leprosy.

Perhaps what is most surprising in this amazing story is that Naaman, in his desperate attempt to be healed, is willing to go on what could be a wild goose chase in enemy territory. He first receives permission from the unnamed king of Aram, who is identified by commentators as Ben-Hadad I (Hobbs), Ben-Hadad II (Barnes, Wray Beal), or Ben-Hadad III (Wiseman).[5] The diversity of these views suggests that conclusions regarding the Aramean ruler's identity must be considered speculative.

While the text is not clear, the extravagance of Naaman's gift (v. 5) suggests that the primary contributor was the king, not the general. If it were a royal gift, it would be another sign of Naaman's favor in the eyes of his master. A talent was about seventy pounds, equivalent to about three thousand shekels (Exod 38:25–26).[6] The ten talents of silver was five times more than Omri paid for the hill that became Samaria (1 Kgs 16:24). The silver and gold alone (not counting the ten sets of clothes) would be roughly equivalent today to "three quarters of a billion dollars."[7]

The letter from Aram's ruler confuses Israel's ruler (presumably Joram), since he assumes he is supposed to cure Naaman's leprosy. While Naaman's servant girl's comment made it clear that the source of the healing would be not the king, there were plenty of opportunities for the original message to get garbled. Her message was already relayed at least three times, from servant to mistress, from wife to husband, from general to king.

The king of Israel asks three rhetorical questions, but the first two do not appear connected to this incident ("Am I God? Can I kill and bring back to

5. T. R. Hobbs, *2 Kings*, WBC (Waco, TX: Word, 1986), 62; Barnes, *1–2 Kings*, 223; Wray Beal, *1 & 2 Kings*, 333; Wiseman, *1 & 2 Kings*, 206. On the identity of Aramean rulers, see also Chapter 16 for the discussion of 1 Kgs 20.

6. See also *ZIBBC* 3:134.

7. *BBCOT*, 391.

life?," 2 Kgs 5:7). With Elijah and Elisha, we have already seen God resurrect young boys (1 Kgs 17:22; 2 Kgs 4:34–35), so perhaps the Israelite king is referring to those incidents? His final question—why his Aramean counterpart sends someone to him to be healed—is certainly relevant but merely displays a lack of faith. If this ruler is Joram, then he has already seen YHWH miraculously provide water in the desert and victory over Moab (3:4–25). While a girl who could feel abandoned by God in her enslavement displays great faith, the ruler of God's people displays great cowardice. Even the king of Aram has more faith in Israel's God than Israel's king. In his anguish that Aram is picking a fight with him, the king of Israel tears his robe, a common practice performed in times of crisis (1 Kgs 21:27; 2 Kgs 2:12; 6:30; 11:14; 19:1; 22:11).

Naaman and Elijah (2 Kings 5:8–19a)

Elisha finds out about the king's irrational response to the Aramean embassy, so he sends a message telling them to send Naaman to him (5:8). Upon his arrival, Naaman is upset about not being invited to a personal healing ceremony with the prophet (vv. 9–11). He had a clear expectation of how it should happen involving prayer and hand waving. His negative response to washing seven times in the Jordan may be due to nationalistic pride. The two rivers that he mentions (Abana, Pharpar; v. 12) were probably cleaner than the Jordan, since their sources were snow-capped mountains. The Abana River is now called Nahr el-Barada and flows southeast through Damascus. The location of the Pharpar River is uncertain, but most scholars think it is the modern Nahr el-Awaj, which runs south of Damascus.

While we could critique Naaman for his pride, anger, and refusal to follow Elisha's simple directions to wash in the Jordan, he had already followed a foreign slave girl's advice, his king's guidance, and Elisha's initial message to come visit. As a man accustomed to giving orders, perhaps he was tired of being guided by others?

Fortunately for Naaman, one of his servants steps in and offers wise counsel, urging him to follow the prophet's prescription, since he would have been willing to do something more rigorous to be healed (v. 14). Just as he listened to a servant at the beginning, here he listens to a servant. As he dips seven times in the Jordan, his skin was restored (v. 14).

We do not know why Elisha and Naaman did not meet face-to-face initially. Was it Elisha's lack of hospitality or Naaman's pride? In any case, after the healing, they finally meet. Naaman then makes a bold monotheistic declaration, "Now I know that there is no God in all the world except in Israel" (v. 15). While the household of Omri and Ahab are propagating idolatry, a foreign general boldly declares the uniqueness of Israel's God and proceeds to take tangible steps to display his faith.

People seeking something from a prophet often bring gifts (1 Sam 9:7; 1 Kgs 14:3; 2 Kgs 8:7–9), and Naaman urges the prophet to accept his (5:15). Just as Abraham refused gifts from the king of Sodom (Gen 14:21–24), Naaman's extravagant gift is refused by Elisha (1 Kgs 5:15–16).[8] While the reason for the rejection is not clear, Elisha's answer suggests that his service to YHWH prevents dependence upon others. We will soon discover the servant Gehazi does not share this view.

Like a good general, Naaman thinks strategically and plans for the future. He first asks for two mule-loads of Israelite dirt (2 Kgs 5:17), presumably to make an altar for YHWH. YHWH had already given him victory while he resided in Aram (v. 1), but he assumes an altar for the God of Israel needed to be constructed with the dirt of Israel. Throughout Scripture YHWH is considered the God of the whole earth (e.g., Gen 1:1; Exod 19:5; Josh 2:11; Isa 6:3; Mic 4:13), but in the ancient Near East gods were often associated with the land.

Naaman anticipates that he will be in a situation where he will appear to be worshiping a god whose existence he has just denied (2 Kgs 5:18). Rimmon is another name for Hadad, the storm god and the national god of Aram. Naaman asks for forgiveness in advance for his action of bowing to Rimmon at the arm of his king. Unlike Israel's kings, Naaman wants to avoid any appearance of unfaithfulness to the God to whom he has just committed himself. Despite the theologically problematic nature of Naaman's remarks, Elisha's two-word benediction lacks any doctrinal correction but merely emphasizes grace: "Go in peace" (*lek leshalom*). While there is a time to emphasize doctrinal purity, correction must be secondary and love primary in our interactions.

Naaman and Gehazi (2 Kings 5:19b–27)

The narrative quickly turns dark as the focus shifts to the actions of Elisha's servant Gehazi, who pursues Naaman and asks for a portion of the gift (5:19–21). To explain his master's change of mind, Gehazi makes up a story about the sudden arrival of two prophetic guests. The general graciously gives to the servant what he asks, doubling the amount of silver requested (vv. 22–23). Upon his return home, Elisha asks three questions (vv. 25–26), giving his

8. But Abraham received a generous gift from Pharaoh for "pimping" his wife (Gen 12:16); see David T. Lamb, "David Was a Rapist, Abraham Was a Sex Trafficker" *Christianity Today*, October 22, 2015, https://www.christianitytoday.com/ct/2015/october-web-only/david-was-rapist-abraham-was-sex-trafficker.html.

servant an opportunity to confess, reminiscent of YHWH's questions to the humans in the garden after they ate the forbidden fruit (Gen 3:9–13). Gehazi fails the test by lying to Elisha (2 Kgs 5:25).

What was the sin of Gehazi? Commentators tend to focus on greed.[9] If greed were Gehazi's primary sin, one might expect him to request more from Naaman; of the original gift, he only asked for 20 percent of the clothes, 10 percent of the silver, and none of the gold. It is conceivable that he planned to use Naaman's gift for hospitality later. It is reasonable to assume that greed motivated his behavior, but there are at least three other sins emphasized here.

First, the sin of nationalism prompts Gehazi to go back for more initially. Gehazi said his master was too easy on Naaman, but then adds "this Aramean" (*ha'arammi hazzeh*; v. 20), suggesting that Naaman's foreignness was a motivating factor. Naaman's conquests probably included Israel, but that did not stop an Israelite slave girl from extending grace to a foreign general, in stark contrast to Gehazi here.

Second, Gehazi practiced deception twice in this incident. He lied first to Naaman about the guests (v. 22), then he lied to Elisha about his whereabouts (v. 25). Elisha calls him out for his deception as he points out he was present in spirit when Naaman descended from his chariot to meet Gehazi (v. 26).

Third, returning to Naaman was an act of rebellion against Gehazi's master. As he spoke to himself, he contradicted Elisha, then when he interacted with Naaman he made Elisha seem fickle or unreliable (vv. 20, 22). As he plots his rebellious act, he even uses the same oath formula, "as surely as the Lord lives" (*hay yhwh*) that Elisha had used to refuse the gift (vv. 16, 20).

Elisha's final rhetorical question to his servant suggests greed was a factor, but Elisha's list of potential gifts go beyond what was offered by Naaman to include trees, livestock, and slaves (v. 26). The appropriate punishment for his deceptive, rebellious servant is leprosy—not just for Gehazi but for his descendants as well (v. 27). Thus, the theme of leprosy forms an inclusio (bookend) for this narrative unit (vv. 1, 27). The text never records what happened to the gift. While Gehazi's sin and punishment could have prevented him from continuing to serve the prophet, Elisha graciously allowed him to remain his servant (8:4–5; see also 6:15–17). Like Gehazi here (5:27), King Azariah of Judah was given leprosy as a punishment by YHWH (2 Kgs 15:5) and neither were banished because of their illness.

9. See for example, Barnes, *1–2 Kings*, 226; House, *1, 2 Kings*, 274.

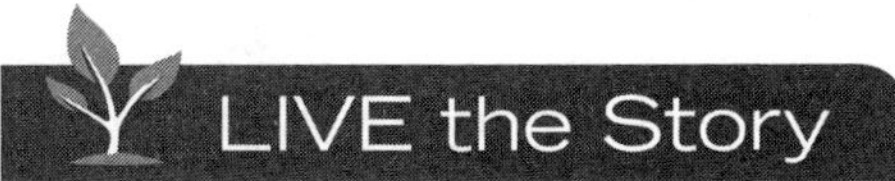

Loving Lepers

The narrative of Naaman, the Aramean general who was healed of leprosy by Elisha, is familiar to many readers of Scripture, not only because it is a great tale but also because of Jesus's reference to it. When speaking to a Sabbath-day crowd at the Nazareth synagogue, Jesus mentions the story of Naaman the leper, along with the widow of Zarephath (1 Kgs 17), at the beginning of his ministry to make the point that God is concerned about foreigners (Luke 4:26–27). But the hometown crowd wasn't ready to hear his message, and they attempted to kill him by throwing him off a cliff (Luke 4:29). Interestingly, the only other person to heal a leper in Scripture is, not surprisingly, Jesus (Luke 5:12–16; 7:22; 17:12–19). Jesus liked the shocking story of Naaman so much that, out of hundreds of Old Testament stories, it is the one he tells at the beginning of his ministry to declare the good news.

Listening to Slaves

When people are young, they tend to receive direction from those who are older (e.g., parents, teachers, and supervisors). As people grow older and move into those roles themselves, they become the ones directing, advising, and guiding, which is what makes Naaman's behavior here so unusual. He is criticized for his nationalistic aversion to the Jordan, but he also should be affirmed for his willingness to listen to people with less status. He is a highly respected commander of the army, but twice here he follows the direction of servants. He listens to the slave girl to go to visit Elisha, and he listens to his servants to actually do what Elisha said to be healed (2 Kgs5:3–4; 13–14). While this second act of listening may be understandable, the first is shocking. All the characteristics that distinguish Naaman from the slave girl should make him less likely to take her seriously. She's young, she's female, she's foreign, and she's a slave. And she suggests he should travel into enemy territory for a miraculous healing. Yet Naaman follows her advice. We should follow his example and listen to people who are younger, who are a different gender, who are foreign, or whom we have authority over. Ignore the wisdom of those "below" you at your peril. If he didn't listen to his servants, Naaman would have missed out on a miraculous healing. In his ministry, Jesus was willing to not only listen to a foreign female—a Syrophoenician—but also to change his mind regarding her request to cast a demon out of her daughter (Mark 7:24–30).

Learning from Faithful Females

During a dark time in Israel's history, while kings are faithless and idolatrous, a series of females provide models of faith, trust, and devotion to YHWH as they interact with and bless the prophets Elijah and Elisha. All four of these faithful females remain anonymous: the widow from Zarephath who fed Elijah (1 Kgs 17:8–24), the prophetic widow whose oil was multiplied (2 Kgs 4:1–7), the Shunammite woman who hosted Elisha (4:8–37), and Israelite slave girl who served Naaman's wife (5:2–3). Even though they lack the honor of a name, the text records their stories and portrays them favorably.

While Israel's rulers were trying to kill God's prophets (1 Kgs 18:4; 19:10, 14), these females were supporting and sustaining God's prophets, even in times of famine (17:8–16; 2 Kgs 4:9–10). While Israel's rulers were looking to false or foreign prophets for assistance (1 Kgs 18:19; 22:5–27; 2 Kgs 1:2–3), these females were crying out in their distress to the prophets of YHWH (1 Kgs 17:18; 2 Kgs 4:1–2, 28). While Israel's rulers were making statements displaying their faithlessness (2 Kgs 3:10; 5:7), these females were making declarations praising the power of God (1 Kgs 17:24; 2 Kgs 5:3). Lest we think this is just a feature of the prophetic narratives of the book of Kings, Jesus consistently held women up as examples to learn from (e.g., Mark 12:43–44; 14:6–9; Luke 10:42; 15:8–10; 18:1–8). As these stories are taught and preached, it is easy to focus exclusively on the prophets—their names and their miracles are recorded—but we must not forget the anonymous women of Scripture who have a lot to teach us about hospitality, prayer, and faithfulness.

Loving Enemies

One lesson that both the slave girl and Elisha can teach us from this story is about loving our enemies. Israel and Aram were neighbors that often fought, and even here we see Aram capturing and enslaving Israelite children (5:2). From Israel's perspective Naaman was a foreign enemy, which is why Jesus's listeners were so mad (in Luke 4) when he spoke of how God healed not an Israelite leper but a foreign one. This slave girl would have many reasons to hate Naaman. She was a slave in a foreign land, cut off from her family and forced to serve the wife of the man who was probably responsible for her predicament. Hatred, anger, repulsion, and bitterness would not be surprising for a person in her situation. And yet she serves as the catalyst for his healing. Elisha may have less reasons than the girl to view Naaman as an enemy, but the general doesn't trust Elisha initially, and Naaman views Aram's river as superior to those of Israel. Gehazi certainly viewed Naaman as an enemy not worthy of favor. While Jesus justifiably gets credit for exhorting his followers to love their enemies in the Sermon on the Mount (Matt 5:44), we see the theme appear frequently in the Old Testament, perhaps most notably several places in the Elisha narratives (here and 6:20–23).

About eight hundred years before Jesus, this Israelite girl was kidnapped in a raid and taken to a foreign country to serve as a slave; about four hundred years after Jesus, a British boy was kidnapped in a raid and taken to a foreign country to serve as a slave. After six years of enslavement, the boy escaped and returned home. While he was home, he saw a vision where the people from the land of his captivity were calling him back, saying, "We appeal to you, holy servant boy, to come and walk among us."[10] Patrick returned to Ireland, the land of his oppression and, just like Naaman's servant girl, told people about God. Love for enemies can lead not only to healing, but also to many people hearing about God.

10. From Saint Patrick's *Confessio*, from the Royal Irish Academy, http://www.confessio.ie/#.

CHAPTER 23

2 Kings 6:1–23

LISTEN to the Story

1The company of the prophets said to Elisha, "Look, the place where we meet with you is too small for us. 2Let us go to the Jordan, where each of us can get a pole; and let us build a place there for us to meet."

And he said, "Go."

3Then one of them said, "Won't you please come with your servants?"

"I will," Elisha replied. 4And he went with them.

They went to the Jordan and began to cut down trees. 5As one of them was cutting down a tree, the iron axhead fell into the water. "Oh no, my lord!" he cried out. "It was borrowed!"

6The man of God asked, "Where did it fall?" When he showed him the place, Elisha cut a stick and threw it there, and made the iron float. 7"Lift it out," he said. Then the man reached out his hand and took it.

8Now the king of Aram was at war with Israel. After conferring with his officers, he said, "I will set up my camp in such and such a place."

9The man of God sent word to the king of Israel: "Beware of passing that place, because the Arameans are going down there." 10So the king of Israel checked on the place indicated by the man of God. Time and again Elisha warned the king, so that he was on his guard in such places.

11This enraged the king of Aram. He summoned his officers and demanded of them, "Tell me! Which of us is on the side of the king of Israel?"

12"None of us, my lord the king," said one of his officers, "but Elisha, the prophet who is in Israel, tells the king of Israel the very words you speak in your bedroom."

13"Go, find out where he is," the king ordered, "so I can send men and capture him." The report came back: "He is in Dothan." 14Then he sent horses and chariots and a strong force there. They went by night and surrounded the city.

[15]When the servant of the man of God got up and went out early the
next morning, an army with horses and chariots had surrounded the city.
"Oh no, my lord! What shall we do?" the servant asked.
[16]"Don't be afraid," the prophet answered. "Those who are with us are
more than those who are with them."
[17]And Elisha prayed, "Open his eyes, LORD, so that he may see." Then
the LORD opened the servant's eyes, and he looked and saw the hills full
of horses and chariots of fire all around Elisha.
[18]As the enemy came down toward him, Elisha prayed to the LORD,
"Strike this army with blindness." So he struck them with blindness, as
Elisha had asked.
[19]Elisha told them, "This is not the road and this is not the city. Follow
me, and I will lead you to the man you are looking for." And he led them
to Samaria.
[20]After they entered the city, Elisha said, "LORD, open the eyes of these
men so they can see." Then the LORD opened their eyes and they looked,
and there they were, inside Samaria.
[21]When the king of Israel saw them, he asked Elisha, "Shall I kill them,
my father? Shall I kill them?"
[22]"Do not kill them," he answered. "Would you kill those you have
captured with your own sword or bow? Set food and water before them
so that they may eat and drink and then go back to their master." [23]So
he prepared a great feast for them, and after they had finished eating and
drinking, he sent them away, and they returned to their master. So the
bands from Aram stopped raiding Israel's territory.

Listening to the Text in the Story: Biblical Texts: Deuteronomy 19:5; Judges 7; 1 Samuel 17; 2 Kings 2:11–12; 13:14, 20; Ancient Near Eastern Texts: The Hittite Laws; The Lachish Letters

In the previous three chapters of 2 Kings, Elisha alternated from assisting his king and country in military contexts to providing miracles for prophets and individuals. This pattern continues in this section as he raises a lost axhead for the prophetic company (6:1–7) and protects Israel's army by providing them with insider information regarding foreign troop movements and by blinding the Arameans (6:8–23).

Not surprisingly, there are no other stories of borrowed axheads miraculously floating elsewhere in Scripture, but the law speaks of axheads flying off the handle—not landing in water but lodging in a neighbor and killing him (Deut 19:5). The law provides a way for the careless lumberjack to be okay if he flees to a city of refuge. Kings here speaks of no rental fee for the borrowed iron axhead, but the Hittite laws state fair prices for ax rentals, to give us a rough idea of the prices.[1] A bronze ax weighing 1.54 kilograms costs one silver shekel per month; a copper ax weighing 0.77 kilograms costs a half silver shekel per month. The lost axhead here was iron and therefore more valuable than bronze or copper ones.[2]

It is not unusual for prophets to give directions to kings about when and where to fight, but the specific nature of Elisha's guidance here is not typical. However, a letter from Lachish describes a situation similar to that of Elisha and Israel here, where the author has discovered information regarding troop movements (2 Kgs 6:9–11) into Egypt and also mentions a word of warning from a prophet:

> Now your servant has received the following information: General Konyahu son of Elnatan has moved south in order to enter Egypt. He has sent (messengers) to fetch Hodavyahu son of Ahiyahu and his men from here. (Herewith) I am also sending to my lord the letter of Tobyahu servant of the king, which came to Shallum son of Yada from the prophet and which says, "Beware."[3]

As Elisha attempts to calm his fearful servant, he declares there are more on their side than on the side of their enemy (6:16). The theme of an underdog overcoming a favored opponent is common in Scripture; for example, Gideon's victory over Midian (Judg 7) and David's victory over Goliath (1 Sam 17). Elisha's servant sees an image of fiery horses and chariots (2 Kgs 6:17). Elisha witnesses a similar spectacle when his master Elijah was taken into heaven (2 Kgs 2:11–12), as did King Jehoash of Israel immediately before Elisha's death (13:14, 20).

EXPLAIN the Story

Elisha Makes an Axhead Float (2 Kings 6:1–7)

When he was last with the company of the prophets ("sons of the prophets"; *bene-hannebiim*), Elisha purified their poisoned stew during a famine (2 Kgs

1. *COS* 2:116
2. For an image of an iron axhead, see *ZIBBC* 3:136.
3. *COS* 3:79; see also *ANET*, 322.

4:38–41). Now they need to construct a bigger building, since their last one was too small to accommodate their numbers when meeting with Elisha. They invite Elisha to join them (6:1–3). Elisha's response, "I will" (v. 3), is literally, "I myself will go," since the pronoun is included for emphasis in the Hebrew. The word translated as "pole" (*qorah*) could also be rendered as "log" (ESV, NRSV) or "beam" (KJV, NASB). Because of the abundant forests of acacia, tamarisk, and willow, the Jordan valley would serve as an excellent source of timber for the new dwelling.[4]

Evidence suggesting that these prophets were poor has already been discussed (see previous chapter), but here their poverty is seen in that they did not own their own tools; when the iron axhead comes unattached and flies into the Jordan, the ax wielder cries out, "It was borrowed!" (v. 5). Archaeologically, Israel at this point in time is well into the Iron Age, so iron weapons and tools should have gradually been becoming more widely available (1 Sam 13:19–22), but an iron axhead would still be a valued possession, comparable to a valuable chain saw today. The loss of this tool could have put the borrower into serious debt. Any of us who have damaged or ruined a borrowed tool should be able to empathize with this man.

Elsewhere, Elisha displays supernatural knowledge of events beyond his purview (2 Kgs 2:16; 5:8, 26; 6:9–10), but here he is ignorant of the axhead's location, so he asks the borrower about it (6:6). The location was deep enough that, long before diving masks, finding the submerged axhead would have been impossible. Elisha uses props in his water miracles; he added salt to the Jericho spring (2:21) and flour to the poisoned stew (4:41), so now he throws a stick into the Jordan (6:6). While iron does not normally float, miraculously the lost axhead followed the example of the floating stick and rose to the surface, allowing it to be retrieved (v. 7) and eventually returned to the owner. In this strange story we see another example of God creatively providing for his people.[5]

Tinker, Tailor, Soldier, Prophet (2 Kings 6:8–23)

The narrative abruptly shifts to the Aramean war room, as Israel's northern neighbor is plotting strategy against Israel (6:8), with curiously no reference to the healing of the Aramean general, Naaman, recorded in the preceding chapter. The text provides no geographical details, but Elisha has supernatural knowledge of the king of Aram's plans, which he relates to the king of Israel.

4. *BBCOT*, 392.

5. Raymond Dillard argues that this story illustrates YHWH's sovereignty over the realm of water, which in their context was thought to be controlled by Baal; *Faith in the Face of Apostasy* (Phillipsburg, NJ: P&R, 1999), 124.

Neither the king of Israel nor the king of Aram are mentioned by name here, but based upon where this text lies in the broader narrative, we could assume the Israelite king is Joram and the king of Aram is named Ben-Hadad (either I, II, or III). Any truce established after Naaman's healing is apparently long gone. Behind the NIV's "such and such" used to describe the indeterminate location of the Aramean campsite (v. 8) is a rhyming phrase in Hebrew, *peloni 'almoni* (see also 1 Sam 21:3; Ruth 4:1).

Elisha is essentially acting as a mole, an embedded spy informing the king of Israel about the Aramean troop movements in advance. The text provides no details, but readers are left to assume that God was his unnamed source. While Elisha was reluctant to help Israel's king against Moab (2 Kgs 3:13–14), here he freely offers vital assistance (6:9). Even though the NIV has "Elisha" in 6:10, the man of God is not identified by name in the Hebrew until spoken by one of the Aramean officers in 6:12. The warning about the Aramean troop movements was so effective and so consistent that the Aramean ruler suspected one of his own officers was acting as a mole (v. 11). He demands that the traitor confess his betrayal. Elisha's intelligence of the Aramean's troop locations is thus contrasted with the king of Aram's ignorance of the mole's identity. But one of his officers informs him that Elisha knows even the words he speaks in his bedroom (v. 12). Readers are left to wonder how this officer knew about Elisha—perhaps it was Naaman or one of his confidants? When the king finds out Elisha is in Dothan, about ten miles north of Samaria, he sends a force of horses and chariots, perhaps overkill to capture a single man (vv. 13–14). But just as the two teams of fifty soldiers sent by Ahaziah failed to seize Elijah (1:9–12), this Aramean force will also fail.

Elisha's servant (possibly Gehazi; see 8:4–5) cries out in terror as he sees that Aramean horses and chariots have surrounded the city (6:15). Elisha's servant uses the same expression "Oh no, my lord" (*'ahah 'adoni*) that the ax borrower used earlier (vv. 5, 15), and Elisha uses the same expression, "Don't be afraid" (*'al-tira'*) to calm his servant (6:16) that Elijah used to comfort the widow of Zarephath (1 Kgs 17:13). Elisha's reason to not fear is based on his supernatural knowledge that, somehow, they were the stronger side. It is easy to be critical of the servant's apparent lack of faith, but in his moment of panic he made a wise choice to cry out to a man of God. At this point Elisha offers the first of three prayers (2 Kgs 6:17, 18, 20), requesting that his servant's eyes would be opened. Elisha's prayer includes the first reference to YHWH in this chapter—he has been working behind the scenes in Elisha's miracles, but now his actions are made explicit as he opens the servant's eyes to see a force of heavenly horses and chariots of fire (v. 17).

Elisha's second prayer is one of imprecation, as he calls down blindness (see Ps 69:23) upon the surrounding Aramean forces (2 Kgs 6:18). Once again, the prophet's prayer is immediately answered. After cursing them, Elisha next deceives them and leads their army into a trap in Samaria, the capital of their enemy (v. 19). Leading a blinded army the ten-mile distance from Dothan to Samaria must have been an arduous endeavor. Upon their arrival, Elisha prays a third time, undoing his second prayer and requesting that the eyes of the blind be opened (v. 20). The joy the Arameans must have experienced at the restoration of their sight was quickly dampened by the realization of their location. The Arameans presumably did not begin a skirmish at this point, because they were already disarmed or obviously outnumbered. The king of Israel, like a child on Christmas morning, could not curb his enthusiasm, "Shall I kill them? Shall I kill them?" (v. 21). The verb used for "strike" with blindness (v. 18) and for "kill" (vv. 21, 22) is the same in Hebrew, *nakah*.

Perhaps because of his debt to the prophet for the great intel, the Israelite ruler displays uncharacteristic deference to Elisha, calling him "My father" (*'abi*), a term Elisha used for Elijah (2:12) and King Jehoash later used for Elisha (13:14). Deuteronomy 20:11–12 allows Israel to enslave a surrendered foreign people, but Elisha tells the king of Israel here to feed his enemies (2 Kgs 6:23). Ahab was condemned by a prophet for not killing the king of Aram (1 Kgs 20:34, 42), but here the Israelite ruler wants to kill the king of Aram and is prevented by a prophet. In both situations, however, the point of the text is that YHWH or YHWH's prophet, not the king, determines the right action.[6] The king of Israel goes the "extra mile" here by not just providing the Arameans with food and water but by preparing a great feast (6:23). This act of peacemaking, performed by Israel's king and YHWH's prophet, effectively stopped the Aramean raiders from attacking Israel (v. 23) for an extended period of time (although, see v. 24).

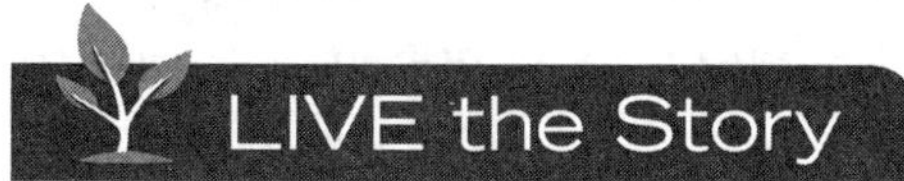

Making Requests

One of the dominant themes of this section is people making requests either to Elisha or to YHWH. At least seven times here someone asks for something from God or the man of God. Four times people make implicit or explicit requests to Elisha. The prophets ask Elisha to join them (2 Kgs 6:3).

6. See Barnes, *1–2 Kings*, 231.

The axhead borrower exclaims, "Oh no, my lord . . . it was borrowed" (v. 5). Elisha's servant cries, "Oh no, my lord . . . what shall we do?" (v. 15). The king of Israel asks, "Shall I kill him?" (v. 21). Three times Elisha prays to YHWH to open or close people's eyes (vv. 17, 18, 20). All of these requests somehow display not only humility on the part of the petitioner but also faith in the ability of the one being petitioned to provide, even miraculously. In each of these instances, the petitioners' request was responded to favorably. Thus, we find support for Jesus's exhortation, "Ask, and it will be given to you" (Matt 7:7).

Generally, three things are asked for. First, the prophets ask for the presence of Elisha. Elisha's presence in their midst was so popular that they needed to construct a new building to hold everyone. As they ask the man of God to join them, they are essentially requesting God's presence. They desperately wanted the representative of God's presence in their midst. As we pray, we should remember to ask for the presence of Jesus to come alongside us in our endeavors (Acts 3:19; 1 Cor 16:22; Rev 22:20).

Second, both the ax borrower and Elisha's servant ask for assistance. Their "Oh, no" prayers were simple cries for help in the midst of a crisis. While these prayers might seem self-serving, God wants to help his people, particularly when they cry out to him in their day of trouble (Ps 50:15; Isa 58:9). Just as God raised an axhead here, and Jesus raised a sinking Peter later (Matt 14:28–33), we can be confident that God will hear and respond to our cries for help when it feels like we are drowning. Many people, when faced with a crisis, attempt to solve their problem on their own. Sometimes it works; often it doesn't. For people of faith, prayer should be an instinctive reaction. Develop habits and disciplines so that the next time you are in an "Oh, no" scenario, your first reaction is to cry to God for help.

Third, the king of Israel asks for guidance from Elisha (2 Kgs 6:21). The king wanted to kill his enemies. Logically, an Aramean slaughter should be the next course of action. But the king waited and deferred to the prophet, and when the prophet told him what he didn't want to hear, he listened and obeyed. And in the spirit of Jesus's command to go the extra mile (Matt 5:41), he graciously provided an ample feast. It's hard, when there is something you really want to do, to stop and ask for guidance from God or from God's people. It takes faith to slow down, to wait, and to potentially hear "no." And yet we can be confident that God can be trusted in all of these situations.

Love Your Enemies (Again)

The theme of loving enemies has appeared several places in Kings (see particularly the previous chapter). While Elisha's initial act of blinding the Arameans doesn't count as love, restoring their sight would, as well as commanding the king of Israel to feed them. Elisha doesn't only love the Arameans, he trains a ruler—who has been taught to fight—how to reconcile and show hospitality toward his enemies.

While Jesus healed blindness on several occasions (e.g, Mark 8:22–26; 10:46–52), the story that shares the most similarities to the blinding of the army of Aram in 2 Kings 6 is that of the conversion of Saul/Paul in Acts 9:1–19. While Saul was seeking to kill Christians, Jesus sent a bright light to blind him; he was then led, while blind, into Damascus, the Aramean capital.[7] Acting like Elisha, a follower of Jesus named Ananias, after hearing from God, was willing to love his enemy, to pray that Saul's sight would be restored, and to feed him (Acts 9:10–19). Just as Elisha used blindness to reconcile Israel and Aram, Jesus used blindness to reconcile Saul and Christians.

The significance of this event went way beyond merely a temporary truce between Israel and its northern neighbor. When Saul was killing Christians, he was acting as an enemy of Jesus ("I am Jesus, whom you are persecuting," Acts 9:5). Jesus's love for his enemy therefore not only led to Saul's conversion in Damascus but also served as a catalyst for Paul's missionary efforts and the gospel spreading throughout the world. We should therefore follow the examples of Elisha and Jesus and love our enemies.

7. While Aram and Syria are not identical, these names refer to comparable kingdoms. The name Aram is used in the Old Testament and Syria in the New Testament. A few chapters after Paul's conversion, Jesus's followers were first called Christians in the Aramean/Syrian city of Antioch (Acts 11:26).

CHAPTER 24

2 Kings 6:24–7:20

LISTEN to the Story

[24]Some time later, Ben-Hadad king of Aram mobilized his entire army and marched up and laid siege to Samaria. [25]There was a great famine in the city; the siege lasted so long that a donkey's head sold for eighty shekels of silver, and a quarter of a cab of seed pods for five shekels.

[26]As the king of Israel was passing by on the wall, a woman cried to him, "Help me, my lord the king!"

[27]The king replied, "If the LORD does not help you, where can I get help for you? From the threshing floor? From the winepress?" [28]Then he asked her, "What's the matter?"

She answered, "This woman said to me, 'Give up your son so we may eat him today, and tomorrow we'll eat my son.' [29]So we cooked my son and ate him. The next day I said to her, 'Give up your son so we may eat him,' but she had hidden him."

[30]When the king heard the woman's words, he tore his robes. As he went along the wall, the people looked, and they saw that, under his robes, he had sackcloth on his body. [31]He said, "May God deal with me, be it ever so severely, if the head of Elisha son of Shaphat remains on his shoulders today!"

[32]Now Elisha was sitting in his house, and the elders were sitting with him. The king sent a messenger ahead, but before he arrived, Elisha said to the elders, "Don't you see how this murderer is sending someone to cut off my head? Look, when the messenger comes, shut the door and hold it shut against him. Is not the sound of his master's footsteps behind him?" [33]While he was still talking to them, the messenger came down to him.

The king said, "This disaster is from the LORD. Why should I wait for the LORD any longer?"

[7:1]Elisha replied, "Hear the word of the LORD. This is what the LORD says: About this time tomorrow, a seah of the finest flour will sell for a shekel and two seahs of barley for a shekel at the gate of Samaria."

[2]The officer on whose arm the king was leaning said to the man of God, "Look, even if the LORD should open the floodgates of the heavens, could this happen?"

"You will see it with your own eyes," answered Elisha, "but you will not eat any of it!"

[3]Now there were four men with leprosy at the entrance of the city gate.
They said to each other, "Why stay here until we die? [4]If we say, 'We'll go
into the city'—the famine is there, and we will die. And if we stay here, we will die. So let's go over to the camp of the Arameans and surrender. If they spare us, we live; if they kill us, then we die."

[5]At dusk they got up and went to the camp of the Arameans. When
they reached the edge of the camp, no one was there, [6]for the Lord had
caused the Arameans to hear the sound of chariots and horses and a great army, so that they said to one another, "Look, the king of Israel has hired
the Hittite and Egyptian kings to attack us!" [7]So they got up and fled in
the dusk and abandoned their tents and their horses and donkeys. They left the camp as it was and ran for their lives.

[8]The men who had leprosy reached the edge of the camp, entered one of the tents and ate and drank. Then they took silver, gold and clothes, and went off and hid them. They returned and entered another tent and took some things from it and hid them also.

[9]Then they said to each other, "What we're doing is not right. This is a day of good news and we are keeping it to ourselves. If we wait until daylight, punishment will overtake us. Let's go at once and report this to the royal palace."

[10]So they went and called out to the city gatekeepers and told them,
"We went into the Aramean camp and no one was there—not a sound of anyone—only tethered horses and donkeys, and the tents left just as they
were." [11]The gatekeepers shouted the news, and it was reported within
the palace.

[12]The king got up in the night and said to his officers, "I will tell you what the Arameans have done to us. They know we are starving; so they have left the camp to hide in the countryside, thinking, 'They will surely come out, and then we will take them alive and get into the city.'"

[13]One of his officers answered, "Have some men take five of the horses

that are left in the city. Their plight will be like that of all the Israelites left here—yes, they will only be like all these Israelites who are doomed. So let us send them to find out what happened."

[14]So they selected two chariots with their horses, and the king sent them after the Aramean army. He commanded the drivers, "Go and find out what has happened." [15]They followed them as far as the Jordan, and they found the whole road strewn with the clothing and equipment the Arameans had thrown away in their headlong flight. So the messengers returned and reported to the king. [16]Then the people went out and plundered the camp of the Arameans. So a seah of the finest flour sold for a shekel, and two seahs of barley sold for a shekel, as the LORD had said.

[17]Now the king had put the officer on whose arm he leaned in charge of the gate, and the people trampled him in the gateway, and he died, just as the man of God had foretold when the king came down to his house. [18]It happened as the man of God had said to the king: "About this time tomorrow, a seah of the finest flour will sell for a shekel and two seahs of barley for a shekel at the gate of Samaria."

[19]The officer had said to the man of God, "Look, even if the LORD should open the floodgates of the heavens, could this happen?" The man of God had replied, "You will see it with your own eyes, but you will not eat any of it!" [20]And that is exactly what happened to him, for the people trampled him in the gateway, and he died.

Listening to the Text in the Story: Biblical Texts: 1 Kings 3:16–28; Deuteronomy 28:53–57; Ancient Near Eastern Texts: The Curse of the Agade; The Kulamuwa Inscription; Seventh-Century Assyrian Treaties; Ashurbanipal's Inscription of his Campaign against Arabia, Josephus's *Jewish War*

The text recorded earlier famines during the ministries of Elijah and Elisha (1 Kgs 18:2; 2 Kgs 4:38), but this chapter describes "a great famine" (*ra'ab gadol*; 6:25) where the consequences appear much worse, with horrific descriptions of inflated prices for disgusting food and mothers eating their own children. The Old Testament includes many stories that could make a reader uncomfortable, but cannibalistic mothers must be near the top. In the midst of this epic tragedy, Elisha speaks a word of judgment for a faithless officer and of hope for an impoverished city (7:1–2). The prophet then disappears from the narrative, as his word of divine provision is fulfilled in a shockingly creative manner involving four lepers.

During times of ancient sieges and famines, the price of food often rises to astronomical levels as it did during the famine recorded in 2 Kings 6–7. A poem called "The Curse of the Agade" from ancient Sumer describes famine food prices: one shekel only bought half a sila of oil, half a sila of grain, or half a mina of wool.[1] In his account of the siege of Jerusalem in AD 70, the Jewish historian Josephus speaks of a measure of wheat being sold for a talent (*J.W.*, 5.13.7).

The incident involving the two cannibalistic women who complain to the king of Israel (6:26–29) shares several similarities to the story of the two prostitutes who approach Solomon at the beginning of his reign (1 Kgs 3:16–28). In both instances two mothers seek wisdom or assistance from a ruler. All four of these women have a young son. The major difference is, unlike Solomon who exercised wisdom to resolve the problem, the ruler of Israel here is helpless and merely blames Elisha for the crisis.

The maternal cannibalism grotesquely depicted here (2 Kgs 6:28–29) is a fulfillment of the curses of Deuteronomy for disobedience: "Because of the suffering your enemy will inflict on you during the siege, you will eat the fruit of the womb, the flesh of the sons and daughters the Lord your God has given you" (Deut 28:53; see also 28:55–57 and Lev 26:29). All these texts portray the horrific consequences of those who chose a life of disobedience.

Assyrian treaties of the seventh century often included cannibalistic curses.[2] An inscription recording Ashurbanipal of Assyria's siege of the stronghold of Hukkuruna in Arabia includes a similar gruesome description:

> Famine broke out among them and they ate the flesh of their children against their own hunger.[3]

To lure the Arameans away from Samaria, God caused them to hear a foreign army. They assume that the Israelites had hired the Hittites and the Egyptians to attack them (2 Kgs 7:6). The practice of hiring a foreign army to assist in battle is not uncommon. Ahaz of Judah hired Tiglath-Pileser III of Assyria to help against Aram and Israel (16:5–9). King Kilamuwa of Y'dy claims to have hired the king of Assyria in his battle against the Danunians.[4]

1. *ANET*, 649.
2. *BBCOT*, 393.
3. *ANET*, 300; see also *ZIBBC* 3:139.
4. *COS* 2:147.

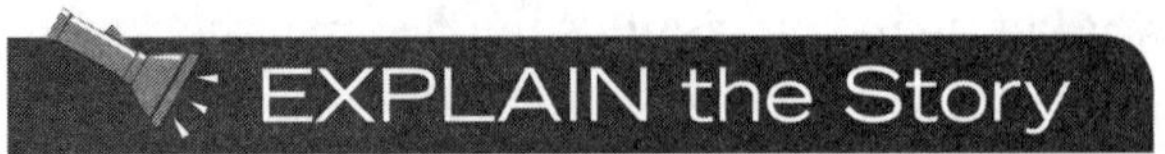

Siege, Famine, and Cannibalistic Mothers (2 Kings 6:24–31)

The truce established between Israel and Aram as a result of Elisha's ministry may have persisted awhile chronologically, but as the text is constructed, it lasted only one verse (6:23–24). Aram and Israel waged warfare earlier in the book of Kings (1 Kgs 11:25; 15:19–20; 20:1–21, 26–33; 22:2–38), but only once before was a siege involved (20:1).[5] The Aramean ruler's name was Ben-Hadad, but we do not know whether he was Ben-Hadad II or III.[6] Based on the context, we could assume the Israelite ruler is Joram, but the text never names him.

To illustrate how bad the siege-induced famine was, prices are given for two items of food not normally be considered edible (2 Kgs 6:25). While measurements and currency values fluctuated over time, prices here are given in shekels: ten shekels was approximately an annual wage for a laborer.[7] A donkey's head was unclean (Lev 11:3) and probably not tasty, but it was selling for eighty shekels, so about eight years wages. Seed pods (or "dove's dung" in the ESV, NAS, NRSV; 2 Kgs 6:25) were primarily used for fuel. However, during a siege, seed pods apparently were eaten. A "cab" (*qab*) is about 1.2 liters, so a quarter of a cab would only be about a third of a liter.[8] Thus a third of a liter of these seed pods cost five shekels, about a half year's salary. In this case, supply cannot meet demand, hence the exorbitant prices, which sets up the interaction between the ruler and the two mothers. These graphic descriptions of famine should remind those of us who experience abundance to be thankful for God's gracious provision.

In response to the cry for "help" (*yasha'*; a plea for justice[9]) from one of the mothers, the Israelite ruler asks four questions (v. 27). The first implies YHWH is not helping; the second and third observe that no produce is coming from the threshing floor or the winepress; the fourth is genuine, "What's the matter?" After hearing her answer, the king probably wished he had not asked. We would expect the mother to be disturbed that she had to consume her own son, but she seemed more upset that her neighbor did not

5. See also "Siege Warfare in the Ancient Near East," *ZIBBC* 3:140–41.

6. On which Ben-Hadad is being referred to here, see *BBCOT*, 393; Cogan and Tadmor, *II Kings*, 78–79.

7. See *BBCOT*, 393; *ZIBBC*, 3:138.

8. The term "cab" only appears here in the Old Testament. See Cogan and Tadmor, *II Kings*, 79.

9. Alter, *The Former Prophets*, 759.

share her son the next day (vv. 28–29). The text is unclear whether she killed him or merely consumed him after he starved to death. Either situation is deeply troubling.

The king's initial response to this news is understandable: tearing his clothes (v. 30; see also 1 Kgs 21:27; 2 Kgs 2:12; 5:7–8; 11:14; 18:37; 19:1; 22:11, 19), which reveals he is wearing sackcloth (2 Kgs 6:30; see also 1 Kgs 20:31–32; 21:27; 2 Kgs 19:1–2). But just as Jezebel swore to kill Elijah (1 Kgs 19:2), the king swears to decapitate Elisha, whom he blames for the famine (2 Kgs 6:31), presumably because he has not done anything yet. While he should know that Elisha could do something dramatic as he has in the past, it would have been better for the king to approach the prophet to humbly ask for assistance rather than putting a hit out on him.

Elisha's Prediction of Deliverance (2 Kings 6:32–7:2)

Despite the king's best wishes, Elisha's head remains on his shoulders as he holds council with the elders at his home (6:32). Just as he knew about the Aramean troop movements (vv. 9–10), Elisha has supernatural knowledge that the king sent someone to decapitate him, so he orders the door to be barred. Elisha also knows that the king will soon follow.

In the Hebrew, the messenger comes and speaks to Elisha's group (v. 33), but some translations (NRSV and NIV) reasonably put the words of lament directly in the mouth of the king. Elisha just said the king will soon follow the messenger (v. 32). The Hebrew words for king (*melek*) and messenger (*mal'ak*) are similar. Elisha's response is clearly heard by the king and the king's right-hand man.

Elisha's reply to the king begins with a two-part prophetic formula (7:1). The second part, "This is what the Lord says" (*koh 'amar yahweh*) appears frequently in Kings (e.g., 1 Kgs 12:24; 13:2, 21; 2 Kgs 1:4, 6, 16), but the first part, "Hear the word of the Lord" (*shema' debar-yahweh*), appears only two other place in Kings, in both instances spoken by a prophet to a ruler (1 Kgs 22:19; 2 Kgs 20:16). Elisha's introduction should cause his audience to heed the message that prices will plummet over the next twenty-four hours. The term used for measuring grain, a seah, is approximately seven and a half quarts, about a week's worth of food for one adult. Elisha predicts that a week's worth of fine flour (one seah) will be purchased with about a month's salary (one shekel) and that two weeks' worth of barley (two seahs) for about a month's salary. Prices will still be higher than normal but will be drastically reduced from famine levels—and would purchase normal food. Typically, it would take an entire season of farming for food prices to come down after a famine.

The price reduction is so dramatic that the king's right-hand man questions YHWH's ability to perform a miracle so great (7:2). The officer's skeptical response elicits an ominous warning from Elisha that he will see it, but he will not eat of it (v. 2), with the clear implication that he will soon be dead.

Why would Elisha pronounce such a harsh punishment for simply asking a question? This officer should have been aware of Elisha's miracles in the past. Elisha's authoritative introduction and his confident assertion of immediate provision should have led the officer to be hopeful, or at least to keep his mouth shut. The incredible doubt of this Israelite officer, on whose arm the king leaned, is contrasted with the incredible faith of Naaman, who performed a similar function for the king of Aram (5:18).

Four Lepers Share Good News (2 Kings 7:3–20)

The narrative shifts again from Elisha (not mentioned again until 8:1) to a group of four lepers living as outcasts outside the city gate (see Lev 13:46; Num 12:14–15). While the text has the lepers speaking to each other in unison (2 Kgs 7:3–4), this literary device is often used in Scripture to briefly summarize the gist of a longer, more complicated interaction. Something similar happens the next time they speak (v. 9). They will soon starve, so they decide they have nothing to lose to surrender to the Arameans, who may treat lepers better than the Israelites; after all, the commander of their army, Naaman, had been a leper (5:1).

When they arrive, the lepers are surprised to find the Aramean camp empty (7:5). To explain their absence, the text includes a flashback. God had caused the Arameans to hear a massive army. Just as Elisha's servant supernaturally saw an army of chariots and horses when Elisha's house was surrounded by an Aramean army (6:17), so now this Aramean army supernaturally hears an army of chariots and horses that they attribute to the Hittites and the Egyptians (7:6). The Arameans abandon all their valuables and their food as they flee in panic at "dusk" (*neshep*; 7:7), leaving just as the threatening horde of four starving lepers arrives at "dusk" (*neshep*; 7:5).

After breaking their famine-induced fast with a feast in one of the tents, they begin to rummage through the plunder, hiding gold, silver, and clothes (see also 5:5) until they realize they need to share their good news with the starving residents of Samaria (7:8–9). These lepers harbor no ill-will toward the city that left them outside the walls during a siege. They report to the city gatekeepers what happened, and their message is relayed to the king. Despite Elisha's hopeful prophecy, the king responds with suspicion, confident that the Arameans are hiding in order to lure them outside the walls (7:10–12).

During the conquest, Joshua used a similar strategy to lure the army of Ai outside the city to defeat them (Josh 8:1–29). Just as Naaman listened to his servants (2 Kgs 5:13), the king of Israel fortunately listened to one of the officers, who comes up with a wise plan to send a small group of men to investigate (two chariots and five horses; 7:13). The officer's logic is similar to that of the lepers (7:3–4); they may be killed by the Arameans, but they would have starved anyway, so they have nothing to lose. The men travel at least twenty miles to the Jordan River and find no waiting army, merely more plunder, clothes, and equipment (7:14–15).

After hearing that there is no danger and the siege has ended, the people rush out to seize the plunder (v. 16). The rest of the chapter narrates (in rather repetitive manner) how the word of Elisha was fulfilled, both about the price reduction and the death of the officer (vv. 16–20). The doubting officer had the unfortunate task of being in charge of the gate as the starving masses rushed out and was trampled (vv. 17, 20). The redundant nature of the conclusion of the chapter could be explained as chiasm,[10] as an addition,[11] as dittography, or as a doublet,[12] but the best explanation is that the text is merely emphasizing that, despite the doubts of the king or the officer, the prophetic word of YHWH was fulfilled exactly as predicted.

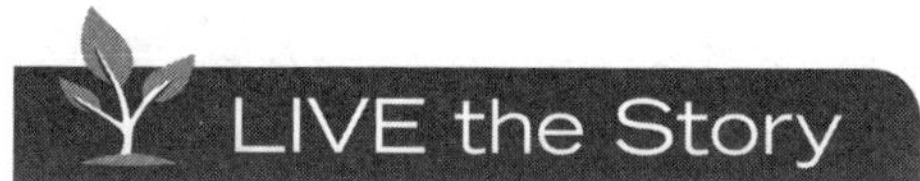

Responding to Crises with Doubt or Hope

As we reflect on how YHWH worked previously in the ministries of Elijah and Elisha, a number of questions arise from this story of the lifting of the Aramean siege. Why does God not blind the Arameans here like he did earlier (2 Kgs 6:18)? Why does God allow a famine to endure here, while he provided food earlier (1 Kgs 17:8–16; 2 Kgs 4:1–7, 38–44)? Why does he not resurrect a young boy like he did earlier (1 Kgs 17:17–24; 2 Kgs 4:18–37)? It is easy to assume that God will work the same way in the present that he did in the past. And yet, just as God first told Moses to strike the rock for water (Exod 17:6) and later told him to speak to the rock (Num 20:7–13), God often chooses to work in different ways at different times. Earlier, to display his power to Elisha's servant, God created a vision of chariots and horses (2 Kgs 6:17);

10. See Cogan and Tadmor, *II Kings*, 83.

11. See Hobbs, *2 Kings*, 88.

12. Wiseman argues that the repetition should not be explained by dittography or a doublet, *1 & 2 Kings*, 212.

now, to frighten the Aramean army, he created a sound of chariots and horses (7:6). His miraculous creativity is evidenced here not only in horses but also in his ability to work through leprous outcasts to deliver the gospel to a starving city (vv. 9–10).

As we see God work in unexpected ways to provide for us, it stretches our faith. Even though we want him to provide now, God often makes us wait, as he did for the Israelites in the city of Samaria. How people respond during times of waiting will be determined by their faith and their ability to trust in God. The characters in this story who lack faith express doubt and blame God and others (the king, the two women, and king's right-hand officer). The ones with faith express hope and take initiative to make a difference (the prophet, the four lepers, and the officer who suggested sending out a small party).

While the king never prays but merely blames YHWH and Elisha, the prophet of God speaks words of hope, confident in God's provision. Both the two mothers and the four lepers take desperate steps to solve the problem. But one of the mothers has no shame talking about her cannibalism and blames her friend for not sharing. The lepers could have blamed the residents of the city for keeping them outside the gates during a famine, but once they discover the plunder, they decide to share the good news. The king's right-hand officer has seen and heard God at work through the ministry of Elisha, but he can only doubt and question God's ability to provide. The king's other officer offers a plan based on hope. Fortunately, the king listened to this officer, and the city was saved. In the midst of a crisis, it is tempting to give into doubt and blame like the king, these women, and the first officer. And yet, Scripture includes many stories like this one, showing us how to remain hopeful during dark times like Elisha, the lepers, and the second officer.

In many ways, Christians are like these lepers: we have good news about God, God's grace, and God's Son, but for a variety of reasons we enjoy the abundant blessings with no concern to inform others. Ironically, it is the faithless woman and the faithless ruler who point us in the right direction as they speak of God's "help" (6:26, 27). The Hebrew word translated as "help" is *yasha'*, the verb from which the name Joshua is based, which means "YHWH helps" or "YHWH saves." And Joshua is, of course, the Old Testament equivalent of Jesus. In this regard, the king was correct: only God can save, and fortunately, he provided something much better than food—a savior. We should respond like the lepers. It's not right if we don't share the good news.

CHAPTER 25

2 Kings 8:1–29

LISTEN to the Story

1Now Elisha had said to the woman whose son he had restored to life, "Go away with your family and stay for a while wherever you can, because the LORD has decreed a famine in the land that will last seven years." 2The woman proceeded to do as the man of God said. She and her family went away and stayed in the land of the Philistines seven years.

3At the end of the seven years she came back from the land of the Philistines and went to appeal to the king for her house and land. 4The king was talking to Gehazi, the servant of the man of God, and had said, "Tell me about all the great things Elisha has done." 5Just as Gehazi was telling the king how Elisha had restored the dead to life, the woman whose son Elisha had brought back to life came to appeal to the king for her house and land.

Gehazi said, "This is the woman, my lord the king, and this is her son whom Elisha restored to life." 6The king asked the woman about it, and she told him.

Then he assigned an official to her case and said to him, "Give back everything that belonged to her, including all the income from her land from the day she left the country until now."

7Elisha went to Damascus, and Ben-Hadad king of Aram was ill. When the king was told, "The man of God has come all the way up here," 8he said to Hazael, "Take a gift with you and go to meet the man of God. Consult the LORD through him; ask him, 'Will I recover from this illness?'"

9Hazael went to meet Elisha, taking with him as a gift forty camel-loads of all the finest wares of Damascus. He went in and stood before him, and said, "Your son Ben-Hadad king of Aram has sent me to ask, 'Will I recover from this illness?'"

10Elisha answered, "Go and say to him, 'You will certainly recover.' Nevertheless, the LORD has revealed to me that he will in fact die."

[11]He stared at him with a fixed gaze until Hazael was embarrassed. Then the man of God began to weep.

[12]"Why is my lord weeping?" asked Hazael.

"Because I know the harm you will do to the Israelites," he answered. "You will set fire to their fortified places, kill their young men with the sword, dash their little children to the ground, and rip open their pregnant women."

[13]Hazael said, "How could your servant, a mere dog, accomplish such a feat?"

"The LORD has shown me that you will become king of Aram," answered Elisha.

[14]Then Hazael left Elisha and returned to his master. When Ben-Hadad asked, "What did Elisha say to you?" Hazael replied, "He told me that you would certainly recover." [15]But the next day he took a thick cloth, soaked it in water and spread it over the king's face, so that he died. Then Hazael succeeded him as king.

[16]In the fifth year of Joram son of Ahab king of Israel, when Jehoshaphat was king of Judah, Jehoram son of Jehoshaphat began his reign as king of Judah. [17]He was thirty-two years old when he became king, and he reigned in Jerusalem eight years. [18]He followed the ways of the kings of Israel, as the house of Ahab had done, for he married a daughter of Ahab. He did evil in the eyes of the LORD. [19]Nevertheless, for the sake of his servant David, the LORD was not willing to destroy Judah. He had promised to maintain a lamp for David and his descendants forever.

[20]In the time of Jehoram, Edom rebelled against Judah and set up its own king. [21]So Jehoram went to Zair with all his chariots. The Edomites surrounded him and his chariot commanders, but he rose up and broke through by night; his army, however, fled back home. [22]To this day Edom has been in rebellion against Judah. Libnah revolted at the same time.

[23]As for the other events of Jehoram's reign, and all he did, are they not written in the book of the annals of the kings of Judah? [24]Jehoram rested with his ancestors and was buried with them in the City of David. And Ahaziah his son succeeded him as king.

[25]In the twelfth year of Joram son of Ahab king of Israel, Ahaziah son of Jehoram king of Judah began to reign. [26]Ahaziah was twenty-two years old when he became king, and he reigned in Jerusalem one year. His mother's name was Athaliah, a granddaughter of Omri king of Israel.

[27]He followed the ways of the house of Ahab and did evil in the eyes of the LORD, as the house of Ahab had done, for he was related by marriage to Ahab's family.

[28]Ahaziah went with Joram son of Ahab to war against Hazael king of Aram at Ramoth Gilead. The Arameans wounded Joram; [29]so King Joram returned to Jezreel to recover from the wounds the Arameans had inflicted on him at Ramoth in his battle with Hazael king of Aram.

Then Ahaziah son of Jehoram king of Judah went down to Jezreel to see Joram son of Ahab, because he had been wounded.

Listening to the Text in the Story: Biblical Texts: Genesis 41:27–31; Numbers 27:1–11; 1 Kings 11:36; 15:4; 17:1; 19:15–17; 2 Kings 4:33–35; 9:1–3; Ancient Near Eastern Texts: The Ugaritic Epic of Aqhat; The Royal Inscriptions of Shalmaneser III of Assyria; The Lachish Ostraca; The Hazael Aramaic Dedication Inscriptions; The Inscription of Zakkur

The four short passages that make up 2 Kings 8 (each less than ten verses) are a dramatic change from the long story of the Aramean siege and famine that spanned the previous chapter and a half (6:24–7:20). These four passages record the restoration of the Shunammite woman's land (8:1–6), the murder of Ben-Hadad and succession of Hazael (vv. 7–15), and the regnal formulas for two Judean rulers: Jehoram (vv. 16–24) and Ahaziah (vv. 25–29).

Elisha charges the Shunammite woman, whose son he had brought back to life (4:33–35), to leave the land, because he was predicting a seven-year famine (8:1). Ancient Near Eastern famines apparently often lasted seven years. In his dream interpretation, the patriarch Joseph also predicted a seven-year famine in the land of Egypt (Gen 41:27–31). The Ugaritic Epic of Aqhat describes a seven-year famine: "Seven years has Ba'lu failed . . . no dew, no showers, no upsurging (of waters) from the deeps."[1]

The Shunammite's request to the king for her land upon her return from Philistia (2 Kgs 8:3–6) is comparable to the request from the daughters of Zelophehad to Moses to give them a tribal portion since their father had no sons (Num 27:1–11). In both instances a man in power grants the property right request of a woman with no man to advocate for her.

1. *COS* 1:351.

When Ben-Hadad of Aram hears that Elisha has come to Damascus, he sends a messenger (Hazael) to inquire from YHWH via his prophet whether he would recover (2 Kgs 8:7–8). Ahaziah of Israel does something similar, seeking direction about his health from Baal-Zebub, the god of Ekron (1:2). Despite their desire for a hopeful diagnosis, in both cases the ruler does not recover and soon dies.

The text records no reason for Elisha's long trip to Damascus, the capital of Aram (8:7). A roundtrip from Samaria to Damascus was over two hundred miles and could have taken Elisha several weeks. Elisha's journey may have been intended to fulfill the spirit of the prediction that YHWH gave to Elijah to anoint Hazael king over Aram (1 Kgs 19:15–16). The next act Elisha does is to commission a young prophet to anoint Jehu (2 Kgs 9:1–3), also part of YHWH's commission to Elijah at Horeb (1 Kgs 19:16). No actual anointing takes place in Damascus, but Elisha's words serve as a catalyst for Hazael's usurpation of the Aramean throne (2 Kgs 8:13–15). Elisha's prediction that Hazael would slaughter many Israelites (v. 12) is consistent with YHWH's prediction of death coming from Hazael's sword (1 Kgs 19:17).

Hazael appears surprised by Elisha's prediction that he would seize the throne, because in his own words, he is merely a "dog" (*keleb*; 8:13). This humble self-assessment is consistent with the description of Hazael in Assyrian inscriptions. In the Assur Basalt Statue of Shalmaneser III, Hazael is called "the son of a nobody",[2] suggesting he did not have royal blood.

Despite lacking a royal lineage, Hazael features prominently in ancient Near Eastern inscriptions, suggesting he was a well-known ruler. Numerous Assyrian royal inscriptions proclaim Shalmaneser's victories over Hazael.[3] Several West Semitic Aramaic dedication inscriptions mention "our lord Hazael."[4] Both Hazael and his son, Bar-Hadad III, are mentioned in the Inscription of Zakkur.[5]

In the regnal formula for Jehoram king of Judah, the text mentions the third and final "lamp oracle" (8:19; see also 1 Kgs 11:36; 15:4), explaining why YHWH did not wipe out Judah. In each of the three references, the Judean ruler is evaluated as evil, but because of YHWH's promise to David (2 Sam 7), he will allow a "lamp" (*nir*) to remain for David's descendants (2 Kgs 8:19).[6]

2. *COS* 2:270; for an image, see *ZIBBC* 3:144.
3. *COS* 2:267, 268, 269, 270.
4. *COS* 2:162–63.
5. *COS* 2:155.
6. For a longer discussion of lamp oracles, see Lamb, *Righteous Jehu*, 228–30.

EXPLAIN the Story

The Shunammite Woman's Land Is Restored (2 Kings 8:1–6)

Most stories in Scripture include at least one character portrayed negatively, making the thoroughly positive narrative of the restoration of the Shunammite woman's land unusual. The text never reveals the name of the woman from Shunem who had provided for Elisha (4:8–37), and here she is merely referred to as "the woman whose son (Elisha) had restored to life" (8:1). The famine mentioned here is one of several in Kings (1 Kgs 17:1; 18:2; 2 Kgs 4:38; 6:25; 7:4; 8:1; 25:3). During famines in the time of the patriarchs, Abraham went to Egypt (Gen 12:10), and Isaac, like the Shunammite here, moved to what became Philistine territory (Gen 26:1). The land of Philistia was located along the coastal plain, so it received more rainfall, was less prone to droughts, and was therefore a reasonable destination for her family.[7] The Shunammite's story is comparable to Ruth's—an Israelite family moves to a foreign land during a famine and eventually returns under the leadership of a woman (Ruth 1).

The Shunammite faithfully obeys Elisha's directive to leave (2 Kgs 8:1–2). She is probably a widow since her husband was described as old (4:14), and she makes the appeal to the king (8:3; see also 6:26). As a widow in a patriarchal society, she would have little status or power. In her absence, her land was presumably taken by the king (see 1 Kgs 21:1–16). The context suggests the unnamed ruler is Joram, but Wiseman thinks he could be Jehu, because the king does not seem familiar with Elisha.[8]

With her approach, the Shunammite interrupts a discussion between the king and Elisha's servant Gehazi, whose leprosy (see 2 Kgs 5:27) is not mentioned here. The Israelite king asks Gehazi about all the great things Elisha has done (8:4). Just as Gehazi is narrating about the resurrection of her son, she appears (v. 5). She gets to finish the story, which makes the king sympathetic to her cause (v. 6). During a landowner's absence, the income would normally go to those who worked the land, so the fact that the Shunammite's income was returned to her is unusual.[9]

We are not surprised for Elisha and the Shunammite to be viewed favorably here, but for Gehazi and the king it is unexpected. When we last saw Gehazi, he was deceiving Naaman and Elisha (5:20–27). In previous interactions between Elisha and Israel's ruler, the king is occasionally portrayed positively

---

7. Hobbs, *2 Kings*, 100.
8. See Wiseman, *1 & 2 Kings*, 213.
9. See *BBCOT*, 395.

(6:10, 23) but is more frequently portrayed negatively (3:10, 14; 5:7–8; 6:27, 31–33; 7:12).[10] Each of these four characters contributes to the happy ending of this story; the subsequent story, however, has a Machiavellian tone.

Hazael Kills Ben-Hadad and Seizes the Throne (2 Kings 8:7–15)

The narrative jumps from the capital of Israel to the capital of Aram (8:7). The Aramean ruler here, whose throne name was Ben-Hadad (probably the second), had a personal name of Hadadezer and was called Adad-idri by the Assyrians.[11] Like a modern celebrity, Elisha cannot travel inconspicuously, so word reaches Ben-Hadad in Damascus that the prophet was on his way. He sends his faithful (thus far) servant Hazael to find out from YHWH's prophet if he will recover from the illness from which he is currently suffering (v. 8).

Like Naaman's gift to Elisha, which was refused (5:5, 15–16), Ben-Hadad offers an exorbitant gift of forty camels loaded with Aramean valuables (8:9), which we assume was also refused by the prophet. This gift was not meant merely to thank him for his prophetic services but also to elicit a favorable response, assuming that the prophet could influence the behavior of his god. Ben-Hadad was trying to hire a healing. In contrast to the king of Israel's threats toward Elisha (6:31), Hazael's initial comments are highly deferential ("your son," 8:9; "my lord," 8:12).

In response to Hazael's question regarding his master's health, Elisha offers a contradictory answer. He says Hazael should tell the king that he will recover; but to Hazael Elisha says the king will die (8:9–10). There are a number of problems, both textual and theological, that arise here. For Elisha's message to Ben-Hadad, the written Hebrew text (the *ketiv*) has "you will not recover," but the spoken tradition (the *qere*) is followed by most translations, "you will certainly recover." Barnes summarizes well the various ways commentators attempt to explain that Elisha is not lying when the text seems to suggest otherwise.[12] But careful readers of Kings should recall two other incidents when prophetic deception seemed acceptable (1 Kgs 13:11–25; 22:1–28). Elisha knows what will happen, but unlike Elijah with Ahaziah earlier (2 Kgs 1:4, 6, 16), he decides honesty is not the best policy for the message to the king, only for the message to the king's messenger.

Elisha next begins a stare down with Hazael, forcing the Aramean to blink first with embarrassment (8:11). Elisha begins to weep, the only incident of

---

10. Since the ruler in most of these texts is unnamed, several different northern rulers may be being referred to, even though the context suggests Joram of Israel.

11. Wiseman, *1 & 2 Kings*, 213. See also *COS* 2:270.

12. Barnes, *1–2 Kings*, 246–48.

prophetic weeping in the book. Emotional expressions like Elisha's here are consistently viewed positively in Kings, as illustrated in the examples of the three weeping rulers (13:14; 20:3; 22:19).

Hazael asks a reasonable question regarding the cause of the prophet's tears (8:12). Just as Elisha read the minds of earlier Aramean rulers (6:8–10), here he sees Hazael's plans and knows what devastation he will wreak upon Israel: burning fortresses and killing young men, children, and pregnant women (8:12); similar atrocities were performed by King Menahem of Israel (2 Kings 15:16) and the king of the Ammonites (Amos 1:13; see also Hos 13:16). After hearing what Elisha is predicting, Hazael continues to use deferential language to describe himself (2 Kgs 8:13: "your servant" and "a mere dog") as he asks Elisha how these things could happen. The interaction ends with Elisha informing Hazael that YHWH said he would become king (v. 13), which hearkens back to YHWH's word to Elijah at Horeb (1 Kgs 19:15).

Hazael leaves and dutifully delivers the optimistic, but deceptive, message to his master that he will recover (2 Kgs 8:14). While scholars debate what happens the next day, since the pronouns and the details are vague, the narrative is still sufficiently clear—Hazael suffocated his master (v. 15). The regicidal assassination thus allowed Hazael to succeed Ben-Hadad, which we know from other sources took place in 842 BC.[13] It took a while, but the word from YHWH to Elijah was finally fulfilled (1 Kgs 19:15).

The Reigns of Jehoram and Ahaziah of Judah (2 Kings 8:16–29)

The book of Kings pays far more attention to Israel than to Judah during the period of the divided monarchy, primarily due to the long prophetic narratives of Elijah and Elisha (1 Kgs 12–2 Kgs 17). After focusing on the Northern Kingdom of Israel for almost eight chapters (from 1 Kgs 22:51), at this point the narrative shifts back to the Southern Kingdom of Judah for fourteen verses (8:16–29), before heading north again for two more chapters (2 Kgs 9–10).

Jehoshaphat finally dies, and his son, Jehoram, comes to power (8:16) while another Jehoram (called "Joram" in the NIV) of Israel reigns in Samaria. For eight years both Israel and Judah were ruled by men named Jehoram (which means "YHWH is exalted"). To make it more confusing, both were also called Joram (8:16, 21). Following the NIV, I will call the king of Judah, Jehoram, and the king of Israel, Joram. Joram of Israel was preceded by his brother Ahaziah (1:17), and Jehoram of Judah was succeeded by his son, Ahaziah (8:24). All of these Jehorams and Ahaziahs were evaluated as evil (1 Kgs 22:52;

13. *BBCOT*, 395.

2 Kgs 3:2; 8:18, 27). The text records that the two Judean rulers here have short reigns; Jehoram reigned for eight years (8:17) and his son, Ahaziah, for only one (8:26), since he will soon be killed by Jehu (9:27).

Within these two southern regnal formulas, the northern king Ahab is curiously mentioned nine times (8:16, 18 [2x], 25, 27 [3x], 28, 29). Ahab is arguably the most famous northern ruler (mentioned seventy-six times in Kings, more than any other northern ruler). Ahab appears here for two reasons. First, Ahab is mentioned to distinguish his son, Joram of Israel, from Jehoram of Judah (the NIV gives them different names, but in the Hebrew they are the same). Second, Ahab was evil, and his familial connections with them seemed to contribute to the evil of the Judean royal family. Just as foreign marriage alliances adversely affected Solomon and Ahab (1 Kgs 11:1–8; 16:31–34), the marriage between Ahab's daughter Athaliah and Jehoshaphat's son, Jehoram, is blamed for the idolatry during the reigns of Jehoram and Ahaziah (2 Kgs 8:18).

Several commentators assume that Jezebel was the mother of Athaliah,[14] presumably because, as we will discover in 2 Kings 11, her behavior is "Jezebelian," but the text never clearly states who her mother is. The text does not mention Jehoram's wife in his regnal formula, and Ahaziah's regnal formula says that Athaliah is literally the "daughter" (*bat*) of Omri (Ahab's father). But *bat* can also mean female offspring, so the NIV's translation here as "granddaughter" is reasonable. Later, the text clarifies that Athaliah is the mother of Ahaziah (11:1), which means she is the wife of Jehoram and, therefore, also the daughter of Ahab (8:18).

The union between the royal houses of Israel and Judah is highly problematic, since David's heirs and Ahab's heirs now overlap. A tension is thus created between the promise that David would always have an heir on the throne (2 Sam 7:12–16) and the judgment that all the male descendants of Ahab will be killed (1 Kgs 21:20–26; 2 Kgs 9:7–10).[15] We will revisit this topic when Athaliah comes to power and David's royal dynasty is nearly cut off (11:1–3).

Both of these regnal formulas include brief notices about military campaigns. It is reasonable to assume that Judah's losses in these campaigns were a result of their evil actions, following in the ways of their northern neighbors. Edom rebelled against Judah and set up their own ruler (8:20). Jehoram attempted to quash the rebellion with his chariots but was surrounded and barely was able to escape (v. 21). Edom and Libnah remain independent until "this day" (v. 22). The alliance established between Jehoshaphat and Ahab

14. See Cogan and Tadmor, *II Kings*, 98; Barnes, *1–2 Kings*, 251; August Konkel, *1 & 2 Kings*, NIVAC (Grand Rapids: Zondervan, 2006), 475.

15. For a discussion of this tension, see Lamb, "The 'Eternal' Curse," 315–25.

continued as Judah fought alongside Israel against Aram (v. 28). Few battle details are included, except that Joram was wounded and withdrew to Jezreel, while Ahaziah joined him there (v. 29). Neither will survive much longer, but the new threat does not come from Aram.

Unlike Kings, Chronicles focuses more on Judah than Israel, and it provides additional information about Jehoram of Judah. Jehoram killed all his brothers when he came to power (2 Chr 21:4), just as his wife Athaliah later does to the Judean royal family (2 Kgs 11:1–2). Jehoram receives a letter from Elijah (even though Elijah has been gone awhile; 2:11) condemning his alliance with Israel (2 Chr 21:11–15). The letter predicted the capture of his family and an incurable intestinal disease. Fortunately, the text provides graphic details: "his bowels came out because of his disease and he died in great pain" (2 Chr 21:19).

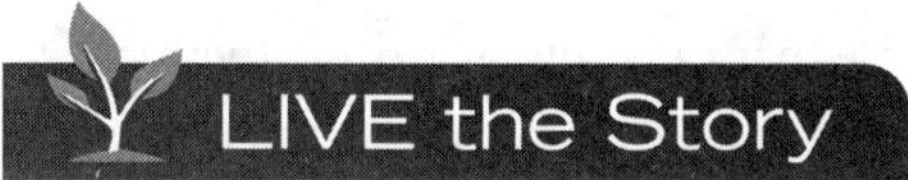

Working through Flawed People

We may be tempted to focus our attention upon the prophetic heroes here, but there are other individuals who also deserve our attention. It is difficult to find fault with Elijah and Elisha, making it hard for readers to identify with them. In 2 Kings 8 we see several people who are clearly flawed, and yet God still works powerfully through them.

Greedy Gehazi is now sharing good news with the king about what God has done through the ministry of Elisha, the man of God. As Elisha's servant introduces the Shunammite woman to the king, he plays a role in the restoration of her property. We can't be certain the king of Israel is Joram here, but the vast majority of Israelite rulers (except Jehu) were evil. If he were Joram (as the context suggests), he was recently attempting to kill Elisha, but now he's listening to Gehazi's stories, restoring the Shunammite's land, and returning her income. James would say the king is performing "pure and faultless religion" as he cares for a widow in her distress (Jas 1:27). Hazael's mission is far less commendable, but he is still used here as an instrument of God to bring judgment upon his people (2 Kgs 8:12; 10:32–33).

Thus, we see here how God is able to use both the righteous and the unrighteous to accomplish his purposes. For any of us who have performed deeds comparable to, or perhaps worse than, the characters in these narratives, these stories can give us hope and inspire us to get involved in God's mission. The retelling of the Shunammite's story motivated the king to help her.

Find a widow, or some other distressed person near you, listen to their story, and then do something to help them.

Waiting for God's Word

One of the major themes of the book of Kings is the fulfillment of prophecy. Within 2 Kings 8 we see four different prophetic words being fulfilled. One, the seven-year famine came as Elisha told the Shunammite (8:1–2). Two, Ben-Hadad of Aram dies as Elisha predicted (8:10, 15). Three, Hazael becomes ruler over Aram as YHWH told Elijah (1 Kgs 19:15; 2 Kgs 8:15). Four, David's descendants remain on the throne of Judah as YHWH had promised him through his prophet Nathan (2 Sam 7:12–16; 2 Kgs 8:19). Thus, this chapter reemphasizes one of the central truths of Scripture—God's word comes to pass. This message should be a source of comfort and hope to any of us who are struggling with doubt about God's faithfulness in the midst of a crisis.

However, God often allows his people to wait before he works. Two of these prophetic words were fulfilled soon after they were spoken (the famine and Ben-Hadad's death), but two of them had much longer horizons of fulfillment (Hazael's accession and David's dynasty). When we hope or expect God to work now, these times of waiting can be a trial, a testing of our faith. The Shunammite had to wait seven years before she was able to return home (8:2–3). God's people often have to wait on God, but as James reminds us, the testing of our faith is a good thing since it produces endurance (Jas 1:3).

However, the delay from the time of Elijah to that of Elisha for Hazael's "royal anointing" doesn't appear to have a divine explanation. We don't know why these two prophets delayed their obedience to the commission to anoint Hazael as king, but perhaps their hesitation was related to what Elisha foresaw that Hazael would do to the people of Israel. God revealed to his prophet that this leader would perform horrendous acts and his people would be the victims. And the text here doesn't give an explanation why this is to take place. God allows his people to suffer. While this realization may not make the suffering magically disappear, it helps to realize that God is still somehow in control in the midst of it and that many of his people throughout the Bible also suffered (e.g., Job).

Just as he does with Hazael here, sometimes God puts an evil leader in a position of power, even over an entire country, and many people suffer as a result. Elsewhere in Scripture political leaders, more often evil than good, are used by God to oppress or judge Israel (several pharaohs, several Ben-Hadads, Tiglath-Pileser III, Shalmaneser V, and Nebuchadnezzar). When we find ourselves suffering under an unrighteous ruler, what are we to do?

Weeping in the Face of Suffering

Elisha provides us a model of how to respond to suffering, violence, and oppression. He wept (2 Kgs 8:11). The man who parted a mighty river (2:14), purified poisoned water (2:19–22), sicced bears on a young gang (2:24), provided water for a thirsty army (3:16–20) and food for a starving widow and for a company of prophets (4:3–7, 42–44), healed a foreign general (5:10–14), and prevented a war (6:8–23) had nothing left in his miraculous arsenal here except tears. Sometimes that's all one can do when faced with massive evil.[16]

When Jesus looked over the city of Jerusalem, knowing the persecution and oppression that it would suffer, he also wept (Luke 19:41–44). Jesus had more power at his disposal than Elisha. He was the ultimate fulfillment of this final lamp oracle (2 Kgs 8:19) as the Davidic descendant destined to reign on his ancestor's throne forever. He knew that not only would his people suffer but that he himself would also suffer. So, he wept. As we face sufferings, trials, and persecutions of our world, sometimes the only response is to follow the examples of Elisha and Jesus and weep, waiting for God to work.

---

16. However, God often calls his people to resist oppression and oppressive rulers (e.g., 2 Kgs 21:17–26; Isa 14:3–23; Amos 1–2; Matt 23; Mark 6:18).

CHAPTER 26

2 Kings 9:1–37

LISTEN to the Story

[1]The prophet Elisha summoned a man from the company of the prophets and said to him, "Tuck your cloak into your belt, take this flask of olive oil with you and go to Ramoth Gilead. [2]When you get there, look for Jehu son of Jehoshaphat, the son of Nimshi. Go to him, get him away from his companions and take him into an inner room. [3]Then take the flask and pour the oil on his head and declare, 'This is what the LORD says: I anoint you king over Israel.' Then open the door and run; don't delay!"

[4]So the young prophet went to Ramoth Gilead. [5]When he arrived, he found the army officers sitting together. "I have a message for you, commander," he said.

"For which of us?" asked Jehu.

"For you, commander," he replied.

[6]Jehu got up and went into the house. Then the prophet poured the oil on Jehu's head and declared, "This is what the LORD, the God of Israel, says: 'I anoint you king over the LORD's people Israel. [7]You are to destroy the house of Ahab your master, and I will avenge the blood of my servants the prophets and the blood of all the LORD's servants shed by Jezebel. [8]The whole house of Ahab will perish. I will cut off from Ahab every last male in Israel—slave or free. [9]I will make the house of Ahab like the house of Jeroboam son of Nebat and like the house of Baasha son of Ahijah. [10]As for Jezebel, dogs will devour her on the plot of ground at Jezreel, and no one will bury her.'" Then he opened the door and ran.

[11]When Jehu went out to his fellow officers, one of them asked him, "Is everything all right? Why did this maniac come to you?"

"You know the man and the sort of things he says," Jehu replied.

[12]"That's not true!" they said. "Tell us."

Jehu said, "Here is what he told me: 'This is what the LORD says: I anoint you king over Israel.'"

[13]They quickly took their cloaks and spread them under him on the bare steps. Then they blew the trumpet and shouted, "Jehu is king!"

[14]So Jehu son of Jehoshaphat, the son of Nimshi, conspired against Joram. (Now Joram and all Israel had been defending Ramoth Gilead against Hazael king of Aram, [15]but King Joram had returned to Jezreel to recover from the wounds the Arameans had inflicted on him in the battle with Hazael king of Aram.) Jehu said, "If you desire to make me king, don't let anyone slip out of the city to go and tell the news in Jezreel." [16]Then he got into his chariot and rode to Jezreel, because Joram was resting there and Ahaziah king of Judah had gone down to see him.

[17]When the lookout standing on the tower in Jezreel saw Jehu's troops approaching, he called out, "I see some troops coming."

"Get a horseman," Joram ordered. "Send him to meet them and ask, 'Do you come in peace?'"

[18]The horseman rode off to meet Jehu and said, "This is what the king says: 'Do you come in peace?'"

"What do you have to do with peace?" Jehu replied. "Fall in behind me."

The lookout reported, "The messenger has reached them, but he isn't coming back."

[19]So the king sent out a second horseman. When he came to them he said, "This is what the king says: 'Do you come in peace?'"

Jehu replied, "What do you have to do with peace? Fall in behind me."

[20]The lookout reported, "He has reached them, but he isn't coming back either. The driving is like that of Jehu son of Nimshi—he drives like a maniac."

[21]"Hitch up my chariot," Joram ordered. And when it was hitched up, Joram king of Israel and Ahaziah king of Judah rode out, each in his own chariot, to meet Jehu. They met him at the plot of ground that had belonged to Naboth the Jezreelite. [22]When Joram saw Jehu he asked, "Have you come in peace, Jehu?"

"How can there be peace," Jehu replied, "as long as all the idolatry and witchcraft of your mother Jezebel abound?"

[23]Joram turned about and fled, calling out to Ahaziah, "Treachery, Ahaziah!"

[24]Then Jehu drew his bow and shot Joram between the shoulders. The arrow pierced his heart and he slumped down in his chariot. [25]Jehu

said to Bidkar, his chariot officer, "Pick him up and throw him on the field that belonged to Naboth the Jezreelite. Remember how you and I were riding together in chariots behind Ahab his father when the LORD spoke this prophecy against him: [26]'Yesterday I saw the blood of Naboth and the blood of his sons, declares the LORD, and I will surely make you pay for it on this plot of ground, declares the LORD.' Now then, pick him up and throw him on that plot, in accordance with the word of the LORD."

[27]When Ahaziah king of Judah saw what had happened, he fled up the road to Beth Haggan. Jehu chased him, shouting, "Kill him too!" They wounded him in his chariot on the way up to Gur near Ibleam, but he escaped to Megiddo and died there. [28]His servants took him by chariot to Jerusalem and buried him with his ancestors in his tomb in the City of David. [29](In the eleventh year of Joram son of Ahab, Ahaziah had become king of Judah.)

[30]Then Jehu went to Jezreel. When Jezebel heard about it, she put on eye makeup, arranged her hair and looked out of a window. [31]As Jehu entered the gate, she asked, "Have you come in peace, you Zimri, you murderer of your master?"

[32]He looked up at the window and called out, "Who is on my side? Who?" Two or three eunuchs looked down at him. [33]"Throw her down!" Jehu said. So they threw her down, and some of her blood spattered the wall and the horses as they trampled her underfoot.

[34]Jehu went in and ate and drank. "Take care of that cursed woman," he said, "and bury her, for she was a king's daughter." [35]But when they went out to bury her, they found nothing except her skull, her feet and her hands. [36]They went back and told Jehu, who said, "This is the word of the LORD that he spoke through his servant Elijah the Tishbite: On the plot of ground at Jezreel dogs will devour Jezebel's flesh. [37]Jezebel's body will be like dung on the ground in the plot at Jezreel, so that no one will be able to say, 'This is Jezebel.'"

Listening to the Text in the Story: Biblical Texts: Deuteronomy 28:25–26; 1 Kings 19:16–17; 21:19–24; 22:38; Ancient Near Eastern Texts: The Royal Inscriptions of Shalmaneser III of Assyria; The Black Obelisk; The Amarna Letters; The Kirta Epic; The Tel Dan Inscription; The Egyptian Tale of the Two Brothers; The Sippur Boundary Stone

Jehu in Assyrian Inscriptions

Jehu's anointing, rebellion, and royal assassinations make for a great, albeit bloody, story. As we move into the narrative of Jehu, the nation of Israel begins to be mentioned far more frequently in external sources, particularly Neo-Assyrian ones. Ahab appears once in Assyrian royal inscriptions,[1] but Jehu is mentioned on four inscriptions associated with Shalmaneser III of Assyria: the Calah Bulls, the Kurba'il Statue, the Marble Slab, and the Black Obelisk.[2] In each of these descriptions Jehu is listed briefly among a group of rulers who gave tribute to Shalmaneser.[3] Hazael of Aram is also mentioned on these four inscriptions, but not among the tributaries. These inscriptions were erected in prominent locations and served as royal propaganda, the ancient equivalent of a campaign ad—"Look how impressive I am since all these foreign rulers pay homage to me!"

The Black Obelisk of Shalmaneser III (located at the British Museum in London) is one of the most significant ancient artifacts for the field of biblical studies. The Black Obelisk not only mentions Jehu but also includes a relief of Jehu bowing down before Shalmaneser as he offers tribute. This image of Jehu is the oldest pictorial representation of a biblical character and the only one of an Israelite ruler that dates to their reign.[4] According to the four panels depicting Jehu's tribute, thirteen individuals were required to transport it. The adjacent inscription lists the contents of the tribute:

> I received the tribute of Jehu, son of Omri: silver, gold, a golden bowl, a golden goblet, golden cups, golden buckets, tin, a staff of the king's hand, and javelins.[5]

In Kings Jehu is described as a son of Jehoshaphat and Nimshi, not Omri as the Black Obelisk states, but scholars speculate this inscription is meant to be saying Jehu comes from the land of Omri, Ahab's father.[6] While the Assyrian tribute of several other Israelite and Judean rulers is mentioned in both biblical and Assyrian sources (Menahem of Israel, Ahaz of Judah, Hoshea of Israel, and Hezekiah of Judah),[7] Jehu's tribute only appears in Assyrian sources. We cannot

1. *COS* 2:263; see 1 Kings 16:29–34.
2. *COS* 2:267, 268, 270.
3. For an extended discussion of Jehu's Assyrian tribute and his depiction on the Black Obelisk, see Lamb, *Righteous Jehu*, 124–28.
4. For images see *ZIBBC* 3:149; *ANEP*, 120–122; #351–55.
5. *COS* 2:270.
6. For a longer discussion of Jehu's ancestry, see Lamb, *Righteous Jehu*, 33–47.
7. For these references to these tributes, see Lamb, *Righteous Jehu*, 122.

be sure why Kings does not record Jehu's tribute, but the text clearly states other information from the reign of Jehu is omitted (2 Kgs 10:34). These Assyrian records mentioning Jehu and Hazael provide external validation for the historicity of the biblical account during this period.

External References to Anointing and Divine Election

At Mount Horeb YHWH told Elijah to anoint Jehu as king over Israel (1 Kgs 19:16–17), but he never performed this task. Apparently Elijah delegated it to Elisha, who then delegated it to the young prophet, who finally anoints and commissions Jehu here (2 Kgs 9:1–13). YHWH predicted the swords of Hazael, Jehu, and Elisha would kill many (1 Kgs 19:17), and Jehu's violent rebellion is narrated in 2 Kings 9–10.

In addition to Jehu, the book of Kings only mentions anointings for six other rulers of Israel and Judah (Saul, David, Absalom, Solomon, Jehoash of Judah, and Jehoahaz of Judah). I argue elsewhere that "royal anointing was not typically practiced in the [ancient Near East] outside of Israel and Judah."[8] Perhaps the closest extrabiblical parallel appears in one of the Amarna Letters, when Pharaoh Thutmose III anoints a Canaanite ruler, Taku, as his vassal king over Nuhasse.[9]

While anointing was unusual in the ancient Near East, claims of divine election were common.[10] Rulers wanted their subjects to know that they were selected by the gods, so they would publicize their divine election on inscriptions, establishing their royal legitimacy since potential usurpers would hesitate to resist the will of the gods. Shalmaneser III was one of many Assyrian rulers who claimed divine election. The author of the Tel Dan Inscription (see also "The Tel Dan Inscription and the Death of Two Kings" below), which most scholars assume was Hazael, claims that Hadad (the primary god of Aram) made him king.[11]

For Jehu, his anointing was synonymous with his divine election. The young prophet made it clear that YHWH had chosen him to rule (2 Kgs 9:3, 6). Four other Israelite rulers were selected by God to reign; two were anointed (Saul and David), and two were not (Jeroboam I and Baasha). For usurpers like Hazael and Jehu, a claim of divine election was particularly important to

8. See Lamb, *Righteous Jehu*, 48.

9. William L. Moran, *The Amarna Letters* (Baltimore: Johns Hopkins University Press, 1992), 122 (EA 51).

10. For a discussion of divine election in the ancient Near East and in the Old Testament, see Lamb, *Righteous Jehu*, 57–81.

11. *COS* 2:161.

maintain a royal dynasty. Jehu's dynasty of five rulers was the longest over the Northern Kingdom.[12]

Canines, Curses, and Corpses

While the young prophet was anointing Jehu, he delivered a message (2 Kgs 9:6–10) that recalled Elijah's prophetic judgment against the house of Ahab, specifically that it would be cut off and that dogs would consume the body of Jezebel (1 Kgs 21:19–24). Ahab's blood was licked by dogs earlier (1 Kgs 22:38), and Jezebel's corpse will be consumed by dogs (9:35–37). Here Jehu kills both Ahab's son, Joram of Israel (2 Kgs 9:24–26), and his grandson, Ahaziah of Judah (9:27), but the rest of Ahab's royal family is slaughtered later (10:1–17).

The fates of Jezebel and Ahab's house are paralleled in several ancient texts. The young prophet declares that Ahab's house will be cut off (9:7), and the Kirta Epic similarly describes a royal house being cut off.[13] Just as Jezebel is consumed by dogs (9:10, 35–37), in the Egyptian tale of The Two Brothers, the wife of the older brother is killed and cast to the dogs.[14] The young prophet here states that Jezebel's body is to remain unburied (9:10; 35–37), and the Sippur Boundary Stone includes a similar curse, "May his corpse fall down, and may it not have someone to bury it."[15] Other biblical texts describe corpses remaining unburied or consumed by animals (Deut 28:25–26; see also Jer 16:4).

The Tel Dan Inscription and the Death of Two Kings

Another important ancient inscription for biblical studies comes from the Tel Dan Stele, which is written from the perspective of an Aramean king (probably Hazael).

> There came up the king of I[s]rael before in the land of my father. Hadad [ma]de [me] king. Hadad went before me [and] I sent from . . . of my kings. I killed kin[gs] who harnessed X [ch]ariots and thousands of horsemen [ ]rm son of [ ] king of Israel and kill[ed]yahu son of [I overthr]ew the house of David.[16]

---

12. According to the regnal formulas, Jehu's dynasty lasted 102 years. The second longest northern dynasty, Omri's, lasted 48 years.

13. *COS* 1:333.

14. *COS* 1:87.

15. *COS* 2:368; for an image, see *ZIBBC* 3:150.

16. *COS* 2:161.

Unfortunately, the stele is badly damaged, but most scholars think that Hazael is claiming here to kill Joram of Israel ("[ ]rm") and Ahaziah ("[. . .] yahu") of Judah ("the house of David"), the same two rulers that 2 Kings 9 claims were killed by Jehu. How do we reconcile this conflict? While Hazael will later attack Israel (10:32–33), it is likely that in their early reigns Hazael and Jehu were allies. Elisha served as the kingmaker for both Hazael and Jehu. Hazael and Jehu both appear in Assyrian inscriptions as enemies of Shalmaneser III and, in 2 Kings 9, as enemies of Joram of Israel. If the enemy of your enemy is your friend, it is reasonable to assume the rulers of Israel and Aram were, at this point, united. If they were allies, Hazael, who was the more powerful partner, could reasonably claim these regicides, comparable to how Jehu receives credit for both Joram and Ahaziah's deaths, even though he did not actually kill Ahaziah (9:27).

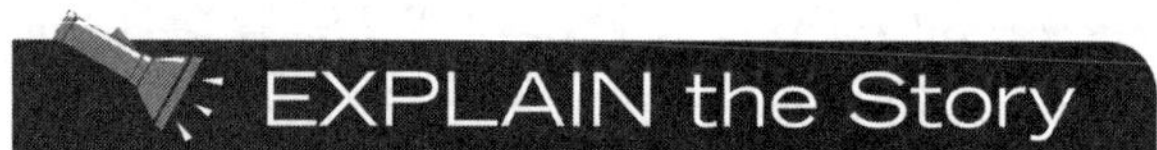

Jehu Is Anointed King over Israel (2 Kings 9:1–13)

While the narrative of Jehu's rebellion makes numerous references to previous prophetic messages, curiously, before Jehu's anointing the text makes no reference to YHWH's commission to Elijah at Mount Horeb (1 Kgs 19:16).[17] The text does, however, include an unusual amount of details in Elisha's directions to the young prophet: tuck your shirt in (sounds like my mother), take this flask, look for Jehu, isolate Jehu, take this flask (again), pour, declare, and flee (2 Kgs 9:1–3).[18] The prophet's destination is Ramoth Gilead, east of the Jordan River in the tribal territory of Gad. A tucked-in shirt ("girded loins" in the KJV) should allow the prophet to arrive there more quickly (see 1 Kgs 18:46; 2 Kgs 4:29). After giving these instructions, Elisha disappears until shortly before his death (13:14).

The anointing details here may have been necessary since this young prophet is, from the perspective of King Joram, committing treason. He is attempting to set up a new ruler. The prophet Samuel, who was normally quite bold (e.g., 1 Sam 15:32–33), when called to anoint David needed to be convinced by YHWH and was allowed to do it surreptitiously (1 Sam 16:1–3).

17. For a narrative analysis of Jehu's rebellion, see L. M. Wray Beal, *The Deuteronomist's Prophet: Narrative Control of Approval and Disapproval in the Story of Jehu (2 Kings 9 and 10)*, LHBOTS 478 (London: T&T Clark, 2007).

18. The ancient Rabbinic text *Seder Olam* identifies the young prophet as Jonah (2 Kgs 14:25); see Wiseman, *1 & 2 Kings*, 218.

To help the young prophet quickly identify the right man, an unusual double patronymic is given: "son of Jehoshaphat, son of Nimshi" (2 Kgs 9:2, 14); in two other texts Jehu is just a "son of Nimshi" (1 Kgs 19:16; 2 Kgs 9:20). The instructions to anoint privately and flee immediately could save the prophet's life, should there be opposition.

Jehu shares many similarities with Israel's most famous ruler, David: prophetic anointing, divine election, and military background.[19] Jehu's anointing, however, is unusual for several reasons. He is the only northern ruler anointed, and his anointing is emphasized by repetition. It is foretold twice (1 Kgs 19:16; 2 Kgs 9:3), narrated once (9:6), and retold one final time (v. 12).

While the message Elisha told the young prophet to deliver was quite short (seven words in Hebrew; v. 3), the actual message privately delivered was much longer (fifty-eight words in Hebrew). He inserts two phrases into Elisha's original message, "the God of Israel" and "the Lord's people" (v. 6), and then he tacks on details regarding the judgment against the house of Ahab (vv. 7–10). The young prophet recalls the first two northern dynasties (v. 9), of Jeroboam I and Baasha, which were both cut off in the second generation as prophesied (1 Kgs 14:10–14; 15:27–30; 16:1–7, 11–13). The term used here for male descendants is translated literally in the KJV as "him that pisseth against the wall" (*mashtin beqir*; 2 Kgs 9:8). This crass idiom is used exclusively in the book of Kings in contexts of dynastic judgments (1 Kgs 14:10; 16:11; 21:21; 2 Kgs 9:8).

After the prophet obediently fled (9:3, 10), Jehu's fellow officers ask the officer in charge, Jehu (9:5), what the message was (v. 11). Jehu is reluctant to share its contents, but they persist. Reluctance is a common feature of biblical call narratives (Moses: Exod 3:11; 4:1, 10, 13; Gideon: Judg 6:13, 15; Isaiah: Isa 6:5; Jeremiah: Jer 1:6), suggesting that the primary inspiration for the call was not human but divine. After hearing what the young prophet did and said, Jehu's companions feel no reluctance. They quickly blow the trumpet and declare him king (2 Kgs 9:13). The only other time a trumpet is blown in Kings is at Solomon's royal anointing (1 Kgs 1:34, 39, 41).

Jehu Kills Joram of Israel and Ahaziah of Judah (2 Kings 9:14–29)

Jehu is a man of action, and he knows that, to become king, Joram and his ally (and nephew) Ahaziah both need to be killed. The text states Jehu "conspired" (*qashar*) against Joram (9:14), a term used to describe the rebellions of most

19. See the discussion of the parallels between Jehu and David in Lamb, *Righteous Jehu*, 130–54.

other northern usurpers (Baasha, Zimri, Shallum, Pekah, Hoshea; 1 Kgs 15:27; 16:9, 16, 20; 2 Kgs 9:14; 10:9; 14:19; 15:10, 15, 25, 30). Fortunately for Jehu, Joram is already injured (perhaps explaining the lack of resistance from Jehu's companions), so Jehu travels quickly to Jezreel, Joram's secondary palace. The parenthetical summary of Joram's convalescence in 9:15 is a repetition of 8:29. Jehu orders his colleagues to keep silent, gathers a small mobile unit together, and drives his chariot to Jezreel (9:15–16).

The narrative shifts to the lookout on the wall at Jezreel, who calls out a warning (v. 17). Joram sends two messengers to ask if they come in peace (literally, "Is it peace?" *hashalom*; vv. 18, 19). Over the course of Jehu's bloody rebellion, ironically, forms of the word "peace" (*shalom*) appear ten times in the Hebrew (vv. 11, 17, 18 [2x], 19 [2x], 22 [2x], 31; 10:13). Both times Jehu asks back, "What do you have to do with peace?" (literally, "What to you and to peace?" *mah-lleka uleshalom*; 9:18, 19). Joram may want peace, but that is not what Jehu's bringing. Jehu commands both messengers to get behind him as his inexorable approach continues. Perhaps like someone you know, Jehu had a reputation as a crazy driver, so much so that Mr. Jehu's wild ride revealed his identity to the lookout, who informs Joram. The word used for Jehu's "mad" driving (*shigga'on*) is related to the verb used to describe the "mad" prophet (*shaga'*; 9:11). Madness is contagious.

Despite Jehu's furious approach and the lack of solid intel, Joram assumes Jehu can be trusted, so he and Ahaziah leave the walled city (a fatal mistake) to meet with Jehu. Kings who leave fortified cities to meet with opposing forces typically do not live long. Joram asks the same question (*hashalom*), now a third time, to Jehu. Jehu flips the question (*hashalom*), implying peace is not possible while his mother Jezebel's idolatries (literally, "whoredoms") and witchcraft persist (v. 22), essentially calling Joram's mother a whore and a witch. In the realm of modern trash talking, maternal insults like these are normally off-limits,[20] but Jezebel's history of dragging both Israelite rulers and subjects into idolatry warrants the harsh language. Instead of fighting for the honor of his mother, Joram flees and warns his ally Ahaziah, assuming that his previously loyal commander is now threatening him (v. 23). As the two kings run away, Jehu's arrow pierces Joram's heart. As Jehu is directing his chariot officer, Bidkar, to leave the body of Joram in the field that used to belong to Naboth (1 Kgs 21:1–16), he recalls a prophecy given to Jehu that is not recorded elsewhere (2 Kgs 9:26). It is, however, similar to the one spoken by Elijah to Ahab (1 Kgs 21:17–24), as it describes how Ahab's house will be

20. For a discussion of biblical trash talking, see Lamb, "Trash Talking," 111–30.

punished for killing Naboth and stealing his field. The dynastic judgment is finally meted out against the house of Ahab. Ahab's humility after hearing Elijah's condemnation had delayed the fulfillment until the days of his son (21:27–29).

As Ahaziah is fleeing toward Beth Haggan, Jehu commands his men to kill him (2 Kgs 9:27). They wound him, presumably with an arrow, but he manages to escape to Megiddo, where he dies. His servants returned Ahaziah's body to Jerusalem for burial (v. 28).

Jehu Kills Jezebel (2 Kings 9:30–37)

Jehu has finished off the kings of Israel and Judah, but one more cursed royal figure remains: Jezebel, introduced as the wife of Ahab sixteen chapters earlier (1 Kgs 16:31). As Jehu approaches her tower, Jezebel applies makeup and arranges her hair (2 Kgs 9:31). The text does not state why she does this. She asks Jehu the same question her son did, if he comes in peace (*hashalom*), but her question appears sarcastic. Then she insults him by accusing him of murder and disloyalty. While calling Jehu "Zimri" may seem strange, it was a clever insult. (He had already called her a witch and a whore.) Zimri was Israel's shortest-reigning monarch (seven days; 1 Kgs 16:15), and he was killed by Jezebel's father-in-law, Omri (16:17–18). And Zimri, like Jehu, was a military commander (16:9). Jezebel is predicting a short reign by Jehu, perhaps even to be cut off by one of Omri and Ahab's descendants, which may explain why Jehu is so thorough to make sure none of them survive.

Jehu calls out to see if anyone there is on his side (reminiscent of Moses's call to the Israelites post-golden calf; Exod 32:26). Two or three eunuchs stick out their heads (2 Kgs 9:32). When Jehu commands them to toss her from the window, her eunuchs display as much loyalty to Jezebel as Jehu did to Joram. They quickly comply to Jehu's request (v. 33). We are not sure what the pathologist would say was the cause of her death, but the text lists several options. First, it could have been the fall, which was sufficiently high for her blood to spatter on the tower walls. Second, it could have been horses that trampled her post-fall. Third, it could have been the dogs who devoured her mangled, bloody body. I prefer the first option. As a mother of adult children, she probably would not have survived the fall. After Jehu's celebration, he has second thoughts about leaving her body to decompose, so he charges his men to bury her; but the dogs have already made quick work of her corpse, fulfilling Elijah's prophetic judgment as they excrete her remains on the ground at Jezreel (9:34–37).

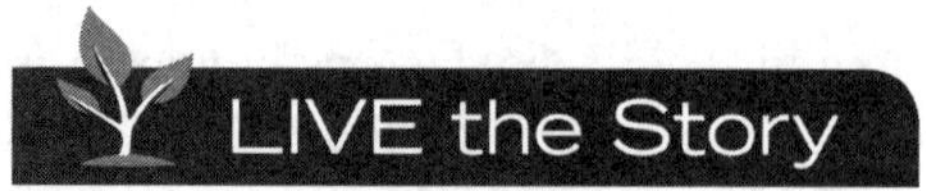

Fascinated by Scripture

In 2002, as I was finishing up my masters degree at the University of Oxford, I was faced with a difficult decision. I needed to decide upon a focus for my doctoral dissertation. I examined dynastic succession in the book of Samuel for my masters, so examining the theme of dynasty in the book of Kings seemed a logical next step. I began to read through Kings, past the narrative of Solomon (too familiar), past the early divided monarchy (too boring), past the prophetic narratives (no dynasties), and I finally arrived at the narrative of Jehu's dynasty (just right). I thought, "What a fascinating collection of kings! This is it. I could study these rulers for years." Three years later, I submitted my doctoral dissertation with the short title: "'Righteous' Jehu and his 'Evil' Heirs."[21] I hope you also find portions of Scripture that you could enjoying studying for years and not lose interest.

Peace and Violence

Even though I found Jehu's narrative fascinating, I was still troubled by it, particularly the violence. The dual themes of violence and peace dominate this chapter. Jeremiah describes a situation where the people say "peace, peace" when there is no peace because of rampant idolatry, greed, injustice, and deception (Jer 6:14; 8:11). Even though he came two centuries after Jehu, the prophet's words are particularly relevant to 2 Kings 9. The Hebrew word *shalom*, translated in the NIV usually as "peace," appears more frequently in 2 Kings 9 than in any other chapter in the book of Kings (9:11, 17, 18 [2x], 19 [2x], 22 [2x], 31). It always appears in dialogue, six times in the form of a question to Jehu (9:11, 17, 18, 19, 22, 31) and three times in Jehu's response asking how peace is possible (9:18, 19, 22).

Terms of violence also permeate the chapter: "blood" (9:7 [2x], 26 [2x], 33), "destroy" (9:7), "perish" (9:8), "cut off" (9:8), "devour" (9:10), "conspired" (9:14), "pierced" (9:24), "kill" (9:27), "wounded" (9:27), and "throw" (referring to bodies; 9:25, 33 [2x]). Jehu essentially kills three royals here (Joram, Ahaziah, and Jezebel), and the slaughter is ratcheted up a level in the next chapter.

For many readers of this narrative, the gruesome violence is highly disturbing. But the reason there is no peace, according to Jehu, is that Joram's

21. See Lamb, *Righteous Jehu.*

mother Jezebel led the nation into idolatry and Joram's father Ahab led the nation into oppression and injustice, as seen in the seizure of Naboth's vineyard (1 Kgs 21). Into these situations of widespread idolatry and injustice, divine judgment comes in the form of a conspiring usurper named Jehu, who was commissioned by a prophet of YHWH for this task.

YHWH gave the house of Ahab plenty of time to change, to recommit to YHWH, and to practice justice. YHWH is slow to judgment, and he waited a long time to bring final judgment against the house of Ahab. Through his prophets YHWH made it clear to Ahab and his family that judgment was coming. This chapter repeatedly emphasizes that God's word will be fulfilled (9:3, 6, 12, 25, 26, 36). He delayed the judgment because of Ahab's repentance (1 Kgs 21:27–29), but when it finally arrived, it came fast and furious.

Many things haven't changed since the time of Jehu. We are surrounded by idols as people (often Christians) look for security in wealth, materialism, sports, appearance, nationalism, fame, and other things. We may not be bowing down to altars, but worshiping anything other than God is still idolatry and will ultimately result in disaster, as it did for the house of Ahab. Only God can offer us any form of reliable security. Just as it did for Ahab and Jezebel, often our idolatries can lead us into unjust practices: greed, taking things that belong to others, or not sharing what God has generously given to us. There can be no peace while idolatry and injustice are rampant.

Even the prince of peace said that he didn't come to bring peace but a sword (Matt 10:34; Luke 12:51). We may not be comfortable with the violence here, but we can be confident that justice was served and that God's word will always come true. We will revisit the topics of violence and peace in light of Jesus in the Live the Story section of the next chapter.

CHAPTER 27

2 Kings 10:1–36

LISTEN to the Story

1Now there were in Samaria seventy sons of the house of Ahab. So
Jehu wrote letters and sent them to Samaria: to the officials of Jezreel, to
the elders and to the guardians of Ahab's children. He said, 2"You have
your master's sons with you and you have chariots and horses, a fortified
city and weapons. Now as soon as this letter reaches you, 3choose the best
and most worthy of your master's sons and set him on his father's throne.
Then fight for your master's house."

4But they were terrified and said, "If two kings could not resist him,
how can we?"

5So the palace administrator, the city governor, the elders and the
guardians sent this message to Jehu: "We are your servants and we will do
anything you say. We will not appoint anyone as king; you do whatever
you think best."

6Then Jehu wrote them a second letter, saying, "If you are on my side
and will obey me, take the heads of your master's sons and come to me in
Jezreel by this time tomorrow."

Now the royal princes, seventy of them, were with the leading men of
the city, who were rearing them. 7When the letter arrived, these men took
the princes and slaughtered all seventy of them. They put their heads in
baskets and sent them to Jehu in Jezreel. 8When the messenger arrived,
he told Jehu, "They have brought the heads of the princes."

Then Jehu ordered, "Put them in two piles at the entrance of the city
gate until morning."

9The next morning Jehu went out. He stood before all the people and
said, "You are innocent. It was I who conspired against my master and
killed him, but who killed all these? 10Know, then, that not a word the
Lord has spoken against the house of Ahab will fail. The Lord has done
what he announced through his servant Elijah." 11So Jehu killed everyone

in Jezreel who remained of the house of Ahab, as well as all his chief men,
his close friends and his priests, leaving him no survivor.
12Jehu then set out and went toward Samaria. At Beth Eked of the
Shepherds, 13he met some relatives of Ahaziah king of Judah and asked,
"Who are you?"

They said, "We are relatives of Ahaziah, and we have come down to greet the families of the king and of the queen mother."

14"Take them alive!" he ordered. So they took them alive and slaughtered
them by the well of Beth Eked—forty-two of them. He left no survivor.
15After he left there, he came upon Jehonadab son of Rekab, who was
on his way to meet him. Jehu greeted him and said, "Are you in accord
with me, as I am with you?"

"I am," Jehonadab answered.

"If so," said Jehu, "give me your hand." So he did, and Jehu helped
him up into the chariot. 16Jehu said, "Come with me and see my zeal for
the LORD." Then he had him ride along in his chariot.
17When Jehu came to Samaria, he killed all who were left there of
Ahab's family; he destroyed them, according to the word of the LORD
spoken to Elijah.
18Then Jehu brought all the people together and said to them, "Ahab
served Baal a little; Jehu will serve him much. 19Now summon all the
prophets of Baal, all his servants and all his priests. See that no one is
missing, because I am going to hold a great sacrifice for Baal. Anyone who
fails to come will no longer live." But Jehu was acting deceptively in order
to destroy the servants of Baal.
20Jehu said, "Call an assembly in honor of Baal." So they proclaimed it.
21Then he sent word throughout Israel, and all the servants of Baal came;
not one stayed away. They crowded into the temple of Baal until it was full
from one end to the other. 22And Jehu said to the keeper of the wardrobe,
"Bring robes for all the servants of Baal." So he brought out robes for them.
23Then Jehu and Jehonadab son of Rekab went into the temple of Baal.
Jehu said to the servants of Baal, "Look around and see that no one who
serves the LORD is here with you—only servants of Baal." 24So they went
in to make sacrifices and burnt offerings. Now Jehu had posted eighty men
outside with this warning: "If one of you lets any of the men I am placing
in your hands escape, it will be your life for his life."
25As soon as Jehu had finished making the burnt offering, he ordered

the guards and officers: "Go in and kill them; let no one escape." So they cut them down with the sword. The guards and officers threw the bodies out and then entered the inner shrine of the temple of Baal. [26]They brought the sacred stone out of the temple of Baal and burned it. [27]They demolished the sacred stone of Baal and tore down the temple of Baal, and people have used it for a latrine to this day.

[28]So Jehu destroyed Baal worship in Israel. [29]However, he did not turn away from the sins of Jeroboam son of Nebat, which he had caused Israel to commit—the worship of the golden calves at Bethel and Dan.

[30]The LORD said to Jehu, "Because you have done well in accomplishing what is right in my eyes and have done to the house of Ahab all I had in mind to do, your descendants will sit on the throne of Israel to the fourth generation." [31]Yet Jehu was not careful to keep the law of the LORD, the God of Israel, with all his heart. He did not turn away from the sins of Jeroboam, which he had caused Israel to commit.

[32]In those days the LORD began to reduce the size of Israel. Hazael overpowered the Israelites throughout their territory [33]east of the Jordan in all the land of Gilead (the region of Gad, Reuben and Manasseh), from Aroer by the Arnon Gorge through Gilead to Bashan.

[34]As for the other events of Jehu's reign, all he did, and all his achievements, are they not written in the book of the annals of the kings of Israel?

[35]Jehu rested with his ancestors and was buried in Samaria. And Jehoahaz his son succeeded him as king. [36]The time that Jehu reigned over Israel in Samaria was twenty-eight years.

Listening to the Text in the Story: Biblical Texts: Numbers 25; Judges 9:5; 2 Samuel 7:12–16; 1 Kings 21:21–22; 2 Kings 9:7–9; 11:1; Ancient Near Eastern Texts: The Panamuwa Inscription; Ashurnasirpal's Royal Inscriptions; Esarhaddon's Prophetic Oracles

After killing the kings of Israel and Judah, Jehu proceeds to slaughter their extended families. In 2 Kings 9 Jehu has three rulers killed (Joram, Ahaziah, and Jezebel); in 2 Kings 10 Jehu orchestrates three slaughters (Ahab's family, Ahaziah's family, and the worshipers of Baal).

While this brutal bloodshed is shocking to modern readers, as we examine the context, it is less troubling. First, during a royal coup usurpers typically wiped out rivals to the throne (see 2 Kgs 11:1). Just as Jehu orchestrates the killing of seventy sons of Ahab, Abimelech, the son of Gideon, arranged the deaths of seventy of his brothers when he installed himself as ruler over Shechem (Judg 9:5). Similarly, an Aramaic inscription dedicated to Panamuwa king of Y'dy describes how Panamuwa survived a palace coup that killed his father and seventy of his father's brothers.[1] If Jehu had left any members of Ahab's family, they would have attempted a counter-rebellion.

Second, Jehu's actions fulfill prophecies that the house of Ahab would be wiped out (1 Kgs 21:21–22, 29; 2 Kgs 9:7–9). Thus, his violent behavior is divinely authorized because of the wickedness of Ahab's house and their persistent idolatry. YHWH made it clear that he would not tolerate idolatry among his people (Exod 20:3–6).

Jehu's tactic of stacking the heads of the sons of Ahab at the gate of Jezreel may have been something he learned from the Assyrians. Ashurnasirpal (883–859 BC), who ruled Assyria a generation before Jehu, bragged about piling up heads of his enemies, even outside a city gate.

> I cut off their heads and formed a pile. . . . I appointed Azi-ili as my own governor over them. I erected a pile in front of his gate; I flayed as many nobles as had rebelled against me. . . . I gouged out the eyes of many troops. I made one pile of the living and one of the heads. I hung their heads on trees around the city.[2]

This brutal practice sent a clear warning to enemies of Ashurnasirpal and Jehu that anyone who opposed them would experience the same fate.

Jehu did not limit his carnage to royal families. He also orchestrated a scheme to trap and kill the worshipers of Baal. Previously in Israel's history, two similar religious massacres are recorded. During Israel's wandering in the wilderness, Moses commanded the slaughter of any Israelites who worshiped Baal of Peor (Num 25). After his victory on Mount Carmel, Elijah slaughters the prophets of Baal (1 Kgs 18:40).

To reward Jehu for wiping out Ahab's family, YHWH promised the northern ruler that four more generations of Jehuites would rule over the throne of Israel, making them the longest northern dynasty (2 Kgs 10:30). While David was given an eternal dynastic promise (2 Sam 7:12–16), Jehu's limited promise finds a parallel in the two-generational royal promise given to Esarhaddon of

1. *COS* 2:158.

2. A. K. Grayson, *Assyrian Rulers of the Early First Millennium BC 1 (1114–859 BC)*, RIMA 3 (Toronto: University of Toronto Press, 1991), 197–98, 199, 201. For an image of a pile of heads slain by Sennacherib, see *ANEP*, 74 (#236).

Assyria by La-dagil-ili, one of his royal prophets:[3] "Even your son and grandson will exercise kingship in the lap of Ninurta."[4]

The Slaughter of Ahab's Family (2 Kings 10:1–17)

From Jezreel, Jehu corresponds with the leaders of Samaria, where the seventy remaining sons of Ahab reside (10:1). The number seventy need not be hyperbolic, since rulers typically had many wives, but it could be symbolic or rounded, and it apparently included some children (Ahab's grandchildren) since they still required guardians (v. 6). Comparable to Goliath's challenge to Israel to select a man to fight him (1 Sam 17:8–10), Jehu challenges the leaders of Samaria to select a man to replace Joram and lead their army into battle against him (2 Kgs 10:2–3). Jehu points out that they have military advantages (a cavalry, a fortified city, and weapons) but omits the fact that he has the support of the army that had been in the field fighting Aram.

Cowering in fear because of Jehu's recent exploits, the city officials immediately submit to Jehu's authority (vv. 4–5). In his second letter Jehu tells them that they can prove their support by bringing the "heads" (*ra'shim*) of their master's sons to him at Jezreel by tomorrow. Since "head" can mean a leader or the thing normally attached to the top of one's neck, Jehu's command is ambiguous. They interpret him literally, so they kill the seventy Ahabites and ship the bloody heads to Jehu in baskets. When this gruesome sign of their loyalty arrives, Jehu orders the heads stacked in two piles at the city gate. Because of the ambiguity in his request, Jehu claims that he was innocent of their deaths, but then he notes that Elijah's prophecy has been fulfilled, as the house of Ahab is eliminated (vv. 9–10). Jehu goes one step further, killing anyone associated with Ahab: his leaders, friends, and priests (v. 11). Upon his arrival in Samaria he kills any of the remaining members of Ahab's family (v. 17).

As Jehu travels to Samaria to take the northern capital, he encounters members of Ahaziah's family, who are oblivious to recent events (vv. 12–13). They are planning to visit (literally, "to peace"; *leshalom*) the relatives that Jehu has killed. After their capture, Jehu has all forty-two of them slaughtered. Since Ahaziah was a grandson of Ahab (through his mother, Athaliah, Ahab's daughter), these relatives may all be male descendants of Ahab and therefore

3. See Lamb, "Non-Eternal Dynastic Promises," 337–44.
4. Nissinen, *Prophets and Prophecy*, 110–11.

fall under the Ahabite ban. If, however, this group includes non-Ahabites, this bloodshed, along with the additional slaughter of Ahab's friends and priests, could explain Hosea's judgment on the bloodshed of the house of Jehu (Hos 1:4).[5]

The Slaughter of Baal's Worshipers (2 Kings 10:15–28)

Before instigating his third and final slaughter, Jehu encounters Jehonadab, the son of Rekab. Much speculation surrounds this enigmatic figure, but we only know the following. Jehonadab was already coming to meet Jehu (10:15). During the time of Jeremiah, Jehonadab's descendants were part of a religious order that drank no wine (Jer 35:6, 14–16). Jehonadab offers support here to Jehu. Jehu assumes Jehonadab will be excited about his religious zeal, which will be displayed in his scheme to wipe out Baal. Thus, Jehonadab appears to be a spiritual leader who could lend Jehu support. Jehu realizes the importance of securing support from people like Jehonadab, who could add legitimacy to Jehu's reign during the transition.

Jehonadab serves as co-conspirator in Jehu's final purge, against the cult of Baal. In order to trick all the Baal worshipers into coming together, Jehu announces a massive sacrifice for all prophets, servants, and priests of Baal (2 Kgs 10:18–19). The text states that Jehu was acting "deceptively" (*'aqevah*; 10:19; from the same root as Jacob (*ya'qov*); Gen 25:26; 27:36).

After the word spread, a large number of servants of Baal gathered into the Baal temple (2 Kgs 10:20–21), which had been constructed by Ahab and Jezebel (1 Kgs 16:31–32). The fact that this temple was packed was an indictment on the prevalence of idolatry during the time of the Ahabites. Before the slaughter, Jehu and Jehonadab make sure that only true servants of Baal remain (2 Kgs 10:23). As the sacrifice is beginning, Jehu warns his soldiers to not let anyone escape, at penalty of death (10:24; see also Elijah's similar command: 1 Kgs 18:40). After killing every servant of Baal inside with the sword, they demolish the sacred stone and the temple (2 Kgs 10:25–27). Just as the text adds a scatological notice regarding Jezebel's final fate (9:36–37), the text informs us that the holy Baal site is repurposed as a latrine (10:27). The text records that Jehu wiped out Baal worship in Israel (v. 28), but in Judah it persisted for centuries (21:3; 23:4, 5).

Righteous Jehu (2 Kings 10:29–36)

Jehu's religious reforms did not include destroying the golden calf altars at Dan in the north and Bethel in the south (10:29). References to the sins of

5. For a discussion of Hosea's perspective on Jehu's bloodshed, see Lamb, *Righteous Jehu*, 86–88.

Jeroboam (who constructed these altars) continue for each of the remaining northern rulers (e.g., 13:2, 11; 14:24; 15:9), but this is the last time Dan altar is mentioned in Kings. The Bethel altar was destroyed by Josiah (23:15).

Despite not removing Jeroboam's altars, Jehu's zealous purge of the house of Ahab warrants a righteous (*yashar*) regnal evaluation in the eyes of YHWH (10:30). While commentators[6] tend to focus on his connection to Jeroboam's sins to support the idea that Jehu is generally disapproved of, four points suggest otherwise. One, Jehu is the only one of nineteen northern rulers to be evaluated as righteous. Two, Jehu is the only ruler of either kingdom to be told directly by YHWH he is righteous.[7] The last ruler to hear directly from YHWH was Solomon (1 Kgs 11:11). Three, almost all other northern rulers are associated with Jeroboam's sins, so there is nothing distinctive about mentioning Jeroboam here. Four, because of his obedience, Jehu is granted a four-generational dynastic promise, fulfilled in the reigns of his descendants (see 2 Kgs 15:12). Jehu is the only northern ruler to receive an unconditional dynastic promise (like David). Jehu's dynasty was the longest northern dynasty (102 years, based on regnal years). At twenty-eight years, Jehu was the second-longest-reigning northern ruler (10:36), second only to his great-grandson, Jeroboam II, who reigned forty-one years (14:23).

During the reign of Jehu, Israel lost significant territory to Hazael of Aram on the eastern side of the Jordan in the tribal regions of Gad, Reuben, and Manasseh (10:31–32). A theological notice states that YHWH was the reason for Hazael's victories over Israel, an ominous foreshadowing of another northern threat, Assyria, who would later wipe out the Northern Kingdom completely (16:9; 17:5–6). Jehu's regnal formula includes the typical remark that other events from his reign are recorded in the royal annals, which would include his massive tribute to Shalmaneser III, recorded on the Black Obelisk (see Chapter 26 for a discussion of 2 Kgs 9).

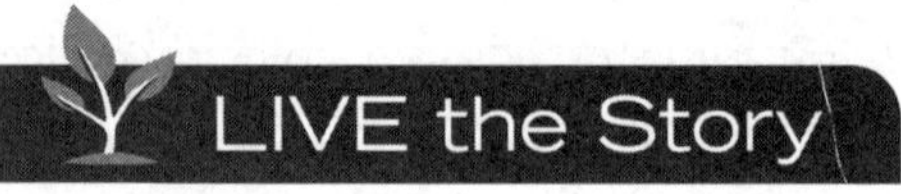

Peace, Not Violence

How are we to understand Jehu's excessive violence? His bloodshed was limited to three individuals in 2 Kings 9, but in chapter 10 it multiplied to include seventy sons of Ahab, forty-two relatives of Ahaziah, other royal figures, and a temple-full of servants of Baal—literally hundreds of individuals.

6. Wiseman, *1 & 2 Kings*, 228–29; Barnes, *1–2 Kings*, 268–69; Wray Beal, *1 & 2 Kings*, 382.
7. See also Lamb, *Righteous Jehu*, 17–27.

As we work to understand Jehu's violent behavior, we can make four points. First, Jehu was initially reluctant. The rebellion was not instigated by Jehu. He didn't think the prophet was coming to speak to him. Even after being commissioned by a prophet of YHWH, he hesitated to talk about it with his companions. It wasn't until his fellow officers declared him king that he began his rebellion.

Two, Jehu involved many others in the completion of his commission: his fellow commanders, his soldiers, Bidkar his chariot officer, Jezebel's eunuchs, the leaders of Samaria, and Jehonadab. While one would expect soldiers under his command to obey orders, many of these individuals would not have been under military obligation to submit. The fact that he received widespread support, even from people who should have opposed him, suggests that people knew the family of Ahab deserved judgment.

Three, Jehu perceived himself to be fulfilling the word of God. The previous chapter of the commentary explains that Jehu was justified because he was fulfilling a divine mandate to wipe out the house of Ahab, and 2 Kings 10 adds further support for this theory. YHWH is silent throughout Jehu's narrative, but both Jehu and the narrator speak of how the word of YHWH was fulfilled at each step (9:3, 6, 12, 25–26, 36; 10:10, 17, 30, 31). When YHWH finally speaks, he offers a word of high praise to this violent usurper for his diligence in performing his mission (10:30).

Four, it appears that Jehu took his violence too far. The text isn't clear on this point, but hints that YHWH was not pleased with Jehu's zealous bloodshed can be seen in YHWH's removal of land east of the Jordan (10:32–33). The prophet Hosea appears to view Jehu's overly zealous commitment to his bloody crusade to be worthy of judgment (Hos 1:4), presumably because he went beyond what was required by his prophetic commission.[8] But God was still gracious to his overly zealous usurper in allowing him to have an ongoing royal dynasty.

I discuss the problem of a violent God elsewhere, but here I will merely point out that the trajectory of Scripture moves not toward violence, but peace.[9] Even in the midst of the many wars of the book of Kings, God and his prophets were still calling for a cessation of warfare and love for enemies (1 Kgs 12:24; 2 Kgs 5:1–19; 6:8–23).

Just as Elisha told Naaman, a man who should have been his enemy, to

---

8. See also Wiseman, *1 & 2 Kings*, 224.

9. See Lamb, *God Behaving Badly*, 93–113; David T. Lamb, "Compassion and Wrath as Motivations for Divine Warfare" in *Holy War in the Bible: Christian Morality and an Old Testament Problem*, ed. H. A. Thomas, J. Evans, and P. Copan (Downers Grove, IL: IVP Academic, 2013), 133–51.

"go in peace" (5:19), Jesus sent two distressed women off with a similar word of blessing (Luke 7:50; 8:48). Jesus also commanded the troubled storm to be at peace (Mark 4:39). Jesus told the argumentative disciples to be at peace with one another (Mark 9:50). When Jesus appeared to his fearful disciples post-resurrection, he blessed three times with the words, "Peace be with you" (John 20:19, 21, 26). The people of God should therefore learn from the obedience of Jehu, not his violence. We follow the peaceful example of Elisha and Jesus. After all, Jesus, the Prince of Peace (Isa 9:6), through his death purchased peace for all his followers (Rom 5:1).

Truth, Not Deception

How are we to understand Jehu's deception, as he lied to lure the servants of Baal into his trap (2 Kgs 10:18–19)? Do the ends justify the means? As we think about the issue of deception, we can make two points.

One, Scripture is clear that bearing false witness is wrong (Exod 20:16; 23:1; Deut 19:18). But this command is speaking into a legal context where honest testimony ensures that a just decision will be made. Naboth's neighbors bore false witness and therefore deserved punishment (1 Kgs 21:9–13). Jehu's isn't bearing false witness here; he is deceiving to root out idolatry from Israel.

Two, there are other examples of deceptive behavior in Scripture by people portrayed positively. The Hebrew midwives deceived Pharaoh and were blessed by YHWH (Exod 1:19–21). Rahab the prostitute lied to the soldiers of Jericho, and she is praised in the New Testament (Josh 2:4–5; Matt 1:5; Heb 11:31; Jas 2:25). In these situations the lie is told to save life. David told Ahimelech he was on a mission from Saul when he was actually fleeing from Saul, and Jesus upholds David's behavior in his interaction with the Pharisees (1 Sam 21:2; Mark 2:26). The prophet Elisha deceives the recently blinded king of Aram and leads him into a trap in Samaria (2 Kgs 6:19).

More problematically, we even see examples of divine behavior that appear deceptive. YHWH told Moses to tell Pharaoh the Israelites were only going for a three-day march, when YHWH clearly intended to deliver his people permanently (Exod 3:18). After telling his brothers that he wasn't going to the festival, Jesus went to the festival anyway in secret (John 7:8–10). The psalmist addresses this type of situation in this description of God: "to the pure you show yourself pure, but to the devious you show yourself shrewd" (Ps 18:26).

In none of these instances is the deceptive behavior praised, but neither is it explicitly condemned. None of these individuals are bearing false witness in order to accuse someone of a crime. In each scenario a greater goal was achieved by misleading someone.

While normally the ends do not justify the means (see Rom 3:7–8), it appears that in certain unusual circumstances deception is warranted. In Jehu's case deception is clearly not as significant a problem as idolatry. Jehu was praised for his obedience and criticized for not removing Jeroboam's altars, but the text is silent about his deception.

However, just as we are called to be people not of violence but of peace, we are also called to be people not of deception but of truth. In the same Gospel where Jesus appears to mislead his brothers, he also declares himself to be "the way, the truth, and the life" (John 14:6). Jesus also promises that the spirit of truth will come upon his followers (John 14:17; 15:26; 16:13). Those of us who have God's spirit, should be people of peace and truth.

CHAPTER 28

2 Kings 11:1–12:21

LISTEN to the Story

[1]When Athaliah the mother of Ahaziah saw that her son was dead, she proceeded to destroy the whole royal family. [2]But Jehosheba, the daughter of King Jehoram and sister of Ahaziah, took Joash son of Ahaziah and stole him away from among the royal princes, who were about to be murdered. She put him and his nurse in a bedroom to hide him from Athaliah; so he was not killed. [3]He remained hidden with his nurse at the temple of the Lord for six years while Athaliah ruled the land.

[4]In the seventh year Jehoiada sent for the commanders of units of a hundred, the Carites and the guards and had them brought to him at the temple of the Lord. He made a covenant with them and put them under oath at the temple of the Lord. Then he showed them the king's son. [5]He commanded them, saying, "This is what you are to do: You who are in the three companies that are going on duty on the Sabbath—a third of you guarding the royal palace, [6]a third at the Sur Gate, and a third at the gate behind the guard, who take turns guarding the temple—[7]and you who are in the other two companies that normally go off Sabbath duty are all to guard the temple for the king. [8]Station yourselves around the king, each of you with weapon in hand. Anyone who approaches your ranks is to be put to death. Stay close to the king wherever he goes."

[9]The commanders of units of a hundred did just as Jehoiada the priest ordered. Each one took his men—those who were going on duty on the Sabbath and those who were going off duty—and came to Jehoiada the priest. [10]Then he gave the commanders the spears and shields that had belonged to King David and that were in the temple of the Lord. [11]The guards, each with weapon in hand, stationed themselves around the king—near the altar and the temple, from the south side to the north side of the temple.

[12]Jehoiada brought out the king's son and put the crown on him; he

presented him with a copy of the covenant and proclaimed him king.
They anointed him, and the people clapped their hands and shouted,
"Long live the king!"

[13]When Athaliah heard the noise made by the guards and the people,
she went to the people at the temple of the LORD. [14]She looked and there
was the king, standing by the pillar, as the custom was. The officers and
the trumpeters were beside the king, and all the people of the land were
rejoicing and blowing trumpets. Then Athaliah tore her robes and called
out, "Treason! Treason!"

[15]Jehoiada the priest ordered the commanders of units of a hundred,
who were in charge of the troops: "Bring her out between the ranks and
put to the sword anyone who follows her." For the priest had said, "She
must not be put to death in the temple of the LORD." [16]So they seized her
as she reached the place where the horses enter the palace grounds, and
there she was put to death.

[17]Jehoiada then made a covenant between the LORD and the king and
people that they would be the LORD's people. He also made a covenant
between the king and the people. [18]All the people of the land went to the
temple of Baal and tore it down. They smashed the altars and idols to
pieces and killed Mattan the priest of Baal in front of the altars.

Then Jehoiada the priest posted guards at the temple of the LORD. [19]He
took with him the commanders of hundreds, the Carites, the guards and
all the people of the land, and together they brought the king down from
the temple of the LORD and went into the palace, entering by way of the
gate of the guards. The king then took his place on the royal throne. [20]All
the people of the land rejoiced, and the city was calm, because Athaliah
had been slain with the sword at the palace.

[21]Joash was seven years old when he began to reign.

[12:1]In the seventh year of Jehu, Joash became king, and he reigned
in Jerusalem forty years. His mother's name was Zibiah; she was from
Beersheba. [2]Joash did what was right in the eyes of the LORD all the years
Jehoiada the priest instructed him. [3]The high places, however, were not
removed; the people continued to offer sacrifices and burn incense there.

[4]Joash said to the priests, "Collect all the money that is brought as
sacred offerings to the temple of the LORD—the money collected in the
census, the money received from personal vows and the money brought
voluntarily to the temple. [5]Let every priest receive the money from

one of the treasurers, then use it to repair whatever damage is found in the temple."

6But by the twenty-third year of King Joash the priests still had not repaired the temple. 7Therefore King Joash summoned Jehoiada the priest and the other priests and asked them, "Why aren't you repairing the damage done to the temple? Take no more money from your treasurers, but hand it over for repairing the temple." 8The priests agreed that they would not collect any more money from the people and that they would not repair the temple themselves.

9Jehoiada the priest took a chest and bored a hole in its lid. He placed it beside the altar, on the right side as one enters the temple of the Lord. The priests who guarded the entrance put into the chest all the money that was brought to the temple of the Lord. 10Whenever they saw that there was a large amount of money in the chest, the royal secretary and the high priest came, counted the money that had been brought into the temple of the Lord and put it into bags. 11When the amount had been determined, they gave the money to the men appointed to supervise the work on the temple. With it they paid those who worked on the temple of the Lord—the carpenters and builders, 12the masons and stonecutters. They purchased timber and blocks of dressed stone for the repair of the temple of the Lord, and met all the other expenses of restoring the temple.

13The money brought into the temple was not spent for making silver basins, wick trimmers, sprinkling bowls, trumpets or any other articles of gold or silver for the temple of the Lord; 14it was paid to the workers, who used it to repair the temple. 15They did not require an accounting from those to whom they gave the money to pay the workers, because they acted with complete honesty. 16The money from the guilt offerings and sin offerings was not brought into the temple of the Lord; it belonged to the priests.

17About this time Hazael king of Aram went up and attacked Gath and captured it. Then he turned to attack Jerusalem. 18But Joash king of Judah took all the sacred objects dedicated by his predecessors—Jehoshaphat, Jehoram and Ahaziah, the kings of Judah—and the gifts he himself had dedicated and all the gold found in the treasuries of the temple of the Lord and of the royal palace, and he sent them to Hazael king of Aram, who then withdrew from Jerusalem.

19As for the other events of the reign of Joash, and all he did, are they not written in the book of the annals of the kings of Judah? [20]His officials conspired against him and assassinated him at Beth Millo, on the road down to Silla. [21]The officials who murdered him were Jozabad son of Shimeath and Jehozabad son of Shomer. He died and was buried with his ancestors in the City of David. And Amaziah his son succeeded him as king.

Listening to the Text in the Story: Biblical Texts: 1 Kings 11; 2 Kings 3:2; 6:25; 9; 10:25–27; 15:20; 18:4; 23:1–25; Ancient Near Eastern Text: The Temple of Yahweh Ostracon

Rebellion, reformation, and reparation characterized the reign of righteous Joash. In the narrative of his reign (2 Kgs 11–12), three other characters play significant roles: Queen Athaliah and the husband-and-wife team who orchestrate her downfall, Jehoiada and Jehosheba. Parallels of three events from this chapter were examined earlier in this commentary. Athaliah purges the royal family to eliminate rivals (11:1; see Chapter 26 for the discussion of royal purges in 2 Kgs 9); Joash is anointed by the people (11:12; see again Chapter 26 for the discussion of royal anointing in 2 Kgs 9); Athaliah tears her garments when Joash is declared king (11:14; see Chapter 9 for a discussion of garment rending in 1 Kgs 11). The unique aspect of Athaliah's slaughter is that it included her own sons and grandsons.

The chapter begins with Athaliah's rebellion, and it ends with rebellion as Joash is assassinated by several of his officials (2 Kgs 11:1; 12:20). While the Northern Kingdom experienced more dynastic chaos than their neighbors to the south, there were just as many rebellions against the house of David (eight rebellions, led by Absalom, Sheba, Adonijah, Jeroboam I, Athaliah, Jehoash's servants, and Amon's servants) as there were against northern rulers (eight rebellions, led by Baasha, Zimri, Omri, Jehu, Shallum, Menahem, Pekah, and Hoshea). However, the eight southern rebellions were extended over a longer period of time, and half of them occurred before the divided monarchy.

After the death of Athaliah, the priest Jehoiada led the people of Judah to reestablish a covenant with YHWH, then they tore down the temple and altars of Baal and killed Mattan, the priest of Baal (11:17–18). Several rulers in the book of Kings instituted similar religious reforms. Jehoram of Israel removed the sacred stone of Baal (3:2). Jehu of Israel slaughtered the worshipers of Baal and destroyed the sacred stone and temple of Baal (10:25–27). Hezekiah of

Judah removed the high places, smashed the sacred stones, cut down the sacred poles, and broke up the bronze serpent (18:4). Josiah of Judah undertook the most extensive reforms as he broke down altars (including Jeroboam's at Bethel) and high places, killed their priests, reinstituted the Passover, and put away mediums and wizards (23:1–25).

Because the priests were not making progress on repairing the temple, Joash sets up a way for the people to directly fund the renovation project. Similarly, in the wilderness Moses established a way for the people to donate to the construction of the tabernacle with gifts of not only precious metals but also precious wood, coverings, and stones (Exod 25:1–7; 35:20–29). An ostracon (an inscribed potsherd) that has been dated to the period of Josiah describes a donation for Yahweh's temple: "As 'Ashyahu[1] the king has commanded you to give in the hand of Zacharyahu silver of Tarshish for the house of Yahweh: three shekels."[2] Three shekels would be a rather modest gift; during the Samarian famine, five shekels bought a cab of seed pods (6:25), and when Menahem taxed the wealthy Israelites he required a payment of fifty shekels (15:20).

Athaliah's Reign and Jehoiada's Rebellion (2 Kings 11:1–21)

In the patriarchal world of the Old Testament, only one female, Athaliah, manages to attain the throne over either Israel or Judah. Unlike the wise and righteous prophetic judge Deborah (Judg 4:4), who led Israel during the period of the judges, Athaliah was foolish and wicked. Athaliah was the daughter of Israel's rulers, Ahab and Jezebel, and she married Jehoshaphat's son, Jehoram, to cement a political alliance between the Northern and Southern Kingdoms. She seized power in Judah for six years by killing off her sons and grandsons (probably from Jehoram's other wives) when she discovers her son, Ahaziah, was killed by Jehu (2 Kgs 9:27). Her brother, Joram, was also killed by Jehu (9:24). Nothing can excuse Athaliah's brutal family slaughter here, but she must have been in a state of deep mourning not only for her son and brother, who were just executed by Jehu, but also for her husband, who had recently passed away (8:24–26).

Athaliah's reign was limited to six years by the clever and risky plan of

1. K. Lawson Younger speculates that the ruler 'Ashyahu could be an inverted form of the name of Joash of Judah (*COS* 2, 174–75, note 3).

2. *COS* 2:174.

Jehosheba and Jehoiada (11:2–12). Jehosheba was the daughter of Athaliah's husband King Jehoram, presumably by another wife.[3] The Chronicler records that Jehosheba was the wife of the priest Jehoiada (2 Chr 22:11). While Athaliah is killing her own family, Jehosheba rescues one-year-old Joash and hides him in the temple. Presumably Jehoram had sufficient children for the absence of one to not be noticed.

As priest in charge of the temple, Jehoiada, along with his wife Jehosheba, raised young Joash, and therefore could be considered traitors (from the perspective of Athaliah) or patriots (from the perspective of the Davidic lineage). Keeping a child, particularly one with royal lineage, hidden in Jerusalem would not have been simple, but fortunately for young Joash, the queen never seemed to visit the temple, another indication of her lack of a concern for YHWH. Joash's interest in the condition of the temple, evidenced in his extensive reforms, must have been established during the years he lived there as a boy.

When Joash was seven his guardians decided it was time to retake the throne (2 Kgs 11:4). As priest, Jehoiada had authority to issue orders to the military commanders, the Carites, and the guards. There are no hints of resistance as Jehoiada sets up his scheme (vv. 5–8), suggesting that the people and the military were not supportive of Athaliah's reign, perhaps because she was foreign (half-Israelite from Ahab and half-Phoenician from Jezebel) or because of the brutal manner she seized power.

Athaliah's earlier rebellion is narrated briefly in one verse (v. 1), while this counter-rebellion is narrated in thirteen verses (vv. 4–16), suggesting that the biblical authors were more interested in how Athaliah lost power than in how she gained it. The description of Jehoiada's plan is elaborate and confusing at points, but four general observations can be stated about the narrative of Joash's transition from hidden boy to reigning king.

First, Jehoiada was the primary force ensuring the success of this rebellion. He organized the temple guards and told them precisely what to do, and he had sufficient authority for them to diligently follow his directions (vv. 4–11). He established covenants with the guards and the people (vv. 4, 12, 17). He presented Joash publicly, set the crown on his head, and declared him to be king (v. 12). He also commanded that the usurper Athaliah be killed (v. 15).

Second, the temple played a crucial role in Joash's rebellion and reign. In the narrative of Joash's reign, the text makes nineteen references to "the temple of the LORD" (*bet yhwh*; vv. 3, 4, 7, 13, 15, 18; 12:4 [2x], 9 [2x], 10, 11 [2x],

---

3. Cogan and Tadmor think Jehosheba was Athaliah's own daughter (*II Kings*, 126), but this is unlikely since the text never links them.

12, 13 [2x], 14, 17, 19). The temple was where Joash was hidden, where he became king, and where he focused his efforts during his reign.

Third, the young king needed to be kept safe until he was no longer in danger (11:7, 8). From the moment when he was revealed as Ahaziah's last surviving son until he was firmly established on the throne, he was extremely vulnerable. The covenant that Jehoiada established with the guards was one way to protect the young king. Jehoiada's decision to stage the coup during the changing of the guard meant that there were five separate companies of guards protecting young Joash (instead of the two or three normally on duty).

Fourth, support for the rebellion was widespread, beyond the primary instigators, and included the commanders, the guards, and the people of the land.[4] No one offered any resistance, but when Jehoiada pronounced Joash as king, they eagerly anointed him, clapped for him, and declared, "Long live the king!" (v. 12; see also 1 Sam 10:24; 2 Sam 16:16; 1 Kgs 1:25, 34, 39). In contrast, Athaliah's cry of "Treason! Treason!" (2 Kgs 11:14) fell on deaf ears. When Jehoiada commanded her to be killed, the guards eagerly obeyed (vv. 15–16).

Just as after Jehu's rebellion he tore down the northern temple of Baal (10:27), so now only a few years later the people of the land tear down the southern temple of Baal, smashing its altars and idols and killing the priest Mattan (11:19). In contrast to the bloody rebellions of Jehu and Athaliah, Joash's coup only results in two deaths (one queen and one priest). After Athaliah is killed, seven-year-old Joash takes his place on the throne, the people rejoice, and the city is calm (vv. 19–21).[5]

Joash's Reign and Repairs (2 Kings 12:1–16)

The regnal formula for Joash (12:1–3) was typical for southern rulers, but three features are noteworthy. First, Joash was the youngest ruler of Judah, coming to power at age seven (11:21), beating out Josiah, who was eight when he took the throne (22:1). Second, Joash's forty-year reign was the fourth longest for a southern ruler (12:1). Third, Joash's righteous regnal evaluation was unusual, not because it was qualified (12:3; see the evaluations of Asa, Jehoshaphat, Amaziah, Azariah and Jotham) but because his piety was explicitly connected to the instruction of an individual, Jehoiada (v. 2). Jehoiada's positive influence in the life of Joash reminds us how important it is for people who come into

4. The phrase "all the people of the land" (*kol-'am ha'arets*) appears four times here (11:14, 18, 19, 20), and they appear to be a distinct group who have sufficient authority to legitimize the rebellion.

5. The Hebrew Masoretic Text begins chapter 12, where English Bibles have 11:21.

positions of power at a young age to be mentored by older leaders who can impart wisdom about how to pursue God faithfully.

Joash is best known for his temple reparations. We do not know if the repairs were necessary because of abuse suffered during the six-year reign of Athaliah or merely because there was a pattern of neglect over the century or so since Solomon completed the temple. The word for "repair" (*hazaq*) is literally "strengthen," and it appears seven times here (12:5, 6, 7, 8, 12 [2x], 14). The word for "damage" (*bedeq*), which could be translated literally as "crack," also appears seven times in the Hebrew (12:5 [2x], 6, 7 [2x], 8, 12).

While the narrative of Solomon's project details the construction of the building itself and the contents (1 Kgs 6–7), the text here does not provide detailed information about which parts of the temple were repaired. It emphasizes what was not done. No temple repairs happened until after Joash's twenty-third year (2 Kgs 12:6), a delay that warranted a rebuke from Joash (v. 7). The priests agreed to not do the repairs themselves (v. 8). The donations were not used to repair or construct precious items of silver and gold (v. 13).

The text does describe how the money was raised. No gifts came from guilt or sin offerings, since those belonged to the priests (v. 16). The initial gifts designated for repairs came from several sources: sacred offerings, the census, personal vows, and voluntary donations (v. 4). After Joash rebuked the priests, a new system was implemented with a chest with a hole on top into which people could drop their coins (like a large piggy bank), which was emptied into bags after it filled up (vv. 9–10).

The text also records how the money was spent. The filled money bags were given to the building supervisors, who paid the wages of the carpenters, builders, masons, and stonecutters (v. 11). They used the offerings to purchase timber, stone, and other supplies. While the priests did not use the earlier gifts as they were intended, the temple workers acted with so much integrity that bookkeeping was unnecessary (vv. 15–16).

Hazael's Threat and Joash's Death (2 Kings 12:17–21)

Just as Solomon the builder of the temple ended his reign poorly (1 Kgs 11), Joash the renovator of the temple ended poorly. After taking territory from the Northern Kingdom (2 Kgs 10:32–33), Hazael of Aram attacked and captured the Philistine city of Gath, then he turned his attention toward Jerusalem (12:17). Hazael's attacks against Israel and Judah were prophesied by Elijah and Elisha (1 Kgs 19:17; 2 Kgs 8:12). In response to the threat, Joash followed the example of Asa and looted the temple to bribe Hazael to withdraw (1 Kgs 15:18; 2 Kgs 12:18). Joash's tribute must have been substantial, since it included sacred objects dedicated not only by Joash, but also by his predecessors (Jehoshaphat, Jehoram, and Ahaziah; v. 18). While the text does not explicitly condemn Joash's behavior here, treaties with foreign nations were generally condemned (Deut 7:2; Josh 9; Isa 31:1; Jer 2:36–37; Hos 7:11). And Joash was not taxing the people to pay a foreign tribute like Menahem of Israel (2 Kgs 15:20), but he was taking gifts dedicated to YHWH and giving them to foreign powers to secure their assistance, an act of idolatry.

The most interesting bit of information from Joash's final regnal notice (12:19–21) concerns the scheme orchestrated by his servants to assassinate him (v. 20). Literally, they "conspired" (*qashar*) a "conspiracy" (*qesher*), as both verb and noun forms of the same root are used. Thus begins a series of conspiratorial royal assassinations: Amaziah of Judah by a group of conspirators (14:19), Zechariah of Israel by Shallum (15:10), Shallum of Israel by Menahem (15:14), Pekahiah of Israel by Pekah (15:25), Pekah of Israel by Hoshea (15:30), Amon of Judah by his own servants (21:23). Unlike northern conspiracies, each of the southern kings was succeeded by his heir. The narrative here suggests that Joash was killed because he looted the treasury to buy off Hazael, but Chronicles states that his officials killed him because Joash condemned Zechariah, the son of Jehoiada, to death, because he rebuked the king for rejecting YHWH (2 Chr 24:20–25).

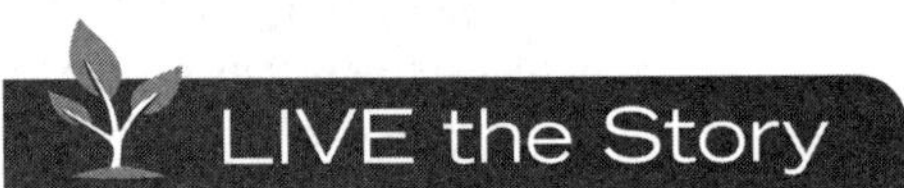

Divine Sovereignty

The story of Athaliah's purge of the Judean royal family may not seem one of the most significant events of the Old Testament, but the implications were potentially catastrophic, since the royal dynasty of David was almost completely cut off. After Jehu slaughtered forty-two of Ahaziah's relatives (2 Kgs 10:12–14), Athaliah killed the remaining members of the royal family, all except young Joash. Thus, David's "eternal" dynasty was nearly exterminated in the eighth generation. Josephus explicitly states that Athaliah intended to cut off the Davidic line.[6]

YHWH promised that David's descendants would rule for ever (2 Sam 7:12–16). But YHWH also declared that all male descendants of Ahab would be killed (1 Kgs 21:20–26; 2 Kgs 9:7–10), and the royal houses of David and Ahab had been intertwined since Jehoram, son of Jehoshaphat of Judah,

---

6. *Ant.* 9.7.1.

married Athaliah, daughter of Ahab of Israel (8:18, 26).[7] Thus, there was a conflict between the judgment to kill all Ahabite males and the promise that Davidides would continue to reign.[8] Joash was a descendant of both David and Ahab. A compromise within the text resolves these two conflicting oracles by having all of Jehoram's sons killed except the infant Joash. David's line survived, but only by a single thread.

While YHWH's role in this story is not made explicit in the narrative, one can perceive divine sovereignty behind the actions of Jehosheba and Jehoiada as they protect and promote young Joash, ensuring that David's legacy continues. For the six years that Athaliah was in power, it appeared that the Davidic dynasty was going to be extinguished. Yet God had a plan to take a boy, who should have been killed by the ruler of Jerusalem, and to make him king over his people.

We see God's sovereign hand at work in the lives of two other important leaders in Israel's history who, like Joash, experienced dramatic deliverances as infants from the threat of death by a ruler in power. Moses was rescued from Pharaoh by a group of women, including Moses's mother, sister, and Pharaoh's daughter (Exod 2:1–10). Jesus, the descendant of Joash, was protected from King Herod when his family traveled to Egypt after his father was warned in a dream (Matt 2:13–15).[9] Jesus's story continues to overlap with that of Joash, as he also spent a lot of time as a boy in the temple (Luke 2:49). Jesus also was involved in temple "renovations," as he predicted that after the temple of his body was to be destroyed (on the cross), he would raise it up after three days (John 2:19). And all of this was part of God's sovereign plan.

The Wise Use of Money

The wise use of money is a significant theme of 2 Kings 12. To illustrate the positive and negative ways, the text focuses on four distinct groups of people. First, the people give expecting their donations to be used for the intended purpose of repairing the temple. They give initially, and they continue to give—even when Jehoiada implements a new system using the slotted chest. From the people we see a positive example of consistent generosity.

Second, the priests don't spend the people's contributions as they were intended. We don't know what the priests were using the money for, but after Joash had ruled for twenty-three years, no repairs had been made, undermining

7. For a longer discussion of Davidic dynastic oracles, see Lamb, "The Eternal Curse."

8. The Ahabite judgment primarily targets the reigning Israelite dynasty, but the sons of Jehoram and Athaliah were also condemned by the ban against all of Ahab's male descendants.

9. Joash is one of three Judean rulers omitted from Jesus's genealogy (Matt 1:8).

trust among donors; this could have resulted in a reduction in donations. One would expect the priests to be more diligent, but their lackadaisical attitude prompts a rebuke from Joash and a loss of responsibility. From the negative example of the priests, we see a need to be diligent with money and to make sure donor requests are being honored in the implementation process.

Third, in contrast to the priests, the construction workers act with honesty, so much so that no bookkeeping was necessary. Presumably, witnesses to the renovations thought that work was being done in a timely and proficient manner. While not requiring accounting is not generally a good idea (human depravity), in this case it highlights the integrity of these workers. From the construction workers we see a great example of serving God with our skills and doing so to the best of our abilities.

Fourth, Joash doesn't trust God when threatened by Aram and uses the temple treasury to bribe Hazael. While the people and the workers trusted God with their money and their time, the leader of the nation panicked and essentially stole money from God's house, handing it over to Judah's enemy. From the negative example of Joash, we are reminded that even though it can sometimes be costly to wait on God, we know he can be trusted.

CHAPTER 29

2 Kings 13:1–25

LISTEN to the Story

[1]In the twenty-third year of Joash son of Ahaziah king of Judah, Jehoahaz son of Jehu became king of Israel in Samaria, and he reigned seventeen years. [2]He did evil in the eyes of the LORD by following the sins of Jeroboam son of Nebat, which he had caused Israel to commit, and he did not turn away from them. [3]So the LORD's anger burned against Israel, and for a long time he kept them under the power of Hazael king of Aram and Ben-Hadad his son.

[4]Then Jehoahaz sought the LORD's favor, and the LORD listened to him, for he saw how severely the king of Aram was oppressing Israel. [5]The LORD provided a deliverer for Israel, and they escaped from the power of Aram. So the Israelites lived in their own homes as they had before. [6]But they did not turn away from the sins of the house of Jeroboam, which he had caused Israel to commit; they continued in them. Also, the Asherah pole remained standing in Samaria.

[7]Nothing had been left of the army of Jehoahaz except fifty horsemen, ten chariots and ten thousand foot soldiers, for the king of Aram had destroyed the rest and made them like the dust at threshing time.

[8]As for the other events of the reign of Jehoahaz, all he did and his achievements, are they not written in the book of the annals of the kings of Israel? [9]Jehoahaz rested with his ancestors and was buried in Samaria. And Jehoash his son succeeded him as king.

[10]In the thirty-seventh year of Joash king of Judah, Jehoash son of Jehoahaz became king of Israel in Samaria, and he reigned sixteen years. [11]He did evil in the eyes of the LORD and did not turn away from any of the sins of Jeroboam son of Nebat, which he had caused Israel to commit; he continued in them.

[12]As for the other events of the reign of Jehoash, all he did and his achievements, including his war against Amaziah king of Judah, are they

not written in the book of the annals of the kings of Israel? [13]Jehoash rested with his ancestors, and Jeroboam succeeded him on the throne. Jehoash was buried in Samaria with the kings of Israel.

[14]Now Elisha had been suffering from the illness from which he died. Jehoash king of Israel went down to see him and wept over him. "My father! My father!" he cried. "The chariots and horsemen of Israel!"

[15]Elisha said, "Get a bow and some arrows," and he did so. [16]"Take the bow in your hands," he said to the king of Israel. When he had taken it, Elisha put his hands on the king's hands.

[17]"Open the east window," he said, and he opened it. "Shoot!" Elisha said, and he shot. "The LORD's arrow of victory, the arrow of victory over Aram!" Elisha declared. "You will completely destroy the Arameans at Aphek."

[18]Then he said, "Take the arrows," and the king took them. Elisha told him, "Strike the ground." He struck it three times and stopped. [19]The man of God was angry with him and said, "You should have struck the ground five or six times; then you would have defeated Aram and completely destroyed it. But now you will defeat it only three times."

[20]Elisha died and was buried.

Now Moabite raiders used to enter the country every spring. [21]Once while some Israelites were burying a man, suddenly they saw a band of raiders; so they threw the man's body into Elisha's tomb. When the body touched Elisha's bones, the man came to life and stood up on his feet.

[22]Hazael king of Aram oppressed Israel throughout the reign of Jehoahaz. [23]But the LORD was gracious to them and had compassion and showed concern for them because of his covenant with Abraham, Isaac and Jacob. To this day he has been unwilling to destroy them or banish them from his presence.

[24]Hazael king of Aram died, and Ben-Hadad his son succeeded him as king. [25]Then Jehoash son of Jehoahaz recaptured from Ben-Hadad son of Hazael the towns he had taken in battle from his father Jehoahaz. Three times Jehoash defeated him, and so he recovered the Israelite towns.

Listening to the Text in the Story: Biblical Texts: Genesis 9:8–17; 15:17–21; 17:1–14; Exodus 24:3–8; Joshua 24:1–28; Judges 2:11–18; 3:7–15; 4:1–3; 2 Samuel 7:1–17; 1 Kings 12:25–33; 14:15, 23; 15:13; 16:33; 18:19; 2 Kings 2:12; 9–10; 23:4; Ancient Near Eastern Texts: The Royal Inscriptions of Adad-nirari III of Assyria

After two chapters focusing on the Southern Kingdom, the narrative shifts back to the Northern Kingdom, recording the reigns of Jehu's royal successors, Jehoahaz and Jehoash. Despite their evil evaluations, their narratives portray them both surprisingly favorably.[1] Jehoahaz prays and is sent a deliverer. Jehoash visits the ailing Elisha, shows compassion toward the prophet, and is rewarded with victory in battle over Aram. Both rulers have relatively long reigns.

They also both share names with Judean counterparts. One of Josiah's sons, also named Jehoahaz, ruled over Judah (2 Kgs 23:30–31). Jehoash of Israel came to power toward the end of the reign of Jehoash of Judah (13:10), and both of these rulers were also sometimes called Joash. In an attempt to reduce the confusion, this commentary consistently calls the southern ruler Joash and the northern ruler Jehoash.

The story of Jehoahaz has many elements of the cyclical pattern found throughout the book of Judges. The sins of the people (Judg 2:11; 3:7, 12; 4:1; 2 Kgs 13:2) cause the anger of YHWH to be kindled against them (Judg 2:14; 3:8; 2 Kgs 13:3). YHWH gives the people into the hands of their enemies (Judg 2:14; 3:8, 12; 4:2; 2 Kgs 13:3). The people of Israel cry to YHWH for help (Judg 2:18; 3:9, 15; 4:3; 2 Kgs 13:4), so he sends a deliverer to rescue them from their oppressors (Judg 2:16; 3:9, 15; 2 Kgs 13:5).[2] For many of us, we are unfortunately like the Israelites from the time of Judges and of Jehoahaz and only seek out divine assistance when things are desperate.

The text details Jehu's efforts to eliminate idolatrous practices (2 Kgs 9–10), but as was often the case in Kings, syncretistic practices and worship of other gods quickly reemerge after reforms. Worship at the altars set up at Dan and Bethel by Jeroboam (1 Kgs 12:25–33) continued during the reign of Jehu's son, Jehoahaz. The "sins of Jeroboam" are emphasized, as they are mentioned both in Jehoahaz's initial regnal formula (2 Kgs 13:2) and in the middle of his narrative (v. 6). Additionally, Asherah worship persisted during this time. Asherah was a Canaanite goddess, considered the consort of the Canaanite god El, and she was worshiped in both kingdoms during the period of the monarchy. The Hebrew word, *'asherah*, can refer to either the goddess (e.g., 1 Kgs 18:19; 2 Kgs 23:4) or the pole associated with her worship (e.g., 1 Kgs 14:15, 23; 15:13; 16:33).

When Jehoash goes to visit the dying prophet Elisha, he exclaims "My father! My father! . . . The chariots and horsemen of Israel!" (2 Kgs 13:14),

1. For a longer discussion of Jehoahaz and Jehoash, see "Jehu's Evil Heirs" in Lamb, *Righteous Jehu*, 155–205.

2. Wray Beal frames her discussion of this section as an analysis of the Judges paradigm, see *1 & 2 Kings*, 408–9.

which are the identical words that Elisha declared as his master Elijah was taken up into heaven (2:12). Since the text merely says "and he said" (*wayyōʾmar*), Wiseman thinks the words may have come not from the king but from the prophet anticipating death, which is possible but not likely.

To explain why YHWH does not use Aram to destroy the Northern Kingdom, the narrator mentions his compassion because of the covenant between YHWH and Abraham, Isaac, and Jacob (13:23). The only other place these three patriarchs are mentioned in Kings is when Elijah is praying on Mount Carmel (1 Kgs 18:36). YHWH had established his covenant with Abraham, that he would give him the land of Canaan and many descendants (Gen 15:17–21; 17:1–14). The theme of covenant is significant in Scripture as God established covenants at key moments in Israel's history (with Noah: Gen 9:8–17; with Moses: Exod 24:3–8; with Joshua: Josh 24:1–28; with David: 2 Sam 7:1–17). More recently, the priest Jehoiada established a covenant between YHWH, the people, and Joash of Judah (2 Kgs 11:17). The "lamp oracles" repeatedly explain why YHWH had not yet destroyed the Southern Kingdom (1 Kgs 11:36; 15:4; 2 Kgs 8:19), but this explanation for the Northern Kingdom's divine protection is unique. However, both of these protective oracles will eventually expire, as Israel is destroyed by Assyria (17:5–18) and Judah by Babylon (25:1–21).

Several royal inscriptions from the reign of Adad-nirari III of Assyria relate to the reigns of Jehoahaz and Jehoash of Israel. In the Tell al-Rimah Stela, Adad-nirari boasts about his military exploits and how he received tribute from various rulers, including from Jehoash of Israel (spelled Joash here).

> I mustered my chariots, troops and camps; I ordered them to mark to the land of Hatti. In a single year, I subdued the entire lands of Amurru and Hatti. I imposed upon them tax and tribute forever. I received 2,000 talents of silver, 1,000 talents of copper, 2,000 talents of iron, 3,000 linen garments with multi-colored trim—the tribute of Mari of the land of Damascus. I received the tribute of Joash the Samarian, of the Tyrian ruler, and of the Sidonian ruler.[3]

Another inscription from Adad-nirari's royal annals (the Calah Orthostat Slab) records the same campaign and many of the same tributaries, mentioning Israel and many of its neighbors, but not Jehoash, by name.[4]

---

3. *COS* 2:276a.
4. *COS* 2:276.

An Evil Praying King: Jehoahaz of Israel (2 Kings 13:1–9)

Jehoahaz, the son of Jehu, came to power in the twenty-third year of Joash of Judah's reign. He reigned seventeen years, the sixth longest for Israelite kings. His name means "YHWH has grasped." The section of Jehoahaz's narrative that does not consist of regnal formulaic material is extremely short (13:4–7). YHWH punishes Israel for their idolatrous worship practices by giving them over to Aram. As was prophesied both by YHWH (to Elijah) and by Elisha, Hazael and his son, Ben-Hadad (III), oppressed Israel from the time of Jehu through the reigns of his successors.

In response to this Aramean oppression, "Jehoahaz sought the Lord's favor" (*wayehal yeho'ahaz 'et-pene yhwh*), language similar to Jeroboam's request to the anonymous man of God to pray for his withered hand (1 Kgs 13:6). The text leaves the identity of Jehoahaz's deliverer uncertain, which has allowed scholars to speculate options: Jehoash of Israel, Elisha, or Jeroboam II of Israel.[5] The text speaks of Jehoahaz's prayer being answered promptly, since the people were allowed to return to their homes (literally, "tents"; *'aholehem*; v. 5), which undermines the idea of a delayed deliverance during the reigns of either Jehoash or Jeroboam. Within the context of this narrative, the most reasonable deliverer for Jehoash is therefore Adad-nirari III of Assyria since, toward the end of Jehoahaz's reign, he attacked Aram. Adad-nirari's campaign would have diverted Aram's attention away from Israel and toward the north. From the perspective of the text, Adad-nirari would play a similar role to Cyrus (Isa 45:1), as a foreign ruler who accomplishes a divinely appointed task. If the deliverer were one of these other characters the text has already named, there is no reason not to name them as the deliverer. However, it makes sense to keep Adad-nirari anonymous, since he never is mentioned in the Hebrew Bible.

Before concluding Jehoahaz's reign in the typical formulaic manner, the text notes that Jehoahaz's army has been reduced to fifty horsemen, ten chariots, and ten thousand foot soldiers due to the Aramean oppression (2 Kgs 13:7). According to the Kurkh Monolith of Shalmaneser III of Assyria, Ahab had two thousand chariots and ten thousand soldiers,[6] so even though the number of Israelite soldiers has not changed since Ahab, the number of chariots has been drastically reduced (99.5 percent).

---

5. For references to scholars who advocate for these perspectives, see Lamb, *Righteous Jehu*, 181–82, and Wray Beal, *1 & 2 Kings*, 408.

6. *COS* 2:263; see also "Ahab, Son of Omri" in Chapter 13 for a discussion of 1 Kgs 16:29–34.

Only Formula for Jehoash of Israel (2 Kings 13:10–13)

Jehoash, the grandson of Jehu, came to power in the thirty-seventh year of Joash of Judah. He reigned sixteen years, the seventh longest for Israelite kings. Typically, a ruler's narrative begins with a formulaic introduction, followed by narrative material, then ends with a formulaic conclusion. Jehoash's concluding death notice has two unusual features. First, it appears in the narrative immediately after his initial notice (13:12–13), before recording his interaction with Elisha (vv. 14–21). Jehoash features prominently in the narratives of Elisha's death (vv. 14–21) and of Amaziah's battle with Israel (14:8–14), but thus far his narrative is all regnal formula.

Second, his formulaic conclusion is repeated, almost verbatim, after the narrative of Jehoash's defeat of Amaziah of Judah (vv. 15–16). Scholars speculate reasons for these unusual aspects, but none of them are particularly compelling.[7] Perhaps Jehoash's narrative is closed prematurely to highlight the dramatic ending of the life of the great prophet Elisha. Like other regnal conclusions, Jehoash's alludes to other events from his reign not recorded in Kings, which for Jehoash would include his tribute to Adad-nirari III, as recorded in the Assyrian royal inscriptions.

The Illness, Death, and Magical Bones of Elisha (2 Kings 13:14–21)

After a ministry that spanned the reigns of six northern rulers (Ahab, Ahaziah, Jehoram, Jehu, Jehoahaz, and Jehoash) and lasted almost sixty years (starting in 1 Kgs 19:16–21), the prophet Elisha is about to die (2 Kgs 13:14). The text records no details regarding his ailment or location, merely that Jehoash came for a visit and greeted the prophet with the same expression that the prophet used to bid farewell to his own master, Elijah (2:12). The outburst reveals both the king's respect for Elisha and his lament that the prophet who had aided (and condemned) so many Israelite rulers will soon be gone.

Elisha has no interest in reminiscing or wallowing in his illness, but he immediately started giving orders to his king, specifically to obtain a bow and arrows (13:15). The prophets Jeremiah and Ezekiel often used symbolic acts involving props (e.g., a loin cloth, an iron yoke, a brick) to illustrate their points (e.g., Jer 13:1–11; 18:1–11; 19:1–15; Ezek 4:1–17; 5:1–12).[8] Similarly, Elisha uses weapons of war here to symbolize a military victory. Once Jehoash has obeyed and has taken up the bow, the prophet places his hands on the king's hands (2 Kgs 13:16), presumably to signify his support

---

7. See, for example, Wiseman, *1 & 2 Kings*, 241, 246.

8. The king of Babylon is described in Ezekiel as using arrows as divination for travel directions (Ezek 21:21).

for the ruler's cause. Any of us who teach on a regular basis would do well to follow the example of these prophets to use tangible props (not merely words or PowerPoint presentations) to dramatically illustrate our points and make them more memorable.

Elisha's prediction has two parts. First, Jehoash is directed to shoot an arrow out the east window, which he promptly does as the prophet proclaims victory over Aram at Aphek (v. 17). Aram is generally northeast of Israel, and Aphek is east of the Sea of Galilee, located in the border region between Aram and Israel.

Second, Jehoash is commanded to strike the ground with his arrows, which he does three times (v. 18).[9] Curiously, the prophet becomes angry that Jehoash did not hit the ground more times. The reason for Elisha's harsh response is not clear since the king has repeatedly obeyed the prophet's commands, but presumably a more extreme display of aggression was warranted given the context of a campaign against Israel's enemy the Arameans. Instead of a complete destruction (five or six ground strikes), a partial victory involving only three defeats will occur (v. 19). Elisha's anger reveals a compassionate attitude toward his people; he hoped that they would achieve ultimate deliverance from Aramean oppression.

Immediately after this final declaration, the prophet dies, and yet his miracles continue. When the body of a dead man is thrown onto Elisha's grave, it touches Elisha's bones and the man came back to life and stood up (v. 21).[10] During their lifetimes both Elijah and Elisha had resurrected a boy (1 Kgs 17:17–24; 2 Kgs 4:8–37), but this supernatural event is more bizarre. The image here of the walking dead is reminiscent of Ezekiel's vision of dry bones that come to life after receiving the breath of God (Ezek 37:1–14; "Dem bones, dem bones, gonna walk around . . .").

YHWH's Compassion for Israel (2 Kings 13:22–25)

The chapter concludes with notices regarding Hazael and the Aramean oppression. While the text states this oppression lasted throughout the reign of Jehoahaz (13:22), it is likely that this claim is hyperbolic.[11] The text earlier suggested that Hazael died during Jehoahaz's reign (v. 3), and YHWH had sent a deliverer in response to the prayer of Jehoahaz (v. 5).

9. While Wiseman thinks Jehoash was meant to fire the arrows into the ground (*1 & 2 Kings*, 242), Alter's perspective of beating the arrows on the ground is more reasonable (*Former Prophets*, 793), since it appears that the king is only holding a bunch of arrows in his hand and no bow (13:18).

10. Reformation commentator Johannes Bugenhagen states emphatically that Elisha's bones' resurrection here should not constitute an endorsement of relic veneration; *1–2 Samuel, 1–2 Kings, 1–2 Chronicles*, ed. Derek Cooper and Martin J. Lohrmann, Reformation Commentary on Scripture, Old Testament V (Downers Grove, IL: InterVarsity, 2016), 459–60.

11. See also Wray Beal, *1 & 2 Kings*, 411.

Because of a covenant that dates back to the time of Abraham, YHWH showed compassion on his people and was unwilling to destroy them. The comment "to this day" (v. 23) suggests that at least this section of the narrative was written before the Assyrian conquest of the Northern Kingdom of Israel (17:6).

It is unusual for the text to record the death and succession notice for a Gentile ruler (13:24), but Hazael was the most famous adversary of Israel during the mid-monarchy, mentioned twenty times in the book of Kings, beginning with YHWH's prediction to Elijah (1 Kgs 19:15, 17; 2 Kgs 8:8, 9, 12, 13, 15, 28, 29; 9:14, 15; 10:32; 12:18 [2x], 19, 13:3 [2x], 22, 24, 25). The chapter concludes by recording the three defeats of Ben-Hadad, son of Hazael, by Jehoahaz, just as the prophet Elisha had predicted (13:19, 25).

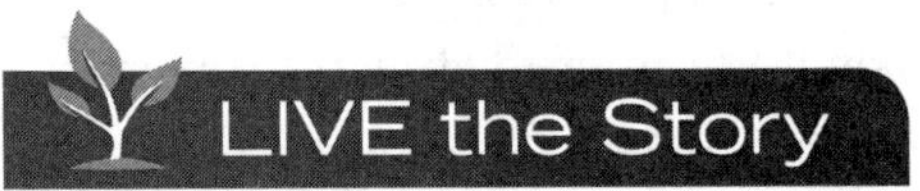

Divine Compassion for an Evil Leader

While this narrative begins with divine anger (2 Kgs 13:3), the theological theme that permeates the chapter is divine compassion. YHWH listens to the prayer of evil Jehoahaz and sends a deliverer to rescue his people (vv. 4–5). Even as Elisha is dying, YHWH allows him to deliver two final messages of hope to Jehoash, another evil ruler (vv. 17, 19), and the narrative ends by noting the fulfillment of these oracles (v. 25). YHWH continues to show compassion for his idolatrous people Israel because he remembers the covenant he established about a thousand years earlier with Abraham, Isaac, and Jacob (v. 23).

It is tempting for any of us who struggle with ongoing sin to give up hope or to think we are beyond the grace of God. Satan would certainly want us to believe that message. This passage reminds us of the good news that, even if we are perceived to be evil, by ourselves or others, God will still listen to our prayers and show us favor in other ways. Jesus used the universal compassion of God to remind his disciples that God "causes his sun to rise on the evil and the good, and sends rain on the righteous and the unrighteous" in his exhortation to love one's enemies (Matt 5:45). Jesus's ministry was characterized by a compassionate and relentless pursuit of sinners and lost sheep (Luke 15:1–7). And the core of the gospel message is that God displays his love for sinners by sending Christ to die for us (Rom 5:8). Yes, the prayers of a righteous man (and woman) "availeth much" (Jas 5:16), but God is so abundantly merciful and compassionate that even unrighteous people's prayers can still "avail" much. Whether we feel holy or unholy, there is nothing that should prevent us from seeking God's favor in prayer.

## CHAPTER 30

2 Kings 14:1–15:7

LISTEN to the Story

1In the second year of Jehoash son of Jehoahaz king of Israel, Amaziah
son of Joash king of Judah began to reign. 2He was twenty-five years old
when he became king, and he reigned in Jerusalem twenty-nine years. His
mother's name was Jehoaddan; she was from Jerusalem. 3He did what was
right in the eyes of the LORD, but not as his father David had done. In
everything he followed the example of his father Joash. 4The high places,
however, were not removed; the people continued to offer sacrifices and
burn incense there.

5After the kingdom was firmly in his grasp, he executed the officials
who had murdered his father the king. 6Yet he did not put the children
of the assassins to death, in accordance with what is written in the Book
of the Law of Moses where the LORD commanded: "Parents are not to be
put to death for their children, nor children put to death for their parents;
each will die for their own sin."

7He was the one who defeated ten thousand Edomites in the Valley
of Salt and captured Sela in battle, calling it Joktheel, the name it has to
this day.

8Then Amaziah sent messengers to Jehoash son of Jehoahaz, the son
of Jehu, king of Israel, with the challenge: "Come, let us face each other
in battle."

9But Jehoash king of Israel replied to Amaziah king of Judah: "A thistle
in Lebanon sent a message to a cedar in Lebanon, 'Give your daughter
to my son in marriage.' Then a wild beast in Lebanon came along and
trampled the thistle underfoot. 10You have indeed defeated Edom and now
you are arrogant. Glory in your victory, but stay at home! Why ask for
trouble and cause your own downfall and that of Judah also?"

11Amaziah, however, would not listen, so Jehoash king of Israel attacked.
He and Amaziah king of Judah faced each other at Beth Shemesh in Judah.

12Judah was routed by Israel, and every man fled to his home. 13Jehoash king of Israel captured Amaziah king of Judah, the son of Joash, the son of Ahaziah, at Beth Shemesh. Then Jehoash went to Jerusalem and broke down the wall of Jerusalem from the Ephraim Gate to the Corner Gate—a section about four hundred cubits long. 14He took all the gold and silver and all the articles found in the temple of the LORD and in the treasuries of the royal palace. He also took hostages and returned to Samaria.

15As for the other events of the reign of Jehoash, what he did and his achievements, including his war against Amaziah king of Judah, are they not written in the book of the annals of the kings of Israel? 16Jehoash rested with his ancestors and was buried in Samaria with the kings of Israel. And Jeroboam his son succeeded him as king.

17Amaziah son of Joash king of Judah lived for fifteen years after the death of Jehoash son of Jehoahaz king of Israel. 18As for the other events of Amaziah's reign, are they not written in the book of the annals of the kings of Judah?

19They conspired against him in Jerusalem, and he fled to Lachish, but they sent men after him to Lachish and killed him there. 20He was brought back by horse and was buried in Jerusalem with his ancestors, in the City of David.

21Then all the people of Judah took Azariah, who was sixteen years old, and made him king in place of his father Amaziah. 22He was the one who rebuilt Elath and restored it to Judah after Amaziah rested with his ancestors.

23In the fifteenth year of Amaziah son of Joash king of Judah, Jeroboam son of Jehoash king of Israel became king in Samaria, and he reigned forty-one years. 24He did evil in the eyes of the LORD and did not turn away from any of the sins of Jeroboam son of Nebat, which he had caused Israel to commit. 25He was the one who restored the boundaries of Israel from Lebo Hamath to the Dead Sea, in accordance with the word of the LORD, the God of Israel, spoken through his servant Jonah son of Amittai, the prophet from Gath Hepher.

26The LORD had seen how bitterly everyone in Israel, whether slave or free, was suffering; there was no one to help them. 27And since the LORD had not said he would blot out the name of Israel from under heaven, he saved them by the hand of Jeroboam son of Jehoash.

28As for the other events of Jeroboam's reign, all he did, and his military achievements, including how he recovered for Israel both Damascus and Hamath, which had belonged to Judah, are they not written in the book of the annals of the kings of Israel? [29]Jeroboam rested with his ancestors, the kings of Israel. And Zechariah his son succeeded him as king.

[15:1]In the twenty-seventh year of Jeroboam king of Israel, Azariah son of Amaziah king of Judah began to reign. [2]He was sixteen years old when he became king, and he reigned in Jerusalem fifty-two years. His mother's name was Jekoliah; she was from Jerusalem. [3]He did what was right in the eyes of the LORD, just as his father Amaziah had done. [4]The high places, however, were not removed; the people continued to offer sacrifices and burn incense there.

[5]The LORD afflicted the king with leprosy until the day he died, and he lived in a separate house. Jotham the king's son had charge of the palace and governed the people of the land.

[6]As for the other events of Azariah's reign, and all he did, are they not written in the book of the annals of the kings of Judah? [7]Azariah rested with his ancestors and was buried near them in the City of David. And Jotham his son succeeded him as king.

Listening to the Text in the Story: Biblical Texts: Judges 9:8–15; 1 Kings 15–16; 17–19; 2 Kings 1–8; 11–12; Hosea; Amos; Jonah; Ancient Near Eastern Texts: The Inscriptions of Tiglath-Pileser III; The Palace of Sennacherib Reliefs of the Siege of Lachish; The Samarian Ostraca; The Shema Servant of Jeroboam Seal

Terence Fretheim states, "Read 1 Kings 15–16 or 2 Kings 15 when you are having trouble getting to sleep."[1] Why are these sections a cure for insomnia? From chapters thirteen to sixteen of 2 Kings, there is a high percentage of regnal formulaic material, with little intervening narrative, making each ruler's section relatively short. The highly formulaic nature of 2 Kings 13–16 is comparable in this regard to 1 Kings 14–16. The narrative also switches back and forth from the north (chapter 13), to the south (14:1–22), to the north (14:23–29), and back to the south (15:1–7), contributing to a sense of textual discontinuity. In contrast, the prophetic narratives of Elijah (1 Kgs 17–19; 2 Kgs 1–2) and Elisha (2 Kgs 2–8) record dramatic stories with familiar characters, which keep our interest.

1. Fretheim, *Kings*, 2.

If you stay awake, you will discover in 2 Kings 14:1–15:7 sophisticated trash talking, a civil war, a northern rout of the south, a plundering of the temple, a conspiratorial assassination, the only appearance of the prophet Jonah outside the book that bears his name, a massive territorial expansion for Israel, and, most significantly, another example of God's amazing compassion for his people. Intrigued? Keep reading.

The most striking aspect of Amaziah's narrative (14:1–22) is the number of parallels between his reign and that of his father, Joash (11:1–12:21). The text makes the comparison between these two rulers explicit, stating that in everything Amaziah followed the example of his father Joash (14:3). Both of their righteous regnal evaluations were qualified, since neither removed the high places (12:3; 14:2–4). Both were defeated by a northern neighbor (Joash by Aram, Amaziah by Israel), who then plundered the temple (12:17–18; 14:11–14). Both were killed in a conspiratorial assassination but were still succeeded on the throne by their own son (12:20–21; 14:19–21).

However, unlike Joash, Amaziah engaged in a civil war with Israel. In response to Amaziah's invitation to battle, Jehoash of Israel tells a fable involving a thistle and a cedar. After his fratricidal brother Abimelech has killed seventy of their brothers, Jotham relates another arboreal fable—involving olive, fig, and cedar trees—as a warning to the lords of Shechem (Judg 9:8–15). Not surprisingly, using images from nature to illustrate a point, even about warfare, was common in the ancient Near East. In one of the Amarna Letters, King Lab'ayu of Shechem writes to Pharaoh, "When an ant is struck, does it not fight back and bite the hand of the man that struck it?"[2]

Perhaps because Amaziah lost to Jehoash of Israel in battle, a group of men conspired against him in Jerusalem. Amaziah's conspirators pursued him to the city of Lachish, located about thirty miles south-west of Jerusalem, where the king was eventually killed (2 Kgs 14:19). We get a glimpse of Lachish in a series of reliefs from the palace of Sennacherib of Assyria (see also Chapter 34 for a discussion of Lachish and Sennacherib in 2 Kings 18).[3]

While we do not know the details, Jeroboam II was more successful in battle than his father, Jehoash. His massive territorial expansion of Israel (14:25, 28) was probably due to the relative weakness of Assyria at this point in their history. We know little of the reigns of the Assyrian kings Shalmaneser IV (783–773 BC), Ashur-dan III (773–755 BC), and Adad-nirari V (755–745 BC), but they appeared to leave Israel alone. This policy would soon

2. Moran, *The Amarna Letters*, 305–6.
3. See images in *ANEP*, 129–32, 293–94; #371–74.

change under Tiglath-Pileser III (see 2 Kgs 15:19, 29; 16:7, 10). Jeroboam's narrative is short, but it focuses on Israel's military success during this period. The patriotic prophet Jonah, who clearly hated the Assyrians (Jonah 1:2–3; 3:4; 4:1–11), lent support to Jeroboam's expansions (2 Kgs 14:25).

Two other prophets, however, took a much more negative view on events during the time of Jeroboam II (Hos 1:1; Amos 1:1; 7:9–11). The books of Hosea and Amos describe the social and economic situation in Israel, where the upper classes thrived at the expense of the poor (similar to our own contemporary situation today). The widespread injustice and oppression that characterized the nation under Jeroboam would be judged by YHWH and end in disaster for Israel: the elimination of the house of Jeroboam (Amos 7:9), death for his people (Amos 8:2–3), and exile for the nation (Amos 9:4). Several ostraca (inscribed potsherds) found in Samaria are dated to the time of Jeroboam II.[4] While they do not provide much information (e.g., #18: "In the tenth year. From Hazeroth to Gaddiyau. A jar of fine oil"), speaking mainly of wine and oil, they generally support the idea that the royal income was expanding under Jeroboam.[5]

The name "Jeroboam" appears in a seal impression (bulla) belonging to a certain "Shema, servant of Jeroboam."[6] While it is difficult to make definitive connections between names on seals and biblical characters, many scholars think Shema's master is Jeroboam II.[7] Most ancient Israelites would not own a seal, but royals and officials needed them to authorize documents. The image on Shema's seal is an impressive roaring lion.[8]

The name "Uzziah" (the alternative name for King Azariah of Judah; 15:1–7) also appears on two seals; one belongs to "Abiah, servant of Uzziah," the other to "Shebaniah, servant of Uzziah."[9] In regard to the seals of Jeroboam and Uzziah, Jeffrey H. Tigay and Alan R. Millard state, "The names of the masters can all be identified with eighth-century kings of Israel and Judah."[10] Some scholars also connect Azariah with a certain individual named "Azriyau," who appears in an Assyrian text from the reign of Tiglath-Pileser III.[11]

---

4. *ANET*, 321.

5. See also *DOTT* 204–8; Wiseman, *1 & 2 Kings*, 248.

6. *COS* 2:200.

7. See Andre Lemaire, "Royal Signature: Name of Israel's Last King Surfaces in a Private Collection," *BAR* 21.6 (1995): 50.

8. *ANEP*, 85, 280; #276.

9. *COS* 2:200.

10. *COS* 2:200.

11. *ANET*, 282–83; *COS* 2:285. For an argument in favor of identifying "Azriyau" with Azariah, see *ZIBBC* 3:168–69; for an argument against this identification, see *COS* 2:285, note 10.

Amaziah of Judah (2 Kings 14:1–22)

The chronological details of Amaziah's reign are curiously identical to those of Hezekiah: both came to power at age twenty-five and reigned for twenty-nine years (14:2; 18:2). These two tie for being the sixth-longest-reigning rulers of Judah. According to the text, Amaziah was good (like his father), but not great (like David), since the high places remained (14:3–4). These syncretistic worship locations survived for at least another century, until they were finally destroyed by Josiah of Judah (23:8).

Amaziah may have faced a power struggle early in his reign (14:5). The language used to describe Amaziah's stabilization of power, "the kingdom was firmly in his grasp" (*hazqah hammamlakah beyado*; v. 5), is comparable to that of Solomon's consolidation of power after killing his rivals Adonijah, Joab, and Shimei (1 Kgs 2:46). Amaziah kills his enemies (the officials who assassinated his father) after he is established on the throne. His execution of justice was restrained, since he did not kill the children of the conspirators, thereby obeying the law in regard to not punishing children for the sins of their parents (2 Kgs 14:6). The quotation from Deuteronomy (24:16) is a rare instance of a verbatim quote from the Pentateuch appearing in the Historical Books.

Amaziah is praised not only for his obedience to the law (*torah*) of Moses but also for his major victory over Edom in the Valley of Salt, south of the Dead Sea (2 Kgs 14:7).[12] No reason is given for Amaziah's campaign, but it was presumably to reestablish Edom as a Judean vassal. David also defeated Edom in the Valley of Salt (2 Sam 8:13).[13] Edom had been the ally of Jehoshaphat of Judah (with Jehoram of Israel) against Moab (2 Kgs 3:8–12), but they successfully rebelled against Jehoram of Judah (8:20–22). Sela, captured here by Amaziah, was located about twenty miles south of the Dead Sea. The renaming of Sela as Joktheel implies Judean control over this important city.

Because of his recent victory over Aram, Amaziah challenged his stronger neighbor to the north, Jehoash of Israel, in battle. The double patronym used for Jehoash (son of Jehoahaz, son of Jehu; 14:8) is unusual in Kings. The connection to his grandfather Jehu reminds readers of the dynastic promise to Jehu (10:30). Amaziah's words to Jehoash could be literally translated as,

12. While this text speaks merely of defeating ten thousand Edomites, the parallel in Chronicles describes the killing of ten thousand soldiers (2 Chr 25:12).

13. Even though the MT of 2 Sam 8:13 has "Aram" as David's defeated foe, most translators have "Edom" instead, based on 1 Chr 18:12.

"Let us look each other in the face" (14:8), which may seem harmless.[14] But they clearly were an invitation to fight, comparable to the overused film trope "Let's dance."[15]

While Amaziah of Judah is evaluated as righteous (v. 3) and Jehoash of Israel as evil (13:11), in this interaction the northern ruler is the one portrayed as wise. First, Jehoash's response is in the form of a fable, a wisdom form used to convey a more subtle message. Second, just as the prophet Shemaiah had warned Rehoboam of Judah not to start a civil war with Jeroboam I of Israel earlier (1 Kgs 12:24), Jehoash's message was a warning to Amaziah to stay home and avoid conflict.

Despite the subtle medium, Jehoash's choice of metaphors was derogatory—Jehoash is a strong cedar and a wild beast, but Amaziah is a thistle that gets trampled upon (2 Kgs 14:9). Jehoash clearly perceives arrogance from his northern neighbor. King Ahab cautioned Ben-hadad of Aram about his premature boasting, "One who puts on his armor should not boast like one who takes it off" (1 Kgs 20:11).[16] In his fable Jehoash makes a prediction of defeat for Amaziah, but he also appears to allude to an offer of marriage alliance that was rejected by Israel (2 Kgs 14:9), which possibly provoked the initial challenge.

Unlike Rehoboam, who heeded the prophetic warning (1 Kgs 12:24), Amaziah followed the example of Ahab, who ignored Micaiah's warning (ch. 22). The two nations met at Beth Shemesh (about fifteen miles west of Jerusalem), where Israel routed Judah (2 Kgs 14:11–12). The results were catastrophic for Judah—Amaziah was captured, six hundred feet of Jerusalem's wall was broken down,[17] and the temple and treasuries of Jerusalem were plundered (vv. 13–14). In this disaster it is hard not to see a foreshadowing of the destruction of Jerusalem and the temple by Nebuchadnezzar of Babylon recorded in 2 Kings 25.

Curiously, the concluding regnal formula of Jehoash is repeated at this point in the text (14:15–16; see also 13:12–13). Amaziah's concluding formula immediately follows Jehoash's and is typical, until it is interrupted by the story of his assassination (14:19–20). The conspirators forced him to flee Jerusalem

---

14. While it may appear that Amaziah's initial words were merely an invitation to meet or perhaps to establish a marriage, a similar expression (facing each other) is used again a few verses later in a military context (14:11), leading most commentators to interpret the first message belligerently (e.g., Wiseman, *1 & 2 Kings*, 245; Wray Beal, *1 & 2 Kings*, 418).

15. The phrase is helpfully explained by the character Deadpool (Ryan Reynolds) in the 2016 film *Deadpool* as "Let's try to kill each other."

16. For a discussion of taunt speech in military contexts generally and these examples from Ahab and Jehoash specifically, see Lamb, "Trash Talking," 118–19.

17. The text speaks of four hundred cubits, and a cubit was about eighteen inches (14:13).

and head to Lachish, a heavily fortified city. Little is known about these regicidal schemers, except that they were persistent, as they chased Amaziah to Lachish, where they finally succeeded in killing the king. The beginning of Amaziah's reign was so successful (Torah obedience and military success; vv. 6–7)—why did they want to kill him? Probably because he was perceived weak after losing to Israel, being captured, and then allowing Jerusalem to be plundered. Leaders be warned; followers are fickle.

Despite the conspiracy, Amaziah's son, Azariah, still succeeded his father (v. 21). Here the text notes that Azariah rebuilt the city of Elath (the northern tip of the Gulf of Aqabah, about one hundred and fifty miles south of Jerusalem; v. 22), information one would expect in his own concluding formula, not his father's.

Jeroboam II of Israel (2 Kings 14:23–29)

Jeroboam II, the fourth Jehuite ruler, was one of divided Israel's greatest rulers, and yet his magnificent reign is recorded in only seven verses (14:23–29). Most of Jeroboam's short narrative involves regnal formula (vv. 23–24, 28–29), but three aspects are distinctive and worthy of comment.

First, Jeroboam was the Northern Kingdom's longest-reigning ruler (forty-one years; v. 23). Only two Judean rulers reigned longer (Manasseh and Azariah). Deuteronomy describes how righteous rulers will reign for a long time (Deut 17:20), but problematically, the longest-reigning rulers of both Israel (Jeroboam II) and Judah (Manasseh) are evaluated as evil (14:24; 21:2). Jeroboam's evil evaluation is based on his continuation of the sins of Jeroboam I (14:24), presumably the ruler he was named after.

Second, Jeroboam restored Israel's borders to those of the Davidic empire, from Lebo Hamath in the north to the Dead Sea in the south (v. 25). He also recaptured the Aramean cities of Damascus and Hamath for Israel (v. 28).[18] It is difficult to be certain about the details of these locations, but he clearly achieved significant military success. The Israelite border contraction under Jehu (10:32–33) ended under his son, Jehoahaz (13:5).[19] His son, Jehoash, retook several Aramean cities (v. 25), and finally his son, Jeroboam, reestablished the ideal northern borders (1 Kgs 4:21; 8:65). Jeroboam's efforts to retake this territory is described as an act of obedience in response to the prophetic word from Jonah (2 Kgs 14:25).

---

18. The Hebrew of 14:28 could be translated, "He restored Damascus and Hamath to Judah in Israel," which is problematic. To make sense of this phrase the NIV adds several words, resulting in "which had belonged to Judah." See also Cogan and Tadmor, *II Kings*, 161–62.

19. For a discussion of Jeroboam's expansion, see Lamb, *Righteous Jehu*, 196–97.

Third, Jeroboam was a recipient of divine compassion (vv. 26–27). How does the text reconcile Jeroboam's territorial expansion with his evil evaluation? The text attributes his success not to Jeroboam's worthiness but to God's mercy. Jeroboam did obey Jonah, but that was not what YHWH noticed. He saw the suffering of his people and that they were alone, so he used Jeroboam to save (*yasha'*) them. Similarly, when Jeroboam's father Jehoash reigned, YHWH showed them compassion and gave them success over Aram (13:23–25). During the reign of Jeroboam II, Amos was shown several visions of destruction by YHWH, and the prophet pleaded for his people; YHWH again showed compassion and relented (Amos 7:1–6). While it is not recalled specifically, another reason for the divine compassion may have been YHWH's dynastic promise to Jeroboam's great-grandfather, Jehu (2 Kgs 10:30), a promise that will soon expire.

Azariah of Judah (2 Kings 15:1–7)

Amaziah's son, Azariah, was sixteen when he came to power, and he reigned fifty-two years, the second-longest-reigning king of Judah (15:2). To address the chronological problems associated with this long reign, scholars suggest co-regencies (twenty-four years overlapping with his father, 791–767 BC, and ten years overlapping with his son, 750–740 BC).[20] His co-regency with Amaziah may have begun when his father was captured by Jehoash (14:13); his co-regency with his son, Azariah, began when Azariah contracted leprosy (15:5).

The book of Kings more frequently calls him by his personal name Azariah (eight times: 14:21; 15:1, 6, 7, 8, 17, 23, 27), but it also refers to him by his throne name Uzziah (four times: 15:13, 30, 32, 34), which is the name he is generally called outside of the book of Kings (2 Chr 26:1–27:2; Ezra 10:21; Isa 1:1; 6:1, 7:1; Neh 11:4; Hos 1:1; Amos 1:1; Zech 14:5).[21] Perhaps the most familiar reference to this ruler appears at the beginning of Isaiah's call narrative (Isa 6:1).

Like Jeroboam, Azariah's long reign is recorded in only seven verses (2 Kgs 15:1–7). Like his father Amaziah, Azariah was righteous, but the people continued to worship at the high places (vv. 3–4). At some point in Azariah's reign, YHWH afflicted him with leprosy, which remained with him until he died (v. 5; for other cases of leprosy in 2 Kings, see 5:1, 11, 27; 7:3). No reason is given for Azariah's leprosy in Kings, but in Chronicles his disease

20. See Wiseman, *1 & 2 Kings*, 250.

21. Barnes, *1 & 2 Kings*, 299.

is a punishment for acting in a priestly role by making an offering on the incense altar (2 Chr 26:16–21).

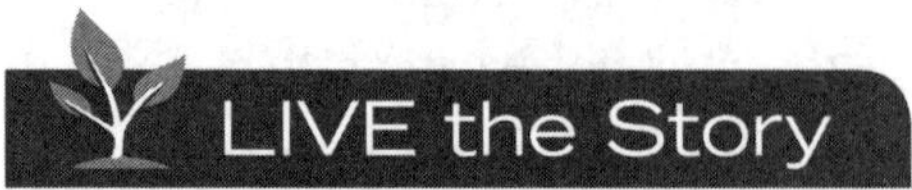

"Everyone Who Exalts Himself . . ."

Amaziah got off to a great start by only executing the conspirators and not their families in accordance with Mosaic law (2 Kgs 14:6) and by defeating Edom dramatically in the Valley of Salt (v. 7), like his ancestor David. His success on his southern border led him to believe he could achieve victory on his northern border against Israel, leading to his invitation to Jehoash. Wisely, Jehoash urged restraint to avoid a downfall. Foolishly, Amaziah ignored his northern contemporary's advice and fought. The personal and national consequences of his arrogance were catastrophic.

The wisdom of Proverbs is apt here: "Pride goes before destruction, a haughty spirit before a fall" (Prov 16:18). After telling the parable of the Pharisee and tax collector, Jesus paraphrases this proverbial truth, "For all those who exalt themselves will be humbled, and those who humble themselves will be exalted" (Luke 18:14). Many of us, like Amaziah, may not be content with or thankful for divinely granted success, so we put ourselves in positions where our arrogance is exposed by putting others down, by competing with rivals, or by bragging about our accomplishments.

When I was a graduate student at Stanford, I was a volunteer staff with the undergraduate InterVarsity chapter. My first opportunity to give a talk at the large-group meeting (about one hundred and fifty students) went really well—people even clapped afterwards. I had received a lot of assistance from my staff worker Greg, but in my mind, I was the one who delivered the talk and therefore deserved the praise. The next time I had an opportunity to give a large-group talk, I spent much less time in preparation, thinking, "I'm a natural speaker, what could go wrong?" I neglected to ask for help from wise, experienced friends. When the time for this second talk finally arrived, I realized I was massively underprepared. I showed up late to the meeting in a frantic state. My talk was a disaster. When it ended there was a long pause (with no clapping)—people were relieved that it was finally over.

The remedy for pride is a focus on God. As the text makes clear in the midst of Jeroboam's narrative, any success we experience is the result of divine compassion, which should lead us to thanksgiving and praise.

Barnes includes a challenging discussion of how Amaziah failed to "count the cost" of going to battle.[22] Jesus warns that a king needs to decide if he is able to go against a larger army (Israel would have had more forces than Judah) before committing his forces (Luke 14:31–32). Barnes concludes, "We disciples of the ultimate Son of David should count the cost carefully as well, for Jesus bids us to contemplate nothing less than the giving of everything we own as the continuing price of following him (Luke 14:33)."[23]

22. Barnes, *1 & 2 Kings*, 295.
23. Barnes, *1 & 2 Kings*, 295.

CHAPTER 31

2 Kings 15:8–31

LISTEN to the Story

[8]In the thirty-eighth year of Azariah king of Judah, Zechariah son of
Jeroboam became king of Israel in Samaria, and he reigned six months.
[9]He did evil in the eyes of the LORD, as his predecessors had done. He
did not turn away from the sins of Jeroboam son of Nebat, which he had
caused Israel to commit.

[10]Shallum son of Jabesh conspired against Zechariah. He attacked him
in front of the people, assassinated him and succeeded him as king. [11]The
other events of Zechariah's reign are written in the book of the annals of
the kings of Israel. [12]So the word of the LORD spoken to Jehu was fulfilled:
"Your descendants will sit on the throne of Israel to the fourth generation."

[13]Shallum son of Jabesh became king in the thirty-ninth year of Uzziah
king of Judah, and he reigned in Samaria one month. [14]Then Menahem
son of Gadi went from Tirzah up to Samaria. He attacked Shallum son of
Jabesh in Samaria, assassinated him and succeeded him as king.

[15]The other events of Shallum's reign, and the conspiracy he led, are
written in the book of the annals of the kings of Israel.

[16]At that time Menahem, starting out from Tirzah, attacked Tiphsah
and everyone in the city and its vicinity, because they refused to open
their gates. He sacked Tiphsah and ripped open all the pregnant women.

[17]In the thirty-ninth year of Azariah king of Judah, Menahem son of
Gadi became king of Israel, and he reigned in Samaria ten years. [18]He
did evil in the eyes of the LORD. During his entire reign he did not turn
away from the sins of Jeroboam son of Nebat, which he had caused Israel
to commit.

[19]Then Pul king of Assyria invaded the land, and Menahem gave him
a thousand talents of silver to gain his support and strengthen his own
hold on the kingdom. [20]Menahem exacted this money from Israel. Every
wealthy person had to contribute fifty shekels of silver to be given to the

king of Assyria. So the king of Assyria withdrew and stayed in the land no longer.

21As for the other events of Menahem's reign, and all he did, are they not written in the book of the annals of the kings of Israel? 22Menahem rested with his ancestors. And Pekahiah his son succeeded him as king.

23In the fiftieth year of Azariah king of Judah, Pekahiah son of Menahem became king of Israel in Samaria, and he reigned two years.
24Pekahiah did evil in the eyes of the LORD. He did not turn away from the sins of Jeroboam son of Nebat, which he had caused Israel to commit.
25One of his chief officers, Pekah son of Remaliah, conspired against him. Taking fifty men of Gilead with him, he assassinated Pekahiah, along with Argob and Arieh, in the citadel of the royal palace at Samaria. So Pekah killed Pekahiah and succeeded him as king.

26The other events of Pekahiah's reign, and all he did, are written in the book of the annals of the kings of Israel.

27In the fifty-second year of Azariah king of Judah, Pekah son of Remaliah became king of Israel in Samaria, and he reigned twenty years.
28He did evil in the eyes of the LORD. He did not turn away from the sins of Jeroboam son of Nebat, which he had caused Israel to commit.

29In the time of Pekah king of Israel, Tiglath-Pileser king of Assyria came and took Ijon, Abel Beth Maakah, Janoah, Kedesh and Hazor. He took Gilead and Galilee, including all the land of Naphtali, and deported
the people to Assyria. 30Then Hoshea son of Elah conspired against Pekah son of Remaliah. He attacked and assassinated him, and then succeeded him as king in the twentieth year of Jotham son of Uzziah.

31As for the other events of Pekah's reign, and all he did, are they not written in the book of the annals of the kings of Israel?

Listening to the Text in the Story: Biblical Texts: 2 Kings 10:30; Hosea 1:4; Amos 1:13; Ancient Near Eastern Texts: The Royal Inscriptions of Tiglath-Pileser III; The Babylonian King List A

While God appears to be absent in this section of Kings, several Israelite rulers are mentioned in extrabiblical texts, making the material fascinating historically. As the Northern Kingdom rapidly approaches its downfall, the text briefly records the narratives of five Israelite rulers (Zechariah, Shallum, Menahem, Pekahiah, and Pekah), whose reigns were characterized by great instability and dynastic chaos. Part of this instability was caused by the arrival of the Assyrians,[1] most notably the great ruler Tiglath-Pileser III, who conquered most of the Northern Kingdom.

While the Judean monarchy was characterized by dynastic stability, the Israelite monarchy had already experienced five non-dynastic rebellions (those of Jeroboam, Baasha, Zimri, Omri, and Jehu). Israel was entering the reign of the fifth and final Jehuite ruler, Zechariah, an almost Judah-esque century of relative dynastic calm (102 years, according to regnal years). The northern peace ended abruptly, and the next thirty years saw five different rulers and four rebellions. After Zechariah's death (2 Kgs 15:10), the text recalls YHWH's dynastic promise to Jehu that four generations (Jehoahaz, Jehoash, Jeroboam II, and Zechariah) would succeed him on the throne of Israel (10:30; 15:12). The end of Jehuite rule fulfills a prophecy from the book of Hosea for the overly violent nature of Jehu's rebellion (2 Kgs 9–10):

> And the LORD said to him, "Name him Jezreel; for yet a little while, and I will punish the house of Jehu for the bloodshed of Jezreel, and I will put an end to the kingdom of the house of Israel." (Hos 1:4)

Often periods of political instability coincide with times of brutal violence. Menahem, who seized the throne from Shallum (who seized the throne from Zechariah), attacked the city of Tiphsah and ripped open all the pregnant women (2 Kgs 15:16). This horrific practice appears in two other biblical contexts: in Elisha's prediction to Hazael (8:12) and in Amos's description of the crimes of Ammon (Amos 1:13).[2] Human depravity knows no bounds.

Perhaps the ancient Near Eastern empire most infamous for excessive brutality was Assyria. The Assyrian army was massive and technologically advanced. But what made the Assyrians distinctive was their effective use of propaganda, as they terrorized their opponent by bragging about what they had done to their previous victims. Ashurnasirpal II (883–859 BC), in his annals of his military campaigns, not only recorded but boasted about what today would be considered war crimes:

---

1. For an extended discussion of the Assyrians, see Christopher. B. Hays and Peter Machinist, "Assyria and the Assyrians" in *The World around the Old Testament: The People and Places of the Ancient Near East*, ed. Bill T. Arnold and Brent A. Strawn (Grand Rapids: Baker Academic, 2016): 31–105.

2. Assyrian examples of this brutal practice are discussed in Mordechai Cogan, "'Ripping Open Pregnant Women' in Light of an Assyrian Analogue," *JAOS* 103 (1983): 755–57; and Peter Dubosky, "Ripping Open Pregnant Arab Women: Reliefs in Room L of Ashurbanipal's North Palace," *Orientalia* 78.3 (2009): 394–419.

> I burnt many captives from them. I captured many troops alive: from some I cut off their arms and hands; from others I cut off their noses, ears and extremities. I gouged out the eyes of many troops. I made one pile of the living and one of the heads. I hung their heads on trees around the city. I burnt their adolescent boys and girls. I razed, destroyed, burnt, and consumed the city.[3]

We receive few details of the Assyrians' violent deeds here, as the text briefly records their taking tribute from and deportation of the Israelites. Assyria's ruler during the reigns of Menahem, Pekahiah, and Pekah was Tiglath-Pileser III (745–727 BC).[4] He first appears in the biblical text as "Pul" (2 Kgs 15:19), a shortened form of "Pileser."[5] He is called Pulu in the Babylonian King List A.[6]

Three Israelite rulers appear in Tiglath-Pileser's royal inscriptions (Menahem, Pekah, and Hoshea). In 2 Kings 15 Menahem gives a large tribute to Tiglath-Pileser (15:19), probably the same tribute recorded in two Assyrian inscriptions listing tributaries, including "Menahem, the Samarian" and "Rezin, the Damascene" (i.e., the king of Aram; 15:37; 16:5, 6, 9).

> The Calah Annals: "I received the tribute of Kustaspi, the Kummuhite, Rezin, the Damascene, Menahem, the Samarian, Hiram, the Tyrian . . . gold, silver, tin, iron, elephant hides, elephant tusks (ivory) . . . *colored garments* . . . camels and she-camels."[7]
>
> The Iran Stela: "The kings of the land of Hatti, and of Aram . . . Rezin, the Damascene, Menahem, the Samarian . . . I imposed on them tribute of silver, gold, tin, iron, elephant hides, elephant tusks (ivory) . . . *colored garments* . . . camels and she-camels." [8]

The biblical text records Pekah's assassination by Hoshea (15:30), who then took the throne, while an inscription of Tiglath-Pileser claims the Assyrian emperor was responsible for the regicide and the succession. Both sources describe Israelites taken into captivity (15:29).

---

3. Grayson, *Assyrian Rulers*, 201.
4. For images of Tiglath-Pileser III, see *ANEP*, 153, 300, #445, for another image, see also *ZIBBC* 3:171.
5. See Cogan and Tadmor, *II Kings*, 172.
6. *COS* 1:462, note 5; *ANET*, 272.
7. *COS* 2:285–86.
8. *COS* 2:287.

> Summary Inscription 4: "I carried off to Assyria the land of Bit-Humria (Israel), . . . all of its people . . . I killed Pekah their king, and I installed Hosea as king over them. I received from them 10 talents of gold, X talents of silver, with their possessions and I carried them to Assyria."[9]

While the discrepancy between the biblical and the Assyrian accounts regarding the killer of Pekah may seem troubling, it is not uncommon for the killing of a royal figure to be attributed to different people in different sources (see "The Tel Dan Inscription and the Death of Two Kings," Chapter 26). However, it is significant historically that the biblical and Assyria records agree about the general chronology during this period, putting the Israelite rulers in the same order (Menahem, then Pekah, then Hosea). Both sources record Menahem giving tribute to Tiglath-Pileser of Assyria (738 BC), and both situate Pekah's death in office (and the succession of Hoshea) to the period when Tiglath-Pileser was campaigning in Israel.

Overview (2 Kings 15:8–31)

Since these five short royal narratives share much in common, an overview of their common features will precede the discussions of their separate narratives. The text records narratives of five consecutive northern rulers (Zechariah, Shallum, Menahem, Pekahiah, and Pekah) because their reigns all overlapped with that of Azariah of Judah (15:8, 13, 17, 23, 27). The overlap is due to Azariah's long, fifty-two-year reign and to the dynastic chaos that characterized their short northern reigns. Only one heir in five succeeded his father, as four of the reigns (Zechariah, Shallum, Pekahiah, and Pekah) ended in conspiratorial assassinations (vv. 10, 14, 25, 30). Since each of the usurpers killed their predecessor, we are introduced to the next king in the previous king's narrative. Four of these five did evil in the eyes of YHWH, and none of them turned from the sins of Jeroboam (vv. 9, 18, 24, 28). Shallum is one of only two northern rulers to lack an evaluation (Elah is the other; 1 Kgs 16:8–14). His short, one-month reign apparently did not warrant an assessment.

9. *COS* 2:288; see a parallel version of this incident in *COS* 2:291.

Zechariah (2 Kings 15:8–12)

Zechariah, whose name means "YHWH has remembered," was the son of Jeroboam II and the fifth and final Jehuite ruler. He only reigned for six months before he was killed by Shallum, making him the third-shortest-reigning northern ruler (15:8). His assassination was noted uniquely for its public nature, "in front of the people" (v. 10), which suggests that either Shallum was trying to send a message about his ruthless nature or that his conspiracy received widespread support. The only interesting theological notice here is the record of the fulfillment of YHWH's direct word to Jehu regarding four more dynastic heirs. Thus ends Israel's longest dynasty.

Shallum (2 Kings 15:13–15)

Shallum only reigned for one month before he was killed by Menahem, making him the second-shortest-reigning northern ruler (15:13–15). Perhaps most striking about his narrative is the missing regnal evaluation, which probably would have been negative. Before assassinating Shallum, Menahem came from Tirzah (v. 14), about ten miles east of Samaria and Israel's capital before Omri moved it to Samaria (1 Kgs 14:17; 15:21, 33; 16:6, 8, 9, 15, 17, 23, 24). Wiseman speculates that Menahem may have been a garrison commander there.[10]

Menahem (2 Kings 15:16–22)

Before recording Menahem's regnal introduction (15:17), the text notes Menahem ripping open pregnant women from the town of Tiphsah (v. 16). As is often the case in wartime, the marginalized (here women and unborn children) bear the brunt of the violence. While it is troubling that this horrific act is not condemned, often the text merely records an incident where the crime is so obvious that no condemnation is necessary (e.g., Judg 11:29–33; 19:22–30). The text includes this heinous act as further evidence of Menahem's evilness.

The brutality of the action is unquestioned, but the location is far from certain. The only city known by the name Tiphsah is three hundred miles north of Tirzah on the Euphrates River, which was on the border of Solomon's empire (1 Kgs 4:24). But this distance seems too far, so some scholars follow the Septuagint's "Tappuah," which was located only about twelve miles south of Tirzah.[11] If it took place at Tappuah, on the border between Ephraim

10. Wiseman, *1 & 2 Kings*, 253.
11. See Wray Beal, *1 & 2 Kings*, 429.

and Manasseh, then Menahem would have committed this crime against fellow Israelites.

At this point the biblical text mentions the first Assyrian ruler by name, Pul (2 Kgs 15:19), whom we know from other sources—and a few verses later (v. 29)—as Tiglath-Pileser III. He will do more damage during the reign of Pekah, but here his invasion results only in a tribute from Menahem (see Listen to the Story above). The tribute was sizeable, a thousand silver talents (v. 19)—roughly three million shekels, thirty-seven tons, involving sixty thousand taxpayers each contributing fifty shekels (v. 20).[12] The previous two northern rulers reigned for only a total of seven months (vv. 8, 13), so Menahem's decision to pay up and not resist was a pragmatic one that appeared to pay off in the short term. He was able to survive for ten years on the throne, die a natural death, and be succeeded by his own heir, Pekahiah (v. 22), a feat neither his two predecessors nor his two successors were able to achieve.

Pekahiah (2 Kings 15:23–26)

Menahem's son, Pekahiah, was one of four northern rulers to reign for only two years (15:23; the other three were Nadab, Elah, and Ahaziah); given the historical context, he should have been merely content to succeed his father. While the text only records the identity of the assassin (Pekah, one of Pekahiah's officers; v. 25) and not the motive, the fact that Pekah was able to easily recruit fifty co-conspirators from Gilead suggests that the rebellion was politically motivated, perhaps to punish Pekahiah for the pro-Assyrian tendencies of his father, Menahem. Tiglath-Pileser soon conquers and exiles much of Israel, lending further support to this theory.

Pekah (2 Kings 15:27–31)

The name of the next ruler, Pekah, is basically a shortened form of the name Pekahiah, the man he assassinated.[13] In contrast to many of his recent northern predecessors, Pekah reigned twenty years, the sixth-longest-reigning ruler of Israel (15:27). Pekah of Israel and Rezin of Aram formed an alliance and threatened Ahaz of Judah (v. 37; 16:5; Isa 7:1), a move that may have been intended to force Judah to join their anti-Assyrian coalition (see "Ahaz of Judah," Chapter 32). Presumably because of his concern to quickly quash any resistance to Assyrian hegemony, Tiglath-Pileser reappears (2 Kgs 15:29). No tribute is mentioned in the biblical account, but the Assyrian record describes a tribute of gold and

12. See Wiseman, *1 & 2 Kings*, 255.

13. See Barnes, *1 & 2 Kings*, 305.

silver from Israel.[14] The biblical text does, however, record the first (and perhaps largest, geographically) deportation for either Israel or Judah (v. 29; usually dated to 733 BC). Tiglath-Pileser's conquest included both cities (Ijon, Abel Beth Maakah, Janoah, Kedesh, and Hazor) as well as regions (Gilead, Galilee, and Naphtali). Pekah's territory was drastically reduced to the Ephraimite highlands surrounding Samaria, often called the "rump state of Ephraim."[15] The vast majority of Israel's territory and population was lost as a result of this massive Assyrian campaign.[16] This initial exile was significant historically, since it broke centuries of continuous independent rule in Palestine. After the final downfall of the Northern Kingdom about ten years later (17:6), the text provides a theological explanation for the tragedy, but none is given at this point. The Assyrian deportation strategy allowed them to use subjugated people in labor camps in Assyria and decreased the likelihood of rebellion in conquered territories as new peoples are "imported" who lack a unified national identity.[17]

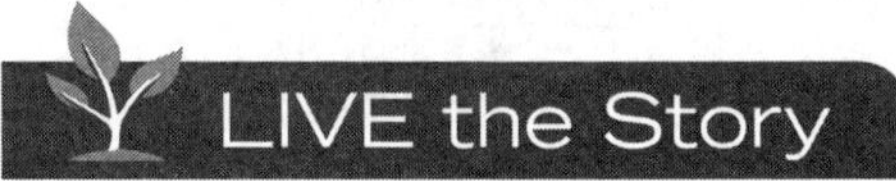

Where Is God?

In the final years of the Northern Kingdom of Israel, both their political and spiritual realms devolve into chaos. The idolatrous worship sites established at the outset of the divided monarchy persist (15:9, 18, 24, 28), and new forms of evil behavior emerge. Depraved behavior that elsewhere was performed by foreigners (by Hazael of Aram, 8:12; by Ammon, Amos 1:13) is now committed by Israel's ruler as Menahem rips open pregnant women (2 Kgs 15:16). Ambition for power leads to a series of four conspiratorial assassinations in rapid succession (vv. 10, 14, 25, 30). Tiglath-Pileser of Assyria conquers most of the land as he takes captive most of the people.

Curiously, in the midst of this chaos YHWH appears to be absent, as he is mentioned only five times in 15:8–31, and these occurrences are mainly in the contexts of formulaic evaluations (rulers doing evil in his eyes). YHWH never appears as an active agent here, and none of his prophets speak to condemn the rulers or the people for their evil behavior. Where is God?[18]

---

14. *COS* 2:288b.

15. See Jones, *1 and 2 Kings*, 2:529.

16. A badly damaged royal inscription of Tiglath-Pileser III (Calah Annals #24; *COS* 2:286) mentions a figure of deported people (13,520) that scholars assume is the number of Israelites taken from Galilee; see Cogan and Tadmor, *II Kings*, 174–75.

17. See also *ZIBBC* 3:172.

18. We will revisit this question in Chapter 40.

The longer answer to this question appears in 2 Kings 17, in the theological explanation for the northern exile by Assyria. But at this point the text suggests that YHWH is allowing his people who have rejected him to experience the natural consequences of their independence (see Romans 1:24–32). Just as the Israelites during the period of the judges or the reign of King Jehoahaz (2 Kgs 13:4–5) cried out to YHWH for help, we would hope that Israel would do the same here. Alas, there is no repentance or cry for help from the ruler or the people. They don't cry for help here, but we see elsewhere in Scripture that God is quick to show mercy and forgive his people. Even as Jesus was dying on a cross, when the thief, who presumably deserved death, asked to be remembered, Jesus was eager to speak to him a word of hope and grace, "Truly I tell you, today you will be with me in paradise" (Luke 23:42–43). Even at the darkest of times, for Israel and for this thief, God remains present and is eager to move with compassion. The darkness of death will soon be followed by the dawn of new life for those who desire to join Jesus in paradise.

CHAPTER 32

2 Kings 15:32–16:20

LISTEN to the Story

[32]In the second year of Pekah son of Remaliah king of Israel, Jotham son
of Uzziah king of Judah began to reign. [33]He was twenty-five years old when
he became king, and he reigned in Jerusalem sixteen years. His mother's
name was Jerusha daughter of Zadok. [34]He did what was right in the eyes
of the LORD, just as his father Uzziah had done. [35]The high places, however,
were not removed; the people continued to offer sacrifices and burn incense
there. Jotham rebuilt the Upper Gate of the temple of the LORD.

[36]As for the other events of Jotham's reign, and what he did, are they
not written in the book of the annals of the kings of Judah? [37](In those days
the LORD began to send Rezin king of Aram and Pekah son of Remaliah
against Judah.) [38]Jotham rested with his ancestors and was buried with
them in the City of David, the city of his father. And Ahaz his son succeeded him as king.

[16:1]In the seventeenth year of Pekah son of Remaliah, Ahaz son of
Jotham king of Judah began to reign. [2]Ahaz was twenty years old when
he became king, and he reigned in Jerusalem sixteen years. Unlike David
his father, he did not do what was right in the eyes of the LORD his God.
[3]He followed the ways of the kings of Israel and even sacrificed his son in
the fire, engaging in the detestable practices of the nations the LORD had
driven out before the Israelites. [4]He offered sacrifices and burned incense
at the high places, on the hilltops and under every spreading tree.

[5]Then Rezin king of Aram and Pekah son of Remaliah king of Israel
marched up to fight against Jerusalem and besieged Ahaz, but they could
not overpower him. [6]At that time, Rezin king of Aram recovered Elath
for Aram by driving out the people of Judah. Edomites then moved into
Elath and have lived there to this day.

[7]Ahaz sent messengers to say to Tiglath-Pileser king of Assyria, "I am
your servant and vassal. Come up and save me out of the hand of the king

of Aram and of the king of Israel, who are attacking me." [8]And Ahaz took the silver and gold found in the temple of the LORD and in the treasuries of the royal palace and sent it as a gift to the king of Assyria. [9]The king of Assyria complied by attacking Damascus and capturing it. He deported its inhabitants to Kir and put Rezin to death.

[10]Then King Ahaz went to Damascus to meet Tiglath-Pileser king of Assyria. He saw an altar in Damascus and sent to Uriah the priest a sketch of the altar, with detailed plans for its construction. [11]So Uriah the priest built an altar in accordance with all the plans that King Ahaz had sent from Damascus and finished it before King Ahaz returned. [12]When the king came back from Damascus and saw the altar, he approached it and presented offerings on it. [13]He offered up his burnt offering and grain offering, poured out his drink offering, and splashed the blood of his fellowship offerings against the altar. [14]As for the bronze altar that stood before the LORD, he brought it from the front of the temple—from between the new altar and the temple of the LORD—and put it on the north side of the new altar.

[15]King Ahaz then gave these orders to Uriah the priest: "On the large new altar, offer the morning burnt offering and the evening grain offering, the king's burnt offering and his grain offering, and the burnt offering of all the people of the land, and their grain offering and their drink offering. Splash against this altar the blood of all the burnt offerings and sacrifices. But I will use the bronze altar for seeking guidance." [16]And Uriah the priest did just as King Ahaz had ordered.

[17]King Ahaz cut off the side panels and removed the basins from the movable stands. He removed the Sea from the bronze bulls that supported it and set it on a stone base. [18]He took away the Sabbath canopy that had been built at the temple and removed the royal entryway outside the temple of the LORD, in deference to the king of Assyria.

[19]As for the other events of the reign of Ahaz, and what he did, are they not written in the book of the annals of the kings of Judah? [20]Ahaz rested with his ancestors and was buried with them in the City of David. And Hezekiah his son succeeded him as king.

Listening to the Text in the Story: Biblical Text: Isaiah 7:1–15; Ancient Near Eastern Texts: West Semitic Seal Inscriptions; The Royal Inscriptions of Tiglath-Pileser III; The Panamuwa Aramaic Inscription

The text shifts focus from Israel back to Judah to record two southern rulers who overlapped with Pekah of Israel: Jotham and Ahaz. The Northern Kingdom is about to be exiled, but its influence will linger as southern rulers are now described as following its example.

As we move into the late eighth century BC, an increasing number of extrabiblical sources mention characters from the biblical text. Five rulers mentioned in this section (Jotham, Ahaz, Pekin, Rezin, and Tiglath-Pileser III) appear in Assyrian royal inscriptions or in West Semitic seal inscriptions.

Seals were used in the ancient Near East to authorize legal documents, like a notarized signature is today. They would not typically be owned by common folk but only by rulers and royal officials. While the identification of seals and seal impressions is difficult, the scholars associated with the publications of these inscriptions conclude that each of them is genuine and refer to the respective rulers of Judah. One seal impression (bulla) is particularly significant: it mentions two southern kings, and it appears to be the oldest known royal seal inscription. It belongs to King Ahaz, but it also mentions his father, King Jotham:

> Belonging to Ahaz, *son of* Jehotham (=Jotham), king of Judah.[1]

Another royal seal inscription also mentions two rulers, Ahaz and his son, King Hezekiah:

> Hezekiah, son of Ahaz, king of Judah.[2]

A more elaborate seal appears to belong to Ushna, a servant of Ahaz:

> Ushna, servant of Ahaz.[3]

Ushna is not mentioned in the biblical text, but he appears in another royal seal inscription associated with Hezekiah (see 2 Kgs 18). Thus, these seal inscriptions mention three generations of Davidic rulers from this period (Jotham, father of Ahaz, father of Hezekiah).

Both the biblical text (16:8) and a royal Assyrian inscription speak of Ahaz's

1. Robert Deutsch, "First Impression: What We Learn from King Ahaz's Seal," *BAR* 24.3 (1998): 54–56, 62.

2. Frank Moore Cross, "King Hezekiah's Seal," *BAR* 25.2 (1994): 42–45, 60, states, "There can be little or no doubt as to its authenticity."

3. Jeffrey H. Tigay and Alan R. Millard conclude the Ahaz here is the Judean ruler (*COS* 2:200).

tribute to Tiglath-Pileser III of Assyria in 734 BC. Ahaz's tribute is intended to convince the Assyrian emperor to give assistance to Judah against Aram and Israel.

> Summary 7 Inscription: "I received the tribute of Kustaspi, the Kummuhite . . . *other tributaries* . . . Panammuwa, the Sam'alite . . . *other tributaries* . . . Jehoahaz, the Judahite . . . *other tributaries* . . . : gold, silver, tin, multi-colored garments."[4]

Among this list of Assyrian tributaries, Ahaz is identified by his full name, Jehoahaz the Judahite. One of the tributaries from the Summary 7 inscription, Panamuwa of Sam'al, appears in an Aramaic inscription that also describes his tribute to Tiglath-Pileser:

> Then my father, Panamuwa, son of Barsur, brought a gift to the king of Assyria. And he made him king of the house of his father. . . . And his lord, the king of Assyria, positioned him over powerful kings . . . and he ran at the wheel of his lord, Tiglath-Pileser, king of Assyria.[5]

As was noted in the previous chapter, Rezin king of Aram (16:5) is mentioned alongside Menahem and other tributaries in several royal inscriptions of Tiglath-Pileser.[6] From these sources we see that Judah is not unique in giving tribute to Assyria.

Jotham of Judah (2 Kings 15:32–38)

After five brief northern regnal accounts, we have one short southern account for Jotham (seven verses), followed by a much longer one for his son, Ahaz (twenty verses). Jotham, whose name means "YHWH is perfect," succeeded his father Azariah (called here Uzziah; 15:32) when he was twenty-five (v. 33). His sixteen-year reign (v. 33) was average among southern kings. Based on 2 Kings 15:5, scholars assume his reign included a ten-year co-regency with his father Azariah.[7] Like his father, Jotham's righteous evaluation was qualified

4. *COS* 2:289.
5. *COS* 2:159.
6. *COS* 2:284, 285, 287.
7. See Wiseman, *1 & 2 Kings*, 258.

because the high places remained (vv. 34–35). The text provides little distinctive information about Jotham except that he rebuilt the Upper Gate of the temple (v. 35), which was probably on the north side and perhaps synonymous with the Benjamin Gate (Jer 20:2). Before recording his death and succession by Ahaz (2 Kgs 15:38), the text includes a theological explanation for the aggression of Aram and Israel—Rezin and Pekah were sent by YHWH (v. 37).

Ahaz of Judah (2 Kings 16:1–20)

Jotham's son Ahaz came to power at age twenty and reigned for sixteen years, like his father (16:2). Ahaz is evaluated as not doing right like David (v. 3), breaking a streak of four righteous Judean rulers (Joash, Amaziah, Azariah, and Jotham). He is one of only two southern rulers with no record of his mother (v. 2; also Jehoram, 8:16). The text lists the crimes of Ahaz. He offered sacrifices on the high places, "on the hilltops and under every spreading tree" (v. 4), language found several places in Jeremiah (Jer 2:20; 3:6; 17:2). He followed the appalling examples of the kings of Israel and the nations who were in Canaan before Israel (2 Kgs 16:3). Specifically, he appears to have sacrificed his own son (v. 3). A literal translation here would be, "he made his son pass through the fire" (*wegam 'et-beno he'ebir ba'esh*), but scholars believe this expression is a euphemism for child sacrifice.[8]

After noting that the siege campaign of Rezin of Aram and Pekah of Israel does not initially succeed (v. 5), the text includes a brief note regarding control of the Edomite city of Elath on the northern tip of the Gulf of Aqabah (v. 6). The Hebrew text says that Rezin recovered Elath for Aram, but some scholars replace Aram with Edom, since Elath is a great distance from Aram, and the Hebrew words for these two nations differ by only one consonant (*dalet* in Edom and *resh* in Aram, two letters that are easily confused).[9]

Rezin's campaign in the south to recover Elath meant the siege of Jerusalem had ended, which allowed Ahaz to send messengers to Tiglath-Pileser III of Assyria asking for help (v. 7). In becoming a tributary of Assyria, Ahaz followed the example of Menahem of Israel (15:19; 16:7). In Isaiah 7 the prophet exhorted Ahaz to trust in YHWH exclusively and not fear Aram and Israel (Isa 7:4–17). YHWH consistently called his people to depend exclusively on him and not foreign powers (Deut 7:2; Isa 30:2–3; 31:1; 36:6, 9).

---

8. See Barnes, *1 & 2 Kings*, 311.

9. For an argument for keeping "Aram," see Wiseman, *1 & 2 Kings*, 261. For an argument for reading "Edom," see Wray Beal, *1 & 2 Kings*, 434–35.

Ahaz's fear of the looming threat of Aram and Israel, however, led him to abandon YHWH.

Ahaz looted the temple and royal treasuries in order to purchase protection from Tiglath-Pileser (2 Kgs 16:8–9), comparable to other southern kings (Asa: 15:18; Joash: 2 Kgs 12:18; Hezekiah: 18:16). After receiving the gift from his new vassal, Tiglath-Pileser promptly displayed the power of his military by attacking Damascus, Aram's capital, deporting its inhabitants to Kir (probably in Mesopotamia), and killing its ruler, Rezin (v. 9). For Ahaz, problem solved.

Often rulers deliver their gifts in person to their lord.[10] Ahaz, who had already given tribute, went to visit Tiglath-Pileser in Damascus after the Assyrian conquest of the city to deliver a second gift or to express his vassalage in person. During his visit he saw an altar he admired so much that he sent plans back to Uriah the priest (see also Isa 8:2), who finished its construction before Ahaz returned from Damascus (2 Kgs 16:10–11). Ahaz then offered sacrifices (burnt, grain, drink, and fellowship) and repositioned the bronze altar to the north side of the new altar (vv. 12–14). The king gave detailed instructions to Uriah regarding the offerings he had given, directing him specifically to splash blood against the new altar; Uriah diligently obeyed (vv. 15–16).

Ahaz next arranged renovations to the temple that included removing the side panels, the basins, the bronze bulls that had supported the bronze sea (now on a stone base; v. 17), the Sabbath canopy, and the royal entryway. These actions may have been motivated by a desire to conform the temple to the style of the Aramean altar, but the phrase "in deference to the king of Assyria" (*mippene melek 'ashur*; v. 18) suggests Ahaz needed metal from these objects to continue paying tribute to Assyria.

Ahaz's closing comment includes nothing distinctive, merely that his son, Hezekiah, succeeded him. The story of Hezekiah will continue after the chapter's long theological explanation for Israel's demise (17:1–41). Hezekiah's long narrative (chs. 18–20) will reveal that an evil father can produce a righteous child.

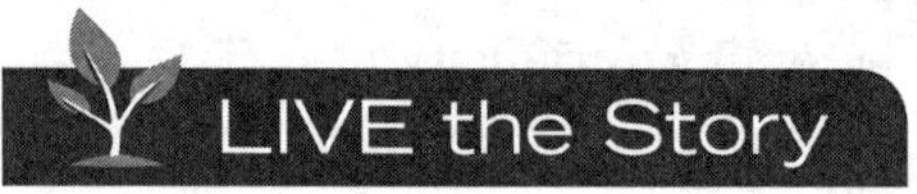

Immanuel

The alliance between Rezin of Aram and Pekah of Israel against Ahaz of Judah described here (2 Kgs 16:5) is the focus of the famous "Immanuel" narrative

10. See Jehu of Israel delivering tribute to Shalmaneser III of Assyria on the Black Obelisk; *ANEP*, 120–22, 290–91; #351–55; *ZIBBC* 3:149.

of Isaiah 7. In Isaiah 7:1 and 2 Kings 16:5, Pekah and Rezin marched against Jerusalem and Ahaz, but in 2 Kings 15:37 we discover that YHWH sent these two rulers. Presumably, Aram and Israel wanted Judah to join them in an anti-Assyrian alliance. Ahaz is fearful because of the northern threat, so YHWH sends the prophet Isaiah (not mentioned in the book of Kings until the reign of Hezekiah; 19:2) to encourage him and ask for a sign. Ahaz refuses to ask, but Isaiah says he will receive one anyway: a young woman will give birth to a son, he'll be called Immanuel—literally, "with-us-God," a sign of divine presence, and the threat of Pekah and Rezin will soon be gone because of the king of Assyria (Isa 7:1–17).

When Isaiah 7 is taught at Christmas time, Ahaz's historical context is often ignored. Matthew's Gospel appropriately connects the Immanuel prophecy (Isa 7:14) to the birth of Jesus (Matt 1:23—a virgin birth!), but Isaiah also had a more contemporary sign for Ahaz. It would not be good news if Ahaz needed to "wait" over seven centuries until Jesus was born for his deliverance from Rezin and Pekah.

While God was with King Ahaz at the birth of "Immanuel" centuries before Jesus, in a far more dramatic manner God was with us at the birth of Jesus, the Word who became flesh (John 1:14). Jesus's birth was a powerful sign that the promise to the "house of David" (repeated in Isa 7:2, 13) would be fulfilled in the Christ, the son of David. We can be confident that the God who was Immanuel for evil Ahaz in Isaiah 7 and who was Immanuel in Matthew 1 will continue to be present with us today. The promise of divine presence bookends Matthew's Gospel. It was manifested at Jesus's birth, and it is reiterated at Jesus's departure as he commissions his disciples, declaring that he will be with them "to the very end of the age" (Matt 28:20).

Dealing with Ambiguity

There is a lot of textual ambiguity in this section (2 Kgs 15:32–16:20), which records the narrative of a good king who isn't very good (Jotham) and a bad king who isn't very bad (Ahaz). It may seem hard to find spiritual points from the stories of these two rulers, but there are still lessons to be learned about divine grace in the midst of this ambiguity.

While Ahaz is condemned for following in the ways of the northern kings, not removing the high places, and apparently sacrificing his son (16:2–4), he does other things that he isn't condemned for, many of which one might expect him to be judged negatively for. He offers tribute to Assyria, plundering the temple to do so, although several other righteous rulers do the same (Asa, Joash, Amaziah, and Hezekiah), so this act in itself shouldn't be viewed highly negatively. If the text doesn't rebuke Ahaz, it should cause us to also be slow to judgment. The lack of textual clarity regarding Ahaz is exposed by an insightful comment by Barnes, who notes that the ambiguity here allows Wiseman to view Ahaz's temple renovations positively, like those of Solomon, but also allows Leithart to view them negatively, comparing them to those of Jeroboam I.[11]

Curiously, two characters the text views favorably, Uriah and Isaiah, engage with Ahaz. Uriah the priest, whom YHWH deemed as honest (Isa 8:2), follows Ahaz's directions diligently to renovate the temple and offer sacrifices, which could suggest that there were good motivations behind Ahaz's actions. Isaiah, who speaks critical words to Ahaz, still engages with him and offers him a sign of hope (Isa 7:3–17). Perhaps the best thing to be said about Ahaz was that he was the father of righteous Hezekiah (2 Kgs 16:20).

There is a time in the midst of morally ambiguous actions and behaviors to condemn. But from the life of Ahaz we see another example of God and God's people continuing to display patience and even compassion toward people who are literally not righteous (v. 2). God will soon judge both the nations of Israel and Judah, but at this point he is still slow to anger. I can be quick to judge behavior that is clearly not in line with God, but I am always grateful when I realize that God is slow to judge me. As we deal with the ambiguity of life, we need to remember to err on the side of grace, just as God's priest, God's prophet, and God himself do here. After all, the promise given from God to evil Ahaz focused on a hopeful sign of God's compassion and God's presence: the birth of a son, one who would be called "Immanuel" (Isa 7:14: Matt 1:23).

---

11. Barnes, *1 & 2 Kings*, 313–15.

CHAPTER 33

2 Kings 17:1–41

LISTEN to the Story

[1]In the twelfth year of Ahaz king of Judah, Hoshea son of Elah became king of Israel in Samaria, and he reigned nine years. [2]He did evil in the eyes of the LORD, but not like the kings of Israel who preceded him.

[3]Shalmaneser king of Assyria came up to attack Hoshea, who had been Shalmaneser's vassal and had paid him tribute. [4]But the king of Assyria discovered that Hoshea was a traitor, for he had sent envoys to So king of Egypt, and he no longer paid tribute to the king of Assyria, as he had done year by year. Therefore Shalmaneser seized him and put him in prison. [5]The king of Assyria invaded the entire land, marched against Samaria and laid siege to it for three years. [6]In the ninth year of Hoshea, the king of Assyria captured Samaria and deported the Israelites to Assyria. He settled them in Halah, in Gozan on the Habor River and in the towns of the Medes.

[7]All this took place because the Israelites had sinned against the LORD their God, who had brought them up out of Egypt from under the power of Pharaoh king of Egypt. They worshiped other gods [8]and followed the practices of the nations the LORD had driven out before them, as well as the practices that the kings of Israel had introduced. [9]The Israelites secretly did things against the LORD their God that were not right. From watchtower to fortified city they built themselves high places in all their towns. [10]They set up sacred stones and Asherah poles on every high hill and under every spreading tree. [11]At every high place they burned incense, as the nations whom the LORD had driven out before them had done. They did wicked things that aroused the LORD's anger. [12]They worshiped idols, though the LORD had said, "You shall not do this." [13]The LORD warned Israel and Judah through all his prophets and seers: "Turn from your evil ways. Observe my commands and decrees, in accordance with the entire Law that I commanded your ancestors to obey and that I delivered to you through my servants the prophets."

14But they would not listen and were as stiff-necked as their ancestors, who did not trust in the LORD their God. 15They rejected his decrees and the covenant he had made with their ancestors and the statutes he had warned them to keep. They followed worthless idols and themselves became worthless. They imitated the nations around them although the LORD had ordered them, "Do not do as they do."

16They forsook all the commands of the LORD their God and made for themselves two idols cast in the shape of calves, and an Asherah pole. They bowed down to all the starry hosts, and they worshiped Baal. 17They sacrificed their sons and daughters in the fire. They practiced divination and sought omens and sold themselves to do evil in the eyes of the LORD, arousing his anger.

18So the LORD was very angry with Israel and removed them from his presence. Only the tribe of Judah was left, 19and even Judah did not keep the commands of the LORD their God. They followed the practices Israel had introduced. 20Therefore the LORD rejected all the people of Israel; he afflicted them and gave them into the hands of plunderers, until he thrust them from his presence.

21When he tore Israel away from the house of David, they made Jeroboam son of Nebat their king. Jeroboam enticed Israel away from following the LORD and caused them to commit a great sin. 22The Israelites persisted in all the sins of Jeroboam and did not turn away from them 23until the LORD removed them from his presence, as he had warned through all his servants the prophets. So the people of Israel were taken from their homeland into exile in Assyria, and they are still there.

24The king of Assyria brought people from Babylon, Kuthah, Avva, Hamath and Sepharvaim and settled them in the towns of Samaria to replace the Israelites. They took over Samaria and lived in its towns. 25When they first lived there, they did not worship the LORD; so he sent lions among them and they killed some of the people. 26It was reported to the king of Assyria: "The people you deported and resettled in the towns of Samaria do not know what the god of that country requires. He has sent lions among them, which are killing them off, because the people do not know what he requires."

27Then the king of Assyria gave this order: "Have one of the priests you took captive from Samaria go back to live there and teach the people what the god of the land requires." 28So one of the priests who had been exiled

from Samaria came to live in Bethel and taught them how to worship
the Lord.
29Nevertheless, each national group made its own gods in the several
towns where they settled, and set them up in the shrines the people of
Samaria had made at the high places. 30The people from Babylon made
Sukkoth Benoth, those from Kuthah made Nergal, and those from
Hamath made Ashima; 31the Avvites made Nibhaz and Tartak, and the
Sepharvites burned their children in the fire as sacrifices to Adrammelek
and Anammelek, the gods of Sepharvaim. 32They worshiped the Lord,
but they also appointed all sorts of their own people to officiate for them
as priests in the shrines at the high places. 33They worshiped the Lord,
but they also served their own gods in accordance with the customs of the
nations from which they had been brought.
34To this day they persist in their former practices. They neither
worship the Lord nor adhere to the decrees and regulations, the laws
and commands that the Lord gave the descendants of Jacob, whom he
named Israel. 35When the Lord made a covenant with the Israelites, he
commanded them: “Do not worship any other gods or bow down to
them, serve them or sacrifice to them. 36But the Lord, who brought you
up out of Egypt with mighty power and outstretched arm, is the one you
must worship. To him you shall bow down and to him offer sacrifices.
37You must always be careful to keep the decrees and regulations, the laws
and commands he wrote for you. Do not worship other gods. 38Do not
forget the covenant I have made with you, and do not worship other gods.
39Rather, worship the Lord your God; it is he who will deliver you from
the hand of all your enemies.”
40They would not listen, however, but persisted in their former practices. 41Even while these people were worshiping the Lord, they were
serving their idols. To this day their children and grandchildren continue
to do as their ancestors did.

Listening to the Text in the Story: Biblical Texts: Exodus 20:2–5; Deuteronomy 4:19; 5:7–9; 2 Kings 15:29; 16:7, 10; 1 Chronicles 5:6, 26; 2 Chronicles 28:20; Isaiah 7:17; 8:4; 20:1; Hosea 10:14; Ancient Near Eastern Texts: The Royal Inscriptions of Tiglath-Pileser III; The Hoshea Seal; The Babylonian Chronicle; The Royal Inscriptions of Sargon II

The Northern Kingdom of Israel endured as a separate nation for two centuries, beginning with Jeroboam I's rebellion against Rehoboam. The rulers of Israel, from Jeroboam to Hoshea, were consistently evaluated negatively in the text (with the exception of Jehu).[1] Throughout this period numerous prophets of YHWH, unnamed and named (Ahijah, Jehu, Elijah, Elisha, Micaiah, and Jonah), confronted northern rulers, rebuking them for idolatry and calling them to repentance. But the sins of the nation and its rulers finally caught up to them, and in 722 BC the empire of Assyria completed its conquest of the Northern Kingdom, captured Samaria, and deported many of its people. This chapter provides a theological explanation for the tragedy; put succinctly, "All this took place because the Israelites had sinned against the LORD their God" (2 Kgs 17:7).

Several of the rulers in 2 Kings 17 appear in extrabiblical texts, providing helpful background. Hoshea of Israel is mentioned (with his predecessor Pekah) in an inscription from the annals of Tiglath-Pileser III describing the Assyrian ruler's conquests and installation of Hoshea:

> I carried off to Assyria the land of Bit-Humria (Israel) . . . all of its people, I killed Pekah, their king, and I installed Hoshea as king over them. I received from them 10 talents of gold, X talents of silver with their possessions and I carried them to Assyria.[2]

This inscription describes the first Assyrian conquest and deportation narrated earlier (15:29). The events from 2 Kings 17 were orchestrated by the sons of Tiglath-Pileser.

Hoshea of Israel also appears in a seal inscription from one of his servants, "Belonging to Abdi servant of Hoshea."[3] The story of the seal's sale in 1993 at Sotheby's in New York and the description of its translucent brown carnelian appearance are fascinating, but the seal itself provides little additional information about Hoshea or his servant.

The Shalmaneser who attacked Hoshea in this text (17:3) was the fifth Assyrian ruler of that name and the only one mentioned in the Old Testament (see also 18:9; Hos 10:14?). He was the son and successor of Tiglath-Pileser III (2 Kgs 15:29; 16:7, 10; 1 Chr 5:6, 26; 2 Chr 28:20). Shalmaneser's brother and successor was Sargon II.[4] Sargon II is only mentioned once in the Old Testament, in Isaiah 20:1.

1. Elah and Shallum received no regnal evaluation.
2. *COS* 2:288.
3. Lemaire, "Royal Signature."
4. For an image of Sargon II, see *ANEP*, 154, 300; #446.

While Shalmaneser began the Israelite conquest, his brother Sargon finally captured Samaria and deported the Israelites to Assyria. Apparently Shalmaneser died about the time Samaria was falling. The Babylonian Chronicle describes the destruction of Samaria (727 BC) and the succession of the Assyrian throne to Sargon II (722 BC).

> On 27th Tebet Shalmaneser (V) ascended the throne in Assyria and Babylonia. He shattered Samaria.
>
> Year 5: Shalmaneser died in Tebet. Five years Shalmaneser ruled Babylonia and Assyria. On 12th Tebet Sargon ascended the throne in Assyria.[5]

In one of his summary inscriptions Sargon describes his conquest and deportation of Samaria ("Samarina" in the quote below), even listing the number of Israelite exiles.

> I besieged and conquered Samarina. I took as booty 27,290 people who lived there. I gathered 50 chariots from them. I taught the rest (of the deportees) their skills. I set my eunuch over them, and I imposed upon them the (same) tribute as the previous king (i.e., Shalmaneser V).[6]

The biblical text speaks of Shalmaneser initially (2 Kgs 17:3–4), but then it merely calls him the "king of Assyria" (vv. 5, 6), suggesting that his brother Sargon may have finished what Shalmaneser began, which is consistent with the extrabiblical accounts that attribute the event both to Shalmaneser (Babylonian Chronicle) and to Sargon (Sargon's royal inscriptions).

Hoshea of Israel sent envoys to an Egyptian ruler named "So" (v. 4), but there is no record of an Egyptian ruler with this name, so it is difficult to clearly identify him.[7] The two most viable options are Osorkon IV (727–716 BC), assuming that "So" was a shortening of this name, or Tefnakte (726–716 BC), understanding "So" as Sais, the city where Tefnakte ruled.[8]

The biblical text attributes the fall of Samaria and deportation of Israel to the wrath of YHWH for their many sins (vv. 11, 17, 18). Similarly, the Mesha Inscription describes how the Moabite god Kemosh was angry with his people allowing them to be oppressed by Omri, the king of Israel.

---

5. *COS* 1:467.
6. *COS* 2:296; see also 298.
7. For a longer discussion of the identity of this ruler, see John Day, "The Problem of 'So, King of Egypt' in 2 Kings 17:4," *VT* 42 (1992): 289–301.
8. For the problems associated with each of these options, see Wiseman, *1 & 2 Kings*, 265; Cogan and Tadmor, *II Kings*, 196; Wray Beal, *1 & 2 Kings*, 446.

Omri was the king of Israel,
and he oppressed Moab for many days,
for Kemosh was angry with his land.[9]

In contrast to 2 Kings 17, the Mesha Inscription gives no explanation of why Chemosh was angry with the people of Moab. However, both texts describe how the respective deities (Chemosh and YHWH) allowed a foreign nation (Israel and Assyria) to conquer his people (Moabites and Israelites) and oppress them.

The primary cause of YHWH's anger was the idolatry of his people (vv. 11–12, 15–17). Their worship of other gods was a blatant violation of the prohibition in the Decalogue against idolatry (Exod 20:2–5; Deut 5:7–9). One of the specific idolatrous acts Israel is accused of is worshiping the stars (2 Kgs 17:16), which is condemned in Deuteronomy, "[W]hen you look up to the sky and see the sun, the moon and the stars—all the heavenly array—do not be enticed into bowing down to them" (Deut 4:19).

The idolatry in the land continued after the Israelite deportation. The Assyrians imported foreign peoples into Israel, and they were attacked by lions because they did not know how to worship YHWH (2 Kgs 17:26). The Weidner Chronicle describes a comparable situation: "The Gutians were unhappy people unaware how to revere the gods, ignorant of the right cultic practices."[10]

The Conquest of Israel (2 Kings 17:1–6)

This chapter divides into three sections: (1) the conquest (17:1–6); (2) the punishment (17:7–23); and (3) the resettlement of Israel (17:24–41). Hoshea, Israel's final ruler, was also the eighth one to usurp the throne (15:30). Thus, the Northern Kingdom ended as it began. Hoshea's name is the same as the original name of Joshua (Num 13:8), meaning "salvation." Hoshea reigned for nine years, and, like his predecessors, "He did evil in the eyes of the Lord" (2 Kgs 17:1–2). But the text also includes a unique notice that he was "not like the kings of Israel who preceded him" (v. 2). No reason is given for his qualified negative assessment, and no mention is made of the sins of Jeroboam

9. *COS* 2:137.
10. *COS* 1:469.

(i.e., worshiping the golden calves he set up; 1 Kgs 12:25–32). Perhaps Hoshea instituted reforms the text did not record.

The short-reigning Shalmaneser V of Assyria (727–722 BC) attacked Hoshea and forced him to pay tribute like several earlier northern kings (Jehu, Jehoash, and Menahem). To punish Hoshea for seeking assistance from Egypt and for ceasing to pay tribute, Shalmaneser imprisoned him (see also 2 Kgs 24:12). The Assyrian king (probably Shalmaneser) invaded and besieged the capital, Samaria. The text does not explain how Hoshea was captured before the invasion began, but it suggests that Hoshea remained in prison for the duration of the siege. Just as the siege of Nebuchadnezzar against Jerusalem would eventually succeed (24:10–12), the siege of the Assyrian ruler (Sargon II) would succeed against Samaria after three years (17:5–6). The locations for the Israelite resettlements (Halah, Gozan, and Median towns) were far removed from Samaria, northeast and northwest of Nineveh, making the possibility of an eventual return of the "ten lost tribes of Israel" unlikely.[11]

The Punishment of Israel (2 Kings 17:7–23)

The middle section of chapter 17 gives an explanation in language that is typically described as Deuteronomistic, echoing themes and terms repeated in the book of Deuteronomy.[12] To explain why YHWH would allow his covenant people to be defeated and deported, an extensive list of sins is recorded that primarily involves disobedience and idolatry. While YHWH is slow to anger (e.g., Exod 34:6; Num 14:18), over their course of the Northern Kingdom's history the extreme wickedness of their sin provoked great anger from YHWH (2 Kgs 17:11, 17, 18).

Hoshea had most recently looked to Egypt for deliverance from Assyria (v. 4), so appropriately the judgment against Israel begins and ends with reminders of how YHWH delivered Israel from oppression in Egypt (vv. 7, 36). Three negative influences upon Israel are emphasized throughout this section: they followed the sinful examples of their kings (vv. 8, 21, 22), of their ancestors (vv. 13, 14, 15, 41), and of the Canaanite nations who occupied the land before them (vv. 8, 11, 15, 33, 41).

YHWH had repeatedly warned his people about their sins through his servants the prophets (vv. 13, 23), although none of the prophets is mentioned by name here. The prophets' message to the people was a call to observe the

11. See Barnes, *1 & 2 Kings*, 318.

12. See Jones, *1 and 2 Kings*, 2:542–45.

"Law" (*torah*), the "commands" (*mitswot*), the "decrees" (*huqqim*), and the "covenant" (*berit*) of YHWH (vv. 13, 15, 16). The prophets' warnings were consistently unheeded.

The text speaks generically about idolatry (vv. 7, 12, 15, 16), but it also mentions specifically which gods are being worshiped. Except for the end of the Solomon narrative (1 Kgs 11:5–10), most of the Israelite idolatry has focused thus far in Kings on Baal and Asherah (1 Kgs 14:15, 23; 16:31–33; 18:19, 21, 25; 2 Kgs 13:6), but a virtual pantheon of foreign gods is mentioned here. In addition to Baal and Asherah, the Israelites and the people who replaced them in the land worshiped the starry host (17:16), Sukkoth Benoth, Nergal, Ashima (v. 30), Nibhaz, Tartak, Adrammelek, and Anammelek (v. 31). Idolatrous worship is manifested in a wide variety of idolatrous Canaanite practices involving high places (vv. 9, 11, 29, 32), sacred stones (v. 10), child sacrifice, divination, and omens (v. 17).

As the text piles up evidence against Israel, it emphasizes the comprehensiveness of their sins. They built high places in all their towns (v. 9). They set up pillars on every high hill and under every green tree (v. 10). They made offerings on all the high places (v. 11). They ignored warnings by every prophet and every seer (vv. 13, 23). They abandoned all the commandments, and they worshiped all the host of heaven (v. 16). They walked in all the sins of Jeroboam (v. 22).

The result of ignoring YHWH, YHWH's law, and YHWH's prophets was devastating for the nation. The military and political events recorded earlier (defeat and deportation; vv. 5–6) are now given a theological explanation. They followed worthless idols and therefore became worthless (v. 15). They were removed from YHWH's presence (vv. 18, 20, 23). YHWH afflicted them and gave them into the hands of plunderers (v. 20). YHWH rejected all the people of Israel (v. 20). They were taken from their homeland and remain there (v. 23).

The consequence of Israel's persistent disobedience means that Judah alone remains (vv. 18–19). But the text includes an ominous warning to Israel's southern neighbors who are also not keeping the commands of YHWH. And just as Israel followed the negative example of the Canaanite nations and their stiff-necked ancestors, so Judah follows the sinful practices of Israel. Judah survives over a hundred years beyond the downfall of their northern neighbors, but tragically they will also reap the consequences of disobedience.

Before concluding the theological explanation, the text recalls the rebellion of Jeroboam I, which began the Northern Kingdom of Israel (17:21; 1 Kgs 12:1–19). It reminds readers that throughout Israel's two-hundred-year history, Jeroboam's sins (i.e., the golden calves set up in Dan and Bethel; 1 Kgs 12:25–33) consistently led the nation into sin (2 Kgs 17:22).

As readers, we serve in the capacity of the jury. Israel stands accused in the dock. Like an experienced prosecuting attorney, the text has brought forth witnesses and evidence (the law and the prophets). The weight of evidence leaves us no other option but to deliver a guilty verdict. The punishment fits the crime.

The Resettlement of Israel (2 Kings 17:24–41)

Readers of the Gospels may be familiar with Samaritans (e.g., the traveler who showed mercy in Jesus's parable: Luke 10:33; the leper who thanked Jesus: Luke 17:16; the woman at the well who spoke to Jesus: John 4:9). This section explains how the new residents of the cities surrounding Israel's capital, Samaria, became what the New Testament calls Samaritans.

Just as he deported the Israelites and settled them in remote lands (2 Kgs 17:6), so now the king of Assyria (probably Sargon II) takes people from distant lands (Babylon, Kuthah, Avva, Hamath, and Sepharvaim) and imports them into the region around Samaria (v. 24). The book of Ezra describes how later Assyrian rulers (Esarhaddon and Ashurbanipal) continued this practice (Ezra 4:2, 9–10). The Assyrians deported and resettled subjugated peoples in order both to display their power and to reduce the likelihood of rebellion.

Several lion attacks were recorded earlier in Kings (1 Kgs 13:22–26; 20:36), and now YHWH sends lions to attack the new residents (2 Kgs 17:25). While the text is not clear, the message given to the Assyrian ruler blames the attacks on the people's ignorance of Israel's God (v. 26). So he sends one of the Israelite priests back to teach them how to worship YHWH.

The text records that the people begin to worship YHWH (vv. 28, 32, 33), but they also continue to worship their old national gods (vv. 29–33). Confusingly, the text also says they did not worship YHWH (v. 34). Worship of YHWH was combined with syncretistic other practices involving worship of foreign gods (vv. 32–33). They set up shrines on the high places (v. 29) and established their own people to serve as priests at these shrines (v. 32). The new Samaritans repeated the sins of the old Samaritans, who had repeated the sins of the Canaanites who had lived in the land previously.

The chapter concludes by reemphasizing themes from the beginning of the theological explanation. The new residents disobey the laws and commands that were given to the descendants of Jacob (v. 34). The text then recalls a command from YHWH to his people prohibiting worship of other gods, reminding them how YHWH delivered them from Egypt and established a covenant with them (vv. 35–39). These people refused to listen, continuing their syncretistic practices until the writing of this narrative (vv. 40–41).

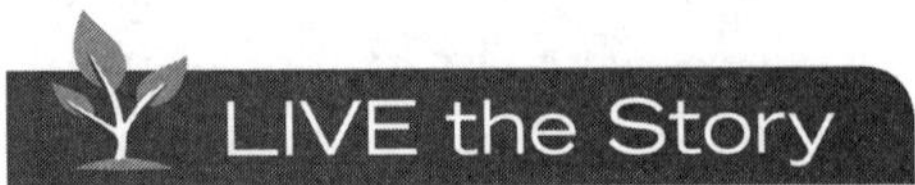

What Went Wrong?

The catastrophe of the conquest and deportation of the Northern Kingdom prompts the text to pause and ask the question, "What went wrong?" At this juncture the narrative stops its succession of regnal formulas and reflects upon the spiritual condition of the Northern Kingdom over the course of its history. YHWH features prominently in this reflection. This chapter has the highest concentration of references to YHWH in the entire book (twenty-five of forty-one verses [60.9 percent] mention YHWH).

In times of personal or national crisis, it is good to reflect on the question, "What went wrong?" After a natural disaster, well-known religious figures often make an announcement about why they think God caused it (e.g., God punished the US with the destruction of 9/11 or God punished the Haitians with the earthquake of 2010). While these dogmatic declarations are problematic for many reasons, the impetus toward theological reflection after tragedy is still valid. Instead of following the example of self-righteous quasi-political religious leaders, we need to learn how to engage in post-crisis theological reflection from texts like 2 Kings 17.

I see three lessons here. **First, remember that God sends his prophets.** One reason things went wrong was that God's people ignored God's prophets. Anyone can place blame after a catastrophe (like these religious leaders), but only God gives a warning beforehand. He not only sends his prophets, but he also gives commands to make it clear he expects his people to obey him and to worship him alone. When times are good, it is easy to ignore God's prophets. But after judgment has come, one should realize that the judgment could have been anticipated. The key is listening to prophetic voices, especially when they call us to repent. Unfortunately, Judah didn't learn from the tragedy of their northern neighbors.

Second, remember that God judges his own people. God had established a covenant with Israel and had set up Jeroboam I to rule over them (1 Kgs 11:31–39), but when they continued to sin and worship other gods, he was willing to punish them even though they were his own people. It is easy to blame other people for the problems of our culture: the poor, the wealthy, urban folk, rural folk, immigrants, people of other ethnicities, or people from other parts of the world. But God and his prophets condemned their own people.[13] Israelite prophets were condemning Israelite rulers and Israelite people. The prophets in the book of Kings are not like wealthy, megachurch pastors in the US blaming Haitians for a catastrophic earthquake. Israel's own story condemns its own leaders and its own ancestors. When we ask, "What went wrong?" let's avoid the temptation to blame others and instead ask, "What did we do wrong to contribute to the problem?" Throughout US history, the twin idolatries of greed and money have led to great injustices and have contributed to the tragedies associated with slavery, civil war, racism, and oppression. Tragically, the church still hasn't learned to listen to its own prophetic voices regarding these subjects.

Third, remember that God is sovereign. God controls the fates of Israel and Assyria, and later we see he controls the fates of Judah and Babylon. It is easy in the midst of political unrest to be focused on the politicians who appear to be either running or ruining the country, thinking that they are either saviors or anti-Christs. Political leaders can make a difference, particularly as they are concerned about God, God's law, God's prophets, and God's justice. But ultimately, praying for our nation and our leaders is going to be more powerful than writing our congressional representatives (ideally, we do both) because God is sovereign over nations and history.

Jesus tells a parable about wicked tenants in Luke 20:9–19 that both recalls the song of the vineyard from Isaiah 5:1–7 and encapsulates Israel's history as seen generally in the Old Testament and specifically here in 2 Kings 17. Just as God repeatedly sent his prophets to Israel to call them to repentance, the vineyard owner in the parable, who represents God, repeatedly sent his servants to collect fruit from the vineyard, but the owner's servants are beaten and sent back empty-handed. Just as God judged his people by sending Assyria, the owner in the parable eventually comes in judgment against his tenants. The vineyard owner appears naïve, but in reality, he is sovereign. In telling this parable Jesus not only summarizes their history and warns his listeners, but he also predicts his own death, as the son of the vineyard owner who is sent to die, and his own resurrection, as the rejected stone becomes the cornerstone in a glorious new building.

13. In other contexts, God's prophets also condemn people from other nations. Many prophetic books include oracles condemning other nations (e.g., Isa 13–23; Jer 46–49; Ezek 25–29; Amos 1:3–2:3).

CHAPTER 34

2 Kings 18:1–37

LISTEN to the Story

1In the third year of Hoshea son of Elah king of Israel, Hezekiah son of Ahaz king of Judah began to reign. 2He was twenty-five years old when he became king, and he reigned in Jerusalem twenty-nine years. His mother's name was Abijah daughter of Zechariah. 3He did what was right in the eyes of the LORD, just as his father David had done. 4He removed the high places, smashed the sacred stones and cut down the Asherah poles. He broke into pieces the bronze snake Moses had made, for up to that time the Israelites had been burning incense to it. (It was called Nehushtan.)

5Hezekiah trusted in the LORD, the God of Israel. There was no one like him among all the kings of Judah, either before him or after him. 6He held fast to the LORD and did not stop following him; he kept the commands the LORD had given Moses. 7And the LORD was with him; he was successful in whatever he undertook. He rebelled against the king of Assyria and did not serve him. 8From watchtower to fortified city, he defeated the Philistines, as far as Gaza and its territory.

9In King Hezekiah's fourth year, which was the seventh year of Hoshea son of Elah king of Israel, Shalmaneser king of Assyria marched against Samaria and laid siege to it. 10At the end of three years the Assyrians took it. So Samaria was captured in Hezekiah's sixth year, which was the ninth year of Hoshea king of Israel. 11The king of Assyria deported Israel to Assyria and settled them in Halah, in Gozan on the Habor River and in towns of the Medes. 12This happened because they had not obeyed the LORD their God, but had violated his covenant—all that Moses the servant of the LORD commanded. They neither listened to the commands nor carried them out.

13In the fourteenth year of King Hezekiah's reign, Sennacherib king of Assyria attacked all the fortified cities of Judah and captured them. 14So Hezekiah king of Judah sent this message to the king of Assyria at

Lachish: "I have done wrong. Withdraw from me, and I will pay whatever
you demand of me." The king of Assyria exacted from Hezekiah king
of Judah three hundred talents of silver and thirty talents of gold. 15So
Hezekiah gave him all the silver that was found in the temple of the LORD
and in the treasuries of the royal palace.

16At this time Hezekiah king of Judah stripped off the gold with which
he had covered the doors and doorposts of the temple of the LORD, and
gave it to the king of Assyria.

17The king of Assyria sent his supreme commander, his chief officer and
his field commander with a large army, from Lachish to King Hezekiah
at Jerusalem. They came up to Jerusalem and stopped at the aqueduct of
the Upper Pool, on the road to the Washerman's Field. 18They called for
the king; and Eliakim son of Hilkiah the palace administrator, Shebna the
secretary, and Joah son of Asaph the recorder went out to them.

19The field commander said to them, "Tell Hezekiah:

"'This is what the great king, the king of Assyria, says: On what
are you basing this confidence of yours? 20You say you have the counsel
and the might for war—but you speak only empty words. On whom
are you depending, that you rebel against me? 21Look, I know you are
depending on Egypt, that splintered reed of a staff, which pierces the
hand of anyone who leans on it! Such is Pharaoh king of Egypt to all
who depend on him. 22But if you say to me, "We are depending on
the LORD our God"—isn't he the one whose high places and altars
Hezekiah removed, saying to Judah and Jerusalem, "You must worship
before this altar in Jerusalem"?

23"'Come now, make a bargain with my master, the king of Assyria:
I will give you two thousand horses—if you can put riders on them!
24How can you repulse one officer of the least of my master's officials,
even though you are depending on Egypt for chariots and horsemen?
25Furthermore, have I come to attack and destroy this place without
word from the LORD? The LORD himself told me to march against this
country and destroy it.'"

26Then Eliakim son of Hilkiah, and Shebna and Joah said to the field
commander, "Please speak to your servants in Aramaic, since we understand
it. Don't speak to us in Hebrew in the hearing of the people on the wall."

[27]But the commander replied, "Was it only to your master and you that my master sent me to say these things, and not to the people sitting on the wall—who, like you, will have to eat their own excrement and drink their own urine?"

[28]Then the commander stood and called out in Hebrew, "Hear the word of the great king, the king of Assyria! [29]This is what the king says: Do not let Hezekiah deceive you. He cannot deliver you from my hand. [30]Do not let Hezekiah persuade you to trust in the LORD when he says, 'The LORD will surely deliver us; this city will not be given into the hand of the king of Assyria.'

[31]"Do not listen to Hezekiah. This is what the king of Assyria says: Make peace with me and come out to me. Then each of you will eat fruit from your own vine and fig tree and drink water from your own cistern, [32]until I come and take you to a land like your own—a land of grain and new wine, a land of bread and vineyards, a land of olive trees and honey. Choose life and not death!

"Do not listen to Hezekiah, for he is misleading you when he says, 'The LORD will deliver us.' [33]Has the god of any nation ever delivered his land from the hand of the king of Assyria? [34]Where are the gods of Hamath and Arpad? Where are the gods of Sepharvaim, Hena and Ivvah? Have they rescued Samaria from my hand?[35]Who of all the gods of these countries has been able to save his land from me? How then can the LORD deliver Jerusalem from my hand?"

[36]But the people remained silent and said nothing in reply, because the king had commanded, "Do not answer him."

[37]Then Eliakim son of Hilkiah the palace administrator, Shebna the secretary, and Joah son of Asaph the recorder went to Hezekiah, with their clothes torn, and told him what the field commander had said.

Listening to the Text in the Story: Biblical Texts: Numbers 21:4–9; Isaiah 7:14; 36–39; Ancient Near Eastern Texts: The Babylonian Chronicle; The Royal Inscriptions of Sargon II and Sennacherib; The Hezekiah Seals

From the division of the monarchy in 1 Kings 12 to the fall of the Northern Kingdom in 2 Kings 17, the narrative has primarily focused on Israel. The narratives of Judah's rulers are intertwined with those of Israel, but because the long prophetic narratives of Elijah and Elisha are located in the north, the nation of Israel dominates this long middle section of Kings. Now that Israel as a separate kingdom has ceased to exist, the remainder of the book shifts focus to the Southern Kingdom (2 Kings 18–25). Judah alone survives.

Fortunately, Judah's ruler at this critical juncture was one of their best, Hezekiah. Some scholars even perceive him to be the original "Immanuel" of Isaiah 7:14.[1] While there are chronological problems with this idea, the argument is compelling.[2] The young woman (*'almah*) would be the queen, King Ahaz's wife (Abijah; 2 Kgs 18:2), the child born would be named Immanuel by his father Ahaz, and Hezekiah grows up to be a reforming ruler who trusts God during a dark time of Israel's history.

The story of Hezekiah was important enough for the biblical writers to repeat it in the book of Isaiah.[3] Most of Hezekiah's narrative (2 Kgs 18:13, 17–20:19) is retold at the end of what is often called "First Isaiah" (Isa 36:1–39:8). While it is difficult to be certain which account came first, most scholars assume that the older account is 2 Kings, used as a source for Isaiah.[4] Why was Hezekiah's story repeated? Perhaps it was retold to highlight a positive example of a reforming, praying ruler in contrast to Hezekiah's evil father Ahaz (Isa 7:1–12; 14:28).

While Jehu had dramatically attacked Baal worship in Israel (2 Kgs 10:18–27), and Joash had performed significant renovations in the Jerusalem temple (12:4–16), no previous ruler had undertaken as many actions to reform worship practices as Hezekiah. The bronze snake (called the Nehushtan) that Moses had lifted up in the wilderness for the people to look at in order to recover from venemous snake bites (Num 21:4–9; see also John 3:14) had become an object of worship, so it was among the many cultic objects that Hezekiah destroyed (2 Kgs 18:4).[5] A recent archaeological find of a gate shrine near Lachish could be viewed as support for Hezekiah's reforms since the horns on the altar are intentionally cut off, which would be consistent with Hezekiah's destruction of sacred shrines (v. 4).[6]

---

1. John McHugh ("The Date of Hezekiah's Birth," *VT* 14 [1964]: 446–53) argues that Isa 7:14 could be viewed as an oracle of the birth of Hezekiah.

2. Matthew perceives the title "Immanuel" as also referring to Jesus (Matt 1:23).

3. Much of the Judean royal narratives are included in 1 and 2 Chronicles, but Hezekiah's narrative alone is included in Isaiah. The Chronicler includes extensive information not included in 2 Kings regarding Hezekiah's cleansing of the temple, reinstituting the Passover, and reorganizing the priests (2 Chr 29–31).

4. See, for example, Barnes, *1 & 2 Kings*, 330–31.

5. For images of snakes associated with the worship of Asherah, see *ANEP*, 163–64, 304–5; #470–74.

6. Laura Geggel, "Ancient City Gate and Shrine from Hebrew Bible Uncovered," *LiveScience*, September 28, 2016, http://www.livescience.com/56300-gate-shrine-excavated-in-israel.html.

Hezekiah's foreign enemy here is Assyria, who first appears in Kings during the reign of Menahem of Israel shortly before the final collapse of the Northern Kingdom (15:19, 20, 29). After wreaking havoc up north, destroying cities, and deporting residents, Assyria shifts focus south to Judah.

Sargon II, the Assyrian ruler who completed the destruction of Samaria and exiled its people, also claims (in the Nimrud Inscription) to be "the subduer of Judah, which lies far away."[7] It is difficult to know what event this inscription is referring to, but it may be describing events from the early reign of Hezekiah.[8] Sennacherib, son of Sargon, is the Assyrian ruler orchestrating the attack on Jerusalem (18:13; 19:16, 20, 36). The Babylonian Chronicle records that Sennacherib ruled Assyria for twenty-four years.[9]

Sennacherib sends three officials to convey his threatening message to Hezekiah (v. 17). We see clues concerning their respective roles in other biblical and extrabiblical texts where the terms are used. The term "supreme commander" (*tartan*; v. 17) refers to a military leader. The term appears in only one other place in the Hebrew Bible, where this individual is sent by Sargon II to attack the Philistine city of Ashdod (Isa 20:1). The Akkadian equivalent, *turtanu,* appears in Assyrian texts describing military conquests and is usually translated as "commander-in-chief."[10] The term "chief officer" (*rab-saris*; 2 Kgs 18:17) refers to an administrative figure, without an obvious military function. It appears only in one other text in the Hebrew Bible, to describe two Babylonian royal officials who were serving in Jerusalem (Jer 39:3, 13). A similar term (*rab-saresi*) is used to describe Nebuchadnezzar's chief eunuch, who serves in an administrative, or perhaps educational, capacity in Babylon (Dan 1:3). In 2 Kings 18 the term "field commander" (*rab-shakeh*) refers to an individual who is gifted in speech and rhetoric, like a spokesperson. The term is mentioned eight times in this chapter and the next (18:17, 19, 26, 27, 28, 37; 19:4, 8; see also the parallels in Isa 36:2–37:8), and it appears in a royal inscription from Sennacherib in the context of his campaign against Babylon.[11]

Sennacherib's annals narrate his military conquests and specifically mention Judah, Jerusalem, and Hezekiah. The Azekah Inscription describes a campaign (perhaps by Sennacherib) against Judah. It clearly mentions the Judean fortress at Azekah (Jer 34:7), but the references to Hezekiah are both

7. *COS* 2:298.
8. See *ZIBBC* 3:183–84.
9. *COS* 1:467.
10. *COS* 2:272; 278; 284; 296.
11. *COS* 2:301.

badly damaged.[12] Probably the most relevant Neo-Assyrian inscription records several of Sennacherib's military campaigns, including his conquests of Judah, his siege of Jerusalem, and the tribute of Hezekiah. It was deemed sufficiently important to be repeated in three six-sided clay prisms.[13] Most other ancient Near Eastern inscriptions mentioning Israelite or Judean rulers do so briefly, making this inscription's extended focus on Hezekiah unique.[14]

> As for Hezekiah, the Judean, I besieged forty-six of his fortified walled cities and surrounding smaller towns, which were without number. Using packed-down ramps and applying battering rams, infantry attacks by mines, breeches, and siege machines, I conquered (them). I took out 200,150 people, young and old, male and female, horses, mules, donkeys, camels, cattle, and sheep, without number, and counted them as spoil. He himself, I locked up within Jerusalem, his royal city, like a bird in a cage. I surrounded him with earthworks, and made it unthinkable for him to exit by the city gate. His cities which I had despoiled I cut off from his land and gave them to Mitinti, king of Ashdod, Padi, king of Ekron and Ṣilli-bel, king of Gaza, and thus diminished his land.[15]

Both this quotation and the biblical text describe Sennacherib's conquest of much of Judah (2 Kgs 18:13), including the major fortified cities. Sennacherib's inscription adds details regarding the siege, the large number of deportees, and how Hezekiah was trapped "like a bird in a cage." The most notable absence is any record of a final conquest of the city of Jerusalem, which surely would have been included if the event had taken place. In this regard, the biblical and Assyrian accounts agree. Sennacherib did not conquer Jerusalem. His inscription continues to describe Hezekiah's extensive tribute.

> I imposed dues and gifts for my lordship upon him, in addition to the former tribute, their yearly payment. He, Hezekiah, was overwhelmed by the awesome splendor of my lordship, and he sent me after my departure to Nineveh, my royal city, his elite troops (and) his best soldiers, which he had brought in as reinforcements to strengthen Jerusalem, with 30 talents

12. *COS* 2:304.

13. The Taylor Prism is located at the British Museum in London, the Oriental Institute Prism at the Oriental Institute of Chicago, and the Jerusalem Prism at the Israel Museum in Jerusalem.

14. See also my discussion of eighteen ancient Near Eastern inscriptions mentioning rulers of Israel and Judah in Leuchter and Lamb, *The Historical Writings*, 299–301.

15. *COS* 2:303.

> of gold, 800 talents of silver, choice antimony, large blocks of carnelian, beds (inlaid) with ivory, armchairs (inlaid) with ivory, elephant hides, ivory, ebony-wood, boxwood, multicolored garments, garments of linen, wool (dyed) red-purple and blue-purple, vessels of copper, iron, bronze and tin, chariots, siege shields, lances, armor, daggers for the belt, bows and arrows, countless trappings and implements of war, together with his daughters, his palace women, his male and female singers. He (also) dispatched his messenger to deliver the tribute and to do obeisance.[16]

Both the biblical text and Sennacherib's inscription describe a major tribute. They agree that Hezekiah gave thirty talents of gold (v. 14), but the Assyrian source has a greater number of silver talents (eight hundred instead of three hundred; v. 14), and it includes many non-monetary gifts (hides, woods, weapons, etc.) not mentioned in 2 Kings 18. The difference in silver could be explained by the additional weight of silver taken from the temple and the treasuries. Either way, the amounts are enormous: thirty talents of gold would be approximately one ton, and three hundred talents of silver would be approximately eleven tons. Hezekiah gave a massive gift in an attempt to buy Judean independence, but it did not work as Sennacherib's officials demanded complete surrender (v. 31).

Sennacherib set up his headquarters about thirty miles southwest of Jerusalem at the city of Lachish (vv. 14, 17), the location of King Amaziah's demise (see "Amaziah of Judah," Chapter 30). We get a glimpse of Sennacherib's siege of Lachish in a series of reliefs from his palace at Nineveh.[17] In one image the inhabitants of Lachish are bringing tribute to Sennacherib. Other images portray the attack, with siege engines, archers, and victims impaled. One of the adjacent inscriptions reads, "Sennacherib, king of the world, king of Assyria, sat upon *nimedu*-throne and passed in review the booty (taken) from Lachish."[18]

Additionally, numerous seals or seal impressions (bulla) mention Hezekiah or one of his officials. Because they are often not found in official archaeological sites, it is difficult to make definitive conclusions regarding identification, but it is still reasonable to assume that many of these seals and bulla mention actual people from the biblical text. Perhaps the most significant one mentions both Hezekiah and his father, King Ahaz.

---

16. *COS* 2:303.
17. *ANEP*, #371–74; pp. 129–32, 293–94.
18. *ANET*, 288.

Hezekiah, son of Ahaz, king of Judah.[19]

Hezekiah is mentioned in four other seals belonging to his royal servants.

Amariah, son of Hananiah, servant of Hezekiah.

Yhozarah, son of Hilkiah, servant of Hezekiah.[20]

Domla, servant of Hezekiah.[21]

Ushna, servant of Hezekiah.[22]

Ushna is probably the same individual who appears on a seal as the servant of Hezekiah's father, Ahaz. Hilkiah also appears in this chapter as the father of Eliakim the palace administrator (18:37). Since these individuals have seals mentioning Hezekiah, they were probably high-ranking royal officials. Hezekiah's secretary, Shebna, who is mentioned three times (vv. 18, 26, 37), also appears in a seal (spelled "Shebaniah").

Shebaniah, servant of the king.[23]

Shebna is condemned by the prophet Isaiah for cutting his own tomb in a rock (Isa 22:15–19). A tomb cut into the rock on the eastern slope of the Kidron valley just outside of Jerusalem is widely believed to belong to Shebna. Here is the tomb inscription:

This is [the tomb of Sheban]iah who is over the house.[24]

In both Assyrian royal annals and in Judean royal seals, we find numerous ancient references to events and people from 2 Kings 18.

---

19. Cross, "Hezekiah's Seal," 42.
20. *COS* 2:200.
21. Robert Deutsch, "Lasting Impressions: New Bullae Reveal Egyptian-Style Emblems on Judah's Royal Seals" BAR 28.4 (2002): 43–51, 60.
22. R. Deutsch, *Biblical Period Bullae*, The Joseph Chaim Kaufman Collection 1 (Tel Aviv: Archaeological Center Publications, 2003): 13a–c.
23. Robert Deutsch, "Tracking Down Shebnayahu, Servant of the King," *BAR* 35.3 (2009): 45–49, 67.
24. *COS* 2:180.

Hezekiah's Reforms and Reign (2 Kings 18:1–8)

Hezekiah has the longest narrative of any ruler of the divided monarchy (ninety-five verses in 2 Kgs 18–20).[25] Just like his great, great-grandfather Amaziah of Judah (14:2), Hezekiah, son of Ahaz, came to the throne at age twenty-five and ruled for twenty-nine years (v. 2).[26] The text praises Solomon for his wisdom and wealth (1 Kgs 3:12–13), it condemns Omri, Ahab, and Manasseh for their wickedness (1 Kgs 16:25, 30; 21:25; 2 Kgs 21:11), and it praises Hezekiah and Josiah for their righteousness (18:5; 23:25). These assessments use hyperbolic language, as several different rulers are described as unique in similar aspects. Even though Josiah was uniquely righteous (23:25), the text also praises Hezekiah: "there was no one like him among all the kings of Judah" (18:5).

The reforms of Hezekiah were extensive. He removed the high places that had survived since the time of Solomon (1 Kgs 3:2). He smashed the sacred stones (*matsevot*), the Asherah poles, and the bronze snake (Nehushtan) that Moses had set up (2 Kgs 18:4). In addition to his acts of cultic purification, Hezekiah is praised for his obedience to the law of Moses (v. 6). Because of his piety, YHWH gave him victory in his rebellion against Assyria and his campaign against Philistia (vv. 6–8). However, his success must have been fleeting since Hezekiah was forced to give a massive tribute and was besieged by Sennacherib of Assyria (vv. 15–17).

Shalmaneser and Sennacherib's Campaigns (2 Kings 18:9–16)

The text next recalls (from 17:3–6) Shalmaneser V's attack and conquest of the Northern Kingdom (18:9–12). This retelling includes additional information: the beginning of the siege of Samaria occurred in Hezekiah's fourth year (v. 9) and the end in his sixth year (18:10). The theological explanation for the Northern Kingdom's demise is shortened from seventeen verses (17:7–23) down to one (18:12)—they disobeyed YHWH and violated the covenant. Why does the text include this review? Perhaps to show a contrast between the respective rulers. While both Hoshea and Hezekiah rebelled and gave tribute,

25. Various commentators discuss the different sources and somewhat confusing timetable associated with Hezekiah's narrative; see, for example, Wray Beal, *1 & 2 Kings*, 462–64.

26. There are numerous chronological problems associated with the reign of Hezekiah; see Cogan and Tadmor, *II Kings*, 216; Barnes, *1 & 2 Kings*, 323–27.

only Hezekiah reformed worship practices (vv. 3–6) and prayed (19:4, 15, 20), the reason he survived the Assyrian threat.

In spite of Hezekiah's piety and presumably because of his rebellion, Sennacherib of Assyria attacks Judah in the fourteenth year of Hezekiah's reign (18:13). The domain of his conquest is vast, including "all the fortified cities of Judah" (except Jerusalem; v. 13). In stark contrast to the man who defied the might of Assyria a few verses earlier (v. 7), Hezekiah now grovels and pleads for mercy (v. 14).[27] And like many Judean tributaries before him (Rehoboam, Asa, Jehoash, Amaziah, and Ahaz), Hezekiah plunders the treasuries and the temple (even stripping gold off the doors) to pay his massive tribute to Sennacherib: a ton of gold and over ten tons of silver (vv. 15–16; see discussion in Listen to the Story above).[28]

Sennacherib's Three Messengers (2 Kings 18:17–18)

It is difficult to understand why the king of Assyria, who appeared to be appeased by Hezekiah's tribute, would now attack and besiege Jerusalem (18:17). It is possible that 18:13–16 is a shorter, annalistic account of the same campaign of Sennacherib that is told in a longer, more theological version in 18:17–19:37. To avoid allowing issues of chronology and sources to dominate the discussion, I will refer interested readers to the discussions of these issues in other commentaries and will examine Hezekiah's narrative in its canonical order.[29]

Sennacherib remains in Lachish and sends three officials with a large army to demand Jerusalem's surrender (see discussion in Listen to the Story above). The location of their demand outside Jerusalem (the aqueduct on the road to the Washerman's Field) is where the prophet Isaiah exhorted Hezekiah's father Ahaz to trust in YHWH, not Assyria (Isa 7:3). Sennacherib's three officials are met by Hezekiah's three officials: Eliakim the palace administer, Shebna the secretary, and Joah the recorder (2 Kgs 18:18).

The Rabshakeh's First Speech (2 Kings 18:19–25)

The Rabshakeh (NIV: "field commander") serves as Sennacherib's spokesperson in the negotiations. He was a gifted communicator, making a brilliant use of rhetoric, even speaking the language of the Judeans (NIV: "Hebrew"). Wiseman

---

27. Presumably because 18:14–16 portrays Hezekiah so negatively, these three verses are omitted in Isa 36.

28. See my discussion of Israelite and Judean kings who give tribute in Lamb, *Righteous Jehu*, 121–24.

29. See, for example, Cogan and Tadmor, *II Kings*, 240–44; Barnes, *1 & 2 Kings*, 329–31; Wray Beal, *1 & 2 Kings*, 462–64.

describes his communication as "a masterpiece of deception and psychological warfare."[30] His two speeches to Hezekiah's officials are some of the longest in Kings (sixteen verses in English; 18:19–25, 27–35). The Rabshakeh starts and ends his speech with rhetorical questions (he asked twelve total) in his attempt to undermine their confidence in their allies, their army, their ruler, and their God.

He calls Egypt a splintered reed of a staff (v. 21), presumably because of the abundant reeds in Egypt's marshy waters. We are not sure which Pharaoh is referred to here, but it could be Tirhakah, the king of Cush, who appears in the next chapter (19:9). The Rabshakeh predicts the "reed" of Egypt will prove an unstable staff, inflicting injury upon any who rely upon it (see also Ezek 29:6–7).

Apparently, the Rabshakeh heard of Hezekiah's reforms, and he portrays them negatively (2 Kgs 18:22), arguing that YHWH was offended that his high places were removed (he clearly had not been reading the book of Kings), so YHWH will not support Hezekiah. The Rabshakeh not only claims YHWH was upset over the destroyed high places, but he also claims YHWH told him to attack and destroy Judah (v. 25). Was YHWH behind Assyria's attack? There is no biblical record of YHWH speaking directly to Sennacherib, but YHWH had sent Assyria to destroy Israel earlier (17:6–7), and the implication in that context was that YHWH was punishing Judah as well (vv. 19–20). Isaiah declared that YHWH used Assyria as a rod of his anger (Isa 10:5–6). YHWH was also behind Judah's ultimate downfall under Nebuchadnezzar of Babylon (2 Kgs 20:16–18; 24:1–2, 13, 20; Jer 29:3–4).

To insult the Judeans further, the Rabshakeh makes a wager that even if Sennacherib were to give Hezekiah two thousand horses, he could not produce riders for them (2 Kgs18:23). The Rabshakeh continues to taunt them by suggesting Judah's army could not even resist one of the weakest of the Assyrian officers (v. 24). The Rabshakeh's threat is supported by the fact that Sennacherib's army had encountered little resistance as they attacked and captured all the fortified cities of Judah (v. 13).

The Rabshakeh's Second Speech (2 Kings 18:26–37)

Hezekiah's three servants, Eliakim, Shebna, and Joah, have a brief interlude to recover from the Rabshakeh's first rhetorical onslaught. They request a shift to the language of Aramaic to prevent residents of Jerusalem on the wall from listening in on their diplomatic negotiations (18:26).

Just as a good boxer does not let up when he realizes his foe is weak, in his second speech the Rabshakeh intensifies his verbal barrage, predicting that the

30. Wiseman, *1 & 2 Kings*, 277.

residents of Jerusalem, because of the severity of their siege-induced famine, will be forced to eat their own excrement and drink their own urine (v. 27). As is typical of trash talking, the vulgarity of his speech is intended to intimidate people into submission as they envision horrific fates.[31]

The Rabshakeh calls out louder in the language of the people with two sets of negative imperatives: do not let Hezekiah deceive/persuade you (vv. 29, 30); do not listen to Hezekiah (vv. 31, 32). He repeatedly ridicules the idea that YHWH could possibly deliver, rescue, or save them from this crisis (vv. 29, 30, 32, 33, 34, 35).

Saying essentially, "Let's make a deal," he switches momentary from the stick to the carrot, as he dangles the idea of making peace with Sennacherib before them. They would be able to eat their own fruit and drink their own water (instead of the less attractive previously mentioned dietary alternatives; vv. 27, 31). He piles on the positives: grain, wine, bread, vineyards, olives, honey (v. 32)—like a new promised land. Then, in language reminiscent of Deuteronomy, he challenges them to "Choose life and not death" (v. 32; see also Deut 30:19).

The Rabshakeh's last tactic is to review how the gods of Israel's neighbors did not help in their defense against the Assyrian juggernaut (2 Kgs 18:33–35). Hamath and Arpad are to the west, Hena to the east; the locations of Sepharvaim and Ivvah are uncertain.[32] The text earlier reviewed the Assyrian conquest of Samaria, and now the Rabshakeh reminds Hezekiah's team that Samaria's God did not save them earlier (vv. 34–35), although readers of the text know it was not because of a lack of ability (17:7–12; 18:12). The Rabshakeh concludes that YHWH cannot save Jerusalem now. YHWH will get a chance to respond to this insult later (19:21–28), but the Rabshakeh's final barrage of six rhetorical questions (18:33–35) leaves Hezekiah's officials silent as they return with torn clothes to give their report to the king (vv. 36–37).[33]

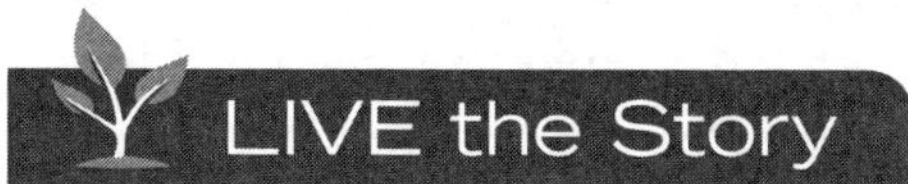

Trust and Obey

Perhaps more so than any other king in the book, Hezekiah trusted and obeyed God. He didn't have a recent positive example of what it looked like; David

31. See also, Lamb, "Trash Talking," 111–30.

32. See Wray Beal, *1 & 2 Kings*, 469.

33. On torn clothes during times of mourning or crisis, see 1 Kgs 11:30–31; 21:27; 2 Kgs 2:12; 5:7–8; 6:30; 11:14; 19:1; 22:11, 19.

(2 Kgs 18:3) lived almost three centuries earlier. The text doesn't specify which ones, but it states he was obeying commands given to Moses by YHWH (v. 6). The most obvious of these were the prohibitions against idol worship in the Decalogue (Exod 20:3–6; Deut 5:7–10), commands that many of the previous rulers have blatantly broken (e.g., 1 Kgs 16:26; 21:26; 2 Kgs 13:6; 17:12, 15). Hezekiah didn't merely trust YHWH generically, but his trust led him to acts of destruction against structures that contributed to syncretistic worship practices (high places, sacred stones, Asherah poles, and the Nehushtan).

While Hezekiah's actions here are clearly righteous and perceived positively in the text, it is likely that they were not viewed positively in his context, particularly by those who had been utilizing these objects. Asherah poles were clearly idols, but the Nehushtan pole was originally God's idea (Num 21:4–9). What caused the shift from perceiving the bronze snake as a tangible image of God's deliverance to an idolatrous image of false worship?

The problem with any image, object, or location is that it can quickly become the focus of worship instead of God himself. The people thought they needed to worship at a high place, near a sacred stone, or with a bronze snake. YHWH wanted his people to worship at the temple, but even his temple had a limited time span, as God himself allowed it to be destroyed (2 Kgs 25:9). Hezekiah was modeling for his people how to trust and obey by removing their precious sacred objects to force them to trust in God alone.

Many churches or ministries today have seen God work in the past through a location or a program. But just as the bronze snake was no longer helpful and became harmful, many popular programs or structures can outlive their useful purpose. But like these familiar objects in the time of Hezekiah, people are comfortable with these structures because they are familiar with them, and this familiarity means people don't need to trust God as much.

For several years my church held a very popular outdoor expo in the spring. Thousands of people would come every year to learn about hunting, fishing, and outdoor adventure activities, and children could be entertained by zip lines, ropes courses, face painting, and so on. One year my wife and I signed up for a course in scuba diving, and now we're certified divers. Many of those who came to the expo were not regular church attenders, so the expo gave them an opportunity to visit a church in a low-key way and to be served in a way they really appreciated. It became so popular over the years that there was a growing temptation to depend upon this familiar structure instead of the God who had originally inspired it. Just as the Nehushtan was no longer helping people depend on God during the time of Hezekiah, the outdoor expo had ceased being a way to trust God and needed to end. So, a few years ago the leaders of the church decided to stop holding this popular program in order to trust God in new ways. Not surprisingly, the decision was not popular, but by being willing to remove a structure that was becoming an idol, they, like Hezekiah, modeled a costly dependence upon God. Trust and obey, there's no other way.

Tell and Retell

Certain stories bear repeating. The book of Chronicles retells much of the book of Kings (particularly material related to Judah). Most of Hezekiah's narrative is repeated in the book of Isaiah (in chapters 36–39). Even though it had just been recorded in the previous chapter (2 Kgs 17:1–6), the fall of Samaria is retold before narrating Sennacherib's campaign (18:9–12). The Assyrians knew the importance of retelling stories, as they recorded Sennacherib's annals on three separate prisms (see Listen to the Story above).

Israel's calendar emphasizes the value of retelling stories. The story of Esther was remembered in the annual festival of Purim (Est 9:18–32). The story of the Exodus was recalled annually in the observance of the Passover (Exod 13:3–10). The story of creation was "retold" weekly in the commemoration of the Sabbath (Exod 20:8–11).

While we may groan when a family member begins to tell a very familiar story, the divinely inspired biblical authors clearly thought that some stories needed to be retold. Why? Pragmatically, stories are entertaining because they are enjoyable to listen to. As stories are retold, they are less likely to be forgotten—they become part of us. Stories that remind us of how God has been at work in the past can give us hope for how he can be at work in the future. Stories that are important need to be repeated.

Be a person that is willing to endure the occasional groans from family members to tell important stories of how God has been at work in your life. The story of Hezekiah's descendant Jesus is repeated in four Gospels. Each of them has their own unique perspective on Jesus's birth, life, ministry, death, and resurrection, but, particularly in the Synoptic Gospels (Matthew, Mark and Luke), much of the material is repeated. Why? Because the story of Jesus is one that bears repeating.

CHAPTER 35

2 Kings 19:1–37

LISTEN to the Story

[1]When King Hezekiah heard this, he tore his clothes and put on sackcloth and went into the temple of the LORD. [2]He sent Eliakim the palace
administrator, Shebna the secretary and the leading priests, all wearing
sackcloth, to the prophet Isaiah son of Amoz. [3]They told him, "This is
what Hezekiah says: This day is a day of distress and rebuke and disgrace,
as when children come to the moment of birth and there is no strength to
deliver them. [4]It may be that the LORD your God will hear all the words
of the field commander, whom his master, the king of Assyria, has sent to
ridicule the living God, and that he will rebuke him for the words the LORD
your God has heard. Therefore pray for the remnant that still survives."

[5]When King Hezekiah's officials came to Isaiah, [6]Isaiah said to them,
"Tell your master, 'This is what the LORD says: Do not be afraid of what
you have heard—those words with which the underlings of the king of
Assyria have blasphemed me. [7]Listen! When he hears a certain report, I will
make him want to return to his own country, and there I will have him
cut down with the sword.'"

[8]When the field commander heard that the king of Assyria had left
Lachish, he withdrew and found the king fighting against Libnah.

[9]Now Sennacherib received a report that Tirhakah, the king of Cush, was
marching out to fight against him. So he again sent messengers to Hezekiah
with this word: [10]"Say to Hezekiah king of Judah: Do not let the god you
depend on deceive you when he says, 'Jerusalem will not be given into the
hands of the king of Assyria.' [11]Surely you have heard what the kings of
Assyria have done to all the countries, destroying them completely. And
will you be delivered? [12]Did the gods of the nations that were destroyed by
my predecessors deliver them—the gods of Gozan, Harran, Rezeph and the
people of Eden who were in Tel Assar? [13]Where is the king of Hamath or the
king of Arpad? Where are the kings of Lair, Sepharvaim, Hena and Ivvah?"

14Hezekiah received the letter from the messengers and read it. Then
he went up to the temple of the LORD and spread it out before the LORD.
15And Hezekiah prayed to the LORD: "LORD, the God of Israel, enthroned
between the cherubim, you alone are God over all the kingdoms of the
earth. You have made heaven and earth. 16Give ear, LORD, and hear; open
your eyes, LORD, and see; listen to the words Sennacherib has sent to
ridicule the living God.

17"It is true, LORD, that the Assyrian kings have laid waste these nations
and their lands. 18They have thrown their gods into the fire and destroyed
them, for they were not gods but only wood and stone, fashioned by
human hands. 19Now, LORD our God, deliver us from his hand, so that
all the kingdoms of the earth may know that you alone, LORD, are God."

20Then Isaiah son of Amoz sent a message to Hezekiah: "This is what
the LORD, the God of Israel, says: I have heard your prayer concerning
Sennacherib king of Assyria. 21This is the word that the LORD has spoken
against him:

"'Virgin Daughter Zion
despises you and mocks you.
Daughter Jerusalem
tosses her head as you flee.
22Who is it you have ridiculed and blasphemed?
Against whom have you raised your voice
and lifted your eyes in pride?
Against the Holy One of Israel!
23By your messengers
you have ridiculed the Lord.
And you have said,
"With my many chariots
I have ascended the heights of the mountains,
the utmost heights of Lebanon.
I have cut down its tallest cedars,
the choicest of its junipers.
I have reached its remotest parts,
the finest of its forests.
24I have dug wells in foreign lands
and drunk the water there.

With the soles of my feet
    I have dried up all the streams of Egypt."

25"'Have you not heard?
    Long ago I ordained it.
In days of old I planned it;
    now I have brought it to pass,
that you have turned fortified cities
    into piles of stone.
26Their people, drained of power,
    are dismayed and put to shame.
They are like plants in the field,
    like tender green shoots,
like grass sprouting on the roof,
    scorched before it grows up.

27"'But I know where you are
    and when you come and go
    and how you rage against me.
28Because you rage against me
    and because your insolence has reached my ears,
I will put my hook in your nose
    and my bit in your mouth,
and I will make you return
    by the way you came.'

29"This will be the sign for you, Hezekiah:

"This year you will eat what grows by itself,
    and the second year what springs from that.
But in the third year sow and reap,
    plant vineyards and eat their fruit.
30Once more a remnant of the kingdom of Judah
    will take root below and bear fruit above.
31For out of Jerusalem will come a remnant,
    and out of Mount Zion a band of survivors.

"The zeal of the LORD Almighty will accomplish this.

32"Therefore this is what the LORD says concerning the king of Assyria:

"'He will not enter this city
  or shoot an arrow here.
He will not come before it with shield
  or build a siege ramp against it.
33By the way that he came he will return;
  he will not enter this city,
  declares the LORD.
34I will defend this city and save it,
  for my sake and for the sake of David my servant.'"

35That night the angel of the LORD went out and put to death a hundred and eighty-five thousand in the Assyrian camp. When the people got up the next morning—there were all the dead bodies! 36So Sennacherib king of Assyria broke camp and withdrew. He returned to Nineveh and stayed there.

37One day, while he was worshiping in the temple of his god Nisrok, his sons Adrammelek and Sharezer killed him with the sword, and they escaped to the land of Ararat. And Esarhaddon his son succeeded him as king.

Listening to the Text in the Story: Biblical Texts: Ezra 4:2; Isaiah 36–39; Ancient Near Eastern Texts: The Babylonian Chronicle; The Royal Inscriptions of Esarhaddon and Ashurbanipal; The Victory Stele of Esarhaddon; The Prophet Isaiah Bulla

Previously in Kings, Sennacherib's army had surrounded Jerusalem, and his officials were taunting Hezekiah's officials and tempting Hezekiah to surrender the city. According to the Rabshakeh ("the field commander"), if they did not give up, the residents of Jerusalem would soon be eating their own dung and drinking their own urine (18:27). Hezekiah responds in this chapter with prayer, a model for all people of faith in times of crisis. The prophet Isaiah delivers messages of encouragement to Hezekiah, predicting that Sennacherib would soon be dead. The chapter ends with the slaughter of Sennacherib's army and the death of the ruler at the hands of his own sons back in his capital city, Nineveh (19:37).

The catalyst for Sennacherib's departure from Jerusalem is a report that Tirhakah, the king of Cush, was marching toward him. Tirhakah (in Nubian sources Taharqa) did not become ruler of Egypt until later (689–664 BC), but at this point he was probably the commander-in-chief for his brother, Shebitku.[1] Tirhakah is mentioned in Assyrian inscriptions as a foe of Sennacherib's son, Esarhaddon, and his grandson, Ashurbanipal.[2] Esarhaddon, whose ascension is reported at the end of this chapter (19:37), is also mentioned in Ezra, as a group of residents spoke of living in the land since Esarhaddon brought them there (Ezra 4:2).

Sennacherib's inscription that described Hezekiah as a "bird in a cage" (discussed in the previous chapter) also records the officials of the Philistine city of Ekron overthrowing their ruler Padi and handing him over to Hezekiah. It also mentions a conflict between Egypt and Assyria that may be alluded to in this chapter (19:9).

> The officials, the nobles, and the people of Ekron who had thrown Padi, their king, (who was) under oath and obligation to Assyria, into iron fetters and handed him over in a hostile manner to Hezekiah, the Judean, took fright because of the offense they had committed. The kings of Egypt, (and) the bowmen, chariot corps and cavalry of the kings of Ethiopia assembled a countless force and came to their (i.e. the Ekronites') aid. In the plain of Eltekeh, they drew up their ranks against me and sharpened their weapons. Trusting in the god Ashur, my lord, I fought with them and inflicted a defeat upon them. . . . I besieged and conquered Eltekeh and Timnah and carried off their spoil. I advanced to Ekron and slew its officials and nobles who had stirred up rebellion and hung their bodies on watchtowers all about the city. . . . I freed Padi, their king, from Jerusalem and set him on the throne as king over them and imposed tribute for my lordship over him.[3]

The Egyptian army came to the aid of the rebels of Ekron. But since Padi (their ruler) was an Assyrian vassal, Assyria retaliated against the rebels. Egypt supported the rebels, so the forces of Sennacherib engaged those of Egypt at

1. Wiseman, *1 & 2 Kings*, 280.
2. *ANET*, 290, 292, 293, 294, 295, 296.
3. *COS* 2:303.

Eltekah. Sennacherib claims to defeat the Egyptian forces. Hezekiah then apparently released Padi, perhaps in an attempt to appease the Assyrians who were threatening Jerusalem.[4]

In 2 Kings 19 the Israelites are delivered from the Assyrians by an angel of YHWH (19:35). Similarly, the Greek historian Herodotus mentions how an Egyptian army facing an overwhelming Assyrian army led by Sennacherib was miraculously delivered at Pelusium (a city on the eastern Nile delta) when "thousands of field-mice swarmed over the Assyrians during the night, and ate their quivers, their bowstrings, and the leader handles of their shields, so that on the following day, having no arms to fight with, they abandoned their position and suffered severe losses during their retreat."[5] It is difficult to say if the story in 2 Kings 19 and Herodotus are referring to the same event, yet both clearly speak of a divine deliverance from an Assyrian army led by Sennacherib.[6]

The language of Isaiah's oracle to Sennacherib (vv. 21–28) suggests a familiarity with Assyrian practices recorded in their own sources. YHWH quotes Sennacherib's boast about cutting down the tallest cedars (v. 23), and Sennacherib's distant predecessor Ashurnasirpal II (883–859 BC) is described in a hymn as having cut down "beams of Cedar from the Amantus" and taken them to a temple at Esharna.[7] YHWH declares that he would put a hook in Sennacherib's nose to lead him back home (v. 28). The Victory Stele of Esarhaddon depicts Sennacherib's son leading two captives, each with a ring through their lips; the first is Tirhakah of Egypt (v. 9), and the second is Baal I of Tyre.[8]

Two of Sennacherib's sons kill him while he worships at the temple of Nisrok. This assassination took place on the twentieth day of the tenth month in 681 BC.[9] Ironically, in one of his inscriptions Sennacherib prays for the long life of his sons; perhaps he should have prayed instead that they would not commit patricidal regicide.[10] The Babylonian Chronicle records that the sons of Sennacherib killed him and that his son Esarhaddon succeed him on the throne:

4. See also *ZIBBC* 3:191.

5. Herodotus, *The Histories*, trans. Aubrey de Sélincourt (Penguin Books: New York, 1996), 2.141.

6. For possible interpretations of this event, see Barnes, *1 & 2 Kings*, 341.

7. *COS* 1:471.

8. *ZIBBC* 3:193; *ANEP*, 154, 300–301; #447.

9. *BBCOT*, 407.

10. See the discussion of this inscription and of royal prayers for longevity in Lamb, *Righteous Jehu*, 164–66.

> 681 BCE On 20th Tebet Sennacherib king of Assyria—his son killed him in a revolt. For [24] years Sennacherib ruled over Assyria . . . On [1/2]8th of Adar Esarhaddon, his son, ascended the throne of Assyria.[11]

In one of his inscriptions Esarhaddon describes how his father Sennacherib had selected him to be his successor, despite the fact that he was the youngest son, and how his brothers attempted to take the throne.[12] A damaged letter from Esarhaddon also appears to report on this incident, specifically naming one of the co-conspirators, his brother Arad-Mullissu,[13] who is called Adrammelek in the biblical text (v. 37).

One of the most interesting archaeological finds of 2018 involved the prophet Isaiah. A small bulla (a stamp seal impression) with the name Isaiah was found at the foot of the southern wall of the temple mount in Jerusalem.[14] While we cannot be sure it belonged to the famous prophet, two factors suggest it is likely. The bulla was found only ten feet from where the King Hezekiah bulla was found (see previous chapter), and the inscription, which is unfortunately damaged, appears to include the word "prophet."

Hezekiah's Message to Isaiah (2 Kings 19:1–4)

Sending and receiving messages is a major theme of 2 Kings 19. The chapter mentions nine messages: six are recorded and the other three are merely received as reports (vv. 7, 8, 9). The six recorded messages are exchanged between Hezekiah, Isaiah, Sennacherib, and YHWH in the chapter, each of whom sends and receives a message. Five of the six involve Hezekiah.

There is no real dialogue here, but the text states that each character hears before replying. Forms of the verb "hear" (*shema'*) appear twelve times in the chapter (vv. 1, 4 [2x], 6, 7, 8, 9, 11, 16 [2x], 20, 25).

The chapter begins with Hezekiah hearing the news of the Assyrian threat, tearing his clothes, and putting on sackcloth (v. 1), practices that are associated elsewhere with crisis or mourning (see 1 Kgs 11:30–31; 21:27; 2 Kgs 2:12; 5:7–8; 6:30; 11:14; 22:11, 19). He goes to the temple of YHWH; later the text makes it explicit that he is praying in the temple (19:14–15).

11. *COS* 1:467.
12. *ANET*, 289.
13. *COS* 3:244.
14. Eliat Mazar, "Is This the Prophet Isaiah's Signature?," *BAR* 42.2 (March–June 2018): 64–73, 92.

Hezekiah's first message is to the great prophet Isaiah, the son of Amoz (v. 2). While we know that Isaiah ministered during the reign of Hezekiah's father, Ahaz, and interacted with him directly (Isa 1:1; 7:1, 2, 3, 10, 12; 14:28), Isaiah has not been mentioned previously in Kings. Isaiah is the first prophet mentioned by name since Jonah, during the reign of Jeroboam II (14:25). While Amos, Hosea, Micah, Zephaniah, Jeremiah, Nahum, and Habakkuk all presumably ministered during the period of the monarchy, Isaiah and Jonah are the only prophets with books named after them who are mentioned in Kings.

To deliver his message to Isaiah, Hezekiah sends a similar group of people that he had sent to the Rabshakeh earlier (18:18), without Joah the recorder but with some priests (19:2), perhaps thinking that they are more likely to be taken seriously by the prophet than administrators would be.

In his message Hezekiah cries words of lament (distress, rebuke, disgrace, ridicule) and compares their situation to that of a woman who, at the moment of birth, has no strength to deliver (v. 3). Motherhood thus far in Kings has been brutal and tragic: experiencing the deaths of sons (1 Kgs 17:17; 2 Kgs 4:20), being forced to eat sons during a famine (6:29), and being ripped open during pregnancy (15:16). Hezekiah identifies YHWH twice, not as his own God but as the God of Isaiah ("your God"; *'eloheyka*; 19:4), suggesting he feels abandoned in the midst of the crisis.

Hezekiah wonders if YHWH was listening to the Rabshakeh's words as the Assyrian was ridiculing Judah's God. He requests a divine rebuke for the Rabshakeh and a prophetic prayer for the Judeans who have survived the Assyrian campaign (v. 4).

YHWH's First Message to Hezekiah (2 Kings 19:5–7)

Isaiah responds to Hezekiah's message with a message from YHWH, using the divine messenger formula, "This is what the Lord says" (*koh 'amar yhwh*; 19:6), an expression used frequently in the book (thirty-three times) to introduce a prophetic oracle. Sennacherib has the Rabshakeh as his spokesperson; YHWH has Isaiah.

YHWH tells Hezekiah to not fear (v. 6), words that both YHWH spoke to Elijah (1:15) and Elisha spoke to his servant (6:16). To inspire hope in the anxious ruler, he insults Sennacherib's messengers—instead of NIV's "underlings of the king" (*na'are melek*; 19:6), Alter has the appropriately disparaging "flunkies of the king."[15] YHWH accuses them of blasphemy and then predicts he'll hear a message prompting his return, where he will be killed (v. 7).

15. Alter, *Former Prophets*, 819. Perhaps "minions" would have been more contemporary?

Sennacherib's Message to Hezekiah (2 Kings 19:8–13)

The text records no response from Hezekiah to YHWH's oracle but shifts to the Rabshakeh's response to the message that Sennacherib had moved from Lachish to Libnah, prompting the departure of the Assyrian embassy that had been harassing and threatening the residents of Jerusalem (19:8). Next, Sennacherib receives another message that Tirhakah, king of Cush, was marching to fight Assyria (v. 9). We know from Assyrian sources that Tirhakah and Assyrian rulers engaged in numerous conflicts during this period (see Listen to the Story above). Sennacherib wants to deliver a parting shot to Hezekiah, so he sends a letter in the hands of his messengers, reiterating several of the themes the Rabshakeh (who may have delivered it) had said earlier (18:19–25, 27–35).

Sennacherib's letter begins with two exhortations (19:10) and ends with four rhetorical questions (19:11–13). He argues that YHWH cannot deliver Jerusalem from Assyria, just as the gods of these other places did not deliver them. His list of Assyrian conquests includes five locations mentioned earlier: Hamath, Arpad, Sepharvaim, Hena, and Ivvah (18:34) and five new ones: Gozan, Harran, Rezeph, Eden, and Lair (19:12–13). This impressive list was meant to further intimidate the king. The Assyrians were uniquely gifted at psychological warfare.[16]

Hezekiah's Message to YHWH (2 Kings 19:14–19)

Upon reading Sennacherib's threatening letter, the text records no immediate emotional response from Hezekiah (see 20:3). He merely goes to the temple, as he did when his officials reported the words of the Rabshakeh (19:1, 14). But this time Hezekiah speaks directly to YHWH, and he uses a visual aid—spreading out the letter. The text states that he prayed, and it records his prayer (vv. 15–19). Scripture includes a wide variety of different types and patterns of prayer, but many of them begin with praise, as does Hezekiah's here (v. 15).

While Sennacherib claims power over nations, Hezekiah declares that YHWH alone is king as he sits on his cherubic throne over all nations, including Assyria (v. 15). Hezekiah's reference is presumably inspired by the two cherubim in the inner sanctuary (1 Kgs 6:23), or perhaps by the two that rest on the cover of the mercy seat of the ark of the covenant (Exod 25:18–22).

Before his ultimate request (2 Kgs 19:19), Hezekiah gives YHWH a series of five commands (give ear, hear, open, see, listen; v. 16), which appears audacious—things one should not say to God. But Scripture is full

16. For more on psychological warfare, see Lamb, "Trash Talking."

of surprisingly bold prayers like these (e.g., 1 Kgs 8:28–30; Pss 17:6; 31:2; 102:2; Dan 9:18). Hezekiah's imperatives focus on the senses of hearing and seeing. Hezekiah wants to make sure YHWH knows what the ruler of Assyria has said and done, because, ultimately, he is ridiculing YHWH (2 Kgs 19:16).

Hezekiah acknowledges that Assyria has conquered the areas mentioned in the letter, but that is not surprising, because their gods were powerless, merely wood and stone, made by humans (see also Isa 40:20; 44:19). Hezekiah's ultimate request—divine deliverance—would prove a sign for not just Hezekiah but for all kingdoms of the earth that YHWH alone was God (2 Kgs 19:19).

YHWH's Message to Sennacherib (2 Kings 19:20–28)

Unlike the book of Samuel (e.g., 1 Sam 2:1–10; 15:22–23; 2 Sam 1:19–27; 22:2–51), the book of Kings includes very little poetry, making Isaiah's second oracle of this chapter by far the longest section of poetry in the book. While the NIV formats 19:21–34 poetically, several other English translations (ESV, NRSV, and NASB) have the poetry ending at 19:28. In any case, this poetic section, while unique in Kings, is much more typical of the book of Isaiah.

The beginning and end of Isaiah's oracle is a message from YHWH to Hezekiah (vv. 20, 29–34). Before speaking to the Assyrian ruler, YHWH wants to reassure the Judean ruler that his prayer has been heard. While most of this oracle is addressed to Sennacherib (vv. 21–28), Hezekiah is allowed to overhear the message to the Assyrian ruler, presumably to encourage the Judean king in the crisis. The message to Sennacherib is a taunt song, giving back to the Assyrians a taste of what they were dishing out before (18:23, 27).

While Sennacherib's officers were mocking Jerusalem earlier, as they flee, Assyria is mocked by a young girl, as Jerusalem is personified as a virgin daughter (19:21). Previously, Hezekiah said the Rabshakeh ridiculed YHWH (v. 4), and YHWH said he blasphemed YHWH (v. 6); now YHWH asks Sennacherib who he was ridiculing and blaspheming (v. 22). YHWH then accuses the Assyrian of attacking none other than the "Holy One of Israel" (*qedosh yisra'el*), a title that the book of Isaiah distinctively uses for YHWH (e.g., Isa 1:4; 5:19; 10:20; 12:6; 17:7).

YHWH then reviews the many boasts of Sennacherib (see Listen to the Story above) regarding his geographic conquests—not over specific cities (Gozan, Harran, etc), but to high mountains, remote forests, and distant lands, ranging from Lebanon to Egypt (2 Kgs 19:23–24). Sennacherib has bragged about his mighty achievements, including chopping down tall trees, digging deep wells, and drying up the streams of Egypt (presumably the delta of the Nile). YHWH intends to chop down Sennacherib's ego by informing him that he has already ordained all of these events in the distant past (vv. 25–26). YHWH does not deny Assyria has conquered these regions, he merely notes that it was part of his sovereign plan.

YHWH began the taunt oracle by describing girls mocking Sennacherib in his flight (v. 21) and ends it with an image of the Assyrian ruler with a hook in his nose and bit in his mouth as YHWH leads him home (v. 28; see Listen to the Story above). Just as the Assyrians humiliated their foes, YHWH would do the same to the foes of his people Judah.

YHWH's Second Message to Hezekiah (2 Kings 19:29–34)

The presence of parallelism throughout this section explains why the NIV continues to format 19:29–34 poetically, although other translations format it as prose (ESV, NRSV, and NASB). Starting at verse 29, there is a shift in address from Sennacherib to Hezekiah (although the Hebrew text omits the Hezekiah's name here).

The prophet Isaiah gave Hezekiah's father, Ahaz, the sign (*'ot*) of the birth of the Immanuel child (Isa 7:11, 14), and now Isaiah gives Hezekiah a sign (*'ot*; see also 2 Kgs 20:8, 9) of a quick recovery for the harvests (19:29; see also 7:1–20). After an extended siege, many years are required for normal harvests to return, since everything has been consumed (no seeds for sowing), but by the third year they will be sowing, reaping, planting, and eating (19:29). This sign will not just serve as a reminder of divine provision, but it will also symbolize hope that the remnant of Israel and Judah that has been devastated by the Assyrians will take root, be fruitful, survive, and thrive (vv. 30–31). All will be accomplished by the zeal of "the LORD almighty" (*yhwh tseba'ot*).

Only the first verse of this message to Hezekiah focuses directly on the king (v. 29). The final three verses speak about Sennacherib in third-person language, describing his ultimate fate. YHWH declares Sennacherib will not do four things. He will not enter Jerusalem, shoot an arrow there, approach with a shield, or build a siege ramp (v. 32). Sennacherib will return home to Nineveh via the same road he arrived on (v. 33), but presumably with a nose hook (v. 28), while the daughters of Jerusalem taunt him (v. 21). YHWH declares that, just as Hezekiah prayed for deliverance, YHWH would defend and save his city for the sake of Hezekiah's distant ancestor, David (19:34; see 20:6).

YHWH's Prediction Fulfilled (2 Kings 19:35–37)

The same night that Hezekiah prayed and Isaiah delivered the oracle, "the angel of the LORD" (*mal'ak yhwh*) killed 185,000 Assyrian soldiers at their camp (19:35). Three questions arise here. First, what can we determine about "the angel of the Lord" (*mal'ak yhwh*; 19:35) by examining his actions elsewhere? In the two other places this divine angel appears in Kings, he feeds Elijah (1 Kgs 19:7) and encourages Elijah to meet with King Ahaz (2 Kgs 1:15). Elsewhere in the Old Testament the angel of YHWH does not usually slaughter people but commissions them (e.g., Gen 16:9; Exod 3:2; Judg 6:11) or gives them good news (e.g., Gen 16:10; 22:11–18; Judg 13:3). While this messenger brought bad news to the Assyrians, it was good news for the Judeans. The people who were going to force them to eat their own dung and drink their own urine (2 Kgs 18:27) are now dead.

Second, where is the Assyrian camp? The camp could be just outside of Jerusalem, meaning the people who saw all the bodies would be the residents of the city. It could be near Libnah, where Sennacherib was last fighting and was joined by the Rabshakeh's embassy (19:8). It could also be located somewhere on the way toward Egypt, as Sennacherib was marching toward the Egyptian forces of Tirhakah (v. 9). In any case, Sennacherib will not be able to fulfill his threat (v. 10)—YHWH did deliver Jerusalem.

Third, why the massive slaughter of 185,000? I discuss this troubling question in more depth elsewhere,[17] but at this point we can make three points. One, the Hebrew word translated as "thousand" (*aleph*) need not imply a strict numeric value. Wiseman suggests the phrase could be "185 officers."[18] Two, large numbers of people often get killed in contexts of war, and the Assyrians were the ones instigating the conflict. Three, the destruction of the Assyrian army meant the people of YHWH were delivered from this horrific threat. After all his boasting and taunting, Sennacherib returned quietly to Nineveh, where he remained (v. 36; see discussion of the Herodotus parallel in Listen to the Story above).

The chapter concludes with a report of the death of Sennacherib, which occurred many years later (681 BC). The delay is here suggested by the phrase "one day" (v. 37). The assassination took place in the temple of Nisrok, a god who does not appear in other ancient sources. The co-conspirators flee to Ararat, while one of Sennacherib's younger sons, Esarhaddon, succeeds him (see Listen to the Story above). As YHWH predicted (v. 7), Sennacherib the mighty emperor was cut down with the sword.

17. See Lamb, *God Behaving Badly*, 102–4.

18. Wiseman, *1 & 2 Kings*, 284.

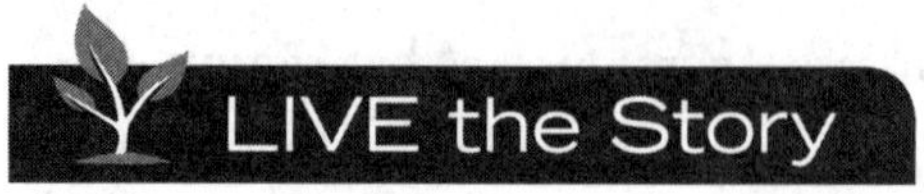

The theme of communication dominates 2 Kings 19. People send messages, and the recipients listen and respond. Nine messages are sent, three merely noted, but the six that are recorded make up most of the chapter. The Assyrians knew that words were powerful, and they used them effectively in their messages to intimidate their enemies. Earlier, Hezekiah responded with a message directly to Sennacherib (18:14), and it resulted in him giving a massive tribute (vv. 15–16). Here, Hezekiah gives no response to Sennacherib's verbal attacks. Instead of replying, he communicates with the prophet of YHWH (19:3–4) and then YHWH himself (vv. 15–19). What can we learn about prayer from Hezekiah's response here? I see three lessons.

Praise God

Hezekiah praises God (2 Kgs 19:15). He begins this chapter with lament, as he rips his clothes and complains of disgrace in his message to Isaiah (vv. 1, 3), but when he prays directly to YHWH, he begins with praise. Praise God in your prayers, particular at the beginning. Praise shifts our focus from ourselves and our problems to God and his sovereignty. When the disciples asked Jesus to teach them how to pray, he began his prayer with praise (Matt 6:9; Luke 11:2).

For most of my life I have found it difficult to praise God. It was much easier to thank God for what he had done than to honor him for who he is. The author who has helped me the most in this area is C. S. Lewis. He describes how he found it troubling that God himself demanded that we praise him: "we despise the man who demands continued assurance of his own virtue, intelligence or delightfulness; we despise still more the crowd of people round every dictator, every millionaire, every celebrity, who gratify that demand."[19] Lewis continues narrating his struggles with praise until the realization hit him: "I had never noticed that all enjoyment spontaneously overflows into praise . . . the world rings with praise—lovers praising their mistresses, readers their favorite poet, walkers praising the countryside, players praising their favorite game . . . praise of . . . even sometimes politicians and scholars."[20]

Whether it is sports, food, books, or films—we praise what we love. Hezekiah loved God and therefore praised God. If you find it hard to praise

19. C. S. Lewis, *Reflections on the Psalms* (New York: Harcourt Brace Jovanovich, 1958), 90.
20. Lewis, *Reflections*, 94.

God, allow the psalmist to inspire you by reading psalms of praise (Pss 8, 19, 33, 66, 100, 103, 104, 105, 111, 113, 114, 117, 145–150). Hezekiah was clearly affected by the surroundings of the temple, particularly the cherubim, so put yourself in a place conducive to praise. Go outside and experience the creator in his creation, which should naturally lead us to praise.

Command God

After praising God, Hezekiah commanded God (2 Kgs 19:16). We may not naturally praise God, but we know we should. Commanding God, however, feels wrong. It shouldn't, because that's how people pray in Scripture.

We often qualify our requests in prayer with expressions like "please, God" or "if it be your will," but we rarely do we string together a series of commands to God like Hezekiah does here (give ear, hear, open, see, listen; 19:16). The book of Psalms is full of prayers, but none of them use "please" to compel God to answer. If you fell overboard on a boat at sea during a storm, would you say to the people standing back on the boat with the life jacket, "Oh, person on the boat, please, if it be your will, person on the boat, would you be willing to toss me that life jacket, person on the boat, please." There's no time for politeness—"Help! Save me!" If we truly believe God is the only source of our salvation, our prayers should be more like Hezekiah's.

Giving God commands requires boldness and trust that he is actually listening and that he is able to respond. When Jesus taught the disciples to pray, after praising God, he gave God two direct commands (give us, forgive us; Matt 6:11–12; Luke 11:3–4). Jesus wants us to command God.

It may feel awkward at your church prayer meeting to start giving God a series of bold commands, but perhaps that will help keep our fellow prayers awake. It is easy for prayer to feel like a passive experience, almost boring, when it should feel like an incredible encounter with the king of the whole earth (2 Kgs 19:19). Be bold—command God in prayer.

Listen to God

Hezekiah commands God to listen to him and to listen to Sennacherib (2 Kgs 19:4, 16). From YHWH's response, we know that he has listened to the words of not just his king but also his king's enemy (vv. 6, 22–23, 28, 34). God listens to both prayers and taunts. But God isn't the only one listening here. Hezekiah also listens to God.

God delivers three messages, two to Hezekiah (19:6–7; 29–34) and one to Sennacherib (vv. 21–28). The second oracle delivered by Isaiah is the longest message from YHWH in the book of Kings (fourteen verses). The text here makes it clear that God is speaking, reiterating five times that these are God's words (vv. 6, 20, 21, 32, 33).

But we don't really see Hezekiah respond. Even though the chapter includes many verbs of hearing, none of them have Hezekiah as the subject. How do we know Hezekiah is listening? In Hebrew the literal expression to "listen to the voice of" (*shama' beqol*) someone is often translated as "to obey" (e.g., 18:12). In the world of the Bible, true listening is revealed not in merely hearing words but in resulting behavior.

As we look at the process Hezekiah goes through in his responses to the various threats from Sennacherib, we see evidence he is listening. First, he capitulates in fear (18:14). Then he says nothing to the Assyrian but sends his messages to ask Isaiah the prophet to pray for help (19:2–4). Finally, he goes to the temple and prays (v. 14). He had heard the word of God delivered by Isaiah (vv. 5–7), and he responded in faith by praying, by praising, and by commanding God to act to deliver.

Jesus frequently told his audience to listen to his words (e.g., Mark 4:3, 9, 12, 23; 7:14). On the Mount of Transfiguration God himself spoke from heaven, commanding Peter, James, and John to listen to Jesus (Mark 9:7). Likewise, we need to follow the examples of both Hezekiah and Jesus as we pray and listen to God. And we will see in the next chapter that Hezekiah again responds to a crisis with prayer, another sign that the ruler is listening to God.

CHAPTER 36

2 Kings 20:1–21

LISTEN to the Story

[1]In those days Hezekiah became ill and was at the point of death. The prophet Isaiah son of Amoz went to him and said, "This is what the LORD says: Put your house in order, because you are going to die; you will not recover."

[2]Hezekiah turned his face to the wall and prayed to the LORD, [3]"Remember, LORD, how I have walked before you faithfully and with wholehearted devotion and have done what is good in your eyes." And Hezekiah wept bitterly.

[4]Before Isaiah had left the middle court, the word of the LORD came to him: [5]"Go back and tell Hezekiah, the ruler of my people, 'This is what the LORD, the God of your father David, says: I have heard your prayer and seen your tears; I will heal you. On the third day from now you will go up to the temple of the LORD. [6]I will add fifteen years to your life. And I will deliver you and this city from the hand of the king of Assyria. I will defend this city for my sake and for the sake of my servant David.'"

[7]Then Isaiah said, "Prepare a poultice of figs." They did so and applied it to the boil, and he recovered.

[8]Hezekiah had asked Isaiah, "What will be the sign that the LORD will heal me and that I will go up to the temple of the LORD on the third day from now?"

[9]Isaiah answered, "This is the LORD's sign to you that the LORD will do what he has promised: Shall the shadow go forward ten steps, or shall it go back ten steps?"

[10]"It is a simple matter for the shadow to go forward ten steps," said Hezekiah. "Rather, have it go back ten steps."

[11]Then the prophet Isaiah called on the LORD, and the LORD made the shadow go back the ten steps it had gone down on the stairway of Ahaz.

[12]At that time Marduk-Baladan son of Baladan king of Babylon sent

Hezekiah letters and a gift, because he had heard of Hezekiah's illness.
[13]Hezekiah received the envoys and showed them all that was in his
storehouses—the silver, the gold, the spices and the fine olive oil—his
armory and everything found among his treasures. There was nothing in
his palace or in all his kingdom that Hezekiah did not show them.
[14]Then Isaiah the prophet went to King Hezekiah and asked, "What
did those men say, and where did they come from?"
"From a distant land," Hezekiah replied. "They came from Babylon."
[15]The prophet asked, "What did they see in your palace?"
"They saw everything in my palace," Hezekiah said. "There is nothing
among my treasures that I did not show them."
[16]Then Isaiah said to Hezekiah, "Hear the word of the LORD: [17]The
time will surely come when everything in your palace, and all that your
predecessors have stored up until this day, will be carried off to Babylon.
Nothing will be left, says the LORD. [18]And some of your descendants, your
own flesh and blood who will be born to you, will be taken away, and they
will become eunuchs in the palace of the king of Babylon."
[19]"The word of the LORD you have spoken is good," Hezekiah replied.
For he thought, "Will there not be peace and security in my lifetime?"
[20]As for the other events of Hezekiah's reign, all his achievements and
how he made the pool and the tunnel by which he brought water into the
city, are they not written in the book of the annals of the kings of Judah?
[21]Hezekiah rested with his ancestors. And Manasseh his son succeeded
him as king.

Listening to the Text in the Story: Biblical Texts: Deuteronomy 17:19–20; 1 Kings 3:14; Isaiah 38:1–8; 39:1–8; Jeremiah 50:2; Ancient Near Eastern Texts: Nebuchadnezzar's Ziggurat Inscription; The Babylonian Chronicle; The Babylonian King List; Sennacherib's First Campaign Inscription; The Siloam Tunnel Inscription

Two final stories from the life of Hezekiah conclude his narrative. First, his emotional prayer after being told he would soon die prompts YHWH to change his mind and extend his life (2 Kgs 20:1–11). Second, his naïve decision to show the Babylonian embassy all the temple treasures elicits a rebuke and a dire prediction from the prophet Isaiah (vv. 12–21). There are clues that these events may have taken place before some of the events in 2 Kings 18–19.

Kings Praying for Long Life

While Hezekiah does not actually ask YHWH for healing or for a longer life, the context suggests that was the implication of his prayer as he reminds YHWH of his righteous lifestyle (2 Kgs 20:3). Hezekiah's request is consistent with Deuteronomy's law of the king (Deut 17:19–20), which promise longevity to righteous rulers. After granting his wish for wisdom, YHWH tells young Solomon that if he walks faithfully and in obedience to YHWH's commands, then he will have a long life (1 Kgs 3:14). YHWH's promise to Solomon and Hezekiah's prayer to YHWH use similar (Deuteronomistic) language of walking in faithful obedience.

Many ancient Near Eastern rulers prayed for long life, often basing their request on their pious behavior (like Hezekiah here).[1] A ziggurat inscription includes a prayer from King Nebuchadnezzar of Babylon to the god Nabu requesting long life based on his acceptable deeds:

> O Nabû, legitimate heir, exalted vizier, preeminent one, beloved by Marduk, look joyfully (and) favorably upon my deeds and grant me as a gift a long life, satiety with extreme old age, stability of throne, long duration of reign, defeat of adversaries, (and) conquest of the land of the enemies. On your reliable writing board which establishes the border of heaven and the netherworld, decree the lengthening of my days, inscribe for me extreme old age.[2]

Healing Figs

Isaiah's prescription for Hezekiah's healing involved a poultice of figs (2 Kgs 20:7). If you have not used a poultice recently, you are not unique. A poultice consists of a moist mass of flour and plant material in a cloth placed on a wound or inflamed part of the body to aid healing. Figs were used in other ancient remedies, including a hippiatric (related to the healing of horses) text that seems to describe a concoction of figs, raisins, and flour:

> If <a horse> [meaning of two verbs uncertain] incessantly, old fig-cakes and old raisins and flour of groats should be pulverized together, and it (the remedy) should (then) be poured into his nose.[3]

1. For examples of ancient Near Eastern rulers (e.g., Hammurabi, Kamose, Thutmose III, Ramesses II, Ashurnasirpal II, Sargon II, Sennacherib) praying for longevity, see Lamb, *Righteous Jehu*, 164–66.
2. *COS* 2:310.
3. *COS* 1:362.

You may ask, "How did they discover this method worked?" Good question. Presumably they shoved different types of crushed fruit into the nostrils of horses until they found the right formula.

Marduk-Baladan

The ruler of Babylon sends a "get-well" gift to King Hezekiah to encourage him during his time of recovery, to curry favor with the Judean to possibly assist him in gaining autonomy from Assyrian hegemony. This incident is the first place Babylon shows up as a major player in Kings (excluding 2 Kgs 17:24, 30).[4] Babylon's role will just get larger, particularly at the end of the book (e.g., 24:1, 7; 25:27, 28).

The name of the Babylonian ruler who sent the gifts to Hezekiah (20:12) is transliterated into English in a variety of ways: Berodach-baladan (NASB, KJV, based on the Hebrew of 20:12), Merodach-baladan (ESV, NRSV, based on the Hebrew of Isa 39:1), Marduk-apla-iddin (based on cuneiform sources) and, the name used here, Marduk-Baladan (NIV, following the Hebrew of Isa 39:1 but using the more familiar "Marduk").

Just as many rulers of Israel and Jerusalem had theophoric names, where the name of the deity forms part of their name (e.g., Hezekiah, Josiah, Jehoiachin),[5] so did many Babylonian rulers like Marduk-Baladan. The Babylonian ruler who releases Jehoiachin from prison at the end of Kings is named Awel-Marduk (25:27; Jer 52:31). Marduk was the primary god of Babylon and the object of an oracle from Jeremiah against the kingdom, "Babylon will be captured; Bel will be put to shame, Marduk filled with terror" (Jer 50:2).

After Sargon II became the ruler of Assyria, Marduk-Baladan seized power in Babylon (721 BC) and was able to maintain control until Sargon retook the city (710 BC). He bided his time until Sargon died (705 BC), which may have been when he sent an embassy to Hezekiah, and then he re-took power (704 BC).

Marduk-Baladan is mentioned in several ancient sources. In the Babylonian King List Marduk-Baladan appears twice (called Marduk-apla-iddin) because his reign over Babylon was interrupted; the first reign was twelve years, and the second was nine months. Two rulers we discussed earlier appear in the list between his two reigns, Sargon and Sennacherib. Comparable to the regnal

---

4. For an extended discussion of the Babylonians, see David S. Vanderhooft, "Babylon and the Babylonians" in *The World around the Old Testament*, ed. Arnold and Strawn, 107–37.

5. In English both the "Je-" at the beginning, and the "iah" at the end of many Old Testament names are based on shortened forms of YHWH.

formula of Kings, the source merely lists the regnal years, the ruler's name, and perhaps additional information.

12 [years] Marduk-apla-iddin, dynasty of the Sea-Land,
5 [years] Sargon
2 [years] Sennacherib, dynasty of Habigal
1 month Maduk-zakir-shumi, son of Ardu
9 months Marduk-apla-iddin.[6]

Marduk-Baladan is also mentioned in the Babylonian Chronicle between Sargon II and Sennacherib: "In Nisan [the first year of Sargon II, 722 BC] Merodach-baladan ascended the throne in Babylon."[7] An inscription recording Sennacherib's first campaign mentions Marduk-Baladan and records how he gave a gift to another ruler looking for help, similar to what the Babylon ruler does here with Hezekiah (2 Kgs 20:12):

> At the beginning of my reign, when I had majestically ascended the throne and ruled the people of Assyria with obedience and peace, Merodach-baladan, king of Karduniash (i.e., Babylonia), an evil rebel, of treacherous mind, doer of evil, for whom truth is sinful, turned to Shutur-Nahhunte, the Elamite, for help, sent him gold and silver and precious stones, requesting his help.[8]

The inscription continues to describe how Sennacherib raged like a lion, the soldiers of Merodach-baladan (i.e., Marduk-Baladan) were slaughtered like sheep in a rout, and Bel-ibni was installed over Babylon.

Hezekiah's Tunnel

Hezekiah's narrative ends with a brief reference to the pool and tunnel he constructed to bring water from the Gihon Spring to the Pool of Siloam inside the wall of Jerusalem (2 Kgs 20:20).[9] The tunnel survives to this day, and I walked through it in the spring of 2014 with a friend from my seminary. It was a fantastic experience, but I wouldn't recommend it for the claustrophobic, since the walls are narrow, you walk in six–twelve inches of water, and unless

6. *COS* 1:462.
7. *COS* 1:467.
8. *COS* 2:300.
9. For images of Hezekiah's Siloam Tunnel, see *ANEP*, 232; #744; *ZIBBC* 3:197; for an image of the Siloam Tunnel Inscription, see *ANEP*, 85; #275; *ZIBBC* 3:198.

you are short (5'), you will need to stoop for much of the walk. A Hebrew inscription was found at the entrance to the tunnel describing its construction, its length (1200 cubits = about 1800 feet, about a third of a mile), and its dramatic completion.

> This is the record of how the tunnel was breached. While the excavators were wielding their pick-axes, each man towards his co-worker, and while there were yet three cubits for the breach, a voice was heard each man calling to his co-worker . . . the excavators struck, each man to meet his co-worker, pick-axe against pick-axe. Then the water flowed from the spring to the pool, a distance of one thousand and two hundred cubits.[10]

YHWH Heals Hezekiah (2 Kings 20:1–7)

As a signal that the subsequent events do not necessarily follow the preceding ones chronologically, the chapter begins, "In those days . . ." (*bayyamim hahem*; 20:1; see also 10:32; 15:37). Hezekiah's illness appears to precede the deliverance of 19:35–36, since YHWH speaks of delivering Jerusalem from the hand of Assyria (20:6), even though, from the narrative's perspective, that has already occurred. Hezekiah is so sick he is at the point of death. The only other time this form (*lamed* with the infinitive of *mut*, "to death") appears in Kings for a ruler is when David gives his final charge to Solomon immediately before his death (1 Kgs 2:1). At this point the prophet Isaiah appears, announcing, "You are going to die"; and if that were not clear enough, he adds, "You will not recover" (20:1). Isaiah's message was harsh but honest, and it gave Hezekiah the opportunity to prepare for the inevitable, like a good doctor who informs a cancer patient their condition is terminal.

In response to Isaiah's dire message, Hezekiah prays (vv. 2–3). We can observe four things about his prayer. First, he appears to disobey YHWH's command to put his "house in order." We may not be sure what God intended, but the text records Hezekiah doing nothing to order his house. Second, Hezekiah begins by giving God a command—"Remember" (the imperative of *zakar*)—which is ironic, since he seems to disobey God's command to him. He reminds God by laying out his spiritual CV, how he had walked faithfully and had done what is good in God's eyes (v. 3). Third, Hezekiah never directly

10. *COS* 2:145–46.

asks YHWH for healing or for an extension of his life. However, Wray Beal's conclusion that his command implies a "petition for healing" is reasonable.[11] Fourth, like Josiah the righteous king who followed him (22:2, 19), Hezekiah wept bitterly—literally, "Hezekiah wept a great weeping" (20:3; both the verb *baka* and the related noun *beki* are used). Earlier, Hezekiah tore his clothes and put on sackcloth (19:1). Hezekiah was an emotional ruler who freely expressed himself to God in prayer.

YHWH responds to Hezekiah immediately, before Isaiah leaves the palace complex (20:4).[12] YHWH sends his prophet back, informing the ruler his prayer was heard, his tears were seen, his life would be extended, and his city would be defended (vv. 5–6). YHWH remembered Hezekiah. Even though Hezekiah disobeyed YHWH's command, YHWH obeyed Hezekiah's command. Thus, it appears that Hezekiah's prayer changed the mind of YHWH (see "Does God Change?" in Live the Story below).

We discover that Hezekiah's primary ailment was a boil, which Isaiah heals with a fig poultice (v. 7; see Listen to the Story above). Hezekiah's son Manasseh was apparently born during his father's fifteen-year extension, since Manasseh was twelve when he came to power after his father died (20:21; 21:1). One could argue that YHWH should not have listened to Hezekiah's prayer because Manasseh turned out to be an extremely evil ruler (21:2, 6, 11), but this type of speculative logic finds no warrant in Scripture.

In 2 Kings 20 the cure immediately follows Isaiah's message (v. 7); however, in Isaiah the cure comes after the sign and a long psalm of thanksgiving (Isa 38:7–8, 9–20). The psalm is omitted from 2 Kings 20.

YHWH's Sign for Hezekiah (2 Kings 20:8–11)

His father Ahaz refused to seek a "sign" (*'ot*; Isa 7:12), but Hezekiah has no qualms about requesting one (2 Kgs 20:8). His boil had been healed (v. 7), but he apparently desired further evidence that he would fully recover and survive another fifteen years. Isaiah offers Hezekiah a choice, and the ruler suggests having the sun's shadow move back ten steps, because moving forward would be the sun's natural progression (vv. 9–10). Some commentators think the "stairway of Ahaz" (v. 11) was some type of sundial,[13] but the word here for "steps" (*ma'alot*) typically just means "stairs," which in this instance merely serves as a convenient method to mark the progress of the sun's shadow. The details of how this miracle happened may not be clear, but God's ability to

11. Wray Beal, *1 & 2 Kings*, 481.
12. The parallel in Isa 38 is much shorter than the account in 2 Kgs 20.
13. See Barnes, *1 & 2 Kings*, 344–45.

work in dramatic ways has been seen in Kings (e.g., 1 Kgs 17:22; 18:38; 2 Kgs 5:14; 7:6), and in relation to the movement of the sun specifically in the book Joshua (Josh 10:12–14).

Envoys from Babylon (2 Kings 20:12–21)

After recording his dramatic reforms and sincere prayers, the narrative of Hezekiah ends on a down note, as he shows too much hospitality toward the Babylonian visitors from Marduk-Baladan (see Listen to the Story above). The biblical text does not provide a political reason for Marduk-Baladan's get-well gift, but Josephus reasonably assumes it was to purchase his loyalty for an alliance against Assyria.[14]

While Solomon's display of wealth to the queen of Sheba is recorded as a sign of blessing from YHWH (1 Kgs 10:4–9), Hezekiah's display to the ruler of Babylon suggests a desire to depend on Babylon and not YHWH for assistance.[15] Hezekiah shows Marduk-Baladan's representatives all the precious metals (silver and gold) and precious spices in his storehouse and treasuries. In 2 Kings 18 Hezekiah gives a massive tribute to Sennacherib, involving all the silver in the temple and the treasuries and the gold from the temple doors (vv. 14–16), which suggests that the Babylonian display here predated the Assyrian tribute that gutted Judah's treasuries.

While prophets in the book of Kings often display supernatural knowledge (1 Kgs 17:1; 18:41; 2 Kgs 5:25–26; 6:10), Isaiah asks the king basic questions about the officials and what they saw (20:14–15). Isaiah's response to hearing Hezekiah's answers does not include an explicit rebuke, but it is clearly implied. Isaiah declares that, at some point in the future, Babylon will return and carry away all those treasures Hezekiah has shown them. Additionally, Hezekiah's own descendants will also be deported, where they will serve as eunuchs in the palace in Babylon. During Nebuchadnezzar's conquests of Judah, he carried off treasures (24:13; 25:13–15), and he deported people, including Hezekiah's great, great, great-grandson, Jehoiachin (24:12–16). The final part of Isaiah's prediction may have been fulfilled by Daniel and his three friends, since they were from royal families (Dan 1:3), they served in the palace of Babylon (Dan 1:4), and they were supervised by the chief of the eunuchs, suggesting that they were made eunuchs (Dan 1:7–9).

Hezekiah's response that YHWH's word is "good" (*tov*) might seem another

14. *Ant.* 10.2.2.

15. See also David T. Lamb, "The Trust of Hezekiah: In YHWH . . . and Assyria, Egypt, and Babylon (2 Kings 18–20)," in *Characters and Characterization in the Book of Kings*, ed. Benjamin J. M. Johnson and Keith Bodner, LHBOTS 670 (New York: T&T Clark, 2019), 214–33.

example of his trusting YHWH for the future (2 Kgs 20:19), but the reason he states (peace and security now) suggests not a trust in YHWH but a selfish concern. And his passive reaction here to Isaiah's dire prediction for his children sits in stark contrast to his emotional reaction to Isaiah's dire prediction for himself a few verses earlier (v. 3). The king who changed YHWH's mind to extend his life now submits to God's will for his exiled descendants.

The prophet Isaiah disappears from the narrative after 20:19. Hezekiah's final achievements are recorded in his concluding regnal note (vv. 20–21). He is succeeded by arguably the worst ruler in Judah's history, his son Manasseh.

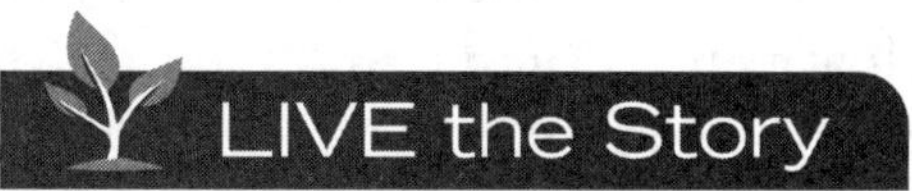

Does God Change?

When Hezekiah's prayer of 2 Kings 20 is discussed, three objections are often raised in response to the idea that God changed his mind.[16] The first objection is, "Isaiah changed his mind, not God."[17] According to this objection, Isaiah's first oracle here was like Nathan's first message to David in 2 Samuel 7 to build the temple, which was later corrected by YHWH (2 Sam 7:3–4). Thus, the first messages—of Nathan to David and of Isaiah to Hezekiah—were not from God but merely the prophet. However, there is a significant difference between Nathan's two oracles in 2 Samuel 7 and Isaiah's two oracles in 2 Kings 20. The prophetic messenger formula used to give authority to Nathan's second message to David to not build is absent for the first one to build (2 Sam 7:3–5). But the prophetic messenger formula is present in both of Isaiah's messages about Hezekiah's extended life in 2 Kings 20:5 and in his initial message about Hezekiah's imminent death in 20:1, suggesting that both of Isaiah's messages to Hezekiah originated from God and had his full endorsement. It was not Isaiah who changed his mind.

The second objection is, "Hezekiah's healing was God's plan." According to this objection, God was already planning to heal Hezekiah, and the reason God told the ruler beforehand was to invite him to intercede in order for YHWH to heal him.[18] However, there are no hints in the text that Hezekiah's healing

---

16. I discuss the topic of divine change generally and Hezekiah's prayer specifically elsewhere: *God Behaving Badly*, 135–52 and "The Immutable Mutability of YHWH," *Southeastern Theological Review*, 2.1 (2011): 21–38.

17. Barnes focuses not on YHWH's change but that of the prophet Isaiah in both 2 Kgs 19 and 20 (*1–2 Kings*, 337, 338, 344).

18. Wiseman states that the "prayer and God's answer are both part of his plan" (*1 & 2 Kings*, 286).

was part of God's plan all along. In fact, the text states the opposite quite clearly. God said in the first message that Hezekiah would die, expressed both positively (you shall die) and negatively (you shall not recover).[19] If God were planning to heal him from the beginning, he should not have said Hezekiah will die. People who think God was planning to heal Hezekiah while God was saying Hezekiah will not recover essentially make God into a liar. Thus, this solution to the problem of a mind-changing God results in a bigger problem of a deceptive God. God states in the second message that he is going to add fifteen years to Hezekiah's life because God heard his prayer and saw his tears. The context therefore suggests that the additional fifteen years are a direct result of Hezekiah's prayer, not a result of a pre-ordained plan.

The third objection is, "God does not change his mind." According to this objection, other Scriptures inform us that God does not change his mind, so he cannot be doing that in 2 Kings 20. However, the issue is more complicated than the advocates for divine immutability here might lead us to think. The witness of Scripture on this issue suggests that God both does not change and that he does, depending upon the context.

There are four primary Old Testament texts supporting the idea that God does not change, and three of them use the verb *naham* ("to relent" / "change one's mind"). Balaam declares that God is not like a human who changes his mind (*naham*), so he will not curse his people (Num 23:19). Samuel tells Saul that YHWH is not like a human that he would change his mind (*naham*) (1 Sam 15:29). YHWH himself declares that he does not change (*shanah*) (Mal 3:6). The psalmist explains that YHWH will not change his mind (*naham*) about his decision to make the addressee a priest forever (Ps 110:4).

However, offsetting these four divine immutability texts are nineteen divine mutability texts supporting the idea that God does change. Most of these references use the same verb, *naham,* that appears in three of the immutability texts.[20] After the golden calf and the refusal to enter the land, Moses intercedes with YHWH, who then twice relents from punishment (Exod 32:14; Num 14:20). After David's census YHWH relents and stops the pestilence (2 Sam 24:16; 1 Chr 21:15). The psalmist narrates how, after his people cried, YHWH relented according to this steadfast love (Ps 106:45). The book of Jeremiah repeatedly describes God as changing his mind, even so much that God gets tired of it (Jer 15:6; 18:8, 10; 26:3, 13, 19; 42:10). Two texts from the Minor Prophets describe how relenting from judgment is a part of God's character

19. Fretheim describes God's initial word to Hezekiah as "not conditional, no ifs ands or buts" (*Kings*, 208).

20. Except Num 14:20 and the Hezekiah prayers in 2 Kgs 20 and Isa 38.

(Joel 2:13–14; Jonah 4:2), and three other prophetic references narrate him relenting (Amos 7:3, 6; Jonah 3:9–10).

Thus, there are far more texts supporting the idea that God does change his mind than those supporting the idea that he does not. The argument that Hezekiah could not change God's mind based on other Scripture is therefore not compelling. In fact, Hezekiah's point-of-death prayer fits a consistent pattern of God relenting in response to prayer.

How do we reconcile texts that describe God as changing with ones that describe him as not changing? In contexts where there is doubt as to whether or not God will be faithful, the text declares that he does not waver in his commitments. It is not simply that God never changes but specifically that he does not change regarding his promises to his covenant people. In contexts of imminent judgment from God, when people repent, he changes his mind and shows mercy. It is not that God always changes and is inconsistent but specifically in situations where people deserve punishment, when they repent, he consistently changes from judgment to grace.

The idea of a God that changes his mind should not be unsettling to us. God is not fickle or unreliable. As we look at the contexts of these passages, we see not a divine contradiction but a consistent pattern. The Old Testament characters themselves understood both the changing and unchanging aspects of God's nature. When he changes, God moves from judgment toward mercy. According to the Old Testament, God is predictably flexible, constantly changeable, and immutably mutable, at least in regard to showing mercy toward repentant sinners.

Prayer: Righteousness, Emotions, and Change

Hezekiah was a man of prayer, so as we conclude his narrative and reflect on prayer from his example, I want to focus on three words: righteousness, emotions, and change. First, righteousness is not as important as we may think in prayer. I believe the prayers of righteous men and righteous women "availeth much" (Jas 5:16 KJV), but in Kings piety does not seem to be a major factor for God, as he answers prayers for both evil and righteous rulers. God is so eager to be compassionate in these contexts that he listens to the prayers of everyone who turns to him and asks for help. Even when King Hezekiah highlights his righteousness, God does not mention it but is merely pleased that he prayed. This conclusion may be considered bad news for all the righteous people out there, that there is not necessarily an inside track toward a favorable response from God, but for those of us who do not perceive ourselves to be particularly righteous, this message is great news.

Second, emotions are more important in prayer than we may think. The text emphasizes Hezekiah's tears. Hezekiah literally "wept a great weeping" (2 Kgs 20:3; author's translation), and God responded favorably when he saw the king's tears (v. 5). For both Hezekiah and Josiah, their tears are mentioned specifically by YHWH himself as a positive factor when he responds to their prayers. God is moved by emotional prayers. While God sees Hezekiah's tears, the vast majority of commentators do not. Alter, Barnes, Cogan and Tadmor, Fretheim, Fritz, Jones, Leithart, Sweeney, and Wiseman completely ignore Hezekiah's tears. One commentator (Wray Beal) mentions Hezekiah's tears briefly.[21] God viewed Hezekiah's expressions of emotions highly positively, but another commentator (Hobbs) views them highly negatively: "the news . . . sent Hezekiah into a sulk! . . . Hezekiah's weeping [was] presumably for himself!"[22] Apparently biblical scholars are either uncomfortable talking about emotions, or they do not think they are significant enough to warrant a comment. YHWH not only talks about them, but they have a profound impact on him, significant enough to get him to change his mind. Perhaps a commentary is not the ideal setting to talk about the value of honest expressions of emotions in prayer, but Hezekiah's point-of-death prayer leaves me no choice. The God of the Bible is swayed by emotional outbursts associated with prayer.

Third, change is something God does in response to prayer. Most commentators on this passage ignore the issue of God changing his mind or explain that it was part of God's sovereign plan (with little textual evidence to support this view). Fretheim, however, states it boldly: "God changes his mind," and then he proceeds to discuss "the power of prayer to effect changes in God's word."[23] If Hezekiah's God-changing prayer was unique in Scripture, then we should be reticent to draw applications for today, but as we have seen, numerous other biblical characters (Moses, David, Jeremiah, Amos, and the psalmist) prompted God, through prayer, to change his mind. Many of you may not need additional motivation to pray. You wake up eager to pray; you go through your day in a constant state of prayerful meditation. But for those of us who find it difficult to make time to pray, or who wonder what difference it makes, an image of a God who listens, responds, and even changes in response to prayer is a powerful motivator. It makes one want to pray, which ultimately should be our goal as we reflect on the life and prayers of Hezekiah.

---

21. Wray Beal, *1 & 2 Kings*, 480.

22. Hobbs, *2 Kings*, 290. Barnes also speaks negatively about Hezekiah's prayer: "It has the quality of a petulant complaint" (Barnes, *1–2 Kings*, 343).

23. Fretheim, *Kings*, 205, 208.

CHAPTER 37

2 Kings 21:1–26

LISTEN to the Story

[1]Manasseh was twelve years old when he became king, and he reigned in Jerusalem fifty-five years. His mother's name was Hephzibah. [2]He did evil in the eyes of the LORD, following the detestable practices of the nations the LORD had driven out before the Israelites. [3]He rebuilt the high places his father Hezekiah had destroyed; he also erected altars to Baal and made an Asherah pole, as Ahab king of Israel had done. He bowed down to all the starry hosts and worshiped them. [4]He built altars in the temple of the LORD, of which the LORD had said, "In Jerusalem I will put my Name." [5]In the two courts of the temple of the LORD, he built altars to all the starry hosts. [6]He sacrificed his own son in the fire, practiced divination, sought omens, and consulted mediums and spiritists. He did much evil in the eyes of the LORD, arousing his anger.

[7]He took the carved Asherah pole he had made and put it in the temple, of which the LORD had said to David and to his son Solomon, "In this temple and in Jerusalem, which I have chosen out of all the tribes of Israel, I will put my Name forever. [8]I will not again make the feet of the Israelites wander from the land I gave their ancestors, if only they will be careful to do everything I commanded them and will keep the whole Law that my servant Moses gave them." [9]But the people did not listen. Manasseh led them astray, so that they did more evil than the nations the LORD had destroyed before the Israelites.

[10]The LORD said through his servants the prophets: [11]"Manasseh king of Judah has committed these detestable sins. He has done more evil than the Amorites who preceded him and has led Judah into sin with his idols. [12]Therefore this is what the LORD, the God of Israel, says: I am going to bring such disaster on Jerusalem and Judah that the ears of everyone who hears of it will tingle. [13]I will stretch out over Jerusalem the measuring line used against Samaria and the plumb line used against

the house of Ahab. I will wipe out Jerusalem as one wipes a dish, wiping it and turning it upside down. [14]I will forsake the remnant of my inheritance and give them into the hands of enemies. They will be looted and plundered by all their enemies; [15]they have done evil in my eyes and have aroused my anger from the day their ancestors came out of Egypt until this day."

[16]Moreover, Manasseh also shed so much innocent blood that he filled Jerusalem from end to end—besides the sin that he had caused Judah to commit, so that they did evil in the eyes of the LORD.

[17]As for the other events of Manasseh's reign, and all he did, including the sin he committed, are they not written in the book of the annals of the kings of Judah? [18]Manasseh rested with his ancestors and was buried in his palace garden, the garden of Uzza. And Amon his son succeeded him as king.

[19]Amon was twenty-two years old when he became king, and he reigned in Jerusalem two years. His mother's name was Meshullemeth daughter of Haruz; she was from Jotbah. [20]He did evil in the eyes of the LORD, as his father Manasseh had done. [21]He followed completely the ways of his father, worshiping the idols his father had worshiped, and bowing down to them. [22]He forsook the LORD, the God of his ancestors, and did not walk in obedience to him.

[23]Amon's officials conspired against him and assassinated the king in his palace. [24]Then the people of the land killed all who had plotted against King Amon, and they made Josiah his son king in his place.

[25]As for the other events of Amon's reign, and what he did, are they not written in the book of the annals of the kings of Judah? [26]He was buried in his tomb in the garden of Uzza. And Josiah his son succeeded him as king.

Listening to the Text in the Story: Biblical Texts: 2 Chronicles 33:10–17; Isaiah 28:17; 34:11; 44:13; Amos 7:7–9; Ancient Near Eastern Texts: Esarhaddon's Prism B; Ashurbanipal's Cylinder C

Sandwiched between two of Judah's best rulers (Hezekiah and Josiah) are two of Judah's worst rulers (Manasseh and Amon). Yet all four are related. With fifty-five years, Manasseh was the longest-reigning ruler of either Israel or Judah, but the book of Kings has nothing positive to say about him. With only two years, Amon was one of the shortest-reigning rulers of Judah (three reigns were shorter); perhaps the most indicting comment about Amon is that "he followed completely the ways of his father" Manasseh (2 Kgs 21:21).

Over much of the history of the divided monarchy, the Assyrian Empire exercised control in the region. A series of both northern and southern rulers have been mentioned in Neo-Assyrian inscriptions, usually as tributaries during this period (from Israel: Omri, Jehu, Jehoash, Menahem, Pekah and Hoshea; from Judah: Ahaz and Hezekiah).[1] As we move into Judah's final century before the Babylonian conquest, Assyria's power begins to wane. Manasseh is the final ruler of Judah to appear in Assyrian inscriptions, in one from each of the two final great Assyrian emperors: Esarhaddon (681–669 BC; 19:37; Ezra 4:2) and Ashurbanipal (668–627 BC; Ezra 4:10).[2]

Esarhaddon mentions Manasseh, king of Judah, among twenty-two rulers forced to contribute construction materials for his palace in Nineveh:

> I called up the kings of the country Hatti and (of the region) on the other side of the river (Euphrates) (to wit): Baʿlu, king of Tyre, Manasseh (*Me-na-si-i*), king of Judah (*Ia-ú-di*), Qaushgabri, king of Edom, Musuri, king of Moab, Sil-Bel, king of Gaza.[3]

The son of Esarhaddon, Ashurbanipal also mentions Manasseh among his royal tributaries who supported Ashurbanipal in his campaigns against two rulers who appear elsewhere in Kings: Tirhakah and Necho (19:9; 23:29–35):

> Baʿal, king of Tyre, Manasseh (*Mi-in-si-e*), king of Judah (*Ia-ú-di*), Qaushgabri, king of Edom, Musuri, king of Moab, Sil-Bel, king of Gaza . . . together 12 kings from the seashore, the islands and the mainland.[4]

Manasseh's name also appears on a Hebrew seal inscription that could have come from the reign of Hezekiah, since Manasseh is described as a royal son, "Manasseh, son of the king."[5]

In the prophetic judgment against Manasseh (21:13), two construction images are used to expose wickedness: a "measuring line" (*qaw*) and a "plumb line" (*mishqelet*). Both of these tools are used to ensure that the building under

1. For references to these inscriptions, see the discussions of these rulers above (chapters 13, 26, 29, 31, 32, 33, 34).
2. In Ezra 4:10 the NIV renders his name as Ashurbanipal, but most English translations transliterate it as "Osnappar" (e.g., ESV, NASB, NRSV).
3. *ANET*, 291; Esarhaddon's Prism B.
4. *ANET*, 294; Ashurbanipal's Cylinder C.
5. For text and image, see *WSS* 55, #16.

construction is straight, true, and consistent with the plans of the builder. Manasseh's "house" is out of line with how YHWH designed it, just as Ahab's was earlier (21:13). Both houses were condemned for their association with idolatrous practices (1 Kgs 21:17–26; 22:17–23; 2 Kgs 1:4; 9:6–10). Just as the "house" of Ahab was destroyed, judgment is coming for Manasseh's descendants. These images are used elsewhere in prophetic texts, specifically in the book of Isaiah: "I will make justice the measuring line (*qaw*) and righteousness the plumb line (*mishqelet*)" (Isa 28:17; see also 34:11; 44:13; Amos 7:7–9).

Among the many other critiques of Manasseh, he is described as shedding much innocent blood (2 Kgs 21:16). In several later traditional sources (the Ascension of Isaiah, the Babylonian Talmud, and the Jerusalem Talmud), Manasseh condemns Isaiah to death, so the prophet hides in a tree, but then Manasseh has the tree sawn in half.[6] The book of Isaiah never records the prophet's death, but his martyrdom is presumably what Hebrews refers to when it describes prophets being sawn in two (Heb 11:37), a reminder that people of God often suffer greatly for their faith.

The Kings's perspective on the reign of Manasseh is exclusively negative, but Chronicles, while still recording his idolatrous practices (2 Chr 33:1–9), narrates Manasseh's repentance and restoration (vv. 10–17).[7] After the forces of the Assyrian ruler (perhaps under Ashurbanipal) capture him and take him to Babylon, he prays (like his father; 2 Kgs 19:15; 20:2–3), and YHWH hears his prayer and allows him to return to Jerusalem. He then removes foreign gods and restores proper worship in the temple.

How do we reconcile Manasseh's exclusively negative account in Kings with that of his mixed but highly positive ending in Chronicles? It is difficult to know why both of these divinely inspired texts would include such diverging perspectives on Manasseh, but history is always told with a perspective. The author of Kings is constantly reminding readers that there is more information about each of these kings found in the royal annals (e.g., 2 Kgs 21:17, 25) that was not selected to be included in the story here. Decisions regarding what is included or omitted, what is highlighted or deemphasized, will dramatically shape the type of story that is told.[8] The author of Kings wanted to make it clear that Judah's eventual tragic fate was caused by the sinfulness of its rulers, in this case Manasseh. However, the Chronicler chose more positive information about Manasseh, presumably to show that repentance is always possible.

---

6. See Cogan and Tadmor, *II Kings*, 269.

7. The apocryphal work, the Prayer of Manasseh, claims to record the ruler's prayer from 2 Chr 33:12–13, 18–19.

8. See Barnes, *1–2 Kings*, 353–54.

EXPLAIN the Story

Manasseh King of Judah (2 Kings 21:1–18)

Manasseh was the longest-reigning ruler of Israel or Judah, but also arguably the worst. Deuteronomy promises long life for righteous rulers (Deut 17:19–20), with the implication that evil ones should have short lives. Why was Manasseh allowed to remain on the throne so long, almost as long as the combined reigns of his righteous father (Hezekiah) and righteous grandson (Josiah)?[9] We'll discuss this question below (see "Why Do the Evil Prosper?" in Live the Story).

Manasseh's narrative offers a blistering critique of the Judean ruler, expressed in classic Deuteronomistic terminology.[10] The text describes how Manasseh did evil, he did much evil, he did more evil than other nations (2 Kgs 21:2, 6, 9, 11, 15). This chapter has the highest concentration of "evil" (*raʿ*) verses in Kings (the word "evil" [*raʿ*] appears in 23 percent of the verses = six out of twenty-six; vv. 2, 6, 9, 15, 16, 20). Manasseh followed the evil practices of the Canaanites, and he was more evil than the Canaanites and the Amorites (vv. 2, 9, 11). His evil was contagious as he led people astray (vv. 9, 16). The sins of leaders often negatively affect the people they lead, a warning to any of us who serve as leaders.

Manasseh was industrious in his idolatry. What Hezekiah destroyed and removed (18:4), his son rebuilt and restored. Manasseh rebuilt high places; he built altars to Baal and to the starry hosts, and he made an Asherah pole (21:3–5). He even situated these idolatrous objects in the temple (vv. 4, 7). The objects of his worship include Baal, Asherah, and the starry hosts (vv. 3–5, 7, 11). In Israel, worship of Baal and Asherah began during the reign of Ahab (21:13), and thus far it has been primarily located in the Northern Kingdom (1 Kgs 16:31–33; 18:19–40; 22:53; 2 Kgs 3:2; 10:18–28; 13:6; 17:16).

Manasseh was also guilty of engaging in many other practices forbidden in the law of Moses (Lev 19:26; Deut 18:10–14), including child sacrifice, divination, omens, and consulting mediums and spiritists (2 Kgs 21:6). The NIV's expression "sacrificed his own son in the fire" (v. 6) could be more literally translated as "he made his son pass through fire," but this euphemism suggests child sacrifice, justifying the NIV's rendering here (see also 16:3; 17:17; 23:10).[11]

---

9. Hezekiah reigned twenty-nine years, Josiah, thirty-one, and Manasseh, fifty-five.

10. See Jones, *1 and 2 Kings*, 2:594.

11. A few scholars are reluctant to conclude child sacrifice (e.g., Wiseman, *1 & 2 Kings*, 291; Cogan and Tadmor, *II Kings*, 266–67), but others make this reasonable assumption (e.g., Barnes, *1–2 Kings*, 311, 351; Wray Beal, *1 & 2 Kings*, 489).

While indictment against Manasseh primarily focuses on improper worship and idolatry, the final condemnation targets his violence, specifically how he shed innocent blood, even (hyperbolically) filling the entire city with blood (21:16). The text concludes that he led the nation into evil behavior (v. 16).

YHWH speaks three times here (vv. 4, 7–8, 10–15). First, a quote from YHWH (v. 4) is a paraphrase of several passages (Deut 12:5; 2 Sam 7:13; 1 Kgs 8:29) declaring he would put his name in Jerusalem, as Manasseh is filling the temple with foreign altars (2 Kgs 21:4).

Second, Manasseh's decision to place an Asherah pole in the temple prompts YHWH to expand on themes from the previous quote (vv. 7–8). YHWH had spoken to David and Solomon about how he had chosen this temple and how he would protect his people if they obeyed the law of Moses, but under Manasseh's leadership Judah did great evil (v. 9).

Third, YHWH speaks through his servants the prophets to pronounce judgment against Manasseh and Judah. The motivation for YHWH's condemnation is his anger over their disobedience (vv. 6, 15). The threatened disaster will cause the ears of anyone who hears it to tingle (v. 12). YHWH will use a measuring line and plumb line to evaluate their wickedness (v. 13). Jerusalem will be wiped clean and turned upside down like a dish (v. 13). Exile for Judah is thus predicted a second time (v. 16) as YHWH's "inheritance" (*nahalah*) will be looted and handed over to their enemies (v. 14). An impressive list of human witnesses (Moses, David, Solomon, and the prophets; vv. 7, 8, 10) all condemn Manasseh for his wickedness. Manasseh's final regnal conclusion offers nothing distinctive except that he was succeeded by his son, Amon (vv. 17–18).

Amon King of Judah (2 Kings 21:19–26)

Manasseh's son, Amon, only reigned for two years before he was assassinated (21:19, 23). His short narrative (eight verses) is dominated by references to his following in the evil ways of his "father" (*'ab*; repeated four times here; 21:20, 21 [2x], 22). He practiced idolatry and did not walk in obedience (vv. 21–22).

A group of his officials assassinated Amon, but the text provides no motivation for their conspiracy (v. 23). Many northern rulers were assassinated by a usurper who then took power (Nadab by Baasha: 1 Kgs 15:27; Elah by Zimri: 16:9; Joram by Jehu: 2 Kgs 9:14; Zechariah by Shallum: 15:10; Shallum by Menahem: 15:14; Pekahiah by Pekah: 15:25; Pekah by Hoshea: 15:30). This regicide is the second Judean one by royal officials, but in both of these incidents the Davidic line continued, as Joash was succeeded by his son, Amaziah, earlier (12:21), and Amon was succeeded by his son, Josiah, here (21:24). Both Manasseh and Amon were buried in the palace garden of Uzza (vv. 18, 26). The most significant and positive thing to be said about Amon is that he fathered righteous Josiah.

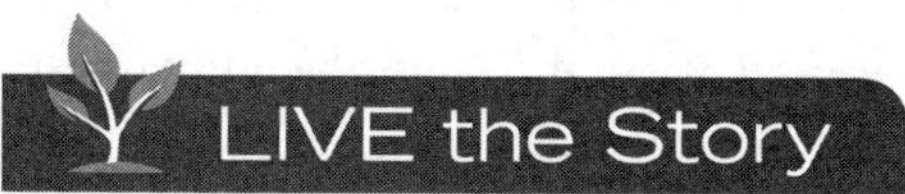

Why Do the Evil Prosper?

Manasseh was the longest-reigning king of Israel or Judah, and he was also arguably the most evil. Deuteronomy speaks of the rewards of faithful obedience to YHWH, specifically that righteous rulers will be blessed with long lives (Deut 17:19–20). Why was an evil ruler like Manasseh allowed to reign for over half a century?

The problem of the persistence of evil arises throughout Scripture.[12] Jeremiah poses a question, "Why does the way of the wicked prosper?" (Jer 12:1). The psalmist addresses the topic in a confession: "For I envied the arrogant when I saw the prosperity of the wicked" (Ps 73:3). Another psalm seems to respond to the confession of Psalm 73 with an admonition: "Do not fret because of those who are evil or be envious of those who do wrong" (Ps 37:1). Job complains about God doing nothing to stop evil: "The groans of the dying rise from the city, and the souls of the wounded cry out for help. But God charges no one with wrongdoing" (Job 24:12). The authors of Scripture were deeply disturbed by the problem of evil.

Moving to modern times, we often encounter leaders like Manasseh in the world of politics, business, and even religion who are corrupt, violent, or oppressive, and for some reason they escape punishment or condemnation as they continue to thrive in their roles and responsibilities for decades.

Why do evil leaders survive so long? Ultimately, we don't know. The text of Kings merely observes Manasseh's wickedness and his long reign but offers no direct answer to the question of why evil persists. However, we can make three points from this passage that might help us understand the problem better.

First, God sees evil. The evil performed by Manasseh and Amon was done in the eyes of YHWH (2 Kgs 21:2, 6, 15, 20). We may be tempted to assume that, since God doesn't act in a manner we expect, he is not aware of the evil going on, but the text makes it clear he knows what is happening. He sees it, and the book of Kings records it. As we remind ourselves that God, despite

12. Here are two books I have found helpful on the problem of evil: Christopher J. H. Wright, *The God I Don't Understand: Reflections on Tough Questions of Faith* (Grand Rapids: Zondervan, 2008) and N. T. Wright, *Evil and the Justice of God* (Downers Grove, IL: InterVarsity Press, 2006).

how it may appear, is aware of evil, we will be able to rest assured that he will do what needs to be done to bring about justice.

Second, God judges evil. Even though Manasseh was allowed to continue to rule, judgment was coming upon the city of Jerusalem and the nation of Judah (vv. 11–15). The two psalms quoted above both address the ultimate fate of the wicked: "for like the grass they will soon wither, like green plants they will soon die away" (Ps 37:2); and "till I entered the sanctuary of God; then I understood their final destiny. Surely you place them on slippery ground; you cast them down to ruin" (Ps 73:17–18). Even when the text doesn't record the details of the judgment, we can be confident that the judge of the world will do what is just (see Gen 18:25). We can pray for justice to be meted out upon the wicked, but we often still have to wait for the timing of God.

Third, there is more to the story. It is humbling to realize that we don't always know the full story. In Kings, Manasseh is completely wicked, but as we turn to Chronicles (see discussion above in Listen to the Story), we see that this wicked ruler repented, prayed, and instigated religious reforms. Manasseh's longevity is not nearly as problematic in the light of the book of Chronicles. As we wonder why evil leaders continue to prosper, it is good to remember that there may be more to the story than what we know. Ultimately, we know Manasseh's story continued—beyond Kings and Chronicles and into the New Testament—as his descendant, Jesus (Matt 1:10), provided the ultimate solution to the problem of evil by living, dying, and rising for all of us who are evil.

CHAPTER 38

2 Kings 22:1–23:30

LISTEN to the Story

[1]Josiah was eight years old when he became king, and he reigned in Jerusalem thirty-one years. His mother's name was Jedidah daughter of Adaiah; she was from Bozkath. [2]He did what was right in the eyes of the LORD and followed completely the ways of his father David, not turning aside to the right or to the left.

[3]In the eighteenth year of his reign, King Josiah sent the secretary, Shaphan son of Azaliah, the son of Meshullam, to the temple of the LORD. He said: [4]"Go up to Hilkiah the high priest and have him get ready the money that has been brought into the temple of the LORD, which the doorkeepers have collected from the people. [5]Have them entrust it to the men appointed to supervise the work on the temple. And have these men pay the workers who repair the temple of the LORD—[6]the carpenters, the builders and the masons. Also have them purchase timber and dressed stone to repair the temple. [7]But they need not account for the money entrusted to them, because they are honest in their dealings."

[8]Hilkiah the high priest said to Shaphan the secretary, "I have found the Book of the Law in the temple of the LORD." He gave it to Shaphan, who read it. [9]Then Shaphan the secretary went to the king and reported to him: "Your officials have paid out the money that was in the temple of the LORD and have entrusted it to the workers and supervisors at the temple." [10]Then Shaphan the secretary informed the king, "Hilkiah the priest has given me a book." And Shaphan read from it in the presence of the king.

[11]When the king heard the words of the Book of the Law, he tore his robes. [12]He gave these orders to Hilkiah the priest, Ahikam son of Shaphan, Akbor son of Micaiah, Shaphan the secretary and Asaiah the king's attendant: [13]"Go and inquire of the LORD for me and for the people and for all Judah about what is written in this book that has been found. Great is the LORD's anger that burns against us because those who have

gone before us have not obeyed the words of this book; they have not acted
in accordance with all that is written there concerning us."
14Hilkiah the priest, Ahikam, Akbor, Shaphan and Asaiah went to
speak to the prophet Huldah, who was the wife of Shallum son of Tikvah,
the son of Harhas, keeper of the wardrobe. She lived in Jerusalem, in the
New Quarter.
15She said to them, "This is what the LORD, the God of Israel, says: Tell
the man who sent you to me, 16'This is what the LORD says: I am going to
bring disaster on this place and its people, according to everything written
in the book the king of Judah has read. 17Because they have forsaken me
and burned incense to other gods and aroused my anger by all the idols
their hands have made, my anger will burn against this place and will not
be quenched.' 18Tell the king of Judah, who sent you to inquire of the
LORD, 'This is what the LORD, the God of Israel, says concerning the words
you heard: 19Because your heart was responsive and you humbled yourself
before the LORD when you heard what I have spoken against this place
and its people—that they would become a curse and be laid waste—and
because you tore your robes and wept in my presence, I also have heard
you, declares the LORD. 20Therefore I will gather you to your ancestors,
and you will be buried in peace. Your eyes will not see all the disaster I am
going to bring on this place.'"

So they took her answer back to the king.

23:1Then the king called together all the elders of Judah and Jerusalem.
2He went up to the temple of the LORD with the people of Judah, the
inhabitants of Jerusalem, the priests and the prophets—all the people
from the least to the greatest. He read in their hearing all the words of the
Book of the Covenant, which had been found in the temple of the LORD.
3The king stood by the pillar and renewed the covenant in the presence
of the LORD—to follow the LORD and keep his commands, statutes and
decrees with all his heart and all his soul, thus confirming the words of
the covenant written in this book. Then all the people pledged themselves
to the covenant.

4The king ordered Hilkiah the high priest, the priests next in rank and
the doorkeepers to remove from the temple of the LORD all the articles
made for Baal and Asherah and all the starry hosts. He burned them
outside Jerusalem in the fields of the Kidron Valley and took the ashes to
Bethel. 5He did away with the idolatrous priests appointed by the kings

of Judah to burn incense on the high places of the towns of Judah and on those around Jerusalem—those who burned incense to Baal, to the sun and moon, to the constellations and to all the starry hosts. [6]He took the Asherah pole from the temple of the Lord to the Kidron Valley outside Jerusalem and burned it there. He ground it to powder and scattered the dust over the graves of the common people. [7]He also tore down the quarters of the male shrine prostitutes that were in the temple of the Lord, the quarters where women did weaving for Asherah.

[8]Josiah brought all the priests from the towns of Judah and desecrated the high places, from Geba to Beersheba, where the priests had burned incense. He broke down the gateway at the entrance of the Gate of Joshua, the city governor, which was on the left of the city gate. [9]Although the priests of the high places did not serve at the altar of the Lord in Jerusalem, they ate unleavened bread with their fellow priests.

[10]He desecrated Topheth, which was in the Valley of Ben Hinnom, so no one could use it to sacrifice their son or daughter in the fire to Molek. [11]He removed from the entrance to the temple of the Lord the horses that the kings of Judah had dedicated to the sun. They were in the court near the room of an official named Nathan-Melek. Josiah then burned the chariots dedicated to the sun.

[12]He pulled down the altars the kings of Judah had erected on the roof near the upper room of Ahaz, and the altars Manasseh had built in the two courts of the temple of the Lord. He removed them from there, smashed them to pieces and threw the rubble into the Kidron Valley. [13]The king also desecrated the high places that were east of Jerusalem on the south of the Hill of Corruption—the ones Solomon king of Israel had built for Ashtoreth the vile goddess of the Sidonians, for Chemosh the vile god of Moab, and for Molek the detestable god of the people of Ammon. [14]Josiah smashed the sacred stones and cut down the Asherah poles and covered the sites with human bones.

[15]Even the altar at Bethel, the high place made by Jeroboam son of Nebat, who had caused Israel to sin—even that altar and high place he demolished. He burned the high place and ground it to powder, and burned the Asherah pole also. [16]Then Josiah looked around, and when he saw the tombs that were there on the hillside, he had the bones removed from them and burned on the altar to defile it, in accordance with the word of the Lord proclaimed by the man of God who foretold these things.

[17]The king asked, "What is that tombstone I see?"

The people of the city said, "It marks the tomb of the man of God
who came from Judah and pronounced against the altar of Bethel the very
things you have done to it."

[18]"Leave it alone," he said. "Don't let anyone disturb his bones." So they
spared his bones and those of the prophet who had come from Samaria.

[19]Just as he had done at Bethel, Josiah removed all the shrines at the
high places that the kings of Israel had built in the towns of Samaria and
that had aroused the LORD's anger. [20]Josiah slaughtered all the priests of
those high places on the altars and burned human bones on them. Then
he went back to Jerusalem.

[21]The king gave this order to all the people: "Celebrate the Passover
to the LORD your God, as it is written in this Book of the Covenant."
[22]Neither in the days of the judges who led Israel nor in the days of the
kings of Israel and the kings of Judah had any such Passover been observed.
[23]But in the eighteenth year of King Josiah, this Passover was celebrated
to the LORD in Jerusalem.

[24]Furthermore, Josiah got rid of the mediums and spiritists, the household gods, the idols and all the other detestable things seen in Judah and
Jerusalem. This he did to fulfill the requirements of the law written in the
book that Hilkiah the priest had discovered in the temple of the LORD.
[25]Neither before nor after Josiah was there a king like him who turned to
the LORD as he did—with all his heart and with all his soul and with all
his strength, in accordance with all the Law of Moses.

[26]Nevertheless, the LORD did not turn away from the heat of his fierce
anger, which burned against Judah because of all that Manasseh had done
to arouse his anger. [27]So the LORD said, "I will remove Judah also from my
presence as I removed Israel, and I will reject Jerusalem, the city I chose,
and this temple, about which I said, 'My Name shall be there.'"

[28]As for the other events of Josiah's reign, and all he did, are they not
written in the book of the annals of the kings of Judah?

[29]While Josiah was king, Pharaoh Necho king of Egypt went up to
the Euphrates River to help the king of Assyria. King Josiah marched out
to meet him in battle, but Necho faced him and killed him at Megiddo.
[30]Josiah's servants brought his body in a chariot from Megiddo to Jerusalem
and buried him in his own tomb. And the people of the land took Jehoahaz
son of Josiah and anointed him and made him king in place of his father.

Listening to the Text in the Story: Biblical Texts: Joshua 12:21; Judges 4:4; 5:19; 1 Kings 12:25–13:32; 22; 2 Kings 9:27; 12:1–21; 18:1–20:21; 2 Chronicles 35:20–27; Jeremiah 1:2; Zephaniah 1:1; Ancient Near Eastern Texts: Seal Inscriptions of Hezekiah's Officials; The Annals of Thutmose III; Herodotus's *The Histories*

Josiah and Hezekiah

Three centuries earlier, an anonymous prophet from Judah predicted the reign and reforms of one of David's descendants, Josiah of Judah (1 Kgs 13:2). After the evil reigns of Manasseh and Amon, the nation of Judah was blessed to be led by a young, righteous ruler, the last good king before the nation begins to spiral into chaos as the Babylonian exile rapidly approaches. Josiah renovated the temple, rediscovered the book of the law, reformed worship, renewed the covenant, and reinstituted the Passover. But he also died tragically in battle at age thirty-nine.

Josiah and his great-grandfather Hezekiah (2 Kgs 18–20) share many similarities as reforming rulers. They are the only two rulers of Israel or Judah who receive unqualified praise as being righteous in the eyes of YHWH (18:3; 22:2).[1] Both removed high places (18:4, 22; 23:5; 8, 9, 13, 15, 20), destroyed idols (18:4; 23:4–6), and petitioned God with tears and torn garments (19:1; 20:3; 22:11, 19). They reign about the same amount of time; Josiah was the fifth-longest-reigning southern king (thirty-one years) and Hezekiah was the sixth (twenty-nine years). Both of their narratives are longer than the average Judean ruler (Hezekiah's is ninety-five verses; Josiah's is fifty verses). Further comparisons between these two rulers will be discussed below.

Josiah and Joash

The other ruler who shares striking similarities to Josiah is Joash of Judah, who reigned about two centuries earlier during the time of Jehu (12:1). Both were righteous and followed particularly evil rulers (12:2; 22:2). They were the two youngest rulers of Judah: Joash coming to the throne at age seven and Josiah at age eight. In the beginning of their narratives, both oversaw significant temple renovations, with similar detailed descriptions (e.g., honest workers; 12:15; 22:7). Both died violent deaths: Joash in an assassination (12:20) and Josiah in battle (23:29).

1. Other southern righteous kings didn't remove high places (Asa, Jehoshaphat, Joash, Amaziah, Azariah, Jotham), and righteous Jehu of Israel didn't remove Jeroboam's altars.

Josiah and His Officials

The name Josiah does not appear in seal inscriptions (thus far), but the names of several officials from Josiah's court and their family members appear in five seal inscriptions. There are two sets of families mentioned in these inscriptions. First, three inscriptions mention four generations of the family of Shaphan, who served as Josiah's secretary and is mentioned repeatedly in the text (22:3, 8, 9, 10, 12, 14; 25:22). These seals mention Shaphan's grandfather, Meshullam (22:3), and his father, Azaliah (22:3; 2 Chr 34:8), as well as his two sons, Ahikam (22:12, 14; 25:22; Jer 26:24; 40:5–16) and Gemariah (Jer 29:3; 36:10, 11, 12, 25).

Azaliah, son of Meshullam.[2]

Ahikam, son of Shaphan.[3]

Gemariah, son of Shaphan.[4]

Second, two seal inscriptions belong to Azariah and Hanan, the sons of Josiah's high priest Hilkiah, who also features prominently in this narrative (22:4, 8, 10, 12, 14; 23:4, 24).

Azariah, son of Hilkiah.[5]

Hanan, son of Hilkiah the priest. [6]

The book of Kings does not mention Azariah, but Chronicles states that Hilkiah is the father of Azariah (1 Chr 6:13). Hanan does not appear to be mentioned in Scripture, but his seal inscription notes that Hilkiah is the priest. These stamp inscriptions provide support for Josiah's efforts to remove idols. Seals from earlier periods often included elaborate iconography related to foreign gods, but these Josianic seals were less elaborate—basically just

2. *WSS* 79, #90. With most seal inscriptions, it is difficult to be certain that they came from the biblical characters, but the family relationships described on these inscriptions are consistent with the biblical record, and most common Judeans would not own a seal. Thus, it is likely the individuals mentioned here were Josiah's officials.

3. *WSS* 181–82, #431.

4. *WSS* 191, #470.

5. The inscriptions of Gemariah, Azaliah, and Azariah are discussed in Tsvi Schneider, "Six Biblical Signatures: Seals and Seal Impressions of Six Biblical Personages Recovered," *BAR* 17.4 (1991): 26–33.

6. *WSS* 59–60, #28.

an inscription of the seal's ownership—suggesting that Josiah's anti-idolatry reforms impacted seal design.[7]

Josiah and Huldah

When Josiah needed guidance regarding the recently found book of the law, he sought out the prophetess Huldah (2 Kgs 22:14). Hezekiah regularly consulted the prophet Isaiah (19:2, 20; 20:1–19); Josiah presumably could have spoken to other prophets whose books are included in the canon, such as Jeremiah or Zephaniah, both of whom ministered during his reign (Jer 1:2; Zeph 1:1). While most of the prophets mentioned thus far in the book of Kings have been male (e.g., Ahijah, Elijah, Elisha), the first and last prophets mentioned by name in the Former Prophets (Joshua, Judges, Samuel, and Kings) were women: Deborah (Judg 4:4) and Huldah. We find several female prophets outside the Historical Books (Exod 15:20; Neh 6:14; Isa 8:3). Even in the patriarchal world of the Bible, God uses godly women to speak powerfully to men (and women).

Nissinen observes that most of the Assyrian prophets were female.[8] Since the existing prophetic sources associated with Assyrian prophecy primarily come from the reigns of Esarhaddon (680–669 BC) and Ashurbanipal (668–627 BC), some of these female Assyrian prophets could have overlapped with the reign of Josiah (640–609 BC) and the ministry of Huldah.

Josiah and Necho

The short account of Josiah's death in battle against the forces of Pharaoh Necho of Egypt in Kings (2 Kgs 23:29) is expanded in the book of Chronicles (2 Chr 35:20–27). While Chronicles portrays Manasseh more positively than Kings (see "Manasseh King of Judah," Chapter 37), Chronicles portrays Josiah more negatively, as he ignores the voice of God speaking through Necho (610–595 BC), telling him not to go to battle. The Chronicles' account of Josiah's death shares striking similarities to Ahab's in Kings (see discussion of 1 Kgs 22 in Chapter 18), as both rulers ignore a warning, wear a disguise, are shot in the field, and command to be removed from the field where they die (although Josiah's blood is not licked up by dogs or bathed in by prostitutes; see 1 Kgs 22:38).

At this point in time Judah was in the midst of a power struggle involving

7. *BBCOT*, 457. For images of Josiah's officials seal inscriptions, see *WSS* #90, #431, #470, #596, #28. For images of earlier seals that included elaborate iconography, see *WSS* #2, #3, #4, #5, #16, #13.

8. Nissinen, *Prophets and Prophecy*, 99.

Egypt, Assyria, and Babylon. After the death of Ashurbanipal in 630 BC, the power of Assyria in the region was waning while that of Babylon was waxing. When Necho's army defeated Josiah's at Megiddo (2 Kgs 23:29; 609 BC), he was marching to assist the Assyrians against Babylon. But the Egypt-Assyrian alliance would lose decisively at Carchemish (605 BC) to the Babylonians under the command of the crown prince, Nebuchadnezzar, who plays a major role in the demise of the Southern Kingdom. In his discussion of Necho, the Greek historian Herodotus appears to mention the Syrian campaign that included the Megiddo conflict:

> He (Necho) then turned his attention to war . . . he attacked the Syrians by land and defeated them at Magdolus, afterwards taking Gaza, a large town in Syria.[9]

Megiddo was a popular place to fight a battle (Josh 12:21; Judg 5:19; 2 Kgs 9:27), since it was strategically located along an important trade route along the western coast of Palestine. A much earlier Egyptian battle of Megiddo was fought by Pharaoh Thutmose III (1490–1436 BC) against a coalition of Canaanite states led by the king of Kadesh.[10]

EXPLAIN the Story

Josiah Repairs the Temple (2 Kings 22:1–7)

Josiah's father, Amon, was killed in a conspiracy by his own officials (21:24), and Josiah came to the throne when he was only eight (22:1). He reigned thirty-one years and was one of eight Judean rulers to do right in the eyes of YHWH, but one of only two to do so without qualification (also Hezekiah), since the other six did not remove the high places. The book of Kings begins with David, the founder of the Judean dynasty, on the throne (1 Kgs 1:1); throughout the book he is the ideal to which other kings are compared (e.g., 14:8; 15:11; 2 Kgs 14:3; 16:2; 18:3). At the end of the book David is mentioned one final time, as Josiah followed in his ways completely (22:2). The language used to describe Josiah's following of David, not turning to the right or to the left (22:2), is classically Deuteronomistic (Deut 5:32; 17:11, 20; 28:14) but is, curiously, applied to no other ruler in Kings.

9. Herodotus, *Histories*, 2:159.
10. See *COS* 2:7–13; *ANET*, 234–38.

The text includes no details about the first seventeen years of Josiah's reign in Kings (22:3), but Chronicles states that he began to seek God when he was sixteen and began his reforms when he was twenty (2 Chr 34:3). In Josiah's eighteenth year (age twenty-six), he sends Shaphan the secretary (*sopher*; 2 Kgs 22:3) to Hilkiah the high priest (*hakkohen haggadol*; v. 4) to begin temple renovations. Both men play crucial roles in Josiah's narrative; in the Hebrew text Shaphan is mentioned by name nine times (vv. 3, 8 [2x], 9, 10 [2x], 12 [2x], 14) and Hilkiah eight (22:4, 8 [2x], 10, 12, 14; 23:4, 24).

The text never records any actual renovations, but we are left to assume that Josiah's orders (vv. 4–7) were implemented. Josiah commissions Hilkiah to collect money, appoint supervisors, and hire an assortment of workers (carpenters, builders, and masons). The temple probably needed repairs desperately. Joash's renovations took place over a century after the temple was completed (about 820 BC) and were necessary after the reign of Athaliah (11:18–12:16). Josiah's repairs took place almost two centuries after Joash (about 620 BC) and fixed many of the problems associated with the corrupt reigns of Manasseh and Amon. Josiah's supervisors apparently were just as honest as Joash's, so that an accounting was unnecessary in both instances (12:15; 22:7).

Josiah Finds the Book of the Law (2 Kings 22:8–13)

While the temple is being renovated, a copy of "the Book of the Law" (*sepher hattorah*) is found and given to Hilkiah, who shows it to Shaphan, who reads it (22:8). Shaphan then goes to Josiah and reports about the renovation progress and how the temple donations have been given to the supervisors (v. 9). He informs the king about the recently discovered book and reads it to him (v. 10).

What is the book of the law? While Shaphan may have only read portions, the text suggests that he read all of this book, both in 22:8 and in 22:10, with the king.[11] Most scholars think the book of the law here was not referring to the entire Torah (i.e., the Pentateuch, Genesis through Deuteronomy). It would take ten to fifteen hours to read the entire Pentateuch. The first place the term "Book of the Law" appears in Scripture is at the end of Deuteronomy (28:61; 29:21; 30:10; 31:26) in reference to itself, suggesting that the newly found book was either Deuteronomy or a portion of it. Deuteronomy's law of the king mandated that Israel's rulers should have a copy of "this law" (*hattorah hazzo't*) with them and that they should read from it all the days of their life (17:18–19). Kings records no rulers reading it, but at least Josiah had it read to him.

11. The NIV has "Shaphan read from it" in 22:10, but the Hebrew is literally "he read it" (*wayyiqra'ehu*; see 22:8).

Upon hearing the book read, Josiah understands its importance and responds in a dramatic fashion. He tears his robes (2 Kgs 22:11), a sign of lament in the midst of tragedy (1 Kgs 11:30; 21:27; 2 Kgs 2:12; 5:7; 6:30; 11:14; 19:1). He sends a contingent of five men, including Hilkiah, Shaphan, and Ahikam, to seek direction from YHWH (22:12–13). As he commissions them, he acknowledges that, because of their ancestor's disobedience, YHWH's anger will be great (v. 13).

Josiah Hears the Response of Huldah (2 Kings 22:14–20)

Josiah's embassy arrives at the home of Huldah, wife of Shallum (perhaps the uncle of Jeremiah; Jer 32:7), in the New Quarter, on the western hill of the city.[12] The text does not record the messengers' words, merely her two-part response (2 Kgs 22:15–17, 18–20). She makes it clear to Josiah's officials that the source of her words is YHWH. Three times she repeats the prophetic messenger formula "This is what the LORD says" (*koh 'amar yhwh*), twice at the beginning of the first oracle (vv. 15, 16) and once at the beginning of the second (v. 18), and she tacks on one more "declares the LORD" (*ne'um-yhwh*) for emphasis (v. 19).

Each message is addressed to "the man who sent you" (i.e., Josiah; vv. 15, 18) and is focused on "this place" (vv. 16, 17, 19, 20), presumably referring not just to Jerusalem but the nation of Judah, since Huldah twice calls Josiah the "king of Judah" (vv. 16, 18). Huldah's first oracle delivers the bad news that disaster is coming, just as the book of the law predicted, because Judah's idolatry has prompted the anger of YHWH. The prophesied disaster is the Babylonian destruction, the focus of the final chapters of Kings.

Huldah's second oracle is more hopeful, particularly for Josiah. Just as YHWH noticed the humble responses of Ahab (tearing his clothes) and Hezekiah (weeping) and extended their lives (1 Kgs 21:29; 2 Kgs 20:5–6), so YHWH has seen the humility of Josiah (torn clothes and weeping). Huldah concludes that Josiah will miss the coming devastation and be buried in peace. However, the end of Huldah's prediction does not appear to come true (see "Josiah Dies in Battle" below for the discussion of Josiah's death; 23:29).

Josiah Renews the Covenant (2 Kings 23:1–3)

He may only be twenty-six, but Josiah is clearly the spiritual leader of Judah. After hearing Huldah's message he calls together the entire nation: all the elders of Judah and Jerusalem, the priests and the prophets, the people of Judah and

12. See Cogan and Tadmor, *II Kings*, 283.

the inhabitants of Jerusalem, from the least to the greatest (23:1–2). The purpose of this temple convocation is a public reading of the book of the covenant, presumably the same book found and read earlier (22:8, 10, 16), and a national renewal of the covenant (23:2–3). Since the people of Israel had repeatedly broken the original blood covenant with YHWH at Mount Sinai (Exod 24:1–8), it was renewed at important transitions in their history. Moses led the nation in a covenant renewal in Moab before they entered the land (Deut 29). After completing the conquest of Canaan, Joshua reviewed Israel's story and renewed the covenant at Shechem (Josh 24). And after the exiles returned and rebuilt the wall of Jerusalem, Ezra read the law of Moses before the gathered nation, which prompted them to sign a covenant (Neh 8:1–18; 9:38). Josiah's covenant renewal is reminiscent of Deuteronomy's Shema, as it speaks of keeping YHWH's commands with one's whole heart and soul (2 Kgs 23:3; Deut 6:5).

Josiah Destroys the Idols and Their Priests (2 Kings 23:4–14)

After the covenant renewal, Josiah begins his religious reforms by clearing out idolatrous artifacts from the temple (23:4). Reformation was an ongoing process since, six centuries later, Jesus would perform a similar act of cleansing on Herod's renovated temple (Matt 21:12–13; Mark 11:15–17; Luke 19:45–46; John 2:13–17). The temple contained objects devoted to the worship of Baal, Asherah, and the starry host. In addition to these deities, people had offered incense to the sun, the moon, and the constellations (2 Kgs 23:4–5; for prohibitions of these objects, see Deut 4:19; 17:3). While the creation narrative makes it clear that Israel's God was the one who created all these celestial objects to serve his purposes to designate times and seasons (Gen 1:14–19), his people continued to worship created objects instead of the creator.

Josiah's agents of reformation were priests under the command of Hilkiah, the high priest (2 Kgs 23:4). In the spirit of the prediction of the anonymous man of God (1 Kgs 13:2), the priests associated with the northern high places were killed (2 Kgs 23:20).[13] While this slaughter is troubling to many modern readers, the law mandated death for worshipers of other gods (Deut 17:2–7). Both Elijah and Jehu engaged in similar slaughters of the priests and the worshipers of Baal (1 Kgs 18:40; 2 Kgs 10:18–27). It is difficult to know what "he did away with" (23:5) means in relation to what Josiah did to the other idolatrous priests. They may have merely been removed from their roles, or they may have been killed like the priests at Bethel.

13. Josiah's slaughter appears to target all northern high places, which would presumably include Jeroboam's.

Josiah's priests destroyed the idolatrous objects in a variety of manners, including obliteration (vv. 6, 12), demolishment (vv. 7, 8, 12, 14), and desecration (vv. 8, 10, 13), but primarily things were burned (vv. 4, 6, 11, 15, 16), with the ashes/dust/rubble dumped at Bethel (v. 4), over graves (v. 6), or into the Kidron Valley (v. 12). Specific idolatrous objects that were destroyed included Asherah poles (v. 6, 15), altars (vv. 12, 15, 16, 17, 20), high places (vv. 8, 13, 15, 19), chariots (v. 11), and sacred stones (v. 14).

The Hebrew behind the term "male shrine prostitutes" (v. 7; also 1 Kgs 14:24; 15:12; 22:46) could be translated literally as "those set apart as holy" (*haqqedeshim*). It is difficult to know exactly what they were doing and why it was condemned, but many scholars associate their behavior with ritual prostitution (see discussion in Chapter 12 of 1 Kgs 14:24).

In his work of reformation Josiah undoes the efforts of earlier idolatrous kings: one from Israel (Jeroboam I: 2 Kgs 23:15–17) and three from Judah (Ahaz: v. 12, Manasseh: v. 12, and Solomon: v. 13). Josiah's priests desecrated three high places devoted to foreign gods (v. 13). These three deities have not been mentioned in the book of Kings since the period of Solomon's apostasy: Ashtoreth of Sidon (1 Kgs 11:5, 33), Chemosh of Moab (11:7, 33), and Molek of Ammon (11:5, 7, 33). In addition to these high places, Josiah desecrated Topheth, the location of child sacrifices to Molek in the Hinnom Valley on the south and west sides of Jerusalem (see also 2 Kgs 16:3; 17:17; 21:6).

Josiah Destroys Jeroboam's Altar (2 Kings 23:15–20)

For over three centuries, the high place established by Jeroboam I at Bethel had been allowed to survive, prompting condemnation for seventeen of nineteen northern rulers (all except Elah and Shallum). Jeroboam had originally set up two golden calves (1 Kgs 12:25–33), but the one at Dan, in the north, has not been mentioned since the reign of Jehu (2 Kgs 10:29). Dan was over a hundred miles north of Jerusalem and would have been under Assyrian or Babylonian control at this point. Bethel, however, was only about ten miles north, a more reasonable target for Josiah's reform. Josiah burned the high place and the Asherah pole (23:15). The text notes that Josiah's altar destruction fulfilled the word proclaimed by the man of God during the time of Jeroboam. Toward the end of 23:16, the Septuagint includes a long insertion between "the man of God" and "who foretold these things," which could be translated "when Jeroboam stood by the altar at the festival; he turned and looked up at the tomb of the man of God." Some English translations omit this addition (e.g., NIV, ESV, NASB), while others include it (e.g., NRSV, NLT, NJB, REB), presumably because it provides details about the actions of the man of God and Josiah. While desecrating Jeroboam's altar with the burned bones of nearby graves, Josiah asks about one of the tombstones (v. 17). When he discovers that it belonged to the man of God from Judah who predicted these actions, Josiah mandates protection for it (v. 18). His grave and the grave of the Samarian prophet who tricked the Judean man of God were not disturbed.

Josiah Celebrates the Passover (2 Kings 23:21–23)

After his initial temple renovations, Josiah's reforms involved death, destruction, and desecration, but now Josiah begins a celebration of the Passover. The Passover commemorates YHWH's deliverance of his people from Egyptian oppression and was to be celebrated annually (Exod 12). Josiah emphasizes to the people that this festival was commanded in the book of the covenant (2 Kgs 23:21; Deut 16:1–8). The text notes that Josiah's Passover celebration was unique; nothing like it has been celebrated during the period of the judges or kings (2 Kgs 23:22). Kings only records one Passover (Josiah's), and the book of Joshua records the only other one in the Former Prophets, after the new generation of Israelites was circumcised at Gilgal (Josh 5:10–11). Chronicles, however, includes a great Passover celebration by Hezekiah (2 Chr 30:1–27). All of Josiah's reformations took place in the eighteenth year of his reign (2 Kgs 22:3; 23:23). It was a busy year for the young ruler.

Josiah Fulfills the Law (2 Kings 23:24–27)

The text includes one final round of reforms, this time targeting the mediums and spiritists (23:24). The law forbade Israelites from engaging in any form of these dark practices (Lev 19:31; 20:6, 27; Deut 18:9–14). Israel's first ruler, Saul, had expelled them from the land, but he also consulted the witch of Endor when he wanted to bring back Samuel from the dead (1 Sam 28:3–25). The only other time mediums and spiritists are mentioned in Kings is during the reign of Manasseh (2 Kgs 21:6). Josiah also removed (23:24) "household gods" (*teraphim*; see also Gen 31:34; Judg 17:5; 1 Sam 19:13), "idols" (*gillulim*; see also Lev 26:30; Deut 29:17; 2 Kgs 21:11), and other "detestable things" (*shiqqutsim*; see also Deut 29:17; 1 Kgs 11:5). While Hezekiah trusted in YHWH more than any other ruler (2 Kgs 18:5), Josiah's incomparable righteousness is expressed in his turning (*shuv*) to YHWH more than any other ruler. The description of his turning is reminiscent of Deuteronomy, with all his heart, soul, and strength (23:25; Deut 6:5; see also Matt 22:37; Mark 12:30; Luke 10:27).

However, even Josiah's wholehearted righteous reformation was not sufficient to overcome his grandfather Manasseh's wholehearted idolatrous corruption (2 Kgs 23:26). The details of the destruction that Huldah's oracle lacked earlier (22:16–20) are provided now by YHWH. YHWH's fierce anger would still lead to judgment—first against Judah, then against Jerusalem, and finally against the location where he chose to place his name, the temple (23:27). YHWH's judgment pronouncement is delivered here with no mention of a prophetic mediator or an intended audience.

Josiah Dies in Battle (2 Kings 23:28–30)

After mentioning that the other events from his reign are recorded in the southern annals, the text records Josiah's death in battle against Necho of Egypt at Megiddo (23:29). His servants return his body to the capital and bury him (v. 30), and then the people of the land anoint his son Jehoahaz as the new king. While some scholars think all rulers of Israel and Judah were anointed,[14] textual evidence suggests otherwise. The book of Kings only records anointings for four of the thirty-eight rulers of Israel and Judah (Solomon: 1 Kgs 1:39; Jehu: 2 Kgs 9:6; Joash: 2 Kgs 11:12; Jehoahaz: 2 Kgs 23:30).[15] Presumably, the people anointed Jehoahaz to give him greater legitimacy, since he was younger than his brother, Jehoiakim. After the short, three-month reign of Jehoahaz, Jehoiakim would succeed him as king (23:31, 36).

How does one reconcile Huldah's prophecy that Josiah would die in peace (22:20) with his apparent death in battle at the hands of Necho of Egypt (23:29)?[16] Several scholars argue that, despite appearances, Huldah's prophecy was fulfilled completely, since the text defines being buried in peace as not being forced to witness the horrors of the Babylonian destruction (22:20), which did not begin until the reigns of his sons.[17] Just as Hezekiah was content to learn that conditions would remain peaceful during his lifetime (20:16–19), Huldah's promise of peace here should be received as good news by Josiah. Other scholars, however, think that this aspect of Huldah's prophecy was not fulfilled, since death in battle is the antithesis of a peaceful death.[18] Barnes believes that Huldah's prophecy may have made Josiah overly confident, leading him to think he could defeat Egypt.[19] The words of prophets have generally

14. See, for example, Cogan and Tadmor, *II Kings*, 106.

15. On royal anointing in Israel and Judah, see Lamb, *Righteous Jehu*, 47–57.

16. For more historical background on the death of Josiah, see Cogan and Tadmor, *II Kings*, 300–2.

17. For example, Hobbs, *2 Kings*, 328; Wiseman, *1 & 2 Kings*, 299; Wray Beal, *1 & 2 Kings*, 505, 510.

18. See, for example, Fretheim, *Kings*, 218; and Alter, *Former Prophets*, 841. Unfortunately, neither of these two scholars provide textual support for their perspective.

19. Barnes, *1–2 Kings*, 370.

been fulfilled in Kings, but even prophetic predictions can be conditioned upon subsequent behavior. Perhaps the most famous example is the royal dynastic promise to David, which in Samuel appears unconditional (2 Sam 7:12–16) but in Kings is conditioned upon obedience (1 Kgs 2:4; 6:12; 8:25; 9:4–5). It is not stated in Kings, but Chronicles makes it clear that Josiah died in battle because he disobeyed the word of YHWH (2 Chr 35:22–24). Curiously, commentators on this subject seem to ignore the prophetic prediction of death for Hezekiah, just a few chapters earlier, that was changed based on the king's prayer and tears (2 Kgs 20:5–6). The authority of God's word is not compromised when the failure of his people to follow their covenantal obligations results in promises being rescinded.

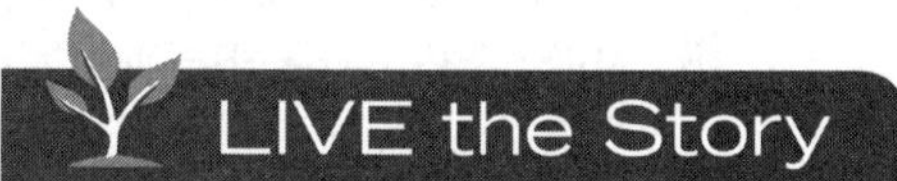

Reforming Worship

As we see throughout Scripture, the people of God need to be constantly reformed. Just like his ancestor Josiah, Jesus also performed a cleansing of the temple (Matt 21:12–13; Mark 11:15–17; Luke 19:45–46; John 2:13–17). Josiah removed cultic objects associated with the worship of Baal and other gods. Jesus's target was primarily idolatry associated with money, as he overturned the tables of the moneychangers and drove out those who were selling livestock. While Josiah got rid of foreign gods, Jesus made room for foreigners to worship God. Jesus quoted from Isaiah: "My house will be called a house of prayer for all nations" (Is 56:7). The moneychangers and livestock sellers were doing business in the court of the Gentiles, making it impossible for them to pray in their designated worship space. Our idols and syncretistic worship practices make it difficult for people to truly worship God. Josiah's reformation culminated in a celebration of the Passover, a time to reminder God's faithfulness in the past. Jesus's reforms focused on prayer, particularly for people from other nations.

Thus, from the reforming examples of Josiah and Jesus, we can make three points to emphasize as we reform worship. First, focus on celebrating God's work of deliverance. Second, prioritize prayer in worship. Third, create spaces of hospitality for people to encounter God, particularly people from other nations. However, we should remember that reformation is not always welcomed. While Josiah's reforms received widespread support (2 Kgs 23:1, 3, 21), Jesus's efforts prompted the chief priests to plot his death (Mark 11:18). But for those who resist reformation, both of these texts offer a warning. Just as

YHWH himself declared that Solomon's Temple would be destroyed, Jesus also ominously predicted the destruction of Herod's Temple (Mark 13:1–2).

Reading the Word of God

Josiah's reformation, the most extensive in the history of Israel or Judah, was inspired by the word of God. God's word, his book, his covenant, his law, his commands, his statutes, his decrees, and his speech are mentioned nineteen times in these two chapters (2 Kgs 22:8, 10, 11, 13 [2x], 15, 16 [2x]), 18, 19; 23:2, 3 [2x], 16, 21, 24, 25, 27 [2x]). The theme of God's word dominates Josiah's narrative. God's word needs to be central in the lives and ministries of God's people. The word "read" (*qara'*) appears four times here, twice with Shaphan as the subject (vv. 8, 10) and twice with Josiah as the subject (v. 16; 23:2), and always with the word of God as the object. The specific catalyst for the events of this chapter was the reading of Scripture. Three points can be made here about reading God's word.

First, reading God's Word should be done publicly. Most reading of Scripture today is done individually. People read books, websites, and emails on their own. I read a book before I fall asleep in bed, while my wife reads a different book next to me. We're both reading, but it is done independently, silently in our heads. However, in the world of ancient Israel reading was done, like many other things, corporately. The word translated as "read" here (*qara'*) literally means "call" or "proclaim." The word of God is not just meant to be read aloud; it is meant to be read loudly, even proclaimed. To begin his ministry (Luke 4:16–30), Jesus reads publicly from the book of Isaiah in the synagogue at Nazareth (Isa 61:1–2) and summarizes two stories from the book of Kings (1 Kgs 17:8–15; 2 Kgs 5:1–19). When Scripture is read out loud in public contexts, the process becomes more dramatic, more experiential. The words are not just being processed in one's head, but our senses are involved. The words are spoken, heard, and seen as the reader moves (ideally) to animate the words. They are more memorable. In every one of my classes, we read Scripture publicly before we discuss a text. As students practice public reading, they become more proficient, more dramatic readers of Scripture. When I was on staff with InterVarsity in the Claremont Colleges in California, one of the college's English professors would invite students to his home for a public reading of *Moby-Dick*. It took twenty-seven hours. If fans of Herman Melville could do it, so could the followers of Jesus. The fellowship decided to read all four Gospels consecutively one Friday evening (over food). We used a variety of alternative translations (J. B. Phillips, the Cotton Patch), and it took about eight hours. As we feasted on the stories of Jesus, we encountered our Lord in new and profound ways.

Second, reading God's word should lead to repentance. No other king turned to YHWH like Josiah; no other king reformed worship like Josiah. Immediately after hearing God's word read aloud, he was quick to repent, tearing his clothes and seeking out God's direction. Josiah then proceeded to destroy idols, altars, and idolatrous objects, actions that were all inspired by Scripture, particularly Deuteronomy. Hezekiah was quick to respond to Isaiah's word about his imminent death; however, Isaiah's message about the castration of his descendants seemed to have no effect on him (2 Kgs 20). When John the Baptist read from Isaiah (40:3–5), unlike Jesus's hostile crowd at Nazareth (Luke 4:28–30), John's hearers at the Jordan were quick to repent, asking how they should change their behavior (Luke 3:3–14). When was the last time anyone you know tore their clothes and repented because they read a convicting passage from Scripture? Josiah's humble response to the reading of Scripture here should serve as a model for all leaders of God's people.

Third, reading God's word should lead to celebration. In his response to Scripture, Josiah's reforms primarily involved stopping negative idolatrous activities. However, he also engaged in positive activities, as he brought the nation together for a covenant renewal ceremony (2 Kgs 23:1–3) and a Passover celebration (vv. 21–23). After reading about the covenant renewal at Moab (Deut 29), Josiah followed their example. While he hadn't seen any examples of it, Josiah read about the Passover celebration from the book of the covenant (Deut 16:1–8), so he decided to reinstitute the practice.

Josiah had received Huldah's message that judgment is coming. Life was going to be very difficult for the people of Judah over the next forty years as they faced a series of Babylonian deportations. The Passover is primarily a reminder that YHWH is a God of deliverance from oppression, a lesson the Judeans will desperately need very soon.

The night before his death, Jesus combined the two ceremonies performed by Josiah. He celebrated Passover with his followers and renewed the covenant with them, as he described how the cup they were drinking contained the blood of the covenant that would be poured out for the sins of many (Mark 14:12–25). Jesus knew that, just like the Judeans pre-exile, his disciples would need hopeful reminders of God's deliverance during the times of persecution ahead. As we respond to public readings of God's word with repentance and celebration, we are actively loving God with our whole heart, our whole soul, and our whole strength—like Josiah modeled and Jesus commanded (2 Kgs 23:25; Deut 6:5; Mark 12:28–30).

CHAPTER 39

2 Kings 23:31–25:7

LISTEN to the Story

31Jehoahaz was twenty-three years old when he became king, and he reigned in Jerusalem three months. His mother's name was Hamutal daughter of Jeremiah; she was from Libnah. 32He did evil in the eyes of the LORD, just as his predecessors had done. 33Pharaoh Necho put him in chains at Riblah in the land of Hamath so that he might not reign in Jerusalem, and he imposed on Judah a levy of a hundred talents of silver and a talent of gold. 34Pharaoh Necho made Eliakim son of Josiah king in place of his father Josiah and changed Eliakim's name to Jehoiakim. But he took Jehoahaz and carried him off to Egypt, and there he died. 35Jehoiakim paid Pharaoh Necho the silver and gold he demanded. In order to do so, he taxed the land and exacted the silver and gold from the people of the land according to their assessments.

36Jehoiakim was twenty-five years old when he became king, and he reigned in Jerusalem eleven years. His mother's name was Zebidah daughter of Pedaiah; she was from Rumah. 37And he did evil in the eyes of the LORD, just as his predecessors had done.

24:1During Jehoiakim's reign, Nebuchadnezzar king of Babylon invaded the land, and Jehoiakim became his vassal for three years. But then he turned against Nebuchadnezzar and rebelled. 2The LORD sent Babylonian, Aramean, Moabite and Ammonite raiders against him to destroy Judah, in accordance with the word of the LORD proclaimed by his servants the prophets. 3Surely these things happened to Judah according to the LORD's command, in order to remove them from his presence because of the sins of Manasseh and all he had done, 4including the shedding of innocent blood. For he had filled Jerusalem with innocent blood, and the LORD was not willing to forgive.

5As for the other events of Jehoiakim's reign, and all he did, are they not written in the book of the annals of the kings of Judah? 6Jehoiakim rested with his ancestors. And Jehoiachin his son succeeded him as king.

7The king of Egypt did not march out from his own country again, because the king of Babylon had taken all his territory, from the Wadi of Egypt to the Euphrates River.

8Jehoiachin was eighteen years old when he became king, and he reigned in Jerusalem three months. His mother's name was Nehushta daughter of Elnathan; she was from Jerusalem. 9He did evil in the eyes of the LORD, just as his father had done.

10At that time the officers of Nebuchadnezzar king of Babylon advanced on Jerusalem and laid siege to it, 11and Nebuchadnezzar himself came up to the city while his officers were besieging it. 12Jehoiachin king of Judah, his mother, his attendants, his nobles and his officials all surrendered to him.

In the eighth year of the reign of the king of Babylon, he took Jehoiachin prisoner. 13As the LORD had declared, Nebuchadnezzar removed the treasures from the temple of the LORD and from the royal palace, and cut up the gold articles that Solomon king of Israel had made for the temple of the LORD. 14He carried all Jerusalem into exile: all the officers and fighting men, and all the skilled workers and artisans—a total of ten thousand. Only the poorest people of the land were left.

15Nebuchadnezzar took Jehoiachin captive to Babylon. He also took from Jerusalem to Babylon the king's mother, his wives, his officials and the prominent people of the land. 16The king of Babylon also deported to Babylon the entire force of seven thousand fighting men, strong and fit for war, and a thousand skilled workers and artisans. 17He made Mattaniah, Jehoiachin's uncle, king in his place and changed his name to Zedekiah.

18Zedekiah was twenty-one years old when he became king, and he reigned in Jerusalem eleven years. His mother's name was Hamutal daughter of Jeremiah; she was from Libnah. 19He did evil in the eyes of the LORD, just as Jehoiakim had done. 20It was because of the LORD's anger that all this happened to Jerusalem and Judah, and in the end he thrust them from his presence.

Now Zedekiah rebelled against the king of Babylon.

25:1So in the ninth year of Zedekiah's reign, on the tenth day of the tenth month, Nebuchadnezzar king of Babylon marched against Jerusalem with his whole army. He encamped outside the city and built siege works all around it. 2The city was kept under siege until the eleventh year of King Zedekiah.

3By the ninth day of the fourth month the famine in the city had become so severe that there was no food for the people to eat. [4]Then the city wall was broken through, and the whole army fled at night through the gate between the two walls near the king's garden, though the Babylonians were surrounding the city. They fled toward the Arabah, [5]but the Babylonian army pursued the king and overtook him in the plains of Jericho. All his soldiers were separated from him and scattered, [6]and he was captured.

He was taken to the king of Babylon at Riblah, where sentence was pronounced on him. [7]They killed the sons of Zedekiah before his eyes. Then they put out his eyes, bound him with bronze shackles and took him to Babylon.

Listening to the Text in the Story: Biblical Texts: Jeremiah 21:3–7; 22:11–30; 25:7; 26:20–23; 36:20–26; 38:14–28; 39:1–10; 40:1–16; 52:1–34; Daniel 1–4; Ancient Near Eastern Texts: The Jehoahaz Seal Inscription; The Babylonian Chronicle; King Adon of Ekron's Appeal to Necho of Egypt; The Babylonian Ration List

After the reforms of righteous Josiah come the reigns of his four evil heirs (Jehoahaz, Jehoiakim, Jehoiachin, and Zedekiah). These thirty-four verses recording the reigns of Judah's final four rulers can be confusing with their short narratives, parallel elements, similar-sounding names, and repeated cycles of evilness, bloodshed, and captivity. To help us understand the contexts of these four Josianic rulers, we will briefly discuss other biblical texts (particularly from Jeremiah) as well as ancient Near Eastern sources.

The book of Chronicles includes significant parallel material from Kings, but for the final chapters of 2 Kings, the book of Jeremiah also records long parallel texts (Jer 39:1–10; 40:1–16; 52:1–34). While the narratives of these four rulers are relatively short in Kings, Jeremiah provides additional details about their reigns, particularly for the two longer-reigning ones, Jehoiakim and Zedekiah (both reigned eleven years), and how they persecuted or killed YHWH's prophets. Jehoiakim is mentioned by name only six times in 2 Kings (23:34, 35, 36; 24:1, 6, 19), but has twenty-two mentions in Jeremiah (e.g., 1:3; 22:18, 24; 24:1; 25:1; 26:1). Jehoiakim hunted down and killed the prophet Uriah, who had prophesied against Jerusalem and Judah (Jer 26:20–23). He burned Jeremiah's scroll and attempted to kill Jeremiah but was thwarted by God (36:20–26). Zedekiah is mentioned by name six times in the Hebrew of 2 Kings (24:17, 18, 20; 25:2, 7 [2x]) but forty-six times in Jeremiah (e.g., 1:3; 21:1; 24:8; 27:1; 28:1; 29:3; 32:1).[1] Zedekiah imprisoned Jeremiah (32:2–3; 37:16–21), consulted with Jeremiah, and kept him alive (38:14–28). Kings records that Zedekiah was blinded and captured by Nebuchadnezzar (2 Kgs 25:7), but Jeremiah adds that he was imprisoned in Babylon, where he died (Jer 52:11).

Josiah and his sons are the focus of a series of Jeremiah's oracles (21:3–7; 22:10–30).[2] One oracle (22:10–12) concerns Josiah and Jehoahaz (called here by his personal name Shallum), urging its audience to not weep over the dead king (Josiah) but rather over the living one (Jehoahaz), who will die in Egypt where he has been carried captive. Another oracle (Jer 22:13–19) concerns Jehoiakim, contrasting the justice of Josiah with the preoccupations of his son: injustice, dishonest gain, and the shedding of innocent blood in the building of his new palace. No one will lament for Jehoiakim; he will be buried with a donkey beyond the gates of Jerusalem (22:19). A third oracle (22:24–30) concerns Jehoiachin (called Coniah), who will be torn off and thrown to the hands of Nebuchadnezzar of Babylon, never to return to Judah, and none of Jehoiachin's offspring will sit on the throne in Judah. A fourth oracle (21:3–7) is a reply to Zedekiah's question about whether YHWH will assist Judah against Nebuchadnezzar of Babylon. Jeremiah informed Zedekiah that YHWH would not help and that he would in fact fight against them, giving them over into the hands of their enemies.

The names of several individuals from these narratives appear in extrabiblical inscriptions. Jehoahaz is mentioned in a seal inscription.

> Jehoahaz, son of the king.[3]

Jehoiachin also appears in the Babylonian Ration List.[4] Pharaoh Necho of Egypt is mentioned in a variety of external sources (see discussion of Josiah and Necho in the previous chapter). A damaged Aramaic letter from King Adon of Ekron requests assistance from the king of Egypt (Necho) against the king of Babylon (Nebuchadnezzar):

> To the Lord of Kings Pharaoh, your servant Adon King of Ekron . . . the force of the King of Babylon has come and reached Aphek. . . . For the

---

1. Not counting other men named Zedekiah in Kings (1 Kgs 22:11, 24) and Jeremiah (Jer 29:21, 22; 36:12).
2. These oracles will be discussed in the order these rulers reigned, not their order in Jeremiah.
3. *WSS* 54, #13.
4. *ANET*, 308.

> Lord of Kings Pharaoh knows that your servant . . . to send a force to rescue me. Let him not abandon me.[5]

Shortly after this letter was written, Ekron was destroyed by Babylon; thus it appears the letter did not achieve its desired result. Necho of Egypt had killed Josiah (2 Kgs 23:29), and he will imprison his son, Jehoahaz (vv. 33–34), but during this period Egyptian hegemony will gradually be replaced by that of Babylon under Nebuchadnezzar.

King Nebuchadnezzar II (605–562 BC) of Babylon makes his first biblical appearance here (24:1). His father, Nabopolassar (626–605 BC), founded the Neo-Babylonian dynasty, but his son was the most significant ruler over the course of the empire (612–539 BC). Nebuchadnezzar is more well-known than any of Josiah's heirs (and perhaps even Josiah)—he is mentioned by name over ninety times in the Bible, more than any other foreign ruler (e.g., 2 Kgs 24:1; 1 Chr 6:15; Ezra 1:7; Neh 7:6; Esth 2:6; Jer 21:2; Ezek 26:7; Dan 1:1).[6] In the books of Jeremiah and Daniel, Nebuchadnezzar plays a more substantial role than he does in Kings.[7] Kings does not state explicitly that Nebuchadnezzar's invasion during the reign of Jehoiakim was caused by YHWH, but texts in Jeremiah and Daniel do (Jer 25:9; Dan 1:2). YHWH even calls Nebuchadnezzar "my servant" in three of Jeremiah's oracles (Jer 25:9; 27:6; 43:10). According to Daniel, early in the reign of Jehoiakim (605 BC), Nebuchadnezzar attacked Jerusalem and took young exiles back to Babylon, giving new Babylonian names to four of them (Daniel and his three friends; Dan 1:1–7), just as he does to Zedekiah here (2 Kgs 24:17). The most familiar stories about Nebuchadnezzar in Daniel involve the troubling dream, the golden image, the fiery furnace, and the period of insanity (Dan 1–4).

The Babylonian Chronicle records the battle of Carchemish (not mentioned in Kings, but elsewhere: 2 Chr 35:20; Isa 10:9; Jer 46:2) where the Babylonian army, under the command of crown prince Nebuchadnezzar, defeated the combined forces of Assyria and Egypt under Necho.

> 605 BCE [Year 21] The king of Babylon (Nabopolassar) was in his country. Nebuchadrezzar, his eldest son, the crown prince, [called] out the [army of Babylon], took the van and went to Carchemish on the bank of the

5. *COS* 3:133.

6. Spelled as both "Nebuchadnezzar" and "Nebuchadrezzar" in the Old Testament.

7. Nebuchadnezzar's name appears six times in Kings (24:1, 10, 11; 25:1, 8, 22), thirty-seven times in Jeremiah (e.g., 21:2, 7; 22:25; 24:1: 25:1), and thirty-two times in Daniel (e.g., 1:1, 18; 2:1, 28, 46; 3:1, 3).

> Euphrates. He crossed the river [to face the army of Egypt] which was camped at Carchemish. [. . .] they fought together and the army of Egypt fled before him. He defeated them utterly. The rest of the army of [Egypt, which] had escaped from the defeat and which the army of Babylon had not conquered, the army defeated in the district of Hamath so that [not] a single man [returned] to his country. At that time Nebuchadrezzar conquered the whole of Hamath. Nabopolassar ruled Babylon for 21 years. On 8th Ab he died. In Elul Nebuchadrezzar returned to Babylon and on 1st Elul he ascended the throne in Babylon.[8]

After his father, Nabopolassar, died, Nebuchadnezzar came to power in 605 BC. The Babylonian Chronicle continues, recording many of the events narrated in this section, including Nebuchadnezzar's siege (2 Kgs 24:10–11), his capture of Jerusalem (v. 12), his plundering of the temple (v. 13), and his appointment of Zedekiah as ruler (v. 17).

> 598/597 BCE [Year 7] In Kislev the king of Babylonia called out his army and marched to Hattu. He set his camp against the city of Judah [*Ya-a-ḫu-du*] and on 2nd Adar he took the city and captured the king. He appointed a king of his choosing there, took heavy tribute and returned to Babylon.[9]

EXPLAIN the Story

The Final Four

A comparison of the narratives of Josiah's four heirs yields a few differences but also a surprising number of similarities. Not surprisingly, however, all four of their introductory regnal formulas include the ruler's name, age at accession in Jerusalem, length of reign, mother's name, and evaluation. They all came to power between the ages of eighteen and twenty-five (2 Kgs 23:31, 36; 24:8, 18). Their closing regnal formulas are unusual, with no reference to the annals of the southern kings or to their deaths and burials (except for Jehoiakim, the only one to die in Jerusalem; 24:5–6).

All the final four rulers receive evil evaluations (23:32, 37; 24:9, 19), but few details are provided to substantiate their evilness (for wicked details

8. *COS* 1:467.
9. *COS* 1:468.

on Jehoiakim and Zedekiah, see Listen to the Story above). Even though their father Josiah was particularly righteous (22:2; 23:25), two of them are described as following in the evil ways of "his fathers" (*'abotayv*; 23:32, 37). The NIV translates the Hebrew here as "his predecessors," assuming that the evil ancestors envisioned were Ahaz, Manasseh, and Amon and not righteous David, Hezekiah, and Josiah. Both Jehoiachin and Zedekiah are compared to evil Jehoiakim (the father of Jehoiachin, 24:9, and brother of Zedekiah, 24:19).

These final four rulers include three sons of Josiah (Jehoahaz, Jehoiakim, and Zedekiah) and one grandson (Jehoiachin). Thus, two successions were normal (father to son), but the other two successions were brother to brother (Jehoahaz to Jehoiakim) and nephew to uncle (Jehoiachin to Zedekiah).

Each of these rulers appears to have their name changed. Two rulers are called multiple names: Jehoahaz was also called Shallum (1 Chr 3:15; Jer 22:11), and Jehoiachin was also called Jeconiah (1 Chr 3:16 [NIV has "Jehoiachin" here], 17; Est 2:6; Jer 24:1, 27:20; 28:4; 29:2; Matt 1:12) or Coniah (Jer 22:24, 28; 37:1). Shallum and Jeconiah (shortened to Coniah) were probably original names, and Jehoahaz and Jehoiachin were throne names taken when they became king.[10] The other two rulers had their names changed by foreign rulers: Eliakim to Jehoiakim by Necho (2 Kgs 23:34), and Mattaniah to Zedekiah by Nebuchadnezzar (24:17). God often changes people's names in Scripture (Abram to Abraham: Gen 17:5; Sarai to Sarah: Gen 17:15; Jacob to Israel: Gen 32:28; Simon to Peter: Matt 16:18). For Jehoiakim and Zedekiah, their name changes presumably involved a declaration of allegiance to a new overlord (see Dan 1:7).[11]

While Davidic rulers were able to maintain power through these final tumultuous years for the Southern Kingdom, the external pressures on the Judean throne led to dramatically reduced reigns. According to the regnal formulas, the average reign length for a Judean ruler over the course of the divided monarchy was 20.4 years, but for these four Josianic rulers it was only 5.6 years.[12] Two rulers reigned eleven years (Jehoiakim, Zedekiah), and two rulers only reigned three months (Jehoahaz, Jehoiachin)—these latter two were the shortest-reigning rulers of Judah. Foreign deportation was a major cause of short reigns. Three rulers were imprisoned and exiled to foreign lands: Jehoahaz by Necho to Egypt (2 Kgs 23:34) and Jehoiachin (24:15) and

10. Wiseman, *1 & 2 Kings*, 306, 309.

11. *BBCOT*, 410.

12. 387.5 years total divided by 19 rulers = 20.4 years as an average (not counting co-regencies). For the final four Judean rulers, 22.5 years total divided by 4 rulers = 5.6 years average reign.

Zedekiah by Nebuchadnezzar to Babylon (25:7). The final two rulers both experienced a siege by Nebuchadnezzar of Babylon (24:10–11; 25:1–2).

Jehoahaz (2 Kings 23:31–34)

Jehoahaz of Judah (609 BC) shares his name ("YHWH has grasped") with a northern ruler, Jehoahaz, the son of Jehu (2 Kgs 13:1–9), who was also evil and oppressed by a foreign nation (then Aram, now Egypt). Scholars speculate how attitudes toward Egypt may have led the people of the land to choose Jehoahaz (23:30) over his brother Jehoiakim, who was two years older (23:31, 36), but the text yields few clues to resolve the problem.[13]

While it might seem unfair for Jehoahaz and his nephew Jehoiachin to be evaluated as evil when they both only reigned three months, three other rulers with short reigns were classified as evil (Zimri of Israel, seven days, 1 Kgs 16:15, 19; Ahaziah of Judah, one year, 2 Kgs 8:26–27; Zechariah of Israel, six months, 2 Kgs 15:8–9). Even in a short time, a ruler can either do great good or great harm. According to the chronological textual notes, all of Josiah's extensive reforms were undertaken within one year (22:3; 23:23). No reforms were recorded during the short reigns of either Jehoahaz or Jehoiachin or the longer reigns of Jehoiakim or Zedekiah.

The ruler who killed Josiah, Necho of Egypt (23:29), imprisoned Jehoahaz and took him to Riblah in Hamath (23:33). Riblah was located in Syria, about seventy miles north of Damascus on the bank of the Orontes River. Riblah served both as field headquarters, for Necho here and later for Nebuchadnezzar, where he imprisoned Jehoahaz's brother Zechariah before killing his sons and plucking out his eyes (25:6–7). The tribute that Necho imposed on Jehoahaz (one hundred silver talents and one gold talent) was significantly less that the Assyrian tribute that Sennacherib imposed upon Hezekiah (three hundred silver talents, thirty gold talents; 18:14). Jehoahaz died in Egypt, explaining his lack of a death and burial notice (23:34).

Jehoiakim (2 Kings 23:35–24:7)

Jehoiakim of Judah (609–598 BC) was made ruler by Necho of Egypt in the first Judean fraternal succession (see also 2 Kgs 1:17). Necho changed his name from Eliakim ("God establishes") to Jehoiakim ("YHWH has established").

Before the text records the regnal introduction of Jehoiakim, it includes an initial comment describing how he paid the tribute imposed by Necho upon his

13. Wiseman thinks Jehoahaz was selected because of Jehoiakim's anti-Egyptian tendencies (*1 & 2 Kings*, 306), while Wray Beal believes that Jehoahaz was anti-Egyptian, since he was removed quickly by Necho (*1 & 2 Kings*, 516).

father by taxing the people of the land (23:33, 35). About 605 BC Jehoiakim exchanged his Egyptian overlords for Babylonian ones when Nebuchadnezzar invaded; Jehoiakim remained a Babylonian vassal for three years (24:1).

Apart from seeing evil (23:32, 37; 24:9, 19), YHWH is largely passive in these four royal narratives, but at this point the text gives a theological explanation for Israel's fate. In response to Jehoiakim's rebellion against Babylon, YHWH sends "bands" (*gedudim*; left untranslated in the NIV but repeated four times in the Hebrew of 24:2) of raiders from Babylon, Aram, Moab, and Ammon (see also 1 Kgs 11:24; 2 Kgs 5:2; 13:20–21). The text explains that these raids fulfilled the word of YHWH and that, because of the sins and bloodshed of Manasseh (21:2–16), YHWH would not forgive his people (24:2–4). Jehoiakim's narrative concludes with a note that Nebuchadnezzar's successful campaign to control the region meant the king of Egypt was forced to remain at home (v. 7). Jehoiakim was the only one of the final five Judean rulers to die in peace in Judah (v. 6; see also Jer 22:18–19).

Jehoiachin (2 Kings 24:8–17)

While it might appear that Jehoiakim of Judah gave his son Jehoiachin ("YHWH will establish"; 598–597 BC)[14] a nearly identical name, neither of these names were birth names. The narrative here includes few details regarding Jehoiachin's evilness during his short reign, but Wiseman perceives an oracle from Ezekiel (17:12–24) explains the judgment against Judah's evil royal house during this period ("Say to this rebellious house . . ."; 17:12 ESV).[15]

Jehoiachin was one of three southern rulers to experience a siege (2 Kgs 24:10–11); the other two were Hezekiah (19:32) and Zedekiah (25:1–2). Sieges had also been used against three northern rulers: Zimri (1 Kgs 16:17), an anonymous king of Israel (2 Kgs 6:24–25), and Hoshea (17:5; 18:9). The siege against Zedekiah lasted about eighteen months, but the siege against Jehoiachin lasted only a few months. In Nebuchadnezzar's eighth year, a teenage Jehoiachin (eighteen years old), his mother, and his officials surrendered to Babylon in March (the 15th?), 597 BC (24:12).

The plunder taken by Nebuchadnezzar included treasures, both from the palace and the temple. The Babylonian booty included gold articles made by Solomon for the temple, which somehow survived the six previous times the temple has been plundered (Rehoboam: 1 Kgs 14:25–26; Asa: 15:18; Joash: 2 Kgs 12:18; Amaziah: 14:14; Ahaz: 16:7–8; Hezekiah: 18:14–16).

---

14. His reign began in the final month of 598 BC and ended after the first two months of 597 BC.
15. Wiseman, *1 & 2 Kings*, 309.

The Hebrew says that "all" (*kol*) the treasures were removed from the temple (24:13), but this "all" is omitted in the NIV (but not the ESV, NASB, NRSV), presumably to explain how some of the temple treasures remained for the final plundering under Zedekiah (25:14).[16] These gold and silver temple vessels were later profaned by Belshazzar during a feast, when Daniel read the writing on the wall immediately before Babylon fell (Dan 5).

The people taken by Nebuchadnezzar included the royal family and large numbers of others including officers, fighting men, skilled laborers, and artisans (24:14–16). While it is likely that this was the largest Babylonian deportation, determining the exact number is difficult since the text here records numbers of ten thousand, seven thousand, and one thousand, with fighting men and skilled workers included in more than one of these totals. Problematically, Jeremiah states the number of exiles for this deportation as 3,023 (Jer 52:28). Jeremiah also includes numbers for the deportation of 586 BC as 832 people (52:29) and the deportation of 581 BC as 745 people (52:30). Scholars harmonize these numerical discrepancies in a variety of ways, assuming the numbers are rounded (ten thousand), or that they include different groups (only men versus all people; only Jerusalemites versus all Judeans).[17] The numbers recorded in Jeremiah do not appear to be rounded, since they include three or four significant digits.

The plunder of the royal treasuries and the deportation of the royal family were both predicted by Isaiah during the reign of Hezekiah (2 Kgs 20:17–18). The prophet Ezekiel was probably also taken to Babylon during this deportation (Ezek 1:1; 17:12). Presumably because Jehoiachin surrendered freely, Nebuchadnezzar was relatively gracious, allowing Jerusalem's wall to survive, a decision he probably regretted ten years later when he had to besiege Jerusalem a second time under the reign of Zedekiah (2 Kgs 25:1–2).

Zedekiah (2 Kings 24:18–25:7)

Nebuchadnezzar took Mattaniah ("Gift of YHWH") and made him king of Judah, changing his name to Zedekiah ("YHWH is righteousness"). Zedekiah was thus the third son of Josiah to rule Judah. His succession was the only nephew-to-uncle one in Israel or Judah. Zedekiah's mother, Hamutal, was also the mother of Jehoahaz (23:31; 24:18).

Earlier the text attributes the judgment on Judah to Manasseh (24:3–4); here the text implies that the people of Jerusalem and Judah are to blame

16. On tribute and plunder during the monarchy, see Lamb, *Righteous Jehu*, 120–24.

17. See discussions of these numbers in Cogan and Tadmor, *II Kings*, 312, and Wray Beal, *1 & 2 Kings*, 519–20.

(24:20). YHWH cast them from his presence (v. 20) because of his anger, mentioned here for the last time in the book (see also 13:3; 17:18, 20, 23; 24:3), giving a theological explanation for the destruction recorded in chapter 25.

While YHWH had repeatedly given his endorsement of Nebuchadnezzar and warned against rebellion (2 Chr 36:12–13; Jer 25:9; 27:6–7, 12–15; 43:10), Zedekiah still rebelled against Babylon (2 Kgs 24:20). The books of Jeremiah and Ezekiel record that Zedekiah sent ambassadors to Egypt, requesting assistance from Pharaoh Hophra (Jer 37:5–7; 44:30; Ezek 29:2), but YHWH had declared that Egypt would not come to their aid (Ezek 17:12–21).

To deal with his rebellious vassal, Nebuchadnezzar returned to Jerusalem in the ninth year, tenth month, tenth day of Zedekiah's reign, January (the 15th?), 588 BC (2 Kgs 25:1). The Babylonians allowed people to leave a city during a siege (Jer 38:19; 39:9), but not to enter it, while residents starved to death (see also 2 Kgs 6:25–29). Over the course of this eighteen-month siege, lasting until the eleventh year of Zedekiah's reign, nothing was left to eat (25:2–3). The Hebrew does not provide the month for the end of the siege, but the NIV adds "the fourth" before "month," based on Jeremiah 52:6, placing the end in July (the 18th?), 587 BC (2 Kgs 25:3).

The northern wall of Jerusalem was finally breached, prompting the Judean army to flee to the south (v. 4). But the Babylonians were expecting a flight, so the Judeans were quickly overtaken near Jericho (v. 5). The king and his sons had fled with the army. The Babylonians were only interested in the royal family; soldiers were allowed to scatter, while Zedekiah and his sons were taken to Nebuchadnezzar's headquarters at Riblah (v. 6). Most prisoners of war were put to work by their captors, so blinding would be counterproductive (although Samson was blinded: Judg 16:21). However, these were no normal prisoners. Nebuchadnezzar's brutal punishment here for vassal insubordination was not uncommon. The brutality of killing Zedekiah's sons before blinding him (2 Kgs 25:7) was intended to send a clear message to any other vassals that the consequences of rebellion would be severe. While he languished in a Babylonian prison, Zedekiah would be forever haunted by his final vision of the deaths of his sons. However, Zedekiah's brother, Jehoiachin, survives (vv. 27–30).

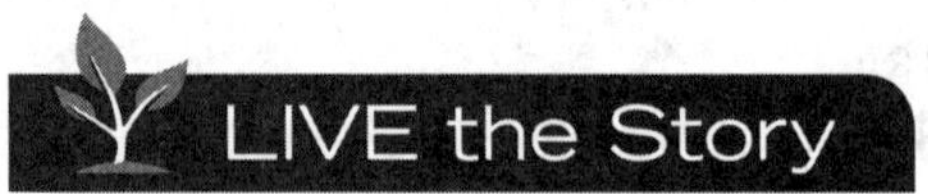

Righteous Parents and Evil Children

The final four rulers of Judah were all evaluated as evil and were all descendants of righteous Josiah, one of the most pious kings in Judah's history. The most evil southern ruler, Manasseh, was the son of righteous Hezekiah. Aren't children supposed to be like their parents (chips off the old block)? Why do righteous kings raise evil children? I asked my sons this question over dinner one night, and they replied, "We think the real question is why do evil fathers have righteous sons?"

These are difficult questions to address for many reasons. Few details are recorded about parenting in the narratives of these four rulers, or even in the book of Kings. Other sections of Scripture address the issue directly (e.g., Exod 20:12; Deut 6:7–9; Prov 1:8–19; Eph 6:1–4), but the only parental advice we find in Kings is given by David to Solomon at the beginning (1 Kgs 2:1–9), and much of it (vv. 5–9) is far too vindictive to be generally applicable. But using these four narratives, the rest of Kings, and other relevant biblical texts, we can still make three points about parenting, evilness, and righteousness.

First, people are evil. Evil children shouldn't surprise us. Many people go to Paul to support the idea of human depravity (Rom 3:10–12, 23), but he got the idea from the Old Testament (Pss 14:1–3; 53:1–3). If everyone is evil, what should surprise us, then, is that some people are considered righteous. Most rulers in Kings were evil (of the rulers of the divided monarchy with evaluations, 27/36 were evil = 75 percent),[18] but a quarter were deemed righteous. How do we reconcile the righteous descriptions of these rulers, or that of Noah (Gen 6:8–9) or Job (Job 1:1), with these statements about the pervasiveness of human sinfulness? Righteousness in these texts is defined not as perfect behavior but as movement toward God. Evilness, particularly in the book of Kings, involves moving away from God and worshiping idols. Even Hezekiah and Josiah do bad things (2 Kgs 18:14–16; 20:12–19; 2 Chr 35:21–22), but as rulers they both turned to God and turned away from idolatry. Some people might cringe at using terms like "good" or "evil" to describe people, but the Bible doesn't shy away from this terminology. We may not like it, but it does get our attention. Parents and children who do not repent from evil and turn to God remain in that state. The responsibility of parents is therefore to help children reconnect to God.

Second, even good leaders may not make good parents. The book of Kings talks more about leadership than parenting. In addition to turning from idolatry, good leaders ask for wisdom (1 Kgs 3:9), they pray (1 Kgs 8:22–53; 2 Kgs 19:15–19; 20:2–3), and they listen to prophets (1 Kgs 21:27–29; 2 Kgs 6:9–10). However, the quality of their parenting doesn't seem to be a factor in determining their evaluation, in contrast to what Paul teaches about

18. See Leuchter and Lamb, *Historical Writings*, 363–65.

the qualifications of leaders (1 Tim 3:4; Titus 1:6). We don't know why the children of Hezekiah and Josiah didn't follow in their father's footsteps. But tragically, in many Christian ministries, spiritual leaders are so caught up in their roles and responsibilities that they are unable to spend quality time with their children. For those of us who are parents, we can learn from the positive examples of good leaders in the book of Kings and help our children ask for wisdom, pray, and listen to others.

Third, being a good parent does not guarantee having a good child. Parenting matters, but the results are not like a mathematical equation: one good parent plus another good parent equals good children. Every parent and every child are different (but separated from God, they are all evil). My wife and I know many parents whose children, for a variety of reasons, aren't where the parents would hope they would be spiritually. Parents in these situations often ask, "What have we done wrong?" I wonder if Josiah asked the same question, if and when he had a sense of what Shallum, Eliakim, and Mattaniah (whose throne names were Jehoahaz, Jehoiakim, and Zedekiah) were going to be like when they grew up. It is possible that Hezekiah and Josiah were great fathers, but, as we just pointed out, people are evil, and good leaders may not be good parents. There are no perfect children and no perfect parents, just evil people who need to follow the example of Josiah and turn to God (2 Kgs 23:25). We've all done many things wrong and right as parents, but parenting isn't like a mathematical equation.

When I talk to friends about their children who somehow have drifted from God, I like to bring up Jesus's parable of the prodigal son (Luke 15:11–32). I proceed with caution here, because parables typically have one main point, but in this case it is relevant because the point of the parable is related to parenting. The father figure in the parable is clearly meant to represent God. If we reflect on him as a father, we must conclude that he, a bit like Josiah, was a righteous father (see Mark 10:18) with evil sons. The younger son, the prodigal, wastes half of his father's estate on, according to his brother, prostitutes. The older son is self-righteous, bitter, angry, and petty. What did the father do wrong to raise such wicked sons? Nothing. He loved his sons by sharing his possessions, by welcoming them, by kissing them, by pursuing them, and by celebrating with them. Whether our children are or are not where we would like them to be spiritually, our responsibility as parents is to continue to show them love like the father of the prodigal, who lavished love on his two boys as a reflection of God's love for us.

## CHAPTER 40

2 Kings 25:8–30

LISTEN to the Story

[8]On the seventh day of the fifth month, in the nineteenth year of Nebuchadnezzar king of Babylon, Nebuzaradan commander of the imperial guard, an official of the king of Babylon, came to Jerusalem. [9]He set fire to the temple of the LORD, the royal palace and all the houses of Jerusalem. Every important building he burned down. [10]The whole Babylonian army under the commander of the imperial guard broke down the walls around Jerusalem. [11]Nebuzaradan the commander of the guard carried into exile the people who remained in the city, along with the rest of the populace and those who had deserted to the king of Babylon. [12]But the commander left behind some of the poorest people of the land to work the vineyards and fields.

[13]The Babylonians broke up the bronze pillars, the movable stands and the bronze Sea that were at the temple of the LORD and they carried the bronze to Babylon. [14]They also took away the pots, shovels, wick trimmers, dishes and all the bronze articles used in the temple service. [15]The commander of the imperial guard took away the censers and sprinkling bowls—all that were made of pure gold or silver.

[16]The bronze from the two pillars, the Sea and the movable stands, which Solomon had made for the temple of the LORD, was more than could be weighed. [17]Each pillar was eighteen cubits high. The bronze capital on top of one pillar was three cubits high and was decorated with a network and pomegranates of bronze all around. The other pillar, with its network, was similar.

[18]The commander of the guard took as prisoners Seraiah the chief priest, Zephaniah the priest next in rank and the three doorkeepers. [19]Of those still in the city, he took the officer in charge of the fighting men, and five royal advisers. He also took the secretary who was chief officer in charge of conscripting the people of the land and sixty of the conscripts who were found in the city. [20]Nebuzaradan the commander took them all

and brought them to the king of Babylon at Riblah. [21]There at Riblah, in the land of Hamath, the king had them executed.

So Judah went into captivity, away from her land.

[22]Nebuchadnezzar king of Babylon appointed Gedaliah son of Ahikam, the son of Shaphan, to be over the people he had left behind in Judah. [23]When all the army officers and their men heard that the king of Babylon had appointed Gedaliah as governor, they came to Gedaliah at Mizpah—Ishmael son of Nethaniah, Johanan son of Kareah, Seraiah son of Tanhumeth the Netophathite, Jaazaniah the son of the Maakathite, and their men. [24]Gedaliah took an oath to reassure them and their men. "Do not be afraid of the Babylonian officials," he said. "Settle down in the land and serve the king of Babylon, and it will go well with you."

[25]In the seventh month, however, Ishmael son of Nethaniah, the son of Elishama, who was of royal blood, came with ten men and assassinated Gedaliah and also the men of Judah and the Babylonians who were with him at Mizpah. [26]At this, all the people from the least to the greatest, together with the army officers, fled to Egypt for fear of the Babylonians.

[27]In the thirty-seventh year of the exile of Jehoiachin king of Judah, in the year Awel-Marduk became king of Babylon, he released Jehoiachin king of Judah from prison. He did this on the twenty-seventh day of the twelfth month. [28]He spoke kindly to him and gave him a seat of honor higher than those of the other kings who were with him in Babylon. [29]So Jehoiachin put aside his prison clothes and for the rest of his life ate regularly at the king's table. [30]Day by day the king gave Jehoiachin a regular allowance as long as he lived.

Listening to the Text in the Story: Biblical Texts: 1 Kings 9:6–9; 1 Chronicles 3:17–18; Ezra 3–7; Nehemiah 1–6; Psalm 79; 137; Lamentations; Haggai 1–2; Ancient Near Eastern Texts: An Elephantine Aramaic Letter; Late Monarchic Period Seal Inscriptions; Babylonian Ration List

The final chapters of Judges repeat the refrain, "In those days Israel had no king . . ." (Judg 17:6; 18:1; 19:1; 21:25). After more than four centuries of Davidic rule, there is now no king in Judah. Josiah, Jehoahaz, and Jehoiakim are dead (2 Kgs 23:29, 34; 24:6),[1] and Jehoiachin and blind Zechariah are

1. Jehoahaz may have survived past the reigns of his brothers, but the text suggests that he died shortly after his arrival in Egypt (23:34).

captives in Babylon (24:15; 25:7). The book of Kings concludes in an unsatisfying manner with a chaotic picture of life in Judah as Nebuchadnezzar's forces destroy the city, deport more people, plunder the temple, slaughter the leaders, and appoint Gedaliah as governor, who is assassinated by his fellow Judeans. Despite the tragedy of the devastation, the record of these losses is terse. The final four verses of the book, however, include a mildly hopeful note, that after thirty-nine years of exile, Jehoiachin is released from prison in Babylon (25:27–30). A variety of biblical and ancient Near Eastern texts provide important context for this dark time in Judah's history.

Since the temple was considered the dwelling place of God, this section devotes more attention to the destruction of the temple (vv. 9, 13–17) than that of the wall, the palace, or other buildings (vv. 9–10). YHWH had warned Solomon that if the people disobeyed his commands, they would be exiled and the temple destroyed (1 Kgs 9:6–9), but the text here doesn't mention a fulfillment of this prophecy.

A large group of Jews fled to Egypt after the killing of Gedaliah (2 Kgs 25:26; see also 23:34 and Jer 41:17; 43:5–7). It is possible that this group ended up settling at Elephantine, an island on the Nile River in southern Egypt. A collection of fifth-century BC papyri records details of the lives of a Jewish community on Elephantine, their customs, and their temple. An Aramaic letter from Jews in Elephantine to Bagayahya, the governor of Judah, describes how their temple was demolished by Egyptian soldiers (the letter is dated 407 BC):

> Afterwards, Nafaina led the Egyptians with the other troops. They came to the fortress of Elephantine with their implements, broke into that Temple, demolished it to the ground, and the pillars of stone which were there—they smashed them. Moreover, it happened (that the) five gateways of stone, built of hewn stone, which were in that Temple, they demolished. And their standing doors, and the pivots of those doors, (of) bronze, and the roof of wood of cedar—all (of these) which, with the rest of the *fittings* and other (things), which were there—all (of these) with fire they burned. But the basins of gold and silver and the (other) things which were in that Temple—all (of these) they took and made their own.[2]

This text continues to describe the devastating effects of this catastrophe on these Elephantine Jews as they mourned their temple's loss.[3]

2. *COS* 3:126–27.
3. *COS* 3:127–29.

The rebuilding of Jerusalem is narrated in the books of Ezra, Nehemiah, and Haggai. Zerubbabel directed the rebuilding of the temple, and, with the support of Haggai and Zechariah (Ezra 3–7; Hag 1–2), it was finally finished in 515 BC. Nehemiah was commissioned by Artaxerxes I to work on the wall (445 BC) and, with the help of Judean residents, eventually finishes it (Neh 1–6).

During the period of Gedaliah's governorship, the text mentions many royal officials (2 Kgs 25:22–25), and four of their names appear on seals and seal impressions (bulla).[4] It is difficult to be certain if these seals actually belonged to these biblical characters, since seals are often not found in official excavations, and people in biblical times often had identical names.[5] But ownership of seals was limited to royals and important officials, so it is very possible these seals belonged to the individuals mentioned in these verses. One seal speaks of Gedaliah, overseer of the royal house, a position that the governor Gedaliah may have held before the palace was destroyed (25:9).

(Belonging) to Gedaliah, "Over(seer of) the (royal) house."[6]

Jaananiah was one of several army commanders who supported Gedaliah (25:23).

Ja'azaniah, servant of the king.[7]

Ishmael was a member of the Judean royal family and leader of the rebels who assassinated the governor, Gedaliah (25:23, 25; Jer 41:1).

Ishmael, son of the king.[8]

Elishama was a member of the Judean royal family and grandfather of the assassin Ishmael (2 Kgs 25:25).

Elishama, son of the king.[9]

---

4. For a brief discussion of late monarchic seals, see *ZIBBC* 3:209.

5. When the source of a seal is an antiquities market, the likelihood of a forgery increases dramatically.

6. *COS* 2:198; *WSS* 172, #405.

7. *WSS* 52, #8; Lemaire, "Royal Signature," 48–52.

8. Gabriel Barkay, "A Bulla of Ishmael, the King's Son," *BASOR* 290–91 (1993): 109–14.

9. *WSS* 53, #11.

Nebuchadnezzar imprisoned Jehoiachin in Babylon in 597 BC, and the ruler who released Jehoiachin from prison in 562 BC was Nebuchadnezzar's son and successor, Awel-Marduk (v. 27). Because of his short, two-year reign (562–560 BC), ancient references only mention him briefly in lists of rulers. His name means "man of Marduk" and is spelled variously as "Evil-merodach" (ESV, NASB, NRSV), "Awel-Marduk" (NIV),[10] or "Awel-Merodach."[11] In August 560 BC Awel-Marduk was assassinated by his own brother-in-law, Neriglissar, who took the throne. According to Jeremiah, Neriglissar contributed to the capture of Jerusalem (Jer 39:3, 13).

Jehoiachin and his sons are mentioned in the Babylonian Rations List,[12] two fragmentary administrative documents recording food rations for prisoners of war or others dependent upon the royal household. These date from the tenth to the thirty-fifth year of Nebuchadnezzar (about 595–570 BC), shortly after Jehoiachin was imprisoned (598 BC).

> 2.5 sila oil to . . . sons of the king of Judah (Ia-a-hu-du)
> 4 sila to 8 men from Judah (Ia-a-hu-da-a-a) . . .
>
> 10 sila to Ia-ku-u-ki-nu (Jehoiachin), the son of the king of Ia-ku-du (i.e., Judah)
> 2.5 sila for the 5 sons of the king of Judah (Ia-ku-du).[13]

EXPLAIN the Story

Destroying the City (2 Kings 25:8–10)

A month after the Babylonian siege ended (August 14(?), 587 BC), Nebuzaradan, commander of Nebuchadnezzar's imperial guard, destroyed the city of Jerusalem and burned its buildings, including the temple (25:8–9). The royal palace and the temple were constructed not merely with quarried stone but also with significant amounts of cedar and juniper wood (1 Kgs 6:9, 10, 15, 16, 18, 20, 34, 36; 7:3, 7, 11, 12), making them highly flammable. The walls around Jerusalem, however, needed to be broken down by the army. It is

10. *ANET,* 219, 309.

11. *ANET,* 561. Marduk (sometimes transliterated Merodach) was originally the city god of Babylon, but as the power of Babylon grew, so did the status of Marduk in the Mesopotamian pantheon.

12. *ANET,* 308c–d. For an image, see *ZIBBC* 3:210.

13. *ANET,* 308c–d.

likely that, instead of leveling the entire wall, gates were destroyed, gaps were expanded, and towers were removed.[14] The result was that Jerusalem had no ability to defend itself against attacks. If there were another Judean rebellion, Nebuchadnezzar would not need a third siege.

Deporting the People (2 Kings 25:11–12)

While many Judeans were deported after Babylon's first siege (2 Kgs 24:14–16), Nebuzaradan takes a second group of exiles, which included soldiers who had deserted (25:11). No numbers are given here, but Jeremiah records 832 people were deported at this time (Jer 52:29). Just as Nebuchadnezzar had done after the last deportation (2 Kgs 24:14), Nebuzaradan allowed poor farmers to remain to work the vineyards and fields (25:12). In addition to this farming community, the Babylonians also allowed certain Judean officials to govern the land under the authority of Babylon (vv. 22–26).

Plundering the Temple (2 Kings 25:13–17)

The temple built by Solomon for YHWH survived over three and half centuries (roughly 955–587 BC), and the final four references to YHWH in the Hebrew of the book of Kings all occur in connection with his temple (25:9, 13 [2x], 16). The text describes in detail how the Babylonians plundered the temple, this being the eighth and final time in the book that a foreign power had taken temple treasures (1 Kgs 14:25–26; 15:18; 2 Kgs 12:18; 14:14; 16:7–8; 18:14–16; 24:13; 25:13–15). Nebuzaradan took some silver and gold censers and bowls (25:15), but most of the plunder was bronze, including pillars, stands, pots, shovels, trimmers, dishes, and capitals (25:13 [3x], 14, 16, 17 [2x]).[15] Because they would not travel well, the Babylonians broke the larger objects into pieces: the pillars, the stands, and the sea (v. 13). Jerusalem will be without a functioning temple for about seventy years, until the Second Temple was completed in 515 BC.

Slaughtering the Leaders (2 Kings 25:18–21)

Nebuzaradan collects a group of over seventy people: religious leaders, military leaders, administrative leaders, and sixty other men (25:18–19). He brings them to Nebuchadnezzar's headquarters at Riblah, where they are all executed (vv. 20–21). Riblah has become a place of punishment, where Jehoahaz was imprisoned (23:33) and Zedekiah was blinded after witnessing the execution of his sons (25:6). The slaughtered religious leaders include the priest Zephaniah,

14. See Barnes, *1 & 2 Kings*, 381.

15. On the construction of these objects, see discussion of 1 Kgs 7:13–47 above.

who relayed messages between Jeremiah and Zedekiah (Jer 21:1; 29:25, 29; 37:3), as well as the chief priest, Seraiah, whose descendants include the exiled Jehozadak (1 Chr 6:14), the high priest Joshua (Hag 1:1), and the priest, scribe, and teacher of the law, Ezra (Ezra 7:1). The text gives no reason why this large group was slaughtered, but they were probably anti-Babylon. The execution of these leaders sent a clear signal that Babylon would not tolerate insubordination. The comment about Judah going into captivity is considered by many scholars to be the original ending of the book (2 Kgs 25:21).[16]

Killing the Governor (2 Kings 25:22–26)

There was no king in Judah, so Nebuchadnezzar appointed Gedaliah ("YHWH is great") as governor (25:22). Gedaliah was the son of Ahikam and grandson of Shaphan, the secretary who delivered the book of the law to King Josiah (22:3–14). Gedaliah set up his new provincial capital at Mizpah, about eight miles north of Jerusalem, because it was spared during the Babylonian destruction of Jerusalem. A group of Judean army officers and soldiers come meet with Gedaliah at Mizpah, and the governor tells them to settle down, serve Babylon, and all will go well (25:23–24). They were not convinced by this advice, so a few months later a group of ten, led by Ishmael (who had royal blood), returned and assassinated Gedaliah before fleeing with many other Judeans to Egypt (vv. 25–26). These rebels were presumably patriots who were offended by the actions of their countrymen, whom they perceived to be Babylonian collaborators and traitors to the house of David.

The book of Jeremiah provides important additional details regarding the narrative of Gedaliah's governorship and assassination. Nebuzaradan gave the prophet Jeremiah the choice to be well taken care of in Babylon or to remain in Judah with Gedaliah; he chose the latter (Jer 40:1–6). In addition to telling the officers and soldiers to serve Babylon, Gedaliah also told them he would represent them before the Babylonians (Jer 40:7–10). Gedaliah was twice warned that Ishmael would try to kill him, but he tragically ignored the threats, believing them to be lies (Jer 40:13–16). Ishmael also killed Gedaliah's Judean officials, the Babylonian soldiers stationed there, and a group from Shechem, Shiloh, and Samaria (Jer 41:1–8).

Releasing the King (2 Kings 25:27–30)

While the events of 587 BC have been dated to the month and day (25:1, 3, 8), here the text skips forward twenty-five years to March/April 562 BC,

16. Wiseman, *1 & 2 Kings*, 315.

when Jehoiachin was released from prison by Awel-Marduk of Babylon (v. 27). This chronological gap leads many scholars to assume these final four verses were added as an appendix to a book that originally ended at 25:21 or 25:26.[17] Other significant events took place during this time; immediately before narrating Jehoiachin's release, the book of Jeremiah records a third deportation to Babylon of 745 people in 582 BC (Jer 52:30).

Awel-Marduk did six things for Jehoiachin: he released him from prison, spoke kindly to him, gave him a seat of honor over other kings, gave him new clothes, allowed him to eat at the king's table, and gave him a regular allowance (25:28–30). Jones cites several examples of similar practices in Mesopotamia, suggesting the amnesty shown to Jehoiachin was normal at the beginning of a new reign.[18]

Why was this appendix added after recording nothing for twenty-five years? Perhaps even a remote glimmer of hope is helpful after such a devastating narrative of destruction and deportation. It is possible also to see hints of hope in two points of connection between Awel-Marduk's actions and the Joseph narrative. The Hebrew behind the phrase "released Jehoiachin" (v. 27) literally means "lifted . . . the head of Jehoiachin" (*nasa' . . . ro'sh yehoyakin*), which is what Joseph predicted would happen to Pharaoh's cupbearer (Gen 40:14). And when Joseph was released from prison and promoted by Pharaoh, he, like Jehoiachin here, was given new clothes (Gen 41:42). Just as Joseph's life in Egypt served as a type for what would eventually happen to his own people (enslavement followed by release from captivity), so does Jehoiachin's life for the nation of Judah (enslavement followed by release from captivity), potentially giving hope to exilic readers of this story.

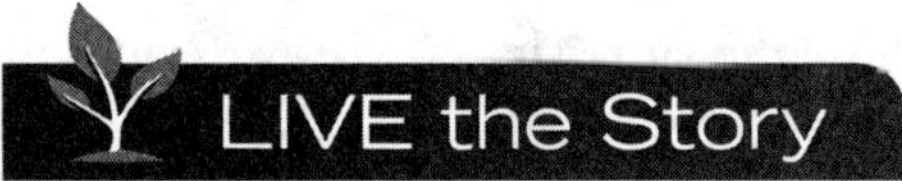

Where Is God?

After experiencing a tragedy one often asks, "Where is God?" This question seems particularly apt since, in the midst of this most painful period in Judah's history, YHWH seems absent. The final chapter of Kings has fewer references to YHWH in the Hebrew than any other in the book (four times; 2 Kgs 25:9, 13(2), 16). YHWH is never the subject of a verb here, and thus he appears passive.

---

17. See Cogan and Tadmor, *II Kings*, 329–30; Wiseman, *1 & 2 Kings*, 308–9; Wray Beal, *1 & 2 Kings*, 525, 529.

18. Jones, *1 and 2 Kings*, 2:649.

Why does the text record no emotional response to this tragedy from the Judeans or the narrator? The text of 2 Kings 24–25 laconically narrates how the Judeans were besieged, deported, imprisoned, and slaughtered. Based on these chapters, it could appear that the appropriate response to calamity is stoic resignation. YHWH had, after all, predicted the destruction (1 Kgs 9:6–9; 2 Kgs 21:11–15).

We don't see language of lament here, but several psalms mourn the destruction of Jerusalem and the loss of the temple.

> O God, the nations have invaded your inheritance;
> they have defiled your holy temple,
> they have reduced Jerusalem to rubble. (Ps 79:1)

> By the rivers of Babylon we sat and wept
> When we remembered Zion. (Ps 137:1)

Lamentations, the book exclusively devoted to the topic, is traditionally attributed to Jeremiah, the prophet who was YHWH's primary mouthpiece predicting the disaster (e.g., Jer 6:1–8; 7:14–15; 21:3–10). The author laments over the city of Jerusalem:

> How deserted lies the city,
> once so full of people. . . .
> Bitterly she weeps at night,
> tears are on her cheeks;
> Among all her lovers
> there is no one to comfort her. (Lam 1:1–2)

and over the temple of YHWH,

> The Lord has rejected his altar
> and abandoned his sanctuary;
> He has given the walls of the palaces
> into the hands of the enemy. (Lam 2:7)

For some of us it is easy in times of tragedy to remain stoic (like 2 Kgs 24–25) and remind ourselves that God is sovereign (which is of course true), and yet Scripture is full of people who respond to disaster with lament and ask, "Where are you, God?" (2 Kgs 2:14; Pss 13:1–2; 22:1–2; 42:3, 10; 79:10;

115:2; Joel 2:17; Mic 7:10; Mal 2:17). Laments are the most common genre of psalm.

Just as Solomon's Temple was destroyed, Herod's would be, too. As he envisioned the future fate of Jerusalem and the temple's destruction, Jesus himself wept and lamented (Luke 19:41–44). What was the tragedy that provoked Jesus to lament in Luke 19? The people of God did not realize that in Jesus, God was present in human form (John 1:14; 2:19–21). A living temple had come to visit them, and they didn't recognize him (Luke 19:44). Perhaps followers of Jesus need to follow his example more closely in this regard and learn to lament?

While we were living in Oxford, England, I remember attending church with my family a few days after 9/11. The service had moved into a time of worship with only a passing reference to the recent tragedies in New York, Pennsylvania, and Washington, DC. I've never considered myself a serious patriot, but at that point in time I wondered, God, where are you, and why did you allow this to happen? During this time of terrible tragedy, I was cut off from my homeland. And the fact that no one else in the congregation seemed to be feeling similarly made me feel further isolated and abandoned. But then the worship leader, moved by the spirit of God, shifted the tone from praise to lament, and many people, including myself, began to weep. As we allow ourselves to grieve, mourn, and lament as a community in times of pain, loss, and disaster, we experience God, God's spirit, and God's comfort—eventually discovering that "the steadfast love (*hesed*) of the Lord never ceases" (Lam 3:22; NRSV).

The ultimate reason that the steadfast love of God never ceases is that Jesus came as Immanuel (Matt 1:23), the word that became flesh and dwelt among us (John 1:14). And as he departed from his followers in a physical form, he promised that he would be with them forever (Matt 28:20). The earthly temples are long gone, but because of Jesus, God will continue to make his home with his people, to dwell with them, to wipe away their tears, and to take away death, mourning, and crying (Rev 21:3–4).

A Dynasty That Never Ceases

YHWH promised not only that his love would never cease but also that the dynasty of David would never end (2 Sam 7:12–16). The Davidic dynasty (David, Solomon, Rehoboam . . . Jehoiakim, Jehoiachin, Zedekiah) was one of the longest in the ancient Near East. According to the regnal formulas, it endured 467.5 years over the throne of Judah. It was longer than any Egyptian dynasty, and only one Babylonian dynasty appears to have been longer.[19] But at the end of the book of Kings, David's dynasty appears to end, as there is no king in Judah. Jehoiachin and his sons may be freed from prison, but they are still in Babylon. No Davidide is on the throne.

However, after a gap of almost six centuries, Matthew's Gospel picks up the story, summarizing the Old Testament by recording a genealogy, from Abraham to David (Matt 1:1–6), from David to Josiah and Jehoiachin (spelled Jeconiah; Matt 1:7–11), from Jehoiachin to Joseph and Mary, the parents of Jesus, the Christ, the Messiah, the anointed King (Matt 1:12–17). According to the New Testament, despite appearances to the contrary, David's dynasty—like the steadfast love of the Lord—never ceases. Israel and Judah never had an opportunity to be subjects under a totally righteous ruler, but we can, as we choose to follow Jesus, the true, perfect, and righteous Davidic ruler.

19. For an extended discussion of ancient Near Eastern dynasties, see Lamb, *Righteous Jehu*, 206–13.

Scripture Index

Genesis

Exodus

Joshua

2 Samuel

1 Kings

2 Kings

1 Chronicles

2 Chronicles

Proverbs

Ecclesiastes

Song of Songs

Isaiah

Amos

Jonah

Micah

Nahum

Habakkuk

Zephaniah

Haggai

Zechariah

Malachi

Matthew

Mark

Luke

John

Acts

Romans

1 Corinthians

Galatians

Ephesians

Subject Index

Author Index